P9-DHP-847

FORD

CONTOUR/MYSTIQUE/COUGAR
1995-99 REPAIR MANUAL

Covers all U.S. and Canadian models of Ford Contour, Mercury Mystique and Cougar Front Wheel Drive

by Eric Michael Mihalyi, A.S.E., S.A.E., S.T.S.

CHILTON *Automotive Books*

PUBLISHED BY **HAYNES NORTH AMERICA, Inc.**

Manufactured in USA
© 1999 Haynes North America, Inc.
ISBN 0-8019-9105-6
Library of Congress Catalog Card No. 99-072293
2345678901 9876543210

Haynes Publishing Group
Sparkford Nr Yeovil
Somerset BA22 7JJ England

Haynes North America, Inc
861 Lawrence Drive
Newbury Park
California 91320 USA

ABCDE
FGHIJ
KLMNO
PQ

Contents

Contents

SAFETY NOTICE

Proper service and repair procedures are vital to the safe, reliable operation of all motor vehicles, as well as the personal safety of those performing repairs. This manual outlines procedures for servicing and repairing vehicles using safe, effective methods. The procedures contain many NOTES, CAUTIONS and WARNINGS which should be followed, along with standard procedures to eliminate the possibility of personal injury or improper service which could damage the vehicle or compromise its safety.

It is important to note that repair procedures and techniques, tools and parts for servicing motor vehicles, as well as the skill and experience of the individual performing the work vary widely. It is not possible to anticipate all of the conceivable ways or conditions under which vehicles may be serviced, or to provide cautions as to all possible hazards that may result. Standard and accepted safety precautions and equipment should be used when handling toxic or flammable fluids, and safety goggles or other protection should be used during cutting, grinding, chiseling, prying, or any other process that can cause material removal or projectiles.

Some procedures require the use of tools specially designed for a specific purpose. Before substituting another tool or procedure, you must be completely satisfied that neither your personal safety, nor the performance of the vehicle will be endangered.

Although information in this manual is based on industry sources and is complete as possible at the time of publication, the possibility exists that some car manufacturers made later changes which could not be included here. While striving for total accuracy, the authors or publishers cannot assume responsibility for any errors, changes or omissions that may occur in the compilation of this data.

PART NUMBERS

Part numbers listed in this reference are not recommendations by Haynes North America, Inc. for any product brand name. They are references that can be used with interchange manuals and aftermarket supplier catalogs to locate each brand supplier's discrete part number.

SPECIAL TOOLS

Special tools are recommended by the vehicle manufacturer to perform their specific job. Use has been kept to a minimum, but where absolutely necessary, they are referred to in the text by the part number of the tool manufacturer. These tools can be purchased, under the appropriate part number, from your local dealer or regional distributor, or an equivalent tool can be purchased locally from a tool supplier or parts outlet. Before substituting any tool for the one recommended, read the SAFETY NOTICE at the top of this page.

ACKNOWLEDGMENTS

This publication contains material that is reproduced and distributed under a license from Ford Motor Company. No further reproduction or distribution of the Ford Motor Company material is allowed without the express written permission from Ford Motor Company.

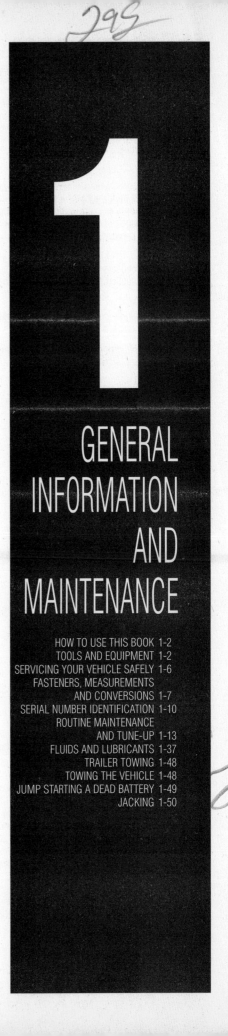

1

GENERAL INFORMATION AND MAINTENANCE

HOW TO USE THIS BOOK

Chilton's Total Car Care manual for the 1995–99 Ford Contour and Mercury Mystique and the 1999 Mercury Cougar is intended to help you learn more about the inner workings of your vehicle while saving you money on its upkeep and operation.

The beginning of the book will likely be referred to the most, since that is where you will find information for maintenance and tune-up. The other sections deal with the more complex systems of your vehicle. Operating systems from engine through brakes are covered to the extent that the average do-it-yourselfer becomes mechanically involved. This book will not explain such things as rebuilding a differential for the simple reason that the expertise required and the investment in special tools make this task uneconomical. It will, however, give you detailed instructions to help you change your own brake pads and shoes, replace spark plugs, and perform many more jobs that can save you money, give you personal satisfaction and help you avoid expensive problems.

A secondary purpose of this book is a reference for owners who want to understand their vehicle and/or their mechanics better. In this case, no tools at all are required.

Where to Begin

Before removing any bolts, read through the entire procedure. This will give you the overall view of what tools and supplies will be required. There is nothing more frustrating than having to walk to the bus stop on Monday morning because you were short one bolt on Sunday afternoon. So read ahead and plan ahead. Each operation should be approached logically and all procedures thoroughly understood before attempting any work.

All sections contain adjustments, maintenance, removal and installation procedures, and in some cases, repair or overhaul procedures. When repair is not considered practical, we tell you how to remove the part and then how to install the new or rebuilt replacement. In this way, you at least save labor costs. "Backyard" repair of some components is just not practical.

Avoiding Trouble

Many procedures in this book require you to "label and disconnect . . ." a group of lines, hoses or wires. Don't be lulled into thinking you can remember where everything goes—you won't. If you hook up vacuum or fuel lines incorrectly, the vehicle may run poorly, if at all. If you hook up electrical wiring incorrectly, you may instantly learn a very expensive lesson.

You don't need to know the official or engineering name for each hose or line. A piece of masking tape on the hose and a piece on its fitting will allow you to assign your own label such as the letter A or a short name. As long as you remember your own code, the lines can be reconnected by matching similar letters or names. Do remember that tape will dissolve in gasoline or other fluids; if a component is to be washed or cleaned, use another method of identification. A permanent felt-tipped marker or a metal scribe can be very handy for marking metal parts. Remove any tape or paper labels after assembly.

Maintenance or Repair?

It's necessary to mention the difference between maintenance and repair. Maintenance includes routine inspections, adjustments, and replacement of parts which show signs of normal wear. Maintenance compensates for wear or deterioration. Repair implies that something has broken or is not working. A need for repair is often caused by lack of maintenance. Example: draining and refilling the automatic transmission fluid is maintenance recommended by the manufacturer at specific mileage intervals. Failure to do this can shorten the life of the transmission/transaxle, requiring very expensive repairs. While no maintenance program can prevent items from breaking or wearing out, a general rule can be stated: MAINTENANCE IS CHEAPER THAN REPAIR.

Two basic mechanic's rules should be mentioned here. First, whenever the left side of the vehicle or engine is referred to, it is meant to specify the driver's side. Conversely, the right side of the vehicle means the passenger's side. Second, screws and bolts are removed by turning counterclockwise, and tightened by turning clockwise unless specifically noted.

Safety is always the most important rule. Constantly be aware of the dangers involved in working on an automobile and take the proper precautions. See the information in this section regarding SERVICING YOUR VEHICLE SAFELY and the SAFETY NOTICE on the acknowledgment page.

Avoiding the Most Common Mistakes

Pay attention to the instructions provided. There are 3 common mistakes in mechanical work:

1. Incorrect order of assembly, disassembly or adjustment. When taking something apart or putting it together, performing steps in the wrong order usually just costs you extra time; however, it CAN break something. Read the entire procedure before beginning disassembly. Perform everything in the order in which the instructions say you should, even if you can't immediately see a reason for it. When you're taking apart something that is very intricate, you might want to draw a picture of how it looks when assembled at one point in order to make sure you get everything back in its proper position. We will supply exploded views whenever possible. When making adjustments, perform them in the proper order. One adjustment possibly will affect another.

2. Overtorquing (or undertorquing). While it is more common for overtorquing to cause damage, undertorquing may allow a fastener to vibrate loose causing serious damage. Especially when dealing with aluminum parts, pay attention to torque specifications and utilize a torque wrench in assembly. If a torque figure is not available, remember that if you are using the right tool to perform the job, you will probably not have to strain yourself to get a fastener tight enough. The pitch of most threads is so slight that the tension you put on the wrench will be multiplied many times in actual force on what you are tightening. A good example of how critical torque is can be seen in the case of spark plug installation, especially where you are putting the plug into an aluminum cylinder head. Too little torque can fail to crush the gasket, causing leakage of combustion gases and consequent overheating of the plug and engine parts. Too much torque can damage the threads or distort the plug, changing the spark gap.

There are many commercial products available for ensuring that fasteners won't come loose, even if they are not torqued just right (a very common brand is Loctite®. If you're worried about getting something together tight enough to hold, but loose enough to avoid mechanical damage during assembly, one of these products might offer substantial insurance. Before choosing a threadlocking compound, read the label on the package and make sure the product is compatible with the materials, fluids, etc. involved.

3. Crossthreading. This occurs when a part such as a bolt is screwed into a nut or casting at the wrong angle and forced. Crossthreading is more likely to occur if access is difficult. It helps to clean and lubricate fasteners, then to start threading the bolt, spark plug, etc. with your fingers. If you encounter resistance, unscrew the part and start over again at a different angle until it can be inserted and turned several times without much effort. Keep in mind that many parts, especially spark plugs, have tapered threads, so that gentle turning will automatically bring the part you're threading to the proper angle. Don't put a wrench on the part until it's been tightened a couple of turns by hand. If you suddenly encounter resistance, and the part has not seated fully, don't force it. Pull it back out to make sure it's clean and threading properly.

Be sure to take your time and be patient, and always plan ahead. Allow yourself ample time to perform repairs and maintenance. You may find maintaining your car a satisfying and enjoyable experience.

TOOLS AND EQUIPMENT

♦ See Figures 1 thru 15

Naturally, without the proper tools and equipment it is impossible to properly service your vehicle. It would also be virtually impossible to catalog every tool that you would need to perform all of the operations in this book. Of course, It

would be unwise for the amateur to rush out and buy an expensive set of tools on the theory that he/she may need one or more of them at some time.

The best approach is to proceed slowly, gathering a good quality set of those tools that are used most frequently. Don't be misled by the low cost of bargain tools. It is far better to spend a little more for better quality. Forged wrenches, 6 or 12-point sockets and fine tooth ratchets are by far preferable to their less expensive counterparts. As any good mechanic can tell you, there are few worse experiences than trying to work on a vehicle with bad tools. Your monetary savings will be far outweighed by frustration and mangled knuckles.

Begin accumulating those tools that are used most frequently: those associated with routine maintenance and tune-up. In addition to the normal assortment of screwdrivers and pliers, you should have the following tools:

• Wrenches/sockets and combination open end/box end wrenches in sizes 3mm–19mm 13/16 in. or 5/8 in. spark plug socket (depending on plug type).

➡️If possible, buy various length socket drive extensions. Universal-joint and wobble extensions can be extremely useful, but be careful when using them, as they can change the amount of torque applied to the socket.

• Jackstands for support.
• Oil filter wrench.

• Spout or funnel for pouring fluids.
• Grease gun for chassis lubrication (unless your vehicle is not equipped with any grease fittings—for details, please refer to information on Fluids and Lubricants, later in this section).
• Hydrometer for checking the battery (unless equipped with a sealed, maintenance-free battery).
• A container for draining oil and other fluids.
• Rags for wiping up the inevitable mess.

In addition to the above items there are several others that are not absolutely necessary, but handy to have around. These include Oil Dry® (or an equivalent oil absorbent gravel—such as cat litter) and the usual supply of lubricants, antifreeze and fluids, although these can be purchased as needed. This is a basic list for routine maintenance, but only your personal needs and desire can accurately determine your list of tools.

After performing a few projects on the vehicle, you'll be amazed at the other tools and non-tools on your workbench. Some useful household items are: a

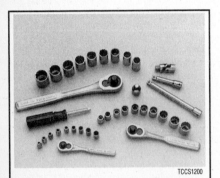

Fig. 1 All but the most basic procedures will require an assortment of ratchets and sockets

TCCS1200

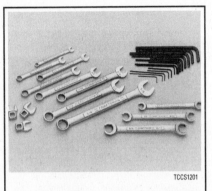

Fig. 2 In addition to ratchets, a good set of wrenches and hex keys will be necessary

TCCS1201

Fig. 3 A hydraulic floor jack and a set of jackstands are essential for lifting and supporting the vehicle

TCCS1202

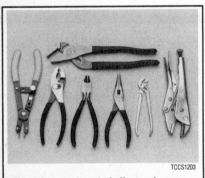

Fig. 4 An assortment of pliers, grippers and cutters will be handy for old rusted parts and stripped bolt heads

TCCS1203

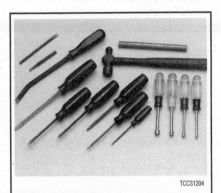

Fig. 5 Various drivers, chisels and prybars are great tools to have in your toolbox

TCCS1204

Fig. 6 Many repairs will require the use of a torque wrench to assure the components are properly fastened

TCCS1205

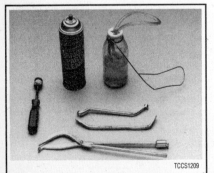

Fig. 7 Although not always necessary, using specialized brake tools will save time

TCCS1209

Fig. 8 A few inexpensive lubrication tools will make maintenance easier

TCCS1210

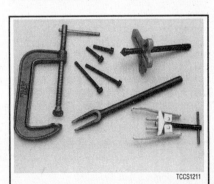

Fig. 9 Various pullers, clamps and separator tools are needed for many larger, more complicated repairs

TCCS1211

Fig. 10 A variety of tools and gauges should be used for spark plug gapping and installation

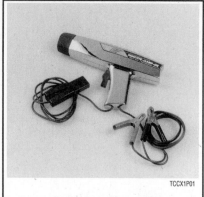

Fig. 11 Inductive type timing light

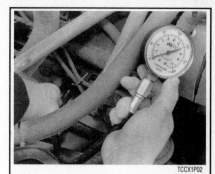

Fig. 12 A screw-in type compression gauge is recommended for compression testing

Fig. 13 A vacuum/pressure tester is necessary for many testing procedures

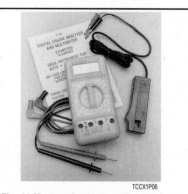

Fig. 14 Most modern automotive multimeters incorporate many helpful features

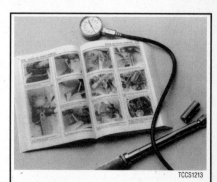

Fig. 15 Proper information is vital, so always have a Chilton Total Car Care manual handy

large turkey baster or siphon, empty coffee cans and ice trays (to store parts), ball of twine, electrical tape for wiring, small rolls of colored tape for tagging lines or hoses, markers and pens, a note pad, golf tees (for plugging vacuum lines), metal coat hangers or a roll of mechanic's wire (to hold things out of the way), dental pick or similar long, pointed probe, a strong magnet, and a small mirror (to see into recesses and under manifolds).

A more advanced set of tools, suitable for tune-up work, can be drawn up easily. While the tools are slightly more sophisticated, they need not be outrageously expensive. There are several inexpensive tach/dwell meters on the market that are every bit as good for the average mechanic as a professional model. Just be sure that it goes to a least 1200–1500 rpm on the tach scale and that it works on 4, 6 and 8-cylinder engines. The key to these purchases is to make them with an eye towards adaptability and wide range. A basic list of tune-up tools could include:

- Tach/dwell meter.
- Spark plug wrench and gapping tool.
- Feeler gauges for valve adjustment.
- Timing light.

The choice of a timing light should be made carefully. A light which works on the DC current supplied by the vehicle's battery is the best choice; it should have a xenon tube for brightness. On any vehicle with an electronic ignition system, a timing light with an inductive pickup that clamps around the No. 1 spark plug cable is preferred.

In addition to these basic tools, there are several other tools and gauges you may find useful..These include:

- Compression gauge. The screw-in type is slower to use, but eliminates the possibility of a faulty reading due to escaping pressure.

- Manifold vacuum gauge.
- 12V test light.
- A combination volt/ohmmeter
- Induction Ammeter. This is used for determining whether or not there is current in a wire. These are handy for use if a wire is broken somewhere in a wiring harness.

As a final note, you will probably find a torque wrench necessary for all but the most basic work. The beam type models are perfectly adequate, although the newer click types (breakaway) are easier to use. The click type torque wrenches tend to be more expensive. Also keep in mind that all types of torque wrenches should be periodically checked and/or recalibrated. You will have to decide for yourself which better fits your pocketbook, and purpose.

Special Tools

Normally, the use of special factory tools is avoided for repair procedures, since these are not readily available for the do-it-yourself mechanic. When it is possible to perform the job with more commonly available tools, it will be pointed out, but occasionally, a special tool was designed to perform a specific function and should be used. Before substituting another tool, you should be convinced that neither your safety nor the performance of the vehicle will be compromised.

Special tools can usually be purchased from an automotive parts store or from your dealer. In some cases special tools may be available directly from the tool manufacturer.

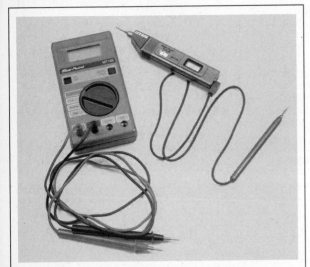

Digital multimeters come in a variety of styles and are a "must-have" for any serious home mechanic. Digital multimeters measure voltage (volts), resistance (ohms) and sometimes current (amperes). These versatile tools are used for checking all types of electrical or electronic components

Modern vehicles equipped with computer-controlled fuel, emission and ignition systems require modern electronic tools to diagnose problems. Many of these tools are designed solely for the professional mechanic and are too costly and difficult to use for the average do-it-yourselfer. However, various automotive aftermarket companies have introduced products that address the needs of the average home mechanic, providing sophisticated information at affordable cost. Consult your local auto parts store to determine what is available for your vehicle.

Trouble code tools allow the home mechanic to extract the "fault code" number from an on-board computer that has sensed a problem (usually indicated by a Check Engine light). Armed with this code, the home mechanic can focus attention on a suspect system or component

Hand-held scanners represent the most sophisticated of all do-it-yourself diagnostic tools. These tools do more than just access computer codes like the code readers above; they provide the user with an actual interface into the vehicle's computer. Comprehensive data on specific makes and models will come with the tool, either built-in or as a separate cartridge

Sensor testers perform specific checks on many of the sensors and actuators used on today's computer-controlled vehicles. These testers can check sensors both on or off the vehicle, as well as test the accompanying electrical circuits

SERVICING YOUR VEHICLE SAFELY

▶ **See Figures 16, 17, 18 and 19**

It is virtually impossible to anticipate all of the hazards involved with automotive maintenance and service, but care and common sense will prevent most accidents.

The rules of safety for mechanics range from "don't smoke around gasoline," to "use the proper tool(s) for the job." The trick to avoiding injuries is to develop safe work habits and to take every possible precaution.

Do's

• Do keep a fire extinguisher and first aid kit handy.

• Do wear safety glasses or goggles when cutting, drilling, grinding or prying, even if you have 20–20 vision. If you wear glasses for the sake of vision, wear safety goggles over your regular glasses.

• Do shield your eyes whenever you work around the battery. Batteries contain sulfuric acid. In case of contact with the eyes or skin, flush the area with water or a mixture of water and baking soda, then seek immediate medical attention.

• Do use safety stands (jackstands) for any undervehicle service. Jacks are for raising vehicles; jackstands are for making sure the vehicle stays raised until you want it to come down. Whenever the vehicle is raised, block the wheels remaining on the ground and set the parking brake.

• Do use adequate ventilation when working with any chemicals or hazardous materials. Like carbon monoxide, the asbestos dust resulting from some brake lining wear can be hazardous in sufficient quantities.

• Do disconnect the negative battery cable when working on the electrical system. The secondary ignition system contains EXTREMELY HIGH VOLTAGE. In some cases it can even exceed 50,000 volts.

• Do follow manufacturer's directions whenever working with potentially hazardous materials. Most chemicals and fluids are poisonous if taken internally.

• Do properly maintain your tools. Loose hammerheads, mushroomed punches and chisels, frayed or poorly grounded electrical cords, excessively worn screwdrivers, spread wrenches (open end), cracked sockets, slipping ratchets, or faulty droplight sockets can cause accidents.

• Likewise, keep your tools clean; a greasy wrench can slip off a bolt head, ruining the bolt and often harming your knuckles in the process.

• Do use the proper size and type of tool for the job at hand. Do select a wrench or socket that fits the nut or bolt. The wrench or socket should sit straight, not cocked.

• Do, when possible, pull on a wrench handle rather than push on it, and adjust your stance to prevent a fall.

• Do be sure that adjustable wrenches are tightly closed on the nut or bolt and pulled so that the force is on the side of the fixed jaw.

• Do strike squarely with a hammer; avoid glancing blows.

• Do set the parking brake and block the drive wheels if the work requires a running engine.

Don'ts

• Don't run the engine in a garage or anywhere else without proper ventilation—EVER! Carbon monoxide is poisonous; it takes a long time to leave the human body and you can build up a deadly supply of it in your system by simply breathing in a little every day. You may not realize you are slowly poisoning yourself. Always use power vents, windows, fans and/or open the garage door.

• Don't work around moving parts while wearing loose clothing. Short sleeves are much safer than long, loose sleeves. Hard-toed shoes with neoprene soles protect your toes and give a better grip on slippery surfaces. Jewelry such as watches, fancy belt buckles, beads or body adornment of any kind is not safe working around a vehicle. Long hair should be tied back under a hat or cap.

• Don't use pockets for toolboxes. A fall or bump can drive a screwdriver deep into your body. Even a rag hanging from your back pocket can wrap around a spinning shaft or fan.

• Don't smoke when working around gasoline, cleaning solvent or other flammable material.

• Don't smoke when working around the battery. When the battery is being charged, it gives off explosive hydrogen gas.

• Don't use gasoline to wash your hands; there are excellent soaps available. Gasoline contains dangerous additives which can enter the body through a cut or through your pores. Gasoline also removes all the natural oils from the skin so that bone dry hands will suck up oil and grease.

• Don't service the air conditioning system unless you are equipped with the necessary tools and training. When liquid or compressed gas refrigerant is released to atmospheric pressure it will absorb heat from whatever it contacts. This will chill or freeze anything it touches.

• Don't use screwdrivers for anything other than driving screws! A screwdriver used as an prying tool can snap when you least expect it, causing injuries. At the very least, you'll ruin a good screwdriver.

• Don't use an emergency jack (that little ratchet, scissors, or pantograph jack supplied with the vehicle) for anything other than changing a flat! These jacks are only intended for emergency use out on the road; they are NOT designed as a maintenance tool. If you are serious about maintaining your vehicle yourself, invest in a hydraulic floor jack of at least a 1½ ton capacity, and at least two sturdy jackstands.

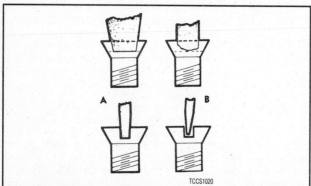

TCCS1020

Fig. 16 Screwdrivers should be kept in good condition to prevent injury or damage which could result if the blade slips from the screw

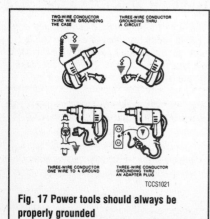

TCCS1021

Fig. 17 Power tools should always be properly grounded

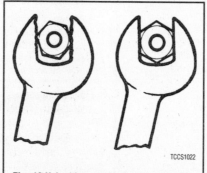

TCCS1022

Fig. 18 Using the correct size wrench will help prevent the possibility of rounding off a nut

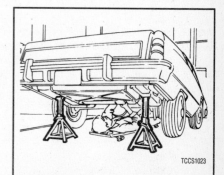

TCCS1023

Fig. 19 NEVER work under a vehicle unless it is supported using safety stands (jackstands)

FASTENERS, MEASUREMENTS AND CONVERSIONS

Bolts, Nuts and Other Threaded Retainers

▶ See Figures 20, 21, 22 and 23

Although there are a great variety of fasteners found in the modern car or truck, the most commonly used retainer is the threaded fastener (nuts, bolts, screws, studs, etc.). Most threaded retainers may be reused, provided that they are not damaged in use or during the repair. Some retainers (such as stretch bolts or torque prevailing nuts) are designed to deform when tightened or in use and should not be reinstalled.

Whenever possible, we will note any special retainers which should be replaced during a procedure. But you should always inspect the condition of a retainer when it is removed and replace any that show signs of damage. Check all threads for rust or corrosion which can increase the torque necessary to achieve the desired clamp load for which that fastener was originally selected. Additionally, be sure that the driver surface of the fastener has not been compromised by rounding or other damage. In some cases a driver surface may become only partially rounded, allowing the driver to catch in only one direction. In many of these occurrences, a fastener may be installed and tightened, but the driver would not be able to grip and loosen the fastener again. (This could lead to frustration down the line should that component ever need to be disassembled again).

If you must replace a fastener, whether due to design or damage, you must ALWAYS be sure to use the proper replacement. In all cases, a retainer of the same design, material and strength should be used. Markings on the heads of most bolts will help determine the proper strength of the fastener. The same material, thread and pitch must be selected to assure proper installation and safe operation of the vehicle afterwards.

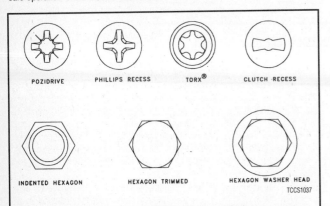

Fig. 20 Here are a few of the most common screw/bolt driver styles

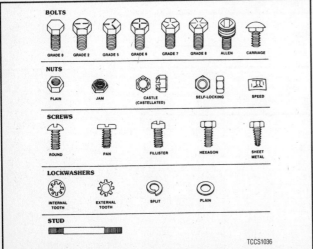

Fig. 21 There are many different types of threaded retainers found on vehicles

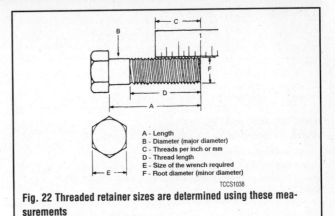

A - Length
B - Diameter (major diameter)
C - Threads per inch or mm
D - Thread length
E - Size of the wrench required
F - Root diameter (minor diameter)

Fig. 22 Threaded retainer sizes are determined using these measurements

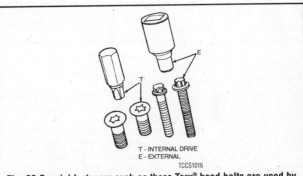

T - INTERNAL DRIVE
E - EXTERNAL

Fig. 23 Special fasteners such as these Torx® head bolts are used by manufacturers to discourage people from working on vehicles without the proper tools

Thread gauges are available to help measure a bolt or stud's thread. Most automotive and hardware stores keep gauges available to help you select the proper size. In a pinch, you can use another nut or bolt for a thread gauge. If the bolt you are replacing is not too badly damaged, you can select a match by finding another bolt which will thread in its place. If you find a nut which threads properly onto the damaged bolt, then use that nut to help select the replacement bolt. If however, the bolt you are replacing is so badly damaged (broken or drilled out) that its threads cannot be used as a gauge, you might start by looking for another bolt (from the same assembly or a similar location on your vehicle) which will thread into the damaged bolt's mounting. If so, the other bolt can be used to select a nut; the nut can then be used to select the replacement bolt.

In all cases, be absolutely sure you have selected the proper replacement. Don't be shy, you can always ask the store clerk for help.

✷✷ WARNING

Be aware that when you find a bolt with damaged threads, you may also find the nut or drilled hole it was threaded into has also been damaged. If this is the case, you may have to drill and tap the hole, replace the nut or otherwise repair the threads. NEVER try to force a replacement bolt to fit into the damaged threads.

Torque

Torque is defined as the measurement of resistance to turning or rotating. It tends to twist a body about an axis of rotation. A common example of this would be tightening a threaded retainer such as a nut, bolt or screw. Measuring torque is one of the most common ways to help assure that a threaded retainer has been properly fastened.

When tightening a threaded fastener, torque is applied in three distinct areas, the head, the bearing surface and the clamp load. About 50 percent of the measured torque is used in overcoming bearing friction. This is the friction between the bearing surface of the bolt head, screw head or nut face and the base material or washer (the surface on which the fastener is rotating). Approximately 40 percent of the applied torque is used in overcoming thread friction. This leaves only about 10 percent of the applied torque to develop a useful clamp load (the force which holds a joint together). This means that friction can account for as much as 90 percent of the applied torque on a fastener.

TORQUE WRENCHES

▶ See Figures 24 and 25

In most applications, a torque wrench can be used to assure proper installation of a fastener. Torque wrenches come in various designs and most automotive supply stores will carry a variety to suit your needs. A torque wrench should be used any time we supply a specific torque value for a fas-

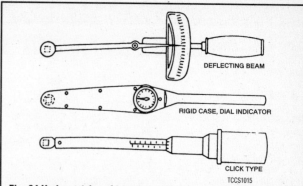

Fig. 24 Various styles of torque wrenches are usually available at your local automotive supply store

Standard Torque Specifications and Fastener Markings

In the absence of specific torques, the following chart can be used as a guide to the maximum safe torque of a particular size/grade of fastener.
- There is no torque difference for fine or coarse threads.
- Torque values are based on clean, dry threads. Reduce the value by 10% if threads are oiled prior to assembly.
- The torque required for aluminum components or fasteners is considerably less.

U.S. Bolts

SAE Grade Number	1 or 2			5			6 or 7		
Number of lines always 2 less than the grade number.									
Bolt Size (Inches)—(Thread)	Maximum Torque			Maximum Torque			Maximum Torque		
	Ft./Lbs.	Kgm	Nm	Ft./Lbs.	Kgm	Nm	Ft./Lbs.	Kgm	Nm
¼ — 20	5	0.7	6.8	8	1.1	10.8	10	1.4	13.5
— 28	6	0.8	8.1	10	1.4	13.6			
⁵/₁₆ — 18	11	1.5	14.9	17	2.3	23.0	19	2.6	25.8
— 24	13	1.8	17.6	19	2.6	25.7			
³/₈ — 16	18	2.5	24.4	31	4.3	42.0	34	4.7	46.0
— 24	20	2.75	27.1	35	4.8	47.5			
⁷/₁₆ — 14	28	3.8	37.0	49	6.8	66.4	55	7.6	74.5
— 20	30	4.2	40.7	55	7.6	74.5			
½ — 13	39	5.4	52.8	75	10.4	101.7	85	11.75	115.2
— 20	41	5.7	55.6	85	11.7	115.2			
⁹/₁₆ — 12	51	7.0	69.2	110	15.2	149.1	120	16.6	162.7
— 18	55	7.6	74.5	120	16.6	162.7			
⅝ — 11	83	11.5	112.5	150	20.7	203.3	167	23.0	226.5
— 18	95	13.1	128.8	170	23.5	230.5			
¾ — 10	105	14.5	142.3	270	37.3	366.0	280	38.7	379.6
— 16	115	15.9	155.9	295	40.8	400.0			
⅞ — 9	160	22.1	216.9	395	54.6	535.5	440	60.9	596.5
— 14	175	24.2	237.2	435	60.1	589.7			
1 — 8	236	32.5	318.6	590	81.6	799.9	660	91.3	894.8
— 14	250	34.6	338.9	660	91.3	849.8			

Metric Bolts

Relative Strength Marking	4.6, 4.8			8.8		
Bolt Markings						
Bolt Size Thread Size x Pitch (mm)	Maximum Torque			Maximum Torque		
	Ft./Lbs.	Kgm	Nm	Ft./Lbs.	Kgm	Nm
6 x 1.0	2–3	.2–.4	3–4	3–6	4–.8	5–8
8 x 1.25	6–8	.8–1	8–12	9–14	1.2–1.9	13–19
10 x 1.25	12–17	1.5–2.3	16–23	20–29	2.7–4.0	27–39
12 x 1.25	21–32	2.9–4.4	29–43	35–53	4.8–7.3	47–72
14 x 1.5	35–52	4.8–7.1	48–70	57–85	7.8–11.7	77–110
16 x 1.5	51–77	7.0–10.6	67–100	90–120	12.4–16.5	130–160
18 x 1.5	74–110	10.2–15.1	100–150	130–170	17.9–23.4	180–230
20 x 1.5	110–140	15.1–19.3	150–190	190–240	26.2–46.9	160–320
22 x 1.5	150–190	22.0–26.2	200–260	250–320	34.5–44.1	340–430
24 x 1.5	190–240	26.2–46.9	260–320	310–410	42.7–56.5	420–550

Fig. 25 Standard and metric bolt torque specifications based on bolt strengths—WARNING: use only as a guide

tener. A torque wrench can also be used if you are following the general guidelines in the accompanying charts. Keep in mind that because there is no worldwide standardization of fasteners, the charts are a general guideline and should be used with caution. Again, the general rule of "if you are using the right tool for the job, you should not have to strain to tighten a fastener" applies here.

Beam Type

▶ See Figure 26

The beam type torque wrench is one of the most popular types. It consists of a pointer attached to the head that runs the length of the flexible beam (shaft) to a scale located near the handle. As the wrench is pulled, the beam bends and the pointer indicates the torque using the scale.

Click (Breakaway) Type

▶ See Figure 27

Another popular design of torque wrench is the click type. To use the click type wrench you pre-adjust it to a torque setting. Once the torque is reached, the wrench has a reflex signaling feature that causes a momentary breakaway of the torque wrench body, sending an impulse to the operator's hand.

Pivot Head Type

▶ See Figures 27 and 28

Some torque wrenches (usually of the click type) may be equipped with a pivot head which can allow it to be used in areas of limited access. BUT, it must be used properly. To hold a pivot head wrench, grasp the handle lightly, and as you pull on the handle, it should be floated on the pivot point. If the handle comes in contact with the yoke extension during the process of pulling, there is a very good chance the torque readings will be inaccurate because this could alter the wrench loading point. The design of the handle is usually such as to make it inconvenient to deliberately misuse the wrench.

➡ It should be mentioned that the use of any U-joint, wobble or extension will have an effect on the torque readings, no matter what type of wrench you are using. For the most accurate readings, install the socket directly on the wrench driver. If necessary, straight extensions (which hold a socket directly under the wrench driver) will have the least effect on the torque reading. Avoid any extension that alters the length of the wrench from the handle to the head/driving point (such as a crow's foot). U-joint or wobble extensions can greatly affect the readings; avoid their use at all times.

Rigid Case (Direct Reading)

▶ See Figure 29

A rigid case or direct reading torque wrench is equipped with a dial indicator to show torque values. One advantage of these wrenches is that they can be held at any position on the wrench without affecting accuracy. These wrenches are often preferred because they tend to be compact, easy to read and have a great degree of accuracy.

TORQUE ANGLE METERS

▶ See Figure 30

Because the frictional characteristics of each fastener or threaded hole will vary, clamp loads which are based strictly on torque will vary as well. In most applications, this variance is not significant enough to cause worry. But, in certain applications, a manufacturer's engineers may determine that more precise clamp loads are necessary (such is the case with many aluminum cylinder heads). In these cases, a torque angle method of installation would be specified. When installing fasteners which are torque angle tightened, a predetermined seating torque and standard torque wrench are usually used first to remove any compliance from the joint. The fastener is then tightened the specified additional portion of a turn measured in degrees. A torque angle gauge (mechanical protractor) is used for these applications.

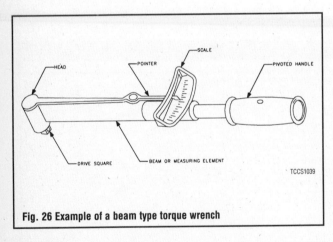

Fig. 26 Example of a beam type torque wrench

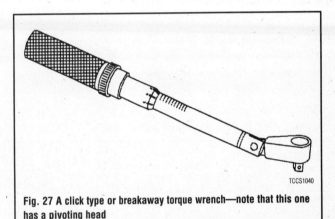

Fig. 27 A click type or breakaway torque wrench—note that this one has a pivoting head

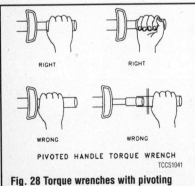

Fig. 28 Torque wrenches with pivoting heads must be grasped and used properly to prevent an incorrect reading

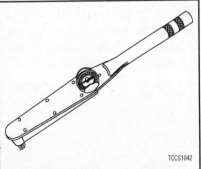

Fig. 29 The rigid case (direct reading) torque wrench uses a dial indicator to show torque

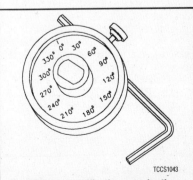

Fig. 30 Some specifications require the use of a torque angle meter (mechanical protractor)

Standard and Metric Measurements

♦ **See Figure 31**

Throughout this manual, specifications are given to help you determine the condition of various components on your vehicle, or to assist you in their installation. Some of the most common measurements include length (in. or cm/mm), torque (ft. lbs., inch lbs. or Nm) and pressure (psi, in. Hg, kPa or mm Hg). In most cases, we strive to provide the proper measurement as determined by the manufacturer's engineers.

Though, in some cases, that value may not be conveniently measured with what is available in your toolbox. Luckily, many of the measuring devices which are available today will have two scales so the Standard or Metric measurements may easily be taken. If any of the various measuring tools which are available to you do not contain the same scale as listed in the specifications, use the accompanying conversion factors to determine the proper value.

The conversion factor chart is used by taking the given specification and multiplying it by the necessary conversion factor. For instance, looking at the first line, if you have a measurement in inches such as "free-play should be 2 in." but your ruler reads only in millimeters, multiply 2 in. by the conversion factor of 25.4 to get the metric equivalent of 50.8mm. Likewise, if the specification was given only in a Metric measurement, for example in Newton Meters (Nm), then look at the center column first. If the measurement is 100 Nm, multiply it by the conversion factor of 0.738 to get 73.8 ft. lbs.

CONVERSION FACTORS

LENGTH-DISTANCE

Inches (in.)	x 25.4	= Millimeters (mm)	x .0394	= Inches
Feet (ft.)	x .305	= Meters (m)	x 3.281	= Feet
Miles	x 1.609	= Kilometers (km)	x .0621	= Miles

VOLUME

Cubic Inches (in3)	x 16.387	= Cubic Centimeters	x .061	= in3
IMP Pints (IMP pt.)	x .568	= Liters (L)	x 1.76	= IMP pt.
IMP Quarts (IMP qt.)	x 1.137	= Liters (L)	x .88	= IMP qt.
IMP Gallons (IMP gal.)	x 4.546	= Liters (L)	x .22	= IMP gal.
IMP Quarts (IMP qt.)	x 1.201	= US Quarts (US qt.)	x .833	= IMP qt.
IMP Gallons (IMP gal.)	x 1.201	= US Gallons (US gal.)	x .833	= IMP gal.
Fl. Ounces	x 29.573	= Milliliters	x .034	= Ounces
US Pints (US pt.)	x .473	= Liters (L)	x 2.113	= Pints
US Quarts (US qt.)	x .946	= Liters (L)	x 1.057	= Quarts
US Gallons (US gal.)	x 3.785	= Liters (L)	x .264	= Gallons

MASS-WEIGHT

Ounces (oz.)	x 28.35	= Grams (g)	x .035	= Ounces
Pounds (lb.)	x .454	= Kilograms (kg)	x 2.205	= Pounds

PRESSURE

Pounds Per Sq. In. (psi)	x 6.895	= Kilopascals (kPa)	x .145	= psi
Inches of Mercury (Hg)	x .4912	= psi	x 2.036	= Hg
Inches of Mercury (Hg)	x 3.377	= Kilopascals (kPa)	x .2961	= Hg
Inches of Water (H₂O)	x .07355	= Inches of Mercury	x 13.783	= H₂O
Inches of Water (H₂O)	x .03613	= psi	x 27.684	= H₂O
Inches of Water (H₂O)	x .248	= Kilopascals (kPa)	x 4.026	= H₂O

TORQUE

Pounds-Force Inches (in-lb)	x .113	= Newton Meters (N·m)	x 8.85	= in-lb
Pounds-Force Feet (ft-lb)	x 1.356	= Newton Meters (N·m)	x .738	= ft-lb

VELOCITY

Miles Per Hour (MPH)	x 1.609	= Kilometers Per Hour (KPH)	x .621	= MPH

POWER

Horsepower (Hp)	x .745	= Kilowatts	x 1.34	= Horsepower

FUEL CONSUMPTION*

Miles Per Gallon IMP (MPG)	x .354	= Kilometers Per Liter (Km/L)		
Kilometers Per Liter (Km/L)	x 2.352	= IMP MPG		
Miles Per Gallon US (MPG)	x .425	= Kilometers Per Liter (Km/L)		
Kilometers Per Liter (Km/L)	x 2.352	= US MPG		

*It is common to covert from miles per gallon (mpg) to liters/100 kilometers (1/100 km), where mpg (IMP) x 1/100 km = 282 and mpg (US) x 1/100 km = 235.

TEMPERATURE

Degree Fahrenheit (°F)   = (°C x 1.8) + 32
Degree Celsius (°C)   = (°F − 32) x .56

TCCS1044

Fig. 31 Standard and metric conversion factors chart

SERIAL NUMBER IDENTIFICATION

Vehicle

♦ **See Figure 32**

VEHICLE IDENTIFICATION NUMBER

♦ **See Figure 33**

The Vehicle Identification Number (VIN) is stamped onto a metal tag mounted in the upper left-hand corner of the instrument panel, visible through the windshield from the outside of the vehicle. The VIN is also presented on various other labels and identifiers found throughout the vehicle.

The VIN is an identification code comprised of a seventeen-digit combination of numbers and letters. Each letter, number or combination represents different items, such as manufacturer, type of restraint system, line, series and body type, engine, model year and consecutive unit number.

The last six digits of the VIN indicate the assembly plant production sequence number of each individual vehicle manufactured at the factory. The unit numbers are divided as follows by manufacturer:
- 000,001 through 599,999—Ford division vehicles
- 600,000 through 999,999—Lincoln and Mercury division vehicles

Refer to the accompanying specifications chart and illustrations for VIN breakdown.

VEHICLE CERTIFICATION LABEL

♦ **See Figures 34 and 35**

The vehicle certification label is affixed to the driver's side door pillar. The vehicle certification label displays various, important information regarding your particular vehicle, such as the following:

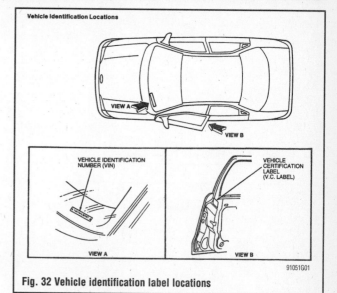

Fig. 32 Vehicle identification label locations

- Name of the manufacturer
- Month and year of manufacture
- Gross Vehicle Weight Rating (GVWR)
- Gross Axle Weight Rating (GAWR)
- Certification statement
- Vehicle Identification Number (VIN)
- Vehicle color

VEHICLE IDENTIFICATION CHART

		Engine Code					Model Year	
Code	Liters	Cu. In. (cc)	Cyl.	Fuel Sys.	Eng. Mfg.		Code	Year
3	2.0	122 (1999)	4	SFI	Ford		S	1995
L	2.5	153 (2507)	6	SFI	Ford		T	1996
							V	1997
							W	1998
							X	1999

SFI - Sequential Fuel Injection

91051C01

Fig. 33 The VIN tag can be viewed from outside the vehicle; it is located on the driver's side of the instrument panel

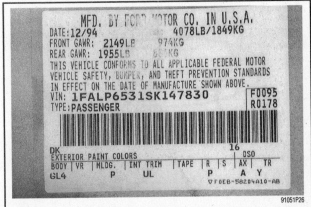

Fig. 34 The vehicle certification label is located on the driver's door pillar

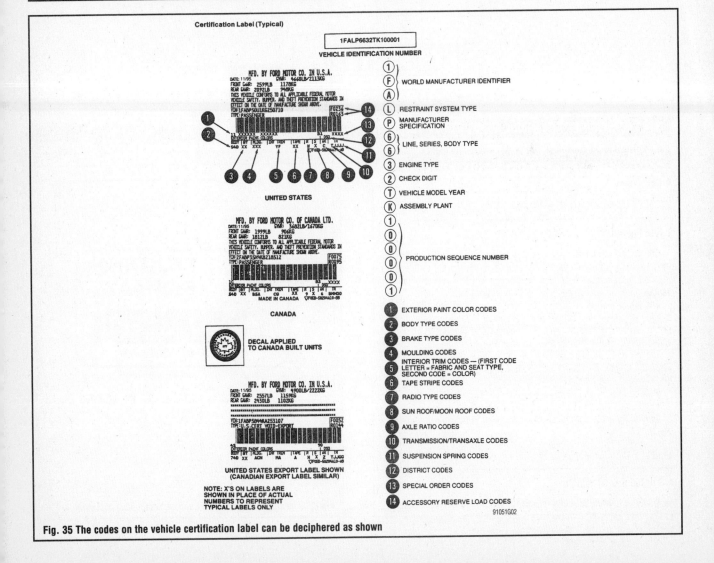

Fig. 35 The codes on the vehicle certification label can be deciphered as shown

- Vehicle body type
- Brake type
- Moulding option (if applicable)
- Tape stripe or paint stripe option (if applicable)
- Interior trim option (if applicable)
- Radio type (if applicable)
- Axle ratio identification
- Transmission identification
- Spring identification
- District sales office
- Special order codes

Engine

▶ See Figures 36, 37 and 38

The engine identification code can be found on a label attached to the engine. On the 2.0L motor it is on the camshaft timing belt cover, and on the 2.5L engine it is located on the left valve cover. The label contains, among other information, the engine calibration number, the engine build date, the engine plant code, and the engine ID number.

Another important label is the emission calibration label, located on the on either the driver's or passenger's door or door jamb. This label identifies the engine calibration, engine code and revision numbers. These numbers are used to determine if parts are unique to specific engines.

➡ **It is imperative that the engine codes and calibration number be used when ordering parts or making inquiries about the engine.**

Transaxle

▶ See Figure 39

The transaxle identification tag is located on the rear of the case. The tag contains the part number, the assembly number, the model number, and the serial number, which includes the build date.

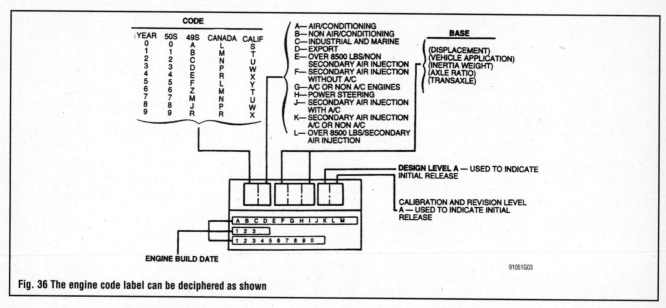

Fig. 36 The engine code label can be deciphered as shown

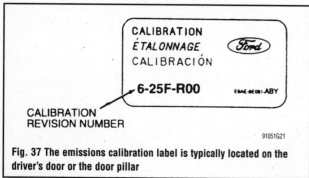

Fig. 37 The emissions calibration label is typically located on the driver's door or the door pillar

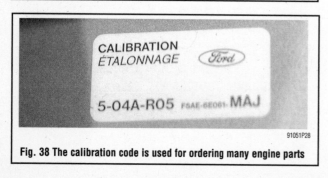

Fig. 38 The calibration code is used for ordering many engine parts

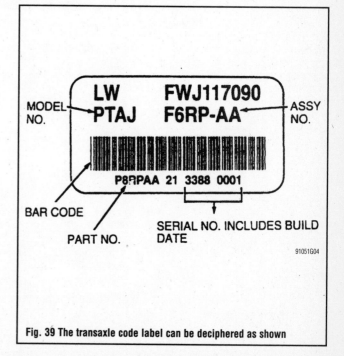

Fig. 39 The transaxle code label can be deciphered as shown

ENGINE IDENTIFICATION AND SPECIFICATIONS

Year	Model	Engine ID/VIN	Engine Displacement Liters (cc)	No. of Cyl.	Engine Type	Fuel System Type	Net Horsepower @ rpm	Net Torque @ rpm (ft. lbs.)	Bore x Stroke (in.)	Compression Ratio	Oil Pressure @ rpm
1995	Contour	3	2.0 (1999)	4	DOHC	SFI	125@5500	130@4500	3.39x3.46	9.6:1	20-45@1500
	Contour	L	2.5 (2507)	6	DOHC	SFI	170@6200	165@4200	3.25x3.13	9.7:1	20-45@1500
	Mystique	3	2.0 (1999)	4	DOHC	SFI	125@5500	130@4500	3.39x3.46	9.6:1	20-45@1500
	Mystique	L	2.5 (2507)	6	DOHC	SFI	170@6200	165@4200	3.25x3.13	9.7:1	20-45@1500
1996	Contour	3	2.0 (1999)	4	DOHC	SFI	125@5500	130@4500	3.39x3.46	9.6:1	20-45@1500
	Contour	L	2.5 (2507)	6	DOHC	SFI	170@6200	165@4200	3.25x3.13	9.7:1	20-45@1500
	Mystique	3	2.0 (1999)	4	DOHC	SFI	125@5500	130@4500	3.39x3.46	9.6:1	20-45@1500
	Mystique	L	2.5 (2507)	6	DOHC	SFI	170@6200	165@4200	3.25x3.13	9.7:1	20-45@1500
1997	Contour	3	2.0 (1999)	4	DOHC	SFI	125@5500	130@4500	3.39x3.46	9.6:1	20-45@1500
	Contour	L	2.5 (2507)	6	DOHC	SFI	170@6200	165@4200	3.25x3.13	9.7:1	20-45@1500
	Mystique	3	2.0 (1999)	4	DOHC	SFI	125@5500	130@4500	3.39x3.46	9.6:1	20-45@1500
	Mystique	L	2.5 (2507)	6	DOHC	SFI	170@6200	165@4200	3.25x3.13	9.7:1	20-45@1500
1998	Contour	3	2.0 (1999)	4	DOHC	SFI	125@5500	130@4500	3.39x3.46	9.6:1	20-45@1500
	Contour	L	2.5 (2507)	6	DOHC	SFI	170@6200	165@4200	3.25x3.13	9.7:1	20-45@1500
	Contour SVT	L①	2.5 (2507)	6	DOHC	SFI	195@6625	165@5600	3.25x3.13	10.0:1	20-45@1500
	Mystique	3	2.0 (1999)	4	DOHC	SFI	125@5500	130@4500	3.39x3.46	9.6:1	20-45@1500
	Mystique	L	2.5 (2507)	6	DOHC	SFI	170@6200	165@4200	3.25x3.13	9.7:1	20-45@1500
1999	Contour	3	2.0 (1999)	4	DOHC	SFI	125@5500	130@4500	3.39x3.46	9.6:1	20-45@1500
	Contour	L	2.5 (2507)	6	DOHC	SFI	170@6200	165@4200	3.25x3.13	9.7:1	20-45@1500
	Contour SVT	L①	2.5 (2507)	6	DOHC	SFI	195@6625	165@5600	3.25x3.13	10.0:1	20-45@1500
	Mystique	3	2.0 (1999)	4	DOHC	SFI	125@5500	130@4500	3.39x3.46	9.6:1	20-45@1500
	Mystique	L	2.5 (2507)	6	DOHC	SFI	170@6200	165@4200	3.25x3.13	9.7:1	20-45@1500
	Cougar	3	2.0 (1999)	4	DOHC	SFI	125@5500	130@4500	3.39x3.46	9.6:1	20-45@1500
	Cougar	L	2.5 (2507)	6	DOHC	SFI	170@6200	165@4200	3.25x3.13	9.7:1	20-45@1500

SFI - Sequential Fuel Injection

DOHC - Double Overhead Camshafts

①The SVT Contour uses the same engine code, the difference is in the body code, which is 68

91051C02

ROUTINE MAINTENANCE AND TUNE-UP

Proper maintenance and tune-up is the key to long and trouble-free vehicle life, and the work can yield its own rewards. Studies have shown that a properly tuned and maintained vehicle can achieve better gas mileage than an out-of-tune vehicle. As a conscientious owner and driver, set aside a Saturday morning, say once a month, to check or replace items which could cause major problems later. Keep your own personal log to jot down which services you performed, how much the parts cost you, the date, and the exact odometer reading at the time. Keep all receipts for such items as engine oil and filters, so that they may be referred to in case of related problems or to determine operating expenses. As a do-it-yourselfer, these receipts are the only proof you have that the required maintenance was performed. In the event of a warranty problem, these receipts will be invaluable.

The literature provided with your vehicle when it was originally delivered includes the factory recommended maintenance schedule. If you no longer have this literature, replacement copies are usually available from the dealer. A maintenance schedule is provided later in this section, in case you do not have the factory literature.

UNDERHOOD MAINTENANCE COMPONENT LOCATIONS—2.0L ENGINE

1. Engine oil fill cap
2. Engine oil dipstick
3. Washer fluid reservoir
4. Coolant recovery tank
5. Power steering reservoir
6. Transaxle dipstick (under air cleaner tube)
7. Master cylinder reservoir
8. Air cleaner
9. Power distribution box
10. Battery

UNDERHOOD MAINTENANCE COMPONENT LOCATIONS—2.5L ENGINE

1. Engine oil dipstick
2. Engine oil fill cap
3. Washer fluid reservoir
4. Coolant recovery tank
5. Power steering reservoir
6. Master cylinder reservoir
7. Transaxle dipstick
8. Air cleaner
9. Power distribution box
10. Battery
11. PVC valve (under cover)

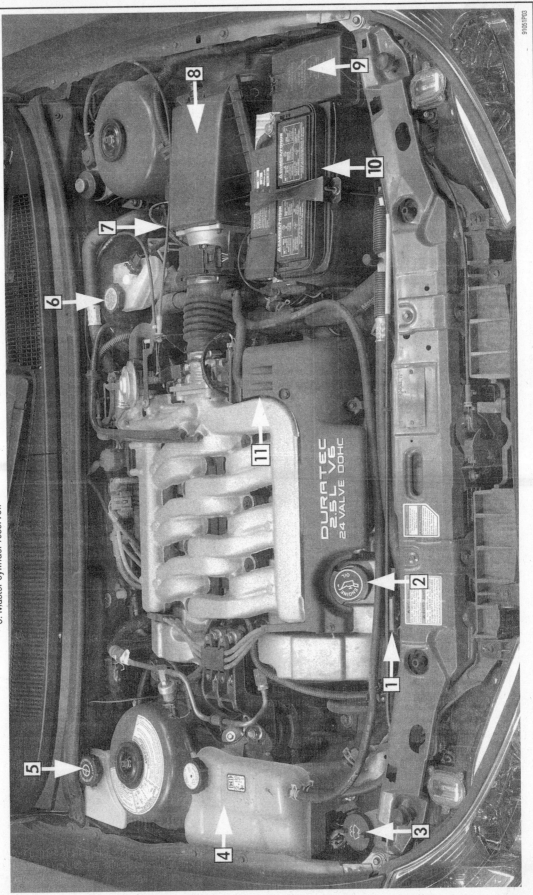

91051P03

Air Cleaner (Element)

REMOVAL & INSTALLATION

▶ See Figures 40, 41, 42 and 43

1. Disconnect the negative battery cable.
2. On the 2.5L engine only:
   a. Loosen the clamps on the air outlet tube from the air cleaner assembly to the mass airflow sensor.
   b. Remove the air outlet tube from the air cleaner assembly.
3. Unplug the MAF sensor connector.
4. Release the retaining clips from the air cleaner housing.
5. Seperate the upper and lower air cleaner housings.
6. Remove the air cleaner element from the housing.
To install:
7. Clean the inside of the air cleaner housing of any dirt and debris that has collected inside.
8. Place a new air cleaner element inside the lower housing. Make sure the seal on the element is fully seated in the groove.
9. Install the upper air cleaner housing onto the lower housing and attach the retaining clips.
10. Plug the connector into the MAF sensor.
11. On the 2.5L engine only:
   a. Install the air outlet tube onto the air cleaner housing.
   b. Tighten the clamps on the tube.
12. Connect the negative battery cable.

Passenger Compartment Air Filter

REMOVAL & INSTALLATION

▶ See Figures 44 thru 55

1. Turn the key to the **ON** position, and turn the windshield wipers on.

When the wipers reach the top of their travel turn the key **OFF**, so they maintain their position there.

2. With the hood closed, remove the plastic covers on the cowl panel cover screws.
3. Remove the screws.
4. Open the hood and pull the weatherstripping on the back of the engine compartment off.
5. Remove the screws under the weatherstripping that retain the cowl panel cover.
6. Seperate the halves of the panel and remove the panel from the vehicle.
7. Remove the two clips that retain the filter housing and remove the housing from the vehicle.
8. Slide the air filter out from the housing.
To install:
9. Clean the housing of any debris and dirt and slide a new filter into the housing.
10. Place the housing into the vehicle and attach the clips.
11. Place the cowl panel into place and install the retaining screws under the weatherstripping.
12. Install the weatherstripping and close the hood.
13. Install the remaining screws and plastic screw covers.
14. Return the windshield wipers to the rest position.

Fuel Filter

REMOVAL & INSTALLATION

▶ See Figures 56 thru 62

➡The in-line fuel filter is located under the vehicle in the rear, near the fuel tank.

✳✳ CAUTION

Observe all applicable safety precautions when working around fuel. Whenever servicing the fuel system, always work in a well

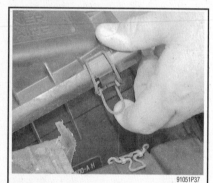

Fig. 40 Grasp and unfasten the retaining clips . . .

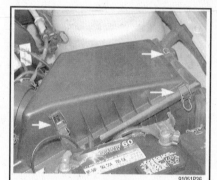

Fig. 41 . . . located at the indicated positions—2.0L engine; 2.5L similar

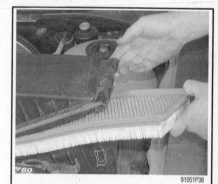

Fig. 42 Lift the lid on the air cleaner box and remove the element

Fig. 43 Pushing the ends of the filter element down enables you to inspect the element's condition

Fig. 44 Place the wiper arms in this position to access the cowl panel cover

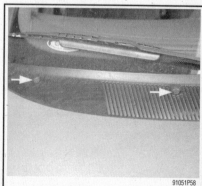

Fig. 45 The two upper trim screws as indicated by the arrows

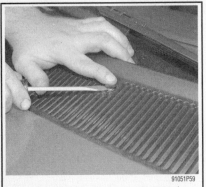

Fig. 46 Gently pry the covers off of the trim screws and . . .

Fig. 47 . . . remove the screws using an appropriate tool

Fig. 48 Grasp the end of the weatherstripping and gently pull up and towards the center of the vehicle to unseat it

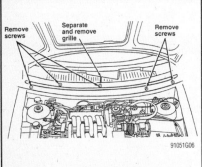

Fig. 49 Remove the panel's three lower retaining bolts as indicated

Fig. 50 Carefully lift the panel up to remove it from the vehicle

Fig. 51 Remove these screws while the hood is closed and . . .

Fig. 52 . . . remove these when the hood is raised and the weatherstripping removed

Fig. 53 The filter element is secured by two retaining clips on the side of the element

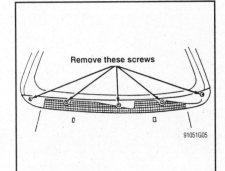

Fig. 54 Unfasten the retaining clips . . .

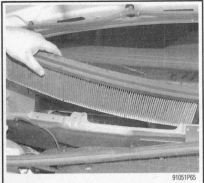

Fig. 55 . . . and remove the air cleaner element

Fig. 56 The fuel filter is located under the vehicle, along the frame rail on the passenger side

Fig. 57 Release the clips holding the fuel lines to the filter by gently prying them from the line. A cotter pin puller works very well for this

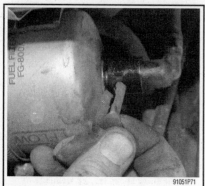

Fig. 58 After the clip's tangs are released, remove the clip from the line

Fig. 59 After the clip is removed, slide the line off of the filter

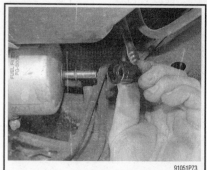

Fig. 60 Inspect the lines for damage, and clean any dirt or build-up around the opening

Fig. 61 Loosen the clamp around the filter and . . .

Fig. 62 . . . remove the filter by sliding it out of the clamp

Fig. 63 Remove the two upper retaining bolts . . .

ventilated area. Do not allow fuel spray or vapors to come in contact with a spark or open flame. Keep a dry chemical fire extinguisher near the work area. Always keep fuel in a container specifically designed for fuel storage; also, always properly seal fuel containers to avoid the possibility of fire or explosion.

1. Disconnect the negative battery cable.
2. Properly relieve the fuel system pressure.
3. Raise and safely support the vehicle securely on jackstands.
4. Remove the two push-connect fittings on the fuel lines. The fittings are removed in the following manner:

   a. Using a small screwdriver or other suitable tool, spread the clip legs outward so that the clip can clear the line.

   b. Using a small screwdriver or other suitable tool (a cotter pin puller works especially well) pull up on the triangular end of the clip to remove the clip.

   c. Pull the connection from the fuel filter and repeat for the other line.

✳✳ CAUTION

Fuel will most likely run out of the line after it is removed from the filter.

5. Loosen the fuel filter retaining clamp.
6. Slide the fuel filter out of the clamp. The fuel filter has a lip on the side facing the filter outlet fitting, always be sure to slide the filter out from this side as the filter will not clear the clamp due to this lip.

To install:

7. Slide the new filter into the clamp and tighten the clamp.
8. Install new clips into the fuel line fittings. The triangular shaped end of the clip should be on the top of the fitting and the point on the clip should face away from the fuel filter.
9. Attach the fuel lines to the filter until an audible click is heard from the connection. Sometimes the click is very quiet, so test the fitting by gently pulling on the line to see if it comes loose.
10. Lower the vehicle

11. Connect the negative battery cable.
12. Start the vehicle and check the filter and lines for leaks.

PCV Valve

REMOVAL & INSTALLATION

➡The dealer will replace your PCV valve at 60,000 miles (except for Canadian and California models) at no charge to ensure the vehicle meets emission standards. After 60,000 miles, the valve is replaced at the cost of the vehicle owner.

2.0L Engine

◗ See Figures 63 thru 78

1. Disconnect the negative battery cable.
2. Raise and support the vehicle.
3. Remove the catalytic converter assembly from the vehicle.

➡The catalytic converter can be removed from the manifold end, moved to access the PCV valve, and supported instead of completely removing it from the vehicle

4. Remove the oil separator retaining bolts and remove the oil separator from the engine.

✳✳ CAUTION

The EPA warns that prolonged contact with used engine oil may cause a number of skin disorders, including cancer! You should make every effort to minimize your exposure to used engine oil. Protective gloves should be worn when changing the oil. Wash your hands and any other exposed skin areas as soon as possible after exposure to used engine oil. Soap and water, or waterless hand cleaner should be used.

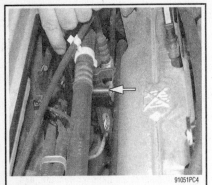

Fig. 64 . . . and the two lower retaining bolts . . .

Fig. 65 . . . then lift the exhaust manifold heat shield up and remove it from the engine

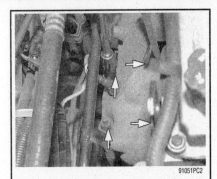

Fig. 66 Remove the four catalytic converter-to-exhaust manifold retaining nuts and bolts

Fig. 67 From under the vehicle, remove the EGR tube from the manifold . . .

Fig. 68 . . . and the rear support bracket retaining bolts . . .

Fig. 69 . . . as well as the front support bracket retaining bolts

Fig. 70 Carefully lower the catalytic converter from the exhaust manifold . . .

Fig. 71 . . . and support the converter using a bungee strap or other suitable device

Fig. 72 The PCV valve connects into the oil separator

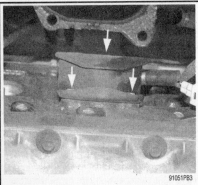

Fig. 73 The oil separator is secured to the engine block by three retaining bolts

Fig. 74 Remove the three retaining bolts . . .

Fig. 75 . . . and remove the oil separator from the engine block

Fig. 76 Pull the PCV valve from the oil separator and disconnect it from the PCV tube

Fig. 77 Inspect the rubber gasket for the PCV valve

Fig. 78 Replace the oil separator gasket before reinstalling the oil separator

5. Remove the PCV valve from the oil separator.

To install:

6. Inspect the grommet on the oil separator. If necessary, replace the grommet.

7. Install a new valve in the oil separator.

8. Place a new gasket on the oil separator and install the oil separator on the engine. Tighten the retaining bolts to 71–97 inch lbs. (8–11 Nm).

9. Install the catalytic converter.

10. Lower the vehicle.

11. Connect the negative battery cable.

2.5L Engine

▶ See Figure 79

1. Disconnect the negative battery cable.

2. Remove the IAC valve tube from the upper intake manifold and the air inlet tube and remove the tube.

3. Remove the EVAP hose from the PCV valve.

4. Remove the vacuum hose from the throttle body.

5. Remove the PCV from the oil separator tube.

To install:

6. Inspect the oil separator tube for wear. Replace if necessary.

7. Install a new valve in the oil separator tube.

8. Replace the hoses and air tubes removed.

9. Connect the negative battery cable.

Evaporative Canister

SERVICING

▶ See Figure 80

The evaporative canister requires no periodic servicing. However, a careful inspection of the canister and hoses should be made frequently. Replace damaged components as required.

The canister is located underneath the vehicle near the fuel tank.

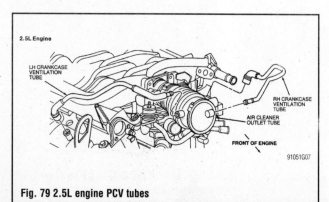

Fig. 79 2.5L engine PCV tubes

Fig. 80 The evaporative canister is inside a protective cover beneath the spare tire well

Battery

PRECAUTIONS

Always use caution when working on or near the battery. Never allow a tool to bridge the gap between the negative and positive battery terminals. Also, be careful not to allow a tool to provide a ground between the positive cable/terminal and any metal component on the vehicle. Either of these conditions will cause a short circuit, leading to sparks and possible personal injury.

Do not smoke, have an open flame or create sparks near a battery; the gases contained in the battery are very explosive and, if ignited, could cause severe injury or death.

All batteries, regardless of type, should be carefully secured by a battery hold-down device. If this is not done, the battery terminals or casing may crack from stress applied to the battery during vehicle operation. A battery which is not secured may allow acid to leak out, making it discharge faster; such leaking corrosive acid can also eat away at components under the hood.

Always visually inspect the battery case for cracks, leakage and corrosion. A white corrosive substance on the battery case or on nearby components would indicate a leaking or cracked battery. If the battery is cracked, it should be replaced immediately.

GENERAL MAINTENANCE

▶ See Figure 81

A battery that is not sealed must be checked periodically for electrolyte level. You cannot add water to a sealed maintenance-free battery (though not all maintenance-free batteries are sealed); however, a sealed battery must also be checked for proper electrolyte level, as indicated by the color of the built-in hydrometer "eye."

Always keep the battery cables and terminals free of corrosion. Check these components about once a year. Refer to the removal, installation and cleaning procedures outlined in this section.

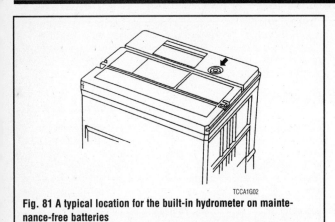

Fig. 81 A typical location for the built-in hydrometer on maintenance-free batteries

Keep the top of the battery clean, as a film of dirt can help completely discharge a battery that is not used for long periods. A solution of baking soda and water may be used for cleaning, but be careful to flush this off with clear water. DO NOT let any of the solution into the filler holes. Baking soda neutralizes battery acid and will de-activate a battery cell.

Batteries in vehicles which are not operated on a regular basis can fall victim to parasitic loads (small current drains which are constantly drawing current from the battery). Normal parasitic loads may drain a battery on a vehicle that is in storage and not used for 6–8 weeks. Vehicles that have additional accessories such as a cellular phone, an alarm system or other devices that increase parasitic load may discharge a battery sooner. If the vehicle is to be stored for 6–8 weeks in a secure area and the alarm system, if present, is not necessary, the negative battery cable should be disconnected at the onset of storage to protect the battery charge.

Remember that constantly discharging and recharging will shorten battery life. Take care not to allow a battery to be needlessly discharged.

BATTERY FLUID

Check the battery electrolyte level at least once a month, or more often in hot weather or during periods of extended vehicle operation. On non-sealed batteries, the level can be checked either through the case on translucent batteries or by removing the cell caps on opaque-cased types. The electrolyte level in each cell should be kept filled to the split ring inside each cell, or the line marked on the outside of the case.

If the level is low, add only distilled water through the opening until the level is correct. Each cell is separate from the others, so each must be checked and filled individually. Distilled water should be used, because the chemicals and minerals found in most drinking water are harmful to the battery and could significantly shorten its life.

If water is added in freezing weather, the vehicle should be driven several miles to allow the water to mix with the electrolyte. Otherwise, the battery could freeze.

Although some maintenance-free batteries have removable cell caps for access to the electrolyte, the electrolyte condition and level on all sealed maintenance-free batteries must be checked using the built-in hydrometer "eye." The exact type of eye varies between battery manufacturers, but most apply a sticker to the battery itself explaining the possible readings. When in doubt, refer to the battery manufacturer's instructions to interpret battery condition using the built-in hydrometer.

➡**Although the readings from built-in hydrometers found in sealed batteries may vary, a green eye usually indicates a properly charged battery with sufficient fluid level. A dark eye is normally an indicator of a battery with sufficient fluid, but one which may be low in charge. And a light or yellow eye is usually an indication that electrolyte supply has dropped below the necessary level for battery (and hydrometer) operation. In this last case, sealed batteries with an insufficient electrolyte level must usually be discarded.**

Checking the Specific Gravity

▶ See Figures 82, 83 and 84

A hydrometer is required to check the specific gravity on all batteries that are not maintenance-free. On batteries that are maintenance-free, the specific gravity is checked by observing the built-in hydrometer eye on the top of the battery case. Check with your battery's manufacturer for proper interpretation of its built-in hydrometer readings.

❋❋ CAUTION

Battery electrolyte contains sulfuric acid. If you should splash any on your skin or in your eyes, flush the affected area with plenty of clear water. If it lands in your eyes, get medical help immediately.

The fluid (sulfuric acid solution) contained in the battery cells will tell you many things about the condition of the battery. Because the cell plates must be kept submerged below the fluid level in order to operate, maintaining the fluid level is extremely important. And, because the specific gravity of the acid is an indication of electrical charge, testing the fluid can be an aid in determining if the battery must be replaced. A battery in a vehicle with a properly operating charging system should require little maintenance, but careful, periodic inspection should reveal problems before they leave you stranded.

As stated earlier, the specific gravity of a battery's electrolyte level can be used as an indication of battery charge. At least once a year, check the specific gravity of the battery. It should be between 1.20 and 1.26 on the gravity scale. Most auto supply stores carry a variety of inexpensive battery testing hydrometers. These can be used on any non-sealed battery to test the specific gravity in each cell.

The battery testing hydrometer has a squeeze bulb at one end and a nozzle at the other. Battery electrolyte is sucked into the hydrometer until the float is lifted from its seat. The specific gravity is then read by noting the position of the float. If gravity is low in one or more cells, the battery should be slowly charged and checked again to see if the gravity has come up. Generally, if after charging, the specific gravity between any two cells varies more than 50 points (0.50), the battery should be replaced, as it can no longer produce sufficient voltage to guarantee proper operation.

Fig. 82 On non-maintenance-free batteries, the fluid level can be checked through the case on translucent models; the cell caps must be removed on other models

Fig. 83 If the fluid level is low, add only distilled water through the opening until the level is correct

Fig. 84 Check the specific gravity of the battery's electrolyte with a hydrometer

CABLES

▶ See Figures 85, 86, 87, 88 and 89

Once a year (or as necessary), the battery terminals and the cable clamps should be cleaned. Loosen the clamps and remove the cables, negative cable first. On batteries with posts on top, the use of a puller specially made for this purpose is recommended. These are inexpensive and available in most auto parts stores. Side terminal battery cables are secured with a small bolt.

Clean the cable clamps and the battery terminal with a wire brush, until all corrosion, grease, etc., is removed and the metal is shiny. It is especially important to clean the inside of the clamp thoroughly (an old knife is useful here), since a small deposit of foreign material or oxidation there will prevent a sound electrical connection and inhibit either starting or charging. Special tools are available for cleaning these parts, one type for conventional top post batteries and another type for side terminal batteries. It is also a good idea to apply some dielectric grease to the terminal, as this will aid in the prevention of corrosion.

After the clamps and terminals are clean, reinstall the cables, negative cable last; DO NOT hammer the clamps onto battery posts. Tighten the clamps securely, but do not distort them. Give the clamps and terminals a thin external coating of grease after installation, to retard corrosion.

Check the cables at the same time that the terminals are cleaned. If the cable insulation is cracked or broken, or if the ends are frayed, the cable should be replaced with a new cable of the same length and gauge.

CHARGING

> **❋❋ CAUTION**
>
> **The chemical reaction which takes place in all batteries generates explosive hydrogen gas. A spark can cause the battery to explode and splash acid. To avoid serious personal injury, be sure there is proper ventilation and take appropriate fire safety precautions when connecting, disconnecting, or charging a battery and when using jumper cables.**

A battery should be charged at a slow rate to keep the plates inside from getting too hot. However, if some maintenance-free batteries are allowed to discharge until they are almost "dead," they may have to be charged at a high rate to bring them back to "life." Always follow the charger manufacturer's instructions on charging the battery.

REPLACEMENT

When it becomes necessary to replace the battery, select one with an amperage rating equal to or greater than the battery originally installed. Deterioration and just plain aging of the battery cables, starter motor, and associated wires makes the battery's job harder in successive years. The slow increase in electrical resistance over time makes it prudent to install a new battery.

Belts

INSPECTION

▶ See Figures 90, 91, 92, 93 and 94

Inspect the belts for signs of glazing or cracking. A glazed belt will be perfectly smooth from slippage, while a good belt will have a slight texture of fabric visible. Cracks will usually start at the inner edge of the belt and run outward. All worn or damaged drive belts should be replaced immediately. It is best to replace all drive belts at one time, as a preventive maintenance measure, during this service operation.

ADJUSTMENT

▶ See Figures 95 and 96

All engines use an automatic drive belt tensioner. No adjustment is necessary. It is recommended that the belt tension indicator mark be inspected with the engine **OFF** at 60,000 mile (96,000 km) intervals. If the indicator

Fig. 85 Maintenance is performed with household items and with special tools like this post cleaner

Fig. 86 The underside of this special battery tool has a wire brush to clean post terminals

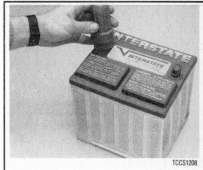

Fig. 87 Place the tool over the battery posts and twist to clean until the metal is shiny

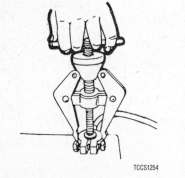

Fig. 88 A special tool is available to pull the clamp from the post

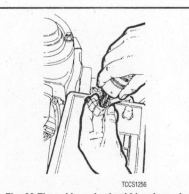

Fig. 89 The cable ends should be cleaned as well

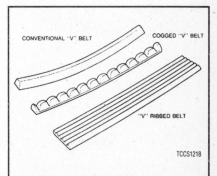

Fig. 90 There are typically 3 types of accessory drive belts found on vehicles today

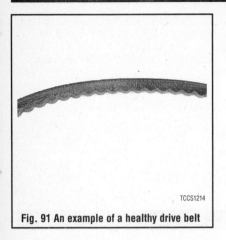

Fig. 91 An example of a healthy drive belt

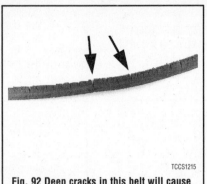

Fig. 92 Deep cracks in this belt will cause flex, building up heat that will eventually lead to belt failure

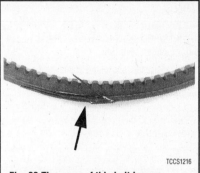

Fig. 93 The cover of this belt is worn, exposing the critical reinforcing cords to excessive wear

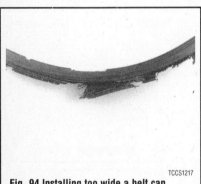

Fig. 94 Installing too wide a belt can result in serious belt wear and/or breakage

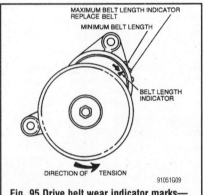

Fig. 95 Drive belt wear indicator marks—2.0L engine

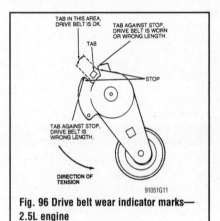

Fig. 96 Drive belt wear indicator marks—2.5L engine

mark is not between the MIN and MAX marks on the tensioner for the 2.0L engine or the indicator mark between the tabs on the front engine cover on the 2.5L engine, the drive belt is worn or an incorrect drive belt has been installed.

REMOVAL & INSTALLATION

▶ See Figure 97

➡On the 2.5L engine, the water pump is located on the back of the engine and is driven by a separate belt. See the procedure for water pump belt for replacement.

Accessory Drive Belt

▶ See Figures 98 thru 103

1. Disconnect the negative battery cable.

➡The proper belt routing is included in this section, however, it is a good idea to make a simple drawing of the belt routing of your engine for installation reference before removing the belt.

2. Rotate the drive belt tensioner to relieve the belt tension. The procedure is as follows:
    a. On the 2.5L engine, use a ⅜ drive tool or a special belt removal tool to rotate the tensioner clockwise.
    b. On the 2.0L engine, use a 13mm socket and drive tool or a special belt removal tool to rotate the tensioner clockwise.
    c. While holding the tensioner back, remove the belt from around one pulley.
3. Remove the belt from around the remaining pulleys.
To install:
4. Position the belt around the pulleys in the proper routing with the exception of one pulley. It is easiest to keep the belt off of the easiest pulley to access. Hold the belt tight with your hands and using the proper tool for your engine, rotate the tensioner clockwise and place the belt around the final pulley.

Fig. 97 The belt routing can be found on a label affixed to the strut tower

Fig. 98 The automatic tensioner pivot bolt (motor mount removed)—2.0L engine

Fig. 99 Due to limited space, a special belt tensioner tool is helpful for reaching the pivot bolt

5. Release the tensioner slowly until it sits firmly against the belt.

➡ **If the tensioner does not touch the belt or the wear indicator marks are not within specification, the belt is routed incorrectly or the wrong belt has been installed.**

6. Connect the negative battery cable.

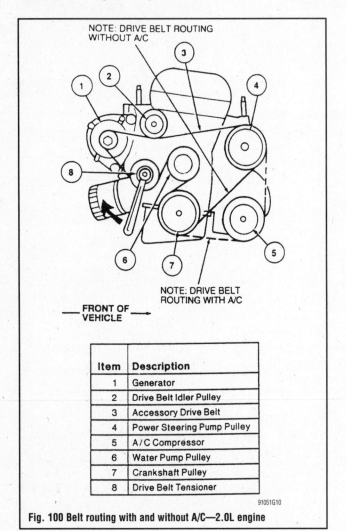

NOTE: DRIVE BELT ROUTING WITHOUT A/C

NOTE: DRIVE BELT ROUTING WITH A/C

→ FRONT OF VEHICLE →

Item	Description
1	Generator
2	Drive Belt Idler Pulley
3	Accessory Drive Belt
4	Power Steering Pump Pulley
5	A/C Compressor
6	Water Pump Pulley
7	Crankshaft Pulley
8	Drive Belt Tensioner

91051G10

Fig. 100 Belt routing with and without A/C—2.0L engine

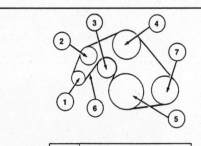

Item	Description
1	Generator
2	Drive Belt Idler Pulley
3	Drive Belt Tensioner
4	Power Steering Pump Pulley
5	Crankshaft Pulley
6	Accessory Drive Belt
7	A/C Compressor

91051G12

Fig. 101 Belt routing with A/C—2.5L engine

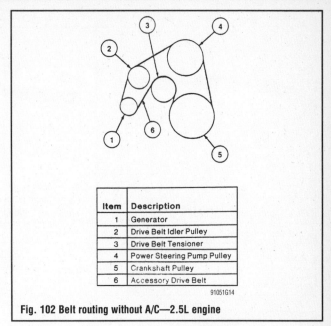

Item	Description
1	Generator
2	Drive Belt Idler Pulley
3	Drive Belt Tensioner
4	Power Steering Pump Pulley
5	Crankshaft Pulley
6	Accessory Drive Belt

91051G14

Fig. 102 Belt routing without A/C—2.5L engine

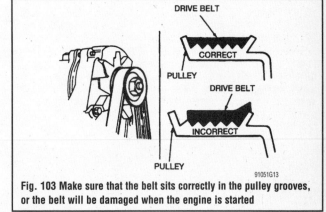

DRIVE BELT

CORRECT

PULLEY

DRIVE BELT

INCORRECT

PULLEY

91051G13

Fig. 103 Make sure that the belt sits correctly in the pulley grooves, or the belt will be damaged when the engine is started

2.5L Water Pump Belt

▶ **See Figure 104**

1. Disconnect the negative battery cable.
2. Remove the water pump drive pulley cover.
3. Rotate the belt tensioner clockwise by hand and remove the belt.

To install:

4. Place the belt around the pulleys except for the tensioner pulley.
5. Rotate the tensioner pulley clockwise by hand and install the belt over the tensioner pulley.
6. Release the tensioner and check the belt tension.
7. Install the water pump pulley.
8. Connect the negative battery cable.

Timing Belts

MAINTENANCE INTERVAL

The 2.0L engine in your Contour/Mystique/Cougar utilizes a timing belt to drive the camshaft from the crankshaft's turning motion, and to maintain proper valve timing. Some manufacturers recommend periodic timing belt replacement to assure optimum engine performance, and to make sure the motorist is never stranded should the belt break (as the engine will stop instantly). On some vehicles (those with interference engines), this is especially important to prevent the possibility of severe internal engine damage, should the belt break.

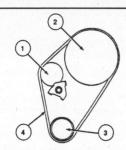

Item	Description
1	Drive Belt Tensioner
2	Water Pump Drive Pulley
3	Water Pump
4	Water Pump Drive Belt

91051G08

Fig. 104 Water pump belt routing—2.5L engine

✳✳ CAUTION

The 2.0L engine is an interference motor. Extending the replacement interval could lead to the belt breaking and severe and costly engine damage. Although Ford does not publish a replacement interval for the 2.0L engine, most belt manufacturers recommend intervals anywhere from 45,000 miles (72,500 km) to 90,000 miles (145,000 km). You will have to decide for yourself if the peace of mind offered by a new belt is worth the effort and expense on higher mileage engines.

Whether or not you do decide to replace the timing belt, you would be wise to check it periodically to make sure it has not become damaged or worn. Generally speaking, a severely worn belt may cause engine performance to drop dramatically, but a damaged belt (which could give out suddenly) may not give as much warning. In general, any time the engine timing cover(s) is (are) removed, you should inspect the belt for premature parting, severe cracks or missing teeth. Also, an access plug may be provided in the upper portion of the timing cover, so that camshaft timing can be checked without cover removal. If timing is found to be off, cover removal and further belt inspection or replacement is necessary. Service and inspection procedures for the timing belt can be found in Section 3.

Hoses

INSPECTION

▶ See Figures 105, 106, 107 and 108

Upper and lower radiator hoses, along with the heater hoses, should be checked for deterioration, leaks and loose hose clamps at least every 15,000 miles (24,000 km). It is also wise to check the hoses periodically in early spring and at the beginning of the fall or winter when you are performing other maintenance. A quick visual inspection could discover a weakened hose which might have left you stranded if it had remained unrepaired.

Whenever you are checking the hoses, make sure the engine and cooling system are cold. Visually inspect for cracking, rotting or collapsed hoses, and replace as necessary. Run your hand along the length of the hose. If a weak or swollen spot is noted when squeezing the hose wall, the hose should be replaced.

REMOVAL & INSTALLATION

▶ See Figure 109

1. Remove the radiator pressure cap.

TCCS1219

Fig. 105 The cracks developing along this hose are a result of age-related hardening

TCCS1220

Fig. 106 A hose clamp that is too tight can cause older hoses to separate and tear on either side of the clamp

TCCS1221

Fig. 107 A soft spongy hose (identifiable by the swollen section) will eventually burst and should be replaced

TCCS1222

Fig. 108 Hoses are likely to deteriorate from the inside if the cooling system is not periodically flushed

91051PC8

Fig. 109 The heater hoses are best accessed from underneath the vehicle

✳✳ CAUTION

Never remove the pressure cap while the engine is running, or personal injury from scalding hot coolant or steam may result. If possible, wait until the engine has cooled to remove the pressure cap. If this is not possible, wrap a thick cloth around the pressure cap and turn it slowly to the stop. Step back while the pressure is released from the cooling system. When you are sure all the pressure has been released, use the cloth to turn and remove the cap.

2. Position a clean container under the radiator and/or engine draincock or plug, then open the drain and allow the cooling system to drain to an appropriate level. For some upper hoses, only a little coolant must be drained. To remove hoses positioned lower on the engine, such as a lower radiator hose, the entire cooling system must be emptied.

✳✳ CAUTION

When draining coolant, keep in mind that cats and dogs are attracted by ethylene glycol antifreeze, and are quite likely to drink any that is left in an uncovered container or in puddles on the ground. This will prove fatal in sufficient quantity. Always drain coolant into a sealable container. Coolant may be reused unless it is contaminated or several years old.

3. Loosen the hose clamps at each end of the hose requiring replacement. Clamps are usually either of the spring tension type (which require pliers to squeeze the tabs and loosen) or of the screw tension type (which require screw or hex drivers to loosen). Pull the clamps back on the hose away from the connection.
4. Twist, pull and slide the hose off the fitting, taking care not to damage the neck of the component from which the hose is being removed.

➡️If the hose is stuck at the connection, do not try to insert a screwdriver or other sharp tool under the hose end in an effort to free it, as the connection and/or hose may become damaged. Heater connections especially may be easily damaged by such a procedure. If the hose is to be replaced, use a single-edged razor blade to make a slice along the portion of the hose which is stuck on the connection, perpendicular to the end of the hose. Do not cut deep so as to prevent damaging the connection. The hose can then be peeled from the connection and discarded.

5. Clean both hose mounting connections. Inspect the condition of the hose clamps and replace them, if necessary.
   To install:
6. Dip the ends of the new hose into clean engine coolant to ease installation.
7. Slide the clamps over the replacement hose, then slide the hose ends over the connections into position.
8. Position and secure the clamps at least ¼ in. (6.35mm) from the ends of the hose. Make sure they are located beyond the raised bead of the connector.
9. Close the radiator or engine drains and properly refill the cooling system with the clean drained engine coolant or a suitable mixture of ethylene glycol coolant and water.
10. If available, install a pressure tester and check for leaks. If a pressure

tester is not available, run the engine until normal operating temperature is reached (allowing the system to naturally pressurize), then check for leaks.

✳✳ CAUTION

If you are checking for leaks with the system at normal operating temperature, BE EXTREMELY CAREFUL not to touch any moving or hot engine parts. Once temperature has been reached, shut the engine OFF, and check for leaks around the hose fittings and connections which were removed earlier.

CV-Boots

INSPECTION

▶ See Figures 110 and 111

The CV (Constant Velocity) boots should be checked for damage each time the oil is changed and any other time the vehicle is raised for service. These boots keep water, grime, dirt and other damaging matter from entering the CV-joints. Any of these could cause early CV-joint failure which can be expensive to repair. Heavy grease thrown around the inside of the front wheel(s) and on the brake caliper/drum can be an indication of a torn boot. Thoroughly check the boots for missing clamps and tears. If the boot is damaged, it should be replaced immediately. Please refer to Section 7 for procedures.

Spark Plugs

▶ See Figure 112

A typical spark plug consists of a metal shell surrounding a ceramic insulator. A metal electrode extends downward through the center of the insulator and protrudes a small distance. Located at the end of the plug and attached to the side of the outer metal shell is the side electrode. The side electrode bends in at a 90° angle so that its tip is just past and parallel to the tip of the center electrode. The distance between these two electrodes (measured in thousandths of an inch or hundredths of a millimeter) is called the spark plug gap.

The spark plug does not produce a spark, but instead provides a gap across which the current can arc. The coil produces anywhere from 20,000 to 50,000 volts (depending on the type and application) which travels through the wires to the spark plugs. The current passes along the center electrode and jumps the gap to the side electrode, and in doing so, ignites the air/fuel mixture in the combustion chamber.

SPARK PLUG HEAT RANGE

▶ See Figure 113

Spark plug heat range is the ability of the plug to dissipate heat. The longer the insulator (or the farther it extends into the engine), the hotter the plug will operate; the shorter the insulator (the closer the electrode is to the block's cooling passages) the cooler it will operate. A plug that absorbs little heat and

Fig. 110 CV-boots must be inspected periodically for damage

Fig. 111 A torn boot should be replaced immediately

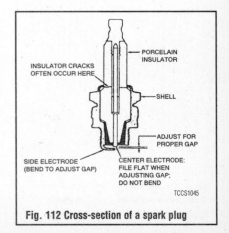

Fig. 112 Cross-section of a spark plug

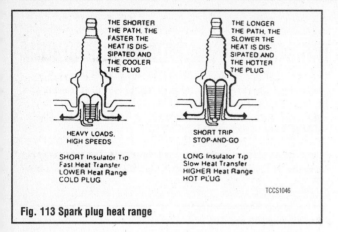

Fig. 113 Spark plug heat range

Within the figure:
THE SHORTER THE PATH, THE FASTER THE HEAT IS DISSIPATED AND THE COOLER THE PLUG

THE LONGER THE PATH, THE SLOWER THE HEAT IS DISSIPATED AND THE HOTTER THE PLUG

HEAVY LOADS, HIGH SPEEDS

SHORT Insulator Tip
Fast Heat Transfer
LOWER Heat Range
COLD PLUG

SHORT TRIP STOP-AND-GO

LONG Insulator Tip
Slow Heat Transfer
HIGHER Heat Range
HOT PLUG

TCCS1046

remains too cool will quickly accumulate deposits of oil and carbon since it is not hot enough to burn them off. This leads to plug fouling and consequently to misfiring. A plug that absorbs too much heat will have no deposits but, due to the excessive heat, the electrodes will burn away quickly and might possibly lead to preignition or other ignition problems. Preignition takes place when plug tips get so hot that they glow sufficiently to ignite the air/fuel mixture before the actual spark occurs. This early ignition will usually cause a pinging during low speeds and heavy loads.

The general rule of thumb for choosing the correct heat range when picking a spark plug is: if most of your driving is long distance, high speed travel, use a colder plug; if most of your driving is stop and go, use a hotter plug. Original equipment plugs are generally a good compromise between the 2 styles and most people never have the need to change their plugs from the factory-recommended heat range.

REMOVAL & INSTALLATION

▶ **See Figures 114 thru 119**

A set of spark plugs usually requires replacement after about 20,000–30,000 miles (32,000–48,000 km), depending on your style of driving. In normal operation plug gap increases about 0.001 in. (0.025mm) for every 2500 miles (4000 km). As the gap increases, the plug's voltage requirement also increases. It requires a greater voltage to jump the wider gap and about two to three times as much voltage to fire the plug at high speeds than at idle. The improved air/fuel ratio control of modern fuel injection, combined with the higher voltage output of modern ignition systems, will often allow an engine to run significantly longer on a set of standard spark plugs, but keep in mind that efficiency will drop as the gap widens (along with fuel economy and power).

When you're removing spark plugs, work on one at a time. Don't start by removing the plug wires all at once, because, unless you number them, they may become mixed up. Take a minute before you begin and number the wires with tape.

1. Disconnect the negative battery cable.
2. If the vehicle has been run recently, allow the engine to thoroughly cool.
3. Remove the spark plug cover(s), if equipped.
4. On the 2.5L engine remove the ignition coil assembly from the rear valve cover. See Section 2 for the procedure. Remove the water pump pulley cover.
5. Carefully twist the spark plug wire boot to loosen it, then pull upward and remove the boot from the plug. Be sure to pull on the boot and not on the wire, otherwise the connector located inside the boot may become separated.
6. Using compressed air, blow any water or debris from the spark plug well to assure that no harmful contaminants are allowed to enter the combustion chamber when the spark plug is removed. If compressed air is not available, use a vacuum to clean the area.

➡ **Remove the spark plugs when the engine is cold, if possible, to prevent damage to the threads. If removal of the plugs is difficult, apply a few drops of penetrating oil or silicone spray to the area around the base of the plug, and allow it a few minutes to work.**

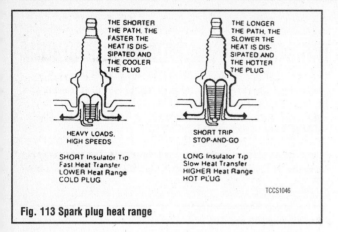

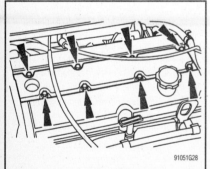

Fig. 114 On some later models, it is necessary to remove a cover to access the spark plugs

91051G28

Fig. 115 Carefully twist the boot end of the spark plug wire . . .

91051P07

Fig. 116 . . . and withdraw the spark plug wire boot from the cylinder head

91051P08

Fig. 117 Using the appropriate sized spark plug socket, necessary extensions and drive tools, remove the plug from the engine—the spark plugs are usually ⅝

91051P09

Fig. 118 After removing the plug from the engine, inspect it using the spark plug condition charts in this section to determine the running condition of your engine

91051P10

Fig. 119 When installing the plugs into the engine, start the plugs by hand. A piece of hose or rubber fuel line makes this job easier

91051P11

7. Using a spark plug socket that is equipped with a rubber insert to properly hold the plug, turn the spark plug counterclockwise to loosen and remove the spark plug from the bore.

❊❊ WARNING

Be sure not to use a flexible extension on the socket. Use of a flexible extension may allow a shear force to be applied to the plug. A shear force could break the plug off in the cylinder head, leading to costly and frustrating repairs.

8. Remove each plug and inspect the plug even if you are replacing them with new ones. An inspection can reveal a great deal of information on the overall condition of an engine. Use the condition charts in this section as a guide.

To install:

9. Inspect the spark plug boot for tears or damage. If a damaged boot is found, the spark plug wire must be replaced.

10. Using a wire feeler gauge, check and adjust the spark plug gap. When using a gauge, the proper size should pass between the electrodes with a slight drag. The next larger size should not be able to pass while the next smaller size should pass freely.

11. Carefully thread the plug into the bore by hand. A handy tool to use to install spark plugs are the flexible rubber installation tools that are available at most auto parts stores, in place of this tool an old plug wire boot or a piece of fuel line long enough to fit to the plug hole is a good alternative. If resistance is felt before the plug is almost completely threaded, back the plug out and begin threading again.

12. Carefully tighten the spark plug. If the plug you are installing is equipped with a crush washer, seat the plug, then tighten about ¼ turn to crush the washer. If you are installing a tapered seat plug, tighten the plug to specifications provided by the vehicle or plug manufacturer.

13. Apply a small amount of silicone dielectric compound to the end of the spark plug lead or inside the spark plug boot to prevent sticking, then install the boot to the spark plug and push until it clicks into place. The click may be felt or heard, then gently pull back on the boot to assure proper contact.

14. On the 2.5L engine, install the coil pack and the water pump pulley.

15. Install the spark plug cover(s), if removed.

16. Connect the negative battery cable.

INSPECTION & GAPPING

◗ See Figures 120, 121, 122, 123 and 124

Check the plugs for deposits and wear. If they are not going to be replaced, clean the plugs thoroughly. Remember that any kind of deposit will decrease the efficiency of the plug. Plugs can be cleaned on a spark plug cleaning machine, which can sometimes be found in service stations, or you can do an acceptable job of cleaning with a stiff brush. If the plugs are cleaned, the electrodes must be filed flat. Use an ignition points file, not an emery board or the like, which will leave deposits. The electrodes must be filed perfectly flat with sharp edges; rounded edges reduce the spark plug voltage by as much as 50%.

Check spark plug gap before installation. The ground electrode (the L-shaped one connected to the body of the plug) must be parallel to the center electrode and the specified size wire gauge (please refer to the Tune-Up Specifications chart for details) must pass between the electrodes with a slight drag.

➡ **NEVER adjust the gap on a used platinum type spark plug.**

Always check the gap on new plugs as they are not always set correctly at the factory. Do not use a flat feeler gauge when measuring the gap on a used plug, because the reading may be inaccurate. A round-wire type gapping tool is the best way to check the gap. The correct gauge should pass through the electrode gap with a slight drag. If you're in doubt, try one size smaller and one larger. The smaller gauge should go through easily, while the larger one shouldn't go through at all. Wire gapping tools usually have a bending tool attached. Use that to adjust the side electrode until the proper distance is obtained. Absolutely never attempt to bend the center electrode. Also, be careful not to bend the side electrode too far or too often as it may weaken and break off within the engine, requiring removal of the cylinder head to retrieve it.

Spark Plug Wires

TESTING

◗ See Figures 125 and 126

At every tune-up/inspection, visually check the spark plug cables for burns cuts, or breaks in the insulation. Check the boots and the nipples on the distributor cap and/or coil. Replace any damaged wiring.

Every 50,000 miles (80,000 km) or 60 months, the resistance of the wires should be checked with an ohmmeter. Wires with excessive resistance will cause misfiring, and may make the engine difficult to start in damp weather.

To check resistance, an ohmmeter should be used on each wire to test resistance between the end connectors. Remove and install/replace the wires in order, one-by-one.

Resistance on these wires should be 4,000–6,000 ohms per foot. To properly measure this, remove the wires from the plugs and the coil pack. Do not pierce any ignition wire for any reason. Measure only from the two ends. Take the length and multiply it by 6,000 to achieve the maximum resistance allowable in each wire, resistance should not exceed this value. If resistance does exceed this value, replace the wire.

➡ **Whenever the high tension wires are removed from the plugs, coil, or distributor, silicone grease must be applied to the boot before reconnection. Coat the entire interior surface with Ford silicone grease D7AZ-19A331-A or its equivalent.**

REMOVAL & INSTALLATION

◗ See Figures 127 thru 135

1. Remove the air cleaner inlet tube.
2. Label each spark plug wire and make a note of its routing.

TCCS1212
Fig. 120 A variety of tools and gauges are needed for spark plug service

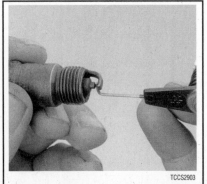
TCCS2903
Fig. 121 Checking the spark plug gap with a feeler gauge

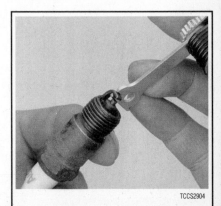
TCCS2904
Fig. 122 Adjusting the spark plug gap

A normally worn spark plug should have light tan or gray deposits on the firing tip.

A carbon fouled plug, identified by soft, sooty, black deposits, may indicate an improperly tuned vehicle. Check the air cleaner, ignition components and engine control system.

This spark plug has been **left in the engine too long,** as evidenced by the extreme gap- Plugs with such an extreme gap can cause misfiring and stumbling accompanied by a noticeable lack of power.

An **oil fouled** spark plug indicates an engine with worn poston rings and/or bad valve seals allowing excessive oil to enter the chamber.

A physically dam-aged spark plug may be evidence of severe detonation in that cylinder. Watch that cylinder carefully between services, as a continued detonation will not only damage the plug, but could also damage the engine.

A bridged or almost bridged spark plug, identified by a build-up between the electrodes caused by excessive carbon or oil build-up on the plug.

TCCA1P40

Fig. 123 Inspect the spark plug to determine engine running conditions

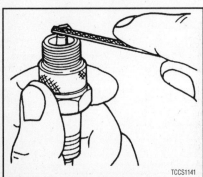
TCCS1141
Fig. 124 If the standard plug is in good condition, the electrode may be filed flat—WARNING: do not file platinum plugs

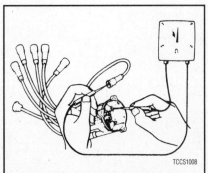
TCCS1008
Fig. 125 Checking plug wire resistance through the distributor cap with an ohmmeter

TCCS1009
Fig. 126 Checking individual plug wire resistance with a digital ohmmeter

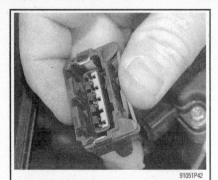

Fig. 127 The MAF connector is released by pressing down on the retaining spring—shown here already disconnected

Fig. 128 Label and disconnect the MAF sensor . . .

Fig. 129 . . . and the IAT sensor

Fig. 130 Loosen the clamp on the air cleaner tube

Fig. 131 Lift the air cleaner inlet tube slightly and slide the retaining tab on the air intake resonator out . . .

Fig. 132 . . . then remove the air cleaner inlet tube from the vehicle

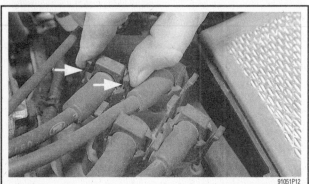

Fig. 133 Press the retaining tabs on the plug wire connections at the coil pack . . .

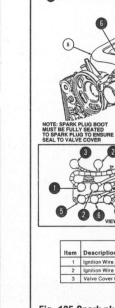

Fig. 134 . . . and lift the plug wire from the coil pack

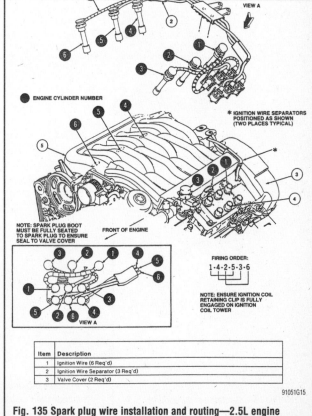

FIRING ORDER:
1-4-2-5-3-6

Item	Description
1	Ignition Wire (6 Req'd)
2	Ignition Wire Separator (3 Req'd)
3	Valve Cover (2 Req'd)

Fig. 135 Spark plug wire installation and routing—2.5L engine

➡Don't rely on wiring diagrams or sketches for spark plug wire routing. Improper arrangement of spark plug wires will induce voltage between wires, causing misfiring and surging. Be careful to arrange spark plug wires properly.

3. Starting with the longest wire, disconnect the spark plug wire from the spark plug and then from the coil pack (2.5L) or distributor cap (2.0L).

4. Disconnect the ignition wire from the coil pack by squeezing the locking tabs and twisting while pulling upward.

To install:

5. If replacing the spark plug wires, match the old wire with an appropriately sized wire in the new set.

6. Lubricate the boots and terminals with dielectric grease and install the wire on the coil pack. Make sure the wire snaps into place.

7. Route the wire in the exact path as the original and connect the wire to the spark plug.

8. Repeat the process for each remaining wire, working from the longest wire to the shortest.

9. Install the air cleaner inlet tube.

Ignition Timing

GENERAL INFORMATION

♦ **See Figures 136, 137 and 138**

Periodic adjustment of the ignition timing is not necessary for any engine covered by this manual. If ignition timing is not within specification, there is a fault in the engine control system. Diagnose and repair the problem as necessary.

Ignition timing is the measurement, in degrees of crankshaft rotation, of the point at which the spark plugs fire in each of the cylinders. It is measured in degrees before or after Top Dead Center (TDC) of the compression stroke.

Ideally, the air/fuel mixture in the cylinder will be ignited by the spark plug just as the piston passes TDC of the compression stroke. If this happens, the piston will be at the beginning of the power stroke just as the compressed and ignited air/fuel mixture forces the piston down and turns the crankshaft. Because it takes a fraction of a second for the spark plug to ignite the mixture in the cylinder, the spark plug must fire a little before the piston reaches TDC. Otherwise, the mixture will not be completely ignited as the piston passes TDC and the full power of the explosion will not be used by the engine.

The timing measurement is given in degrees of crankshaft rotation before the piston reaches TDC (BTDC). If the setting for the ignition timing is 10 BTDC, each spark plug must fire 10 degrees before each piston reaches TDC. This only holds true, however, when the engine is at idle speed. The combustion process must be complete by 23° ATDC to maintain proper engine performance, fuel mileage, and low emissions.

As the engine speed increases, the pistons go faster. The spark plugs have to ignite the fuel even sooner if it is to be completely ignited when the piston reaches TDC. On all engines covered in this manual, spark timing changes are accomplished electronically by the Powertrain Control Module (PCM), based on input from engine sensors.

If the ignition is set too far advanced (BTDC), the ignition and expansion of the fuel in the cylinder will occur too soon and tend to force the piston down while it is still traveling up. This causes pre ignition or "knocking and pinging." If the ignition spark is set too far retarded, or after TDC (ATDC), the piston will have already started on its way down when the fuel is ignited. The piston will be forced down for only a portion of its travel, resulting in poor engine performance and lack of power.

Timing marks or scales can be found on the rim of the crankshaft pulley and the timing cover. The marks on the pulley correspond to the position of the piston in the No. 1 cylinder. A stroboscopic (dynamic) timing light is hooked onto the No. 1 cylinder spark plug wire. Every time the spark plug fires, the timing light flashes. By aiming the light at the timing marks while the engine is running, the exact position of the piston within the cylinder can be easily read (the flash of light makes the mark on the pulley appear to be standing still). Proper timing is indicated when the mark and scale are in specified alignment.

✳✳ WARNING

When checking timing with the engine running, take care not to get the timing light wires tangled in the fan blades and/or drive belts.

INSPECTION

♦ **See Figures 139 and 140**

1. Place the vehicle in **P** or **N** with the parking brake applied and the drive wheels blocked.

2. Start the engine and allow it reach normal operating temperature. Make sure all accessories are off.

3. Connect a suitable tachometer and timing light to the engine, as per the manufacturer's instructions.

4. Check that the idle speed is within the specified rpm range.

5. Disconnect the SPOUT (spark output) connector to set the engine to base timing, so the PCM cannot adjust timing electronically.

6. Following the manufacturer's instructions, aim the timing light and check the ignition timing. As the light flashes, note the position of the mark on the

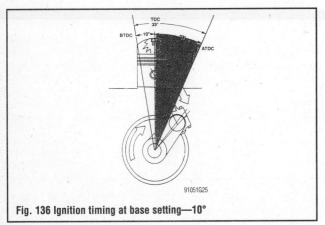

Fig. 136 Ignition timing at base setting—10°

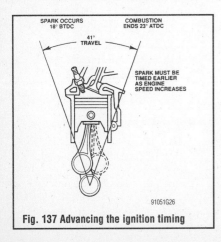

Fig. 137 Advancing the ignition timing

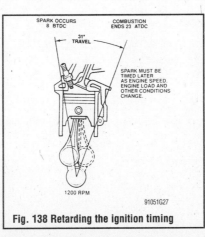

Fig. 138 Retarding the ignition timing

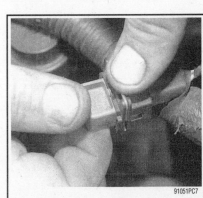

Fig. 139 Press the retaining spring in and . . .

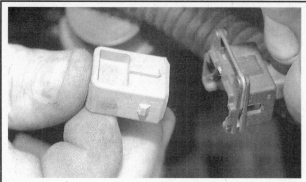

91051PC6

Fig. 140 . . . pull the SPOUT connector from the wiring harness

crankshaft pulley against the scale on the timing cover. Timing should be 8–12 degrees BTDC.

7. If ignition timing is not within specification, there is a fault in the engine control system. Diagnose and repair the problem as necessary.

8. Plug the SPOUT connector in.

9. Stop the engine and remove the tachometer and timing light.

Valve Lash

No periodic valve lash adjustments are necessary or possible on these engines. All engines utilize hydraulic valve trains to automatically maintain proper valve lash. The 2.0L engine has adjustable valve clearance; however, the clearance is set at the factory with shims and only needs to be rechecked if the tappets are removed from the engine.

Idle Speed and Mixture Adjustments

The engines covered by this manual utilize sophisticated Sequential Fuel Injection (SFI) systems in which an engine control computer utilizes information from various sensors to control idle speed and air/fuel mixtures. No periodic adjustments are either necessary or possible on these systems. If a problem is suspected, please refer to Sections 4 of this manual for more information on electronic engine controls and fuel injection.

Air Conditioning System

SYSTEM SERVICE & REPAIR

▶ See Figure 141

➡ It is recommended that the A/C system be serviced by an EPA Section 609 certified automotive technician utilizing a refrigerant recovery/recycling machine.

The do-it-yourselfer should not service his/her own vehicle's A/C system for many reasons, including legal concerns, personal injury, environmental damage and cost. The following are some of the reasons why you may decide not to service your own vehicle's A/C system.

According to the U.S. Clean Air Act, it is a federal crime to service or repair (involving the refrigerant) a Motor Vehicle Air Conditioning (MVAC) system for money without being EPA certified. It is also illegal to vent R-134a refrigerant into the atmosphere.

State and/or local laws may be more strict than the federal regulations, so be sure to check with your state and/or local authorities for further information. For further federal information on the legality of servicing your A/C system, call the EPA Stratospheric Ozone Hotline.

➡ Federal law dictates that a fine of up to $25,000 may be levied on people convicted of venting refrigerant into the atmosphere. Additionally, the EPA may pay up to $10,000 for information or services leading to a criminal conviction of the violation of these laws.

When servicing an A/C system you run the risk of handling or coming in contact with refrigerant, which may result in skin or eye irritation or frostbite. Although low in toxicity (due to chemical stability), inhalation of concentrated refrigerant fumes is dangerous and can result in death; cases of fatal cardiac arrhythmia have been reported in people accidentally subjected to high levels of refrigerant. Some early symptoms include loss of concentration and drowsiness.

Also, refrigerants can decompose at high temperatures (near gas heaters or open flame), which may result in hydrofluoric acid, hydrochloric acid and phosgene (a fatal nerve gas).

R-134a refrigerant is a greenhouse gas which, if allowed to vent into the atmosphere, will contribute to global warming (the Greenhouse Effect).

It is usually more economically feasible to have a certified MVAC automotive technician perform A/C system service to your vehicle. While it is illegal to service an A/C system without the proper equipment, the home mechanic would

GASOLINE ENGINE TUNE-UP SPECIFICATIONS

Year	Engine ID/VIN	Engine Displacement Liters (cc)	Spark Plugs Gap (in.)	Ignition Timing (deg.) MT	Ignition Timing (deg.) AT	Fuel Pump (psi)	Idle Speed (rpm) MT	Idle Speed (rpm) AT	Valve Clearance In.	Valve Clearance Ex.
1995	3	2.0 (1999)	0.050	10B	10B	30-38 ①	880	800	HYD	HYD
	L	2.5 (2507)	0.054	10B	10B	30-36 ①	②	②	HYD	HYD
1996	3	2.0 (1999)	0.050	10B	10B	37-41 ①	②	②	HYD	HYD
	L	2.5 (2507)	0.054	10B	10B	37-41 ①	②	②	HYD	HYD
1997	3	2.0 (1999)	0.050	10B	10B	37-41 ①	②	②	HYD	HYD
	L	2.5 (2507)	0.054	10B	10B	37-41 ①	②	②	HYD	HYD
1998	3	2.0 (1999)	0.050	10B	10B	37-41 ①	②	②	HYD	HYD
	L	2.5 (2507)	0.054	10B	10B	37-41 ①	②	②	HYD	HYD
1999	3	2.0 (1999)	0.050	10B	10B	37-41 ①	②	②	HYD	HYD
	L	2.5 (2507)	0.054	10B	10B	37-41 ①	②	②	HYD	HYD

NOTE: The Vehicle Emission Control Information label often reflects specification changes made during production. The label figures must be used if they differ from those in this chart.

B - Before Top Dead Center

HYD - Hydraulic

① Fuel pressure with engine running, pressure regulator vacuum hose connected

② Refer to Vehicle Emission Control Information label

91051C03

Fig. 141 The A/C certification label has information pertaining to servicing the A/C system

have to purchase an expensive refrigerant recovery/recycling machine to service his/her own vehicle.

PREVENTIVE MAINTENANCE

Although the A/C system should not be serviced by the do-it-yourselfer, preventive maintenance can be practiced and A/C system inspections can be performed to help maintain the efficiency of the vehicle's A/C system. For preventive maintenance, perform the following:

• The easiest and most important preventive maintenance for your A/C system is to be sure that it is used on a regular basis. Running the system for five minutes each month (no matter what the season) will help ensure that the seals and all internal components remain lubricated.

➡**Some newer vehicles automatically operate the A/C system compressor whenever the windshield defroster is activated. When running, the compressor lubricates the A/C system components; therefore, the A/C system would not need to be operated each month.**

• In order to prevent heater core freeze-up during A/C operation, it is necessary to maintain a proper antifreeze protection. Use a hand-held coolant tester (hydrometer) to periodically check the condition of the antifreeze in your engine's cooling system.

➡**Antifreeze should not be used longer than the manufacturer specifies.**

• For efficient operation of an air conditioned vehicle's cooling system, the radiator cap should have a holding pressure which meets manufacturer's specifications. A cap which fails to hold these pressures should be replaced.

• Any obstruction of or damage to the condenser configuration will restrict air flow which is essential to its efficient operation. It is, therefore, a good rule to keep this unit clean and in proper physical shape.

➡**Bug screens that are mounted in front of the condenser (unless they are original equipment) are regarded as obstructions.**

• The condensation drain tube expels any water, which accumulates on the bottom of the evaporator housing, into the engine compartment. If this tube is obstructed, the air conditioning performance can be restricted and condensation buildup can spill over onto the vehicle's floor.

SYSTEM INSPECTION

Although the A/C system should not be serviced by the do-it-yourselfer, preventive maintenance can be practiced and A/C system inspections can be performed to help maintain the efficiency of the vehicle's A/C system. For A/C system inspection, perform the following:

The easiest and often most important check for the air conditioning system consists of a visual inspection of the system components. Visually inspect the air conditioning system for refrigerant leaks, damaged compressor clutch, abnormal compressor drive belt tension and/or condition, plugged evaporator drain tube, blocked condenser fins, disconnected or broken wires, blown fuses, corroded connections and poor insulation.

A refrigerant leak will usually appear as an oily residue at the leakage point in the system. The oily residue soon picks up dust or dirt particles from the surrounding air and appears greasy. Through time, this will build up and appear to be a heavy dirt impregnated grease.

For a thorough visual and operational inspection, check the following:

• Check the surface of the radiator and condenser for dirt, leaves or other material which might block air flow.

• Check for kinks in hoses and lines. Check the system for leaks.

• Make sure the drive belt is properly tensioned. When the air conditioning is operating, make sure the drive belt is free of noise or slippage.

• Make sure the blower motor operates at all appropriate positions, then check for distribution of the air from all outlets with the blower on **HIGH** or **MAX**.

➡**Keep in mind that under conditions of high humidity, air discharged from the A/C vents may not feel as cold as expected, even if the system is working properly. This is because vaporized moisture in humid air retains heat more effectively than dry air, thereby making humid air more difficult to cool.**

• Make sure the air passage selection lever is operating correctly. Start the engine and warm it to normal operating temperature, then make sure the temperature selection lever is operating correctly.

Windshield Wipers

ELEMENT (REFILL) CARE & REPLACEMENT

◆ See Figures 142 thru 151

For maximum effectiveness and longest element life, the windshield and wiper blades should be kept clean. Dirt, tree sap, road tar and so on will cause streaking, smearing and blade deterioration if left on the glass. It is advisable to wash the windshield carefully with a commercial glass cleaner at least once a month. Wipe off the rubber blades with the wet rag afterwards. Do not attempt to move wipers across the windshield by hand; damage to the motor and drive mechanism will result.

To inspect and/or replace the wiper blade elements, place the wiper switch in the **LOW** speed position and the ignition switch in the **ACC** position. When the wiper blades are approximately vertical on the windshield, turn the ignition switch to **OFF**.

Examine the wiper blade elements. If they are found to be cracked, broken or torn, they should be replaced immediately. Replacement intervals will vary with usage, although ozone deterioration usually limits element life to about one year. If the wiper pattern is smeared or streaked, or if the blade chatters across the glass, the elements should be replaced. It is easiest and most sensible to replace the elements in pairs.

If your vehicle is equipped with aftermarket blades, there are several different types of refills and your vehicle might have any kind. Aftermarket blades and arms rarely use the exact same type blade or refill as the original equipment. Here are some typical aftermarket blades; not all may be available for your vehicle:

The Anco® type uses a release button that is pushed down to allow the refill to slide out of the yoke jaws. The new refill slides back into the frame and locks in place.

Some Trico® refills are removed by locating where the metal backing strip or the refill is wider. Insert a small screwdriver blade between the frame and metal backing strip. Press down to release the refill from the retaining tab.

Other types of Trico® refills have two metal tabs which are unlocked by squeezing them together. The rubber filler can then be withdrawn from the frame jaws. A new refill is installed by inserting the refill into the front frame jaws and sliding it rearward to engage the remaining frame jaws. There are usually four jaws; be certain when installing that the refill is engaged in all of them. At the end of its travel, the tabs will lock into place on the front jaws of the wiper blade frame.

Another type of refill is made from polycarbonate. The refill has a simple locking device at one end which flexes downward out of the groove into which the jaws of the holder fit, allowing easy release. By sliding the new refill through all the jaws and pushing through the slight resistance when it reaches the end of its travel, the refill will lock into position.

To replace the Tridon® refill, it is necessary to remove the wiper blade. This refill has a plastic backing strip with a notch about 1 in. (25mm) from the end. Hold the blade (frame) on a hard surface so that the frame is tightly bowed. Grip the tip of the backing strip and pull up while twisting counterclockwise. The backing strip will snap out of the retaining tab. Do this for the remaining tabs until the refill is free of the blade. The length of these refills is molded into the end and they should be replaced with identical types.

Regardless of the type of refill used, be sure to follow the part manufacturer's

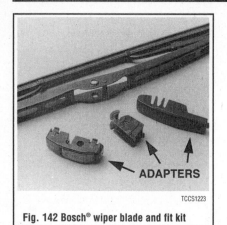

Fig. 142 Bosch® wiper blade and fit kit

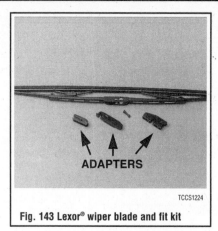

Fig. 143 Lexor® wiper blade and fit kit

Fig. 144 Pylon® wiper blade and adapter

Fig. 145 Trico® wiper blade and fit kit

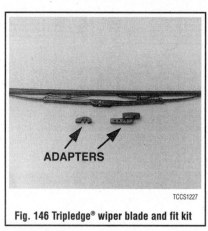

Fig. 146 Tripledge® wiper blade and fit kit

Fig. 147 To remove and install a Lexor® wiper blade refill, slip out the old insert and slide in a new one

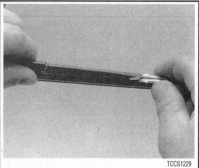

Fig. 148 On Pylon® inserts, the clip at the end has to be removed prior to sliding the insert off

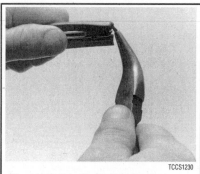

Fig. 149 On Trico® wiper blades, the tab at the end of the blade must be turned up . . .

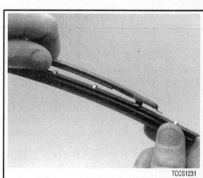

Fig. 150 . . . then the insert can be removed. After installing the replacement insert, bend the tab back

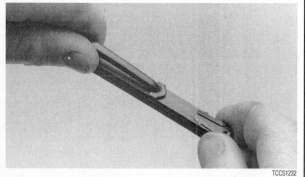
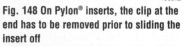

Fig. 151 The Tripledge® wiper blade insert is removed and installed using a securing clip

instructions closely. Make sure that all of the frame jaws are engaged as the refill is pushed into place and locked. If the metal blade holder and frame are allowed to touch the glass during wiper operation, the glass will be scratched.

Tires and Wheels

▶ See Figure 152

Common sense and good driving habits will afford maximum tire life. Fast starts, sudden stops and hard cornering are hard on tires and will shorten their useful life span. Make sure that you don't overload the vehicle or run with incorrect pressure in the tires. Both of these practices will increase tread wear.

➥For optimum tire life, keep the tires properly inflated, rotate them often and have the wheel alignment checked periodically.

Inspect your tires frequently. Be especially careful to watch for bubbles in the tread or sidewall, deep cuts or underinflation. Replace any tires with bubbles in

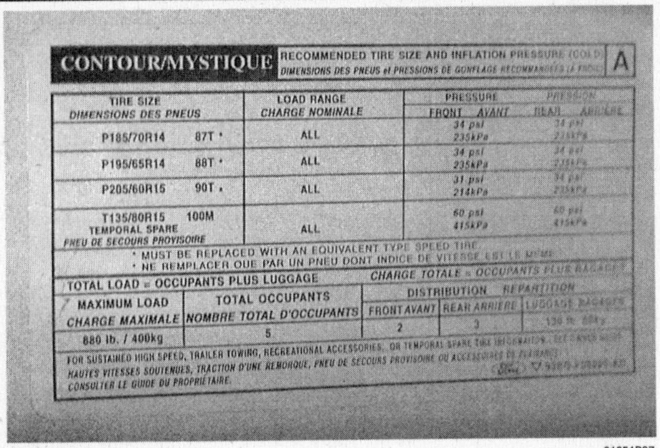

Fig. 152 The tire certification label is usually located on the passenger side front or rear door, and contains information about the tires, including size, inflation pressures and weight capacity

the sidewall. If cuts are so deep that they penetrate to the cords, discard the tire. Any cut in the sidewall of a radial tire renders it unsafe. Also look for uneven tread wear patterns that may indicate the front end is out of alignment or that the tires are out of balance.

TIRE ROTATION

▶ **See Figures 153, 154 and 155**

Tires must be rotated periodically to equalize wear patterns that vary with a tire's position on the vehicle. Tires will also wear in an uneven way as the front steering/suspension system wears to the point where the alignment should be reset.

Rotating the tires will ensure maximum life for the tires as a set, so you will not have to discard a tire early due to wear on only part of the tread. Regular rotation is required to equalize wear.

When rotating "unidirectional tires," make sure that they always roll in the same direction. This means that a tire used on the left side of the vehicle must not be switched to the right side and vice-versa. Such tires should only be rotated front-to-rear or rear-to-front, while always remaining on the same side of the vehicle. These tires are marked on the sidewall as to the direction of rotation; observe the marks when reinstalling the tire(s).

➡**Vehicles equipped with factory wheel locks usually have the key attached to the lug wrench in the trunk.**

Some styled or "mag" wheels may have different offsets front to rear. In these cases, the rear wheels must not be used up front and vice-versa. Furthermore, if these wheels are equipped with unidirectional tires, they cannot be rotated unless the tire is remounted for the proper direction of rotation.

➡**The compact or space-saver spare is strictly for emergency use. It must never be included in the tire rotation or placed on the vehicle for everyday use.**

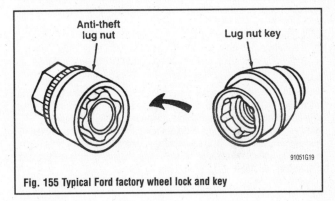

Fig. 154 Unidirectional tires are identifiable by sidewall arrows and/or the word "rotation"

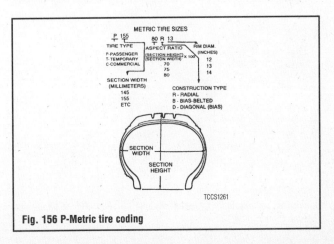

Fig. 155 Typical Ford factory wheel lock and key

TIRE DESIGN

▶ **See Figure 156**

For maximum satisfaction, tires should be used in sets of four. Mixing of different types (radial, bias-belted, fiberglass belted) must be avoided. In most cases, the vehicle manufacturer has designated a type of tire on which the vehicle will perform best. Your first choice when replacing tires should be to use the same type of tire that the manufacturer recommends.

When radial tires are used, tire sizes and wheel diameters should be selected to maintain ground clearance and tire load capacity equivalent to the original specified tire. Radial tires should always be used in sets of four.

✳ CAUTION

Radial tires should never be used on only the front axle.

When selecting tires, pay attention to the original size as marked on the tire. Most tires are described using an industry size code sometimes referred to as P-Metric. This allows the exact identification of the tire specifications, regard-

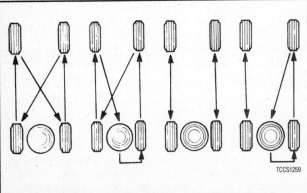

Fig. 153 Common tire rotation patterns for 4 and 5-wheel rotations

Fig. 156 P-Metric tire coding

less of the manufacturer. If selecting a different tire size or brand, remember to check the installed tire for any sign of interference with the body or suspension while the vehicle is stopping, turning sharply or heavily loaded.

Snow Tires

Good radial tires can produce a big advantage in slippery weather, but in snow, a street radial tire does not have sufficient tread to provide traction and control. The small grooves of a street tire quickly pack with snow and the tire behaves like a billiard ball on a marble floor. The more open, chunky tread of a snow tire will self-clean as the tire turns, providing much better grip on snowy surfaces.

To satisfy municipalities requiring snow tires during weather emergencies, most snow tires carry either an M + S designation after the tire size stamped on the sidewall, or the designation "all-season." In general, no change in tire size is necessary when buying snow tires.

Most manufacturers strongly recommend the use of 4 snow tires on their vehicles for reasons of stability. If snow tires are fitted only to the drive wheels, the opposite end of the vehicle may become very unstable when braking or turning on slippery surfaces. This instability can lead to unpleasant endings if the driver can't counteract the slide in time.

Note that snow tires, whether 2 or 4, will affect vehicle handling in all non-snow situations. The stiffer, heavier snow tires will noticeably change the turning and braking characteristics of the vehicle. Once the snow tires are installed, you must re-learn the behavior of the vehicle and drive accordingly.

➡**Consider buying extra wheels on which to mount the snow tires. Once done, the "snow wheels" can be installed and removed as needed. This eliminates the potential damage to tires or wheels from seasonal removal and installation. Even if your vehicle has styled wheels, see if inexpensive steel wheels are available. Although the look of the vehicle will change, the expensive wheels will be protected from salt, curb hits and pothole damage.**

TIRE STORAGE

If they are mounted on wheels, store the tires at proper inflation pressure. All tires should be kept in a cool, dry place. If they are stored in the garage or basement, do not let them stand on a concrete floor; set them on strips of wood, a mat or a large stack of newspaper. Keeping them away from direct moisture is of paramount importance. Tires should not be stored upright, but in a flat position.

INFLATION & INSPECTION

◆ **See Figures 157 thru 164**

➡**The tire identification label is usually attached to the passenger side rear door. It contains information about tire size, weight ratings, and factory recommended inflation levels of all four wheels.**

The importance of proper tire inflation cannot be overemphasized. A tire employs air as part of its structure. It is designed around the supporting strength of the air at a specified pressure. For this reason, improper inflation drastically reduces the tire's ability to perform as intended. A tire will lose some air in day-to-day use; having to add a few pounds of air periodically is not necessarily a sign of a leaking tire.

Two items should be a permanent fixture in every glove compartment: an accurate tire pressure gauge and a tread depth gauge. Check the tire pressure (including the spare) regularly with a pocket type gauge. Too often, the gauge on the end of the air hose at your corner garage is not accurate because it suffers too much abuse. Always check tire pressure when the tires are cold, as pressure increases with temperature. If you must move the vehicle to check the tire inflation, do not drive more than a mile before checking. A cold tire is generally one that has not been driven for more than three hours.

A plate or sticker is normally provided somewhere in the vehicle (door post, hood, tailgate or trunk lid) which shows the proper pressure for the tires. Never counteract excessive pressure build-up by bleeding off air pressure (letting some air out). This will cause the tire to run hotter and wear quicker.

✳✳ CAUTION

Never exceed the maximum tire pressure embossed on the tire! This is the pressure to be used when the tire is at maximum loading, but it is rarely the correct pressure for everyday driving. Consult the owner's manual or the tire pressure sticker for the correct tire pressure.

Once you've maintained the correct tire pressures for several weeks, you'll be familiar with the vehicle's braking and handling personality. Slight adjustments in tire pressures can fine-tune these characteristics, but never change the cold pressure specification by more than 2 psi. A slightly softer tire pressure will give a softer ride but also yield lower fuel mileage. A slightly harder tire will give crisper dry road handling but can cause skidding on wet surfaces. Unless you're fully attuned to the vehicle, stick to the recommended inflation pressures.

All tires made since 1968 have built-in tread wear indicator bars that show up as ½ in. (13mm) wide smooth bands across the tire when 1/16 in. (1.5mm) of tread remains. The appearance of tread wear indicators means that the tires should be replaced. In fact, many states have laws prohibiting the use of tires with less than this amount of tread.

You can check your own tread depth with an inexpensive gauge or by using a Lincoln head penny. Slip the Lincoln penny (with Lincoln's head upside-down) into several tread grooves. If you can see the top of Lincoln's head in 2 adjacent

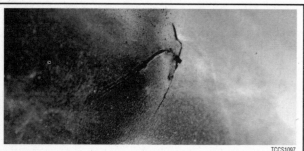

Fig. 157 Tires should be checked frequently for any sign of puncture or damage

Fig. 158 Tires with deep cuts, or cuts which bulge, should be replaced immediately

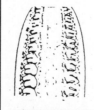

• DRIVE WHEEL HEAVY ACCELERATION
• OVERINFLATION

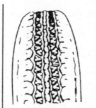

• HARD CORNERING
• UNDERINFLATION
• LACK OF ROTATION

Fig. 159 Examples of inflation-related tire wear patterns

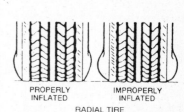

PROPERLY INFLATED   IMPROPERLY INFLATED

RADIAL TIRE

Fig. 160 Radial tires have a characteristic sidewall bulge; don't try to measure pressure by looking at the tire. Use a quality air pressure gauge

CONDITION	RAPID WEAR AT SHOULDERS	RAPID WEAR AT CENTER	CRACKED TREADS	WEAR ON ONE SIDE	FEATHERED EDGE	BALD SPOTS	SCALLOPED WEAR
EFFECT							
CAUSE	UNDER-INFLATION OR LACK OF ROTATION	OVER-INFLATION OR LACK OF ROTATION	UNDER-INFLATION OR EXCESSIVE SPEED*	EXCESSIVE CAMBER	INCORRECT TOE	UNBALANCED WHEEL OR TIRE DEFECT *	LACK OF ROTATION OF TIRES OR WORN OR OUT-OF-ALIGNMENT SUSPENSION.
CORRECTION	ADJUST PRESSURE TO SPECIFICATIONS WHEN TIRES ARE COOL ROTATE TIRES			ADJUST CAMBER TO SPECIFICATIONS	ADJUST TOE-IN TO SPECIFICATIONS	DYNAMIC OR STATIC BALANCE WHEELS	ROTATE TIRES AND INSPECT SUSPENSION

*HAVE TIRE INSPECTED FOR FURTHER USE.

TCCS1267

Fig. 161 Common tire wear patterns and causes

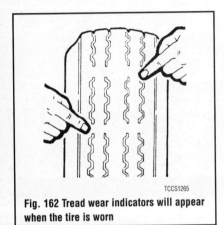

Fig. 162 Tread wear indicators will appear when the tire is worn

TCCS1265

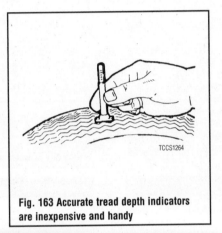

Fig. 163 Accurate tread depth indicators are inexpensive and handy

TCCS1264

Fig. 164 A penny works well for a quick check of tread depth

TCCS1266

grooves, the tire has less than ¹⁄₁₆ in. (1.5mm) tread left and should be replaced. You can measure snow tires in the same manner by using the "tails" side of the Lincoln penny. If you can see the top of the Lincoln memorial, it's time to replace the snow tire(s).

CARE OF SPECIAL WHEELS

If you have invested money in magnesium, aluminum alloy or sport wheels, special precautions should be taken to make sure your investment is not wasted and that your special wheels look good for the life of the vehicle.

Special wheels are easily damaged and/or scratched. Occasionally check the rims for cracking, impact damage or air leaks. If any of these are found, replace the wheel. But in order to prevent this type of damage and the costly replacement of a special wheel, observe the following precautions:

• Use extra care not to damage the wheels during removal, installation, balancing, etc. After removal of the wheels from the vehicle, place them on a mat or other protective surface. If they are to be stored for any length of time, support them on strips of wood. Never store tires and wheels upright; the tread may develop flat spots.

• When driving, watch for hazards; it doesn't take much to crack a wheel.

• When washing, use a mild soap or non-abrasive dish detergent (keeping in mind that detergent tends to remove wax). Avoid cleansers with abrasives or the use of hard brushes. There are many cleaners and polishes for special wheels.

• If possible, remove the wheels during the winter. Salt and sand used for snow removal can severely damage the finish of a wheel.

• Make certain the recommended lug nut torque is never exceeded or the wheel may crack. Never use snow chains on special wheels; severe scratching will occur.

FLUIDS AND LUBRICANTS

Fluid Disposal

Used fluids such as engine oil, transmission fluid, antifreeze and brake fluid are hazardous wastes and must be disposed of properly. Before draining any fluids, consult with your local authorities; in many areas, waste oil, antifreeze, etc. is being accepted as a part of recycling programs. A number of service stations and auto parts stores are also accepting waste fluids for recycling.

Be sure of the recycling center's policies before draining any fluids, as many will not accept different fluids that have been mixed together.

Fuel and Engine Oil Recommendations

▶ See Figures 165 and 166

➡Ford recommends that SAE 5W-30 viscosity engine oil should be used for all climate conditions, however, SAE 10W-30 is acceptable for vehicles operated in moderate-to-hot climates.

When adding oil to the crankcase or changing the oil or filter, it is important that oil of an equal quality to original equipment be used in your car. The use of inferior oils may void the warranty, damage your engine, or both.

The SAE (Society of Automotive Engineers) grade number of oil indicates the viscosity of the oil (its ability to lubricate at a given temperature). The lower the SAE number, the lighter the oil; the lower the viscosity, the easier it is to crank the engine in cold weather but the less the oil will lubricate and protect the engine in high temperatures. This number is marked on every oil container.

Oil viscosity's should be chosen from those oils recommended for the lowest anticipated temperatures during the oil change interval. Due to the need for an oil that embodies both good lubrication at high temperatures and easy cranking in cold weather, multigrade oils have been developed. Basically, a multigrade oil is thinner at low temperatures and thicker at high temperatures. For example, a 10W-40 oil (the W stands for winter) exhibits the characteristics of a 10 weight (SAE 10) oil when the car is first started and the oil is cold. Its lighter weight allows it to travel to the lubricating surfaces quicker and offer less resistance to starter motor cranking than, say, a straight 30 weight (SAE 30) oil. But after the

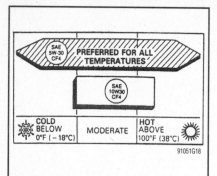

Fig. 165 Recommended oil viscosity usage according to outside air temperature

API SERVICES
SH/CD,SG,SF,CC

DON'T POLLUTE. CONSERVE RESOURCES.
RETURN USED OIL TO COLLECTION CENTERS

TCCS1235

Fig. 166 Look for the API oil identification label when choosing your engine oil

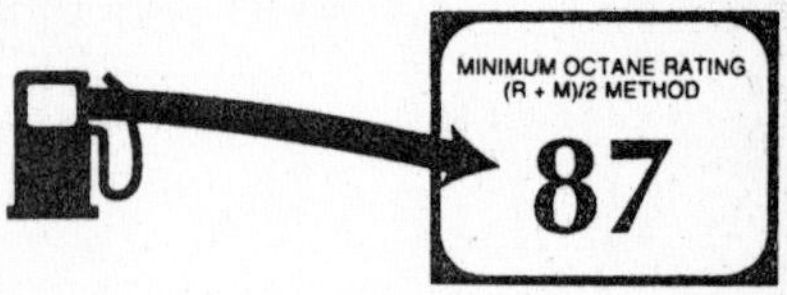

MINIMUM OCTANE RATING
(R + M)/2 METHOD
87

91051G17

Fig. 167 Make sure you use gasoline with at least a rating of 87 octane

engine reaches operating temperature, the 10W-40 oil begins acting like straight 40 weight (SAE 40) oil, its heavier weight providing greater lubrication with less chance of foaming than a straight 30 weight oil.

The API (American Petroleum Institute) designations, also found on the oil container, indicates the classification of engine oil used under certain given operating conditions. Only oils designated for use Service SG heavy duty detergent should be used in your car. Oils of the SG type perform may functions inside the engine besides their basic lubrication. Through a balanced system of metallic detergents and polymeric dispersants, the oil prevents high and low temperature deposits and also keeps sludge and dirt particles in suspension. Acids, particularly sulfuric acid, as well as other by-products of engine combustion are neutralized by the oil. If these acids are allowed to concentrate, they can cause corrosion and rapid wear of the internal engine parts.

❋ CAUTION

Non-detergent motor oils or straight mineral oils should not be used in your Ford gasoline engine.

Synthetic Oil

There are many excellent synthetic and fuel-efficient oils currently available that can provide better gas mileage, longer service life and, in some cases, better engine protection. These benefits do not come without a few hitches, however; the main one being the price of synthetic oil, which is significantly more expensive than conventional oil.

Synthetic oil is not for every car and every type of driving, so you should consider your engine's condition and your type of driving. Also, check your car's warranty conditions regarding the use of synthetic oils.

FUEL

▶ **See Figures 167, 168 and 169**

Your vehicle is designed to operate using regular unleaded fuel with a minimum of 87 octane. Ford warns that using gasoline with an octane rating lower

than 87 can cause persistent and heavy knocking, and may cause internal engine damage.

If your vehicle is having problems with rough idle or hesitation when the engine is cold, it may be caused by low volatility fuel. If this occurs, try a different grade or brand of fuel.

OPERATION IN FOREIGN COUNTRIES

If you plan to drive your car outside the United States or Canada, there is a possibility that fuels will be too low in anti-knock quality and could produce engine damage. It is wise to consult with local authorities upon arrival in a foreign country to determine the best fuels available.

Engine

OIL LEVEL CHECK

▶ **See Figures 170, 171, 172 and 173**

❋ CAUTION

The EPA warns that prolonged contact with used engine oil may cause a number of skin disorders, including cancer! You should make every effort to minimize your exposure to used engine oil. Protective gloves should be worn when changing the oil. Wash your hands and any other exposed skin areas as soon as possible after exposure to used engine oil. Soap and water, or waterless hand cleaner should be used.

The engine oil dipstick is located in front of the engine between the engine and the radiator.

Engine oil level should be checked every time you put fuel in the vehicle or are under the hood performing other maintenance.

1. Park the vehicle on a level surface.

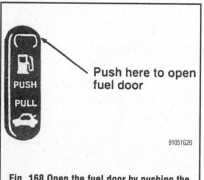

Push here to open fuel door

91051G20

Fig. 168 Open the fuel door by pushing the lever located on the floor, to the left of the driver's seat

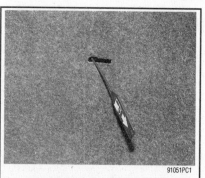

91051PC1

Fig. 169 If the inside handle will not work for some reason, an emergency release is available in the trunk to open the fuel door

91051P14

Fig. 170 Grasp the oil level dipstick and . . .

Fig. 171 . . . pull upward to remove it from the dipstick tube

Fig. 172 Wipe the dipstick clean and reinsert it into the dipstick tube to get the correct oil level

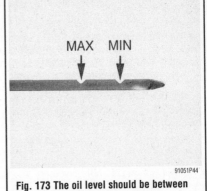

Fig. 173 The oil level should be between the marks/notches on the dipstick

2. The engine may be either hot or cold when checking oil level. However, if it is hot, wait a few minutes after the engine has been turned **OFF** to allow the oil to drain back into the crankcase. If the engine is cold, do not start it before checking the oil level.

3. Open the hood and locate the engine oil dipstick. Pull the dipstick from its tube, wipe it clean, and reinsert it. Make sure the dipstick is fully inserted.

4. Pull the dipstick from its tube again. Holding it horizontally, read the oil level. The oil should be between the MIN and MAX mark. If the oil is below the MIN mark, add oil of the proper viscosity through the capped opening of the valve cover.

5. Replace the dipstick, and check the level again after adding any oil. Be careful not to overfill the crankcase. Approximately one quart of oil will raise the level from the low mark to the high mark. Excess oil will generally be consumed at an accelerated rate even if no damage to the engine seals occurs.

OIL & FILTER CHANGE

▶ See Figures 174 thru 185

The oil and filter should be changed every 5,000 miles (8,000 km) under normal service and every 3,000 miles (5,000 km) under severe service.

✳✳ CAUTION

The EPA warns that prolonged contact with used engine oil may cause a number of skin disorders, including cancer! You should make every effort to minimize your exposure to used engine oil. Protective gloves should be worn when changing the oil. Wash your hands and any other exposed skin areas as soon as possible after exposure to used engine oil. Soap and water, or waterless hand cleaner should be used.

➡The engine oil and oil filter should be changed at the recommended intervals on the Maintenance Chart. Though some manufacturers have at times recommended changing the filter only at every other oil change, Chilton recommends that you always change the filter with the oil. The benefit of fresh oil is quickly lost if the old filter is clogged and

unable to do its job. Also, leaving the old filter in place leaves a significant amount of dirty oil in the system.

The oil should be changed more frequently if the vehicle is being operated in a very dusty area. Before draining the oil, make sure that the engine is at operating temperature. Hot oil will hold more impurities in suspension and will flow better, allowing the removal of more oil and dirt.

It is a good idea to warm the engine oil first so it will flow better. This can be accomplished by 15–20 miles of highway driving. Fluid which is warmed to normal operating temperature will flow faster, drain more completely and remove more contaminants from the engine.

1. Raise and support the vehicle safely on jackstands. Make sure the oil drain plug is at the lowest point on the oil pan. If not, you may have to raise the vehicle slightly higher on one jackstand (side) than the other.

2. Before you crawl under the vehicle, take a look at where you will be working and gather all the necessary tools, such as a few wrenches or a ratchet and strip of sockets, the drain pan, some clean rags and, if the oil filter is more accessible from underneath the vehicle, you will also want to grab a bottle of oil, the new filter and a filter wrench at this time.

3. Position the drain pan beneath the oil pan drain plug. Keep in mind that the fast flowing oil, which will spill out as you pull the plug from the pan, will flow with enough force that it could miss the pan. Position the drain pan accordingly and be ready to move the pan more directly beneath the plug as the oil flow lessens to a trickle.

4. Loosen the drain plug with a wrench (or socket and driver), then carefully unscrew the plug with your fingers. Use a rag to shield your fingers from the heat. Push in on the plug as you unscrew it so you can feel when all of the screw threads are out of the hole (and so you will keep the oil from seeping past the threads until you are ready to remove the plug). You can then remove the plug quickly to avoid having hot oil run down your arm. This will also help assure that have the plug in your hand, not in the bottom of a pan of hot oil.

✳✳ CAUTION

Be careful of the oil; when at operating temperature, it is hot enough to cause a severe burn.

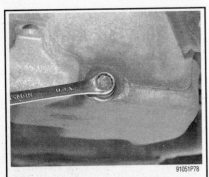

Fig. 174 Loosen the drain plug on the engine oil pan with a wrench. The drain plug's head is usually 16mm

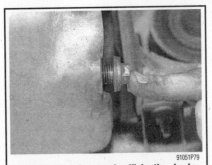

Fig. 175 When loosened sufficiently, slowly turn the drain plug by hand, keeping constant inward pressure on the plug to prevent oil from streaming out until you are ready

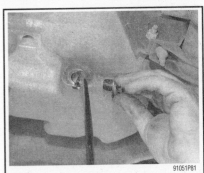

Fig. 176 When you are ready, carefully pull the drain plug out and to the side, out of the way of flowing oil

5. Allow the oil to drain until nothing but a few drops come out of the drain hole. Check the drain plug to make sure the threads and sealing surface are not damaged. Carefully thread the plug into position and tighten it with a torque wrench to 9–11 ft. lbs. (11–16 Nm). If a torque wrench is not available, snug the drain plug and give a slight additional turn. You don't want the plug to fall out (as you would quickly become stranded), but the pan threads are EASILY stripped from overtightening (and this can be time consuming and/or costly to fix).

6. To remove the filter, you may need an oil filter wrench since the filter may have been fitted too tightly and/or the heat from the engine may have made it even tighter. A filter wrench can be obtained at any auto parts store and is well-worth the investment. Loosen the filter with the filter wrench. With a rag wrapped around the filter, unscrew the filter from the boss on the side of the engine. Be careful of hot oil that will run down the side of the filter. Make sure that your drain pan is under the filter before you start to remove it from the engine; should some of the hot oil happen to get on you, there will be a place to dump the filter in a hurry and the filter will usually spill a good bit of dirty oil as it is removed.

7. Wipe the base of the mounting boss with a clean, dry cloth. When you install the new filter, smear a small amount of fresh oil on the gasket with your finger, just enough to coat the entire contact surface. When you tighten the filter, rotate it about a quarter-turn after it contacts the mounting boss (or follow any instructions which are provided on the filter or parts box).

✳✳ WARNING

Operating the engine without the proper amount and type of engine oil will result in severe engine damage.

8. Remove the jackstands and carefully lower the vehicle, then IMMEDIATELY refill the engine crankcase with the proper amount of oil. DO NOT WAIT TO DO THIS because if you forget and someone tries to start the vehicle, severe engine damage will occur.

9. Refill the engine crankcase slowly, checking the level often. You may notice that it usually takes less than the amount of oil listed in the capacity chart

91051P89

Fig. 177 Clean and inspect the threads and the gasket on the drain plug before installing it back into the oil pan

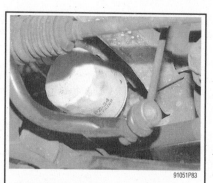
91051P83

Fig. 178 The oil filter is best accessed from the passenger side front wheel well—2.0L engine

91051P84

Fig. 179 A band type filter wrench is used here to loosen the filter

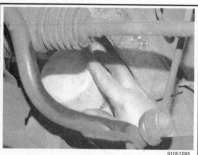
91051P85

Fig. 180 When the filter is sufficiently loosened with the filter wrench, turn the filter by hand, but be careful, as oil will start to run out of the filter

91051P86

Fig. 181 Remove the oil filter from the engine

91051P87

Fig. 182 Make sure the gasket stayed on the oil filter and is not stuck on the engine block, or an oil leak will occur

TCCS1901

Fig. 183 Before installing a new oil filter, lightly coat the rubber gasket with clean oil

91051P22

Fig. 184 Loosen the oil filler cap . . .

91051P23

Fig. 185 . . . insert a funnel, and pour oil directly into the engine to refill the crankcase. But, that is only until the engine is run and the oil filter is filled with oil. To make sure the proper level is obtained, run the engine to normal operating temperature, shut the engine **OFF**, allow the oil to drain back into the oil pan, and recheck the level. Top off the oil at this time to the fill mark.

➡If the vehicle is not resting on level ground, the oil level reading on the dipstick may be slightly off. Be sure to check the level only when the vehicle is sitting level.

10. Drain your used oil in a suitable container for recycling.

Manual Transaxle

FLUID RECOMMENDATIONS

Ford recommends Mercon® Automatic Transmission Fluid (ATF) or its equivalent for use in your manual transaxle.

LEVEL CHECK

1. Park the car on a level surface, turn the engine **OFF** and apply the parking brake.
2. Raise and support the vehicle.
3. Place a suitable drain pan under the transaxle drain plug.
4. Remove the oil level check plug.
5. The oil level in the transaxle should be at or just slightly below the bottom edge of the plug. An easy check if the fluid is not visible is to insert a small screwdriver or pick at a downward angle in the check plug hole. Remove the tool and look for fluid on the tool. The level of the transaxle oil can then be determined.
6. If the fluid is low, add fluid until the fluid slowly begins to seep out of the check/fill plug hole. Let the fluid drain out for a few seconds then insert the plug into the hole.
7. Tighten the plug to 29–43 ft. lbs. (40–58 Nm).
8. Remove the drain pan.
9. Lower the vehicle.

DRAIN & REFILL

1. Park the car on a level surface, turn the engine **OFF** and apply the parking brake.
2. Raise and support the vehicle.
3. Place a suitable drain pan under the transaxle drain plug.
4. Remove the oil drain plug from the transaxle.
5. Let the fluid sufficiently drain out of the transaxle.
6. Install the drain plug and tighten the plug to 29–43 ft. lbs. (40–58 Nm).
7. Remove the oil level check plug.
8. Add fluid until the fluid slowly begins to seep out of the check/fill plug hole. Let the fluid drain out for a few seconds then insert the plug into the hole.
9. Tighten the plug to 29–43 ft. lbs. (40–58 Nm).
10. Remove the drain pan.
11. Lower the vehicle.
12. Road test the car and check for proper transaxle operation.

Automatic Transaxle

FLUID RECOMMENDATIONS

Ford recommends the use of Mercon® automatic transmission fluid.

LEVEL CHECK

▶ **See Figures 186, 187, 188 and 189**

The transmission dipstick is located behind the air inlet hose, towards the firewall.
1. Park the vehicle on a level surface.
2. The transaxle should be at normal operating temperature when checking fluid level. To ensure the fluid is at normal operating temperature, drive the vehicle at least 10 miles.
3. With the selector lever in **P** and the parking brake applied, start the engine.
4. Open the hood and locate the transaxle fluid dipstick. Pull the dipstick from its tube, wipe it clean, and reinsert it. Make sure the dipstick is fully inserted.
5. Pull the dipstick from its tube again. Holding it horizontally, read the fluid level. The fluid should be between the MIN and MAX mark. If the fluid is below the MIN mark, add fluid through the dipstick tube.
6. Insert the dipstick, and check the level again after adding any fluid. Be careful not to overfill the transaxle.

DRAIN & REFILL

▶ **See Figures 190, 191, 192, 193 and 194**

1. Raise and support the vehicle safely.
2. Place a suitable drain pan under the transaxle drain plug.
3. Remove the transaxle drain plug. Let the fluid completely drain out of the transaxle.
4. Install the drain plug and tighten it to 19–21 ft. lbs. (25–29 Nm).
5. Remove the drain pan.
6. Lower the vehicle.
7. Fill the transaxle through the dipstick to the proper level.
8. Place the gear selector lever in **P** and start the engine. Run the engine at idle, engage the emergency brake and hold the brake pedal down. Move the gear selector lever through all transaxle ranges for approximately 5 minutes.
9. Return the selector lever to **P** and leave the engine running at idle.
10. Check the transaxle fluid level. The fluid level at normal operating temperature should read within the crosshatched area of the fluid level dipstick.
11. If the fluid level reads below the crosshatched area, adjust the level by adding fluid in small increments until the correct fluid level is obtained.

PAN & FILTER SERVICE

The CD4E transaxle in the Contour/Mystique/Cougar has no service procedure for the transaxle pan and filter removal. The filter is located in the center of the transaxle and can only be removed at transaxle disassembly. The pan should only be removed when repair or adjustment of the transaxle is necessary.

Fig. 186 The automatic transaxle dipstick is located under the air cleaner inlet tube and near the brake master cylinder

Fig. 187 Pull the dipstick up to remove it from the transaxle

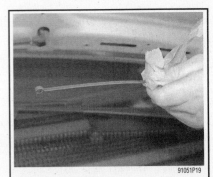

Fig. 188 Wipe the dipstick clean and insert it into the transaxle again to get the correct fluid level reading

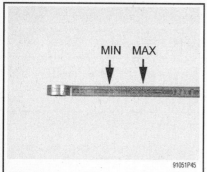

Fig. 189 The fluid level is OK if it is within the crosshatched area. Do not overfill the transaxle or problems could occur

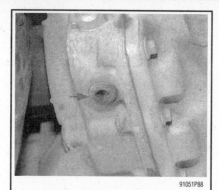

Fig. 190 The transaxle drain plug is located on the bottom of the transaxle

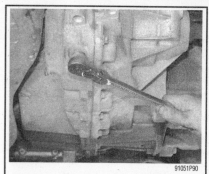

Fig. 191 Insert a ⅜ in. drive ratchet or other ⅜ in. drive tool to loosen the transaxle drain plug

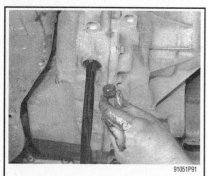

Fig. 192 Carefully pull the drain plug out and to the side, out of the way of flowing transaxle oil

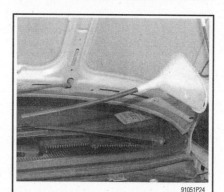

Fig. 193 A long, thin funnel is necessary to access the transaxle dipstick tube

Fig. 194 Pour the fluid directly into the funnel, periodically checking the fluid level to make sure you do not overfill the transaxle

Cooling System

FLUID RECOMMENDATIONS

▶ See Figure 195

Ford recommends the use of a good quality ethylene glycol based or other aluminum compatible antifreeze. It is best to add a 50/50 mix of antifreeze and water to avoid diluting the coolant in the system.

LEVEL CHECK

▶ See Figure 196

The coolant recovery tank is located on the passenger side of the engine compartment, over the front wheel well.

The proper coolant level is slightly above the FULL COLD marking on the recovery tank when the engine is cold. Top off the cooling system using the recovery tank and its marking as a guideline.

➡ Never overfill the recovery tank.

A coolant level that consistently drops is usually a sign of a small, hard to detect leak, although in the worst case it could be a sign of an internal engine leak. In most cases, you will be able to trace the leak to a loose fitting or damaged hose.

Evaporating ethylene glycol antifreeze will have a sweet smell and leave small, white (salt-like) deposits, which can be helpful in tracing a leak.

✳✳ CAUTION

Never open, service or drain the radiator or cooling system when hot; serious burns can occur from the steam and hot coolant. Also, when draining engine coolant, keep in mind that cats and dogs are attracted to ethylene glycol antifreeze and could drink any that is left in an uncovered container or in puddles on the ground. This will prove fatal in sufficient quantities. Always drain coolant into a sealable container. Coolant should be reused unless it is contaminated or is several years old.

TESTING FOR LEAKS

▶ See Figures 197, 198, 199, 200 and 201

If a the fluid level of your cooling system is constantly low, the chances of a leak are probable. There are several ways to go about finding the source of your leak.

The first way should be a visual inspection. During the visual inspection, look around the entire engine area including the radiator and the heater hoses. The interior of the car should be inspected behind the glove box and passenger side floorboard area, and check the carpet for any signs of moisture. The smartest way to go about finding a leak visually is to first inspect any and all joints in the system such as where the radiator hoses connect to the radiator and the engine. Another thing to look for is white crusty stains that are signs of a leak where the coolant has already dried.

If a visual inspection cannot find the cause of your leak, a pressure test is a logical and extremely helpful way to find a leak. A pressure tester will be needed to perform this and if one is not available they can be purchased or even rented at many auto parts stores. The pressure tester usually has a standard size radiator cap adapter on the pressure port, however, other adapters are available based on the size of the vehicle's radiator neck or recovery tank depending on where the pressure tester connects. when pressurizing the cooling system, make sure you do not exceed the pressure rating of the system, which can be found on the top of the radiator cap, however, if you have and aftermarket or replacement cap that does not have the rating on it, 16 psi is a standard to use but some cars are higher. Overpressurizing the system can cause a rupture in a hose or worse in the radiator or heater core and possibly cause an injury or a burn if the coolant is hot. Overpressurizing is normally controlled by the radiator cap which has a vent valve in it which is opened when the system reaches it's maximum pressure rating. To pressure test the system:

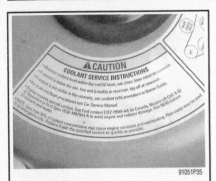

Fig. 195 Service information on the cooling system is located on a label affixed to the strut tower

Fig. 196 The coolant level should be between the MIN and MAX levels on the coolant recovery tank

Fig. 197 Remove the recovery tank cap to allow the pressure tester to be connected to the system

Fig. 198 The Contour/Mystique/Cougar cooling system requires a threaded adapter for the recovery tank to allow the pressure tester to be connected

Fig. 199 Thread the adapter onto the recovery tank

Fig. 200 Pump the cooling system with air pressure, making sure not to overpressurize the system, or damage can occur

Fig. 201 Watch the gauge on the system and observe the pressure reading

➡The pressure test should be performed with the engine OFF.

1. Remove the radiator or recovery tank cap.
2. Using the proper adapter, insert it onto the opening and connect the pressure tester,
3. Begin pressurizing the system by pumping the pressure tester and watching the gauge, when the maximum pressure is reached, stop.
4. Watch the gauge slowly and see if the pressure on the gauge drops, if it does, a leak is definitely present.
5. If the pressure stayed somewhat stable, visually inspect the system for leaks. If the pressure dropped, repressurize the system and then visually inspect the system.
6. If no signs of a leak are noticed visually, pressurize the system to the maximum pressure rating of the system and leave the pressure tester connected for about 30 minutes. Return after 30 minutes and verify the pressure on the gauge, if the pressure dropped more than 20%, a leak definitely exists, if the pressure drop is less than 20%, the system is most likely okay.

Another way coolant is lost is by a internal engine leak, causing the oil to be contaminated or the coolant to be burned in the process of combustion and sent out the exhaust. To check for oil contamination, remove the dipstick and check the condition of the oil in the oil pan. If the oil is murky and has a white or beige "milkshake look to it, the coolant is contaminating the oil through an internal leak and the engine must be torn down to find the leak. If the oil appears okay, the coolant can be burned and going out the tailpipe. A quick test for this is a cloud of white smoke appearing from the tailpipe, especially on start-up. On cold days, the white smoke will appear, this is due to condensation and the outside temperature, not a coolant leak. If the "smoke test does not verify the situation, removing the spark plugs one at a time and checking the electrodes for a green or white tint can verify an internal coolant leak and identify which cylinder(s) is the culprit and aiding your search for the cause of the leak. If the spark plugs appear okay, another method is to use a gas analyzer or emissions tester, or one of several hand-held tools that most professional shops possess. This tools are used to check the cooling system for the presence of Hydrocarbons (HC's) in the coolant.

DRAIN & REFILL

◆ See Figures 202 thru 209

Ensure that the engine is completely cool prior to starting this service.

✳✳ CAUTION

Never open, service or drain the radiator or cooling system when hot; serious burns can occur from the steam and hot coolant. Also, when draining engine coolant, keep in mind that cats and dogs are attracted to ethylene glycol antifreeze and could drink any that is left in an uncovered container or in puddles on the ground. This will prove fatal in sufficient quantities. Always drain coolant into a sealable container. Coolant should be reused unless it is contaminated or is several years old.

Fig. 202 Remove the recovery tank cap, make sure that the engine is cold, or hot coolant could blow out and possibly burn or injure

Fig. 203 The splash shield is held by 6 retaining bolts

Fig. 204 Remove the splash shield retaining bolts using a T25 Torx® driver . . .

Fig. 205 . . . and remove the splash shield from the vehicle

Fig. 206 The radiator drain plug is located on the passenger side of the vehicle, just below the lower radiator hose

Fig. 207 Loosen the drain plug and the coolant will drain out; if the fluid flow is slow, ensure that you have removed the recovery tank cap

Fig. 208 Add coolant/water directly into the coolant recovery tank, to the MAX level, then start the vehicle

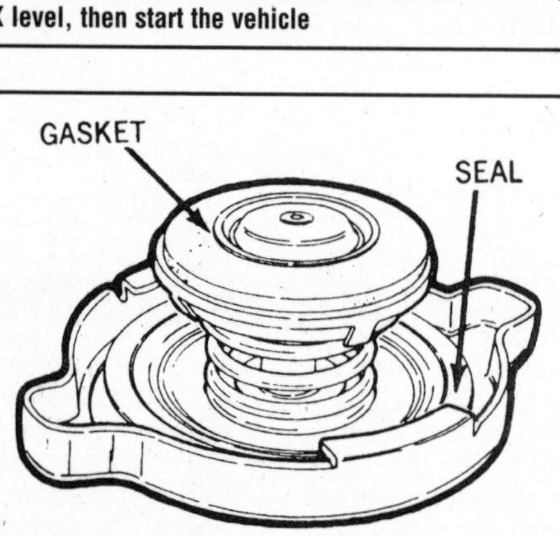

1. Remove the recovery tank cap.
2. Raise and support the vehicle.
3. Remove the splash shield from under the front of the vehicle.
4. Place a drain pan of sufficient capacity under the radiator and open the petcock (drain) on the radiator.

➥Plastic petcocks easily bind. Before opening a plastic radiator petcock, spray it with some penetrating lubricant.

5. Drain the cooling system completely.
6. Close the petcock.
7. Remove the drain pan.
8. Install the splash shield under the vehicle.
9. Lower the vehicle.
10. Determine the capacity of the cooling system, then properly refill the system at the recovery tank with a 50/50 mixture of fresh coolant and water until it reaches the MAX line.
11. Leave the recovery tank cap off to aid in bleeding the system.
12. Start the engine and allow it to idle until the thermostat opens (the upper radiator hose will become hot). The coolant level should go down; this is normal as the system bleeds the air pockets out of the system.
13. Refill the recovery tank until the coolant level is at the MAX line.
14. Turn the engine OFF and check for leaks.

FLUSHING & CLEANING THE SYSTEM

1. Drain the cooling system completely as described earlier.
2. Close the petcock and fill the system with a cooling system flush (clean water may also be used, but is not as efficient).
3. Idle the engine until the upper radiator hose gets hot.
4. Allow the engine to cool completely and drain the system again.
5. Repeat this process until the drained water is clear and free of scale.
6. Flush the recovery tank with water and leave empty.

GASKET

SEAL

Fig. 209 Be sure the rubber gasket on the radiator cap has a tight seal

Never open, service or drain the radiator or cooling system when hot; serious burns can occur from the steam and hot coolant. Also, when draining engine coolant, keep in mind that cats and dogs are attracted to ethylene glycol antifreeze and could drink any that is left in an uncovered container or in puddles on the ground. This will prove fatal in sufficient quantities. Always drain coolant into a sealable container. Coolant should be reused unless it is contaminated or is several years old.

7. Fill and bleed the cooling system as described earlier.

Brake Master Cylinder

The brake master cylinder reservoir is located under the hood, attached to the brake booster and firewall on the driver's side of the engine compartment.

FLUID RECOMMENDATIONS

Brake fluid contains polyglycol ethers and polyglycols. Avoid contact with the eyes and wash your hands thoroughly after handling brake fluid. If you do get brake fluid in your eyes, flush your eyes with clean, running water for 15 minutes. If eye irritation persists, or if you have taken brake fluid internally, IMMEDIATELY seek medical assistance.

Clean, high quality brake fluid is essential to the safe and proper operation of the brake system. You should always buy the highest quality brake fluid that is available. If the brake fluid becomes contaminated, drain and flush the system, then refill the master cylinder with new fluid. Never reuse any brake fluid. Any brake fluid that is removed from the system should be discarded. Also, do not allow any brake fluid to come in contact with a painted surface; it will damage the paint.

When adding fluid to the system, ONLY use fresh DOT 3 brake fluid from a sealed container. DOT 3 brake fluid will absorb moisture when it is exposed to the atmosphere, which will lower its boiling point. A container that has been opened once, closed and placed on a shelf will allow enough moisture to enter over time to contaminate the fluid within. If your brake fluid is contaminated with water, you could boil the brake fluid under hard braking conditions and lose all or some braking ability. Don't take the risk, buy fresh brake fluid whenever you must add to the system.

LEVEL CHECK

▶ See Figures 210, 211, 212 and 213

Brake fluid contains polyglycol ethers and polyglycols. Avoid contact with the eyes and wash your hands thoroughly after handling brake fluid. If you do get brake fluid in your eyes, flush your eyes with clean, running water for 15 minutes. If eye irritation persists, or if you have taken brake fluid internally, IMMEDIATELY seek medical assistance.

Observe the fluid level indicators on the master cylinder; the fluid level should be between the MIN and MAX lines.

Before removing the master cylinder reservoir cap, make sure the vehicle is resting on level ground and clean all dirt away from the top of the master cylinder. Unscrew the cap and fill the master cylinder until the level is between the MIN and MAX lines.

If the level of the brake fluid is less than half the volume of the reservoir, it is advised that you check the brake system for leaks. Leaks in a hydraulic brake system most commonly occur at the wheel cylinder and brake line junction points.

Clutch Master Cylinder

The clutch uses the same reservoir as the brake fluid.

The Contour/Mystique/Cougar is equipped with a hydraulic clutch control system. The system consists of a fluid reservoir, master cylinder, pressure line and a slave cylinder. The hydraulic clutch control system is tapped into the brake master cylinder reservoir and utilizes brake fluid for its operation.

FLUID RECOMMENDATIONS

Use a DOT 3 brake fluid meeting Ford specifications, such as Ford Heavy Duty Brake Fluid.

Fig. 210 The fluid level should be between the MAX and MIN lines; if the fluid level is low, be sure to check the brakes

Fig. 211 Wipe the master cylinder reservoir clean before opening the cap to ensure that no contamination enters the brake fluid

Fig. 212 Unscrew the master cylinder cap and . . .

Fig. 213 . . . carefully pour fresh, approved brake fluid directly into the reservoir

✳ WARNING

Clean, high quality brake fluid is essential to the safe and proper operation of the brake system. You should always buy the highest quality brake fluid that is available. If the brake fluid becomes contaminated, drain and flush the system, then refill the master cylinder with new fluid. Never reuse any brake fluid. Any brake fluid that is removed from the system should be discarded. Also, do not allow any brake fluid to come in contact with a painted surface; it will damage the paint.

FLUID LEVEL CHECK

✳ CAUTION

Brake fluid contains polyglycol ethers and polyglycols. Avoid contact with the eyes and wash your hands thoroughly after handling brake fluid. If you do get brake fluid in your eyes, flush your eyes with clean, running water for 15 minutes. If eye irritation persists, or if you have taken brake fluid internally, IMMEDIATELY seek medical assistance.

Inspect the brake master cylinder fluid level through the translucent master cylinder reservoir. It should be between the **MIN** and **MAX** level marks embossed on the side of the reservoir. If the level is found to be low, remove the reservoir cap and fill to the **MAX** level with DOT 3 brake fluid.

➡**Never reuse brake fluid that has been drained from the hydraulic system or fluid that has been allowed to stand in an open container for an extended period of time.**

Power Steering Pump/Rack and Pinion

FLUID RECOMMENDATIONS

The power steering reservoir is located on the passenger side of the engine compartment behind the strut tower.

Fill the power steering pump reservoir with a good quality power steering fluid or Mercon Type Automatic Transmission Fluid .

LEVEL CHECK

◆ **See Figures 214, 215 and 216**

Position the vehicle on level ground. Run the engine until the fluid is at normal operating temperature. Turn the steering wheel all the way to the left and right several times. Position the wheels in the straight ahead position, then shut off the engine. Check the level in the reservoir; it should be at the **FULL** mark. If fluid is required, remove the cap and add fluid until it reaches the **FULL** mark.

✳ CAUTION

Do not over fill the power steering fluid reservoir, overfilling can cause foaming of the fluid and a reduction in lubrication ability of the fluid. This could lead to wear of the components and expensive repairs.

Chassis Greasing

Ball joints, suspension bushings and driveline joints are permanently lubricated at the factory and require no periodic lubrication. However, many aftermarket parts used to replace these components will contain a provision for lubrication. The easiest way to determine if a component can be lubricated is to look for a grease (Zerk®) fitting.

Although the manufacturer does not recommend an interval, we at Chilton feel the chassis should be lubricated every 10,000 miles (16,000 km).

Body Lubrication and Maintenance

LUBRICATION

Treat the specified components as follows:
- Lock cylinders—apply graphite lubricant sparingly through the key slot. Insert the key and operate the lock several times to be sure that the lubricant is worked into the lock cylinder.
- Hinges—spray a silicone lubricant or white lithium grease on the hinge pivot points to eliminate any binding conditions. Open and close the door several times to be sure that the lubricant is evenly and thoroughly distributed.
- Latches—spray a silicone lubricant or white lithium grease on the latch mechanism and friction surfaces to eliminate squeaks and binding. Operate the latch to distribute the lubricant.
- Door seals—spray a silicone lubricant or a rubber protectant on the door seals and wipe the excess with a rag. This will eliminate squeaks and prevent the rubber from sticking to the metal.

CAR WASHING

The car should be washed at regular intervals to remove dirt, dust, insects, and tar and other possibly damaging stains that can adhere to the paint and may cause damage. Proper exterior maintenance also helps in the resale value of the vehicle by maintaining its like-new appearance.

➡**It is particularly important to frequently wash the car in the wintertime to prevent corrosion, when salt has been used on the roads.**

There are many precautions and tips on washing, including the following:
- When washing the car, do not expose it do direct sunlight.
- Use lukewarm water to soften the dirt before you wash with a sponge, and plenty of water, to avoid scratching.
- A detergent can be used to facilitate the softening of dirt and oil.
- A water-soluble grease solvent may be used in cases of sticky dirt. However, use a washplace with a drainage separator.

Fig. 214 The fluid level should be between the MAX and MIN lines on the reservoir

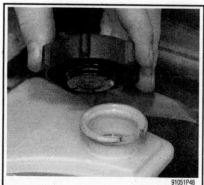

Fig. 215 Unscrew the power steering reservoir cap and . . .

Fig. 216 . . . carefully pour the fluid directly into the power steering reservoir, making sure you do not overfill it

- Dry the car with a clean chamois and remember to clean the drain holes in the doors and rocker panels.
- If equipped with a power radio antenna, it must be dried after washing.

✳✳ CAUTION

Never clean the bumpers with gasoline or paint thinner, always use the same agent as used on the painted surfaces of the vehicle.

- Tar spots can be removed with tar remover or kerosene after the car has been washed.
- A stiff-bristle brush and lukewarm soapy water can be used to clean the wiper blades. Frequent cleaning improves visibility when using the wipers considerably.
- Wash off the dirt from the underside (wheel housings, fenders, etc.).
- In areas of high industrial fallout, more frequent washing is recommended.

✳✳ CAUTION

During high pressure washing the spray nozzle must never be closer to the vehicle than 13 inches (30 cm). Do not spray into the locks.

- When washing or steam cleaning the engine, avoid spraying water or steam directly on the electrical components or near the distributor or ignition components. After cleaning the engine, the spark plug wells should be inspected for water and blown dry if necessary.
- Special car washing detergent is the best to use. Liquid dishwashing detergent can remove wax and leave the car's paint unprotected and in addition some liquid detergents contains abrasives which can scratch the paint.
- Bird droppings should be removed from the paintwork as soon as possible, otherwise the finish may be permanently stained.

✳✳ WARNING

When the car is driven immediately after being washed, apply the brakes several times in order to remove any moisture from the braking surfaces.

✳✳ WARNING

Engine cleaning agents should not be used when the engine is warm, a fire risk is present as most engine cleaning agents are highly flammable.

Automatic car washing is a simple and quick way to clean your car, but it is worth remembering that it is not as thorough as when you yourself clean the car. Keeping the underbody clean is vitally important, and some automatic washers do not contain equipment for washing the underside of the car.

When driving into an automatic was, make sure the following precautions have been taken:
- Make sure all windows are up, and no objects that you do not want to get wet are exposed.
- In some cases, rotating the side view mirrors in can help to avoid possible damage.
- If your car is equipped with a power antenna, lower it. If your vehicle has a solid mounted, non-power antenna, it is best to remove it, but this is not always practical. Inspect the surroundings to reduce the risk of possible damage, and check to see if the antenna can be manually lowered.

✳✳ WARNING

Most manufacturers do not recommend automatic car washing in the first six months due to the possibility of insufficient paint curing; a safe bet is to wait until after six months of ownership (when purchased new) to use an automatic car wash.

WAXING

➡**Before applying wax, the vehicle must be washed and thoroughly dried.**

Waxing a vehicle can help to preserve the appearance of your vehicle. A wide range of polymer-based car waxes are available today. These waxes are easy to use and produce a long-lasting, high gloss finish that protects the body and paint against oxidation, road dirt, and fading.

Sometimes, waxing a neglected vehicle, or one that has sustained chemical or natural element damage (such as acid rain) require more than waxing, and a light-duty compound can be applied. For severely damaged surfaces, it is best to consult a professional to see what would be required to repair the damage.

Waxing procedures differ according to manufacturer, type, and ingredients, so it is best to consult the directions on the wax and/or polish purchased.

INTERIOR CLEANING

Upholstery

Fabric can usually be cleaned with soapy water or a proper detergent. For more difficult spots caused by oil, ice cream, soda, etc., use a fabric cleaner available at most parts stores. Be sure when purchasing the cleaner to read the label to ensure it is safe to use on your type of fabric. A safe method of testing the cleaner is to apply a small amount to an area usually unseen, such as under a seat, or other areas. Wait a while, perhaps even a day to check the spot for fading, discoloring, etc., as some cleaners will only cause these problems after they have dried.

Leather upholstery requires special care, it can be cleaned with a mild soap and a soft cloth. It is recommended that a special leather cleaner be used to clean but also treat the leather surfaces in your vehicle. Leather surfaces can age quickly and can crack if not properly taken care of, so it is vital that the leather surfaces be maintained.

Floor Mats and Carpet

The floor mats and carpet should be vacuumed or brushed regularly. They can be cleaned with a mild soap and water. Special cleaners are available to clean the carpeted surfaces of your vehicle, but take care in choosing them, and again it is best to test them in a usually unseen spot.

Dashboard, Console, Door Panels, Etc.

The dashboard, console, door panels, and other plastic, vinyl, or wood surfaces can be cleaned using a mild soap and water. Caution must be taken to keep water out of electronic accessories and controls to avoid shorts or ruining the components. Again special cleaners are available to clean these surfaces, as with other cleaners care must taken in purchasing and using such cleaners.

There are protectants available which can treat the various surfaces in your car giving them a "shiny new look", however some of these protectants can cause more harm than good in the long run. The shine that is placed on your dashboard attracts sunlight accelerating the aging, fading and possibly even cracking the surfaces. These protectants also attract more dust to stick to the surfaces they treat, increasing the cleaning you must do to maintain the appearance of your vehicle. Personal discretion is advised here.

Wheel Bearings

REPACKING

All vehicles in this manual have permanently lubricated bearings in the front and rear. The wheel bearings are integral to the hub and are sealed.

TRAILER TOWING

General Recommendations

Your vehicle was primarily designed to carry passengers and cargo. It is important to remember that towing a trailer will place additional loads on your vehicles engine, drive train, steering, braking and other systems. However, if you decide to tow a trailer, using the prior equipment is a must.

Local laws may require specific equipment such as trailer brakes or fender mounted mirrors. Check your local laws.

Trailer Weight

The weight of the trailer is the most important factor. A good weight-to-horse-power ratio is about 35:1, 35 lbs. of Gross Combined Weight (GCW) for every horsepower your engine develops. Multiply the engine's rated horsepower by 35 and subtract the weight of the vehicle passengers and luggage. The number remaining is the approximate ideal maximum weight you should tow, although a numerically higher axle ratio can help compensate for heavier weight.

Hitch (Tongue) Weight

▶ See Figure 217

Calculate the hitch weight in order to select a proper hitch. The weight of the hitch is usually 9–11% of the trailer gross weight and should be measured with the trailer loaded. Hitches fall into various categories: those that mount on the frame and rear bumper, the bolt-on type, or the weld-on distribution type used for larger trailers. Axle mounted or clamp-on bumper hitches should never be used.

Check the gross weight rating of your trailer. Tongue weight is usually figured as 10% of gross trailer weight. Therefore, a trailer with a maximum gross weight of 2000 lbs. will have a maximum tongue weight of 200 lbs. Class I trailers fall into this category. Class II trailers are those with a gross weight rating of 2000–3000 lbs., while Class III trailers fall into the 3500–6000 lbs. category. Class IV trailers are those over 6000 lbs. and are for use with fifth wheel trucks, only.

When you've determined the hitch that you'll need, follow the manufacturer's installation instructions, exactly, especially when it comes to fastener torques.

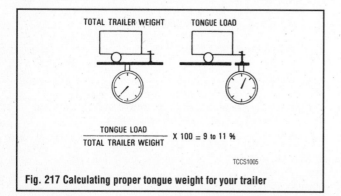

$$\frac{TONGUE\ LOAD}{TOTAL\ TRAILER\ WEIGHT} \times 100 = 9\ to\ 11\ \%$$

TCCS1005

Fig. 217 Calculating proper tongue weight for your trailer

The hitch will subjected to a lot of stress and good hitches come with hardened bolts. Never substitute an inferior bolt for a hardened bolt.

Engine

One of the most common, if not THE most common, problems associated with trailer towing is engine overheating. If you have a cooling system without an expansion tank, you'll definitely need to get an aftermarket expansion tank kit, preferably one with at least a 2 quart capacity. These kits are easily installed on the radiator's overflow hose, and come with a pressure cap designed for expansion tanks.

Aftermarket engine oil coolers are helpful for prolonging engine oil life and reducing overall engine temperatures. Both of these factors increase engine life. While not absolutely necessary in towing Class I and some Class II trailers, they are recommended for heavier Class II and all Class III towing. Engine oil cooler systems usually consist of an adapter, screwed on in place of the oil filter, a remote filter mounting and a multi-tube, finned heat exchanger, which is mounted in front of the radiator or air conditioning condenser.

Transaxle

An automatic transaxle is usually recommended for trailer towing. Modern automatics have proven reliable and, of course, easy to operate, in trailer towing. The increased load of a trailer, however, causes an increase in the temperature of the automatic transaxle fluid. Heat is the worst enemy of an automatic transaxle. As the temperature of the fluid increases, the life of the fluid decreases.

It is essential, therefore, that you install an automatic transaxle cooler. The cooler, which consists of a multi-tube, finned heat exchanger, is usually installed in front of the radiator or air conditioning compressor, and hooked in-line with the transaxle cooler tank inlet line. Follow the cooler manufacturer's installation instructions.

Select a cooler of at least adequate capacity, based upon the combined gross weights of the vehicle and trailer.

Cooler manufacturers recommend that you use an aftermarket cooler in addition to, and not instead of, the present cooling tank in your radiator. If you do want to use it in place of the radiator cooling tank, get a cooler at least two sizes larger than normally necessary.

➡**A transaxle cooler can, sometimes, cause slow or harsh shifting in the transaxle during cold weather, until the fluid has a chance to come up to normal operating temperature. Some coolers can be purchased with or retrofitted with a temperature bypass valve which will allow fluid flow through the cooler only when the fluid has reached above a certain operating temperature.**

Handling a Trailer

Towing a trailer with ease and safety requires a certain amount of experience. It's a good idea to learn the feel of a trailer by practicing turning, stopping and backing in an open area such as an empty parking lot.

TOWING THE VEHICLE

Preferred Towing Method—Flatbed

▶ See Figure 218

For maximum safety to the components of your drive train and chassis, it is most desirable to have your vehicle towed by on a flatbed or whole vehicle trailer. The only way to properly place the vehicle on a flatbed is to have it pulled on from the front.

Alternate Towing Method—T-Hook

If a flatbed is unavailable, your vehicle can be towed using a T-hook wrecker. In this case, the front wheels must be off the ground, as this will prevent wear and tear on the drive train. Tow vehicle speed should not exceed 35 mph (56 km/h) when using this method.

Last Chance Towing Method—Dolly

If absolutely necessary, you can tow your vehicle on a T-Hook from the rear. The front wheels must be placed on a dolly. Tow vehicle speed should not exceed 35 mph (56 km/h) when using this method.

Towing Your Vehicle Behind Another Vehicle

At times, you may want to tow your vehicle behind another vehicle such as a recreational vehicle (R/V), a truck, or another car. Before the vehicle is towed a few steps must be taken:
* Release the parking brake
* Move the gearshift to **N** (Neutral)
* Turn the ignition to the **OFF** position

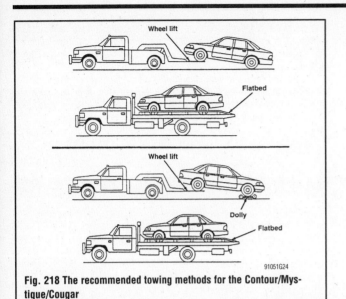

Fig. 218 The recommended towing methods for the Contour/Mystique/Cougar

* Unlock the steering wheel

When towing your vehicle behind another vehicle a few precautions must be taken:

* Do not tow your vehicle at a speed faster than 35 mph (55 km/h) for more than 50 miles (80 km) unless the wheels are placed on dollies
* Do not tow your vehicle at a speed faster than 55 mph (90 km/h) if you have a manual transaxle

JUMP STARTING A DEAD BATTERY

▶ See Figure 219

Whenever a vehicle is jump started, precautions must be followed in order to prevent the possibility of personal injury. Remember that batteries contain a small amount of explosive hydrogen gas which is a by-product of battery charging. Sparks should always be avoided when working around batteries, especially when attaching jumper cables. To minimize the possibility of accidental sparks, follow the procedure carefully.

✳✳ CAUTION

NEVER hook the batteries up in a series circuit or the entire electrical system will go up in smoke, including the starter!

Vehicles equipped with a diesel engine may utilize two 12 volt batteries. If so, the batteries are connected in a parallel circuit (positive terminal to positive terminal, negative terminal to negative terminal). Hooking the batteries up in parallel circuit increases battery cranking power without increasing total battery voltage output. Output remains at 12 volts. On the other hand, hooking two 12 volt batteries up in a series circuit (positive terminal to negative terminal, positive terminal to negative terminal) increases total battery output to 24 volts (12 volts plus 12 volts).

Jump Starting Precautions

* Be sure that both batteries are of the same voltage. Vehicles covered by this manual and most vehicles on the road today utilize a 12 volt charging system.

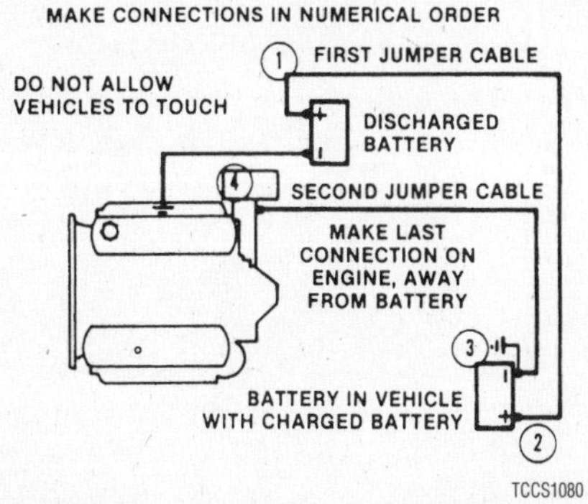

* Be sure that both batteries are of the same polarity (have the same terminal, in most cases NEGATIVE grounded).
* Be sure that the vehicles are not touching or a short could occur.
* On serviceable batteries, be sure the vent cap holes are not obstructed.
* Do not smoke or allow sparks anywhere near the batteries.
* In cold weather, make sure the battery electrolyte is not frozen. This can occur more readily in a battery that has been in a state of discharge.
* Do not allow electrolyte to contact your skin or clothing.

Jump Starting Procedure

1. Make sure that the voltages of the 2 batteries are the same. Most batteries and charging systems are of the 12 volt variety.
2. Pull the jumping vehicle (with the good battery) into a position so the jumper cables can reach the dead battery and that vehicle's engine. Make sure that the vehicles do NOT touch.
3. Place the transmissions/transaxles of both vehicles in **Neutral** (MT) or **P** (AT), as applicable, then firmly set their parking brakes.

➡**If necessary for safety reasons, the hazard lights on both vehicles may be operated throughout the entire procedure without significantly increasing the difficulty of jumping the dead battery.**

4. Turn all lights and accessories OFF on both vehicles. Make sure the ignition switches on both vehicles are turned to the **OFF** position.
5. Cover the battery cell caps with a rag, but do not cover the terminals.
6. Make sure the terminals on both batteries are clean and free of corrosion or proper electrical connection will be impeded. If necessary, clean the battery terminals before proceeding.
7. Identify the positive (+) and negative (-) terminals on both batteries.
8. Connect the first jumper cable to the positive (+) terminal of the dead battery, then connect the other end of that cable to the positive (+) terminal of the booster (good) battery.
9. Connect one end of the other jumper cable to the negative (-) terminal on the booster battery and the final cable clamp to an engine bolt head, alternator bracket or other solid, metallic point on the engine with the dead battery. Try to pick a ground on the engine that is positioned away from the battery in order to minimize the possibility of the 2 clamps touching should one loosen during the procedure. DO NOT connect this clamp to the negative (-) terminal of the bad battery.

✳✳ CAUTION

Be very careful to keep the jumper cables away from moving parts (cooling fan, belts, etc.) on both engines.

MAKE CONNECTIONS IN NUMERICAL ORDER

DO NOT ALLOW VEHICLES TO TOUCH

① FIRST JUMPER CABLE

DISCHARGED BATTERY

SECOND JUMPER CABLE

MAKE LAST CONNECTION ON ENGINE, AWAY FROM BATTERY

③

BATTERY IN VEHICLE WITH CHARGED BATTERY

②

TCCS1080

Fig. 219 Connect the jumper cables to the batteries and engine in the order shown

10. Check to make sure that the cables are routed away from any moving parts, then start the donor vehicle's engine. Run the engine at moderate speed for several minutes to allow the dead battery a chance to receive some initial charge.

11. With the donor vehicle's engine still running slightly above idle, try to start the vehicle with the dead battery. Crank the engine for no more than 10 seconds at a time and let the starter cool for at least 20 seconds between tries. If the vehicle does not start in 3 tries, it is likely that something else is also wrong or that the battery needs additional time to charge.

12. Once the vehicle is started, allow it to run at idle for a few seconds to make sure that it is operating properly.

13. Turn ON the headlights, heater blower and, if equipped, the rear defroster of both vehicles in order to reduce the severity of voltage spikes and subsequent risk of damage to the vehicles' electrical systems when the cables are disconnected. This step is especially important to any vehicle equipped with computer control modules.

14. Carefully disconnect the cables in the reverse order of connection. Start with the negative cable that is attached to the engine ground, then the negative cable on the donor battery. Disconnect the positive cable from the donor battery and finally, disconnect the positive cable from the formerly dead battery. Be careful when disconnecting the cables from the positive terminals not to allow the alligator clips to touch any metal on either vehicle or a short and sparks will occur.

JACKING

▶ See Figures 220 thru 228

Your vehicle was supplied with a jack for emergency road repairs. This jack is fine for changing a flat tire or other short term procedures not requiring you to go beneath the vehicle. If it is used in an emergency situation, carefully follow the instructions provided either with the jack or in your owner's manual. Do not attempt to use the jack on any portions of the vehicle other than specified by the vehicle manufacturer. Always block the diagonally opposite wheel when using a jack.

A more convenient way of jacking is the use of a garage or floor jack. You may use the floor jack to lift the front of the vehicle up by placing it under the front body rail, behind the front suspension. this method will only lift the side the jack is placed on. Another option to lift the front of the vehicle is to place the jack on the front subframe. This enables both front wheel wheels to be lifted off the ground. The rear of the vehicle can be lifted by placing the floor jack on the rear sill, forward of the rear wheel openings. The location is marked by an arrow symbol stamped into the rocker panel. On SE and Contour SVT models, a cover in the rocker panel is removed allowing clearance to the rear sill. If possible, use a cushioned pad to avoid damaging the painted surfaces.

Never place the jack under the radiator, engine or transmission components. Severe and expensive damage will result when the jack is raised. Additionally, never jack under the floorpan or bodywork; the metal will deform.

Whenever you plan to work under the vehicle, you must support it on jackstands or ramps. Never use cinder blocks or stacks of wood to support the vehicle, even if you're only going to be under it for a few minutes. Never crawl under the vehicle when it is supported only by the tire-changing jack or other floor jack.

➡**Always position a block of wood or small rubber pad on top of the jack or jackstand to protect the lifting point's finish when lifting or supporting the vehicle.**

Small hydraulic, screw, or scissors jacks are satisfactory for raising the vehicle. Drive-on trestles or ramps are also a handy and safe way to both raise and support the vehicle. Be careful though, some ramps may be too steep to drive your vehicle onto without scraping the front bottom panels. Never support the vehicle on any suspension member (unless specifically instructed to do so by a repair manual) or by an underbody panel.

91051PD1

Fig. 220 Place a floor jack under the front frame rails to raise the front of the vehicle

91051PD2

Fig. 221 Place the jackstands under the frame rails to support the front of the vehicle

91051PD5

Fig. 222 A piece of wood with a slot in the center will help avoid damaging the drip rails while jacking up the rear of the vehicle

91051PD4

Fig. 223 Raise the rear of the vehicle directly beneath the drip rail

91051PD3

Fig. 224 Place the jackstands beneath the small flat perches on the rear subframe

91051PD6

Fig. 225 The rear of the vehicle as supported on both sides with jackstands

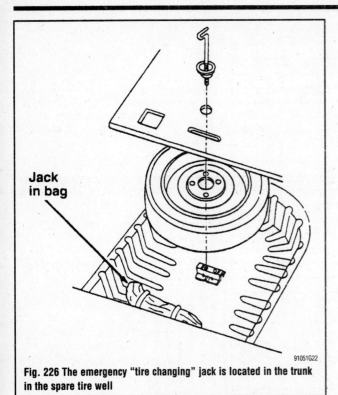

Jack in bag

Fig. 226 The emergency "tire changing" jack is located in the trunk in the spare tire well

91051G22

The following safety points cannot be overemphasized:
• Always block the opposite wheel or wheels to keep the vehicle from rolling off the jack.
• When raising the front of the vehicle, firmly apply the parking brake.
• When the drive wheels are to remain on the ground, leave the vehicle in gear to help prevent it from rolling.
• Always use jackstands to support the vehicle when you are working underneath. Place the stands beneath the vehicle's jacking brackets. Before climbing underneath, rock the vehicle a bit to make sure it is firmly supported.

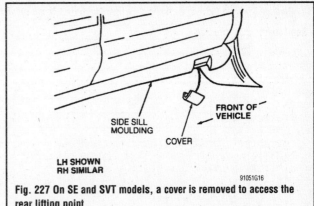

SIDE SILL MOULDING

COVER

FRONT OF VEHICLE

LH SHOWN RH SIMILAR

91051G16

Fig. 227 On SE and SVT models, a cover is removed to access the rear lifting point

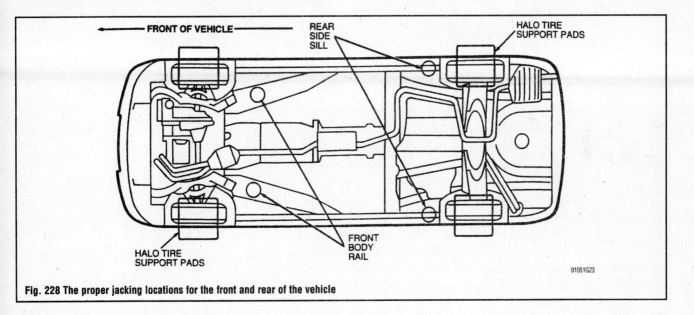

FRONT OF VEHICLE

REAR SIDE SILL

HALO TIRE SUPPORT PADS

HALO TIRE SUPPORT PADS

FRONT BODY RAIL

91051G23

Fig. 228 The proper jacking locations for the front and rear of the vehicle

MANUFACTURER RECOMMENDED NORMAL MAINTENANCE INTERVALS

Component	Type of Service	5	10	15	20	25	30	35	40	45	50	55	60	65	70	75	80
VEHICLE MAINTENANCE INTERVAL — Miles (x1000)		5	10	15	20	25	30	35	40	45	50	55	60	65	70	75	80
km (x1000)		8	16	24	32	40	48	56	64	72	80	88	96	104	112	121	128
Engine oil and filter	Replace	✓	✓	✓	✓	✓	✓	✓	✓	✓	✓	✓	✓	✓	✓	✓	✓
Tires	Rotate	✓		✓		✓		✓		✓		✓		✓		✓	
Air cleaner	Replace						✓						✓				
Passenger compartment air cleaner	Replace				✓				✓				✓				✓
Spark plugs	Replace												✓①				
Drive belts	Inspect												✓			✓	
Cooling system	Inspect			✓			✓			✓			✓			✓	
Coolant	Replace						✓						✓			✓	
PCV valve	Replace												✓				✓
Exhaust heat shields	Inspect						✓						✓				
Brake linings and drums	Inspect		✓		✓		✓		✓		✓		✓		✓		✓
Brake pads and rotors	Inspect		✓		✓		✓		✓		✓		✓		✓		✓
Clutch pedal operation	Inspect						✓						✓				
CV-joint boots	Inspect			✓			✓			✓			✓			✓	
Brake line hoses and connections	Inspect			✓			✓			✓			✓			✓	
Front ball joints	Inspect						✓						✓				
Bolts and nuts on chassis body	Inspect						✓						✓				
Steering linkage operation	Inspect						✓						✓				

Perform maintenance at the same intervals for mileage beyond that on this chart

Follow the normal service interval schedule if the vehicle is driven in the following conditions:

The vehicle is driven more than 10 miles on a daily basis

The vehicle is not used in the following conditions:

  towing a trailer or using a car-top carrier

  operating in severe dust conditions

  extensive idling such as a police car, taxi, or delivery service

  short trips of less than 10 miles when outside temperatures remain below 0°F (-18°C)

① 2.0L engine only, 2.5L at 100,000 miles

91051C05

MANUFACTURER RECOMMENDED SEVERE MAINTENANCE INTERVALS

Component	Type of Service	3	6	9	12	15	18	21	24	27	30	33	36	39	42	45	48	51	54	57	60
VEHICLE MAINTENANCE INTERVAL — Miles (x1000)		3	6	9	12	15	18	21	24	27	30	33	36	39	42	45	48	51	54	57	60
km (x1000)		5	10	15	20	25	30	35	40	45	50	55	60	65	70	75	80	85	90	95	100
Engine oil and filter	Replace	✓	✓	✓	✓	✓	✓	✓	✓	✓	✓	✓	✓	✓	✓	✓	✓	✓	✓	✓	✓
Tires	Rotate		✓		✓		✓		✓		✓		✓		✓		✓		✓		✓
Air cleaner	Replace										✓										✓
Passenger compartment air cleaner	Replace						✓						✓						✓		
Spark plugs	Replace										✓										✓
Drive belts	Inspect																✓				
Cooling system	Inspect					✓					✓					✓					✓
Coolant ①	Replace																✓				
PCV valve	Replace																				✓
Automatic transaxle fluid	Replace					✓					✓					✓					✓
Exhaust heat shields	Inspect										✓										✓
Brake linings and drums	Inspect		✓		✓		✓		✓		✓		✓		✓		✓		✓		✓
Brake pads and rotors	Inspect		✓		✓		✓		✓		✓		✓		✓		✓		✓		✓
Clutch pedal operation	Inspect										✓										✓
CV-joint boots	Inspect				✓				✓				✓			✓					✓
Brake line hoses and connections	Inspect				✓				✓				✓			✓					✓
Front ball joints	Inspect				✓				✓				✓			✓					✓
Bolts and nuts on chassis body	Inspect					✓					✓					✓					✓
Steering linkage operation	Inspect					✓					✓					✓					✓

Perform maintenance at the same intervals for mileage beyond that on this chart

Follow the severe service interval schedule if the vehicle is driven in the following conditions:

  towing a trailer or using a car-top carrier

  operating in severe dust conditions

  extensive idling such as a police car, taxi, or delivery service

  short trips of less than 10 miles when outside temperatures remain below 0°F (-18°C)

① Initially change coolant at 48,000 miles, thereafter change coolant every 30,000 miles

91051C06

ENGLISH TO METRIC CONVERSION: MASS (WEIGHT)

Current mass measurement is expressed in pounds and ounces (lbs. & ozs.). The metric unit of mass (or weight) is the kilogram (kg). Even although this table does not show conversion of masses (weights) larger than 15 lbs, it is easy to calculate larger units by following the data immediately below.

To convert ounces (oz.) to grams (g): multiply th number of ozs. by 28
To convert grams (g) to ounces (oz.): multiply the number of grams by .035
To convert pounds (lbs.) to kilograms (kg): multiply the number of lbs. by .45
To convert kilograms (kg) to pounds (lbs.): multiply the number of kilograms by 2.2

lbs	kg	lbs	kg	oz	kg	oz	kg
0.1	0.04	0.9	0.41	0.1	0.003	0.9	0.024
0.2	0.09	1	0.4	0.2	0.005	1	0.03
0.3	0.14	2	0.9	0.3	0.008	2	0.06
0.4	0.18	3	1.4	0.4	0.011	3	0.08
0.5	0.23	4	1.8	0.5	0.014	4	0.11
0.6	0.27	5	2.3	0.6	0.017	5	0.14
0.7	0.32	10	4.5	0.7	0.020	10	0.28
0.8	0.36	15	6.8	0.8	0.023	15	0.42

ENGLISH TO METRIC CONVERSION: TEMPERATURE

To convert Fahrenheit (°F) to Celsius (°C): take number of °F and subtract 32; multiply result by 5; divide result by 9
To convert Celsius (°C) to Fahrenheit (°F): take number of °C and multiply by 9; divide result by 5; add 32 to total

Fahrenheit (F)	Celsius (C)	Celsius (C)	Fahrenheit (F)	Fahrenheit (F)	Celsius (C)	Celsius (C)	Fahrenheit (F)	Fahrenheit (F)	Celsius (C)	Celsius (C)	Fahrenheit (F)
°F	°C	°C	°F	°F	°C	°C	°F	°F	°C	°C	°F
-40	-40	-38	-36.4	80	26.7	18	64.4	215	101.7	80	176
-35	-37.2	-36	-32.8	85	29.4	20	68	220	104.4	85	185
-30	-34.4	-34	-29.2	90	32.2	22	71.6	225	107.2	90	194
-25	-31.7	-32	-25.6	95	35.0	24	75.2	230	110.0	95	202
-20	-28.9	-30	-22	100	37.8	26	78.8	235	112.8	100	212
-15	-26.1	-28	-18.4	105	40.6	28	82.4	240	115.6	105	221
-10	-23.3	-26	-14.8	110	43.3	30	86	245	118.3	110	230
-5	-20.6	-24	-11.2	115	46.1	32	89.6	250	121.1	115	239
0	-17.8	-22	-7.6	120	48.9	34	93.2	255	123.9	120	248
1	-17.2	-20	-4	125	51.7	36	96.8	260	126.6	125	257
2	-16.7	-18	-0.4	130	54.4	38	100.4	265	129.4	130	266
3	-16.1	-16	3.2	135	57.2	40	104	270	132.2	135	275
4	-15.6	-14	6.8	140	60.0	42	107.6	275	135.0	140	284
5	-15.0	-12	10.4	145	62.8	44	112.2	280	137.8	145	293
10	-12.2	-10	14	150	65.6	46	114.8	285	140.6	150	302
15	-9.4	-8	17.6	155	68.3	48	118.4	290	143.3	155	311
20	-6.7	-6	21.2	160	71.1	50	122	295	146.1	160	320
25	-3.9	-4	24.8	165	73.9	52	125.6	300	148.9	165	329
30	-1.1	-2	28.4	170	76.7	54	129.2	305	151.7	170	338
35	1.7	0	32	175	79.4	56	132.8	310	154.4	175	347
40	4.4	2	35.6	180	82.2	58	136.4	315	157.2	180	356
45	7.2	4	39.2	185	85.0	60	140	320	160.0	185	365
50	10.0	6	42.8	190	87.8	62	143.6	325	162.8	190	374
55	12.8	8	46.4	195	90.6	64	147.2	330	165.6	195	383
60	15.6	10	50	200	93.3	66	150.8	335	168.3	200	392
65	18.3	12	53.6	205	96.1	68	154.4	340	171.1	205	401
70	21.1	14	57.2	210	98.9	70	158	345	173.9	210	410
75	23.9	16	60.8	212	100.0	75	167	350	176.7	215	414

TCCS1C01

CAPACITIES

Year	Model	Engine ID/VIN	Engine Displacement Liters (cc)	Engine Oil with Filter (qts.)	Transmission (pts.) 4-Spd	Transmission (pts.) 5-Spd	Transmission (pts.) Auto.	Drive Axle Front (pts.)	Drive Axle Rear (pts.)	Fuel Tank (gal.)	Cooling System (qts.)
1995	Contour	3	2.0 (1999)	4.5	—	5.5	18.0 ①	②	—	14.5	③
	Contour	L	2.5 (2507)	5.5	—	5.5	20.6 ①	②	—	14.5	③
	Mystique	3	2.0 (1999)	4.5	—	5.5	18.0 ①	②	—	14.5	④
	Mystique	L	2.5 (2507)	5.5	—	5.5	20.6 ①	②	—	14.5	④
1996	Contour	3	2.0 (1999)	4.5	—	5.5	18.0 ①	②	—	14.5	③
	Contour	L	2.5 (2507)	5.8	—	5.5	20.6 ①	②	—	14.5	③
	Mystique	3	2.0 (1999)	4.5	—	5.5	18.0 ①	②	—	14.5	③
	Mystique	L	2.5 (2507)	5.8	—	5.5	20.6 ①	②	—	14.5	③
1997	Contour	3	2.0 (1999)	4.5	—	5.5	18.0 ①	②	—	14.5	③
	Contour	L	2.5 (2507)	5.8	—	5.5	20.6 ①	②	—	14.5	③
	Mystique	3	2.0 (1999)	4.5	—	5.5	18.0 ①	②	—	14.5	③
	Mystique	L	2.5 (2507)	5.8	—	5.5	20.6 ①	②	—	14.5	③
1998	Contour	3	2.0 (1999)	4.5	—	5.5	18.0 ①	②	—	14.5	③
	Contour	L	2.5 (2507)	5.8	—	5.5	20.6 ①	②	—	14.5	③
	Contour SVT	L⑤	2.5 (2507)	5.8	—	5.5	18.0 ①	②	—	14.5	④
	Mystique	3	2.0 (1999)	4.5	—	5.5	18.0 ①	②	—	14.5	③
	Mystique	L	2.5 (2507)	5.8	—	5.5	20.6 ①	②	—	14.5	③
1999	Contour	3	2.0 (1999)	4.5	—	5.5	18.0 ①	②	—	14.5	③
	Contour	L	2.5 (2507)	5.8	—	5.5	20.6 ①	②	—	14.5	③
	Contour SVT	L⑤	2.5 (2507)	5.8	—	5.5	18.0 ①	②	—	14.5	④
	Cougar	3	2.0 (1999)	4.5	—	5.5	18.0 ①	②	—	14.5	③
	Cougar	L	2.5 (2507)	5.8	—	5.5	20.6 ①	②	—	14.5	④
	Mystique	3	2.0 (1999)	4.5	—	5.5	18.0 ①	②	—	14.5	③
	Mystique	L	2.5 (2507)	5.8	—	5.5	20.6 ①	②	—	14.5	④

NOTE: All capacities are approximate. Add fluid gradually and ensure a proper fluid level is obtained.
① Includes torque converter
② Included in transaxle capacity
③ Automatic transaxle: 7.5 qts.
Manual transaxle: 7.0 qts.
④ Automatic transaxle: 9.1 qts.
Manual transaxle: 8.9 qts.
⑤ The SVT Contour uses the same engine code, the difference is in the body code, which is 68

91051C04

ENGLISH TO METRIC CONVERSION: LENGTH

To convert inches (ins.) to millimeters (mm): multiply number of inches by 25.4
To convert millimeters (mm) to inches (ins.): multiply number of millimeters by .04

Inches	Decimals	Milli-meters	Inches	Decimals	Milli-meters	Inches to millimeters (inches)	mm
1/64	0.051625	0.3969	33/64	0.515625	13.0969	0.6	15.24
	0.03125	0.7937	17/32	0.53125	13.4937	0.7	17.78
3/64	0.046875	1.1906	35/64	0.546875	13.8906	0.8	20.32
1/16	0.0625	1.5875	9/16	0.5625	14.2875	0.9	22.86
5/64	0.078125	1.9844	37/64	0.578125	14.6844	1	25.4
	0.09375	2.3812	19/32	0.59375	15.0812	2	50.8
7/64	0.109375	2.7781	39/64	0.609375	15.4781	3	76.2
1/8	0.125	3.1750	5/8	0.625	15.8750	4	101.6
9/64	0.140625	3.5719	41/64	0.640625	16.2719	5	127.0
	0.15625	3.9687	21/32	0.65625	16.6687	6	152.4
11/64	0.171875	4.3656	43/64	0.671875	17.0656	7	177.8
3/16	0.1875	4.7625	11/16	0.6875	17.4625	8	203.2
13/64	0.203125	5.1594	45/64	0.703125	17.8594	9	228.6
	0.21875	5.5562	23/32	0.71875	18.2562	10	254.0
15/64	0.234375	5.9531	47/64	0.734375	18.6531	11	279.4
1/4	0.25	6.3500	3/4	0.75	19.0500	12	304.8
17/64	0.265625	6.7469	49/64	0.765625	19.4469	13	330.2
	0.28125	7.1437	25/32	0.78125	19.8437	14	355.6
19/64	0.296875	7.5406	51/64	0.796875	20.2406	15	381.0
5/16	0.3125	7.9375	13/16	0.8125	20.6375	16	406.4
21/64	0.328125	8.3344	53/64	0.828125	21.0344	17	431.8
	0.34375	8.7312	27/32	0.84375	21.4312	18	457.2
23/64	0.359375	9.1281	55/64	0.859375	21.8281	19	482.6
3/8	0.375	9.5250	7/8	0.875	22.2250	20	508.0
25/64	0.390625	9.9219	57/64	0.890625	22.6219	21	533.4
	0.40625	10.3187	29/32	0.90625	23.0187	22	558.8
27/64	0.421875	10.7156	59/64	0.921875	23.4156	23	584.2
7/16	0.4375	11.1125	15/16	0.9375	23.8125	24	609.6
29/64	0.453125	11.5094	61/64	0.953125	24.2094	25	635.0
	0.46875	11.9062	31/32	0.96875	24.6062	26	660.4
31/64	0.484375	12.3031	63/64	0.984375	25.0031	27	690.6
1/2	0.5	12.7000					

ENGLISH TO METRIC CONVERSION: TORQUE

To convert foot-pounds (ft. lbs.) to Newton-meters: multiply the number of ft. lbs. by 1.3
To convert inch-pounds (in. lbs.) to Newton-meters: multiply the number of in. lbs. by .11

in lbs	N-m	in lbs	N-m	in lbs	N-m	in lbs	N-m	in lbs	N-m
0.1	0.01	1	0.11	10	1.13	19	2.15	28	3.16
0.2	0.02	2	0.23	11	1.24	20	2.26	29	3.28
0.3	0.03	3	0.34	12	1.36	21	2.37	30	3.39
0.4	0.04	4	0.45	13	1.47	22	2.49	31	3.50
0.5	0.06	5	0.56	14	1.58	23	2.60	32	3.62
0.6	0.07	6	0.68	15	1.70	24	2.71	33	3.73
0.7	0.08	7	0.78	16	1.81	25	2.82	34	3.84
0.8	0.09	8	0.90	17	1.92	26	2.94	35	3.95
0.9	0.10	9	1.02	18	2.03	27	3.05	36	4.0

ENGLISH TO METRIC CONVERSION: TORQUE

Torque is now expressed as either foot-pounds (ft./lbs.) or inch-pounds (in./lbs.). The metric measurement unit for torque is the Newton-meter (Nm). This unit—the Nm—will be used for all SI metric torque references, both the present ft. lbs. and in./lbs.

ft lbs	N-m	ft lbs	N-m	ft lbs	N-m	ft lbs	N-m
0.1	0.1	33	44.7	74	100.3	115	155.9
0.2	0.3	34	46.1	75	101.7	116	157.3
0.3	0.4	35	47.4	76	103.0	117	158.6
0.4	0.5	36	48.8	77	104.4	118	160.0
0.5	0.7	37	50.7	78	105.8	119	161.3
0.6	0.8	38	51.5	79	107.1	120	162.7
0.7	1.0	39	52.9	80	108.5	121	164.0
0.8	1.1	40	54.2	81	109.8	122	165.4
0.9	1.2	41	55.6	82	111.2	123	166.8
1	1.3	42	56.9	83	112.5	124	168.1
2	2.7	43	58.3	84	113.9	125	169.5
3	4.1	44	59.7	85	115.2	126	170.8
4	5.4	45	61.0	86	116.6	127	172.2
5	6.8	46	62.4	87	118.0	128	173.5
6	8.1	47	63.7	88	119.3	129	174.9
7	9.5	48	65.1	89	120.7	130	176.2
8	10.8	49	66.4	90	122.0	131	177.6
9	12.2	50	67.8	91	123.4	132	179.0
10	13.6	51	69.2	92	124.7	133	180.3
11	14.9	52	70.5	93	126.1	134	181.7
12	16.3	53	71.9	94	127.4	135	183.0
13	17.6	54	73.2	95	128.8	136	184.4
14	18.9	55	74.6	96	130.2	137	185.7
15	20.3	56	75.9	97	131.5	138	187.1
16	21.7	57	77.3	98	132.9	139	188.5
17	23.0	58	78.6	99	134.2	140	189.8
18	24.4	59	80.0	100	135.6	141	191.2
19	25.8	60	81.4	101	136.9	142	192.5
20	27.1	61	82.7	102	138.3	143	193.9
21	28.5	62	84.1	103	139.6	144	195.2
22	29.8	63	85.4	104	141.0	145	196.6
23	31.2	64	86.8	105	142.4	146	198.0
24	32.5	65	88.1	106	143.7	147	199.3
25	33.9	66	89.5	107	145.1	148	200.7
26	35.2	67	90.8	108	146.4	149	202.0
27	36.6	68	92.2	109	147.8	150	203.4
28	38.0	69	93.6	110	149.1	151	204.7
29	39.3	70	94.9	111	150.5	152	206.1
30	40.7	71	96.3	112	151.8	153	207.4
31	42.0	72	97.6	113	153.2	154	208.8
32	43.4	73	99.0	114	154.6	155	210.2

TCCS1C02
TCCS1C03

ENGLISH TO METRIC CONVERSION: FORCE

Force is presently measured in pounds (lbs.). This type of measurement is used to measure spring pressure, specifically how many pounds it takes to compress a spring. Our present force unit (the pound) will be replaced in SI metric measurements by the Newton (N). This term will eventually see use in specifications for electric motor brush spring pressures, valve spring pressures, etc.

To convert pounds (lbs.) to Newton (N): multiply the number of lbs. by 4.45

lbs	N	lbs	N	lbs	N	oz	N
0.01	0.04	21	93.4	59	262.4	1	0.3
0.02	0.09	22	97.9	60	266.9	2	0.6
0.03	0.13	23	102.3	61	271.3	3	0.8
0.04	0.18	24	106.8	62	275.8	4	1.1
0.05	0.22	25	111.2	63	280.2	5	1.4
0.06	0.27	26	115.6	64	284.6	6	1.7
0.07	0.31	27	120.1	65	289.1	7	2.0
0.08	0.36	28	124.6	66	293.6	8	2.2
0.09	0.40	29	129.0	67	298.0	9	2.5
0.1	0.4	30	133.4	68	302.5	10	2.8
0.2	0.9	31	137.9	69	306.9	11	3.1
0.3	1.3	32	142.3	70	311.4	12	3.3
0.4	1.8	33	146.8	71	315.8	13	3.6
0.5	2.2	34	151.2	72	320.3	14	3.9
0.6	2.7	35	155.7	73	324.7	15	4.2
0.7	3.1	36	160.1	74	329.2	16	4.4
0.8	3.6	37	164.6	75	333.6	17	4.7
0.9	4.0	38	169.0	76	338.1	18	5.0
1	4.4	39	173.5	77	342.5	19	5.3
2	8.9	40	177.9	78	347.0	20	5.6
3	13.4	41	182.4	79	351.4	21	5.8
4	17.8	42	186.8	80	355.9	22	6.1
5	22.2	43	191.3	81	360.3	23	6.4
6	26.7	44	195.7	82	364.8	24	6.7
7	31.1	45	200.2	83	369.2	25	7.0
8	35.6	46	204.6	84	373.6	26	7.2
9	40.0	47	209.1	85	378.1	27	7.5
10	44.5	48	213.5	86	382.6	28	7.8
11	48.9	49	218.0	87	387.0	29	8.1
12	53.4	50	224.4	88	391.4	30	8.3
13	57.8	51	226.9	89	395.9	31	8.6
14	62.3	52	231.3	90	400.3	32	8.9
15	66.7	53	235.8	91	404.8	33	9.2
16	71.2	54	240.2	92	409.2	34	9.4
17	75.6	55	244.6	93	413.7	35	9.7
18	80.1	56	249.1	94	418.1	36	10.0
19	84.5	57	253.6	95	422.6	37	10.3
20	89.0	58	258.0	96	427.0	38	10.6

TCCS1C04

ENGLISH TO METRIC CONVERSION: LIQUID CAPACITY

Liquid or fluid capacity is presently expressed as pints, quarts or gallons, or a combination of all of these. In the metric system the liter (l) will become the basic unit. Fractions of a liter would be expressed as deciliters, centiliters, or most frequently (and commonly) as milliliters.

To convert pints (pts.) to liters (l): multiply the number of pints by .47
To convert liters (l) to pints (pts.): multiply the number of liters by 2.1
To convert quarts (qts.) to liters (l): multiply the number of quarts by .95

To convert liters (l) to quarts (qts.): multiply the number of liters by 1.06
To convert gallons (gals.) to liters (l): multiply the number of gallons by 3.8
To convert liters (l) to gallons (gals.): multiply the number of liters by .26

gals	liters	qts	liters	pts	liters
0.1	0.38	0.1	0.10	0.1	0.05
0.2	0.76	0.2	0.19	0.2	0.10
0.3	1.1	0.3	0.28	0.3	0.14
0.4	1.5	0.4	0.38	0.4	0.19
0.5	1.9	0.5	0.47	0.5	0.24
0.6	2.3	0.6	0.57	0.6	0.28
0.7	2.6	0.7	0.66	0.7	0.33
0.8	3.0	0.8	0.76	0.8	0.38
0.9	3.4	0.9	0.85	0.9	0.43
1	3.8	1	1.0	1	0.5
2	7.6	2	1.9	2	1.0
3	11.4	3	2.8	3	1.4
4	15.1	4	3.8	4	1.9
5	18.9	5	4.7	5	2.4
6	22.7	6	5.7	6	2.8
7	26.5	7	6.6	7	3.3
8	30.3	8	7.6	8	3.8
9	34.1	9	8.5	9	4.3
10	37.8	10	9.5	10	4.7
11	41.6	11	10.4	11	5.2
12	45.4	12	11.4	12	5.7
13	49.2	13	12.3	13	6.2
14	53.0	14	13.2	14	6.6
15	56.8	15	14.2	15	7.1
16	60.6	16	15.1	16	7.6
17	64.3	17	16.1	17	8.0
18	68.1	18	17.0	18	8.5
19	71.9	19	18.0	19	9.0
20	75.7	20	18.9	20	9.5
21	79.5	21	19.9	21	9.9
22	83.2	22	20.8	22	10.4
23	87.0	23	21.8	23	10.9
24	90.8	24	22.7	24	11.4
25	94.6	25	23.6	25	11.8
26	98.4	26	24.6	26	12.3
27	102.2	27	25.5	27	12.8
28	106.0	28	26.5	28	13.2
29	110.0	29	27.4	29	13.7
30	113.5	30	28.4	30	14.2

TCCS1C05

ENGLISH TO METRIC CONVERSION: PRESSURE

The basic unit of pressure measurement used today is expressed as pounds per square inch (psi). The metric unit for psi will be the kilopascal (kPa). This will apply to either fluid pressure or air pressure, and will be frequently seen in tire pressure readings, oil pressure specifications, fuel pump pressure, etc.

To convert pounds per square inch (psi) to kilopascals (kPa): multiply the number of psi by 6.89

Psi	kPa	Psi	kPa	Psi	kPa	Psi	kPa
0.1	0.7	37	255.1	82	565.4	127	875.6
0.2	1.4	38	262.0	83	572.3	128	882.5
0.3	2.1	39	268.9	84	579.2	129	889.4
0.4	2.8	40	275.8	85	586.0	130	896.3
0.5	3.4	41	282.7	86	592.9	131	903.2
0.6	4.1	42	289.6	87	599.8	132	910.1
0.7	4.8	43	296.5	88	606.7	133	917.0
0.8	5.5	44	303.4	89	613.6	134	923.9
0.9	6.2	45	310.3	90	620.5	135	930.8
1	6.9	46	317.2	91	627.4	136	937.7
2	13.8	47	324.0	92	634.3	137	944.6
3	20.7	48	331.0	93	641.2	138	951.5
4	27.6	49	337.8	94	648.1	139	958.4
5	34.5	50	344.7	95	655.0	140	965.2
6	41.4	51	351.6	96	661.9	141	972.2
7	48.3	52	358.5	97	668.8	142	979.0
8	55.2	53	365.4	98	675.7	143	985.9
9	62.1	54	372.3	99	682.6	144	992.8
10	69.0	55	379.2	100	689.5	145	999.7
11	75.8	56	386.1	101	696.4	146	1006.6
12	82.7	57	393.0	102	703.3	147	1013.5
13	89.6	58	399.9	103	710.2	148	1020.4
14	96.5	59	406.8	104	717.0	149	1027.3
15	103.4	60	413.7	105	723.9	150	1034.2
16	110.3	61	420.6	106	730.8	151	1041.1
17	117.2	62	427.5	107	737.7	152	1048.0
18	124.1	63	434.4	108	744.6	153	1054.9
19	131.0	64	441.3	109	751.5	154	1061.8
20	137.9	65	448.2	110	758.4	155	1068.7
21	144.8	66	455.0	111	765.3	156	1075.6
22	151.7	67	461.9	112	772.2	157	1082.5
23	158.6	68	468.8	113	779.1	158	1089.4
24	165.5	69	475.7	114	786.0	159	1096.3
25	172.4	70	482.6	115	792.9	160	1103.2
26	179.3	71	489.5	116	799.8	161	1110.0
27	186.2	72	496.4	117	806.7	162	1116.9
28	193.0	73	503.3	118	813.6	163	1123.8
29	200.0	74	510.2	119	820.5	164	1130.7
30	206.8	75	517.1	120	827.4	165	1137.6
31	213.7	76	524.0	121	834.3	166	1144.5
32	220.6	77	530.9	122	841.2	167	1151.4
33	227.5	78	537.8	123	848.0	168	1158.3
34	234.4	79	544.7	124	854.9	169	1165.2
35	241.3	80	551.6	125	861.8	170	1172.1
36	248.2	81	558.5	126	868.7	171	1179.0

TCCS1C06

ENGLISH TO METRIC CONVERSION: PRESSURE

The basic unit of pressure measurement used today is expressed as pounds per square inch (psi). The metric unit for psi will be the kilopascal (kPa). This will apply to either fluid pressure or air pressure, and will be frequently seen in tire pressure readings, oil pressure specifications, fuel pump pressure, etc.

To convert pounds per square inch (psi) to kilopascals (kPa): multiply the number of psi by 6.89

Psi	kPa	Psi	kPa	Psi	kPa	Psi	kPa
172	1185.9	216	1489.3	260	1792.6	304	2096.0
173	1192.8	217	1496.2	261	1799.5	305	2102.9
174	1199.7	218	1503.1	262	1806.4	306	2109.8
175	1206.6	219	1510.0	263	1813.3	307	2116.7
176	1213.5	220	1516.8	264	1820.2	308	2123.6
177	1220.4	221	1523.7	265	1827.1	309	2130.5
178	1227.3	222	1530.6	266	1834.0	310	2137.4
179	1234.2	223	1537.5	267	1840.9	311	2144.3
180	1241.0	224	1544.4	268	1847.8	312	2151.2
181	1247.9	225	1551.3	269	1854.7	313	2158.1
182	1254.8	226	1558.2	270	1861.6	314	2164.9
183	1261.7	227	1565.1	271	1868.5	315	2171.8
184	1268.6	228	1572.0	272	1875.4	316	2178.7
185	1275.5	229	1578.9	273	1882.3	317	2185.6
186	1282.4	230	1585.8	274	1889.2	318	2192.5
187	1289.3	231	1592.7	275	1896.1	319	2199.4
188	1296.2	232	1599.6	276	1903.0	320	2206.3
189	1303.1	233	1606.5	277	1909.8	321	2213.2
190	1310.0	234	1613.4	278	1916.7	322	2220.1
191	1316.9	235	1620.3	279	1923.6	323	2227.0
192	1323.8	236	1627.2	280	1930.5	324	2233.9
193	1330.7	237	1634.1	281	1937.4	325	2240.8
194	1337.6	238	1641.0	282	1944.3	326	2247.7
195	1344.5	239	1647.8	283	1951.2	327	2254.6
196	1351.4	240	1654.7	284	1958.1	328	2261.5
197	1358.3	241	1661.6	285	1965.0	329	2268.4
198	1365.2	242	1668.5	286	1971.9	330	2275.3
199	1372.0	243	1675.4	287	1978.8	331	2282.2
200	1378.9	244	1682.3	288	1985.7	332	2289.1
201	1385.8	245	1689.2	289	1992.6	333	2295.9
202	1392.7	246	1696.1	290	1999.5	334	2302.8
203	1399.6	247	1703.0	291	2006.4	335	2309.7
204	1406.5	248	1709.9	292	2013.3	336	2316.6
205	1413.4	249	1716.8	293	2020.2	337	2323.5
206	1420.3	250	1723.7	294	2027.1	338	2330.4
207	1427.2	251	1730.6	295	2034.0	339	2337.3
208	1434.1	252	1737.5	296	2040.8	240	2344.2
209	1441.0	253	1744.4	297	2047.7	341	2351.1
210	1447.9	254	1751.3	298	2054.6	342	2358.0
211	1454.8	255	1758.2	299	2061.5	343	2364.9
212	1461.7	256	1765.1	300	2068.4	344	2371.8
213	1468.7	257	1772.0	301	2075.3	345	2378.7
214	1475.5	258	1778.8	302	2082.2	346	2385.6
215	1482.4	259	1785.7	303	2089.1	347	2392.5

TCCS1C07

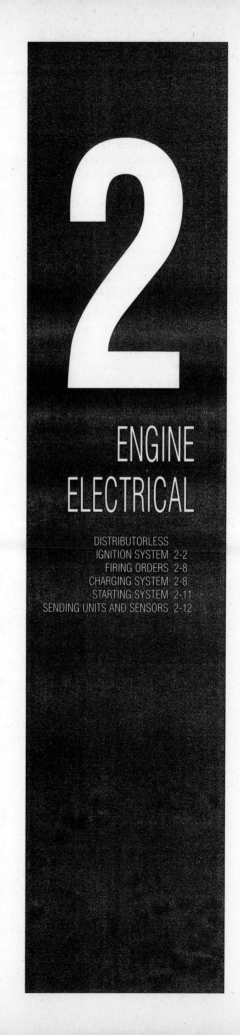

2

ENGINE ELECTRICAL

DISTRIBUTORLESS IGNITION SYSTEM

➡For information on understanding electricity and troubleshooting electrical circuits, please refer to Section 6 of this manual.

General Information

The ignition system used on the 1995–99 Cougar/Mystique and 1999 Cougar is an electronic distributorless ignition system known as the High Data Rate ignition system. There are two control systems used on these models. The system used on 1995 vehicles differs slightly from the 1996–99 vehicles in that it utilizes an Ignition Control Module (ICM). The 1996–99 vehicles utilize what is known as an integrated ignition system in which the Powertrain Control Module (PCM) performs all the control functions and the ICM is eliminated.

The system used on 1995 vehicles consists of the PCM, ICM, crankshaft position sensor (CKP), CKP trigger wheel, and a coil pack. The system operates as follows: The CKP sensor produces a signal generated from the induced voltage created as the trigger wheel on the crankshaft or flywheel passes the sensor. This signal is received at the ICM and sends the signal to the PCM as a Profile Ignition Pickup (PIP) signal. The PCM processes the PIP signal along with signals received from other sensors on engine speed, engine temperature, and engine load, and determines the correct ignition timing and generates a Spark Output (SPOUT) signal which is sent to the ICM. The ICM grounds the proper ignition coils in the coil pack firing the coil and sending voltage to the spark plugs. When the ignition coil is grounded, an Ignition Diagnostic Monitor (IDM) signal is sent from the ICM to the PCM. This signal provides the PCM with diagnostic information and confirms that the coil fired and is also used to operate the vehicle's tachometer.

The integrated ignition system consists of the powertrain control module (PCM), crankshaft position sensor (CKP), CKP trigger wheel, and a coil pack. The system operates as follows: The CKP sensor produces a signal generated from the induced voltage created as the trigger wheel on the crankshaft or flywheel passes the sensor. This signal is received at the PCM as a Profile Ignition Pickup (PIP) signal. The PCM processes the PIP signal along with signals received from other sensors on engine speed, engine temperature, and engine load, and determines the correct ignition timing and grounds the proper ignition coils in the coil pack. When the ignition coil is grounded, an Ignition Diagnostic Monitor (IDM) signal is sent to the PCM. This signal provides the PCM with diagnostic information and confirms that the coil fired and is also used to operate the vehicle's tachometer.

Diagnosis and Testing

▶ See Figure 1

SECONDARY SPARK TEST

▶ See Figures 2, 3, 4 and 5

The best way to perform this procedure is to use a spark tester (available at most automotive parts stores). Three types of spark testers are commonly available. The Neon Bulb type is connected to the spark plug wire and flashes with each ignition pulse. The Air Gap type must be adjusted to the individual spark plug gap specified for the engine. The last type of spark plug tester looks like a spark plug with a grounding clip on the side, but there is no side electrode for the spark to jump to. The last two types of testers allows the user to not only detect the presence of spark, but also the intensity (orange/yellow is weak, blue is strong).

1. Disconnect a spark plug wire at the spark plug end.
2. Connect the plug wire to the spark tester and ground the tester to an appropriate location on the engine.
3. Crank the engine and check for spark at the tester.
4. If spark exists at the tester, the ignition system is functioning properly.
5. If spark does not exist at the spark plug wire, perform diagnosis of the ignition system using individual component diagnosis procedures.

CYLINDER DROP TEST

▶ See Figures 6, 7 and 8

The cylinder drop test is performed when an engine misfire is evident. This test helps determine which cylinder is not contributing the proper power. The easiest way to perform this test is to remove the plug wires one at a time from the cylinders with the engine running.

1. Place the transaxle in **P**, engage the emergency brake, and start the engine and let it idle.
2. Using a spark plug wire removing tool, preferably the plier type, carefully remove the boot from one of the cylinders.

❊❊ WARNING

Make sure your body is free from touching any part of the car which is metal. The secondary voltage in the ignition system is high and although it cannot kill you, it will shock you and it does hurt.

		CONDITIONS		
	No Spark	Loss of Spark	Weak Spark	Timing
No Start	✔		✔	✔
Hard Start			✔	✔
Quits After Start		✔		
Stalls		✔		✔
Idle-Fast/slow				✔
Misses/Rough Run		✔	✔	
Buck/Jerk		✔	✔	
Stumble			✔	
Induction Backfire				✔
Loss of Power			✔	✔
Spark Knock				✔
Poor Fuel Economy*		✔	✔	✔
Excessive Emissions*		✔	✔	✔

91052G13

Fig. 1 Chart of Symptoms and possible ignition related causes

Fig. 2 This spark tester looks just like a spark plug, attach the clip to ground and crank the engine to check for spark

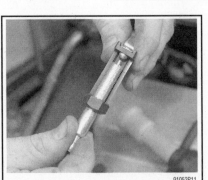

Fig. 3 This spark tester has an adjustable air-gap for measuring spark strength and testing different voltage ignition systems

Fig. 4 Attach the clip to ground and crank the engine to check for spark

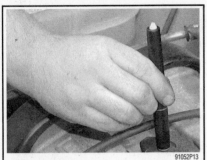

Fig. 5 This spark tester is the easiest to use just place it on a plug wire and the spark voltage is detected and the bulb on the top will flash with each pulse

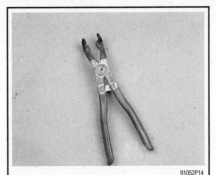

Fig. 6 These pliers are insulated and help protect the user from shock as well as the plug wires from being damaged

Fig. 7 To perform the cylinder drop test, remove one wire at a time and . . .

Fig. 8 . . . note the idle speed and idle characteristics of the engine. the cylinder(s) with the least drop is the non-contributing cylinder(s)

3. The engine will sputter, run worse, and possibly nearly stall. If this happens reinstall the plug wire and move to the next cylinder. If the engine runs no differently, or the difference is minimal, shut the engine off and inspect the spark plug wire, spark plug, and if necessary, perform component diagnostics as covered in this section. Perform the test on all cylinders to verify the which cylinders are suspect.

Adjustments

All adjustments in the ignition system are controlled by the Powertrain Control Module (PCM) for optimum performance. No adjustments are possible.

Ignition Control Module

REMOVAL & INSTALLATION

⬦ **See Figures 9 thru 21**

This procedure applies only to 1995 models.
1. Disconnect the negative battery cable.
2. On the 2.0L engine, remove the air intake resonators from the vehicle.
3. Unplug the Ignition Control Module (ICM) connector.
4. Remove the two ICM retaining screws and remove the ICM from the vehicle.
To install:
5. Place the ICM into position and tighten the retaining screws to 24–35 inch lbs (3–4 Nm).
6. Plug the ICM connector in.
7. On the 2.0L engine, install the air intake resonators.
8. Connect the negative battery cable.

Ignition Coil Pack

TESTING

2.0L Engine

⬦ **See Figures 9 thru 16, 22**

PRIMARY WINDING RESISTANCE

⬦ **See Figure 23**

1. Turn the ignition **OFF**.
2. Disconnect the negative battery cable.

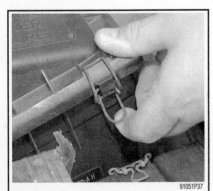

Fig. 9 Grasp and unfasten the retaining clips . . .

Fig. 10 . . . located in the following positions —2.0L engine, 2.5L similar

Fig. 11 The MAF connector is released by pressing down on the retaining spring— shown here already disconnected

Fig. 12 Label and disconnect the MAF sensor . . .

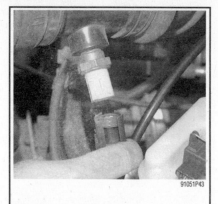

Fig. 13 . . . and the IAT sensor

Fig. 14 Loosen the clamp on the air cleaner tube

Fig. 15 Lift the air cleaner inlet tube slightly and slide the retaining tab on the air intake resonator out . . .

Fig. 16 . . . then remove the air cleaner inlet tube from the vehicle

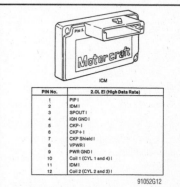

PIN No.	2.0L EI (High Data Rate)
1	PIP I
2	IDM I
3	SPOUT I
4	IGN GND I
5	CKP-I
6	CKP+I
7	CKP Shield I
8	VPWR I
9	PWR GND I
10	Coil 1 (CYL 1 and 4) I
11	IDM I
12	Coil 2 (CYL 2 and 3) I

Fig. 17 ICM pin-out of vehicles with 2.0L engines

PIN No.	2.5L
1	PIP I
2	IDM I
3	SPOUT I
4	IGN GND I
5	CKP-I
6	CKP+I
7	CKP Shield
8	VPWR I
9	PWR GND I
10	Coil 1 (CYL 1 and 5) I
11	Coil 3 (CYL 2 and 6) I
12	Coil 2 (CYL 3 and 4) I

Fig. 18 ICM pin-out of vehicles with 2.5L engines

Fig. 19 Unplug the connector from the ICM

Fig. 20 Remove the ICM retaining bolts and . . .

Fig. 21 . . . carefully remove the ICM from the firewall

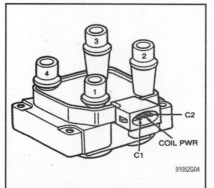

Fig. 22 2.0L engine coil pack pin location and coil towers

Fig. 23 Testing coil primary winding resistance

3. Remove the air intake resonators.

4. Disconnect the wiring harness from the ignition coil.

5. Check for dirt, corrosion or damage on the terminals and repair as necessary.

6. Measure coil primary resistance between the center ignition coil pin (B+) and pins 1 (coil 1) and 3 (coil 2).

7. Resistance should be 0.3–1.0 ohms. If resistance is out of specifications, replace the coil pack. If resistance is within specifications, proceed to secondary windings testing.

SECONDARY WINDING RESISTANCE

▶ See Figures 24 and 25

1. Measure coil secondary resistance between the corresponding spark plug wire towers on the coil.
   - Coil 1—cylinders 1 and 4
   - Coil 2—cylinders 2 and 3

2. Resistance should be 12.8–13.1 kilohms. If secondary resistance is not within specification, replace the coil pack.

2.5L Engine

▶ See Figure 26

PRIMARY WINDING RESISTANCE

▶ See Figure 27

1. Turn the ignition **OFF**.
2. Disconnect the negative battery cable.
3. Disconnect the wiring harness from the ignition coil.

4. Check for dirt, corrosion or damage on the terminals and repair as necessary.

5. Measure coil primary resistance between ignition coil pin 4 (B+) and pins 1 (coil 2), 2 (coil 3) and 3 (coil 1).

6. Resistance should be 0.3–1.0 ohms. If resistance is out of specifications, replace the coil pack. If resistance is within specifications, proceed to secondary windings testing.

SECONDARY WINDING RESISTANCE

▶ See Figure 28

1. Measure coil secondary resistance between the corresponding spark plug wire towers on the coil.
   - Coil 1—cylinders 1 and 5
   - Coil 3—cylinders 2 and 6
   - Coil 2—cylinders 3 and 4

2. Resistance should be 12.8–13.1 kilohms. If secondary resistance is not within specification, replace the coil pack.

REMOVAL & INSTALLATION

2.0L Engine

▶ See Figures 9 thru 15, 29 thru 33

1. Disconnect the negative battery cable.
2. Remove the air intake resonators from the vehicle.
3. Unplug the ignition coil pack connector.
4. Label and remove the spark plug wires from the coil by squeezing the locking tabs and twisting while gently pulling upward.
5. Remove the four ignition coil pack retaining screws and remove the ignition coil.

Fig. 24 Testing coil secondary resistance of coil 1—2.0L engine

91052P01

Fig. 25 Testing coil secondary resistance of coil 2—2.0L engine

91052P02

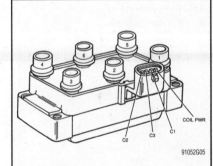

COIL PWR

C2   C3   C1

91052G05

Fig. 26 2.5L engine coil pack pin location and coil towers

89692P04

Fig. 27 Testing the coil primary resistance using a multimeter—2.5L engine

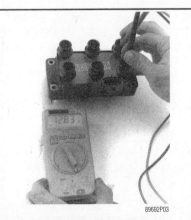

89692P03

Fig. 28 Testing the coil secondary resistance between the ignition wire terminals—2.5L engine

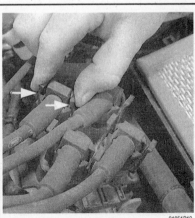

91051P12

Fig. 29 Press the retaining tabs on the plug wire connections at the coil pack and . . .

To install:

6. Position the coil pack into place and tighten the retaining screws.

7. Install the spark plug wires. The plug wire boots are fully seated when a click is heard.

8. Attach the coil pack connector.

9. Install the air intake resonators.

10. Connect the negative battery cable.

2.5L Engine

▶ **See Figures 34, 35 and 36**

1. Disconnect the negative battery cable.

2. Unplug the ignition coil pack connector and unplug the radio interference capacitor located on the coil pack.

3. Remove the EGR vacuum regulator solenoid from the upper intake manifold.

4. Label and remove the spark plug wires from the coil by squeezing the locking tabs and twisting while gently pulling upward.

5. Remove the coil pack retaining bolts, the radio interference capacitor, and the ground wire from the bracket and remove the coil pack.

To install:

6. Position the coil pack into place, attach the radio interference capacitor and ground wire and tighten the retaining bolts to 40–61 inch lbs. (5–7 Nm).

7. Install the spark plug wires. The plug wire boots are fully seated when a click is heard.

8. Install the EGR vacuum regulator solenoid onto the upper intake manifold.

9. Attach the coil pack connector and the radio interference capacitor connector.

10. Connect the negative battery cable.

OPERATION

The Crankshaft Position (CKP) sensor is a variable reluctance sensor that uses a trigger wheel to induce voltage. The CKP sensor is a fixed magnetic sensor mounted to the engine block and monitors the trigger or "pulse" wheel. As the pulse wheel rotates by the CKP sensor, teeth on the pulse wheel induce voltage inside the sensor through magnetism. The pulse wheel has a missing tooth, in the case of the 2.5L engine, and a high spot located on the flywheel on the 2.0L engine, that changes the reading of the sensor. This is used for the Cylinder Identification (CID) function to properly monitor and adjust engine timing by locating the number 1 cylinder.

The pulse wheel on the 2.0L engine is actually the flywheel, while on the 2.5L engine the pulse wheel is located on the front of the crankshaft behind the damper and just inside the front cover. The voltage created by the CKP sensor is alternating current (A/C). This voltage reading is sent to the PCM and is used to determine engine RPM, engine timing, and is used to fire the ignition coils.

TESTING

1. Measure the voltage between the sensor CKP sensor terminals by backprobing the sensor connector.

➡**If the connector cannot be backprobed, fabricate or purchase a test harness.**

2. Sensor voltage should be more than 0.1 volt AC with the engine running and should vary with engine RPM.

3. If voltage is not within specification, the sensor may be faulty.

Fig. 30 . . . lift the plug wire from the coil pack

Fig. 31 Unplug the connector on the coil pack by depressing the retaining spring and gently sliding it off

Fig. 32 Remove the coil pack retaining bolts

Fig. 33 Lift the coil pack from it's mounting bracket

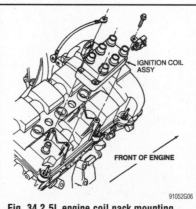

IGNITION COIL ASSY

FRONT OF ENGINE

Fig. 34 2.5L engine coil pack mounting

Fig. 35 Unplug the ignition coil connector

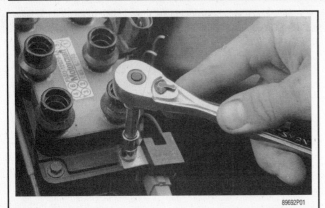

Fig. 36 The coil pack is attached to a bracket with four small bolts

REMOVAL & INSTALLATION

▶ See Figures 37, 38, 39 and 40

The CKP sensor is located on the rear of the engine and is triggered by the flywheel on the 2.0L engine, and it is located on the front of the engine and is triggered by a pulse wheel behind the crankshaft damper and inside the front cover on the 2.5L engine.

1. Disconnect the negative battery cable.
2. Raise and support the vehicle.
3. On 2.5L engine equipped models, remove the splash shield from the passenger side fenderwell.
4. Unplug the sensor connector.
5. Remove the CKP sensor retaining bolt and remove the sensor.

To install:

6. Place the CKP sensor into position and tighten the retaining bolt to 53–80 inch lbs. (6–9 Nm) on the 2.0L engine, and 71–106 inch lbs. (8–12 Nm) on the 2.5L engine.
7. Attach the sensor connector.
8. On vehicles equipped with the 2.5L engine, install the splash shield.
9. Lower the vehicle.
10. Connect the negative battery cable.

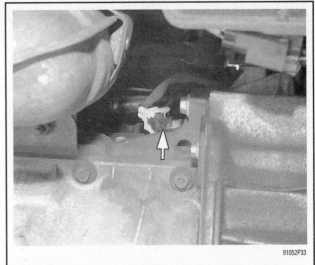

Fig. 38 The CKP sensor as viewed from underneath the vehicle

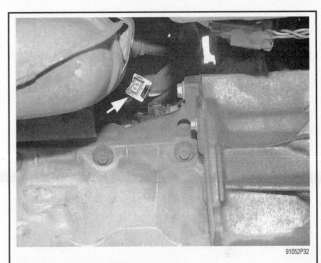

Fig. 39 Unplug the CKP sensor connector

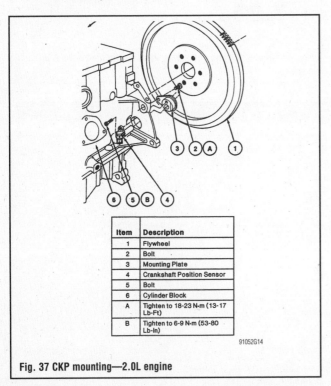

Item	Description
1	Flywheel
2	Bolt
3	Mounting Plate
4	Crankshaft Position Sensor
5	Bolt
6	Cylinder Block
A	Tighten to 18-23 N·m (13-17 Lb-Ft)
B	Tighten to 6-9 N·m (53-80 Lb-In)

Fig. 37 CKP mounting—2.0L engine

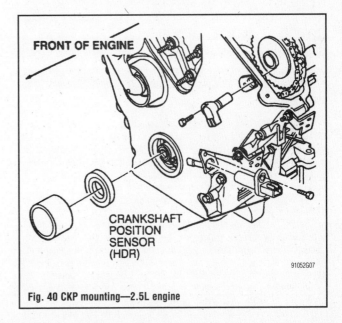

FRONT OF ENGINE

CRANKSHAFT POSITION SENSOR (HDR)

Fig. 40 CKP mounting—2.5L engine

FIRING ORDERS

♦ See Figures 41 and 42

➡To avoid confusion, remove and tag the spark plug wires one at a time, for replacement.

If a distributor is not keyed for installation with only one orientation, it could have been removed previously and rewired. The resultant wiring would hold the correct firing order, but could change the relative placement of the plug towers in relation to the engine. For this reason it is imperative that you label all wires before disconnecting any of them. Also, before removal, compare the current wiring with the accompanying illustrations. If the current wiring does not match, ake notes in your book to reflect how your engine is wired.

The engine firing order for the 2.0L engine is: 1–3–4–2
The engine firing order for the 2.5L engine is: 1–4–2–5–3–6

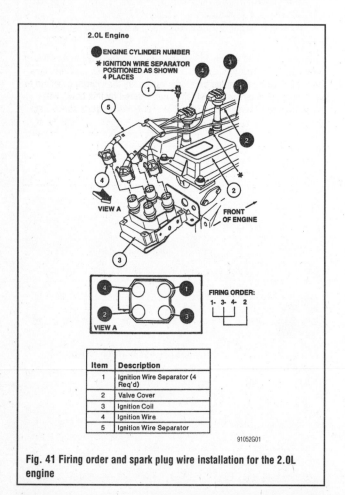

Item	Description
1	Ignition Wire Separator (4 Req'd)
2	Valve Cover
3	Ignition Coil
4	Ignition Wire
5	Ignition Wire Separator

91052G01

Fig. 41 Firing order and spark plug wire installation for the 2.0L engine

91052G02

Fig. 42 Firing order and spark plug wire installation for the 2.5L engine

CHARGING SYSTEM

General Information

♦ See Figure 43

The automobile charging system provides electrical power for operation of the vehicle's ignition and starting systems and all the electrical accessories. The battery serves as an electrical surge or storage tank, storing (in chemical form) the energy originally produced by the engine driven alternator. The system also provides a means of regulating generator output to protect the battery from being overcharged and to avoid excessive voltage to the accessories.

The storage battery is a chemical device incorporating parallel lead plates in a tank containing a sulfuric acid/water solution. Adjacent plates are slightly dissimilar, and the chemical reaction of the 2 dissimilar plates produces electrical energy when the battery is connected to a load such as the starter motor. The chemical reaction is reversible, so that when the generator is producing a voltage (electrical pressure) greater than that produced by the battery, electricity is forced into the battery, and the battery is returned to its fully charged state.

The vehicle's alternator is driven mechanically, by a belt(s) that is driven by the engine crankshaft. In an alternator, the field rotates while all the current produced passes only through the stator winding. The brushes bear against continuous slip rings rather than a commutator. This causes the current produced to

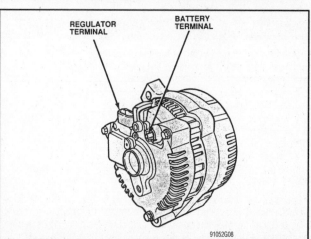

91052G08

Fig. 43 The alternator on the Contour/Mystique/Cougar is an internal fan/integral regulator type

periodically reverse the direction of its flow creating alternating current (A/C). Diodes (electrical one-way switches) block the flow of current from traveling in the wrong direction. A series of diodes is wired together to permit the alternating flow of the stator to be converted to a pulsating, but unidirectional flow at the alternator output. The alternator's field is wired in series with the voltage regulator.

The regulator consists of several circuits. Each circuit has a core, or magnetic coil of wire, which operates a switch. Each switch is connected to ground through one or more resistors. The coil of wire responds directly to system voltage. When the voltage reaches the required level, the magnetic field created by the winding of wire closes the switch and inserts a resistance into the generator field circuit, thus reducing the output. The contacts of the switch cycle open and close many times each second to precisely control voltage.

Alternator Precautions

Several precautions must be observed when performing work on alternator equipment.
- If the battery is removed for any reason, make sure that it is reconnected with the correct polarity. Reversing the battery connections may result in damage to the one-way rectifiers.
- Never operate the alternator with the main circuit broken. Make sure that the battery, alternator, and regulator leads are not disconnected while the engine is running.
- Never attempt to polarize an alternator.
- When charging a battery that is installed in the vehicle, disconnect the negative battery cable.
- When utilizing a booster battery as a starting aid, always connect it in parallel; negative to negative, and positive to positive.
- When arc (electric) welding is to be performed on any part of the vehicle, disconnect the negative battery cable and alternator leads.
- Never unplug the PCM while the engine is running or with the ignition in the **ON** position. Severe and expensive damage may result within the solid state equipment.

Alternator

TESTING

Voltage Test

1. Make sure the engine is **OFF**, and turn the headlights on for 15–20 seconds to remove any surface charge from the battery.
2. Using a DVOM set to volts DC, probe across the battery terminals.
3. Measure the battery voltage.
4. Write down the voltage reading and proceed to the next test.

No-Load Test

1. Connect a tachometer to the engine.

❖❖ CAUTION

Ensure that the transmission is in PARK and the emergency brake is set. Blocking a wheel is optional and an added safety measure.

2. Turn off all electrical loads (radio, blower motor, wipers, etc.)
3. Start the engine and increase engine speed to approximately 1500 rpm.
4. Measure the voltage reading at the battery with the engine holding a steady 1500 rpm. Voltage should have raised at least 0.5 volts, but no more than 2.5 volts.
5. If the voltage does not go up more than 0.5 volts, the alternator is not charging. If the voltage goes up more than 2.5 volts, the alternator is overcharging.

➡**Usually under and overcharging is caused by a defective alternator, or its related parts (regulator), and replacement will fix the problem; however, faulty wiring and other problems can cause the charging system to malfunction. Further testing, which is not covered by this book, will reveal the exact component failure. Many automotive parts stores have alternator bench testers available for use by customers. An alternator**

bench test is the most definitive way to determine the condition of your alternator.

6. If the voltage is within specifications, proceed to the next test.

Load Test

1. With the engine running, turn on the blower motor and the high beams (or other electrical accessories to place a load on the charging system).
2. Increase and hold engine speed to 2000 rpm.
3. Measure the voltage reading at the battery.
4. The voltage should increase at least 0.5 volts from the voltage test. If the voltage does not meet specifications, the charging system is malfunctioning.

➡**Usually under and overcharging is caused by a defective alternator, or its related parts (regulator), and replacement will fix the problem; however, faulty wiring and other problems can cause the charging system to malfunction. Further testing, which is not covered by this book, will reveal the exact component failure. Many automotive parts stores have alternator bench testers available for use by customers. An alternator bench test is the most definitive way to determine the condition of your alternator.**

REMOVAL & INSTALLATION

2.0L Engine

◗ See Figures 44, 45, 46 and 47

1. Disconnect the negative battery cable.
2. Remove air intake resonators.
3. Remove the air cleaner-to-throttle body tube and the mass airflow sensor.
4. Unplug the connectors and remove the cables from the alternator.
5. Raise and support the vehicle.
6. Release the drive belt tensioner and remove the drive belt from around the alternator.

➡**It is not necessary to remove the drive belt from the engine.**

7. Remove the alternator mounting bracket bolts and remove the mounting bracket.
8. Lower the vehicle.
9. Remove the power steering pressure hose bracket retaining nut and bolt and remove the bracket with the hose from the engine lifting eye.
10. Remove the alternator mounting bolts and remove the alternator from the vehicle.
   To install:
11. Place the alternator into position and install the mounting bolts finger tight.
12. Install the power steering hose bracket and tighten the retaining nut and bolt to 70–106 inch lbs. (8–12 Nm).
13. Raise and support the vehicle.
14. Install the alternator mounting bracket and retaining bolts and tighten to 15–22 ft. lbs. (20–30 Nm).

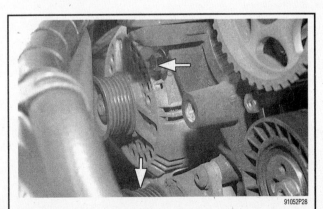

91052P28

Fig. 44 Remove the two mounting bolts on the front of the alternator

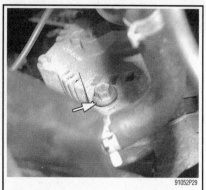

Fig. 45 Remove the rear alternator mounting bolt

Fig. 46 Pull the alternator forward and unplug the connectors on the back

Fig. 47 Carefully remove the alternator from the vehicle

15. Release the drive belt tensioner and install the drive belt pulley over the alternator pulley.

16. Lower the vehicle.

17. Tighten the alternator mounting bolts to 15–22 ft. lbs. (20–30 Nm).

18. Install the alternator connectors and the cables. Tighten the terminal nut to 80–97 inch lbs. (9–11 Nm).

19. Install the air cleaner-to-throttle body tube, mass airflow sensor, and the air intake resonators.

20. Connect the negative battery cable.

2.5L Engine

▶ See Figure 48

1. Disconnect the negative battery cable.

2. Release the drive belt tensioner and remove the drive belt from around the alternator.

3. Raise and support the vehicle.

4. Remove the passenger side front wheel and fender well splash guard.

5. Disconnect the passenger side outer tie rod end from the spindle. See Section 8.

6. Remove the exhaust system Y-pipe.

7. Unplug the connectors and remove the cables from the alternator.

8. Remove the alternator brace retaining bolts and the brace from the vehicle.

9. Remove the passenger side halfshaft. See Section 7.

10. Remove the alternator mounting bolts and remove the alternator from the passenger side fenderwell.

To install:

11. Install the alternator on the bracket and tighten the mounting bolts to 29–40 ft. lbs. (40–55 Nm).

12. Install the passenger side halfshaft. See Section 7.

13. Install the alternator brace and tighten the retaining bolts to 15–22 ft. lbs. (20–30 Nm).

14. Install the alternator connectors and the cables. Tighten the terminal nut to 80–97 inch lbs. (9–11 Nm).

15. Install the exhaust system Y-pipe.

16. Install the passenger side outer tie rod end to the spindle. See Section 8.

17. Install the passenger side fender well splash guard and front wheel.

18. Lower the vehicle.

19. Release the drive belt tensioner and install the drive belt pulley over the alternator pulley.

20. Connect the negative battery cable.

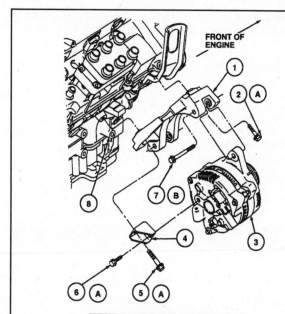

Item	Description
1	Generator Mounting Bracket
2	Bolt (M8 X 1.25 X 49.3) (2 Req'd)
3	Generator
4	Generator Brace
5	Bolt
6	Bolt
7	Bolt (M10 x 1.5 x 83.5) (2 Req'd)
8	Cylinder Block
A	Tighten to 20-30 N·m (15-22 Lb-Ft)
B	Tighten to 40-55 N·m (29-40 Lb-Ft)

Fig. 48 Alternator mounting—2.5L engine

STARTING SYSTEM

General Information

▶ See Figure 49

The starting system includes the battery, starter motor, solenoid, ignition switch, circuit protection and wiring connecting the components. An inhibitor switch located in the Transmission Range (TR) sensor is included in the starting system to prevent the vehicle from being started with the vehicle in gear.

When the ignition key is turned to the START position, current flows and energizes the starter's solenoid coil. The solenoid plunger and clutch shift lever are activated and the clutch pinion engages the ring gear on the flywheel. The switch contacts close and the starter cranks the engine until it starts.

To prevent damage caused by excessive starter armature rotation when the engine starts, the starter incorporates an over-running clutch in the pinion gear.

Starter

TESTING

Voltage Drop Test

▶ See Figures 50 and 51

➡The battery must be in good condition and fully charged prior to performing this test.

1. Disable the ignition system by unplugging the coil pack. Verify that the vehicle will not start.
2. Connect a voltmeter between the positive terminal of the battery and the starter **B+** circuit.
3. Turn the ignition key to the START position and note the voltage on the meter.

4. If voltage reads 0.5 volts or more, there is high resistance in the starter cables or the cable ground, repair as necessary. If the voltage reading is ok proceed to the next step.
5. Connect a voltmeter between the positive terminal of the battery and the starter **M** circuit.
6. Turn the ignition key to the START position and note the voltage on the meter.
7. If voltage reads 0.5 volts or more, there is high resistance in the starter. Repair or replace the starter as necessary.

➡Many automotive parts stores have starter bench testers available for use by customers. A starter bench test is the most definitive way to determine the condition of your starter.

REMOVAL & INSTALLATION

2.0L Engine

▶ See Figures 52 and 53

1. Disconnect the negative battery cable.
2. Remove air intake resonators.
3. Remove starter motor upper mounting bolts.
4. Raise and support the vehicle.
5. Remove the nuts on the starter terminals and remove the cables from the terminals.
6. Remove the two starter lower retaining bolts and remove the starter.

To install:

7. Place the starter into position and tighten the 2 lower retaining bolts to 15–20 ft. lbs (20–27 Nm).
8. Place the starter cables onto the terminals and tighten the retaining nuts to 80–124 inch lbs. (5–7 Nm).
9. Lower the vehicle.

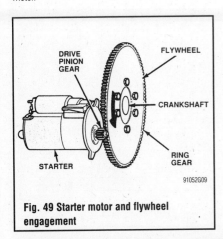

Fig. 49 Starter motor and flywheel engagement

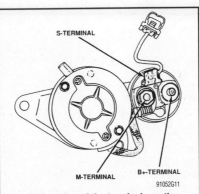

Fig. 50 Location of the terminals on the starter motor

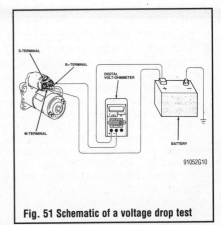

Fig. 51 Schematic of a voltage drop test

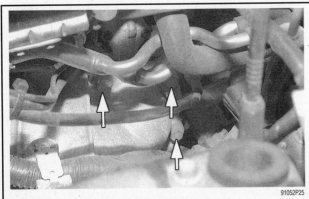

Fig. 52 Remove the three starter mounting bolts

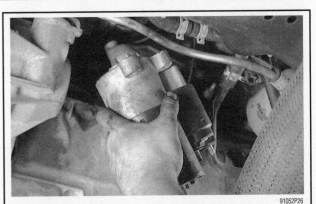

Fig. 53 Carefully lower the starter out of the vehicle

10. Install and tighten the upper retaining bolt to 15–20 ft. lbs (20–27 Nm).
11. Install the air intake resonators.
12. Connect the negative battery cable.

2.5L Engine

♦ See Figure 54

1. Disconnect the negative battery cable.
2. Remove the engine air cleaner assembly.
3. Remove the fuel feed and return lines from the support bracket located on the accelerator cable bracket, and remove the fuel line bracket.
4. On vehicles equipped with a automatic transaxle, remove the gear selector and the gear shift cable bracket from the transaxle.
5. Remove the air cleaner support bracket from the engine and transaxle mount.
6. Remove the nuts on the starter terminals and remove the cables from the terminals.
7. Remove the starter motor-to-transaxle case retaining bolt at the rear of the starter.
8. Remove the two starter retaining bolts and carefully lift the starter from the transaxle case while disengaging the alignment pins.

To install:

9. Position the starter onto the alignment pins and onto the transaxle case.
10. Install the two starter retaining bolts and the rear retaining bolt and tighten them to 15–21 ft. lbs. (21–29 Nm).
11. Place the starter cables onto the terminals and tighten the retaining nuts to 80–124 inch lbs. (5–7 Nm).
12. Install the air cleaner support bracket.
13. If removed, install the gear shift selector and bracket.
14. Install the fuel line bracket and install the fuel lines in the bracket.
15. Install the air cleaner assembly.
16. Connect the negative battery cable.

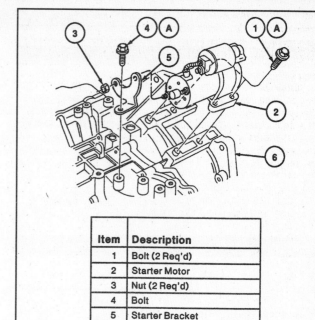

Item	Description
1	Bolt (2 Req'd)
2	Starter Motor
3	Nut (2 Req'd)
4	Bolt
5	Starter Bracket
6	Engine
A	Tighten to 21-29 N·m (15-21 Lb-Ft)

91052G16

Fig. 54 Starter mounting—2.5L engine

SENDING UNITS AND SENSORS

➥This section describes the operating principles of sending units, warning lights and gauges. Sensors which provide information to the Electronic Control Module (ECM) are covered in Section 4 of this manual.

Instrument panels contain a number of indicating devices (gauges and warning lights). These devices are composed of two separate components. One is the sending unit, mounted on the engine or other remote part of the vehicle, and the other is the actual gauge or light in the instrument panel.

Several types of sending units exist, however most can be characterized as being either a pressure type or a resistance type. Pressure type sending units convert liquid pressure into an electrical signal which is sent to the gauge. Resistance type sending units are most often used to measure temperature and use variable resistance to control the current flow back to the indicating device. Both types of sending units are connected in series by a wire to the battery (through the ignition switch). When the ignition is turned **ON**, current flows from the battery through the indicating device and on to the sending unit.

Temperature Gauge Sending Unit

♦ See Figure 55

The sending unit is located on the thermostat housing on the 2.0L engine and on the water crossover tube on the 2.5L engine.

TESTING

1. Check the appropriate fuse before attempting any other diagnostics.
2. Disconnect the sending unit electrical harness.

❋❋ CAUTION

Never open, service or drain the radiator or cooling system when hot; serious burns can occur from the steam and hot coolant. Also, when draining engine coolant, keep in mind that cats and dogs are attracted to ethylene glycol antifreeze and could drink any that is

91052P20

Fig. 55 The temperature sending unit location—2.0L engine

left in an uncovered container or in puddles on the ground. This will prove fatal in sufficient quantities. Always drain coolant into a sealable container. Coolant should be reused unless it is contaminated or is several years old.

3. Remove the radiator cap and place a mechanic's thermometer in the coolant.
4. Using an ohmmeter, check the resistance between the sending unit terminals.
5. Resistance should be high (74 ohms) with engine coolant cold and low (9.7 ohms) with engine coolant hot.

➥It is best to check resistance with the engine cool, then start the engine and watch the resistance change as the engine warms.

6. If resistance does not drop as engine temperature rises, the sending unit is faulty.

REMOVAL & INSTALLATION

✳✳ CAUTION

Never open, service or drain the radiator or cooling system when hot; serious burns can occur from the steam and hot coolant. Also, when draining engine coolant, keep in mind that cats and dogs are attracted to ethylene glycol antifreeze and could drink any that is left in an uncovered container or in puddles on the ground. This will prove fatal in sufficient quantities. Always drain coolant into a sealable container. Coolant should be reused unless it is contaminated or is several years old.

1. Disconnect the negative battery cable.
2. On the 2.5L engine, remove the air cleaner-to-throttle body hose.
3. Disconnect the sending unit electrical harness.
4. Drain the engine coolant below the level of the switch.
5. Remove the sending unit from the engine using the proper size socket (Usually an ¾ inch or 17mm).
   To install:
6. Coat the new sending unit with Teflon® tape or electrically conductive sealer.
7. Install the sending unit and tighten to 62–89 inch lbs. (7–10 Nm) on the 2.0L engine and 13–18 ft. lbs. (18–24 Nm).
8. Attach the sending unit's electrical connector.
9. Fill the engine with coolant.
10. Start the engine, allow it to reach operating temperature ,bleed the cooling system and check for leaks.
11. Check for proper sending unit operation.

Oil Pressure Sensor

▶ See Figure 56

The oil pressure sensor is located on the engine block and operates the oil pressure warning lamp, not a gauge.

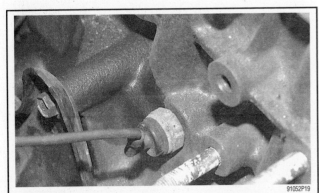

Fig. 56 The oil pressure sensor is located under the intake manifold—2.0L engine

TESTING

▶ See Figure 57

1. Test and verify the engine oil pressure. See Section 3 for more information. If no or insufficient pressure exists, oil pressure problem exists and gauge and sensor are operational, repair oil pressure problem.
2. Check the appropriate fuse before attempting any other diagnostics.
3. Unplug the sensor electrical harness.
4. Using an ohmmeter, check continuity between the sensor terminals.
5. With the engine stopped, continuity should not exist.

➡The switch inside the oil pressure sensor opens at 6 psi or less of pressure.

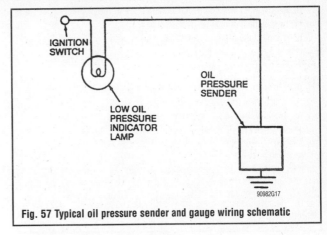

Fig. 57 Typical oil pressure sender and gauge wiring schematic

6. With the engine running, continuity should exist.
7. If continuity does not exist as stated, the sensor is faulty.

REMOVAL & INSTALLATION

✳✳ CAUTION

The EPA warns that prolonged contact with used engine oil may cause a number of skin disorders, including cancer! You should make every effort to minimize your exposure to used engine oil. Protective gloves should be worn when changing the oil. Wash your hands and any other exposed skin areas as soon as possible after exposure to used engine oil. Soap and water, or waterless hand cleaner should be used.

1. Locate the oil pressure sensor on the engine.
2. Disconnect the sensor electrical harness.
3. Unfasten and remove the sensor from the engine.
   To install:
4. Coat the new sensor with Teflon® tape or electrically conductive sealer.
5. Install the sensor and tighten to 11–15 ft. lbs. (15–20 Nm).
6. Attach the sensor's electrical connector.
7. Start the engine, allow it to reach operating temperature and check for leaks.
8. Check for proper sensor operation.

Fuel Level Sending Unit

The fuel level sending unit is located on the fuel pump inside the fuel tank.

TESTING

✳✳ CAUTION

Observe all applicable safety precautions when working around fuel. Whenever servicing the fuel system, always work in a well ventilated area. Do not allow fuel spray or vapors to come in contact with a spark or open flame. Keep a dry chemical fire extinguisher near the work area. Always keep fuel in a container specifically designed for fuel storage; also, always properly seal fuel containers to avoid the possibility of fire or explosion.

➡An assistant is recommended and extremely helpful for this testing procedure.

1. Check the appropriate fuse before attempting any other diagnostics.
2. Raise and support the vehicle.
3. Unplug the fuel level sending unit connector from the top of the fuel tank.
4. Insert the leads of the Rotunda gauge tester number 021-00055 or equivalent into the fuel level sender connector and set the scale to 145 ohms.

➡Although a gauge tester is recommended for the testing of the fuel

level sending unit, you can purchase resistors of the equivalent value at any electrical store and form your own tool.

5. Turn the ignition to the **ON** position and verify that the fuel gauge reads **EMPTY**. If the gauge reads **EMPTY**, proceed to the next step, if it does not, repair gauge and/or wiring as necessary.

➡ **It may take as long as 60 seconds for the gauge to move.**

6. Slowly turn the resistance level on the gauge tester to 22 ohms and verify that the gauge reading moves to **FULL**. If the gauges moves to **FULL**, the gauge and wiring are operating as designed, most likely the sending unit is faulty, repair as necessary. If the gauge does not read **FULL**, repair gauge and/or wiring as necessary.

An alternative method requiring no special testers is to remove the fuel pump from the tank. Connect the wiring to the pump and sending unit and manually operate the sending unit arm while an assistant observes the gauge.

REMOVAL & INSTALLATION

The fuel level sending unit is attached to the fuel pump. Refer to Section 5 and the fuel pump removal and installation procedure.

Coolant Level Sensor

The coolant level sensor is located in the recovery tank and operates a warning lamp on the instrument cluster when the coolant level reaches below a specified level.

TESTING

1. Check the appropriate fuse before attempting any other diagnostics.
2. Check the level of the coolant recovery tank, if it is low, fill it to the appropriate level and check the status of the warning lamp.
3. Remove the coolant level sensor as described below.

4. Place the sensor into a full container of a fluid (preferably water) with the sensor tip submerged into the fluid. Using an ohmmeter, check for continuity of the sensor, if no continuity exists, replace the sensor and retest. If continuity exists, repair the wiring and/or warning lamp as necessary.

REMOVAL & INSTALLATION

1. Disconnect the negative battery cable.
2. Drain and recycle the engine coolant.

✳✳ CAUTION

Never open, service or drain the radiator or cooling system when hot; serious burns can occur from the steam and hot coolant. Also, when draining engine coolant, keep in mind that cats and dogs are attracted to ethylene glycol antifreeze and could drink any that is left in an uncovered container or in puddles on the ground. This will prove fatal in sufficient quantities. Always drain coolant into a sealable container. Coolant should be reused unless it is contaminated or is several years old.

3. Unplug the sensor connector.
4. Remove the coolant recovery tank.
5. Remove the coolant level sensor from the tank.
To install:
6. Install the coolant level sensor into the coolant recovery tank.
7. Install the coolant recovery tank.
8. Plug the sensor connector in.
9. Connect the negative battery cable.
10. Fill the engine with coolant.
11. Start the engine, allow it to reach operating temperature, bleed the cooling system and check for leaks.
12. Verify the operation of the warning lamp.

Troubleshooting Basic Starting System Problems

Problem	Cause	Solution
Starter motor rotates engine slowly	• Battery charge low or battery defective	• Charge or replace battery
	• Defective circuit between battery and starter motor	• Clean and tighten, or replace cables
	• Low load current	• Bench-test starter motor. Inspect for worn brushes and weak brush springs.
	• High load current	• Bench-test starter motor. Check engine for friction, drag or coolant in cylinders. Check ring gear-to-pinion gear clearance.
Starter motor will not rotate engine	• Battery charge low or battery defective	• Charge or replace battery
	• Faulty solenoid	• Check solenoid ground. Repair or replace as necessary.
	• Damaged drive pinion gear or ring gear	• Replace damaged gear(s)
	• Starter motor engagement weak	• Bench-test starter motor
	• Starter motor rotates slowly with high load current	• Inspect drive yoke pull-down and point gap, check for worn end bushings, check ring gear clearance
	• Engine seized	• Repair engine
Starter motor drive will not engage (solenoid known to be good)	• Defective contact point assembly	• Repair or replace contact point assembly
	• Inadequate contact point assembly ground	• Repair connection at ground screw
	• Defective hold-in coil	• Replace field winding assembly
Starter motor drive will not disengage	• Starter motor loose on flywheel housing	• Tighten mounting bolts
	• Worn drive end busing	• Replace bushing
	• Damaged ring gear teeth	• Replace ring gear or driveplate
	• Drive yoke return spring broken or missing	• Replace spring
Starter motor drive disengages prematurely	• Weak drive assembly thrust spring	• Replace drive mechanism
	• Hold-in coil defective	• Replace field winding assembly
Low load current	• Worn brushes	• Replace brushes
	• Weak brush springs	• Replace springs

TCCS2C01

Troubleshooting Basic Charging System Problems

Problem	Cause	Solution
Noisy alternator	• Loose mountings • Loose drive pulley • Worn bearings • Brush noise • Internal circuits shorted (High pitched whine)	• Tighten mounting bolts • Tighten pulley • Replace alternator • Replace alternator • Replace alternator
Squeal when starting engine or accelerating	• Glazed or loose belt	• Replace or adjust belt
Indicator light remains on or ammeter indicates discharge (engine running)	• Broken belt • Broken or disconnected wires • Internal alternator problems • Defective voltage regulator	• Install belt • Repair or connect wiring • Replace alternator • Replace voltage regulator/alternator
Car light bulbs continually burn out— battery needs water continually	• Alternator/regulator overcharging	• Replace voltage regulator/alternator
Car lights flare on acceleration	• Battery low • Internal alternator/regulator problems	• Charge or replace battery • Replace alternator/regulator
Low voltage output (alternator light flickers continually or ammeter needle wanders)	• Loose or worn belt • Dirty or corroded connections • Internal alternator/regulator problems	• Replace or adjust belt • Clean or replace connections • Replace alternator/regulator

TCCS2C02

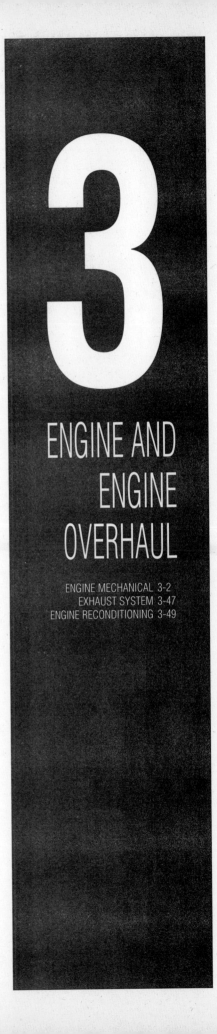

3

ENGINE AND ENGINE OVERHAUL

ENGINE MECHANICAL

2.0L (1999cc) ENGINE MECHANICAL SPECIFICATIONS

Description	English Specifications	Metric Specifications
General Information		
Type	Liquid Cooled, Dual Overhead Camshaft	
Displacement	122 cid	2.0L (1999cc)
Number of cylinders	4	
Bore	3.33in	84.8mm
Stroke	3.46in	88.0mm
Compression ratio	9.6:1	
Firing order	1-3-4-2	
Oil pressure	20-45 psi @1500rpm	
Cylinder Head and Valve Train		
Valve-to-valve guide clearance	0.000662-0.0025196 in.	0.017-0.064mm
Valve clearance-intake valve	0.004331-0.0070787 in.	0.11-0.18mm
Valve clearance-exhaust valve	0.0106299-0.0133858 in.	0.27-0.34mm
Angle degrees run-out (TIR)	90 degrees	
Valve guide bore diameter (ICD)		
Intake	0.23858 in.	6.06mm
Exhaust	0.23858 in.	6.06mm
Head gasket surface flatness	0.003 in.	0.076mm
Head face surface finish	15 microns (max.)	
Valve head diameter		
Intake	1.2598 in.	32mm
Exhaust	1.10236 in.	28mm
Valve face run-out limit		
Intake	0.0013779 in.	0.035mm
Exhaust	0.0013779 in.	0.035mm
Valve face angle	91 degrees	
Valve stem diameter		
Intake	0.23740 in.	6.03mm
Exhaust	0.23740 in.	6.03mm
Valve spring compression		
Intake	82.1 lbs. @ 0.988 in.	365 Nm @ 25.1mm
Exhaust	94.94 lbs. @ 1.0275 in.	422 Nm @ 26.1mm
Free length	1.701 in.	43.2mm
Installed height	1.346 in.	34.2mm
Valve spring assembled	1.346 in.	34.2mm
Height service limit	0.0256 in.	0.65mm
Pressure lost @ specific height		
Intake	32.596 lbs.	145 Nm
Exhaust	40.464 lbs.	180 Nm
Camshaft		
Lobe lift		
Intake	0.3643 in.	9.254mm
Exhaust	0.33858 in.	8.6mm
Theoretical valve maximum lift		
Intake	0.3643 in.	9.254mm
Exhaust	0.33858 in.	8.6mm
End-play service limit	0.00315-0.00866 in.	0.080-0.220mm
Bearing journal diameter	1.0221-1.0227 in.	25.960-25.980mm
Camshaft bearing radial clearance	0.000787-0.002756 in.	0.020-0.070mm
Cylinder Block		
Cylinder bore diameter		
Class-1	3.338576-3.3389697 in.	84.800-84.810mm
Class-2	3.3389697-3.3393634 in.	84.810-84.820mm
Class-3	3.3393634-3.3397571 in.	84.820-84.830mm
Piston-to-cylinder bore clearance	0.0019685 in.	0.05mm
Surface Finish (RA) each bore (min.)	2-6 microns	
Out-of-round limit	0.0009842 in. (max.)	0.025mm (max.)
Taper limit (max.)	+0.0009842-0.0005118 in.	+0.025-0.013mm
Main bearing bores inside diameter	2.28389-2.284966 in.	58.011-58.0380mm
Main bearing bores inside diameter (bearing caps installed)	2.28377749-2.284680 in.	58.008-58.03mm
Bearing caps graded by size	0.000433-0.002833 in.	0.011-0.058mm
Main bearing radial clearance	0.0007716-0.0017322 in.	0.0196-0.044mm
Main bearing bores inside diameter (bearing caps graded by size)		
Crankshaft		
Main bearing journal diameter	2.2826726-2.28346 in.	57.980-58.000mm
Main journal end-play	0.0035433-0.010236 in.	0.09-0.26mm
Connecting rod bearing journal diameter	1.846059-1.850036 in.	46.89-46.91mm

91053C01

2.0L (1999cc) ENGINE MECHANICAL SPECIFICATIONS

Description	English Specifications	Metric Specifications
Connecting Rod		
Connecting rod bearing		
Clearance-to-crankshaft	0.0006299-0.0027599 in.	0.016-0.070mm
Connecting rod piston pin bore diameter	0.810589-0.811379 in.	20.589-20.609mm
Crankshaft bearing bore diameter	1.846059-1.846847 in.	46.89-46.91mm
Pistons		
Piston-to-bore clearance	0.0003937-0.0011811 in.	0.010-0.030mm
Piston diameter		
Class-1	3.337828-3.338637 in.	84.781-84.799mm
Class-2	3.357316-3.3356025 in.	85.276-85.294mm
Piston bore diameter	0.7870063-0.7877937 in.	19.99-20.01mm
Ring width		
Upper compression ring	0.011811-0.019686 in.	0.30-0.50mm
Lower compression ring	0.011811-0.019686 in.	0.30-0.50mm
Oil control ring	0.015748-0.055118 in.	0.40-1.40mm
Ring groove width		
Upper compression ring	0.058425 in.	1.484mm
Lower compression ring	0.0682675 in.	1.734mm
Oil control ring	1.1143698 in.	2.905mm
Piston pin length	2.48031-2.51181 in.	63-63.80mm
Piston pin diameter		
White	0.8134629-0.8120062 in.	20.662-20.625mm
Red	0.8120062-0.8121243 in.	20.625-20.628mm
Blue	0.8121243-0.8122424 in.	20.628-20.631mm
Piston-to-piston clearance	0.0003937-0.00006906 in.	0.010-0.015mm
Piston pin clearance in connecting rod bore	0.0006299-0.0019291 in.	0.016-0.049mm
Lubrication System		
Oil pump type		Gerotor

TIR: Total Indicated Run-out
ICD: Insert Counterbore Diameter
Max.: Maximum
Min.: Minimum

91053C02

2.5L (2507cc) ENGINE MECHANICAL SPECIFICATIONS

Description	English Specifications	Metric Specifications
General Information		
Type	Liquid Cooled, Dual Overhead Camshaft	2.5L (2507cc)
Displacement	153 cid	
Number of cylinders	6	
Bore	3.25in	82.4mm
Stroke	3.13in	79.5mm
Compression ratio	①	
Firing order	1-4-2-5-3-6	
Oil pressure	20-45 psi @1500rpm	
Cylinder Head and Valve Train		
Valve seat width		
Intake	0.043-0.055 in.	1.1-1.4mm
Exhaust	0.055-0.066 in.	1.4-1.7mm
Valve seat angle	44.75 degrees	
Valve seat run-out	0.001 in.	0.04mm
Valve stem-to-guide clearance		
Intake	0.0007-0.0027 in.	0.020-0.069mm
Exhaust	0.0017-0.037 in.	0.045-0.094mm
Valve head diameter		
Intake	1.26 in.	32mm
Exhaust	1.02 in.	26mm
Valve face run-out limit	0.001 in.	0.05mm
Valve face angle	45.5 degrees	
Valve stem diameter		
Intake	0.2355-0.2358 in.	5.975-5.995mm
Exhaust	0.2343-0.2350 in.	5.950-5.970mm
Valve spring compression		
Intake	153 lbs. @ 1.18 in.	680 Nm @ 30.19mm
Exhaust	153 lbs. @ 1.18 in.	680 Nm @ 30.18mm
Free length		
Intake	1.84 in.	46.8mm
Exhaust	1.84 in.	46.8mm
Installed pressure		
Intake	51 lbs. @ 1.57 in.	228 Nm @ 39.99mm
Exhaust	51 lbs. @ 1.57 in.	228 Nm @ 39.99mm
Valve spring assembled	1.346 in.	34.2mm
Service limit	10% pressure loss @ 1.19 in.	10% pressure loss @ 30.09mm
Rocker Arms		
Diameter	0.6290-0.6294 in.	16-15.988mm
Clearance-to-bore	0.0007-0.0027 in.	0.018-0.069mm
Service limit	0.0006 in.	0.016 in.
Hydraulic leakdown rate	5-25 seconds	
Collapsed valve tappet gap-desired	0.019-0.043 in.	0.5-1.11mm
Camshaft		
Lobe lift		
Intake (primary)	0.188 in.	4.79mm
Intake (secondary)	0.188 in.	4.79mm
Exhaust	0.188 in.	4.79mm
Theoretical valve maximum lift		
Intake (primary)	0.388 in.	9.80mm
Intake (secondary)	0.388 in.	9.80mm
Exhaust	0.388 in.	9.80mm
End-play		
Standard	0.001-0.0064 in.	0.025-0.165mm
Service limit	0.00748 in.	0.190mm
Bearing-to-journal clearance		
Standard	0.001-0.0029 in.	0.025-0.076mm
Service limit	0.0047 in.	0121mm
Journal diameter	1.061-1.060 in.	26.962-26.936mm
Bearing inside diameter	1.063-1.062 in.	27.012-26.987mm
Cylinder Block		
Cylinder bore diameter		
Grade-1	3.2441-3.2445 in.	82.4-82.41mm
Grade-2	3.2445-3.2449 in.	82.41-82.42mm
Grade-3	3.2449-3.2453 in.	82.42-82.43mm
Cylinder bore		
Surface Finish (RA) each bore (min.)	2-6 microns	
Out-of-round limit	0.0005 in.	0.015mm
Out-of-round service limit	0.0007 in.	0.020mm
Taper service limit	0.0002 in.	0.006mm

91053C03

2.5L (2507cc) ENGINE MECHANICAL SPECIFICATIONS

Description	English Specifications	Metric Specifications
Crankshaft		
Main bearing journal diameter	2.467-2.479 in.	62.968-62.992mm
Connecting rod journal diameter	1.967-1.968 in.	49.970-49.990mm
Crankshaft free end-play	0.004-0.009 in.	0.110-0.232mm
Crankshaft runout-to-rear face of cylinder block	0.001 in.	0.050mm
Connecting rod bearings		
Clearance to crankshaft	0.001-0.0025 in.	0.028-0.066mm
Bearing wall thickness	0.059 in.	1.503mm
Main bearings		
Clearance to crankshaft- desired	0.0009-0.0017 in.	0.025-0.045mm
Clearance to crankshaft- allowed	0.0009-0.0019 in.	0.025-0.050mm
Bearing wall thickness- Grade 1	0.0984 in.	2.501mm
Bearing wall thickness- Grade 2	0.0986 in.	2.505mm
Bearing wall thickness- Grade 3	0.0988 in.	2.510mm
Connecting Rod		
Connecting rod piston pin bore diameter	0.827-0.828 in.	21.017-21.032mm
Crankshaft bearing bore diameter	2.0872-2.0879 in.	53.015-53.035mm
Length (center-to-center)	5.435-5.448 in.	138.06-138.4mm
Side clearance		
Standard	0.0039-0.0118 in.	0.1-0.3mm
Service limit	0.0137 in.	0.35mm
Pistons		
Piston diameter		
Grade-1	3.2436-3.2444 in.	82.390-82.410mm
Grade-2	3.2440-3.2449 in.	82.398-82.422mm
Grade-3	3.2444-3.2452 in.	82.410-82.430mm
Piston-to-bore clearance	0.0005-0.0009 in.	0.012-0.022mm
Piston bore diameter	0.8270-0.8272 in.	21.008-21.012mm
Ring groove width		
Upper compression ring	0.0484-0.0490 in.	1.230-1.245mm
Lower compression ring	0.0602-0.0608 in.	1.530-1.545mm
Oil control ring	0.1192-0.0120 in.	3.030-3.055mm
Piston pin		
Length	2.1680-2.1839 in.	55.06-55.47mm
Diameter	0.8272-0.8273 in.	21.011-21.013mm
Pin-to-piston clearance	0.0001-0.00003 in.	0.005-0.001mm
Piston-to-rod clearance		
Standard	0.0001-0.0007 in.	0.004-0.020mm
Service limit	0.0013 in.	0.035mm
Side clearance		
Upper compression ring	0.0015-0.0029 in.	0.040-0.075mm
Lower compression ring	0.0015-0.0033 in.	0.040-0.085mm
Oil control ring	Snug fit	
Service limit	0.0039 in.	0.10mm
Piston ring gap		
Upper compression ring- gauge diameter	0.0039-0.0098 in.	0.1-0.25mm
Lower compression ring- gauge diameter	0.0106-0.0165in.	0.27-0.42mm
Oil control ring gauge- diameter	0.0059-0.0255 in.	0.15-0.65mm
Upper compression ring- service limit	0.0196 in.	0.5mm
Lower compression ring- service limit	0.0255 in.	0.65mm
Oil control ring- service limit	0.0354 in.	0.9mm
Lubrication System		
Oil pump type		Gerotor

TIR: Total Indicated Run-out
ICD: Insert Counterbore Diameter
Max: Maximum
Min: Minimum
① 9.7:1 on Contour GL,LX,SE,GS,and LS, 10.0:1 on Contour SVT

91053C04

Engine

REMOVAL & INSTALLATION

◆ **See Figures 1 thru 18**

In the process of removing the engine, you will come across a number of steps which call for the removal of a separate component or system, such as "disconnect the exhaust system" or "remove the radiator." In most instances, a detailed removal procedure can be found elsewhere in this manual.

It is virtually impossible to list each individual wire and hose which must be disconnected, simply because so many different model and engine combinations have been manufactured. Careful observation and common sense are the best possible approaches to any repair procedure.

Removal and installation of the engine can be made easier if you follow these basic points:

- If you have to drain any of the fluids, use a suitable container.

- Always tag any wires or hoses and, if possible, the components they came from before disconnecting them.
- Because there are so many bolts and fasteners involved, store and label the retainers from components separately in muffin pans, jars or coffee cans. This will prevent confusion during installation.
- After unbolting the transmission or transaxle, always make sure it is properly supported.
- If it is necessary to disconnect the air conditioning system, have this service performed by a qualified technician using a recovery/recycling station. If the system does not have to be disconnected, unbolt the compressor and set it aside.
- When unbolting the engine mounts, always make sure the engine is properly supported. When removing the engine, make sure that any lifting devices are properly attached to the engine. It is recommended that if your engine is supplied with lifting hooks, your lifting apparatus be attached to them.
- Lift the engine from its compartment slowly, checking that no hoses, wires or other components are still connected.
- After the engine is clear of the compartment, place it on an engine stand or workbench.
- After the engine has been removed, you can perform a partial or full teardown of the engine using the procedures outlined in this manual.

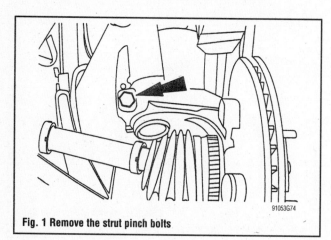

91053G74

Fig. 1 Remove the strut pinch bolts

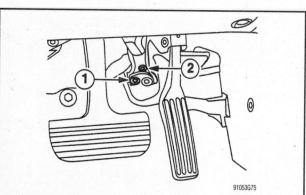

91053G75

Fig. 2 Remove the steering shaft pinch bolt (1), and slide the steering shaft off of the steering column (2)

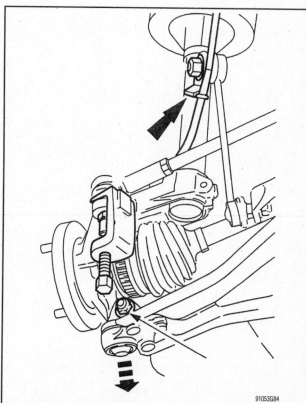

91053G84

Fig. 3 Remove the stabilizer bar link from the strut, the outer tie rod end from the knuckle, and the lower control arm from the knuckle

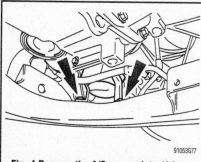

91053G77

Fig. 4 Remove the A/C accumulator/drier bolts

91053G78

Fig. 5 Remove the flywheel access cover and . . .

91053G76

Fig. 6 . . . remove the four torque converter retaining bolts—automatic transaxle only

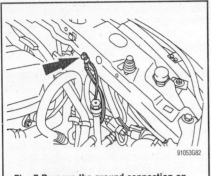

Fig. 7 Remove the ground connection on the radiator support

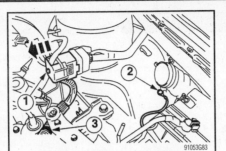

Fig. 8 Remove the main wiring harness connector (1), the transaxle ground cable (2), and cut the wire tie strap on the harness (3)

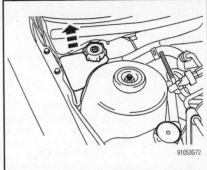

Fig. 9 Remove the power steering reservoir to . . .

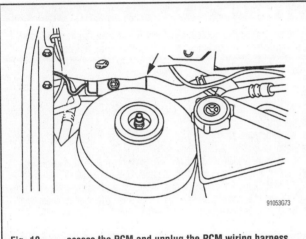

Fig. 10 . . . access the PCM and unplug the PCM wiring harness

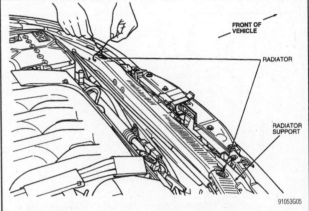

Fig. 11 Support the radiator and condenser assembly with wire on the upper radiator supports

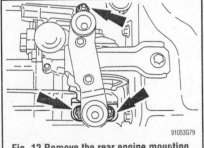

Fig. 12 Remove the rear engine mounting bracket—2.0L engine shown

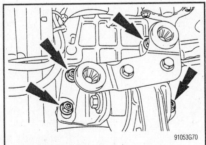

Fig. 13 Remove the transaxle support retaining nuts

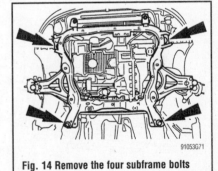

Fig. 14 Remove the four subframe bolts

✳✳ CAUTION

The fuel injection system remains under pressure, even after the engine has been turned OFF. The fuel system pressure MUST BE relieved before disconnecting any fuel lines. Failure to do so may result in fire and/or personal injury.

1. Disconnect the battery cables, negative cable first.
2. Relieve the fuel system pressure using the recommended procedure.

✳✳ CAUTION

Some models covered by this manual may be equipped with a Supplemental Restraint System (SRS), which uses an air bag. Whenever working near any of the SRS components, such as the impact sensors, the air bag module, steering column and instrument panel, properly disable the SRS.

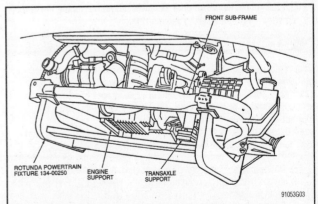

Fig. 15 The engine and transaxle come out together from underneath the vehicle

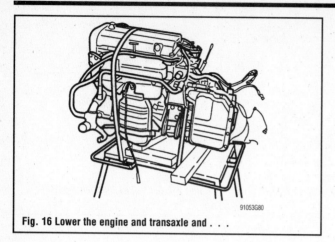

Fig. 16 Lower the engine and transaxle and . . .

91053G80

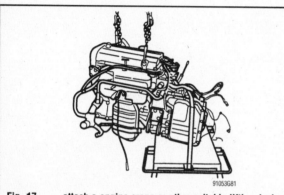

Fig. 17 . . . attach a engine crane or other suitable lifting device to support the engine

91053G81

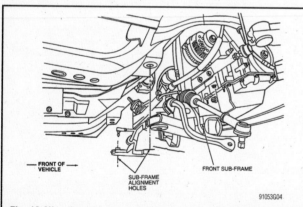

FRONT OF VEHICLE

SUB-FRAME ALIGNMENT HOLES

FRONT SUB-FRAME

91053G04

Fig. 18 Align the subframe with the holes before tightening the bolts

✳✳ CAUTION

Observe all applicable safety precautions when working around fuel. Whenever servicing the fuel system, always work in a well ventilated area. Do not allow fuel spray or vapors to come in contact with a spark or open flame. Keep a dry chemical fire extinguisher near the work area. Always keep fuel in a container specifically designed for fuel storage; also, always properly seal fuel containers to avoid the possibility of fire or explosion.

3. On the 2.5L engine, remove the water pump pulley shield.

4. Remove the pinch bolt and disconnect the steering shaft and joint at the cowl, inside the vehicle.

5. Remove the engine air cleaner and the engine air intake resonators.

6. Properly recover the refrigerant from the A/C system.

7. Raise and safely support the vehicle.

8. Remove the front splash shield from between the front sub-frame and the body.

9. Remove the catalytic converter and the exhaust crossover (2.5L engine only).

✳✳ CAUTION

The EPA warns that prolonged contact with used engine oil may cause a number of skin disorders, including cancer! You should make every effort to minimize your exposure to used engine oil. Protective gloves should be worn when changing the oil. Wash your hands and any other exposed skin areas as soon as possible after exposure to used engine oil. Soap and water, or waterless hand cleaner should be used.

10. Drain the engine cooling system and engine oil.

✳✳ CAUTION

Never open, service or drain the radiator or cooling system when hot; serious burns can occur from the steam and hot coolant.

11. Remove the front wheel and tire assemblies.

12. Separate the left and right stabilizer bar links from the front stabilizer bar.

13. Separate the left and right outer tie rod ends from the front wheel knuckles. Discard the cotter pins.

14. Remove the pinch bolts and separate the front suspension lower control arms from the front wheel knuckles at the ball joints.

15. Remove the left and right wheel hub retainer nuts from the halfshaft ends and remove the halfshafts from the front wheel knuckles.

16. Remove the A/C accumulator retaining screws from the front sub-frame.

17. Disengage the vehicle speed sensor wiring harness at the connector.

18. Disconnect the speedometer drive cable from the transaxle.

19. If the engine is to be separated from the transaxle after removal from the vehicle, and the transaxle is an automatic perform the following steps:

a. Remove the right splash shield from the front fender apron.

b. Remove the access plug from the engine rear plate and remove the four torque converter retaining nuts.

c. Push the torque converter into the transaxle front pump support and gear.

20. Disconnect the wiring to the knock sensor and the oil pressure sensor located on the right side of the cylinder block.

21. Lower the vehicle.

22. Secure the radiator and fan shroud assembly to the radiator support, using safety wire or equivalent.

23. Disconnect the accelerator cable and speed control actuator from the throttle body.

24. Remove the accelerator cable bracket.

25. On vehicles equipped with the 2.5L engine, disengage the three connectors for the engine control wiring from the bracket located on the left-front fender apron and unplug the connectors.

26. Remove the retainer for the engine control wiring from the air cleaner bracket.

27. Remove the ignition control module from the bulkhead, if equipped.

28. Disengage the wiring to the fuel injectors at the connector located near the fuel pressure regulator.

29. Remove the retaining screws from the engine control wiring at the intake manifold.

30. Remove the power steering pump auxiliary reservoir from the bracket and lay on top of the engine assembly using shop towels to absorb the fluid.

31. Disconnect the return hose from the power steering reservoir and plug the hose.

✳✳ WARNING

Do not allow the power steering fluid to come into contact with the accessory drive belts.

32. Disconnect the power steering return hose from the power steering pump.

33. Disconnect the wiring from the power steering pressure switch located on the power steering pressure hose.

34. Disconnect the power steering pressure hose bracket from the upper front engine support bracket. Lay the hose on top of the engine.

35. Disconnect the wiring from the powertrain control module and retainer located on the right side of the dash panel.

36. Remove the ground strap for the engine control wiring at the right fender apron.

37. Disconnect the wiring from the alternator and the grounding strap from the alternator mounting bracket.

38. Disconnect the vacuum supply hose from the fitting on the rear of the intake manifold.

39. Disconnect the coolant hoses from the radiator coolant recovery reservoir.

40. Disconnect the hoses from the A/C compressor and plug.

41. Disconnect the fuel return and supply lines from the fuel rail and plug.

42. Disconnect the vacuum supply hose to the EGR valve, EGR pressure sensor and the EGR valve to exhaust manifold tube.

43. If equipped with automatic transaxle, pry the end of the shift cable from the stud, remove the two retaining bolts and remove shift cable and bracket from the transaxle. Remove the wiring to the transmission range sensor and remove the wire retainers.

44. Disconnect the grounding strap from the transaxle.

45. Disconnect the wiring from the ignition coil and the radio ignition interference capacitor. Move the wiring out of the way.

46. Remove the vacuum supply line from the power brake booster.

47. Disconnect the upper radiator hose from the radiator.

48. Remove the evaporative emission hose from the connector located near the radio ignition interference capacitor.

49. Disconnect the heater hose from the connection located near the EGR valve.

50. Disconnect the positive and negative battery cable retainer from the battery tray.

51. If equipped with manual transaxle, remove the retainer and disconnect the clutch hydraulic line from the clutch actuator pipe at the transaxle case.

52. If equipped, disconnect the block heater power supply wiring from the left side of the radiator support.

53. If equipped with automatic transaxle, remove the transmission oil cooler lines from the transaxle. Remove the oil cooler return line from the bracket on the left-hand side of the transaxle.

54. If equipped with manual transaxle, remove the bolt from the shift rod and the nut from the stabilizer bar and remove from the transaxle.

55. Disconnect the lower radiator hose from the radiator.

56. Remove the four bolts retaining the lower radiator supports to the front sub-frame. Rotate the radiator supports forward.

57. Disconnect the wiring harness from the A/C compressor.

58. Disconnect the A/C suction hose from the A/C condenser core and plug the hose.

59. Disconnect the A/C discharge hose from the A/C accumulator and plug the hose.

60. Position and secure all lines, hoses and components that will be removed with the engine.

61. Disconnect the engine wiring from the heated oxygen sensor, engine coolant temperature sensor and the crankshaft position sensor.

62. Remove the two screws retaining the bumper cover braces to the left and right sides of the front sub-frame and rotate the cover braces forward.

63. Disconnect the power steering oil cooler hoses at the right front sub-frame. Drain the fluid from the hoses.

64. Partially lower the vehicle.

65. Position and secure all lines, hoses and components that will be removed with the engine.

66. Install Powertrain and Sub-frame Support Bracket 134–00250 or equivalent, with Powertrain Lift (hydraulic lift) 134–00251 or equivalent, to support the powertrain assembly for removal from the vehicle.

➡Be sure that the powertrain and sub-frame support bracket and lift are correctly positioned for safe removal of the powertrain assembly.

67. Remove the four sub-frame to body retaining bolts.

68. Remove the upper front engine support bracket and the engine and transmission support insulator retaining nuts.

69. With an assistant, carefully lower the powertrain assembly while checking for body interference.

70. With the powertrain assembly lowered from the vehicle, carefully roll the powertrain lift or equivalent away from the vehicle.

71. Using a appropriate engine crane, and crane lifting sling, support the engine using the engine lifting eyes.

72. Remove the left and the right halfshafts from the transaxle.

73. Remove the left and the right front engine support insulators from the sub-frame and transaxle.

74. Using the floor crane and sling or equivalent, raise the engine and transaxle assembly and remove from the sub-frame.

75. Position the transaxle part of the assembly onto a suitable transmission jack.

76. Remove the two starter retaining bolts and remove the starter motor.

77. Remove the battery ground cable from the engine to transaxle retaining stud bolt.

78. Remove the transaxle to engine retaining bolts and separate the engine from the transaxle.

79. If equipped with manual transaxle, remove the six clutch pressure plate retaining bolts and remove the pressure plate and the clutch disc.

80. Remove the eight flywheel retainer bolts and the flywheel from the crankshaft.

81. Remove the engine rear plate.

82. Install the engine to an engine stand for further service.

To install:

83. Remove the engine from the engine stand using the floor crane and sling or equivalent, attached to the engine lifting eyes.

84. Reinstall the engine rear drive plate and flywheel.

85. Tighten the flywheel retaining bolts.

86. If equipped with manual transaxle, install the clutch disc and the clutch pressure plate.

87. Reinstall the engine to the transaxle. If equipped with automatic transaxle, align the torque converter to the flywheel while positioning the engine to the transaxle.

88. Reinstall the engine to transaxle retaining bolts and tighten to 25–34 ft. lbs. (34–46 Nm).

89. If removed, place the sub-frame onto the powertrain and sub-frame support bracket and hydraulic lift.

90. Using the floor crane and sling, position the engine and transaxle assembly onto the sub-frame keeping the crane attached for support.

91. Install Powertrain Alignment Gauge T94P-6000-AH or equivalent, to the left-hand front engine support bracket and sub-frame. Reinstall the through-bolt. Tighten the retaining bolts and the through-bolt to 20 ft. lbs. (27 Nm).

92. Reinstall the right engine support insulator retaining bolts and through-bolt to the sub-frame. Leave the bolts finger-tight.

93. Reinstall the battery ground cable to the engine at the transaxle stud bolt. Tighten the retaining nut to 15–22 ft. lbs. (20–30 Nm).

94. Reinstall the starter motor.

95. Reinstall the left and right halfshafts into the transaxle.

96. Install Sub-frame Alignment Pin Set 94P-2100-aH or equivalent into the sub-frame.

97. With an assistant, carefully raise the powertrain assembly into the body while checking for body interference.

98. Reinstall the four sub-frame retaining bolts and tighten to 92–100 ft. lbs. (125–135 Nm).

99. Remove the sub-frame alignment pins.

➡Be sure that the engine and transaxle are firmly seated against the front and rear insulator brackets.

100. Using new nuts, install the upper front engine support bracket and the transmission support insulator. Tighten the nuts to 74 inch. lbs. (10 Nm).

101. Remove the sub-frame support bracket and the hydraulic lift.

102. Raise and safely support the vehicle.

103. Tighten the right front engine support insulator to the sub-frame bolts to 30–41 ft. lbs. (41–55 Nm).

➡Check the position of the right front engine support insulator. It must be centered in its bracket and in perfect alignment front to rear.

104. Lower the vehicle.

105. Tighten the front engine support bracket nuts to 52–70 ft. lbs. (70–95 Nm).

106. Tighten the engine and transmission support insulator nuts to 30–41 ft.

lbs. (41–55 Nm) for automatic transaxles and 52–70 ft. lbs. (70–95 Nm) for manual transaxles.

107. Tighten the right front engine support insulator through-bolt to 75–102 ft. lbs. (103–137 Nm).

108. Remove the powertrain alignment gauge.

109. Reinstall the left front engine support insulator to the sub-frame. Toque the retaining bolts to 84 inch. lbs. (10 Nm).

➡ **Check the position of the left front engine support insulator to ensure perfect front to rear alignment.**

110. Retighten the two retaining bolts to 30–41 ft. lbs. (41–55 Nm).

111. Reinstall the left front engine support insulator through-bolt. Tighten the through-bolt to 75–102 ft. lbs. (103–137 Nm).

112. On the remaining steps, installation is the reverse of removal.

Valve Cover

REMOVAL & INSTALLATION

2.0L Engine

▶ **See Figures 19 thru 29, 41 thru 50**

1. Disconnect the negative battery cable.
2. Remove the air intake resonators.
3. Label and remove the ignition wires and separators.
4. Label and unplug the oil feed sensor connector (if equipped).
5. Remove the crankcase ventilation tube from the valve cover.
6. Remove the retaining bolt and nut for the power steering pressure hose bracket-to-engine lifting eye.
7. Position the power steering hose out of the way.
8. Remove the upper timing belt cover.
9. Remove the valve cover retaining bolts, starting from the outside and working in.

10. Remove the valve cover and gasket from the cylinder head.

To install:

11. Clean the valve cover gasket sealing surfaces.
12. Install new valve cover gaskets and O-rings onto the valve covers.
13. Place the valve cover into position and tighten the retaining bolts to 53–71 inch lbs. (6–8 Nm), beginning in the center of the valve cover and working outward.
14. Install the upper timing belt cover.
15. Position the power steering pressure hose and tighten the retaining bolt and nut for the bracket-to-engine lifting eye.
16. Install the ignition wire separators and the ignition wires.
17. Install the crankcase ventilation tubes into both valve covers.
18. Plug the oil feed sensor connector in (if equipped).
19. Install the air intake resonators.
20. Connect the negative battery cable.
21. Run the engine and check for leaks and proper operation.

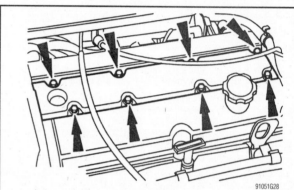

Fig. 19 On some later models, it is necessary to remove a cover to access the spark plugs

Fig. 20 Carefully twist the spark plug wire and . . .

Fig. 21 . . . lift the plug wire out of the cylinder head

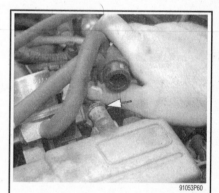

Fig. 22 Remove the crankcase ventilation hose from the back of the valve cover

Fig. 23 Remove the power steering hose bracket-to-engine lifting eye

Fig. 24 Remove the two upper timing belt cover bolts

Fig. 25 After the bolts are removed, lift the upper timing belt cover up and remove it from the engine

Fig. 26 Remove the valve cover retaining bolts

Fig. 27 After the bolts are removed, carefully lift the valve cover off of the cylinder head, if the cover is tight, lightly tap it with a soft-faced hammer

Fig. 28 Thoroughly clean the cylinder head-to-valve cover mating surface before installing the valve cover and new gaskets

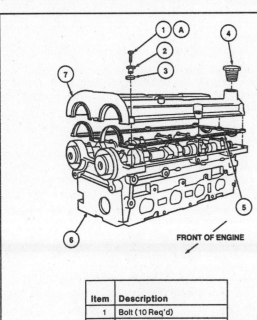

FRONT OF ENGINE

Item	Description
1	Bolt (10 Req'd)
2	Spacer (10 Req'd)
3	O-ring (10 Req'd)
4	Oil Filler Cap
5	Valve Cover Gasket
6	Cylinder Head
7	Valve Cover
A	Tighten to 6-8 N·m (53-71 Lb-In)

Fig. 29 Valve cover and gasket mounting—2.0L engine

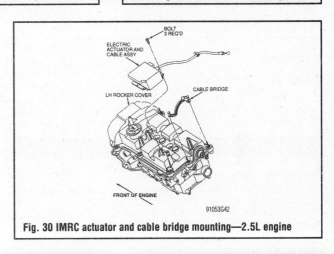

Fig. 30 IMRC actuator and cable bridge mounting—2.5L engine

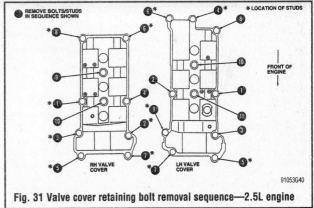

Fig. 31 Valve cover retaining bolt removal sequence—2.5L engine

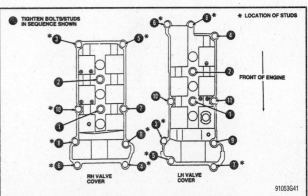

Fig. 32 Valve cover retaining bolt installation sequence—2.5L engine

2.5L Engine

▶ See Figures 30, 31 and 32

1. Disconnect the negative battery cable.
2. Remove the upper intake manifold as described in this Section.
3. Remove the ignition wires and spark plugs.
4. Remove the ignition coil from the rear valve cover.
5. Remove the crankcase ventilation tubes from both valve covers.
6. Remove the wiring harness and bracket to the fuel injectors and move aside.
7. If removing the front valve cover:
    a. Remove the Intake Manifold Runner Control (IMRC) actuator.
    b. Remove the IMRC actuator cable bridge.
8. Remove the retaining nuts and engine wiring from both valve covers and move aside.
9. Remove the valve cover retaining bolts and studs following the correct sequence.

10. Remove both valve covers from the engine.

To install:

11. Clean the valve cover gasket sealing surfaces.

12. Install new valve cover gaskets onto the valve covers.

13. For each valve cover, place a bead of silicone sealant at two places on the valve cover sealing surfaces where the engine front cover and the cylinder heads make contact and at two places on the rear of the cylinder head where the camshaft seal retainer contacts the cylinder head.

14. Place the valve covers into position.

15. Reinstall the valve cover retaining bolts and studs and tighten in sequence to 71–106 inch lbs. (8–12 Nm).

➡The valve covers must be installed and properly tightened within six minutes of applying the silicone sealant.

16. Install the engine wiring and tighten the retaining nuts.

17. Install the fuel injector harness and bracket.

18. If the front valve cover was removed:
   a. Install the IMRC actuator cable bridge.
   b. Install the IMRC actuator.

19. Install the crankcase ventilation tubes into both valve covers.

20. Install the ignition coil onto the rear valve cover.

21. Install the ignition wire separators, the ignition wires, and the spark plugs.

22. Install the upper intake manifold as described in this section.

23. Connect the negative battery cable.

24. Run the engine and check for leaks and proper operation.

Rocker Arms

REMOVAL & INSTALLATION

♦ **See Figure 33**

The 2.5L engine is the only engine covered in this manual with rocker arms. The 2.0L engine's camshaft rides directly on the valve tappets and transfers the motion of the camshaft lobes to the valves.

1. Disconnect both battery cables, negative cable first.

2. Remove the valve covers.

3. Remove the crankshaft pulley retaining bolt.

4. Rotate the crankshaft so that the key-way is at the 11 o'clock position to locate the crankshaft at TDC for No. 1 cylinder.

5. Verify that the alignment arrows on the camshafts are aligned. If not, rotate the crankshaft one complete revolution and recheck.

6. Rotate the crankshaft so that the key-way is at the 3 o'clock position. This positions the right cylinder head camshafts to the neutral position.

7. Remove the accessory drive belts.

8. Remove the battery.

9. Remove the water pump drive pulley from the left intake camshaft using Camshaft Damper Remover/Replacer T94P-6312-AH or equivalent, along with the shaft protector and screw or equivalent.

10. Remove the camshaft rear oil seal retainer bolts and the camshaft rear oil seal retainer and gasket from the left cylinder head.

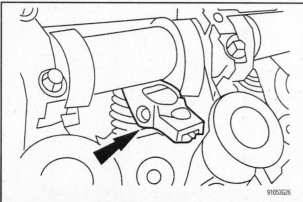

Fig. 33 Rocker arm assembly—2.5L engine

91053G26

➡The camshaft journal caps and cylinder heads are numbered to ensure that they are assembled in their original positions. If removed, keep the camshaft journal caps together with the cylinder head that they were removed from.

11. Remove the right cylinder head camshaft journal thrust cap retaining bolts and thrust caps.

12. Loosen the remaining camshaft journal cap bolts in sequence, releasing the bolts several revolutions at a time by making several passes to allow the camshaft to be raised from the cylinder head evenly. Do not remove the retaining bolts completely.

➡If the valve lifters (tappets) and roller rocker arms are to be reused, mark the positions of the valve lifters and rocker arms so that they are reassembled into their original positions.

13. With the camshafts loose, remove the rocker arms, keeping them in the order that they were removed.

14. If required, remove the valve lifters from the cylinder head.

15. Rotate the crankshaft two revolutions and locate the crankshaft key-way at the 11 o'clock position. This will position the left cylinder head camshafts to their neutral position.

16. Verify that the alignment arrows on the camshafts are aligned.

➡The camshaft journal caps and cylinder heads are numbered to ensure that they are assembled in their original positions. If removed, keep the camshaft journal caps together with the cylinder head that they were removed from.

17. Remove the camshaft journal thrust cap retaining bolts and thrust caps from the left cylinder head.

18. Loosen the remaining camshaft journal cap bolts in sequence, releasing the bolts several revolutions at a time by making several passes to allow the camshaft to be raised from the cylinder head evenly. Do not remove the retaining bolts completely.

➡If the valve lifters (tappets) and roller rocker arms are to be reused, mark the positions of the valve lifters and rocker arms so that they are reassembled into their original positions.

19. With the camshafts loose, remove the rocker arms, keeping them in the order that they were removed.

20. If required, remove the valve lifters from the cylinder head.

21. Inspect the rocker arms and valve lifters for wear and/or damage and replace as necessary.

To install:

22. Be sure that the crankshaft key-way is at the 11 o'clock position.

23. Lubricate the left cylinder head valve lifters with engine assembly lubricant and install into their correct positions in the cylinder head.

24. If the valve lifters are being replaced with new units, soak the lifters in a container of clean engine oil and/or manually pump up the lifters before installing into the cylinder head.

25. Lubricate the left cylinder head rocker arms with engine assembly lubricant and install the left cylinder head rocker arms into their original locations.

➡Do not install the camshaft journal thrust caps until the camshaft journal caps are secured into position.

26. Tighten the left cylinder head camshaft journal cap bolts in sequence (see camshaft procedure for sequence) making several passes to pull the camshafts down evenly. Tighten the bolts to 71–106 inch lbs. (8–12 Nm).

27. Reinstall the left-hand cylinder head thrust caps and bolts. Tighten to 71–106 inch lbs. (8–12 Nm).

28. Rotate the crankshaft two revolutions and position the crankshaft key-way to the 3 o'clock location. This will position the right cylinder head camshafts to the neutral position.

29. Lubricate the right cylinder head valve lifters with engine assembly lubricant and install into their original positions in the cylinder head.

30. If the valve lifters are being replaced with new units, soak the lifters in a container of clean engine oil and/or manually pump the lifters up before installing into the cylinder head.

31. Lubricate the right cylinder head rocker arms with engine assembly lubricant and install the right cylinder head rocker arms into their original locations.

➡Do not install the camshaft journal thrust caps until the camshaft journal caps are secured into position.

32. Tighten the right cylinder head camshaft journal cap bolts in sequence making several passes to pull the camshafts down evenly. Tighten the bolts to 71–106 inch lbs. (8–12 Nm).

33. Reinstall the right-hand cylinder head thrust caps and bolts. Tighten to 71–106 inch lbs. (8–12 Nm).

34. Reinstall the left cylinder head camshaft rear oil seal and retainer with gasket onto the cylinder head. Tighten the retaining bolts to 71–106 inch lbs. (8–12 Nm).

35. Reinstall the water pump drive pulley onto the left intake camshaft using an appropriate power steering pump pulley replacer.

36. Reinstall the accessory drive belts.

37. Reinstall the battery.

38. Reinstall the crankshaft pulley retaining bolt.

39. Tighten the crankshaft pulley retaining bolt as follows:
    a. Tighten to 89 ft. lbs. (120 Nm).
    b. Loosen the bolt at least one full turn.
    c. Tighten the bolt to 35–39 ft. lbs. (47–53 Nm).
    d. Rotate the bolt 85–95 degrees.

40. Reinstall the valve covers.

41. Reconnect both battery cables, negative cable last.

42. Run the engine and check for leaks and proper operation.

Thermostat

REMOVAL & INSTALLATION

2.0L Engine

▶ See Figures 34 thru 39, 41 thru 50

1. Disconnect the negative battery cable.
2. Drain and recycle the engine coolant.
3. Remove the air intake resonators.
4. Remove the upper radiator hose and coolant recovery tank hose from the water outlet.

5. Remove the three retaining bolts from the water outlet and remove the outlet from the thermostat housing.

6. Remove the thermostat and O-ring from the housing.

To install:

7. Thoroughly clean the housing and install the thermostat and new O-ring into the housing.

8. Install the water outlet and tighten the retaining bolts to 71–97 inch lbs. (8–11 Nm).

9. Install the upper radiator and coolant recovery tank hoses to the water outlet.

10. Install the air intake resonators.

11. Connect the negative battery cable.

12. Fill the cooling system with the proper $FR50/50 mixture and start the vehicle.

13. Bleed the cooling system and check for leaks.

2.5L Engine

▶ See Figure 40

1. Drain and recycle the engine coolant.
2. Remove the battery from the vehicle.
3. Remove the radiator hoses from the thermostat housing and remove the housing from the vehicle.
4. Remove the two thermostat housing bolts and separate the housing.
5. Remove the thermostat and O-ring from the housing.

To install:

6. Thoroughly clean the housing and install the thermostat and O-ring into the housing.

7. Place the two thermostat housing halves together and alternatingly tighten the retaining bolts to 15–22 ft. lbs. (20–30 Nm).

8. Place the housing into position and attach the radiator hoses.

9. Install the battery into the vehicle.

10. Fill the cooling system with the proper $FR50/50 mixture and start the vehicle.

11. Bleed the cooling system and check for leaks.

Fig. 34 Remove the coolant recovery tank hose from the water outlet

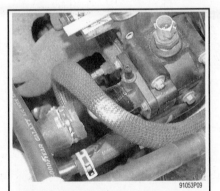

Fig. 35 Remove the upper radiator hose from the water outlet

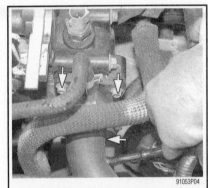

Fig. 36 Remove the three retaining bolts for the water outlet

Fig. 37 Carefully separate the water outlet from the thermostat housing

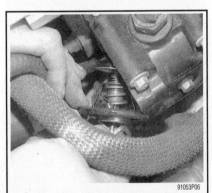

Fig. 38 Remove the thermostat from the housing

Fig. 39 Make sure you replace the O-ring when installing a new thermostat

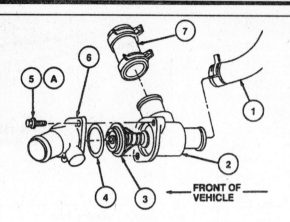

Item	Description
1	Water Bypass Hose
2	Rear Water Thermostat Housing
3	Water Thermostat
4	O-Ring Seal
5	Bolt (2 Req'd)
6	Front Water Thermostat Housing
7	Engine Return Hose
A	Tighten to 20-30 N·m (15-22 Lb-Ft)

91053G02

Fig. 40 Thermostat mounting—2.5L engine

Intake Manifold

REMOVAL & INSTALLATION

2.0L Engine

♦ See Figures 41 thru 64

⁂ CAUTION

The fuel injection system remains under pressure, even after the engine has been turned OFF. The fuel system pressure must be relieved before disconnecting any fuel lines. Failure to do so may result in fire and/or personal injury.

1. Disconnect the negative battery cable.
2. Remove the engine air intake resonators.
3. Relieve the fuel system pressure.
4. Remove the accelerator cable and the speed control actuator from the throttle body.
5. Remove the accelerator cable bracket.
6. Disconnect the main wiring harness connector and move aside.
7. Disconnect the vacuum line at the fuel pressure regulator.
8. Using the proper spring lock coupling disconnect tools (⅜ inch and ½ inch), remove the fuel supply and return hoses from the fuel injection supply manifold (fuel rail).
9. Remove the fuel supply and return hoses from the retaining bracket on the intake manifold and move aside.
10. Disconnect the wiring for the engine coolant temperature sensor and the engine control sensor.
11. Remove the crankcase ventilation tube from the intake manifold fitting.
12. Remove the wiring harness connector at the camshaft position sensor located on the cylinder head.

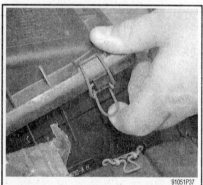

Fig. 41 Grasp and unfasten the retaining clips . . .

Fig. 42 . . . located in the following positions —2.0L engine, 2.5L similar

Fig. 43 The MAF connector is released by pressing down on the retaining spring—shown here already disconnected

Fig. 44 Label and disconnect the MAF sensor and . . .

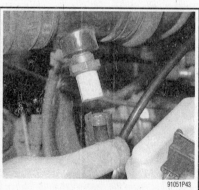

Fig. 45 . . . the IAT sensor

Fig. 46 Loosen the clamp on the air cleaner tube

Fig. 47 Lift the air cleaner inlet tube slightly and slide the retaining tab on the air intake resonator out and . . .

Fig. 48 . . . remove the air cleaner inlet tube from the vehicle

Fig. 49 Remove the four throttle body air intake resonator retaining bolts

Fig. 50 Remove the throttle body air intake resonator from the engine

Fig. 51 Remove the accelerator cable from the throttle body

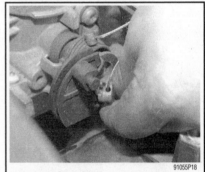

Fig. 52 Remove the transaxle kickdown cable from the throttle body—automatic transaxles only

Fig. 53 Unplug the main wiring harness connector

Fig. 54 Label and remove the vacuum hoses from the back of the intake manifold

Fig. 55 Remove the vacuum hose from the pressure regulator

Fig. 56 Remove the CMP sensor from the cylinder head

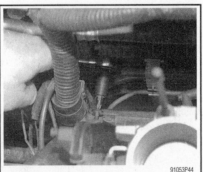

Fig. 57 The wiring harness is held to the bottom of the intake manifold by two T25 torx retaining bolts

Fig. 58 The alternator cable must be disconnected from the mega-fuse connection on the intake manifold

Fig. 59 Remove the two mounting bolts on the front of the alternator

Fig. 60 Remove the rear alternator mounting bolt

Fig. 61 Pull the alternator forward and unplug the connectors on the back

Fig. 62 Carefully remove the alternator from the vehicle

Fig. 63 The alternator and it's bracket aid the removal of the intake manifold

Fig. 64 Pull the intake from the mounting studs on the cylinder head and remove it from the engine

13. Remove the camshaft position sensor retaining screw and remove the sensor.

14. Disconnect the vacuum hose at the EGR valve.

15. Use a 22mm crowfoot wrench to completely loosen the EGR valve to exhaust manifold tube nut.

16. Remove the two EGR valve retaining bolts and remove the EGR valve and gasket.

17. Remove the vacuum supply hoses for the body and brake booster from the bottom of the intake manifold.

18. Remove the retaining bracket screws for the engine control sensor wiring.

➡The intake manifold can be removed without the removal of the alternator and alternator mounting bracket however their removal will make the job easier.

19. Remove the retaining bolts and nuts from the intake manifold.

20. Remove the intake manifold and gasket from the cylinder head.

To install:

21. If the intake manifold is to be replaced, remove the throttle body and idle air control valve from the old manifold and install on the new one.

22. Clean the gasket sealing surfaces on the intake manifold and the cylinder head.

23. Install the intake manifold using a new gasket to the cylinder head.

24. Reinstall the intake manifold retaining nuts and bolts.

25. Tighten the retaining nuts and bolts in several passes to 12–15 ft. lbs. (16–20 Nm), starting at the center and working towards the ends of the cylinder head.

26. Reinstall the alternator mounting bracket and alternator, if removed.

27. Reinstall the retaining screws for the engine control wiring sensor retaining bracket.

28. Reinstall the vacuum supply hoses for the body and brake booster to the bottom of the intake manifold.

29. Reinstall the EGR valve using a new gasket and tighten the two retaining bolts.

30. Reinstall the EGR valve to exhaust manifold tube nut and tighten to 26–33 ft. lbs. (35–45 Nm).

31. Reinstall the EGR valve vacuum hose.

32. Reinstall the camshaft position sensor and its retaining screw and tighten to 13–17 ft. lbs. (18–23 Nm).

33. Reconnect the camshaft position sensor.

34. Reinstall the crankcase ventilation tube to the intake manifold fitting.

35. Reconnect the engine coolant temperature sensor and the engine control sensor wiring.

36. Carefully position the fuel injection supply manifold with injectors into the intake manifold.

37. Reinstall the fuel supply and return hoses to the fuel injection supply manifold.

38. Reinstall the vacuum line to the fuel pressure regulator.

39. Position the wiring harness for the fuel injectors and install.

40. Reinstall the accelerator cable bracket.

41. Reinstall the speed control actuator and the accelerator cable to the throttle body.

42. Reinstall the air cleaner assembly and the air intake resonators.

43. Reconnect the negative battery cable.

44. Run the engine and check for leaks and proper operation.

2.5L Engine

UPPER INTAKE MANIFOLD

◗ See Figures 65 and 66

1. Disconnect the negative battery cable.

✷✷ CAUTION

Observe all applicable safety precautions when working around fuel. Whenever servicing the fuel system, always work in a well ventilated area. Do not allow fuel spray or vapors to come in contact with a spark or open flame. Keep a dry chemical fire extinguisher near the work area. Always keep fuel in a container specifically designed for fuel storage; also, always properly seal fuel containers to avoid the possibility of fire or explosion.

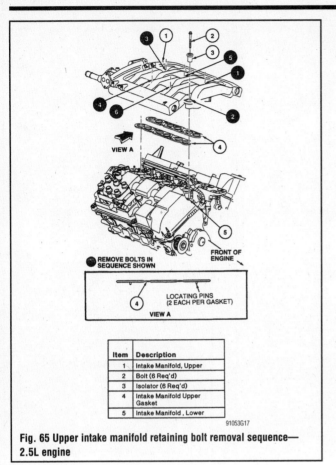

Item	Description
1	Intake Manifold, Upper
2	Bolt (6 Req'd)
3	Isolator (6 Req'd)
4	Intake Manifold Upper Gasket
5	Intake Manifold , Lower

91053G17

Fig. 65 Upper intake manifold retaining bolt removal sequence—2.5L engine

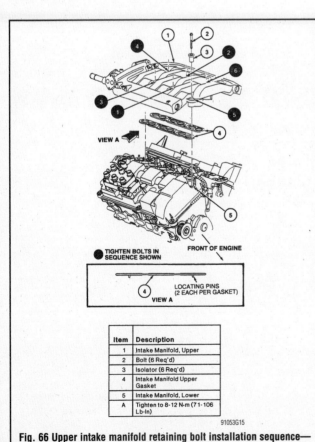

Item	Description
1	Intake Manifold, Upper
2	Bolt (6 Req'd)
3	Isolator (6 Req'd)
4	Intake Manifold Upper Gasket
5	Intake Manifold, Lower
A	Tighten to 8-12 N·m (71-106 Lb-In)

91053G15

Fig. 66 Upper intake manifold retaining bolt installation sequence—2.5L engine

2. Relieve the fuel system pressure.
3. Drain and recycle the engine coolant.
4. Remove the water pump pulley shield.
5. Depress the black retainer with a screwdriver on the upper intake manifold and disconnect the main emission vacuum control and the brake booster vacuum connector from the upper intake manifold.
6. Remove the accelerator cable and speed control actuator from the throttle body.
7. Remove the accelerator cable bracket from the intake manifold and move aside.
8. Remove the idle air control valve fresh air supply hose from the fitting on the upper intake manifold.
9. Disconnect the wiring harnesses from the throttle position sensor, idle air control valve and the EGR vacuum regulator control.
10. Remove the vacuum supply hose from the upper intake manifold to the PCV valve at the upper intake manifold.
11. Disconnect the vacuum supply hoses to the EGR vacuum regulator control and the EGR valve.
12. Loosen and remove the EGR valve to exhaust manifold tube and move aside.
13. Remove the Intake Manifold Runner Control (IMRC) vacuum solenoid linkage rod by carefully prying with a screwdriver.
14. Remove the upper intake manifold retaining bolts in the reverse of the installation sequence illustration.

➡When removing engine components such as manifolds and cylinder heads, always remove the retaining bolts in a reverse order of their tightening sequence to prevent warpage to the component.

15. Remove the upper intake manifold and gaskets from the engine.
To install:
16. Install the upper intake manifold using two new gaskets onto the lower intake manifold.
17. Install the upper manifold retaining bolts and tighten following the proper sequence to 71–106 inch lbs. (8–12 Nm).
18. Install new bushings for the IMRC linkage rod and install the rod.
19. Reinstall the EGR valve to exhaust manifold tube and tighten the nut to 26–33 ft. lbs. (35–45 Nm).
20. Reconnect the vacuum supply hoses to the EGR vacuum regulator control and the EGR valve.
21. Reconnect the throttle position sensor, idle air control valve and the EGR vacuum regulator control.
22. Reinstall the idle air control valve fresh air supply hose to the fitting on the upper intake manifold.
23. Reinstall the accelerator cable bracket to the intake manifold.
24. Reinstall the speed control actuator and the accelerator cable to the throttle body.
25. Reinstall the main emission vacuum control connector and the brake booster vacuum connector to the upper intake manifold.
26. Reinstall the water pump pulley shield.
27. Reconnect the negative battery cable.
28. Run the engine and check for leaks.

LOWER INTAKE MANIFOLD

◆ See Figures 67, 68 and 69

1. Remove the upper intake manifold as outlined in this Section.
2. Disconnect the fuel injector wiring harness and move aside.
3. Disconnect the vacuum line to the fuel pressure regulator and the IMRC valve and set aside.
4. Remove the spring lock coupling retainer clips from the fuel supply and return fittings.
5. Use spring lock coupling disconnect tools (⅜ inch and ½ inch) to disconnect the fuel supply and return hoses from the fuel injection supply manifold.
6. Remove the eight lower intake manifold to cylinder head retaining bolts in reverse of the tighten sequence illustration.
7. Remove the lower intake manifold and gaskets from the vehicle.
8. If the lower intake manifold is to be replaced or machined, remove the fuel injectors and the IMRC vacuum solenoid.
To install:
9. Install the IMRC vacuum solenoid and fuel injectors onto the lower intake manifold. Use a hand vacuum pump to verify operation of the IMRC vacuum solenoid and plate operation at this time.

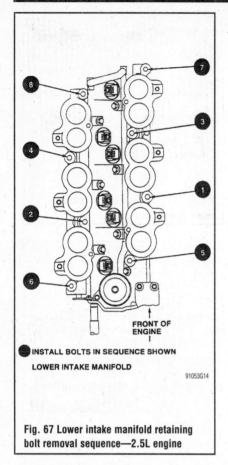

INSTALL BOLTS IN SEQUENCE SHOWN

LOWER INTAKE MANIFOLD

91053G14

Fig. 67 Lower intake manifold retaining bolt removal sequence—2.5L engine

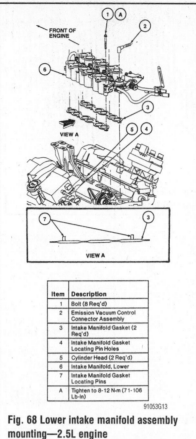

Item	Description
1	Bolt (8 Req'd)
2	Emission Vacuum Control Connector Assembly
3	Intake Manifold Gasket (2 Req'd)
4	Intake Manifold Gasket Locating Pin Holes
5	Cylinder Head (2 Req'd)
6	Intake Manifold, Lower
7	Intake Manifold Gasket Locating Pins
A	Tighten to 8-12 N·m (71-106 Lb-In)

91053G13

Fig. 68 Lower intake manifold assembly mounting—2.5L engine

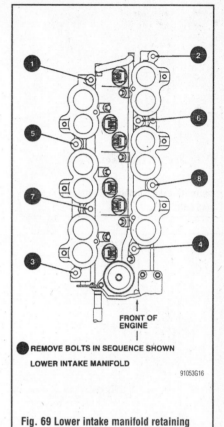

REMOVE BOLTS IN SEQUENCE SHOWN

LOWER INTAKE MANIFOLD

91053G16

Fig. 69 Lower intake manifold retaining bolt installation sequence—2.5L engine

10. Thoroughly clean the gasket sealing areas and place two new intake to cylinder head gaskets into position.

11. Carefully install the lower intake manifold and install the intake manifold to cylinder head retaining bolts.

12. Tighten the retaining bolts in sequence to 71–106 inch lbs. (8–12 Nm).

13. Install the fuel supply and return hoses to the fuel supply manifold and ensure that the spring lock couplings are correctly installed.

14. Install the retaining clips onto the spring lock couplings.

15. Reconnect the vacuum line to the fuel pressure regulator and the IMRC vacuum solenoid.

16. Temporarily connect the negative battery cable.

17. Reconnect the fuel pressure gauge to the fuel pressure relief valve located on the fuel injection supply manifold.

18. Cycle the ignition key several times to the **RUN** position to pressurize the fuel system.

19. Watch the fuel pressure gauge for signs of leakage. If the gauge holds pressure, remove the gauge and continue with the installation of the upper

intake manifold. If the pressure gauge loses pressure, remove the fuel injection supply manifold and replace the leaking O-ring(s) before continuing.

20. Disconnect the negative battery cable.

21. Reposition and install the fuel injector wiring harness.

22. Install the upper intake manifold as outlined in this Section.

Exhaust Manifold

REMOVAL & INSTALLATION

2.0L Engine

▶ See Figures 70 thru 90

1. Disconnect the negative battery cable.
2. Remove the engine air intake resonators.

91051PC5

Fig. 70 Remove the two upper retaining bolts and . . .

91051PC4

Fig. 71 . . . the two lower retaining bolts and . . .

91051PC3

Fig. 72 . . . lift the exhaust manifold heat shield up and remove it from the engine

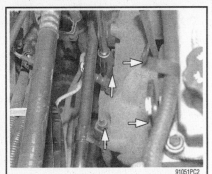

Fig. 73 Remove the four catalytic converter-to-exhaust manifold retaining nuts and bolts

Fig. 74 From under the vehicle, remove the EGR tube from the manifold and . . .

Fig. 75 . . . the rear support bracket retaining bolts and . . .

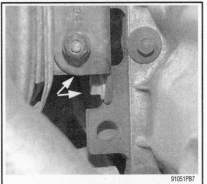

Fig. 76 . . . the front support bracket retaining bolts

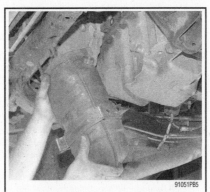

Fig. 77 Carefully lower the catalytic converter from the exhaust manifold and . . .

Fig. 78 . . . support the converter using a bungee strap or other suitable device

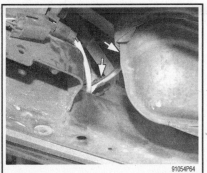

Fig. 79 Remove the HO2 sensor harness from the retaining clip and . . .

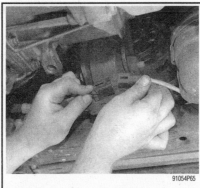

Fig. 80 . . . unplug the connector

Fig. 81 HO2 sensor is located on the exhaust manifold—1995 2.0L engine

Fig. 82 A special socket is recommended to remove the HO2 sensor(s). It can be purchased at most auto parts stores

Fig. 83 Place the harness into the slot in the socket and slide the socket down onto the sensor until the socket engages the sensor

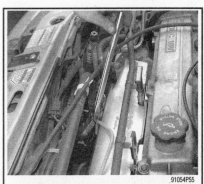

Fig. 84 Carefully loosen the sensor by turning the socket counterclockwise with an appropriate drive tool

Fig. 85 After the sensor is removed from the manifold, take care in handling it if you plan to use it, if dropped they easily break

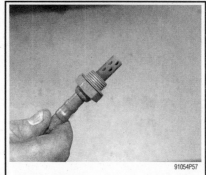

Fig. 86 Inspect the sensor for damage and build-up, replace if necessary

Fig. 87 Remove the engine oil dipstick tube

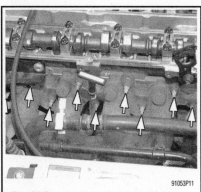

Fig. 88 Remove the exhaust manifold retaining nuts

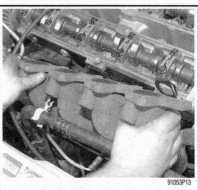

Fig. 89 Carefully lift the manifold off of the cylinder head studs

Fig. 90 Remember to remove the gasket, since it will probably stay on the cylinder head after the manifold is removed

3. Disconnect the heated oxygen sensor.
4. Remove the oil level indicator tube.
5. Remove the exhaust manifold heat shield retainers and the exhaust manifold heat shield.
6. Remove the heated oxygen sensor from the exhaust manifold.
7. Remove the four catalytic converter retaining nuts.
8. Raise and safely support the vehicle.
9. Remove the EGR valve to exhaust manifold tube, retaining bracket and clamp.
10. Remove the catalytic converter.

➡The catalytic converter does not have to be removed, the converter must be supported if it is not removed or damage may occur.

11. Lower the vehicle.
12. Remove the nine exhaust manifold retaining nuts from the cylinder head studs.
13. Remove the exhaust manifold and gasket.
14. Remove the exhaust manifold from the vehicle.
15. Clean all gasket mating surfaces.

To install:
16. Position a new exhaust manifold gasket and the exhaust manifold onto the cylinder head studs.
17. Reinstall the exhaust manifold retaining nuts and tighten to 13–16 ft. lbs. (14–17 Nm).
18. Raise and safely support the vehicle.
19. Reinstall the catalytic converter using a new exhaust converter inlet gasket.
20. Reinstall the EGR valve to exhaust manifold tube, retaining bracket and clamp.
21. Tighten the EGR valve to exhaust manifold tube nut to 26–33 ft. lbs. (35–45 Nm).
22. Lower the vehicle.
23. Reinstall the catalytic converter to exhaust manifold retaining nuts.
24. Reinstall the heated oxygen sensor to the exhaust manifold and tighten to 44 ft. lbs. (60 Nm).
25. Reinstall the exhaust manifold heat shield and heat shield retainers.

26. Tighten the heat shield retainers to 71–106 inch lbs. (8–11 Nm).
27. Reinstall the oil level indicator tube.
28. Reconnect the heated oxygen sensor.
29. Reinstall the air intake resonators.
30. Reconnect the negative battery cable.
31. Run the engine and check for leaks and proper operation.

2.5L Engine

RIGHT SIDE

♦ See Figures 91 and 92

1. Disconnect the negative battery cable.
2. Disconnect the wiring harness from the oxygen sensor.
3. Raise and safely support the vehicle.
4. Remove the alternator and the alternator mounting bracket.
5. Remove the retaining nuts from the outlet flange on the catalytic converter.
6. Remove the muffler and the exhaust converter outlet gasket from the catalytic converter.
7. Remove the catalytic converter retaining nuts and the exhaust pipe flange hold-down springs.
8. Remove the catalytic converter.
9. Remove the halfshaft support bearing retainer bracket from the support bearing and cylinder block.
10. Remove the oxygen sensor from the exhaust manifold.
11. Loosen the EGR valve to exhaust manifold tube nuts and remove the tube.
12. Remove the exhaust manifold retaining nuts from the cylinder head studs.
13. Remove the exhaust manifold and gasket from the engine.
14. Clean all gasket mating surfaces.

To install:
15. Install the exhaust manifold with a new exhaust manifold gasket.
16. Reinstall the exhaust manifold retaining studs and tighten to 13–16 ft. lbs. (18–22 Nm) in the proper sequence.

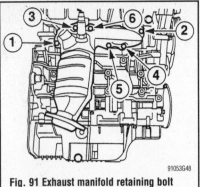

Fig. 91 Exhaust manifold retaining bolt removal sequence—right hand side

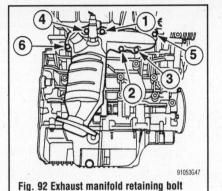

Fig. 92 Exhaust manifold retaining bolt installation sequence—right hand side

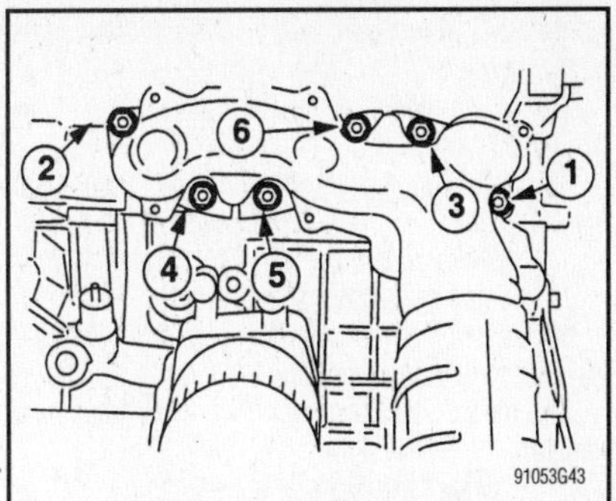

Fig. 93 Exhaust manifold retaining bolt removal sequence—left hand side

17. Reinstall the EGR valve to exhaust manifold tube and tighten the nuts to 26–33 ft. lbs. (35–45 Nm).

18. Reinstall the oxygen sensor into the exhaust manifold and tighten to 26–34 ft. lbs. (35–46 Nm).

19. Reinstall the halfshaft support bearing retainer bracket to the support bearing and the cylinder block.

20. Reinstall the catalytic converter using a new exhaust converter inlet gasket.

21. Position the muffler and a new exhaust converter outlet gasket onto the catalytic converter and loosely install the retaining nuts.

22. Align the exhaust system and tighten all nuts and bolts.

23. Reinstall the alternator mounting bracket and the alternator.

24. Lower the vehicle.

25. Reconnect the wiring harness to the oxygen sensor.

26. Reconnect the negative battery cable.

27. Run the engine and check for exhaust leaks and proper operation.

LEFT SIDE

▶ See Figures 93 and 94

1. Disconnect the negative battery cable.
2. Disconnect the oxygen sensor.
3. Raise and safely support the vehicle.
4. Remove the front and rear exhaust crossover tube flange fasteners from the exhaust manifolds.
5. Remove the stud and nut retainer from the engine oil pan.
6. Remove the two remaining nuts and bolts from the exhaust crossover tubes outlet connection.
7. Remove the exhaust crossover tube.
8. Remove the lower radiator hose tube retaining bracket nuts.
9. Remove the six exhaust manifold retaining nuts from the cylinder head studs.
10. Move the lower radiator hose tube to gain access for removal of the exhaust manifold.
11. Remove the exhaust manifold. If the manifold is being replaced, remove the oxygen sensor.
12. Clean all gasket mating surfaces.

To install:

13. If removed, install the oxygen sensor in the new manifold.
14. Place a new exhaust manifold to cylinder block gasket onto the cylinder head studs.
15. Move the lower radiator hose to allow installing the exhaust manifold.
16. Place the exhaust manifold onto the cylinder head studs and install the six retaining nuts.
17. Tighten the retaining nuts to 13–16 ft. lbs. (18–22 Nm), in sequence.
18. Reinstall the lower radiator hose tube retaining bracket.
19. Reinstall the exhaust crossover tube.
20. Reinstall two nuts and bolts to the exhaust crossover tube outlet connection.
21. Reinstall the stud and nut retainer at the engine oil pan.
22. Reinstall the front and rear exhaust crossover tube flange fasteners at the exhaust manifolds.
23. Lower the vehicle.
24. Reconnect the oxygen sensor.

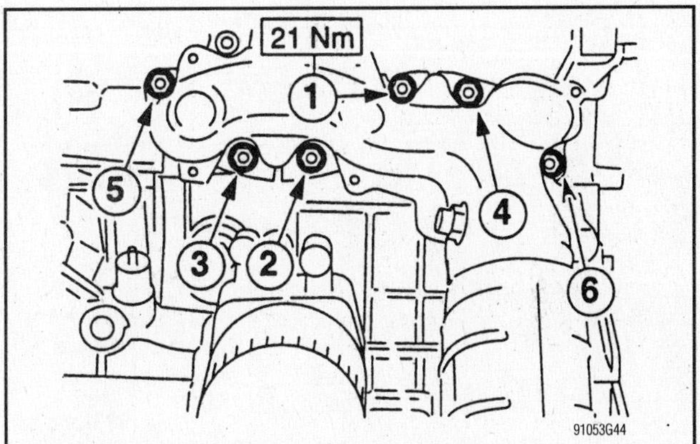

Fig. 94 Exhaust manifold retaining bolt installation sequence—left hand side

25. Reconnect the negative battery cable.
26. Run the engine and check for exhaust leaks and proper operation.

Radiator

REMOVAL & INSTALLATION

▶ See Figures 95 thru 101

1. Disconnect the negative battery cable.
2. Drain and recycle the engine coolant.
3. Remove the upper radiator hose from the radiator.
4. On 2.5L equipped vehicles, remove the radiator overflow hose from the radiator.
5. On vehicles equipped with an automatic transaxle only, remove the transmission cooler line from the cooler inlet fitting and plug the line and the fitting.
6. Remove the engine fan.
7. Raise and support the vehicle.
8. Remove the lower radiator hose from the radiator.
9. On vehicles equipped with an automatic transaxle only, remove the transmission cooler line from the cooler outlet fitting and plug the line and the fitting.

➡Remove the cooler lines while holding the radiator connector with a back-up wrench.

10. Support the radiator, and A/C condenser with a jackstand or other suitable device.
11. Remove the lower radiator supports from the front of the subframe.
12. Remove the two retaining bolts for the A/C condenser from the brackets at the bottom of the radiator.
13. Position the jackstand aside and remove the radiator out the bottom of the vehicle.

To install:

14. Carefully raise the radiator into place and support the radiator with a

jackstand or other suitable device. Install the two retaining bolts for the A/C condenser into the brackets at the bottom of the radiator.

15. Install the lower radiator supports and tighten the bolts to 71–97 inch lbs. (8–11 Nm).

16. Remove the jackstand and install the transmission cooler outlet line (if equipped) and the lower radiator hose to the radiator.

17. Lower the vehicle.

18. Install and tighten the fan shroud nuts.

19. Install the transmission cooler inlet line (if equipped) and the upper radiator hose to the radiator.

20. On 2.5L equipped vehicles, install the radiator overflow hose from the radiator.

21. Connect the negative battery cable.

22. Fill the cooling system with the proper 50/50 mixture and start the vehicle.

23. Bleed the cooling system and check for leaks.

Engine Fan

REMOVAL & INSTALLATION

▶ See Figures 102, 103, 104, 105 and 106

1. Disconnect the negative battery cable.
2. Remove the air intake resonator.
3. Remove the front air intake resonator support bracket.
4. Unplug the fan connector and remove the retaining clips on the wiring harness and move the harness out of the way.
5. Remove the cooling fan ground cable from the passenger side fender apron.
6. Remove the cooling fan assembly from the radiator.

To install:

7. Lower the cooling fan assembly onto the radiator and tighten the cooling fan retaining bolts.

Fig. 95 Remove the upper radiator hose from the radiator

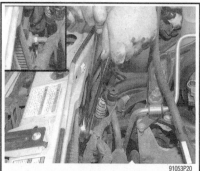

Fig. 96 Use a back-up wrench to remove the transaxle cooler line connections—automatic transaxle only

Fig. 97 the lower transaxle cooler line connection

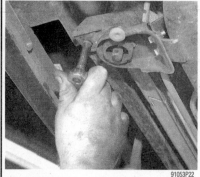

Fig. 98 Remove the passenger side radiator mount and . . .

Fig. 99 . . . and the driver's side radiator mount

Fig. 100 The condenser can be support using mechanic's wire as shown here, or another suitable device

Fig. 101 Carefully lower the radiator out the bottom of the vehicle

Fig. 102 Remove the front air intake resonator support bracket

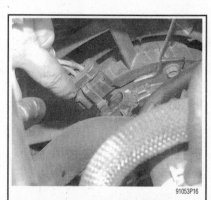

Fig. 103 Unplug the fan connector

Fig. 104 Remove the wiring harnesses from the clip on the top of the fan

Fig. 105 Remove the fan shroud retaining bolts

Fig. 106 Carefully remove the fan from the vehicle

8. Install the fan ground cable.
9. Properly route the wiring harness and install the retaining clips. Plug the fan connector in.
10. Install the front air intake resonator support bracket.
11. Install the air intake resonator.
12. Connect the negative battery cable.
13. Check the fan operation.

Water Pump

REMOVAL & INSTALLATION

2.0L Engine

▶ See Figures 107, 108 and 109

1. Disconnect the negative battery cable.

✳✳ CAUTION

Never open, service or drain the radiator or cooling system when hot; serious burns can occur from the steam and hot coolant.

2. Drain the engine cooling system.
3. Raise and safely support the vehicle.
4. Remove the lower radiator hose from the water pump.

➡If the lower radiator hose is hard to reach on the back of the water pump, remove the hose at the radiator and after the water pump is ready to be removed, pull the water pump away from the engine block until there is enough room to remove the hose from the pump.

5. Lower the vehicle.
6. Remove the accessory drive belt.
7. Remove the timing belt covers and the timing belt as outlined in this Section.

8. Remove the four water pump retaining bolts.
9. Remove the water pump.
To install:
10. Thoroughly clean all sealing surfaces.
11. Install a new water pump gasket and the water pump onto the cylinder block.
12. Tighten the retaining bolts to 12–15 ft. lbs. (16–20 Nm).
13. Reinstall the timing belt and the timing belt covers as outlined in this Section.
14. Reinstall the accessory drive belt.
15. Raise and safely support the vehicle.
16. Reinstall the lower radiator hose.
17. Lower the vehicle.
18. Fill the engine cooling system.
19. Reconnect the negative battery cable.
20. Start the engine and top off the coolant as necessary. Check for leaks.

2.5L Engine

▶ See Figures 110 and 111

➡Before continuing with this procedure, be sure three new water pump retaining bolts (W701544) are available. Due to their torque-to-yield design, the bolts stretch and cannot be reused.

1. Disconnect the negative battery cable.

✳✳ CAUTION

Never open, service or drain the radiator or cooling system when hot; serious burns can occur from the steam and hot coolant.

2. Drain the engine cooling system.
3. Remove the water pump pulley shield.
4. Remove the water pump drive belt.
5. Remove the water pump inlet and outlet hoses from the water pump.
6. Remove the three water pump to left cylinder head retaining bolts.
7. Remove the water pump and water pump housing from the vehicle.

Fig. 107 Remove the lower radiator hose from the back of the water pump

Fig. 108 The water pump is retained by four bolts

Fig. 109 Carefully remove the water pump from the engine block

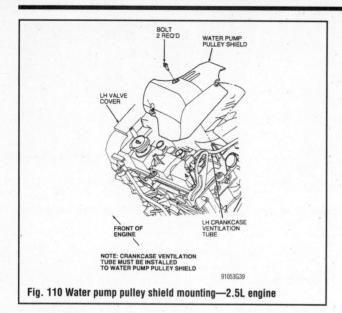

Fig. 110 Water pump pulley shield mounting—2.5L engine

8. Remove the water pump to water pump housing retaining bolts and separate the water pump from the water pump housing.

To install:

9. Thoroughly clean all sealing surfaces.

10. Install the water pump to the water pump housing using a new gasket and install the retaining bolts. Tighten the retaining bolts to 16–18 ft. lbs. (22–25 Nm).

11. Position the water pump and water pump housing and install three new torque-to-yield retaining bolts into the left cylinder head.

12. Tighten the new retaining bolts to 11–13 ft. lbs. (15–18 Nm), then rotate the retaining bolts 85–95 degrees.

13. Reinstall the water pump inlet and outlet hoses to the water pump.

14. Reinstall the water pump drive belt.

15. Reinstall the water pump shield.

16. Fill the engine cooling system.

17. Reconnect the negative battery cable.

18. Start the engine and top off the coolant as necessary. Check for leaks.

Cylinder Head

REMOVAL & INSTALLATION

2.0L Engine

▶ **See Figures 112 thru 130**

➡ The cylinder head bolts are a torque-to-yield design and cannot be reused. Be sure new cylinder head bolts are available before beginning this procedure. If the cylinder head bolts are reused, engine damage may occur.

1. Disconnect the negative battery cable.

❋❋ CAUTION

Never open, service or drain the radiator or cooling system when hot; serious burns can occur from the steam and hot coolant. Coolant should be reused unless it is contaminated or is several years old.

2. Drain the engine coolant from the radiator and the cylinder block drain plugs.

3. Remove the intake manifold.

4. Remove the exhaust manifold.

5. Remove the camshafts and valve tappets.

6. Support the engine with a wood block between the crankshaft pulley and the front sub-frame.

7. Remove the engine support device previously installed for the timing belt cover removal.

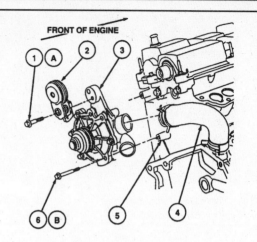

Item	Description
1	Bolt
2	Water Pump Drive Belt Tensioner
3	Water Pump
4	Water Pump Outlet Hose
5	Cylinder Head, LH
6	Bolt (3 Req'd)
A	Tighten to 8-12 N·m (71-106 Lb-In)
B	Tighten to 15-18 N·m (11-13 Lb-Ft), Then Rotate 85-95 Degrees

Fig. 111 Water pump mounting—2.5L engine

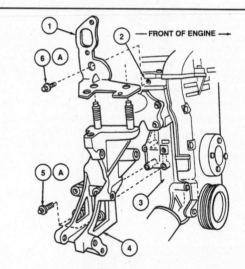

Item	Description
1	Engine Lifting Eye (RH)
2	Cylinder Head
3	Cylinder Block
4	Generator Mounting Bracket
5	Bolt (4 Req'd)
6	Bolt
A	Tighten to 41-55 N·m (30-41 Lb-Ft)

Fig. 112 Upper engine mount and accessory mounting brackets—2.0L engine

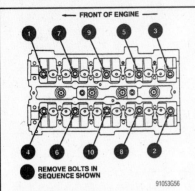

Fig. 113 Cylinder head bolt removal sequence—2.0L engine

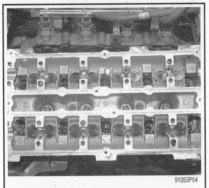

Fig. 114 Once the camshafts are removed, the cylinder head bolts are accessible

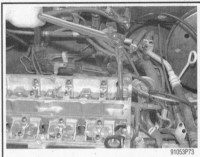

Fig. 115 Loosen the head bolts in sequence, using the appropriate tools. The head bolts on the 2.0L engine require a T55 Torx

Fig. 116 Lift the cylinder head off the engine block

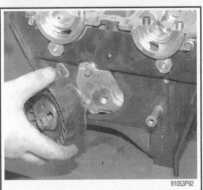

Fig. 117 Remove the head bolts with a magnet once the head is placed on a suitable worksurface

Fig. 118 The thermostat housing is held by three retaining bolts

Fig. 119 Loosen the bolts and remove the housing from the head

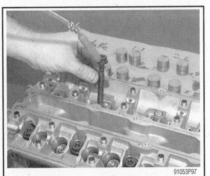

Fig. 120 Remove the timing belt tensioner pulley from the head

Fig. 121 The front cover is held by four retaining bolts, remove the bolts and . . .

Fig. 122 . . . remove the cover from the cylinder head, the head will now lay flat

Fig. 123 Using a suitable tool, remove the gasket material and build-up from the cylinder head and the . . .

Fig. 124 . . . engine block

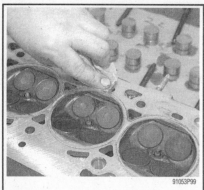

Fig. 125 Wipe the head and the . . .

Fig. 126 . . . block with a rag and solvent to remove any residue to ensure a suitable sealing surface for the gasket

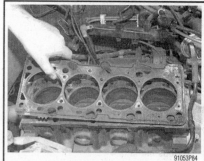

Fig. 127 Place the new head gasket onto the engine block, aligning the holes in the gasket with . . .

Fig. 128 . . . the dowels in the block

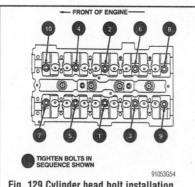

Fig. 129 Cylinder head bolt installation sequence—2.0L engine

Fig. 130 The cylinder head bolts must be tightened in sequence, to the proper torque using a torque wrench

8. Remove the right-hand engine lifting eye retaining bolt and the lifting eye.

9. Remove the support bracket from the power steering pump mounting bracket and cylinder head.

10. Remove the timing belt covers.

11. Remove the camshaft timing belt tensioner pulley.

12. Remove the thermostat housing from the rear of the cylinder head.

13. Remove the ignition coil and bracket from the cylinder head.

14. Remove the spark plugs if not already removed.

15. Remove the cylinder head retaining bolts in the reverse of the installation sequence.

16. Remove the cylinder head and gasket from the engine.

17. If the cylinder head is to be serviced, remove the left-hand engine lifting eye.

To install:

18. Clean the cylinder head and cylinder block gasket surfaces and check for flatness. Refer to the Engine Reconditioning Section for procedures.

19. Install a new cylinder head gasket onto the cylinder block. Be sure the head gasket is properly positioned on the dowels.

✳✳ WARNING

Use care when positioning the cylinder head to prevent damage to the head gasket or dowels.

20. Place a light coating of engine oil onto the threads of the new cylinder head bolts and install.

21. Tighten the cylinder head bolts in sequence and in the following steps:
- Tighten all bolts to 15–22 ft. lbs. (20–30 Nm)
- Tighten all bolts to 30–37 ft. lbs. (40–50 Nm)
- Rotate all bolts 90–120 degrees.

22. Reinstall the ignition coil bracket and the ignition coil.

23. Reinstall the water thermostat housing.

24. Reinstall the timing belt covers.

25. Reinstall the camshaft timing belt tensioner pulley and retaining bolt onto the front of the cylinder head.

26. Reinstall the support bracket to the power steering pump mounting bracket and the cylinder head.

27. Tighten the support bracket to 29–41 ft. lbs. (39–55 Nm).

28. Reinstall the right engine lifting eye to the cylinder head and the alternator mounting bracket. Tighten the retaining bolts to 30–41 ft. lbs. (41–55, Nm).

29. If removed, install the left-hand engine lifting eye to the cylinder head and tighten to 10–13 ft. lbs. (14–18 Nm).

30. Install the engine support device to the engine lifting eyes and support the engine.

31. Remove the wood block from between the sub-frame and the crankshaft pulley.

32. Reinstall the valve tappets and camshaft into their original locations.

33. Reinstall the exhaust manifold.

34. Reinstall the intake manifold.

35. Reinstall the spark plugs.

✳✳ CAUTION

The EPA warns that prolonged contact with used engine oil may cause a number of skin disorders, including cancer! You should make every effort to minimize your exposure to used engine oil. Protective gloves should be worn when changing the oil. Wash your hands and any other exposed skin areas as soon as possible after exposure to used engine oil. Soap and water, or waterless hand cleaner should be used.

36. Drain the engine oil and remove the engine oil filter.

✳✳ WARNING

Operating the engine without the proper amount and type of engine oil will result in severe engine damage.

37. Reinstall the drain plug and tighten to 15–21 ft. lbs. (21–28 Nm).

38. Reinstall a new engine oil filter and fill the crankcase with the proper amount and grade of oil.

39. Fill the engine cooling system.

40. Reconnect the negative battery cable.

41. Run the engine and check for oil and coolant leaks. Check for proper engine operation.

2.5L Engine

▶ See Figures 131, 132, 133, 134 and 135

➡The cylinder head bolts are a torque-to-yield design and cannot be reused. Be sure new cylinder head bolts are available before beginning this procedure.

1. Disconnect the negative battery cable.

❊❊ CAUTION

Never open, service or drain the radiator or cooling system when hot; serious burns can occur from the steam and hot coolant.

2. Drain the engine coolant from the radiator and cylinder block drain plugs.

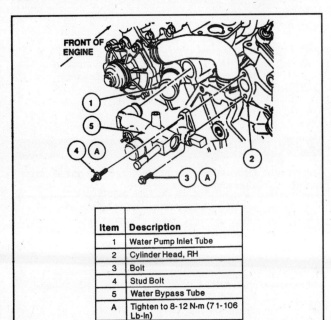

Item	Description
1	Water Pump Inlet Tube
2	Cylinder Head, RH
3	Bolt
4	Stud Bolt
5	Water Bypass Tube
A	Tighten to 8-12 N·m (71-106 Lb-In)

91053G20

Fig. 131 Water bypass tube mounting—2.5L engine

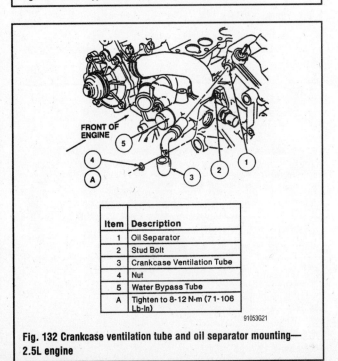

Item	Description
1	Oil Separator
2	Stud Bolt
3	Crankcase Ventilation Tube
4	Nut
5	Water Bypass Tube
A	Tighten to 8-12 N·m (71-106 Lb-In)

91053G21

Fig. 132 Crankcase ventilation tube and oil separator mounting—2.5L engine

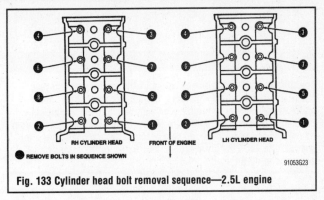

Fig. 133 Cylinder head bolt removal sequence—2.5L engine

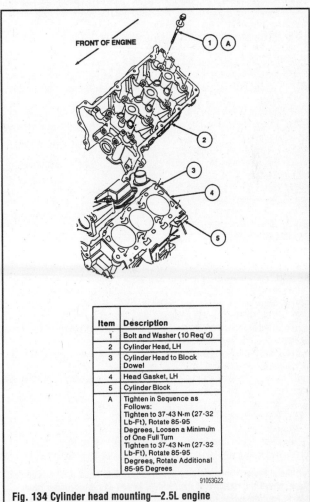

Item	Description
1	Bolt and Washer (10 Req'd)
2	Cylinder Head, LH
3	Cylinder Head to Block Dowel
4	Head Gasket, LH
5	Cylinder Block
A	Tighten in Sequence as Follows: Tighten to 37-43 N·m (27-32 Lb-Ft), Rotate 85-95 Degrees, Loosen a Minimum of One Full Turn Tighten to 37-43 N·m (27-32 Lb-Ft), Rotate 85-95 Degrees, Rotate Additional 85-95 Degrees

91053G22

Fig. 134 Cylinder head mounting—2.5L engine

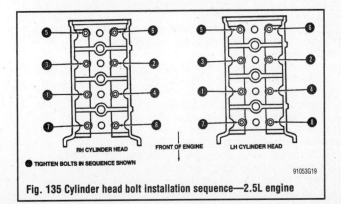

Fig. 135 Cylinder head bolt installation sequence—2.5L engine

3. Close the radiator draincock and install the drain plugs into the cylinder block.

4. Remove the upper and lower intake manifolds.

✳✳ CAUTION

The EPA warns that prolonged contact with used engine oil may cause a number of skin disorders, including cancer! You should make every effort to minimize your exposure to used engine oil. Protective gloves should be worn when changing the oil. Wash your hands and any other exposed skin areas as soon as possible after exposure to used engine oil. Soap and water, or waterless hand cleaner should be used.

5. Drain the engine oil and remove the oil pan.

6. Remove the alternator and the alternator mounting bracket.

7. Remove the heated oxygen sensor from the right cylinder head exhaust manifold.

8. Remove the left cylinder head exhaust manifold.

9. Remove the water pump.

10. Remove the engine front cover.

11. Install the upper front engine mount (support insulator) and the upper front engine support bracket to the front of the engine and the right front fender apron.

12. Remove engine support device.

13. Remove the camshafts and valve tappets from both cylinder heads.

14. Disconnect the hoses from the EGR pressure sensor at the EGR valve, to the exhaust manifold tube.

15. Disengage the EGR pressure sensor.

16. Disconnect the interior vacuum source hose from the main emission vacuum harness.

17. Disconnect the fuel vapor hose from the PCV valve.

18. Disconnect the EGR transducer.

19. Remove the EGR valve to exhaust manifold tube from the right exhaust manifold and remove from the vehicle.

20. Remove the wiring retaining bracket from the EGR transducer bracket.

21. Remove the engine air cleaner.

22. Remove the crankcase ventilation tube from the water crossover and oil separator.

23. Remove the water crossover retaining bolt and stud bolt from the right cylinder head. Set the water crossover aside.

24. Remove the oil level dipstick from the left cylinder head.

25. Remove the cylinder head retaining bolts from the cylinder heads in the reverse of the sequence illustration.

26. Remove the right cylinder head with the exhaust manifold and the EGR transducer bracket attached.

27. If required, remove the exhaust manifold and the EGR transducer bracket from the right cylinder head.

28. Remove the left cylinder head.

29. Inspect the cylinder heads and cylinder block.

To install:

30. Clean the cylinder head and cylinder block gasket surfaces and check for flatness. Refer to the Engine Reconditioning Section for procedures.

➡**If the cylinder heads were removed for cylinder head gasket replacement, check the flatness of the cylinder heads and the cylinder block gasket sealing surfaces.**

31. If removed, install the right exhaust manifold and EGR transducer bracket to the right cylinder head.

32. Install new cylinder head gaskets onto the dowels of the cylinder block.

33. Position the cylinder heads into their original positions using care not to damage the heads, block or gaskets.

34. Be sure that the cylinder heads are correctly positioned on the dowels.

35. Lightly oil the threads of the new cylinder head retaining bolts and install into the cylinder heads.

36. Tighten the new cylinder head retaining bolts as follows:
- Tighten the bolts, in sequence, to 27–32 ft. lbs. (37–43 Nm)
- Rotate the bolts, in sequence, 85–95 degrees
- Loosen the bolts, in sequence, a minimum of one full turn
- Tighten the bolts, in sequence, to 27–32 ft. lbs. (37–43 Nm)
- Rotate the bolts, in sequence, 85–95 degrees
- Rotate the bolts, in sequence, an additional 85–95 degrees

37. Inspect the water crossover O-rings and replace if required.

38. Reinstall the water crossover to the cylinder heads and tighten the retaining bolts to 71–106 inch lbs. (8–12 Nm).

39. Reinstall the crankcase ventilation tube. Tighten the tube to 44–62 inch lbs. (5–7 Nm).

40. Reinstall the oil level dipstick to the left cylinder head.

41. Reinstall the engine air cleaner.

42. Reinstall the wiring retaining bracket onto the EGR transducer bracket.

43. Reinstall the EGR to exhaust manifold tube onto the right exhaust manifold.

44. Reconnect the EGR transducer and the EGR pressure sensor.

45. Reconnect the fuel vapor hose to the PCV valve.

46. Reconnect the interior vacuum source hoses to the main emission vacuum harness.

47. Reconnect the hoses from the EGR pressure sensor and EGR valve to the exhaust manifold tube.

48. Reinstall the camshafts and valve tappets.

49. Install the engine support device to the engine lifting eyes and support the engine.

50. Reinstall the engine front cover.

51. Reinstall the left exhaust manifold.

52. Reinstall the water pump.

53. Reinstall the heated oxygen sensor to the right exhaust manifold.

54. Reinstall the alternator mounting bracket and the alternator.

55. Reinstall the engine oil pan.

56. Reinstall the lower and upper intake manifolds.

57. Replace the engine oil filter.

58. Fill the engine with the proper amount and grade of engine oil.

✳✳ WARNING

Operating the engine without the proper amount and type of engine oil will result in severe engine damage.

59. Fill the engine cooling system.

60. Reconnect the negative battery cable.

61. Run the engine and check for oil and coolant leaks. Check for proper engine operation.

Oil Pan

REMOVAL & INSTALLATION

2.0L Engine

▶ **See Figures 136 thru 148**

1. Disconnect the negative battery cable.

2. Install an engine support device to the engine lifting eyes and support the engine.

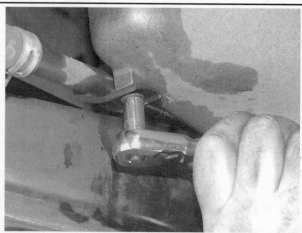

91053P29

Fig. 136 Remove the heater hose tube bracket bolt and position the tube out of the way

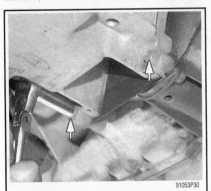

Fig. 137 Remove the oil pan-to-transaxle retaining bolts

Fig. 138 Remove the retaining bolts for the bellhousing cover and . . .

Fig. 139 . . . and remove the cover from the engine

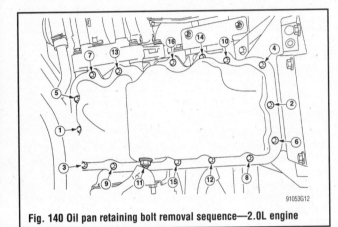

Fig. 140 Oil pan retaining bolt removal sequence—2.0L engine

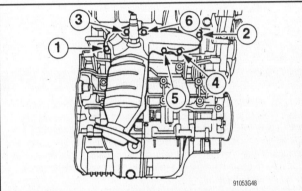

Fig. 141 Exhaust manifold retaining bolt installation sequence—right hand side

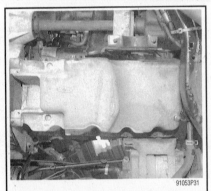

Fig. 142 Remove the oil pan-to-engine block retaining bolts

Fig. 143 Lower the oil pan and remove it from the engine

Fig. 144 Remove the gasket from the oil pan and . . .

Fig. 145 . . . clean the oil pan and the gasket grooves with a wire brush or other suitable tool

Fig. 146 Wipe the oil pan and . . .

Fig. 147 . . . the engine block surfaces with a clean rag and solvent to remove any residue and ensure a good sealing surface

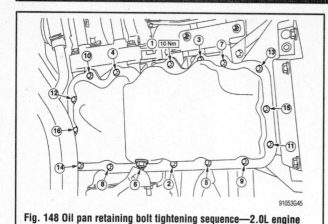

Fig. 148 Oil pan retaining bolt tightening sequence—2.0L engine

3. Raise and safely support the vehicle.
4. Remove the catalytic converter system.
5. Disconnect the wiring to the low oil level sensor, if equipped.
6. Remove the heater water bolt from the bottom of the oil pan and position the tube out of the way.

✳ CAUTION

The EPA warns that prolonged contact with used engine oil may cause a number of skin disorders, including cancer! You should make every effort to minimize your exposure to used engine oil. Protective gloves should be worn when changing the oil. Wash your hands and any other exposed skin areas as soon as possible after exposure to used engine oil. Soap and water, or waterless hand cleaner should be used.

7. Drain the engine oil.
8. Reinstall the oil pan drain plug and tighten to 15–21 ft. lbs. (21–28 Nm).
9. Remove the oil pan retaining bolts from the transaxle housing.
10. Remove the lower engine rear plate.
11. Remove the through-bolt for the left and right support insulators.
12. Lower the vehicle to work on the top side of the engine but keep on the hoist.

→**Mark the location of the upper front engine support bracket before removing from the front engine support bracket.**

13. Remove the upper front engine support bracket retaining nuts from the upper front engine support insulator.
14. Raise the engine to allow room for removal of the engine oil pan, using the engine support device.
15. Raise and safely support the vehicle.
16. Remove the oil pan retaining bolts from the cylinder block, working from the ends of the block toward the center.
17. Loosen and remove the oil pan and gasket.
18. Inspect the oil pump pick-up tube and screen and clean or replace as necessary.
To install:
19. If removed, install the oil pump pick-up tube and screen. Tighten the retaining bolts to 71–97 inch lbs. (8–11 Nm). Install a new self-locking oil pump pick-up tube support nut to the crankshaft main bearing cap retaining stud bolt. Tighten to 13–15 ft. lbs. (17–21 Nm).
20. Clean the gasket sealing surfaces for the oil pan at the cylinder block.
21. Clean the oil pan thoroughly leaving no traces of gasket material, grease or solvents.
22. Apply a bead of silicone gasket sealer to the oil pump parting lines and at the crankshaft rear main seal retainer on the cylinder block.
23. Install the oil pan and a new gasket into position and hold with several oil pan retaining screws.
24. Reinstall the rest of the retaining bolts and push the oil pan flush against the transaxle case before tightening the retaining bolts.
25. Tighten the 10 oil pan retaining bolts, in several passes, to 15–18 ft. lbs. (20–24 Nm), working from the center of the block towards the ends.
26. Reinstall the lower engine rear plate.

27. Reinstall the oil pan to transaxle housing retaining bolts.
28. Tighten the retaining bolts to 25–34 ft. lbs. (34–46 Nm).
29. Lower the vehicle but keep on the hoist.
30. Lower the engine into position by adjusting the Three Bar Engine Support or equivalent.
31. Reinstall the upper front engine support bracket retaining nuts onto the upper front engine support insulator.
32. Raise and safely support the vehicle.
33. Reinstall the through-bolts for the left and the right insulators.
34. Reconnect the low oil level sensor, if equipped.
35. Position the heater water tube and retaining bolt to the bottom of the oil pan.
36. Reinstall the catalytic converter system.
37. Lower the vehicle.
38. Remove the engine support device.

✳✳ WARNING

Operating the engine without the proper amount and type of engine oil will result in severe engine damage.

39. Fill the crankcase with the proper amount of engine oil.
40. Reconnect the negative battery cable.
41. Run the engine and check for leaks and proper operation.

2.5L Engine

♦ **See Figures 149 and 150**

1. Disconnect the negative battery cable.
2. Remove the water pump pulley shield.
3. Install engine support device to the engine lifting eyes and support the engine.
4. Raise and safely support the vehicle.
5. Remove the exhaust crossover and the exhaust retaining bracket located on the right side of the oil pan.

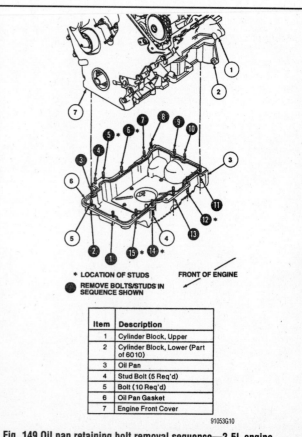

* LOCATION OF STUDS   **FRONT OF ENGINE**
⬤ REMOVE BOLTS/STUDS IN SEQUENCE SHOWN

Item	Description
1	Cylinder Block, Upper
2	Cylinder Block, Lower (Part of 60 10)
3	Oil Pan
4	Stud Bolt (5 Req'd)
5	Bolt (10 Req'd)
6	Oil Pan Gasket
7	Engine Front Cover

Fig. 149 Oil pan retaining bolt removal sequence—2.5L engine

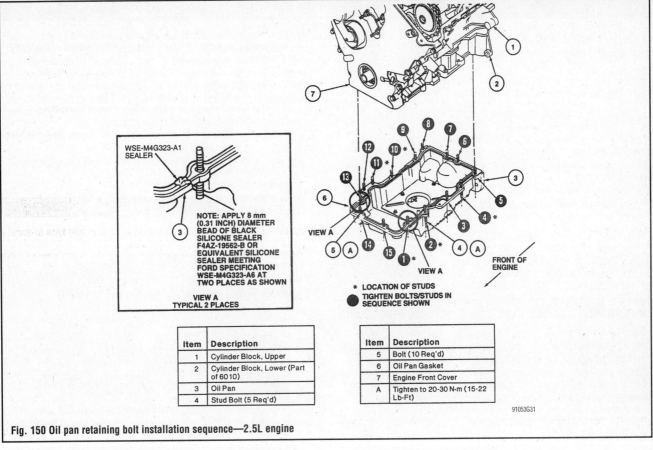

Fig. 150 Oil pan retaining bolt installation sequence—2.5L engine

WSE-M4G323-A1 SEALER

NOTE: APPLY 8 mm (0.31 INCH) DIAMETER BEAD OF BLACK SILICONE SEALER F4AZ-19562-B OR EQUIVALENT SILICONE SEALER MEETING FORD SPECIFICATION WSE-M4G323-A6 AT TWO PLACES AS SHOWN

VIEW A
TYPICAL 2 PLACES

* LOCATION OF STUDS
● TIGHTEN BOLTS/STUDS IN SEQUENCE SHOWN

FRONT OF ENGINE

Item	Description
1	Cylinder Block, Upper
2	Cylinder Block, Lower (Part of 6010)
3	Oil Pan
4	Stud Bolt (5 Req'd)

Item	Description
5	Bolt (10 Req'd)
6	Oil Pan Gasket
7	Engine Front Cover
A	Tighten to 20-30 N·m (15-22 Lb-Ft)

91053G31

6. Remove the exhaust heat shield retaining nuts and the exhaust heat shields from the left side of the oil pan.

✳✳ CAUTION

The EPA warns that prolonged contact with used engine oil may cause a number of skin disorders, including cancer! You should make every effort to minimize your exposure to used engine oil. Protective gloves should be worn when changing the oil. Wash your hands and any other exposed skin areas as soon as possible after exposure to used engine oil. Soap and water, or waterless hand cleaner should be used.

7. Drain the engine oil.
8. Reinstall the oil pan drain plug using a new gasket and tighten to 16–22 ft. lbs. (22–30 Nm).
9. Remove the oil pan retaining bolts from the transaxle housing.
10. If equipped with automatic transaxle, remove the access plug from the engine rear plate.
11. Remove the through-bolt for the left and right front engine support insulators.
12. Partially lower the vehicle on the hoist.

➡ **Mark the location of the upper front engine support bracket before it is removed.**

13. Remove the upper front engine support bracket retaining nuts and remove the upper front engine support bracket.
14. Using the three bar engine support or equivalent, raise the engine to allow room for removal of the engine oil pan.
15. Raise and safely support the vehicle.
16. Remove the oil pan retaining bolts and studs from the lower cylinder block following the bolt removal sequence.
17. Remove the oil pan and the oil pan gasket from the vehicle.
To install:
18. Clean the oil pan to lower cylinder block gasket sealing surfaces.

19. Thoroughly clean the oil pan.
20. Install a new oil pan gasket into the groove of the oil pan.
21. Apply a bead of silicone sealer to the gasket area where the pan meets the parting lines of the lower cylinder block and the front engine cover.
22. Carefully install the oil pan with gasket to the lower cylinder block.
23. Reinstall the bolts and studs but do not tighten.
24. Push the oil pan against the transaxle case and tighten the oil pan bolts and studs.
25. Reinstall the oil pan to transaxle case bolts and tighten to 25–34 ft. lbs. (34–46 Nm).
26. Tighten the oil pan bolts and studs in the proper sequence to 15–22 ft. lbs. (20–30 Nm).
27. If equipped with automatic transaxle, install the access plug into the engine rear plate.
28. Lower the vehicle but keep it on the hoist.
29. Using the three bar engine support or equivalent, lower the engine into its proper position.
30. Reinstall the upper front engine support bracket and its retaining nuts onto the upper front engine support insulator.
31. Raise and safely support the vehicle.
32. Reinstall the through-bolts for the left and right front engine support insulators.
33. Reinstall the exhaust crossover, exhaust retaining bracket and heat shield.
34. Replace the engine oil filter.
35. Lower the vehicle.
36. Remove the three bar engine support or equivalent.

✳✳ WARNING

Operating the engine without the proper amount and type of engine oil will result in severe engine damage.

37. Fill the crankcase with the correct amount and grade of engine oil.
38. Reconnect the negative battery cable.
39. Run the engine and check for leaks and proper operation.

Oil Pump

REMOVAL & INSTALLATION

2.0L Engine

▶ See Figures 151 thru 161

1. Disconnect the negative battery cable.
2. Remove the accessory drive belt.
3. Remove the camshaft timing belt covers, camshaft timing belt and the crankshaft sprocket.
4. Install engine support device to the engine lifting eyes and support the engine.
5. Raise and safely support the vehicle.
6. Remove the catalytic converter system.

7. Remove the oil pan.
8. Remove the oil pump screen cover and tube retaining nut from the crankshaft main bearing cap stud bolt.
9. Remove the oil pump screen cover and tube retaining bolts from the oil pump and remove from the engine.
10. Remove the engine oil filter.
11. Remove the oil pump retaining bolts.
12. Remove the oil pump and gasket from the cylinder block.

Fig. 151 Remove the crankshaft timing belt pulley and . . .

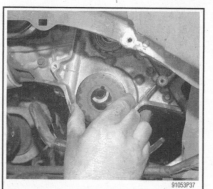

Fig. 152 . . . the seal protector washer from the crankshaft

Fig. 153 Remove the timing belt idler pulley. The pulley is retained by a single bolt in the center

Fig. 154 Remove the two pickup tube-to-oil pump bolts

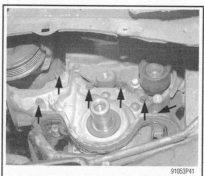

Fig. 155 Remove the six oil pump retaining bolts and . . .

Fig. 156 . . . remove the oil pump from the engine block

Fig. 157 Thoroughly clean the sealing surfaces for the oil pump

Fig. 158 Thoroughly clean the seal bore in the oil pump before replacing the seal, or a leak could occur

Fig. 159 A large socket, roughly the same diameter as the seal can be used to install the seal if the special tool is not available

Fig. 160 Lightly tap the socket with a soft-faced hammer to drive the seal into place and until . . .

Fig. 161 . . . the seal lip is flush with the oil pump

To install:

13. Clean the oil pump gasket sealing surface on the cylinder block and oil pump.

14. Rotate the inner rotor of the oil pump to align with the flats on the crankshaft.

15. Reinstall the oil pump using a new gasket onto the cylinder block.

16. Loosely install the oil pump retaining bolts.

➥Clearance between the cylinder block oil pan sealing surface to the oil pump oil pan sealing surface should not exceed 0.012–0.031 in. (0.3–0.8mm).

17. Use a straight-edge to align the oil pump oil pan sealing surface with the cylinder block oil pan sealing surface.

18. Tighten the oil pump retaining bolts to 71–102 inch lbs. (8–12 Nm).

19. Install a new engine oil filter.

20. Reinstall the oil pump screen cover and tube using a new gasket to the oil pump. Tighten the retaining bolts to 71–97 inch lbs. (8–11 Nm).

21. Reinstall a new self-locking oil pump screen cover and tube support nut to the crankshaft main bearing cap stud bolt. Tighten the retaining nut to 13–15 ft. lbs. (17–21 Nm).

22. Reinstall the engine oil pan.

23. Reinstall the catalytic converter system.

24. Lower the vehicle.

25. Remove the three bar engine support or equivalent.

26. If required, replace the front crankshaft seal at this time. The procedure is as follows:

   a. Use seal remover T92C–6700–CH or equivalent to remove the seal from the oil pump.

   b. Use seal replacer T81P–6292–A or equivalent to install the seal into the oil pump. Lightly coat the seal with engine oil to aid in the installation.

27. Reinstall the crankshaft sprocket, camshaft timing belt and the camshaft timing belt covers.

28. Reinstall the accessory drive belt.

29. Fill the crankcase with the proper amount and grade of engine oil.

✷✷ WARNING

Operating the engine without the proper amount and type of engine oil will result in severe engine damage.

30. Reconnect the negative battery cable.

31. Run the engine and check for leaks and proper operation.

2.5L Engine

◗ **See Figures 162, 163 and 164**

1. Disconnect the negative battery cable.

✷✷ CAUTION

The EPA warns that prolonged contact with used engine oil may cause a number of skin disorders, including cancer! You should make every effort to minimize your exposure to used engine oil. Protective gloves should be worn when changing the oil. Wash your hands and any other exposed skin areas as soon as possible after exposure to used engine oil. Soap and water, or waterless hand cleaner should be used.

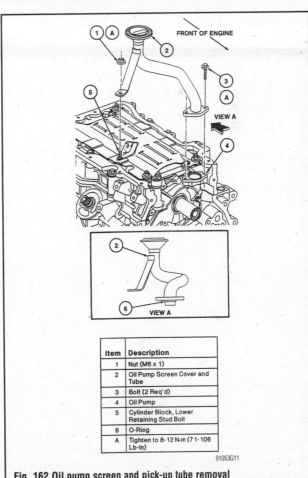

Item	Description
1	Nut (M6 x 1)
2	Oil Pump Screen Cover and Tube
3	Bolt (2 Req'd)
4	Oil Pump
5	Cylinder Block, Lower Retaining Stud Bolt
6	O-Ring
A	Tighten to 8-12 N·m (71-106 Lb-In)

Fig. 162 Oil pump screen and pick-up tube removal

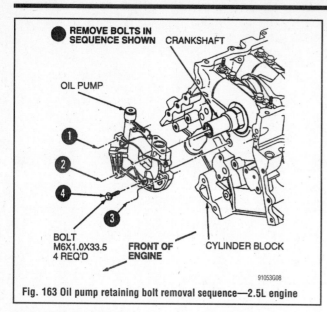

Fig. 163 Oil pump retaining bolt removal sequence—2.5L engine

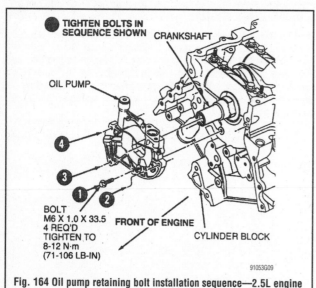

Fig. 164 Oil pump retaining bolt installation sequence—2.5L engine

2. Remove the oil pan and the engine front cover.
3. Remove the timing chains and the crankshaft sprockets.
4. Remove the oil pump screen cover and tube retaining nut from the lower cylinder block stud bolt.

5. Remove the oil pump screen cover and tube retaining bolts from the oil pump and remove the tube from the engine.
6. Remove the four oil pump retaining bolts in reverse of the removal sequence.
7. Remove the oil pump from the vehicle.
To install:
8. Rotate the inner rotor of the oil pump to align with the flats on the crankshaft.
9. Reinstall the oil pump flush to the cylinder block.
10. Reinstall the oil pump retaining bolts and tighten in sequence to 71–106 inch lbs. (8–12 Nm).
11. Inspect the oil pump screen and tube O-ring and replace if needed.
12. Position the oil pump screen and tube with the O-ring to the oil pump. Tighten the retaining bolts to 71–106 inch lbs. (8–12 Nm).
13. Install a new self-locking tube support nut to the lower cylinder block stud. Tighten the nut to 15–22 ft. lbs. (20–30 Nm).
14. Reinstall the crankshaft sprockets and the timing chains.
15. Reinstall the oil pan and the engine front cover.
16. Fill the crankcase with the correct amount of engine oil.

✳✳ WARNING

Operating the engine without the proper amount and type of engine oil will result in severe engine damage.

17. Reconnect the negative battery cable.
18. Run the engine and check for leaks and proper operation.

Crankshaft Damper

REMOVAL & INSTALLATION

2.0L Engine

♦ **See Figures 165, 166 and 167**

1. Disconnect the negative battery cable.
2. Remove the accessory drive belt from around the crankshaft pulley. Refer to Section 1.
3. Raise and support the vehicle.
4. Remove the passenger side front wheel.
5. Remove the passenger side inner fender splash shield to gain access to the crankshaft damper.
6. Remove the crankshaft damper retaining bolt and washer.
7. Remove the damper from the crankshaft.
To install:
8. Place the damper onto the crankshaft, ensuring the key-way is aligned.
9. Install the washer and retaining bolt and tighten the bolt to 81–89 ft. lbs. (110–120 Nm).
10. Install the splash shield.
11. Install the wheel.

Fig. 165 The crankshaft damper is accessible from the passenger side front wheel well opening

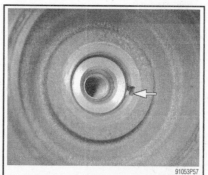

Fig. 166 The crankshaft damper is aligned with a key-way located on the crankshaft, ensure they are aligned before tightening the damper bolt or damage can occur

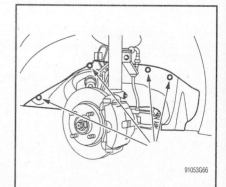

Fig. 167 Remove the 4 retaining bolts for the inner fender splash shield

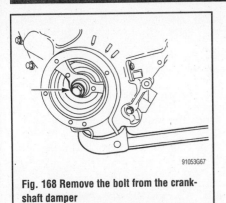

Fig. 168 Remove the bolt from the crank-shaft damper

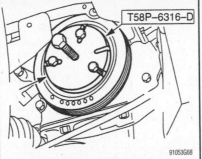

Fig. 169 Use the crankshaft damper puller to remove the damper from the crankshaft

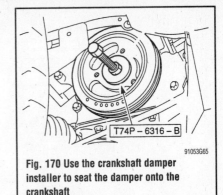

Fig. 170 Use the crankshaft damper installer to seat the damper onto the crankshaft

12. Lower the vehicle.
13. Install the accessory drive belt. Refer to Section 1.
14. Connect the negative battery cable.

2.5L Engine

♦ See Figures 167, 168, 169 and 170

1. Disconnect the negative battery cable.
2. Raise and support the vehicle.
3. Remove the accessory drive belt from around the crankshaft pulley. Refer to Section 1.
4. Remove the passenger side front wheel.
5. Remove the passenger side inner fender splash shield to gain access to the crankshaft damper.
6. Remove the crankshaft damper retaining bolt and washer.
7. Remove the damper from the crankshaft using an appropriate crankshaft damper puller.

To install:

8. Thoroughly clean the surface of the crankshaft around the key-way.
9. Apply an appropriate black silicone rubber sealer on the inside diameter of the key-way slot on the damper.
10. Place the damper onto the crankshaft, ensuring the key-way is aligned.
11. Install the washer and retaining bolt and tighten the bolt in the following sequence:
    a. Tighten to 89 ft. lbs. (120 Nm).
    b. Loosen the bolt a minimum of one full turn.
    c. Tighten the bolt to 35–39 ft. lbs. (47–53 Nm).
    d. Rotate the bolt an additional 85–95 degrees.
12. Install the splash shield.
13. Install the wheel.
14. Install the accessory drive belt. Refer to Section 1.
15. Lower the vehicle.
16. Connect the negative battery cable.

Timing Belt Covers

REMOVAL & INSTALLATION

♦ See Figures 167, 171 thru 185

The 2.0L engine is the only engine covered in this manual driven by a timing belt. The 2.5L engine is driven by timing chains.

When installing a timing belt, tensioner spring (6L277) and retaining bolt (W700001-S309) must be purchased and properly installed on the engine. First check to see if these parts are already installed. The tensioner spring will adjust the timing belts tension and should not require further adjustments.

1. Disconnect the negative battery cable.
2. Remove the engine air intake resonators.
3. Label and remove the ignition wires from the spark plugs. Move the ignition wires aside.
4. Remove the spark plugs.
5. Manually rotate the crankshaft to Top Dead Center (TDC) for the No. 1 piston on its compression stroke. Be sure to align the timing marks.

6. Disconnect the retaining bracket for the power steering pressure hose from the engine lifting eye.
7. Install the engine support device onto the engine lifting eyes and slightly raise the engine.
8. Remove the upper camshaft timing belt cover retaining bolts and the cover from the engine.

➥**Mark the location of the upper front engine support bracket before removing it from the engine support bracket.**

9. Remove the upper front engine support bracket retainer nuts, the bracket and the upper front engine support insulator.
10. If equipped, remove the wiring harness connector from the low coolant level sensor at the radiator coolant recovery reservoir.
11. Remove the radiator coolant recovery reservoir retainers and move the reservoir aside.
12. Remove the upper front engine support insulator.
13. Set the coolant recovery reservoir back into position temporarily.
14. Loosen the water pump pulley retaining bolts. Do not remove the bolts completely.
15. Remove the accessory drive belt.
16. Remove the drive belt idler pulley retaining bolt and pulley from the alternator mounting bracket.
17. Finish removing the water pump retaining bolts and remove the water pump pulley.
18. Remove the center camshaft timing belt cover retaining bolts and the cover from the engine.
19. Raise and safely support the vehicle on jack stands.
20. Remove the crankshaft pulley.
21. Remove the lower camshaft timing belt cover bolts and the cover from the engine.

To install:

22. Position the lower timing belt cover and tighten the retaining bolts to 27–44 inch lbs. (3–5 Nm) .
23. Position the center camshaft timing belt cover.
24. Reinstall the center camshaft timing belt cover retaining bolts and tighten them to 53–71 inch lbs. (6–8 Nm) .
25. Reinstall the water pump pulley and the retaining bolts. Reinstall the bolts, finger-tight.

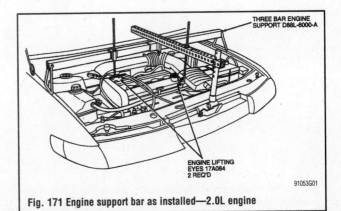

Fig. 171 Engine support bar as installed—2.0L engine

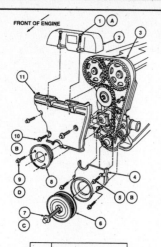

Item	Description
1	Bolt (2 Req'd)
2	Upper Camshaft Timing Belt Cover
3	Cylinder Block
4	Lower Camshaft Timing Belt Cover
5	Bolt (3 Req'd)
6	Crankshaft Pulley
7	Bolt
8	Water Pump Pulley
9	Bolt (4 Req'd)
10	Bolt (3 Req'd)
11	Center Camshaft Timing Belt Cover
A	Tighten to 3-5 N·m (27-44 Lb-In)
B	Tighten to 6-8 N·m (53-71 Lb-In)
C	Tighten to 110-120 N·m (81-89 Lb-Ft)
D	Tighten to 10-14 N·m (89-124 Lb-In)

91053G63

Fig. 172 Timing belt covers—exploded view

26. Reinstall the drive belt idler pulley.
27. Reinstall the drive belt idler pulley retaining bolt and tighten it to 35 ft. lbs. (48 Nm).
28. Reinstall the accessory drive belt.
29. Tighten the water pump pulley retaining bolts to 89–124 inch lbs. (10–14 Nm).
30. Move the radiator coolant recovery reservoir aside.
31. Reinstall the upper front engine support insulator.
32. Position the radiator coolant recovery reservoir and install the retainers.
33. If equipped, install the wiring harness to the low coolant level sensor on the coolant recovery reservoir.

91053P55

Fig. 173 A jackstand with a block of wood under the oil pan is an alternative to the engine support device

91053P45

Fig. 174 Remove the upper motor mount support bracket from the engine

91053P46

Fig. 175 Remove the upper motor mount

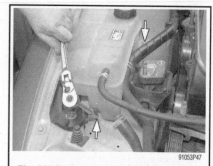

91053P47

Fig. 176 Remove the two retaining bolts and remove the coolant recovery tank for more access

91053P26

Fig. 177 Remove the power steering hose bracket-to-engine lifting eye

91053P48

Fig. 178 Remove the two upper timing belt cover bolts

91053P49

Fig. 179 After the bolts are removed, lift the upper timing belt cover up and remove it from the engine

Fig. 180 Remove the accessory belt idler pulley

Fig. 181 Remove the water pump pulley

Fig. 182 Remove the three center timing belt cover retaining bolts and . . .

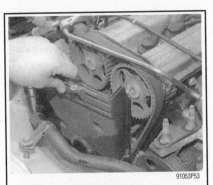

Fig. 183 . . . remove the cover from the engine

Fig. 184 Remove the top retaining bolt for the bottom cover and . . .

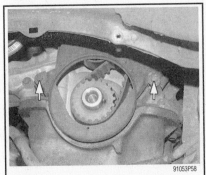

Fig. 185 . . . the two bottom retaining bolts and remove the bottom cover

34. Reinstall the upper front engine support bracket to the engine and the upper front engine support insulator using the mark made during the removal procedure for reference.

35. Install the upper camshaft timing belt cover.

36. Reinstall the upper camshaft timing belt cover retaining bolts and tighten to 27–44 inch lbs. (3–5 Nm) .

37. Remove the engine support.

38. Reinstall the retaining bracket for the power steering pressure hose to the engine lifting eye.

39. Reinstall the spark plugs and the ignition wires.

40. Reinstall the engine air intake resonators.

41. Replace the engine oil.

42. Reconnect the negative battery cable.

43. Run the engine and check for leaks and proper operation.

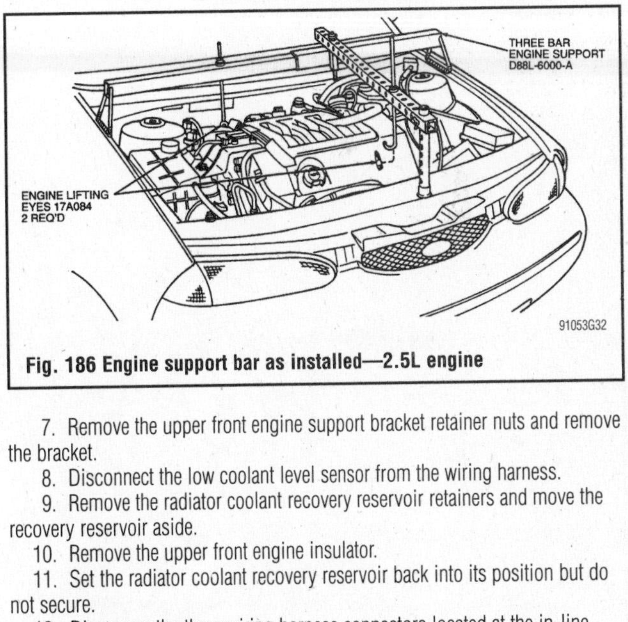

Timing Chain Front Cover and Seal

REMOVAL & INSTALLATION

♦ **See Figures 167, 186, 187, 188 and 189**

The 2.5L engine is the only engine covered by this manual that utilizes a timing chain. The 2.0L engine utilizes a timing belt, see Timing Belt in this Section.

1. Disconnect the negative battery cable.
2. Remove the upper intake manifold.
3. Remove the valve covers.
4. Install an engine support device to the engine lifting eyes and support the engine.
5. Remove the power steering pressure hose bracket retainer bolt from the upper front engine support bracket.
6. Disconnect the power steering pressure hose from the power steering pump and position out of the way.

➡**Mark the position of the upper front engine support bracket before removing.**

Fig. 186 Engine support bar as installed—2.5L engine

7. Remove the upper front engine support bracket retainer nuts and remove the bracket.

8. Disconnect the low coolant level sensor from the wiring harness.

9. Remove the radiator coolant recovery reservoir retainers and move the recovery reservoir aside.

10. Remove the upper front engine insulator.

11. Set the radiator coolant recovery reservoir back into its position but do not secure.

12. Disengage the three wiring harness connectors located at the in-line connector bracket at the front of the right cylinder head and set aside.

13. Loosen the power steering pump pulley retaining bolts but do not remove the bolts completely.

14. Remove the accessory drive belt.

15. Finish removing the power steering pump pulley retaining bolts and remove the pulley.

16. Remove the power steering pump and pump support retaining nuts and bolts and remove the power steering pump and pump support.

17. Raise and safely support the vehicle.

18. Remove the right-front wheel and tire assembly.

19. Remove the alternator from its mounting bracket and move aside.

20. Remove the alternator mounting bracket.
21. Remove the crankshaft pulley.
22. Disconnect the wiring from the Crankshaft Position (CKP) sensor and the Camshaft Position (CMP) sensor.
23. Remove the engine oil pan.
24. Loosen the A/C compressor retaining bolts and move the A/C compressor to gain access to the front cover retaining bolt.
25. Partially lower the vehicle.
26. Remove the bracket retainers and the bracket for the engine wiring and the A/C hose at the engine front cover.

➡️It may be necessary to raise and lower the vehicle several times in order to follow the engine front cover bolt removal sequence.

27. Remove the engine front cover bolts in reverse of the installation sequence illustration.
28. Remove the engine front cover and gasket from the vehicle.
29. Remove the seal from the cover using a suitable seal puller.

To install:

30. Replace the crankshaft seal in the front cover with a new one. Apply clean engine oil to the seal lip.
31. Clean the engine front and the front cover-to-cylinder block gasket sealing surfaces.

➡️The front cover must be installed and properly tightened within six minutes of the application of the sealer.

32. Apply silicone sealer to the six critical areas shown in View **A** , to the cylinder block to prevent oil seepage.
33. Place new front cover gaskets onto the dowel pins on the cylinder block and heads.
34. Place the front cover into position by placing the front cover onto the dowel pins at the cylinder block.
35. Reinstall the six front cover retaining bolts and stud bolts where the silicone sealer was applied.
36. Tighten the bolts and stud bolts until the front cover contacts the cylinder block and heads an, then turn the bolts and stud bolts an additional ¼ turn.
37. Reinstall the remaining front cover retaining bolts and stud bolts.
38. Tighten all of the front cover retaining bolts and stud bolts in proper sequence to 15–22 ft. lbs. (20–30 Nm).
39. Reinstall the bracket and bracket retainers to the front cover. Reinstall the wiring and the A/C hose to the bracket.
40. Raise and safely support the vehicle.
41. Reinstall the A/C compressor and its retaining bolts. Tighten the retaining bolts to 15–22 ft. lbs. (20–30 Nm).
42. If required, replace the crankshaft front seal at this time.
43. Reinstall the engine oil pan.

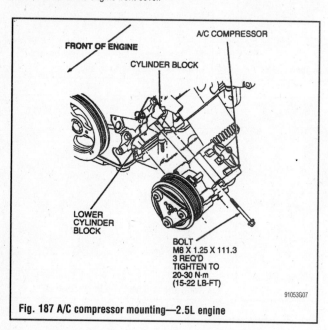

Fig. 187 A/C compressor mounting—2.5L engine

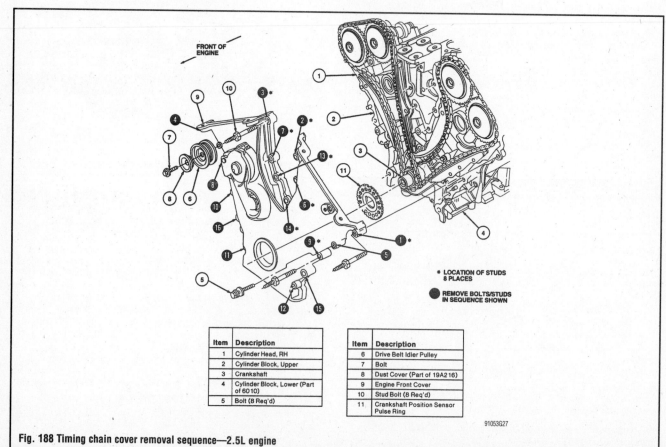

Item	Description
1	Cylinder Head, RH
2	Cylinder Block, Upper
3	Crankshaft
4	Cylinder Block, Lower (Part of 6010)
5	Bolt (8 Req'd)

Item	Description
6	Drive Belt Idler Pulley
7	Bolt
8	Dust Cover (Part of 19A216)
9	Engine Front Cover
10	Stud Bolt (8 Req'd)
11	Crankshaft Position Sensor Pulse Ring

Fig. 188 Timing chain cover removal sequence—2.5L engine

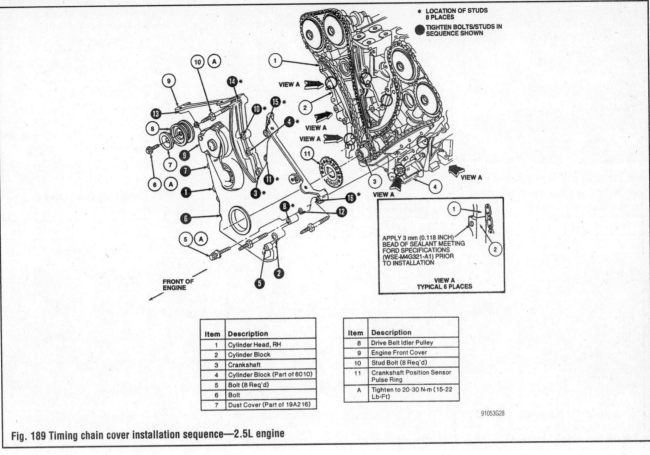

LOCATION OF STUDS 8 PLACES

TIGHTEN BOLTS/STUDS IN SEQUENCE SHOWN

VIEW A

VIEW A

VIEW A

VIEW A

APPLY 3 mm (0.118 INCH) BEAD OF SEALANT MEETING FORD SPECIFICATIONS (WSE-M4G321-A1) PRIOR TO INSTALLATION

VIEW A
TYPICAL 6 PLACES

FRONT OF ENGINE

Item	Description
1	Cylinder Head, RH
2	Cylinder Block
3	Crankshaft
4	Cylinder Block (Part of 6010)
5	Bolt (8 Req'd)
6	Bolt
7	Dust Cover (Part of 19A216)

Item	Description
8	Drive Belt Idler Pulley
9	Engine Front Cover
10	Stud Bolt (8 Req'd)
11	Crankshaft Position Sensor Pulse Ring
A	Tighten to 20-30 N·m (15-22 Lb-Ft)

91053G28

Fig. 189 Timing chain cover installation sequence—2.5L engine

44. Reconnect the wiring harness to the CKP sensor and the CMP sensor.
45. Reinstall the crankshaft pulley.
46. Reinstall the alternator mounting bracket and the alternator.
47. Reinstall the right-front wheel and tire assembly. Tighten the lug nuts to 62 ft. lbs. (85 Nm).
48. Lower the vehicle on the hoist.
49. Lower the engine to its correct position.
50. Reinstall the power steering pump support and the power steering pump to the front of the engine.
51. Reinstall the power steering pump pulley. Loosely install the retaining bolts.
52. Reinstall the accessory drive belt.
53. Tighten the power steering retaining bolts to 15–22 ft. lbs. (20–30 Nm).
54. Position and attach the wiring to the three connectors located on the in-line connector bracket at the front of the right cylinder head.
55. Reinstall the upper front support insulator and the upper front engine support bracket.
56. Loosen and remove the engine support device.
57. Reconnect the power steering pressure hose to the power steering pump.
58. Reconnect the power steering pressure hose bracket and retainer bolt to the upper front engine support bracket.
59. Reinstall both valve covers as follows:
   a. Clean the valve cover gasket sealing surfaces.
   b. Install new valve cover gaskets onto the valve covers.
   c. For each valve cover, place a bead of silicone sealant at two places on the valve cover sealing surfaces where the engine front cover and the cylinder heads make contact and at two places on the rear of the cylinder head where the camshaft seal retainer contacts the cylinder head.
   d. Reinstall the valve cover retaining bolts and studs and tighten in sequence to 71–106 inch lbs. (8–12 Nm).

➡The valve covers must be installed and properly tightened within six minutes of applying the silicone sealant.

60. Reinstall the upper intake manifold.

61. Fill the engine with the proper amount and grade of oil.
62. Replace any lost fluid to the power steering reservoir.
63. Reconnect the negative battery cable.
64. Run the engine and check for leaks and proper operation.
65. Recheck the fluid levels.

Timing Belt and Sprockets

REMOVAL & INSTALLATION

♦ See Figures 190 thru 199

For information on timing belt recommended replacement interval, refer to Section 1.

✷✷ CAUTION

The 2.0L engine is an interference motor. Extending the replacement interval could lead to the belt breaking and severe and costly engine damage. Care must be taken if rotating the crankshaft or camshafts with the belt off, if resistance is felt, do not force them to turn.

1. Disconnect the negative battery cable.
2. Remove the timing belt covers as outlined in this Section.
3. Remove the valve cover.
4. Place Camshaft Alignment Timing Tool T94P-6256-CH or equivalent, into the slots of both camshafts at the rear of the cylinder head to lock the camshafts into position.

➡If the special tool is unavailable, a suitable length and width straight edge can be used to align the camshafts.

5. Loosen the camshaft timing belt tensioner pulley retaining bolt and move the tensioner pulley to relieve the tension on the timing belt.
6. Temporarily tighten the tensioner in this position.

Fig. 190 If you plan on reusing the timing belt, make sure you note the direction of the rotation before removal

Fig. 191 If the special tool is unavailable, a suitable length and width straight edge can be used to align the camshafts

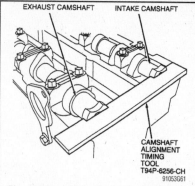

Fig. 192 Camshaft alignment using the special service tool

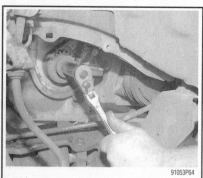

Fig. 193 Insert the crankshaft damper bolt to turn the crankshaft and . . .

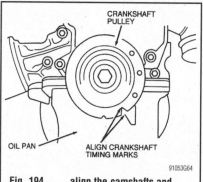

Fig. 194 . . . align the camshafts and the . . .

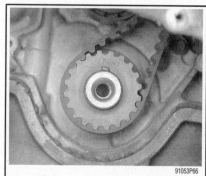

Fig. 195 . . . crankshaft before removing the old belt

Fig. 196 Loosen the timing belt tensioner pulley bolt, slide the tensioner back and . . .

Fig. 197 . . . tighten the bolt to the farthest right hand side as possible to hold the release the tensioner pulley so that the belt can be removed

Fig. 198 . . . remove the belt starting from around the camshaft pulleys

➡ If the timing belt is to be reused, mark the belt for the direction of rotation before removing to prevent premature wear or failure.

7. Remove the timing belt.
8. If required, remove the sprockets as follows:
   a. Hold the camshaft with an appropriate camshaft sprocket holding tool.
   b. Loosen and remove the camshaft sprocket retaining bolt.
   c. Remove the sprocket from the camshaft.
   d. Repeat the procedure for the 2nd camshaft sprocket.
   e. Remove the crankshaft sprocket.
9. Slide the crankshaft sprocket onto the crankshaft aligning the key-way.
10. Align the camshafts using the Camshaft Alignment Timing Tool T94P-6256-CH.

➡ If the special tool is unavailable, a suitable length and width straight edge can be used to align the camshafts.

11. Reinstall the sprockets onto the camshafts and loosely install the camshaft retaining bolts.

12. Tighten the camshaft sprocket retaining bolts to 47–53 ft. lbs. (64–72 Nm) .
13. Loosely install the crankshaft pulley to verify that the engine is at TDC. Realign the marks if they have moved.
14. Verify that the camshafts are aligned.

➡ It is recommended to purchase a tensioner spring and retaining bolt through the dealer parts to apply the proper tension for used or new belt installations. The spring is bolted to the tensioner assembly and becomes a part of the engine. Ignore this notice if the tensioner spring is already installed.

15. Reinstall the retaining bolt (W700001-S309) into the hole provided in the cylinder block and place the tensioner spring (6L277) between the bolt and the camshaft timing belt tensioner pulley.
16. Tighten the retainer bolt to 71–97 inch lbs. (8–11 Nm) .
17. Remove the crankshaft pulley and install the timing belt onto the crankshaft sprocket, then onto the camshaft sprockets working in a counterclockwise direction.

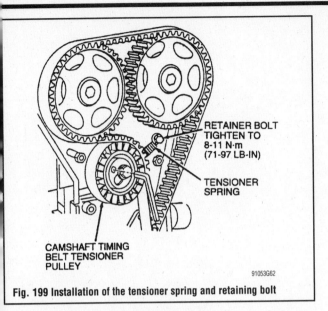

Fig. 199 Installation of the tensioner spring and retaining bolt

RETAINER BOLT TIGHTEN TO 8-11 N·m (71-97 LB-IN)

TENSIONER SPRING

CAMSHAFT TIMING BELT TENSIONER PULLEY

91053G62

18. Tighten the camshaft sprocket retaining bolts to 47–53 ft. lbs. (64–72 Nm) .

19. Be sure that the span of the camshaft timing belt between the crankshaft sprocket and the exhaust camshaft sprocket is not loose.

20. Be sure that the camshaft timing belt is securely aligned on all sprockets.

21. Reinstall the lower timing belt cover and tighten the retaining bolts to 53–71 inch lbs. (6–8 Nm) .

22. Apply silicone sealer to the key-way of the crankshaft pulley and install. Tighten the retaining bolt to 81–89 ft. lbs. (110–120 Nm) .

23. Inspect the timing mark on the crankshaft pulley to verify that the engine is still at TDC.

24. Loosen the camshaft timing belt tensioner pulley retaining bolt and allow the tensioner spring attached to the pulley to draw the tensioner pulley against the camshaft timing belt.

25. Remove the camshaft alignment timing tool from the camshafts at the rear of the engine.

26. Turn the crankshaft two revolutions in a clockwise direction.

27. Tighten the camshaft timing belt tensioner pulley retaining bolt to 26–30 ft. lbs. (35–40 Nm).

28. Recheck that the crankshaft timing mark is at TDC for the No. 1 piston, and that both camshafts are in alignment using the camshaft alignment timing tool.

➡A slight adjustment of the camshafts to allow the insertion of the camshaft alignment timing tool is permissible as long as the crankshaft stays at the TDC location.

29. An appropriate camshaft sprocket holding tool can be used to move the camshaft sprocket (s) if a slight adjustment is required.

30. If a camshaft is not properly aligned, perform the following procedure:

a. Loosen the retaining bolt securing the sprocket to the camshaft while holding the camshaft sprocket from turning with the sprocket holding tool.

b. Turn the camshaft until the camshaft alignment timing tool can be installed.

c. Verify that the crankshaft timing mark is at TDC for the No. 1 cylinder.

d. While holding the camshaft sprocket with the camshaft sprocket holding tool, tighten the retaining bolt to 47–53 ft. lbs. (64–72 Nm) .

e. Remove the tool and rotate the crankshaft two revolutions (clockwise) .

f. Verify that the camshafts are aligned and that the crankshaft is at TDC for the No. 1 cylinder.

31. Install the valve cover.

32. Install the timing belt covers.

33. Connect the negative battery cable.

INSPECTION

♦ See Figures 200 thru 207

An inspection of the timing belt should be performed at least any time the upper timing belt cover is off. If the timing belt shows any signs of failure, it should be replaced. Recommended timing belt replacement intervals can be found in Section 1 of this manual.

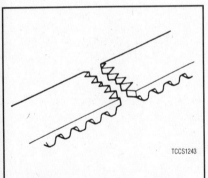

TCCS1243

Fig. 200 Check for premature parting of the belt

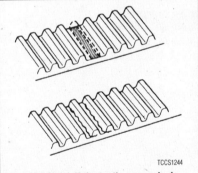

TCCS1244

Fig. 201 Check if the teeth are cracked or damaged

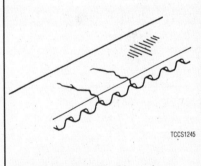

TCCS1245

Fig. 202 Look for noticeable cracks or wear on the belt face

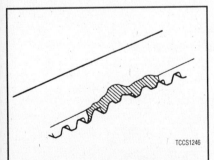

TCCS1246

Fig. 203 You may only have damage on one side of the belt; if so, the guide could be the culprit

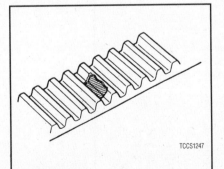

TCCS1247

Fig. 204 Foreign materials can get in between the teeth and cause damage

TCCS1300

Fig. 205 Inspect the timing belt for cracks, fraying, glazing or damage of any kind

Fig. 206 Damage on only one side of the timing belt may indicate a faulty guide

TCCS1301

Fig. 207 ALWAYS replace the timing belt at the interval specified by the manufacturer

TCCS1302

Timing Chains and Sprockets

The 2.5L engine is the only engine covered by this manual that utilizes a timing chain. The 2.0L engine utilizes a timing belt, see Timing Belt in this Section.

REMOVAL & INSTALLATION

▶ **See Figures 208 thru 213**

1. Disconnect the negative battery cable.
2. Remove the timing chain cover as outlined in this section.
3. Rotate the crankshaft so that the key-way is at the 11 o'clock position to locate the crankshaft at TDC for No. 1 cylinder.
4. Verify that the alignment arrows on the camshafts are aligned. If not, rotate the crankshaft one complete revolution and recheck.
5. Rotate the crankshaft so that the key-way is at the 3 o'clock position. This positions the right cylinder head camshafts to the neutral position.
6. Remove the right cylinder head timing chain tensioner retaining bolts and the timing chain tensioner.

➡ **The camshaft journal caps and cylinder heads are numbered to ensure that they are assembled in their original positions. If removed, keep the camshaft journal caps together with the cylinder head that they were removed from.**

7. Remove the right cylinder head camshaft journal thrust cap retaining bolts and thrust caps.
8. Loosen the remaining camshaft journal cap bolts in sequence, releasing the bolts several revolutions at a time by making several passes to allow the camshaft to be raised from the cylinder head evenly. Do not remove the retaining bolts completely.

➡ **If the valve tappets and roller rocker arms are to be reused, mark the positions of the valve tappets and rocker arms so that they are reassembled into their original positions.**

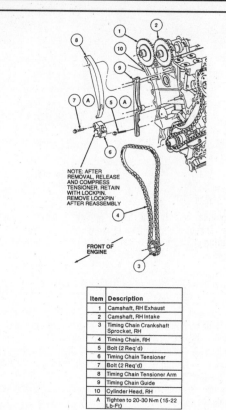

NOTE: AFTER REMOVAL, RELEASE AND COMPRESS TENSIONER. RETAIN WITH LOCKPIN. REMOVE LOCKPIN AFTER REASSEMBLY

FRONT OF ENGINE

Item	Description
1	Camshaft, RH Exhaust
2	Camshaft, RH Intake
3	Timing Chain Crankshaft Sprocket, RH
4	Timing Chain, RH
5	Bolt (2 Req'd)
6	Timing Chain Tensioner
7	Bolt (2 Req'd)
8	Timing Chain Tensioner Arm
9	Timing Chain Guide
10	Cylinder Head, RH
A	Tighten to 20-30 N·m (15-22 Lb-Ft)

91053G37

Fig. 208 Exploded view of the right hand side timing chain and tensioner assembly

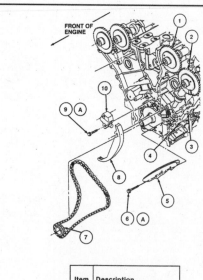

FRONT OF ENGINE

Item	Description
1	Camshaft, LH Intake
2	Camshaft, LH Exhaust
3	LH Cylinder Head
4	Cylinder Block
5	Timing Chain Guide
6	Bolt (2 Req'd)
7	Crankshaft Sprocket, LH Timing Chain
8	Timing Chain Tensioner Arm
9	Bolt (2 Req'd)
10	Timing Chain Tensioner
A	Tighten to 20-30 N·m (15-22 Lb-Ft)

91053G35

Fig. 209 Exploded view of the left hand side timing chain and tensioner assembly

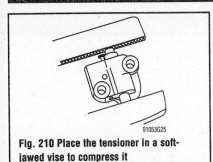

Fig. 210 Place the tensioner in a soft-jawed vise to compress it

Fig. 211 Lock pin installation on the timing chain tensioner

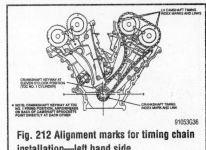

Fig. 212 Alignment marks for timing chain installation—left hand side

9. With the camshafts loose, remove the rocker arms, keeping them in the order that they were removed.

➡️If the right cylinder head timing chain tensioner arm and timing chain guide are to be reused, mark the position of the timing chain tensioner arm and the timing chain guide so that they are reassembled into their original positions.

10. Remove the right cylinder head timing chain tensioner arm and the timing chain.

11. Remove the right cylinder head timing chain guide retaining bolts and the timing chain guide.

12. If worn, replace the timing chain guide.

13. Remove the right crankshaft timing chain sprocket.

14. Remove the right cylinder head camshaft timing chain sprockets if they are to be replaced.

15. Rotate the crankshaft two revolutions and locate the crankshaft key-way at the 11 o'clock position. This will position the left cylinder head camshafts to their neutral position.

16. Verify that the alignment arrows on the camshafts are aligned.

17. Remove the left cylinder head timing chain tensioner retaining bolts and the timing chain tensioner.

➡️The camshaft journal caps and cylinder heads are numbered to ensure that they are assembled in their original positions. If removed, keep the camshaft journal caps together with the cylinder head that they were removed from.

18. Remove the camshaft journal thrust cap retaining bolts and thrust caps from the left cylinder head.

19. Loosen the remaining camshaft journal cap bolts in sequence, releasing the bolts several revolutions at a time by making several passes to allow the camshaft to be raised from the cylinder head evenly. Do not remove the retaining bolts completely.

➡️If the valve tappets and roller rocker arms are to be reused, mark the positions of the valve tappets and rocker arms so that they are reassembled into their original positions.

20. With the camshafts loose, remove the rocker arms, keeping them in the order that they were removed.

➡️If the left cylinder head timing chain tensioner arm and timing chain guide are to be reused, mark the position of the timing chain tensioner arm and the timing chain guide so that they are reassembled into their original positions.

21. Remove the left cylinder head timing chain tensioner arm and the timing chain.

22. Remove the left cylinder head timing chain guide retaining bolts and the timing chain guide.

23. If worn, replace the timing chain guide.

24. Remove the left crankshaft timing chain sprocket.

25. If required, the left cylinder head camshaft sprockets may be removed at this time.

To install:

➡️Inspect the timing chains, tensioners, tensioner arms, guides and sprockets for wear or damage. If any components are to be replaced for premature wear or damage, the camshaft damper should also be replaced.

26. Reinstall or replace the camshaft sprockets, if removed.

27. Be sure that the crankshaft key-way is still at the 11 o'clock position.

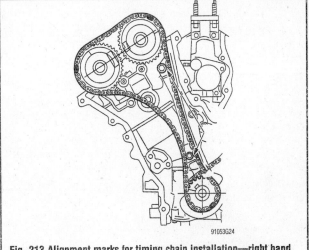

Fig. 213 Alignment marks for timing chain installation—right hand side

28. Reinstall the left timing chain crankshaft sprocket onto the crankshaft.

29. Reinstall the left timing chain guide and retaining bolts to the engine. Tighten the retaining bolts to 15–22 ft. lbs. (20–30 Nm).

30. Verify that the alignment arrows on the left cylinder head camshafts are aligned before proceeding.

31. Reinstall the left timing chain over the left crankshaft sprocket and the left camshaft sprockets.

32. Align the timing index marks on the left cylinder head timing chain with the timing index marks on the crankshaft sprocket and the camshaft sprockets.

33. Reinstall the left timing chain tensioner arm over the alignment dowel on the left cylinder head.

➡️Before installing the timing chain tensioner, it must be properly compressed and locked.

34. Using a small screwdriver, release the timing chain tensioner ratchet/pawl mechanism through the access hole in the timing chain tensioner as follows:

    a. Insert a small piece of wire into the top of the piston and gently unseat the oil check ball.

    b. Compress the timing chain tensioner by hand.

    c. With the tensioner compressed, install a 0.060 inch (1.5mm) drill bit or wire into the small hole above the ratchet, engaging the lock groove in the rack of the timing chain tensioner.

35. Reinstall the compressed and locked left cylinder head timing chain tensioner and retaining bolts onto the cylinder block. Tighten the retaining bolts to 15–22 ft. lbs. (20–30 Nm).

36. Verify that the timing index marks on the left timing chain are in alignment with the timing index marks on the crankshaft sprocket and the camshaft sprockets.

37. Reinstall or replace the camshaft sprockets if removed.

38. Reinstall the right timing chain crankshaft sprocket onto the crankshaft.

39. Reinstall the right timing chain guide and retaining bolts to the engine. Tighten the retaining bolts to 15–22 ft. lbs. (20–30 Nm).

40. Verify that the alignment arrows on the right cylinder head camshafts are aligned before proceeding.

41. Reinstall the right timing chain over the right crankshaft sprocket and the right camshaft sprockets.

42. Align the timing index marks on the right cylinder head timing chain with the timing index marks on the crankshaft sprocket and the camshaft sprockets.

43. Reinstall the right timing chain tensioner arm over the alignment dowel on the right cylinder head.

➡ **Before installing the timing chain tensioner, it must be properly compressed and locked.**

44. Using a small screwdriver, release the timing chain tensioner ratchet/pawl mechanism through the access hole in the timing chain tensioner as follows:

   a. Insert a small wire into the top of the piston and gently unseat the oil check ball.

   b. Compress the timing chain tensioner by hand.

   c. With the tensioner compressed, install a 0.060 inch (1.5mm) drill bit or wire into the small hole above the ratchet, engaging the lock groove in the rack of the timing chain tensioner.

45. Reinstall the compressed and locked right cylinder head timing chain tensioner and retaining bolts onto the cylinder block. Tighten the retaining bolts to 15–22 ft. lbs. (20–30 Nm).

46. Verify that the timing index marks on the right timing chain are in alignment with the timing index marks on the crankshaft sprocket and the camshaft sprockets.

47. Be sure that the crankshaft key-way is at the 11 o'clock position.

48. Lubricate the left-side rocker arms with engine assembly lubricant and install the left cylinder head rocker arms into their original locations.

➡ **Do not install the camshaft journal thrust caps until the camshaft journal caps are secured into position.**

49. Tighten the left cylinder head camshaft journal cap bolts in sequence making several passes to pull the camshafts down evenly. Tighten the bolts to 71–106 inch lbs. (8–12 Nm).

50. Reinstall the left cylinder head thrust caps and bolts. Tighten to 71–106 inch lbs. (8–12 Nm).

51. Rotate the crankshaft two revolutions and position the crankshaft key-way to the 3 o'clock location. This will position the right cylinder head camshafts to the neutral position.

52. Lubricate the right-side rocker arms with engine assembly lubricant and install the right cylinder head rocker arms into their original locations.

➡ **Do not install the camshaft journal thrust caps until the camshaft journal caps are secured.**

53. Tighten the right cylinder head camshaft journal cap bolts in sequence making several passes to pull the camshafts down evenly. Tighten the bolts to 71–106 inch lbs. (8–12 Nm).

54. Reinstall the right cylinder head thrust caps and bolts. Tighten to 71–106 inch lbs. (8–12 Nm).

55. Remove the lock pins from the timing chain tensioners.

56. Verify that the timing index marks on the timing chains are in alignment with the timing index marks on the crankshaft sprocket and the camshaft sprockets.

57. Install the crankshaft position sensor pulse ring, be sure to use the key-way for the 2.5L engine as shown.

58. Install the timing chain cover.

59. Connect the negative battery cable.

Crankshaft Front Oil Seal

REMOVAL & INSTALLATION

2.0L Engine

The front seal is located in the oil pump. For the replacement procedure, see the 2.0L engine oil pump procedure in this Section.

2.5L Engine

The front seal is located in the timing chain cover. For the replacement procedure, see the timing chain cover and seal procedure in this Section.

Camshaft, Bearings and Lifters

REMOVAL & INSTALLATION

2.0L Engine

▶ **See Figures 214 thru 223**

1. Disconnect the negative battery cable.
2. Remove the valve cover.
3. Remove the camshaft timing belt and sprockets.

➡ **Mark the camshaft journal caps to the cylinder head for installation. Do not mix the caps between the two camshafts or from another cylinder head.**

4. Loosen all of the camshaft journal cap bolts in pairs and in sequence one turn at a time starting at the rear cap. This will allow the camshaft to raise up from the cylinder head evenly.

➡ **Remove the camshaft journal thrust caps last.**

5. Remove all of the camshaft journal caps making sure that they are marked so that they can be reassembled to their original positions.

6. Remove the intake and exhaust camshafts and the camshaft front seals from the cylinder head.

7. Inspect the camshafts and cylinder head for wear.

➡ **If the valve lifters (tappets) are to be reused, mark their locations to ensure that they will be installed into their correct positions.**

8. If required, remove the valve lifters from the cylinder head.

9. Inspect the valve lifters for wear.

To install:

➡ **Before installing the camshafts, the crankshaft must be positioned so that No. 1 cylinder is at TDC on its compression stroke.**

10. If removed, lubricate the valve lifters with engine assembly lubricant and install into the lifter bores that they were removed from.

11. If the valve lifters are new, soak the lifters in a container of clean engine oil or manually pump up the lifters before installation.

12. Lubricate the camshafts with engine assembly lubricant and place the camshafts into the cylinder head.

➡ **The intake and exhaust camshafts are marked for identification, also the intake camshaft has an extra cam lobe for the Camshaft Position (CMP) sensor.**

13. Loosely install the camshaft journal caps and retaining bolts into their original positions.

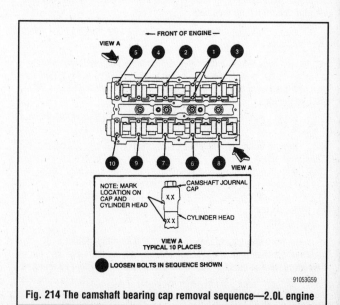

Fig. 214 The camshaft bearing cap removal sequence—2.0L engine

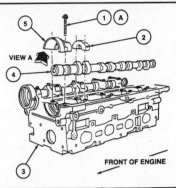

VIEW A

NOTE: APPLY A 3 mm (0.25 INCH) BEAD
OF SILICONE GASKET AND SEALANT
F1AZ-19562-A OR EQUIVALENT MEETING
FORD SPECIFICATION WSE-M4G320-A2 TO
SEALING SURFACES OF THE CAMSHAFT
JOURNAL THRUST CAPS AS SHOWN.

VIEW A

Item	Description
1	Bolt (20 Req'd)
2	Camshaft Journal Cap (8 Req'd, Part of 6049)
3	Cylinder Head
4	Camshaft
5	Camshaft Journal Thrust Cap (2 Req'd) (Part of 6049)
A	Tighten to 13 N·m (115 Lb-In)

91053G60

Fig. 215 The camshafts and bearing cap assembly—2.0L engine

14. Install the camshaft journal thrust caps and retaining bolts last. Apply a bead of silicone sealant to the sealing surfaces of the camshaft journal thrust caps.

15. Tighten all of the camshaft journal caps in several steps pulling the camshaft down evenly following the proper sequence.

16. Once the camshaft journal caps are fully seated, tighten the retaining bolts to 13–15 ft. lbs. (17–21 Nm).

17. Install new camshaft front seals using the an appropriate camshaft seal replacer.

18. Reinstall the camshaft sprockets and the camshaft timing belt.

19. Reinstall the valve cover as follows:
    a. Clean the gasket sealing surfaces.
    b. Inspect the valve cover gasket and O-rings, replace as required.
    c. Reinstall the valve cover retaining bolts and tighten in a standard sequence starting from the center and working towards the outside of the valve cover to 53–71 inch lbs. (6–8 Nm).
    d. Reinstall the upper camshaft timing belt cover and tighten the retaining bolts to 27–44 inch lbs. (3–5 Nm).
    e. Reinstall the power steering hose retaining bracket and the power steering hose.
    f. Reinstall the ignition wires.
    g. Reinstall the crankcase ventilation tube to the valve cover.
    h. Reinstall the engine air intake resonators.
20. Reconnect the negative battery cable.
21. Run the engine and check for leaks and proper operation.

2.5L Engine

◆ See Figures 224, 225 and 226

1. Disconnect the negative battery cable.
2. Remove both valve covers as follows:
    a. Remove the ignition wires and spark plugs.
    b. Remove the ignition coil from the right valve cover.
    c. Remove the crankcase ventilation tubes from both valve covers.
    d. Remove the wiring harness and bracket to the fuel injectors and move aside.

91053P87

Fig. 216 The camshafts are held by five bearing caps on each camshaft

91053P75

Fig. 217 Remove the camshaft bearing cap bolts in sequence

91053P88

Fig. 218 After the bolts are removed, the bearing caps lift off of the dowel pins on the head

91053P74

Fig. 219 After all the bearing caps are removed, remove the camshafts by lifting them upward, remember to mark the camshafts for reassembly

91053P95

Fig. 220 Remove the valve tappets from the cylinder head by carefully lifting them up out of their bores

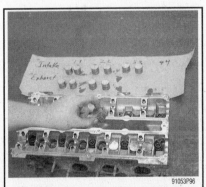

91053P96

Fig. 221 Make sure you place the tappets in an organized way to ensure they go back in their original location

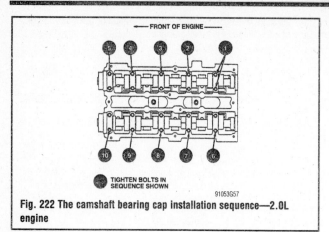

Fig. 222 The camshaft bearing cap installation sequence—2.0L engine

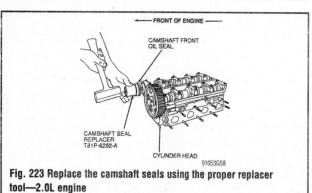

Fig. 223 Replace the camshaft seals using the proper replacer tool—2.0L engine

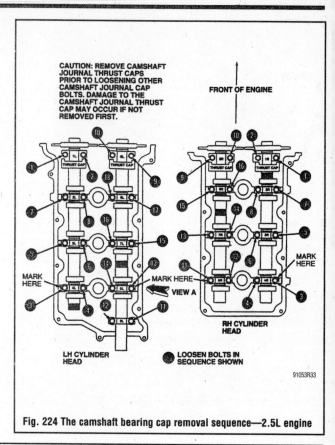

Fig. 224 The camshaft bearing cap removal sequence—2.5L engine

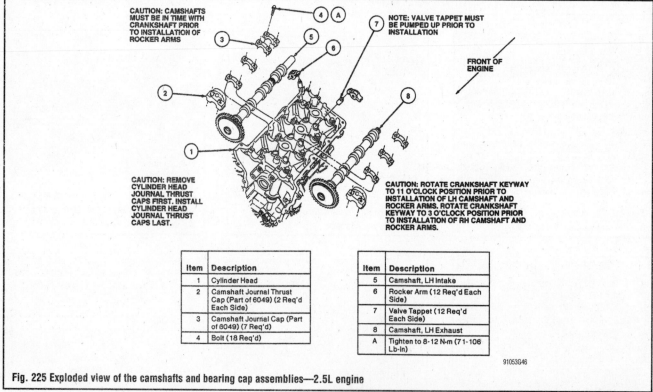

Fig. 225 Exploded view of the camshafts and bearing cap assemblies—2.5L engine

Item	Description
1	Cylinder Head
2	Camshaft Journal Thrust Cap (Part of 6049) (2 Req'd Each Side)
3	Camshaft Journal Cap (Part of 6049) (7 Req'd)
4	Bolt (18 Req'd)

Item	Description
5	Camshaft, LH Intake
6	Rocker Arm (12 Req'd Each Side)
7	Valve Tappet (12 Req'd Each Side)
8	Camshaft, LH Exhaust
A	Tighten to 8-12 N·m (71-106 Lb-In)

e. Remove the retaining nuts and engine wiring from both valve covers and move aside.

f. Loosen the valve cover retaining bolts and studs, in sequence.

g. Remove both valve covers from the engine.

3. Remove the engine front cover.

4. Remove the timing chains.

⁂ WARNING

The camshaft journal thrust caps must be removed first, before loosening the remaining camshaft journal cap bolts, to ensure that the camshaft journal thrust caps are not damaged.

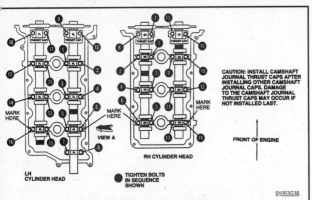

Fig. 226 The camshaft bearing cap installation sequence—2.5L engine

5. Remove the camshaft journal thrust caps.

6. Loosen the camshaft journal cap bolts in sequence, in several passes, to allow the camshaft to raise off of the cylinder head evenly.

✳✳ WARNING

The camshaft journal caps and cylinder heads are numbered to ensure that they are assembled in their original positions. Keep the camshaft journal caps from each cylinder head together; do not mix them with caps from another cylinder head. Failure to do so may result in engine damage.

7. Remove the camshaft journal caps with the retaining bolts installed.

8. Remove the camshafts from the cylinder head. If necessary, remove the rocker arms, marking their position so they can be reinstalled in their original locations.

9. Repeat the procedure for both cylinder heads.

10. Inspect the camshafts and bearing journals for wear or damage.

To install:

✳✳ WARNING

The crankshaft key-way must be at the 11 o'clock position before reassembly. Failure to do so may lead to engine damage.

11. Rotate the crankshaft so that the key-way is at the 11 o'clock position for installation of the camshafts.

12. Reinstall the rocker arms, if removed.

13. Lubricate the camshafts with engine assembly lubricant.

14. Reinstall the camshafts into their correct positions into each cylinder head with the timing marks on the camshaft sprockets aligned.

15. Loosely install the camshaft journal caps and retaining bolts into their correct positions.

➡**Do not install the camshaft journal thrust caps until the rocker arms and timing chains have been installed and the camshaft journal caps are secured into position.**

16. Reinstall the rocker arms.

17. Reinstall the timing chains.

18. Tighten the camshaft journal cap bolts, in the opposite order of the removal sequence, to 71–106 inch lbs. (8–12 Nm). Reinstall the thrust caps and tighten the retaining bolts to 71–106 inch lbs. (8–12 Nm).

19. Reinstall the engine front cover.

20. Reinstall both valve covers as follows:

a. Clean the valve cover gasket sealing surfaces.

b. Reinstall new valve cover gaskets onto the valve covers.

c. For each valve cover, place a bead of silicone sealant at the two places on the valve cover sealing surfaces where the engine front cover and the cylinder heads make contact and at two places on the rear of the cylinder head where the camshaft seal retainer contacts the cylinder head.

d. Reinstall the valve cover retaining bolts and studs and tighten in sequence to 71–106 inch lbs. (8–12 Nm).

➡**The valve covers must be installed and properly tightened within six minutes of applying the silicone sealant.**

21. Reconnect the negative battery cable.

22. Run the engine and check for leaks and proper engine operation.

INSPECTION

Camshaft Lobe Lift

Camshaft lobe lift is the amount (measured in inches or millimeters) that the camshaft is capable of LIFTING the valve train components in order to open the valves. The lobe lift is a measure of how much taller the "egg shaped" portion of the camshaft lobe is above the base or circular portion of the shaft lobe. Lift is directly proportional to how far the valves can open and a worn camshaft (with poor lobe lift) cannot fully open the valves. The lobe lift therefore can be directly responsible for proper or poor engine performance.

Lobe lift can be measured in 2 ways, depending on what tools are available and whether or not the camshaft has been removed from the engine. A dial gauge can be used to measure the lift with the camshaft installed, while a micrometer is normally only used once the shaft has been removed from the engine.

DIAL GAUGE METHOD

Lobe lift may be checked with the camshaft installed. In all cases, a dial gauge is positioned somewhere on the valve train (pushrod, lifter, or camshaft itself) and the camshaft is then turned to measure the lift.

Check the lift of each lobe in consecutive order and make a note of the reading.

1. Remove the valve cover for access to the camshaft.

2. Install a dial indicator so that the actuating point of the indicator is directly placed on the camshaft.

➡**A remote starter can be used to turn the engine over during the next steps. If a remote starter is not available, remove the spark plugs in order to relieve engine compression, and turn the engine over using a large wrench or socket on the crankshaft damper bolt. BE SURE to only turn the engine in the normal direction of rotation.**

3. Turn the crankshaft over until the tappet is on the base circle of the camshaft lobe.

4. Zero the dial indicator. Continue to rotate the crankshaft slowly until the pushrod (or camshaft lobe) is in the fully raised position.

5. Compare the total lift recorded on the dial indicator with the elevation specification shown in the Engine Specification chart.

To check the accuracy of the original indicator reading, continue to rotate the crankshaft until the indicator reads zero. If the lift on any lobe is below specified wear limits listed, the camshaft and the valve tappets must be replaced.

6. Install the valve cover(s).

MICROMETER

▶ See Figure 227

A micrometer may used to measure camshaft lobe lift, but this is usually only after it has been removed from the engine. Once the valve cover is removed from the, access may be possible (though a little awkward) to measure the camshaft lobes using a micrometer.

In any case, two measurements are necessary for each lobe. Measurement **Y** or the total LOBE HEIGHT and measurement **X** or the total LOBE WIDTH. To find the lobe lift, you simply subtract **X** from **Y** (subtract the width from the height).

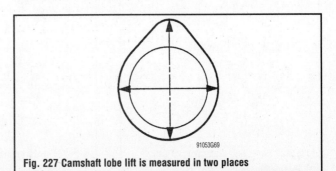

Fig. 227 Camshaft lobe lift is measured in two places

Note each measurement, then make your calculation to determine the lift. Note the final results and repeat the process on the remaining camshaft lobes. Finally, you should compare your results to the specifications charts and decide if a new camshaft is in your future.

Rear Main Seal

REMOVAL & INSTALLATION

♦ See Figures 228, 229, 230, 231 and 232

The procedure for rear main seal removal and installation is the same for both engines.

➡The following procedure requires a specific Ford design seal remover, or equivalent aftermarket version.

1. Disconnect the negative battery cable.
2. Remove transaxle and flexplate/flywheel using the recommended procedure.
3. Using a sharp awl, punch a hole in the rear oil seal metal surface between the oil seal lip and the oil seal retainer.
4. Screw the threaded end of a seal remover into the oil seal, then install a slide hammer and remove the seal from the crankshaft oil seal retainer.

To install:
5. Clean all sealing surfaces.
6. Lubricate the crankshaft, oil seal bore and the lip of the seal with Engine Assembly Lubricant D9AZ-19579-D or equivalent meeting Ford specification ESR-M99C80-A.

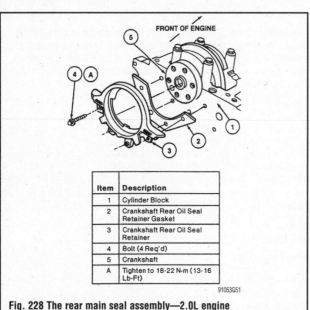

Item	Description
1	Cylinder Block
2	Crankshaft Rear Oil Seal Retainer Gasket
3	Crankshaft Rear Oil Seal Retainer
4	Bolt (4 Req'd)
5	Crankshaft
A	Tighten to 18-22 N·m (13-16 Lb-Ft)

91053G51

Fig. 228 The rear main seal assembly—2.0L engine

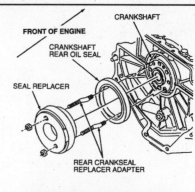

NOTE: LUBRICATE CRANKSHAFT FLANGE AND REAR OIL SEAL BORE WITH ENGINE ASSY LUBRICANT D9AZ-19579-D OR EQUIVALENT MEETING FORD SPECIFICATION ESR-M99C80-A PRIOR TO INSTALLATION OF SEAL

91053G06

Fig. 232 Installing the rear main seal—2.5L engine

7. Install the oil seal using an appropriate seal installer. Seat the seal flush to the rear of the crankshaft oil seal retainer.
8. Reinstall the transaxle and flexplate/flywheel using the recommended procedure.
9. Reconnect the negative battery cable.
10. Start the engine and check for leaks.

Flywheel/Flexplate

REMOVAL & INSTALLATION

2.0L Engine

♦ See Figure 233

1. Disconnect the negative battery cable.
2. Remove the transaxle. Refer to Section 7.
3. If equipped with a manual transaxle, remove the clutch disc and pressure plate. Refer to Section 7.
4. Mark the position of the flywheel on the crankshaft and remove the flywheel retaining bolts.
5. Remove the flywheel and reinforcement plate (on automatic transaxles only).

To install:
6. Coat the threads of the flywheel retaining bolts with thread locking compound.
7. Position the flywheel on the crankshaft flange and install the reinforcement plate (on automatic transaxles only).
8. Install and tighten the bolts in a alternating star pattern to 79–86 ft. lbs. (107–117 Nm) on automatic transaxles, and 81–89 ft. lbs. (110–120 Nm) on manual transaxles.

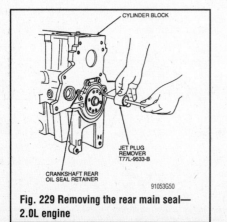

91053G50

Fig. 229 Removing the rear main seal—2.0L engine

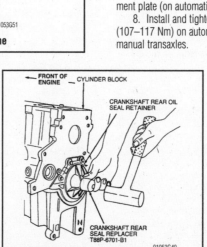

91053G49

Fig. 230 Installing the rear main seal—2.0L engine

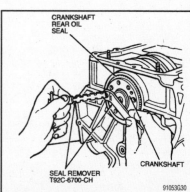

91053G30

Fig. 231 Removing the rear main seal—2.5L engine

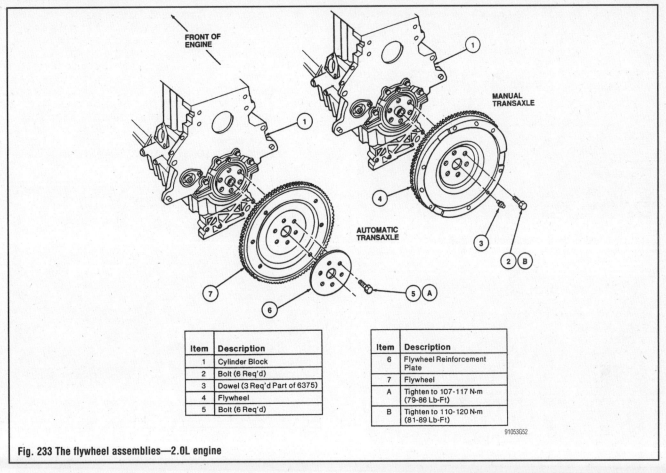

Item	Description
1	Cylinder Block
2	Bolt (6 Req'd)
3	Dowel (3 Req'd Part of 6375)
4	Flywheel
5	Bolt (6 Req'd)

Item	Description
6	Flywheel Reinforcement Plate
7	Flywheel
A	Tighten to 107-117 N·m (79-86 Lb-Ft)
B	Tighten to 110-120 N·m (81-89 Lb-Ft)

91053G52

Fig. 233 The flywheel assemblies—2.0L engine

9. If equipped with a manual transaxle, install the clutch and pressure plate.
10. Install the transaxle. Refer to Section 7.
11. Connect the negative battery cable.

2.5L Engine

▶ See Figure 234

1. Disconnect the negative battery cable.
2. Remove the transaxle. Refer to Section 7.
3. If equipped with a manual transaxle, remove the clutch disc and pressure plate. Refer to Section 7.
4. Mark the position of the flywheel on the crankshaft and remove the flywheel retaining bolts leaving one bolt loosely tightened to retain the flywheel.
5. Install removed flywheel retaining bolts into the two holes in the center of the flywheel. Slowly tighten the bolts until the flywheel is unseated from the crankshaft.
6. Remove the bolts and remove the flywheel from the vehicle.

To install:

7. Coat the threads of the flywheel retaining bolts with thread locking compound.
8. Position the flywheel on the crankshaft flange and tighten the retaining bolts in a alternating star pattern to 54–64 ft. lbs. (73–87 Nm).

9. If equipped with a manual transaxle, install the clutch and pressure plate.
10. Install the transaxle. Refer to Section 7.
11. Connect the negative battery cable.

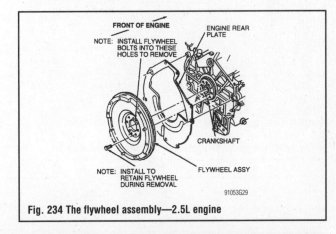

Fig. 234 The flywheel assembly—2.5L engine

EXHAUST SYSTEM

Inspection

▶ See Figures 235 thru 241

➡ Safety glasses should be worn at all times when working on or near the exhaust system. Older exhaust systems will almost always be covered with loose rust particles which will shower you when disturbed. These particles are more than a nuisance and could injure your eye.

※※ CAUTION

DO NOT perform exhaust repairs or inspection with the engine or exhaust hot. Allow the system to cool completely before attempting any work. Exhaust systems are noted for sharp edges, flaking metal and rusted bolts. Gloves and eye protection are required. A healthy supply of penetrating oil and rags is highly recommended.

Your vehicle must be raised and supported safely to inspect the exhaust system properly. By placing 4 safety stands under the vehicle for support should provide enough room for you to slide under the vehicle and inspect the system completely. Start the inspection at the exhaust manifold or turbocharger pipe where the header pipe is attached and work your way to the back of the vehicle. On dual exhaust systems, remember to inspect both sides of the vehicle. Check the complete exhaust system for open seams, holes loose connections, or other deterioration which could permit exhaust fumes to seep into the passenger compartment. Inspect all mounting brackets and hangers for deterioration, some models may have rubber O-rings that can be overstretched and non-supportive. These components will need to be replaced if found. It has always been a practice to use a pointed tool to poke up into the exhaust system where the deterio-

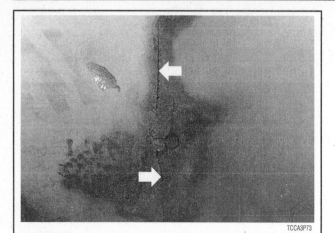

Fig. 235 Cracks in the muffler are a guaranteed leak

TCCA3P73

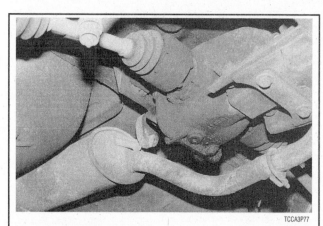

Fig. 237 Make sure the exhaust components are not contacting the body or suspension

TCCA3P77

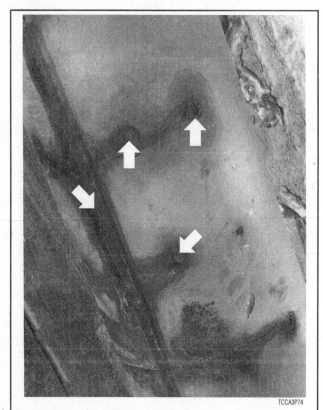

Fig. 236 Check the muffler for rotted spot welds and seams

TCCA3P74

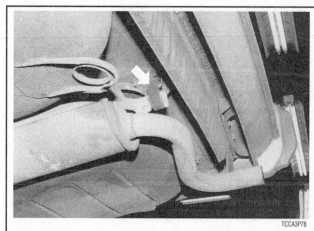

Fig. 238 Check for overstretched or torn exhaust hangers

TCCA3P78

Fig. 239 Example of a badly deteriorated exhaust pipe

TCCA3P75

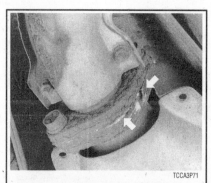

Fig. 240 Inspect flanges for gaskets that have deteriorated and need replacement

TCCA3P71

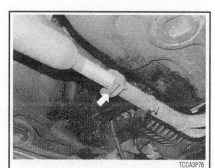

Fig. 241 Some systems, like this one, use large O-rings (doughnuts) in between the flanges

TCCA3P76

ration spots are to see whether or not they crumble. Some models may have heat shield covering certain parts of the exhaust system , it will be necessary to remove these shields to have the exhaust visible for inspection also.

REPLACEMENT

▶ See Figure 242

There are basically two types of exhaust systems. One is the flange type where the component ends are attached with bolts and a gasket in-between. The other exhaust system is the slip joint type. These components slip into one another using clamps to retain them together.

☀ CAUTION

Allow the exhaust system to cool sufficiently before spraying a solvent exhaust fasteners. Some solvents are highly flammable and could ignite when sprayed on hot exhaust components.

Before removing any component of the exhaust system, ALWAYS squirt a liquid rust dissolving agent onto the fasteners for ease of removal. A lot of knuckle skin will be saved by following this rule. It may even be wise to spray the fasteners and allow them to sit overnight.

Flange Type

▶ See Figure 243

☀ CAUTION

Do NOT perform exhaust repairs or inspection with the engine or exhaust hot. Allow the system to cool completely before attempting any work. Exhaust systems are noted for sharp edges, flaking metal and rusted bolts. Gloves and eye protection are required. A healthy supply of penetrating oil and rags is highly recommended. Never spray liquid rust dissolving agent onto a hot exhaust component.

Before removing any component on a flange type system, ALWAYS squirt a liquid rust dissolving agent onto the fasteners for ease of removal. Start by unbolting the exhaust piece at both ends (if required). When unbolting the headpipe from the manifold, make sure that the bolts are free before trying to remove them. if you snap a stud in the exhaust manifold, the stud will have to be removed with a bolt extractor, which often means removal of the manifold itself. Next, disconnect the component from the mounting; slight twisting and turning may be required to remove the component completely from the vehicle. You may need to tap on the component with a rubber mallet to loosen the component. If all else fails, use a hacksaw to separate the parts. An oxy-acetylene cutting torch may be faster but the sparks are DANGEROUS near the fuel tank, and at the very least, accidents could happen, resulting in damage to the undercar parts, not to mention yourself.

Slip Joint Type

▶ See Figure 244

Before removing any component on the slip joint type exhaust system, ALWAYS squirt a liquid rust dissolving agent onto the fasteners for ease of removal. Start by unbolting the exhaust piece at both ends (if required). When unbolting the headpipe from the manifold, make sure that the bolts are free before trying to remove them. if you snap a stud in the exhaust manifold, the stud will have to be removed with a bolt extractor, which often means removal of the manifold itself. Next, remove the mounting U-bolts from around the exhaust pipe you are extracting from the vehicle. Don't be surprised if the U-bolts break while removing the nuts. Loosen the exhaust pipe from any mounting brackets retaining it to the floor pan and separate the components.

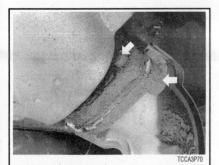

Fig. 242 Nuts and bolts will be extremely difficult to remove when deteriorated with rust

Fig. 243 Example of a flange type exhaust system joint

Fig. 244 Example of a common slip joint type system

ENGINE RECONDITIONING

Determining Engine Condition

Anything that generates heat and/or friction will eventually burn or wear out (for example, a light bulb generates heat, therefore its life span is limited). With this in mind, a running engine generates tremendous amounts of both; friction is encountered by the moving and rotating parts inside the engine and heat is created by friction and combustion of the fuel. However, the engine has systems designed to help reduce the effects of heat and friction and provide added longevity. The oiling system reduces the amount of friction encountered by the moving parts inside the engine, while the cooling system reduces heat created by friction and combustion. If either system is not maintained, a break-down will be inevitable. Therefore, you can see how regular maintenance can affect the service life of your vehicle. If you do not drain, flush and refill your cooling system at the proper intervals, deposits will begin to accumulate in the radiator, thereby reducing the amount of heat it can extract from the coolant. The same applies to your oil and filter; if it is not changed often enough it becomes laden with contaminates and is unable to properly lubricate the engine. This increases friction and wear.

There are a number of methods for evaluating the condition of your engine. A compression test can reveal the condition of your pistons, piston rings, cylinder bores, head gasket(s), valves and valve seats. An oil pressure test can warn you of possible engine bearing, or oil pump failures. Excessive oil consumption, evidence of oil in the engine air intake area and/or bluish smoke from the tailpipe may indicate worn piston rings, worn valve guides and/or valve seals. As a general rule, an engine that uses no more than one quart of oil every 1000 miles is in good condition. Engines that use one quart of oil or more in less than 1000 miles should first be checked for oil leaks. If any oil leaks are present, have them fixed before determining how much oil is consumed by the engine, especially if blue smoke is not visible at the tailpipe.

COMPRESSION TEST

▶ See Figure 245

A noticeable lack of engine power, excessive oil consumption and/or poor fuel mileage measured over an extended period are all indicators of internal

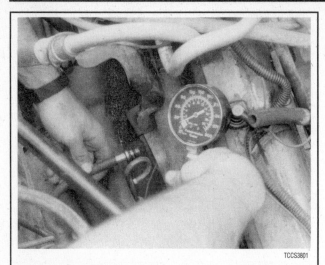

Fig. 245 A screw-in type compression gauge is more accurate and easier to use without an assistant

engine wear. Worn piston rings, scored or worn cylinder bores, blown head gaskets, sticking or burnt valves, and worn valve seats are all possible culprits. A check of each cylinder's compression will help locate the problem.

➡ **A screw-in type compression gauge is more accurate than the type you simply hold against the spark plug hole. Although it takes slightly longer to use, it's worth the effort to obtain a more accurate reading.**

1. Make sure that the proper amount and viscosity of engine oil is in the crankcase, then ensure the battery is fully charged.
2. Warm-up the engine to normal operating temperature, then shut the engine **OFF**.
3. Disable the ignition system.
4. Label and disconnect all of the spark plug wires from the plugs.
5. Thoroughly clean the cylinder head area around the spark plug ports, then remove the spark plugs.
6. Set the throttle plate to the fully open (wide-open throttle) position. You can block the accelerator linkage open for this, or you can have an assistant fully depress the accelerator pedal.
7. Install a screw-in type compression gauge into the No. 1 spark plug hole until the fitting is snug.

❊❊ WARNING

Be careful not to crossthread the spark plug hole.

8. According to the tool manufacturer's instructions, connect a remote starting switch to the starting circuit.
9. With the ignition switch in the **OFF** position, use the remote starting switch to crank the engine through at least five compression strokes (approximately 5 seconds of cranking) and record the highest reading on the gauge.
10. Repeat the test on each cylinder, cranking the engine approximately the same number of compression strokes and/or time as the first.
11. Compare the highest readings from each cylinder to that of the others. The indicated compression pressures are considered within specifications if the lowest reading cylinder is within 75 percent of the pressure recorded for the highest reading cylinder. For example, if your highest reading cylinder pressure was 150 psi (1034 kPa), then 75 percent of that would be 113 psi (779 kPa). So the lowest reading cylinder should be no less than 113 psi (779 kPa).
12. If a cylinder exhibits an unusually low compression reading, pour a tablespoon of clean engine oil into the cylinder through the spark plug hole and repeat the compression test. If the compression rises after adding oil, it means that the cylinder's piston rings and/or cylinder bore are damaged or worn. If the pressure remains low, the valves may not be seating properly (a valve job is needed), or the head gasket may be blown near that cylinder. If compression in any two adjacent cylinders is low, and if the addition of oil doesn't help raise compression, there is leakage past the head gasket. Oil and coolant in the combustion chamber, combined with blue or constant white smoke from the tailpipe,

are symptoms of this problem. However, don't be alarmed by the normal white smoke emitted from the tailpipe during engine warm-up or from cold weather driving. There may be evidence of water droplets on the engine dipstick and/or oil droplets in the cooling system if a head gasket is blown.

OIL PRESSURE TEST

Check for proper oil pressure at the sending unit passage with an externally mounted mechanical oil pressure gauge (as opposed to relying on a factory installed dash-mounted gauge). A tachometer may also be needed, as some specifications may require running the engine at a specific rpm.

1. With the engine cold, locate and remove the oil pressure sending unit.
2. Following the manufacturer's instructions, connect a mechanical oil pressure gauge and, if necessary, a tachometer to the engine.
3. Start the engine and allow it to idle.
4. Check the oil pressure reading when cold and record the number. You may need to run the engine at a specified rpm, so check the specifications chart located earlier in this section.
5. Run the engine until normal operating temperature is reached (upper radiator hose will feel warm).
6. Check the oil pressure reading again with the engine hot and record the number. Turn the engine **OFF**.
7. Compare your hot oil pressure reading to that given in the chart. If the reading is low, check the cold pressure reading against the chart. If the cold pressure is well above the specification, and the hot reading was lower than the specification, you may have the wrong viscosity oil in the engine. Change the oil, making sure to use the proper grade and quantity, then repeat the test.

Low oil pressure readings could be attributed to internal component wear, pump related problems, a low oil level, or oil viscosity that is too low. High oil pressure readings could be caused by an overfilled crankcase, too high of an oil viscosity or a faulty pressure relief valve.

Buy or Rebuild?

Now that you have determined that your engine is worn out, you must make some decisions. The question of whether or not an engine is worth rebuilding is largely a subjective matter and one of personal worth. Is the engine a popular one, or is it an obsolete model? Are parts available? Will it get acceptable gas mileage once it is rebuilt? Is the car it's being put into worth keeping? Would it be less expensive to buy a new engine, have your engine rebuilt by a pro, rebuild it yourself or buy a used engine from a salvage yard? Or would it be simpler and less expensive to buy another car? If you have considered all these matters and more, and have still decided to rebuild the engine, then it is time to decide how you will rebuild it.

➡ **The editors at Chilton feel that most engine machining should be performed by a professional machine shop. Don't think of it as wasting money, rather, as an assurance that the job has been done right the first time. There are many expensive and specialized tools required to perform such tasks as boring and honing an engine block or having a valve job done on a cylinder head. Even inspecting the parts requires expensive micrometers and gauges to properly measure wear and clearances. Also, a machine shop can deliver to you clean, and ready to assemble parts, saving you time and aggravation. Your maximum savings will come from performing the removal, disassembly, assembly and installation of the engine and purchasing or renting only the tools required to perform the above tasks. Depending on the particular circumstances, you may save 40 to 60 percent of the cost doing these yourself.**

A complete rebuild or overhaul of an engine involves replacing all of the moving parts (pistons, rods, crankshaft, camshaft, etc.) with new ones and machining the non-moving wearing surfaces of the block and heads. Unfortunately, this may not be cost effective. For instance, your crankshaft may have been damaged or worn, but it can be machined undersize for a minimal fee.

So, as you can see, you can replace everything inside the engine, but, it is wiser to replace only those parts which are really needed, and, if possible, repair the more expensive ones. Later in this section, we will break the engine down into its two main components: the cylinder head and the engine block. We will discuss each component, and the recommended parts to replace during a rebuild on each.

Engine Overhaul Tips

Most engine overhaul procedures are fairly standard. In addition to specific parts replacement procedures and specifications for your individual engine, this section is also a guide to acceptable rebuilding procedures. Examples of standard rebuilding practice are given and should be used along with specific details concerning your particular engine.

Competent and accurate machine shop services will ensure maximum performance, reliability and engine life. In most instances it is more profitable for the do-it-yourself mechanic to remove, clean and inspect the component, buy the necessary parts and deliver these to a shop for actual machine work.

Much of the assembly work (crankshaft, bearings, piston rods, and other components) is well within the scope of the do-it-yourself mechanic's tools and abilities. You will have to decide for yourself the depth of involvement you desire in an engine repair or rebuild.

TOOLS

The tools required for an engine overhaul or parts replacement will depend on the depth of your involvement. With a few exceptions, they will be the tools found in a mechanic's tool kit (see Section 1 of this manual). More in-depth work will require some or all of the following:

- A dial indicator (reading in thousandths) mounted on a universal base
- Micrometers and telescope gauges
- Jaw and screw-type pullers
- Scraper
- Valve spring compressor
- Ring groove cleaner
- Piston ring expander and compressor
- Ridge reamer
- Cylinder hone or glaze breaker
- Plastigage®
- Engine stand

The use of most of these tools is illustrated in this section. Many can be rented for a one-time use from a local parts jobber or tool supply house specializing in automotive work.

Occasionally, the use of special tools is called for. See the information on Special Tools and the Safety Notice in the front of this book before substituting another tool.

OVERHAUL TIPS

Aluminum has become extremely popular for use in engines, due to its low weight. Observe the following precautions when handling aluminum parts:

- Never hot tank aluminum parts (the caustic hot tank solution will eat the aluminum.
- Remove all aluminum parts (identification tag, etc.) from engine parts prior to the tanking.
- Always coat threads lightly with engine oil or anti-seize compounds before installation, to prevent seizure.
- Never overtighten bolts or spark plugs especially in aluminum threads.

When assembling the engine, any parts that will be exposed to frictional contact must be prelubed to provide lubrication at initial start-up. Any product specifically formulated for this purpose can be used, but engine oil is not recommended as a prelube in most cases.

When semi-permanent (locked, but removable) installation of bolts or nuts is desired, threads should be cleaned and coated with Loctite® or another similar, commercial non-hardening sealant.

CLEANING

▶ See Figures 246, 247, 248, 249 and 250

Before the engine and its components are inspected, they must be thoroughly cleaned. You will need to remove any engine varnish, oil sludge and/or carbon deposits from all of the components to insure an accurate inspection. A crack in the engine block or cylinder head can easily become overlooked if hidden by a layer of sludge or carbon.

Most of the cleaning process can be carried out with common hand tools and readily available solvents or solutions. Carbon deposits can be chipped away using a hammer and a hard wooden chisel. Old gasket material and varnish or sludge can usually be removed using a scraper and/or cleaning solvent. Extremely stubborn deposits may require the use of a power drill with a wire brush. If using a wire brush, use extreme care around any critical machined surfaces (such as the gasket surfaces, bearing saddles, cylinder bores, etc.). USE OF A WIRE BRUSH IS NOT RECOMMENDED ON ANY ALUMINUM COMPONENTS. Always follow any safety recommendations given by the manufacturer of the tool and/or solvent. You should always wear eye protection during any cleaning process involving scraping, chipping or spraying of solvents.

An alternative to the mess and hassle of cleaning the parts yourself is to drop them off at a local garage or machine shop. They will, more than likely, have the necessary equipment to properly clean all of the parts for a nominal fee.

✳✳ CAUTION

Always wear eye protection during any cleaning process involving scraping, chipping or spraying of solvents.

Remove any oil galley plugs, freeze plugs and/or pressed-in bearings and carefully wash and degrease all of the engine components including the fasteners and bolts. Small parts such as the valves, springs, etc., should be placed in a metal basket and allowed to soak. Use pipe cleaner type brushes, and clean all passageways in the components. Use a ring expander and remove the rings from the pistons. Clean the piston ring grooves with a special tool or a piece of broken ring. Scrape the carbon off of the top of the piston. You should never use a wire brush on the pistons. After preparing all of the piston assemblies in this manner, wash and degrease them again.

✳✳ WARNING

Use extreme care when cleaning around the cylinder head valve seats. A mistake or slip may cost you a new seat.

When cleaning the cylinder head, remove carbon from the combustion chamber with the valves installed. This will avoid damaging the valve seats.

Fig. 246 Use a gasket scraper to remove the old gasket material from the mating surfaces

Fig. 247 After the gasket material is scraped off, wipe the head clean using a solvent and a rag

Fig. 248 Use a ring expander tool to remove the piston rings

Fig. 249 Clean the piston ring grooves using a ring groove cleaner tool, or . . .

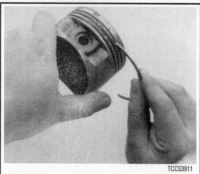

Fig. 250 . . . use a piece of an old ring to clean the grooves. Be careful, the ring can be quite sharp

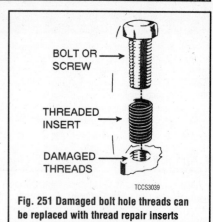

Fig. 251 Damaged bolt hole threads can be replaced with thread repair inserts

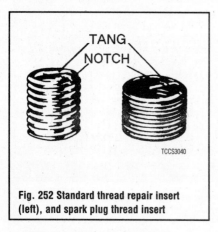

Fig. 252 Standard thread repair insert (left), and spark plug thread insert

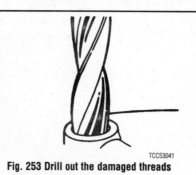

Fig. 253 Drill out the damaged threads with the specified size bit. Be sure to drill completely through the hole or to the bottom of a blind hole

Fig. 254 Using the kit, tap the hole in order to receive the thread insert. Keep the tap well oiled and back it out frequently to avoid clogging the threads

REPAIRING DAMAGED THREADS

▶ See Figures 251, 252, 253, 254 and 255

Several methods of repairing damaged threads are available. Heli-Coil® (shown here), Keenserts® and Microdot® are among the most widely used. All involve basically the same principle—drilling out stripped threads, tapping the hole and installing a prewound insert—making welding, plugging and oversize fasteners unnecessary.

Two types of thread repair inserts are usually supplied: a standard type for most inch coarse, inch fine, metric course and metric fine thread sizes and a spark lug type to fit most spark plug port sizes. Consult the individual tool manufacturer's catalog to determine exact applications. Typical thread repair kits will contain a selection of prewound threaded inserts, a tap (corresponding to the outside diameter threads of the insert) and an installation tool. Spark plug inserts usually differ because they require a tap equipped with pilot threads and a combined reamer/tap section. Most manufacturers also supply blister-packed thread repair inserts separately in addition to a master kit containing a variety of taps and inserts plus installation tools.

Before attempting to repair a threaded hole, remove any snapped, broken or damaged bolts or studs. Penetrating oil can be used to free frozen threads. The offending item can usually be removed with locking pliers or using a screw/stud extractor. After the hole is clear, the thread can be repaired, as shown in the series of accompanying illustrations and in the kit manufacturer's instructions.

Engine Preparation

To properly rebuild an engine, you must first remove it from the vehicle, then disassemble and diagnose it. Ideally you should place your engine on an engine stand. This affords you the best access to the engine components. Follow the manufacturer's directions for using the stand with your particular engine. Remove the flywheel or flexplate before installing the engine to the stand.

Now that you have the engine on a stand, and assuming that you have drained the oil and coolant from the engine, it's time to strip it of all but the necessary components. Before you start disassembling the engine, you may want to

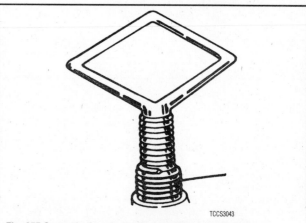

Fig. 255 Screw the insert onto the installer tool until the tang engages the slot. Thread the insert into the hole until it is ¼–½ turn below the top surface, then remove the tool and break off the tang using a punch

take a moment to draw some pictures, or fabricate some labels or containers to mark the locations of various components and the bolts and/or studs which fasten them. Modern day engines use a lot of little brackets and clips which hold wiring harnesses and such, and these holders are often mounted on studs and/or bolts that can be easily mixed up. The manufacturer spent a lot of time and money designing your vehicle, and they wouldn't have wasted any of it by haphazardly placing brackets, clips or fasteners on the vehicle. If it's present when you disassemble it, put it back when you assemble, you will regret not remembering that little bracket which holds a wire harness out of the path of a rotating part.

You should begin by unbolting any accessories still attached to the engine, such as the water pump, power steering pump, alternator, etc. Then, unfasten any manifolds (intake or exhaust) which were not removed during the engine removal procedure. Finally, remove any covers remaining on the engine such as the rocker arm, front or timing cover and oil pan. Some front covers may require the vibration damper and/or crank pulley to be removed beforehand. The idea is to reduce the engine to the bare necessities (cylinder head(s), valve train, engine block, crankshaft, pistons and connecting rods), plus any other 'in block' components such as oil pumps, balance shafts and auxiliary shafts.

Finally, remove the cylinder head(s) from the engine block and carefully place on a bench. Disassembly instructions for each component follow later in this section.

Cylinder Head

There are two basic types of cylinder heads used on today's automobiles: the Overhead Valve (OHV) and the Overhead Camshaft (OHC). The latter can also be broken down into two subgroups: the Single Overhead Camshaft (SOHC) and the Dual Overhead Camshaft (DOHC). Generally, if there is only a single camshaft on a head, it is just referred to as an OHC head. Also, an engine with an OHV cylinder head is also known as a pushrod engine.

Most cylinder heads these days are made of an aluminum alloy due to its light weight, durability and heat transfer qualities. However, cast iron was the material of choice in the past, and is still used on many vehicles today. Whether made from aluminum or iron, all cylinder heads have valves and seats. Some use two valves per cylinder, while the more hi-tech engines will utilize a multi-valve configuration using 3, 4 and even 5 valves per cylinder. When the valve contacts the seat, it does so on precision machined surfaces, which seals the combustion chamber. All cylinder heads have a valve guide for each valve. The guide centers the valve to the seat and allows it to move up and down within it. The clearance between the valve and guide can be critical. Too much clearance and the engine may consume oil, lose vacuum and/or damage the seat. Too little, and the valve can stick in the guide causing the engine to run poorly if at all, and possibly causing severe damage. The last component all cylinder heads have are valve springs. The spring holds the valve against its seat. It also returns the valve to this position when the valve has been opened by the valve train or camshaft. The spring is fastened to the valve by a retainer and valve locks (sometimes called keepers). Aluminum heads will also have a valve spring shim to keep the spring from wearing away the aluminum.

An ideal method of rebuilding the cylinder head would involve replacing all of the valves, guides, seats, springs, etc. with new ones. However, depending on how the engine was maintained, often this is not necessary. A major cause of valve, guide and seat wear is an improperly tuned engine. An engine that is running too rich, will often wash the lubricating oil out of the guide with gasoline, causing it to wear rapidly. Conversely, an engine which is running too lean will place higher combustion temperatures on the valves and seats allowing them to wear or even burn. Springs fall victim to the driving habits of the individual. A driver who often runs the engine rpm to the redline will wear out or break the springs faster then one that stays well below it. Unfortunately, mileage takes it toll on all of the parts. Generally, the valves, guides, springs and seats in a cylinder head can be machined and re-used, saving you money. However, if a valve is burnt, it may be wise to replace all of the valves, since they were all operating in the same environment. The same goes for any other component on the cylinder head. Think of it as an insurance policy against future problems related to that component.

Unfortunately, the only way to find out which components need replacing, is to disassemble and carefully check each piece. After the cylinder head(s) are disassembled, thoroughly clean all of the components.

DISASSEMBLY

▶ See Figures 256 and 257

Whether it is a single or dual overhead camshaft cylinder head, the disassembly procedure is relatively unchanged. One aspect to pay attention to is careful labeling of the parts on the dual camshaft cylinder head. There will be an intake camshaft and followers as well as an exhaust camshaft and followers and they must be labeled as such. In some cases, the components are identical and could easily be installed incorrectly. DO NOT MIX THEM UP! Determining which is which is very simple; the intake camshaft and components are on the same side of the head as was the intake manifold. Conversely, the exhaust camshaft and components are on the same side of the head as was the exhaust manifold.

TCCA3P54

Fig. 256 Exploded view of a valve, seal, spring, retainer and locks from an OHC cylinder head

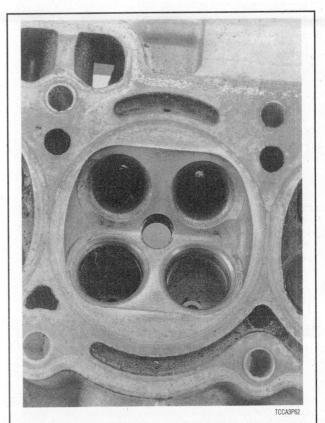

TCCA3P62

Fig. 257 Example of a multi-valve cylinder head. Note how it has 2 intake and 2 exhaust valve ports

2.0L Engine

▶ See Figures 258, 259, 260, 261 and 262

Most cylinder heads with cup type camshaft followers will have the valve spring, retainer and locks recessed within the follower's bore. You will need a C-clamp style valve spring compressor tool, an OHC spring removal tool (or equivalent) and a small magnet to disassemble the head.

1. If not already removed, remove the camshaft(s) and/or followers. Mark their positions for assembly.
2. Position the cylinder head to allow use of a C-clamp style valve spring compressor tool.

➡ **It is preferred to position the cylinder head gasket surface facing you with the valve springs facing the opposite direction and the head laying horizontal.**

Fig. 258 Remove the valve tappets from the cylinder head by carefully lifting them up out of their bores

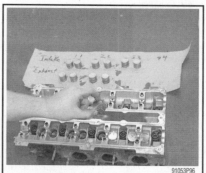

Fig. 259 Make sure you place the tappets in an organized way to ensure they go back in their original location

Fig. 260 C-clamp type spring compressor and an OHC spring removal tool (center) for cup type followers

Fig. 261 Most cup type follower cylinder heads retain the camshaft using bolt-on bearing caps

3. With the OHC spring removal adapter tool positioned inside of the follower bore, compress the valve spring using the C-clamp style valve spring compressor.
4. Remove the valve locks. A small magnetic tool or screwdriver will aid in removal.
5. Release the compressor tool and remove the spring assembly.
6. Withdraw the valve from the cylinder head.
7. If equipped, remove the valve seal.

➡ **Special valve seal removal tools are available. Regular or needlenose type pliers, if used with care, will work just as well. If using ordinary pliers, be sure not to damage the follower bore. The follower and its bore are machined to close tolerances and any damage to the bore will effect this relationship.**

8. If equipped, remove the valve spring shim. A small magnetic tool or screwdriver will aid in removal.
9. Repeat Steps 3 through 8 until all of the valves have been removed.

2.5L Engine

▶ See Figures 263 thru 271

Most cylinder heads with rocker arm-type camshaft followers are easily disassembled using a standard valve spring compressor. However, certain models may not have enough open space around the spring for the standard tool and may require you to use a C-clamp style compressor tool instead.

1. If not already removed, remove the rocker arms and/or shafts and the camshaft. If applicable, also remove the hydraulic lash adjusters. Mark their positions for assembly.
2. Position the cylinder head to allow access to the valve spring.

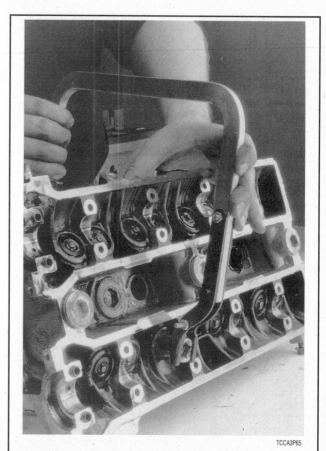

Fig. 262 Position the OHC spring tool in the follower bore, then compress the spring with a C-clamp type tool

3. Use a valve spring compressor tool to relieve the spring tension from the retainer.

➡ **Due to engine varnish, the retainer may stick to the valve locks. A gentle tap with a hammer may help to break it loose.**

4. Remove the valve locks from the valve tip and/or retainer. A small magnet may help in removing the small locks.

5. Lift the valve spring, tool and all, off of the valve stem.

6. If equipped, remove the valve seal. If the seal is difficult to remove with the valve in place, try removing the valve first, then the seal. Follow the steps below for valve removal.

7. Position the head to allow access for withdrawing the valve.

➡ **Cylinder heads that have seen a lot of miles and/or abuse may have mushroomed the valve lock grove and/or tip, causing difficulty in removal of the valve. If this has happened, use a metal file to carefully remove the high spots around the lock grooves and/or tip. Only file it enough to allow removal.**

8. Remove the valve from the cylinder head.

9. If equipped, remove the valve spring shim. A small magnetic tool or screwdriver will aid in removal.

10. Repeat Steps 3 though 9 until all of the valves have been removed.

INSPECTION

Now that all of the cylinder head components are clean, it's time to inspect them for wear and/or damage. To accurately inspect them, you will need some specialized tools:

- A 0–1 in. micrometer for the valves
- A dial indicator or inside diameter gauge for the valve guides
- A spring pressure test gauge

If you do not have access to the proper tools, you may want to bring the components to a shop that does.

Fig. 263 Example of the shaft mounted rocker arms on some OHC heads

Fig. 264 Another example of the rocker arm type OHC head. This model uses a follower under the camshaft

Fig. 265 Before the camshaft can be removed, all of the followers must first be removed . . .

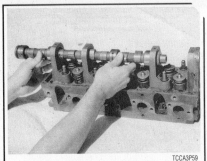

Fig. 266 . . . then the camshaft can be removed by sliding it out (shown), or unbolting a bearing cap (not shown)

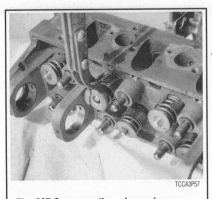

Fig. 267 Compress the valve spring . . .

Fig. 268 . . . then remove the valve locks from the valve stem and spring retainer

Fig. 269 Remove the valve spring and retainer from the cylinder head

Fig. 270 Remove the valve seal from the guide. Some gentle prying or pliers may help to remove stubborn ones

Fig. 271 All aluminum and some cast iron heads will have these valve spring shims. Remove all of them as well

Valves

▶ See Figures 272 and 273

The first thing to inspect are the valve heads. Look closely at the head, margin and face for any cracks, excessive wear or burning. The margin is the best place to look for burning. It should have a squared edge with an even width all around the diameter. When a valve burns, the margin will look melted and the edges rounded. Also inspect the valve head for any signs of tulipping. This will show as a lifting of the edges or dishing in the center of the head and will usually not occur to all of the valves. All of the heads should look the same, any that seem dished more than others are probably bad. Next, inspect the valve lock grooves and valve tips. Check for any burrs around the lock grooves, especially if you had to file them to remove the valve. Valve tips should appear flat, although slight rounding with high mileage engines is normal. Slightly worn valve tips will need to be machined flat. Last, measure the valve stem diameter with the micrometer. Measure the area that rides within the guide, especially towards the tip where most of the wear occurs. Take several measurements along its length and compare them to each other. Wear should be even along the length with little to no taper. If no minimum diameter is given in the specifications, then the stem should not read more than 0.001 in. (0.025mm) below the specification. Any valves that fail these inspections should be replaced.

Springs, Retainers and Valve Locks

▶ See Figures 274 and 275

The first thing to check is the most obvious, broken springs. Next check the free length and squareness of each spring. If applicable, insure to distinguish between intake and exhaust springs. Use a ruler and/or carpenter's square to measure the length. A carpenter's square should be used to check the springs

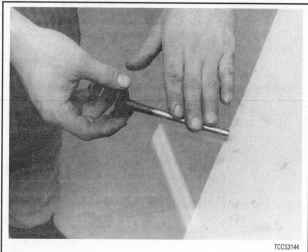

Fig. 272 Valve stems may be rolled on a flat surface to check for bends

for squareness. If a spring pressure test gauge is available, check each springs rating and compare to the specifications chart. Check the readings against the specifications given. Any springs that fail these inspections should be replaced.

The spring retainers rarely need replacing, however they should still be checked as a precaution. Inspect the spring mating surface and the valve lock retention area for any signs of excessive wear. Also check for any signs of cracking. Replace any retainers that are questionable.

Valve locks should be inspected for excessive wear on the outside contact area as well as on the inner notched surface. Any locks which appear worn or broken and its respective valve should be replaced.

Cylinder Head

There are several things to check on the cylinder head: valve guides, seats, cylinder head surface flatness, cracks and physical damage.

VALVE GUIDES

▶ See Figure 276

Now that you know the valves are good, you can use them to check the guides, although a new valve, if available, is preferred. Before you measure anything, look at the guides carefully and inspect them for any cracks, chips or breakage. Also if the guide is a removable style (as in most aluminum heads), check them for any looseness or evidence of movement. All of the guides should appear to be at the same height from the spring seat. If any seem lower (or higher) from another, the guide has moved. Mount a dial indicator onto the spring side of the cylinder head. Lightly oil the valve stem and insert it into the cylinder head. Position the dial indicator against the valve stem near the tip and zero the gauge. Grasp the valve stem and wiggle towards and away from the dial indicator and observe the readings. Mount the dial indicator 90 degrees from the initial point and zero the gauge and again take a reading. Compare the two readings for a out of round condition. Check the readings against the specifications given. An Inside Diameter (I.D.) gauge designed for valve guides will give you an accurate valve guide bore measurement. If the I.D. gauge is used, compare the readings with the specifications given. Any guides that fail these inspections should be replaced or machined.

VALVE SEATS

A visual inspection of the valve seats should show a slightly worn and pitted surface where the valve face contacts the seat. Inspect the seat carefully for severe pitting or cracks. Also, a seat that is badly worn will be recessed into the cylinder head. A severely worn or recessed seat may need to be replaced. All cracked seats must be replaced. A seat concentricity gauge, if available, should be used to check the seat run-out. If run-out exceeds specifications the seat must be machined (if no specification is given use 0.002 in. or 0.051mm).

CYLINDER HEAD SURFACE FLATNESS

▶ See Figures 277 and 278

After you have cleaned the gasket surface of the cylinder head of any old gasket material, check the head for flatness.

Place a straightedge across the gasket surface. Using feeler gauges, determine the clearance at the center of the straightedge and across the cylinder head

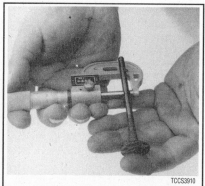

Fig. 273 Use a micrometer to check the valve stem diameter

Fig. 274 Use a caliper to check the valve spring free-length

Fig. 275 Check the valve spring for squareness on a flat surface; a carpenter's square can be used

Fig. 276 A dial gauge may be used to check valve stem-to-guide clearance; read the gauge while moving the valve stem

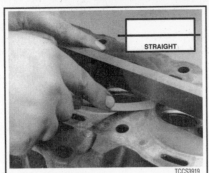

Fig. 277 Check the head for flatness across the center of the head surface using a straightedge and feeler gauge

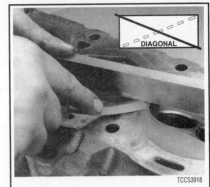

Fig. 278 Checks should also be made along both diagonals of the head surface

at several points. Check along the centerline and diagonally on the head surface. If the warpage exceeds 0.003 in. (0.076mm) within a 6.0 in. (15.2cm) span, or 0.006 in. (0.152mm) over the total length of the head, the cylinder head must be resurfaced. After resurfacing the heads of a V-type engine, the intake manifold flange surface should be checked, and if necessary, milled proportionally to allow for the change in its mounting position.

CRACKS AND PHYSICAL DAMAGE

Generally, cracks are limited to the combustion chamber, however, it is not uncommon for the head to crack in a spark plug hole, port, outside of the head or in the valve spring/rocker arm area. The first area to inspect is always the hottest: the exhaust seat/port area.

A visual inspection should be performed, but just because you don't see a crack does not mean it is not there. Some more reliable methods for inspecting for cracks include Magnaflux®, a magnetic process or Zyglo®, a dye penetrant. Magnaflux® is used only on ferrous metal (cast iron) heads. Zyglo® uses a spray on fluorescent mixture along with a black light to reveal the cracks. It is strongly recommended to have your cylinder head checked professionally for cracks, especially if the engine was known to have overheated and/or leaked or consumed coolant. Contact a local shop for availability and pricing of these services.

Physical damage is usually very evident. For example, a broken mounting ear from dropping the head or a bent or broken stud and/or bolt. All of these defects should be fixed or, if unrepairable, the head should be replaced.

Camshaft and Followers

Inspect the camshaft(s) and followers as described earlier in this section.

REFINISHING & REPAIRING

Many of the procedures given for refinishing and repairing the cylinder head components must be performed by a machine shop. Certain steps, if the inspected part is not worn, can be performed yourself inexpensively. However, you spent a lot of time and effort so far, why risk trying to save a couple bucks if you might have to do it all over again?

Valves

Any valves that were not replaced should be refaced and the tips ground flat. Unless you have access to a valve grinding machine, this should be done by a machine shop. If the valves are in extremely good condition, as well as the valve seats and guides, they may be lapped in without performing machine work.

It is a recommended practice to lap the valves even after machine work has been performed and/or new valves have been purchased. This insures a positive seal between the valve and seat.

LAPPING THE VALVES

➡Before lapping the valves to the seats, read the rest of the cylinder head section to insure that any related parts are in acceptable enough condition to continue.

➡Before any valve seat machining and/or lapping can be performed, the guides must be within factory recommended specifications.

1. Invert the cylinder head.
2. Lightly lubricate the valve stems and insert them into the cylinder head in their numbered order.
3. Raise the valve from the seat and apply a small amount of fine lapping compound to the seat.
4. Moisten the suction head of a hand-lapping tool and attach it to the head of the valve.
5. Rotate the tool between the palms of both hands, changing the position of the valve on the valve seat and lifting the tool often to prevent grooving.
6. Lap the valve until a smooth, polished circle is evident on the valve and seat.
7. Remove the tool and the valve. Wipe away all traces of the grinding compound and store the valve to maintain its lapped location.

✳✳ WARNING

Do not get the valves out of order after they have been lapped. They must be put back with the same valve seat with which they were lapped.

Springs, Retainers and Valve Locks

There is no repair or refinishing possible with the springs, retainers and valve locks. If they are found to be worn or defective, they must be replaced with new (or known good) parts.

Cylinder Head

Most refinishing procedures dealing with the cylinder head must be performed by a machine shop. Read the sections below and review your inspection data to determine whether or not machining is necessary.

VALVE GUIDE

➡If any machining or replacements are made to the valve guides, the seats must be machined.

Unless the valve guides need machining or replacing, the only service to perform is to thoroughly clean them of any dirt or oil residue.

There are only two types of valve guides used on automobile engines: the replaceable-type (all aluminum heads) and the cast-in integral-type (most cast iron heads). There are four recommended methods for repairing worn guides.
- Knurling
- Inserts
- Reaming oversize
- Replacing

Knurling is a process in which metal is displaced and raised, thereby reducing clearance, giving a true center, and providing oil control. It is the least expensive way of repairing the valve guides. However, it is not necessarily the best, and in some cases, a knurled valve guide will not stand up for more than a short time. It requires a special knurlizer and precision reaming tools to obtain proper clearances. It would not be cost effective to purchase these tools, unless you plan on rebuilding several of the same cylinder head.

Installing a guide insert involves machining the guide to accept a bronze insert. One style is the coil-type which is installed into a threaded guide. Another is the thin-walled insert where the guide is reamed oversize to accept a split-sleeve insert. After the insert is installed, a special tool is then run through the guide to expand the insert, locking it to the guide. The insert is then reamed to the standard size for proper valve clearance.

Reaming for oversize valves restores normal clearances and provides a true valve seat. Most cast-in type guides can be reamed to accept an valve with an oversize stem. The cost factor for this can become quite high as you will need to purchase the reamer and new, oversize stem valves for all guides which were reamed. Oversizes are generally 0.003 to 0.030 in. (0.076 to 0.762mm), with 0.015 in. (0.381mm) being the most common.

To replace cast-in type valve guides, they must be drilled out, then reamed to accept replacement guides. This must be done on a fixture which will allow centering and leveling off of the original valve seat or guide, otherwise a serious guide-to-seat misalignment may occur making it impossible to properly machine the seat.

Replaceable-type guides are pressed into the cylinder head. A hammer and a stepped drift or punch may be used to install and remove the guides. Before removing the guides, measure the protrusion on the spring side of the head and record it for installation. Use the stepped drift to hammer out the old guide from the combustion chamber side of the head. When installing, determine whether or not the guide also seals a water jacket in the head, and if it does, use the recommended sealing agent. If there is no water jacket, grease the valve guide and its bore. Use the stepped drift, and hammer the new guide into the cylinder head from the spring side of the cylinder head. A stack of washers the same thickness as the measured protrusion may help the installation process.

VALVE SEATS

➡Before any valve seat machining can be performed, the guides must be within factory recommended specifications.

➡If any machining or replacements were made to the valve guides, the seats must be machined.

If the seats are in good condition, the valves can be lapped to the seats, and the cylinder head assembled. See the valves section for instructions on lapping.

If the valve seats are worn, cracked or damaged, they must be serviced by a machine shop. The valve seat must be perfectly centered to the valve guide, which requires very accurate machining.

CYLINDER HEAD SURFACE

If the cylinder head is warped, it must be machined flat. If the warpage is extremely severe, the head may need to be replaced. In some instances, it may be possible to straighten a warped head enough to allow machining. In either case, contact a professional machine shop for service.

➡Any OHC cylinder head that shows excessive warpage should have the camshaft bearing journals align bored after the cylinder head has been resurfaced.

✳✳ WARNING

Failure to align bore the camshaft bearing journals could result in severe engine damage including but not limited to: valve and piston damage, connecting rod damage, camshaft and/or crankshaft breakage.

CRACKS AND PHYSICAL DAMAGE

Certain cracks can be repaired in both cast iron and aluminum heads. For cast iron, a tapered threaded insert is installed along the length of the crack. Aluminum can also use the tapered inserts, however welding is the preferred method. Some physical damage can be repaired through brazing or welding. Contact a machine shop to get expert advice for your particular dilemma.

ASSEMBLY

◗ See Figure 279

The first step for any assembly job is to have a clean area in which to work. Next, thoroughly clean all of the parts and components that are to be assembled. Finally, place all of the components onto a suitable work space and, if necessary, arrange the parts to their respective positions.

2.0L Engine

To install the springs, retainers and valve locks on heads which have these components recessed into the camshaft follower's bore, you will need a small

Fig. 279 Once assembled, check the valve clearance and correct as needed

screwdriver-type tool, some clean white grease and a lot of patience. You will also need the C-clamp style spring compressor and the OHC tool used to disassemble the head.

1. Lightly lubricate the valve stems and insert all of the valves into the cylinder head. If possible, maintain their original locations.
2. If equipped, install any valve spring shims which were removed.
3. If equipped, install the new valve seals, keeping the following in mind:
• If the valve seal presses over the guide, lightly lubricate the outer guide surfaces.
• If the seal is an O-ring type, it is installed just after compressing the spring but before the valve locks.
4. Place the valve spring and retainer over the stem.
5. Position the spring compressor and the OHC tool, then compress the spring.
6. Using a small screwdriver as a spatula, fill the valve stem side of the lock with white grease. Use the excess grease on the screwdriver to fasten the lock to the driver.
7. Carefully install the valve lock, which is stuck to the end of the screwdriver, to the valve stem then press on it with the screwdriver until the grease squeezes out. The valve lock should now be stuck to the stem.
8. Repeat Steps 6 and 7 for the remaining valve lock.
9. Relieve the spring pressure slowly and insure that neither valve lock becomes dislodged by the retainer.
10. Remove the spring compressor tool.
11. Repeat Steps 2 through 10 until all of the springs have been installed.
12. Install the followers, camshaft(s) and any other components that were removed for disassembly.

2.5L Engine

1. Lightly lubricate the valve stems and insert all of the valves into the cylinder head. If possible, maintain their original locations.
2. If equipped, install any valve spring shims which were removed.
3. If equipped, install the new valve seals, keeping the following in mind:
• If the valve seal presses over the guide, lightly lubricate the outer guide surfaces.
• If the seal is an O-ring type, it is installed just after compressing the spring but before the valve locks.
4. Place the valve spring and retainer over the stem.
5. Position the spring compressor tool and compress the spring.
6. Assemble the valve locks to the stem.
7. Relieve the spring pressure slowly and insure that neither valve lock becomes dislodged by the retainer.
8. Remove the spring compressor tool.
9. Repeat Steps 2 through 8 until all of the springs have been installed.
10. Install the camshaft(s), rockers, shafts and any other components that were removed for disassembly.

Engine Block

GENERAL INFORMATION

A thorough overhaul or rebuild of an engine block would include replacing the pistons, rings, bearings, timing belt/chain assembly and oil pump. For OHV engines also include a new camshaft and lifters. The block would then have the cylinders bored and honed oversize (or if using removable cylinder sleeves, new sleeves installed) and the crankshaft would be cut undersize to provide new wearing surfaces and perfect clearances. However, your particular engine may not have everything worn out. What if only the piston rings have worn out and the clearances on everything else are still within factory specifications? Well, you could just replace the rings and put it back together, but this would be a very rare example. Chances are, if one component in your engine is worn, other components are sure to follow, and soon. At the very least, you should always replace the rings, bearings and oil pump. This is what is commonly called a "freshen up".

Cylinder Ridge Removal

Because the top piston ring does not travel to the very top of the cylinder, a ridge is built up between the end of the travel and the top of the cylinder bore.

Pushing the piston and connecting rod assembly past the ridge can be difficult, and damage to the piston ring lands could occur. If the ridge is not removed before installing a new piston or not removed at all, piston ring breakage and piston damage may occur.

→It is always recommended that you remove any cylinder ridges before removing the piston and connecting rod assemblies. If you know that new pistons are going to be installed and the engine block will be bored oversize, you may be able to forego this step. However, some ridges may actually prevent the assemblies from being removed, necessitating its removal.

There are several different types of ridge reamers on the market, none of which are inexpensive. Unless a great deal of engine rebuilding is anticipated, borrow or rent a reamer.
1. Turn the crankshaft until the piston is at the bottom of its travel.
2. Cover the head of the piston with a rag.
3. Follow the tool manufacturers instructions and cut away the ridge, exercising extreme care to avoid cutting too deeply.
4. Remove the ridge reamer, the rag and as many of the cuttings as possible. Continue until all of the cylinder ridges have been removed.

DISASSEMBLY

▶ **See Figures 280, 281 and 282**

The engine disassembly instructions following assume that you have the engine mounted on an engine stand. If not, it is easiest to disassemble the engine on a bench or the floor with it resting on the bell housing or transmission mounting surface. You must be able to access the connecting rod fasteners and turn the crankshaft during disassembly. Also, all engine covers (timing, front, side, oil pan, whatever) should have already been removed. Engines which are seized or locked up may not be able to be completely disassembled, and a core (salvage yard) engine should be purchased.

If not done during the cylinder head removal, remove the timing chain/belt and/or gear/sprocket assembly. Remove the oil pick-up and pump assembly and, if necessary, the pump drive. If equipped, remove any balance or auxiliary shafts. If necessary, remove the cylinder ridge from the top of the bore. See the cylinder ridge removal procedure earlier in this section.

Rotate the engine over so that the crankshaft is exposed. Use a number punch or scribe and mark each connecting rod with its respective cylinder num-

ber. The cylinder closest to the front of the engine is always number 1. However, depending on the engine placement, the front of the engine could either be the flywheel or damper/pulley end. Generally the front of the engine faces the front of the vehicle. Use a number punch or scribe and also mark the main bearing caps from front to rear with the front most cap being number 1 (if there are five caps, mark them 1 through 5, front to rear).

✳✳ WARNING

Take special care when pushing the connecting rod up from the crankshaft because the sharp threads of the rod bolts/studs will score the crankshaft journal. Insure that special plastic caps are installed over them, or cut two pieces of rubber hose to do the same.

Again, rotate the engine, this time to position the number one cylinder bore (head surface) up. Turn the crankshaft until the number one piston is at the bot-

Fig. 281 Place rubber hose over the connecting rod studs to protect the crankshaft and cylinder bores from damage

TCCS3803

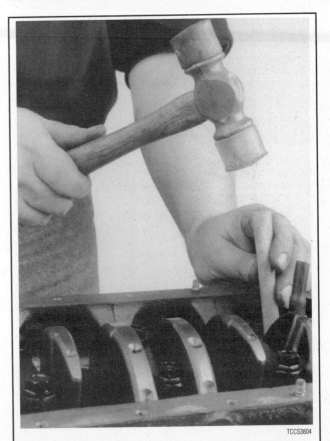

TCCS3804

Fig. 282 Carefully tap the piston out of the bore using a wooden dowel

91053P39

Fig. 280 The baffle is retained by four nuts, remove them to access the crankshaft and main bearings

tom of its travel, this should allow the maximum access to its connecting rod. Remove the number one connecting rods fasteners and cap and place two lengths of rubber hose over the rod bolts/studs to protect the crankshaft from damage. Using a sturdy wooden dowel and a hammer, push the connecting rod up about 1 in. (25mm) from the crankshaft and remove the upper bearing insert. Continue pushing or tapping the connecting rod up until the piston rings are out of the cylinder bore. Remove the piston and rod by hand, put the upper half of the bearing insert back into the rod, install the cap with its bearing insert installed, and hand-tighten the cap fasteners. If the parts are kept in order in this manner, they will not get lost and you will be able to tell which bearings came form what cylinder if any problems are discovered and diagnosis is necessary. Remove all the other piston assemblies in the same manner. On V-style engines, remove all of the pistons from one bank, then reposition the engine with the other cylinder bank head surface up, and remove that banks piston assemblies.

The only remaining component in the engine block should now be the crankshaft. Loosen the main bearing caps evenly until the fasteners can be turned by hand, then remove them and the caps. Remove the crankshaft from the engine block. Thoroughly clean all of the components.

INSPECTION

Now that the engine block and all of its components are clean, it's time to inspect them for wear and/or damage. To accurately inspect them, you will need some specialized tools:

- Two or three separate micrometers to measure the pistons and crankshaft journals
- A dial indicator
- Telescoping gauges for the cylinder bores
- A rod alignment fixture to check for bent connecting rods

If you do not have access to the proper tools, you may want to bring the components to a shop that does.

Generally, you shouldn't expect cracks in the engine block or its components unless it was known to leak, consume or mix engine fluids, it was severely over-heated, or there was evidence of bad bearings and/or crankshaft damage. A visual inspection should be performed on all of the components, but just because you don't see a crack does not mean it is not there. Some more reliable methods for inspecting for cracks include Magnaflux®, a magnetic process or Zyglo®, a dye pen-etrant. Magnaflux® is used only on ferrous metal (cast iron). Zyglo® uses a spray on fluorescent mixture along with a black light to reveal the cracks. It is strongly rec-ommended to have your engine block checked professionally for cracks, especially if the engine was known to have overheated and/or leaked or consumed coolant. Contact a local shop for availability and pricing of these services.

Engine Block

ENGINE BLOCK BEARING ALIGNMENT

Remove the main bearing caps and, if still installed, the main bearing inserts. Inspect all of the main bearing saddles and caps for damage, burrs or high spots. If damage is found, and it is caused from a spun main bearing, the block will need to be align-bored or, if severe enough, replacement. Any burrs or high spots should be carefully removed with a metal file.

Place a straightedge on the bearing saddles, in the engine block, along the centerline of the crankshaft. If any clearance exists between the straightedge and the saddles, the block must be align-bored.

Align-boring consists of machining the main bearing saddles and caps by means of a flycutter that runs through the bearing saddles.

DECK FLATNESS

The top of the engine block where the cylinder head mounts is called the deck. Insure that the deck surface is clean of dirt, carbon deposits and old gasket mater-ial. Place a straightedge across the surface of the deck along its centerline and, using feeler gauges, check the clearance along several points. Repeat the checking procedure with the straightedge placed along both diagonals of the deck surface. If the reading exceeds 0.003 in. (0.076mm) within a 6.0 in. (15.2cm) span, or 0.006 in. (0.152mm) over the total length of the deck, it must be machined.

CYLINDER BORES

♦ See Figure 283

The cylinder bores house the pistons and are slightly larger than the pistons themselves. A common piston-to-bore clearance is 0.0015–0.0025 in.

(0.0381mm–0.0635mm). Inspect and measure the cylinder bores. The bore should be checked for out-of-roundness, taper and size. The results of this inspection will determine whether the cylinder can be used in its existing size and condition, or a rebore to the next oversize is required (or in the case of removable sleeves, have replacements installed).

The amount of cylinder wall wear is always greater at the top of the cylinder than at the bottom. This wear is known as taper. Any cylinder that has a taper of 0.0012 in. (0.305mm) or more, must be rebored. Measurements are taken at a number of positions in each cylinder: at the top, middle and bottom and at two points at each position; that is, at a point 90 degrees from the crankshaft center-line, as well as a point parallel to the crankshaft centerline. The measurements are made with either a special dial indicator or a telescopic gauge and microme-ter. If the necessary precision tools to check the bore are not available, take the block to a machine shop and have them mike it. Also if you don't have the tools to check the cylinder bores, chances are you will not have the necessary devices to check the pistons, connecting rods and crankshaft. Take these components with you and save yourself an extra trip.

For our procedures, we will use a telescopic gauge and a micrometer. You will need one of each, with a measuring range which covers your cylinder bore size.

1. Position the telescopic gauge in the cylinder bore, loosen the gauges lock and allow it to expand.

➡Your first two readings will be at the top of the cylinder bore, then proceed to the middle and finally the bottom, making a total of six mea-surements.

2. Hold the gauge square in the bore, 90 degrees from the crankshaft center-line, and gently tighten the lock. Tilt the gauge back to remove it from the bore.
3. Measure the gauge with the micrometer and record the reading.
4. Again, hold the gauge square in the bore, this time parallel to the crank-shaft centerline, and gently tighten the lock. Again, you will tilt the gauge back to remove it from the bore.
5. Measure the gauge with the micrometer and record this reading. The differ-ence between these two readings is the out-of-round measurement of the cylinder.
6. Repeat steps 1 through 5, each time going to the next lower position, until you reach the bottom of the cylinder. Then go to the next cylinder, and con-tinue until all of the cylinders have been measured.

The difference between these measurements will tell you all about the wear in your cylinders. The measurements which were taken 90 degrees from the crank-shaft centerline will always reflect the most wear. That is because at this position is where the engine power presses the piston against the cylinder bore the hard-est. This is known as thrust wear. Take your top, 90 degree measurement and compare it to your bottom, 90 degree measurement. The difference between them is the taper. When you measure your pistons, you will compare these readings to your piston sizes and determine piston-to-wall clearance.

Crankshaft

Inspect the crankshaft for visible signs of wear or damage. All of the journals should be perfectly round and smooth. Slight scores are normal for a used crankshaft, but you should hardly feel them with your fingernail. When measur-ing the crankshaft with a micrometer, you will take readings at the front and rear of each journal, then turn the micrometer 90 degrees and take two more read-ings, front and rear. The difference between the front-to-rear readings is the journal taper and the first-to-90 degree reading is the out-of-round measure-ment. Generally, there should be no taper or out-of-roundness found, however, up to 0.0005 in. (0.0127mm) for either can be overlooked. Also, the readings should fall within the factory specifications for journal diameters.

If the crankshaft journals fall within specifications, it is recommended that it be polished before being returned to service. Polishing the crankshaft insures that any minor burrs or high spots are smoothed, thereby reducing the chance of scoring the new bearings.

Pistons and Connecting Rods

PISTONS

♦ See Figure 284

The piston should be visually inspected for any signs of cracking or burning (caused by hot spots or detonation), and scuffing or excessive wear on the skirts. The wrist pin attaches the piston to the connecting rod. The piston should move freely on the wrist pin, both sliding and pivoting. Grasp the con-necting rod securely, or mount it in a vise, and try to rock the piston back and

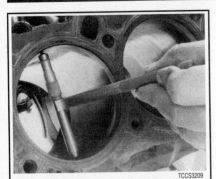

Fig. 283 Use a telescoping gauge to measure the cylinder bore diameter—take several readings within the same bore

Fig. 284 Measure the piston's outer diameter, perpendicular to the wrist pin, with a micrometer

Fig. 285 Use a ball type cylinder hone to remove any glaze and provide a new surface for seating the piston rings

forth along the centerline of the wrist pin. There should not be any excessive play evident between the piston and the pin. If there are C-clips retaining the pin in the piston then you have wrist pin bushings in the rods. There should not be any excessive play between the wrist pin and the rod bushing. Normal clearance for the wrist pin is approx. 0.001–0.002 in. (0.025mm–0.051mm).

Use a micrometer and measure the diameter of the piston, perpendicular to the wrist pin, on the skirt. Compare the reading to its original cylinder measurement obtained earlier. The difference between the two readings is the piston-to-wall clearance. If the clearance is within specifications, the piston may be used as is. If the piston is out of specification, but the bore is not, you will need a new piston. If both are out of specification, you will need the cylinder rebored and oversize pistons installed. Generally if two or more pistons/bores are out of specification, it is best to rebore the entire block and purchase a complete set of oversize pistons.

CONNECTING ROD

You should have the connecting rod checked for straightness at a machine shop. If the connecting rod is bent, it will unevenly wear the bearing and piston, as well as place greater stress on these components. Any bent or twisted connecting rods must be replaced. If the rods are straight and the wrist pin clearance is within specifications, then only the bearing end of the rod need be checked. Place the connecting rod into a vice, with the bearing inserts in place, install the cap to the rod and torque the fasteners to specifications. Use a telescoping gauge and carefully measure the inside diameter of the bearings. Compare this reading to the rods original crankshaft journal diameter measurement. The difference is the oil clearance. If the oil clearance is not within specifications, install new bearings in the rod and take another measurement. If the clearance is still out of specifications, and the crankshaft is not, the rod will need to be reconditioned by a machine shop.

➥You can also use Plastigage® to check the bearing clearances. The assembling section has complete instructions on its use.

Camshaft

Inspect the camshaft and lifters/followers as described earlier in this section.

Bearings

All of the engine bearings should be visually inspected for wear and/or damage. The bearing should look evenly worn all around with no deep scores or pits. If the bearing is severely worn, scored, pitted or heat blued, then the bearing, and the components that use it, should be brought to a machine shop for inspection. Full-circle bearings (used on most camshafts, auxiliary shafts, balance shafts, etc.) require specialized tools for removal and installation, and should be brought to a machine shop for service.

Oil Pump

➥The oil pump is responsible for providing constant lubrication to the whole engine and so it is recommended that a new oil pump be installed when rebuilding the engine.

Completely disassemble the oil pump and thoroughly clean all of the components. Inspect the oil pump gears and housing for wear and/or damage. Insure that the pressure relief valve operates properly and there is no binding or stick-ing due to varnish or debris. If all of the parts are in proper working condition, lubricate the gears and relief valve, and assemble the pump.

REFINISHING

▶ See Figure 285

Almost all engine block refinishing must be performed by a machine shop. If the cylinders are not to be rebored, then the cylinder glaze can be removed with a ball hone. When removing cylinder glaze with a ball hone, use a light or penetrating type oil to lubricate the hone. Do not allow the hone to run dry as this may cause excessive scoring of the cylinder bores and wear on the hone. If new pistons are required, they will need to be installed to the connecting rods. This should be performed by a machine shop as the pistons must be installed in the correct relationship to the rod or engine damage can occur.

Pistons and Connecting Rods

▶ See Figure 286

Only pistons with the wrist pin retained by C-clips are serviceable by the home-mechanic. Press fit pistons require special presses and/or heaters to remove/install the connecting rod and should only be performed by a machine shop.

All pistons will have a mark indicating the direction to the front of the engine and the must be installed into the engine in that manner. Usually it is a notch or arrow on the top of the piston, or it may be the letter F cast or stamped into the piston.

C-CLIP TYPE PISTONS

1. Note the location of the forward mark on the piston and mark the connecting rod in relation.
2. Remove the C-clips from the piston and withdraw the wrist pin.

➥Varnish build-up or C-clip groove burrs may increase the difficulty of removing the wrist pin. If necessary, use a punch or drift to carefully tap the wrist pin out.

3. Insure that the wrist pin bushing in the connecting rod is usable, and lubricate it with assembly lube.
4. Remove the wrist pin from the new piston and lubricate the pin bores on the piston.
5. Align the forward marks on the piston and the connecting rod and install the wrist pin.
6. The new C-clips will have a flat and a rounded side to them. Install both C-clips with the flat side facing out.
7. Repeat all of the steps for each piston being replaced.

ASSEMBLY

Before you begin assembling the engine, first give yourself a clean, dirt free work area. Next, clean every engine component again. The key to a good assembly is cleanliness.

Mount the engine block into the engine stand and wash it one last time using water and detergent (dishwashing detergent works well). While washing it, scrub the cylinder bores with a soft bristle brush and thoroughly clean all of the oil passages. Completely dry the engine and spray the entire assembly down with

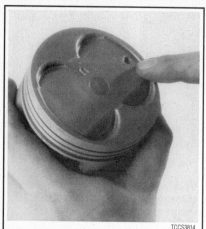

Fig. 286 Most pistons are marked to indicate positioning in the engine (usually a mark means the side facing the front)

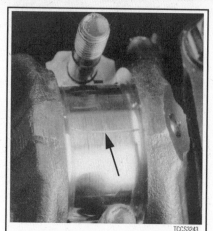

Fig. 287 Apply a strip of gauging material to the bearing journal, then install and torque the cap

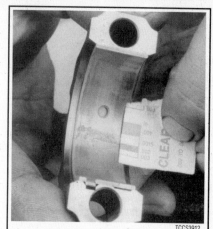

Fig. 288 After the cap is removed again, use the scale supplied with the gauging material to check the clearance

an anti-rust solution such as WD-40® or similar product. Take a clean lint-free rag and wipe up any excess anti-rust solution from the bores, bearing saddles, etc. Repeat the final cleaning process on the crankshaft. Replace any freeze or oil galley plugs which were removed during disassembly.

Crankshaft

♦ **See Figures 287, 288, 289 and 290**

1. Remove the main bearing inserts from the block and bearing caps.
2. If the crankshaft main bearing journals have been refinished to a definite undersize, install the correct undersize bearing. Be sure that the bearing inserts and bearing bores are clean. Foreign material under inserts will distort bearing and cause failure.
3. Place the upper main bearing inserts in bores with tang in slot.

➡The oil holes in the bearing inserts must be aligned with the oil holes in the cylinder block.

4. Install the lower main bearing inserts in bearing caps.
5. Clean the mating surfaces of block and rear main bearing cap.
6. Carefully lower the crankshaft into place. Be careful not to damage bearing surfaces.
7. Check the clearance of each main bearing by using the following procedure:
   a. Place a piece of Plastigage® or its equivalent, on bearing surface across full width of bearing cap and about ¼ in. off center.
   b. Install cap and tighten bolts to specifications. Do not turn crankshaft while Plastigage® is in place.
   c. Remove the cap. Using the supplied Plastigage® scale, check width of Plastigage® at widest point to get maximum clearance. Difference between readings is taper of journal.
   d. If clearance exceeds specified limits, try a 0.001 in. or 0.002 in. undersize bearing in combination with the standard bearing. Bearing clearance must be within specified limits. If standard and 0.002 in. undersize bearing does not bring clearance within desired limits, refinish crankshaft journal, then install undersize bearings.
8. After the bearings have been fitted, apply a light coat of engine oil to the journals and bearings. Install the rear main bearing cap. Install all bearing caps except the thrust bearing cap. Be sure that main bearing caps are installed in original locations. Tighten the bearing cap bolts to specifications.
9. Install the thrust bearing cap with bolts finger-tight.
10. Pry the crankshaft forward against the thrust surface of upper half of bearing.
11. Hold the crankshaft forward and pry the thrust bearing cap to the rear. This aligns the thrust surfaces of both halves of the bearing.
12. Retain the forward pressure on the crankshaft. Tighten the cap bolts to specifications.
13. Measure the crankshaft end-play as follows:
   a. Mount a dial gauge to the engine block and position the tip of the gauge to read from the crankshaft end.
   b. Carefully pry the crankshaft toward the rear of the engine and hold it there while you zero the gauge.
   c. Carefully pry the crankshaft toward the front of the engine and read the gauge.
   d. Confirm that the reading is within specifications. If not, install a new thrust bearing and repeat the procedure. If the reading is still out of specifications with a new bearing, have a machine shop inspect the thrust surfaces of the crankshaft, and if possible, repair it.
14. Rotate the crankshaft so as to position the first rod journal to the bottom of its stroke.
15. Install the rear main seal.

Pistons and Connecting Rods

♦ **See Figures 291, 292, 293 and 294**

1. Before installing the piston/connecting rod assembly, oil the pistons, piston rings and the cylinder walls with light engine oil. Install connecting rod bolt protectors or rubber hose onto the connecting rod bolts/studs. Also perform the following:
   a. Select the proper ring set for the size cylinder bore.
   b. Position the ring in the bore in which it is going to be used.
   c. Push the ring down into the bore area where normal ring wear is not encountered.
   d. Use the head of the piston to position the ring in the bore so that the ring is square with the cylinder wall. Use caution to avoid damage to the ring or cylinder bore.
   e. Measure the gap between the ends of the ring with a feeler gauge. Ring gap in a worn cylinder is normally greater than specification. If the ring gap is greater than the specified limits, try an oversize ring set.
   f. Check the ring side clearance of the compression rings with a feeler gauge inserted between the ring and its lower land according to specification. The gauge should slide freely around the entire ring circumference without binding. Any wear that occurs will form a step at the inner portion of the lower land. If the lower lands have high steps, the piston should be replaced.
2. Unless new pistons are installed, be sure to install the pistons in the cylinders from which they were removed. The numbers on the connecting rod and bearing cap must be on the same side when installed in the cylinder bore. If a connecting rod is ever transposed from one engine or cylinder to another, new bearings should be fitted and the connecting rod should be numbered to correspond with the new cylinder number. The notch on the piston head goes toward the front of the engine.
3. Install all of the rod bearing inserts into the rods and caps.
4. Install the rings to the pistons. Install the oil control ring first, then the second compression ring and finally the top compression ring. Use a piston ring expander tool to aid in installation and to help reduce the chance of breakage.
5. Make sure the ring gaps are properly spaced around the circumference of the piston. Fit a piston ring compressor around the piston and slide the piston and connecting rod assembly down into the cylinder bore, pushing it in with the wooden hammer handle. Push the piston down until it is only slightly below

Fig. 289 A dial gauge may be used to check crankshaft end-play

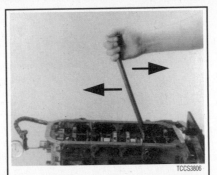

Fig. 290 Carefully pry the crankshaft back and forth while reading the dial gauge for end-play

Fig. 291 Checking the piston ring-to-ring groove side clearance using the ring and a feeler gauge

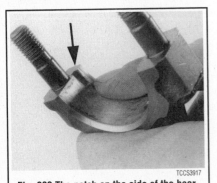

Fig. 292 The notch on the side of the bearing cap matches the tang on the bearing insert

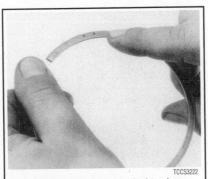

Fig. 293 Most rings are marked to show which side of the ring should face up when installed to the piston

Fig. 294 Install the piston and rod assembly into the block using a ring compressor and the handle of a hammer

the top of the cylinder bore. Guide the connecting rod onto the crankshaft bearing journal carefully, to avoid damaging the crankshaft.

6. Check the bearing clearance of all the rod bearings, fitting them to the crankshaft bearing journals. Follow the procedure in the crankshaft installation above.

7. After the bearings have been fitted, apply a light coating of assembly oil to the journals and bearings.

8. Turn the crankshaft until the appropriate bearing journal is at the bottom of its stroke, then push the piston assembly all the way down until the connecting rod bearing seats on the crankshaft journal. Be careful not to allow the bearing cap screws to strike the crankshaft bearing journals and damage them.

9. After the piston and connecting rod assemblies have been installed, check the connecting rod side clearance on each crankshaft journal.

10. Prime and install the oil pump and the oil pump intake tube.

Cylinder Head(S)

1. Install the cylinder head(s) using new gaskets.
2. Install the timing sprockets/gears and the belt/chain assemblies.

Engine Covers and Components

Install the timing cover(s) and oil pan. Refer to your notes and drawings made prior to disassembly and install all of the components that were removed. Install the engine into the vehicle.

Engine Start-up and Break-in

STARTING THE ENGINE

Now that the engine is installed and every wire and hose is properly connected, go back and double check that all coolant and vacuum hoses are connected. Check that you oil drain plug is installed and properly tightened. If not already done, install a new oil filter onto the engine. Fill the crankcase with the proper amount and grade of engine oil. Fill the cooling system with a 50/50 mixture of coolant/water.

1. Connect the vehicle battery.
2. Start the engine. Keep your eye on your oil pressure indicator; if it does not indicate oil pressure within 10 seconds of starting, turn the vehicle off.

✵ WARNING

Damage to the engine can result if it is allowed to run with no oil pressure. Check the engine oil level to make sure that it is full. Check for any leaks and if found, repair the leaks before continuing. If there is still no indication of oil pressure, you may need to prime the system.

3. Confirm that there are no fluid leaks (oil or other).
4. Allow the engine to reach normal operating temperature (the upper radiator hose will be hot to the touch).
5. If necessary, set the ignition timing.
6. Install any remaining components such as the air cleaner (if removed for ignition timing) or body panels which were removed.

BREAKING IT IN

Make the first miles on the new engine, easy ones. Vary the speed but do not accelerate hard. Most importantly, do not lug the engine, and avoid sustained high speeds until at least 100 miles. Check the engine oil and coolant levels frequently. Expect the engine to use a little oil until the rings seat. Change the oil and filter at 500 miles, 1500 miles, then every 3000 miles past that.

KEEP IT MAINTAINED

Now that you have just gone through all of that hard work, keep yourself from doing it all over again by thoroughly maintaining it. Not that you may not have maintained it before, heck you could have had one to two hundred thousand miles on it before doing this. However, you may have bought the vehicle used, and the previous owner did not keep up on maintenance. Which is why you just went through all of that hard work. See?

2.0L (1999cc) ENGINE TORQUE SPECIFICATIONS

Components	English Specifications	Metric Specifications
A/C compressor bolts	15-22 ft. lbs.	20-30 Nm
Alternator bolts	34 ft. lbs.	47 Nm
Camshaft journal cap bolts ①	13-15 ft. lbs.	17-21 Nm
Camshaft position sensor retaining screw	13-17 ft. lbs.	18-23 Nm
Camshaft sprocket bolts	47-53 ft. lbs.	64-72 Nm
Connecting rod bolts		
Step 1	26 ft. lbs.	35 Nm
Step 2	Tighten the bolts an additional 85-95°	
Crankshaft main bearing cap bolts ①	59-66 ft. lbs.	80-90 Nm
Crankshaft position sensor retaining bolt	53-80 inch lbs.	6-9 Nm
Crankshaft pulley bolt	81-89 ft. lbs.	110-120 Nm
Cylinder head bolts ①		
1st step	15-22 ft. lbs.	20-30 Nm
2nd step	30-37 ft. lbs.	40-50 Nm
3rd step	Tighten the bolts an additional 90-120°	
EGR valve-to-exhaust manifold tube nut	26-33 ft. lbs.	35-45 Nm
Engine lifting eyes		
Rear	10-13 ft. lbs.	14-18 Nm
Front	29-40 ft. lbs.	39-55 Nm
Engine oil dipstick tube bolt	71-97 inch lbs.	8-11 Nm
Engine-to-automatic transaxle bolts	28-38 ft. lbs.	38-51 Nm
Engine-to-manual transaxle bolt	41-59 ft. lbs.	55-80 Nm
Exhaust manifold heat shield bolts	71-106 inch lbs.	8-12 Nm
Exhaust manifold nuts	13-16 ft. lbs.	17-21 Nm
Flywheel bolts		
Automatic transaxle	79-86 ft. lbs.	107-117 Nm
Manual transaxle	81-89 ft. lbs.	110-120 Nm
Front engine support insulator nuts and bolt	50-68 ft. lbs.	67-93 Nm
Heater tube bolts	79 inch lbs.	9 Nm
Intake manifold nuts	12-15 ft. lbs.	16-20 Nm
Lower radiator support	71-97 inch lbs.	8-11 Nm
Lower timing belt cover bolts	27-44 inch lbs.	3-5 Nm
Middle timing belt cover bolts	53-71 inch lbs.	6-8 Nm
Oil pan bolts	15-18 ft. lbs.	20-24 Nm
Oil pan drain plug	-15-21 ft. lbs.	21-28 Nm
Oil pan-to-transaxle bolts	25-34 ft. lbs.	34-46 Nm
Oil pressure sender	19 ft. lbs.	27 Nm
Oil pump bolts	71-102 inch lbs.	8-12 Nm
Oil pump screen cover and tube bolts	71-97 inch lbs.	8-11 Nm
Oil pump screen cover and tube support-main bearing retaining nut	13-15 ft. lbs.	17-21 Nm
Oil separator bolt	71-97 inch lbs.	8-11 Nm
Power steering pump bolts	15 ft. lbs.	20 Nm
Spark plugs	9-13 ft. lbs.	13-17 Nm
Spark plug cover bolts	62 inch lbs.	7 Nm
Splash shield assembly	62-97 inch lbs.	7-11 Nm
Thermostat water outlet	71-97 inch lbs.	8-11 Nm
Throttle body bolts	71-106 inch lbs.	8-12 Nm
Timing belt backplate bolts	80-97 inch lbs.	9-11 Nm
Timing belt idler pulley bolt	35 ft. lbs.	48 Nm
Timing belt tensioner bolt	26-30 ft. lbs.	35-40 Nm
Torque converter inspection cover bolt	28-38 ft. lbs.	38-51 Nm
Transaxle oil cooler line bolts	71-106 inch lbs.	8-12 Nm
Upper timing cover bolts	27-44 inch lbs.	3-5 Nm
Valve cover bolts	53-71 inch lbs.	6-8 Nm
Water pump bolts	12-15 ft. lbs.	16-20 Nm
Water pump pulley bolts	89-124 inch lbs.	10-24 Nm

VCT: Variable Cam Timing
① Refer to the procedure for the tightening sequence

91053C05A

2.5L (2507cc) ENGINE TORQUE SPECIFICATIONS

Components	English Specifications	Metric Specifications
A/C compressor bolts	15-22 ft. lbs.	20-30 Nm
Alternator bolts	34 ft. lbs.	47 Nm
Camshaft journal cap bolts ①	71-106 inch lbs.	8-12 Nm
Camshaft position sensor retaining screw	71-106 inch lbs.	8-12 Nm
Camshaft rear oil seal retainer bolts	71-106 inch lbs.	8-12 Nm
Connecting rod bolts		
Step 1	26-33 ft. lbs.	35-45 Nm
Step 2	Tighten the bolts an additional 85-95°	
Crankshaft position sensor retaining screw	71-106 inch lbs.	8-12 Nm
Crankshaft pulley bolt		
Step 1	89 ft. lbs.	120 Nm
Step 2	Loosen the bolt one full turn	
Step 3	35-39 ft. lbs.	47-53 Nm
Step 4	Tighten the bolts an additional 85-95°	
Cylinder head bolts ①		
Step 1	27-32 ft. lbs.	37-43 Nm
Step 2	Tighten the bolts an additional 85-95°	
Step 3	Loosen the bolts 85-95°	
Step 4	27-32 ft. lbs.	37-43 Nm
Step 5	Tighten the bolts an additional 85-95°	
Step 6	Tighten the bolts an additional 85-95°	
EGR valve	15-22 ft. lbs.	20-30 Nm
EGR valve-to-exhaust manifold tube nut	26-33 ft. lbs.	35-45 Nm
Engine lifting eye bolts	29-40 ft. lbs.	40-55 Nm
Engine oil dipstick tube bolt	71-106 inch lbs.	8-12 Nm
Engine-to-transaxle bolts	25-34 ft. lbs.	34-46 Nm
Exhaust manifold heat shield bolts	71-106 inch lbs.	8-12 Nm
Exhaust manifold nuts ①	13-16 ft. lbs.	17-21 Nm
Flywheel bolts	54-64 ft. lbs.	73-87 Nm
Front engine support isolator nuts and bolt	50-68 ft. lbs.	67-93 Nm
Lower cylinder block ①	②	
Lower intake manifold bolts ①	71-106 inch lbs.	8-12 Nm
Lower radiator support	71-97 inch lbs.	8-11 Nm
Oil pan baffle nuts	15-22 ft. lbs.	20-30 Nm
Oil pan bolts ①	15-22 ft. lbs.	20-30 Nm
Oil pan drain plug	16-22 ft. lbs.	22-30 Nm
Oil pan-to-transaxle bolts	25-34 ft. lbs.	34-46 Nm
Oil pressure sender	9-12 ft. lbs.	12-16 Nm
Oil pump bolts ①	71-106 inch lbs.	8-12 Nm
Oil pump screen cover and tube bolts	71-106 inch lbs.	8-12 Nm
Oil pump screen cover and tube support-main bearing retaining nut	15-22 ft. lbs.	20-30 Nm
Oil separator bolt	71-106 inch lbs.	8-12 Nm
Power steering pump bolts	15-22 ft. lbs.	20-30 Nm
Spark plugs	7-15 ft. lbs.	9-20 Nm
Spark plug cover bolts	62 inch lbs.	7 Nm
Splash shield assembly	62-97 inch lbs.	7-11 Nm
Thermostat water outlet	15-22 ft. lbs.	20-30 Nm
Throttle body bolts	71-106 inch lbs.	8-12 Nm
Timing chain guide retaining bolts	15-22 ft. lbs.	20-30 Nm
Timing chain tensioner retaining bolts	15-22 ft. lbs.	20-30 Nm
Timing cover bolts ①	15-22 ft. lbs.	20-30 Nm

91053C07

2.5L (2507cc) ENGINE TORQUE SPECIFICATIONS

Components	English Specifications	Metric Specifications
Torque converter inspection cover bolt	28-38 ft. lbs.	38-51 Nm
Transaxle oil cooler line bolts	71-106 inch lbs.	8-12 Nm
Upper intake manifold bolts ①	71-106 inch lbs.	8-12 Nm
Valve cover bolts ①	71-106 inch lbs.	8-12 Nm
Water crossover bolts	71-106 inch lbs.	9-12 Nm
Water pump-to-housing bolts	16-18 ft. lbs.	22-25 Nm
Water pump housing-to-cylinder head bolts		
Step 1	11-13 ft. lbs.	15-18 Nm
Step 2	Tighten the bolts an additional 85-95°	

VCT: Variable Cam Timing
① Refer to the procedure for the tightening sequence
② Step 1:Tighten the bolts in sequence to 26-44 inch lbs. (3-5 Nm)
  Step 2:Push the crankshaft rearward and seat the thrust washer
  Step 3: Tighten fasteners 1-8 to 16-21 ft. lbs. (22-28 Nm)
  Step 4: Tighten fasteners 9-16 to 27-32 ft. lbs. (37-43 Nm)
  Step 5: Rotate fasteners 1-16 an additional 85-95 degrees
  Step 6: Tighten fasteners 17-22 to 15-22 ft. lbs. (20-30 Nm)

91063C08

USING A VACUUM GAUGE

White needle = steady needle   Dark needle = drifting needle

The vacuum gauge is one of the most useful and easy-to-use diagnostic tools. It is inexpensive, easy to hook up, and provides valuable information about the condition of your engine.

Indication: Normal engine in good condition

Gauge reading: Steady, from 17-22 in./Hg.

Indication: Late ignition or valve timing, low compression, stuck throttle valve, leaking carburetor or manifold gasket.

Gauge reading: Low (15-20 in./Hg.) but steady

Indication: Weak valve springs, worn valve stem guides, or leaky cylinder head gasket (vibrating excessively at all speeds).

NOTE: A plugged catalytic converter may also cause this reading.

Gauge reading: Needle fluctuates as engine speed increases

Indication: Choked muffler or obstruction in system. Speed up the engine. Choked muffler will exhibit a slow drop of vacuum to zero.

Gauge reading: Gradual drop in reading at idle

Indication: Sticking valve or ignition miss

Gauge reading: Needle fluctuates from 15-20 in./Hg. at idle

Indication: Improper carburetor adjustment, or minor intake leak at carburetor or manifold

NOTE: Bad fuel injector O-rings may also cause this reading.

Gauge reading: Drifting needle

Indication: Burnt valve or improper valve clearance. The needle will drop when the defective valve operates.

Gauge reading: Steady needle, but drops regularly

Indication: Worn valve guides

Gauge reading: Needle vibrates excessively at idle, but steadies as engine speed increases

TCCS3G01

Troubleshooting Engine Mechanical Problems

Problem	Cause	Solution
External oil leaks	Cylinder head cover RTV sealant broken or improperly seated	Replace sealant; inspect cylinder head cover sealant flange and cylinder head sealant surface for distortion and cracks
	Oil filler cap leaking or missing	Replace cap
	Oil filter gasket broken or improperly seated	Replace oil filter
	Oil pan side gasket broken, improperly seated or opening in RTV sealant	Replace gasket or repair opening in sealant; inspect oil pan gasket flange for distortion
	Oil pan front oil seal broken or improperly seated	Replace seal; inspect timing case cover and oil pan seal flange for distortion
	Oil pan rear oil seal broken or improperly seated	Replace seal; inspect oil pan rear oil seal flange; inspect rear main bearing cap for cracks, plugged oil return channels, or distortion in seal groove
	Timing case cover oil seal broken or improperly seated	Replace seal
	Excess oil pressure because of restricted PCV valve	Replace PCV valve
	Oil pan drain plug loose or has stripped threads	Repair as necessary and tighten
	Rear oil gallery plug loose	Use appropriate sealant on gallery plug and tighten
	Rear camshaft plug loose or improperly seated	Seat camshaft plug or replace and seal, as necessary
Excessive oil consumption	Oil level too high	Drain oil to specified level
	Oil with wrong viscosity being used	Replace with specified oil
	PCV valve stuck closed	Replace PCV valve
	Valve stem oil deflectors (or seals) are damaged, missing, or incorrect type	Replace valve stem oil deflectors
	Valve stems or valve guides worn	Measure stem-to-guide clearance and repair as necessary
	Poorly fitted or missing valve cover baffles	Replace valve cover
	Piston rings broken or missing	Replace broken or missing rings
	Scuffed piston	Replace piston
	Incorrect piston ring gap	Measure ring gap, repair as necessary
	Piston rings sticking or excessively loose in grooves	Measure ring side clearance, repair as necessary
	Compression rings installed upside down	Repair as necessary
	Cylinder walls worn, scored, or glazed	Repair as necessary

TCCS3C02

Troubleshooting Engine Mechanical Problems

Problem	Cause	Solution
Excessive oil consumption (cont.)	Piston ring gaps not properly staggered	Repair as necessary
	Excessive main or connecting rod bearing clearance	Measure bearing clearance, repair as necessary
No oil pressure	Low oil level	Add oil to correct level
	Oil pressure gauge, warning lamp or sending unit inaccurate	Replace oil pressure gauge or warning lamp
	Oil pump malfunction	Replace oil pump
	Oil pressure relief valve sticking	Remove and inspect oil pressure relief valve assembly
	Oil passages on pressure side of pump obstructed	Inspect oil passages for obstruction
	Oil pickup screen or tube obstructed	Inspect oil pickup for obstruction
	Loose oil inlet tube	Tighten or seal inlet tube
Low oil pressure	Low oil level	Add oil to correct level
	Inaccurate gauge, warning lamp or sending unit	Replace oil pressure gauge or warning lamp
	Oil excessively thin because of dilution, poor quality, or improper grade	Drain and refill crankcase with recommended oil
	Excessive oil temperature	Correct cause of overheating engine
	Oil pressure relief spring weak or sticking	Remove and inspect oil pressure relief valve assembly
	Oil inlet tube and screen assembly has restriction or air leak	Remove and inspect oil inlet tube and screen assembly. (Fill inlet tube with lacquer thinner to locate leaks.)
High oil pressure	Excessive oil pump clearance	Measure clearances
	Excessive main, rod, or camshaft bearing clearance	Measure bearing clearances, repair as necessary
	Improper oil viscosity	Drain and refill crankcase with correct viscosity oil
	Oil pressure gauge or sending unit inaccurate	Replace oil pressure gauge
	Oil pressure relief valve sticking closed	Remove and inspect oil pressure relief valve assembly
Main bearing noise	Insufficient oil supply	Inspect for low oil level and low oil pressure
	Main bearing clearance excessive	Measure main bearing clearance, repair as necessary
	Bearing insert missing	Replace missing insert
	Crankshaft end-play excessive	Measure end-play, repair as necessary
	Improperly tightened main bearing cap bolts	Tighten bolts with specified torque
	Loose flywheel or drive plate	Tighten flywheel or drive plate attaching bolts
	Loose or damaged vibration damper	Repair as necessary

TCCS3C03

Troubleshooting Engine Mechanical Problems

Problem	Cause	Solution
Connecting rod bearing noise	• Insufficient oil supply	• Inspect for low oil level and low oil pressure
	• Carbon build-up on piston	• Remove carbon from piston crown
	• Bearing clearance excessive or bearing missing	• Measure clearance, repair as necessary
	• Crankshaft connecting rod journal out-of-round	• Measure journal dimensions, repair or replace as necessary
	• Misaligned connecting rod or cap	• Repair as necessary
	• Connecting rod bolts tightened improperly	• Tighten bolts with specified torque
Piston noise	• Piston-to-cylinder wall clearance excessive (scuffed piston)	• Measure clearance and examine piston
	• Cylinder walls excessively tapered or out-of-round	• Measure cylinder wall dimensions, rebore cylinder
	• Piston ring broken	• Replace all rings on piston
	• Loose or seized piston pin	• Measure piston-to-pin clearance, repair as necessary
	• Connecting rods misaligned	• Measure rod alignment, straighten or replace
	• Piston ring side clearance excessively loose or tight	• Measure ring side clearance, repair as necessary
	• Carbon build-up on piston is excessive	• Remove carbon from piston
Valve actuating component noise	• Insufficient oil supply	• Check for: (a) Low oil level (b) Low oil pressure (c) Wrong hydraulic tappets (d) Restricted oil gallery (e) Excessive tappet to bore clearance
	• Rocker arms or pivots worn	• Replace worn rocker arms or pivots
	• Foreign objects or chips in hydraulic tappets	• Clean tappets
	• Excessive tappet leak-down	• Replace valve tappet
	• Tappet face worn	• Replace tappet; inspect corresponding cam lobe for wear
	• Broken or cocked valve springs	• Properly seat cocked springs; replace broken springs
	• Stem-to-guide clearance excessive	• Measure stem-to-guide clearance, repair as required
	• Valve bent	• Replace valve
	• Loose rocker arms	• Check and repair as necessary
	• Valve seat runout excessive	• Regrind valve seat/valves
	• Missing valve lock	• Install valve lock
	• Excessive engine oil	• Correct oil level

TCCS3004

Troubleshooting Engine Performance

Problem	Cause	Solution
Hard starting (engine cranks normally)	• Faulty engine control system component	• Repair or replace as necessary
	• Faulty fuel pump	• Replace fuel pump
	• Faulty fuel system component	• Repair or replace as necessary
	• Faulty ignition coil	• Test and replace as necessary
	• Improper spark plug gap	• Adjust gap
	• Incorrect ignition timing	• Adjust timing
	• Incorrect valve timing	• Check valve timing; repair as necessary
Rough idle or stalling	• Incorrect curb or fast idle speed	• Adjust curb or fast idle speed (If possible)
	• Incorrect ignition timing	• Adjust timing to specification
	• Improper feedback system operation	• Refer to Chapter 4
	• Faulty EGR valve operation	• Test EGR system and replace as necessary
	• Faulty PCV valve air flow	• Test PCV valve and replace as necessary
	• Faulty TAC vacuum motor or valve	• Repair as necessary
	• Air leak into manifold vacuum	• Inspect manifold vacuum connections and repair as necessary
	• Faulty distributor rotor or cap	• Replace rotor or cap (Distributor systems only)
	• Improperly seated valves	• Test cylinder compression, repair as necessary
	• Incorrect ignition wiring	• Inspect wiring and correct as necessary
	• Faulty ignition coil	• Test coil and replace as necessary
	• Restricted air vent or idle passages	• Clean passages
	• Restricted air cleaner	• Clean or replace air cleaner filter element
Faulty low-speed operation	• Restricted idle air vents and passages	• Clean air vents and passages
	• Restricted air cleaner	• Clean or replace air cleaner filter element
	• Faulty spark plugs	• Clean or replace spark plugs
	• Dirty, corroded, or loose ignition secondary circuit wire connections	• Clean or tighten secondary circuit wire connections
	• Improper feedback system operation	• Refer to Chapter 4
	• Faulty ignition coil high voltage wire	• Replace ignition coil high voltage wire (Distributor systems only)
	• Faulty distributor cap	• Replace cap (Distributor systems only)
Faulty acceleration	• Incorrect ignition timing	• Adjust timing
	• Faulty fuel system component	• Repair or replace as necessary
	• Faulty spark plug(s)	• Clean or replace spark plug(s)
	• Improperly seated valves	• Test cylinder compression, repair as necessary
	• Faulty ignition coil	• Test coil and replace as necessary

TCCS3005

Troubleshooting Engine Performance

Problem	Cause	Solution
Faulty acceleration (cont.)	Improper feedback system operation	Refer to Chapter 4
Faulty high speed operation	Incorrect ignition timing	Adjust timing (if possible)
	Faulty advance mechanism	Check advance mechanism and repair as necessary (Distributor systems only)
	Low fuel pump volume	Replace fuel pump
	Wrong spark plug air gap or wrong plug	Adjust air gap or install correct plug
	Partially restricted exhaust manifold, exhaust pipe, catalytic converter, muffler, or tailpipe	Eliminate restriction
	Restricted vacuum passages	Clean passages
	Restricted air cleaner	Cleaner or replace filter element as necessary
	Faulty distributor rotor or cap	Replace rotor or cap (Distributor systems only)
	Faulty ignition coil	Test coil and replace as necessary
	Improperly seated valve(s)	Test cylinder compression, repair as necessary
	Faulty valve spring(s)	Inspect and test valve spring tension, replace as necessary
	Incorrect valve timing	Check valve timing and repair as necessary
	Intake manifold restricted	Remove restriction or replace manifold
	Worn distributor shaft	Replace shaft (Distributor systems only)
	Improper feedback system operation	Refer to Chapter 4
Misfire at all speeds	Faulty spark plug(s)	Clean or relace spark plug(s)
	Faulty spark plug wire(s)	Replace as necessary
	Faulty distributor cap or rotor	Replace cap or rotor (Distributor systems only)
	Faulty ignition coil	Test coil and replace as necessary
	Primary ignition circuit shorted or open intermittently	Troubleshoot primary circuit and repair as necessary
	Improperly seated valve(s)	Test cylinder compression, repair as necessary
	Faulty hydraulic tappet(s)	Clean or replace tappet(s)
	Improper feedback system operation	Refer to Chapter 4
	Faulty valve spring(s)	Inspect and test valve spring tension, repair as necessary
	Worn camshaft lobes	Replace camshaft
	Air leak into manifold	Check manifold vacuum and repair as necessary
	Fuel pump volume or pressure low	Replace fuel pump
	Blown cylinder head gasket	Replace gasket
	Intake or exhaust manifold passage(s) restricted	Pass chain through passage(s) and repair as necessary
Power not up to normal	Incorrect ignition timing	Adjust timing
	Faulty distributor rotor	Replace rotor (Distributor systems only)

TCCS3C06

Troubleshooting Engine Performance

Problem	Cause	Solution
Power not up to normal (cont.)	Incorrect spark plug gap	Adjust gap
	Faulty fuel pump	Replace fuel pump
	Faulty fuel pump	Replace fuel pump
	Incorrect valve timing	Check valve timing and repair as necessary
	Faulty ignition coil	Test coil and replace as necessary
	Faulty ignition wires	Test wires and replace as necessary
	Improperly seated valves	Test cylinder compression and repair as necessary
	Blown cylinder head gasket	Replace gasket
	Leaking piston rings	Test compression and repair as necessary
	Improper feedback system operation	Refer to Chapter 4
Intake backfire	Improper ignition timing	Adjust timing
	Defective EGR component	Repair as necessary
	Defective TAC vacuum motor or valve	Repair as necessary
Exhaust backfire	Air leak into manifold vacuum	Check manifold vacuum and repair as necessary
	Faulty air injection diverter valve	Test diverter valve and replace as necessary
	Exhaust leak	Locate and eliminate leak
Ping or spark knock	Incorrect ignition timing	Adjust timing
	Distributor advance malfunction	Inspect advance mechanism and repair as necessary (Distributor systems only)
	Excessive combustion chamber deposits	Remove with combustion chamber cleaner
	Air leak into manifold vacuum	Check manifold vacuum and repair as necessary
	Excessively high compression	Test compression and repair as necessary
	Fuel octane rating excessively low	Try alternate fuel source
	Sharp edges in combustion chamber	Grind smooth
	EGR valve not functioning properly	Test EGR system and replace as necessary
Surging (at cruising to top speeds)	Low fuel pump pressure or volume	Replace fuel pump
	Improper PCV valve air flow	Test PCV valve and replace as necessary
	Air leak into manifold vacuum	Check manifold vacuum and repair as necessary
	Incorrect spark advance	Test and replace as necessary
	Restricted fuel filter	Replace fuel filter
	Restricted air cleaner	Clean or replace air cleaner filter element
	EGR valve not functioning properly	Test EGR system and replace as necessary
	Improper feedback system operation	Refer to Chapter 4

TCCS3C07

Troubleshooting the Serpentine Drive Belt

Problem	Cause	Solution
Tension sheeting fabric failure (woven fabric on outside circumference of belt has cracked or separated from body of belt)	• Grooved or backside idler pulley diameters are less than minimum recommended • Tension sheeting contacting (rubbing) stationary object • Excessive heat causing woven fabric to age • Tension sheeting splice has fractured	• Replace pulley(s) not conforming to specification • Correct rubbing condition • Replace belt • Replace belt
Noise (objectional squeal, squeak, or rumble is heard or felt while drive belt is in operation)	• Belt slippage • Bearing noise • Belt misalignment • Belt-to-pulley mismatch • Driven component inducing vibration • System resonant frequency inducing vibration	• Adjust belt • Locate and repair • Align belt/pulley(s) • Install correct belt • Locate defective driven component and repair • Vary belt tension within specifications. Replace belt.
Rib chunking (one or more ribs has separated from belt body)	• Foreign objects imbedded in pulley grooves • Installation damage • Drive loads in excess of design specifications • Insufficient internal belt adhesion	• Remove foreign objects from pulley grooves • Replace belt • Adjust belt tension • Replace belt
Rib or belt wear (belt ribs contact bottom of pulley grooves)	• Pulley(s) misaligned • Mismatch of belt and pulley groove widths • Abrasive environment • Rusted pulley(s) • Sharp or jagged pulley groove tips • Rubber deteriorated	• Align pulley(s) • Replace belt • Replace belt • Clean rust from pulley(s) • Replace pulley • Replace belt
Longitudinal belt cracking (cracks between two ribs)	• Belt has mistracked from pulley groove • Pulley groove tip has worn away rubber-to-tensile member	• Replace belt • Replace belt
Belt slips	• Belt slipping because of insufficient tension • Belt or pulley subjected to substance (belt dressing, oil, ethylene glycol) that has reduced friction • Driven component bearing failure • Belt glazed and hardened from heat and excessive slippage	• Adjust tension • Replace belt and clean pulleys • Replace faulty component bearing • Replace belt
"Groove jumping" (belt does not maintain correct position on pulley, or turns over and/or runs off pulleys)	• Insufficient belt tension • Pulley(s) not within design tolerance • Foreign object(s) in grooves	• Adjust belt tension • Replace pulley(s) • Remove foreign objects from grooves

TCCS3C09

Troubleshooting the Serpentine Drive Belt

Problem	Cause	Solution
"Groove jumping" (belt does not maintain correct position on pulley, or turns over and/or runs off pulleys)	• Excessive belt speed • Pulley misalignment • Belt-to-pulley profile mismatched • Belt cordline is distorted	• Avoid excessive engine acceleration • Align pulley(s) • Install correct belt • Replace belt
Belt broken (Note: identify and correct problem before replacement belt is installed)	• Excessive tension • Tensile members damaged during belt installation • Belt turnover • Severe pulley misalignment • Bracket, pulley, or bearing failure	• Replace belt and adjust tension to specification • Replace belt • Replace belt • Align pulley(s) • Replace defective component and belt
Cord edge failure (tensile member exposed at edges of belt or separated from belt body)	• Excessive tension • Drive pulley misalignment • Belt contacting stationary object • Pulley irregularities • Improper pulley construction • Insufficient adhesion between tensile member and rubber matrix	• Adjust belt tension • Align pulley • Correct as necessary • Replace pulley • Replace pulley • Replace belt and adjust tension to specifications
Sporadic rib cracking (multiple cracks in belt ribs at random intervals)	• Ribbed pulley(s) diameter less than minimum specification • Backside bend flat pulley(s) diameter less than minimum • Excessive heat condition causing rubber to harden • Excessive belt thickness • Belt overcured • Excessive tension	• Replace pulley(s) • Replace pulley(s) • Correct heat condition as necessary • Replace belt • Replace belt • Adjust belt tension

TCCS3C10

Troubleshooting the Cooling System

Problem	Cause	Solution
High temperature gauge indication—overheating	• Coolant level low	• Replenish coolant
	• Improper fan operation	• Repair or replace as necessary
	• Radiator hose(s) collapsed	• Replace hose(s)
	• Radiator airflow blocked	• Remove restriction (bug screen, fog lamps, etc.)
	• Faulty pressure cap	• Replace pressure cap
	• Ignition timing incorrect	• Adjust ignition timing
	• Air trapped in cooling system	• Purge air
	• Heavy traffic driving	• Operate at fast idle in neutral intermittently to cool engine
	• Incorrect cooling system component(s) installed	• Install proper component(s)
	• Faulty thermostat	• Replace thermostat
	• Water pump shaft broken or impeller loose	• Replace water pump
	• Radiator tubes clogged	• Flush radiator
	• Cooling system clogged	• Flush system
	• Casting flash in cooling passages	• Repair or replace as necessary. Flash may be visible by removing cooling system components or removing core plugs.
	• Brakes dragging	• Repair brakes
	• Excessive engine friction	• Repair engine
	• Antifreeze concentration over 68%	• Lower antifreeze concentration percentage
	• Missing air seals	• Replace air seals
	• Faulty gauge or sending unit	• Repair or replace faulty component
	• Loss of coolant flow caused by leakage or foaming	• Repair or replace leaking component, replace coolant
	• Viscous fan drive failed	• Replace unit
Low temperature indication—undercooling	• Thermostat stuck open	• Replace thermostat
	• Faulty gauge or sending unit	• Repair or replace faulty component
Coolant loss—boilover	• Overfilled cooling system	• Reduce coolant level to proper specification
	• Quick shutdown after hard (hot) run	• Allow engine to run at fast idle prior to shutdown
	• Air in system resulting in occasional "burping" of coolant	• Purge system
	• Insufficient antifreeze allowing coolant boiling point to be too low	• Add antifreeze to raise boiling point
	• Antifreeze deteriorated because of age or contamination	• Replace coolant
	• Leaks due to loose hose clamps, loose nuts, bolts, drain plugs, faulty hoses, or defective radiator	• Pressure test system to locate source of leak(s) then repair as necessary

TCCS3C11

Troubleshooting the Cooling System

Problem	Cause	Solution
Coolant loss—boilover	• Faulty head gasket	• Replace head gasket
	• Cracked head, manifold, or block	• Replace as necessary
	• Faulty radiator cap	• Replace cap
Coolant entry into crankcase or cylinder(s)	• Faulty head gasket	• Replace head gasket
	• Crack in head, manifold or block	• Replace as necessary
Coolant recovery system inoperative	• Coolant level low	• Replenish coolant to FULL mark
	• Leak in system	• Pressure test to isolate leak and repair as necessary
	• Pressure cap not tight or seal missing, or leaking	• Repair as necessary
	• Pressure cap defective	• Replace cap
	• Overflow tube clogged or leaking	• Repair as necessary
	• Recovery bottle vent restricted	• Remove restriction
Noise	• Fan contacting shroud	• Reposition shroud and inspect engine mounts (on electric fans inspect assembly)
	• Loose water pump impeller	• Replace pump
	• Glazed fan belt	• Apply silicone or replace belt
	• Loose fan belt	• Adjust fan belt tension
	• Rough surface on drive pulley	• Replace pulley
	• Water pump bearing worn	• Remove belt to isolate. Replace pump.
	• Belt alignment	• Check pulley alignment. Repair as necessary.
No coolant flow through heater core	• Restricted return inlet in water pump	• Remove restriction
	• Heater hose collapsed or restricted	• Remove restriction or replace hose
	• Restricted heater core	• Remove restriction or replace core
	• Restricted outlet in thermostat housing	• Remove flash or restriction
	• Intake manifold bypass hole in cylinder head restricted	• Remove restriction
	• Faulty heater control valve	• Replace valve
	• Intake manifold coolant passage restricted	• Remove restriction or replace intake manifold

NOTE: *Immediately after shutdown, the engine enters a condition known as heat soak. This is caused by the cooling system being inoperative while engine temperature is still high. If coolant temperature rises above boiling point, expansion and pressure may push some coolant out of the radiator overflow tube. If this does not occur frequently it is considered normal.*

TCCS3C12

4

DRIVEABILITY AND EMISSIONS CONTROLS

AIR POLLUTION

The earth's atmosphere, at or near sea level, consists approximately of 78 percent nitrogen, 21 percent oxygen and 1 percent other gases. If it were possible to remain in this state, 100 percent clean air would result. However, many varied sources allow other gases and particulates to mix with the clean air, causing our atmosphere to become unclean or polluted.

Some of these pollutants are visible while others are invisible, with each having the capability of causing distress to the eyes, ears, throat, skin and respiratory system. Should these pollutants become concentrated in a specific area and under certain conditions, death could result due to the displacement or chemical change of the oxygen content in the air. These pollutants can also cause great damage to the environment and to the many man made objects that are exposed to the elements.

To better understand the causes of air pollution, the pollutants can be categorized into 3 separate types, natural, industrial and automotive.

Natural Pollutants

Natural pollution has been present on earth since before man appeared and continues to be a factor when discussing air pollution, although it causes only a small percentage of the overall pollution problem. It is the direct result of decaying organic matter, wind born smoke and particulates from such natural events as plain and forest fires (ignited by heat or lightning), volcanic ash, sand and dust which can spread over a large area of the countryside.

Such a phenomenon of natural pollution has been seen in the form of volcanic eruptions, with the resulting plume of smoke, steam and volcanic ash blotting out the sun's rays as it spreads and rises higher into the atmosphere. As it travels into the atmosphere the upper air currents catch and carry the smoke and ash, while condensing the steam back into water vapor. As the water vapor, smoke and ash travel on their journey, the smoke dissipates into the atmosphere while the ash and moisture settle back to earth in a trail hundreds of miles long. In some cases, lives are lost and millions of dollars of property damage result.

Industrial Pollutants

Industrial pollution is caused primarily by industrial processes, the burning of coal, oil and natural gas, which in turn produce smoke and fumes. Because the burning fuels contain large amounts of sulfur, the principal ingredients of smoke and fumes are sulfur dioxide and particulate matter. This type of pollutant occurs most severely during still, damp and cool weather, such as at night. Even in its less severe form, this pollutant is not confined to just cities. Because of air movements, the pollutants move for miles over the surrounding countryside, leaving in its path a barren and unhealthy environment for all living things.

Working with Federal, State and Local mandated regulations and by carefully monitoring emissions, big business has greatly reduced the amount of pollutant introduced from its industrial sources, striving to obtain an acceptable level. Because of the mandated industrial emission clean up, many land areas and streams in and around the cities that were formerly barren of vegetation and life, have now begun to move back in the direction of nature's intended balance.

Automotive Pollutants

The third major source of air pollution is automotive emissions. The emissions from the internal combustion engines were not an appreciable problem years ago because of the small number of registered vehicles and the nation's small highway system. However, during the early 1950's, the trend of the American people was to move from the cities to the surrounding suburbs. This caused an immediate problem in transportation because the majority of suburbs were not afforded mass transit conveniences. This lack of transportation created an attractive market for the automobile manufacturers, which resulted in a dramatic increase in the number of vehicles produced and sold, along with a marked increase in highway construction between cities and the suburbs. Multi-vehicle families emerged with a growing emphasis placed on an individual vehicle per family member. As the increase in vehicle ownership and usage occurred, so did pollutant levels in and around the cities, as suburbanites drove daily to their businesses and employment, returning at the end of the day to their homes in the suburbs.

It was noted that a smoke and fog type haze was being formed and at times, remained in suspension over the cities, taking time to dissipate. At first this "smog," derived from the words "smoke" and "fog," was thought to result from

industrial pollution but it was determined that automobile emissions shared the blame. It was discovered that when normal automobile emissions were exposed to sunlight for a period of time, complex chemical reactions would take place.

It is now known that smog is a photo chemical layer which develops when certain oxides of nitrogen (NOx) and unburned hydrocarbons (HC) from automobile emissions are exposed to sunlight. Pollution was more severe when smog would become stagnant over an area in which a warm layer of air settled over the top of the cooler air mass, trapping and holding the cooler mass at ground level. The trapped cooler air would keep the emissions from being dispersed and diluted through normal air flows. This type of air stagnation was given the name "Temperature Inversion."

TEMPERATURE INVERSION

In normal weather situations, surface air is warmed by heat radiating from the earth's surface and the sun's rays. This causes it to rise upward, into the atmosphere. Upon rising it will cool through a convection type heat exchange with the cooler upper air. As warm air rises, the surface pollutants are carried upward and dissipated into the atmosphere.

When a temperature inversion occurs, we find the higher air is no longer cooler, but is warmer than the surface air, causing the cooler surface air to become trapped. This warm air blanket can extend from above ground level to a few hundred or even a few thousand feet into the air. As the surface air is trapped, so are the pollutants, causing a severe smog condition. Should this stagnant air mass extend to a few thousand feet high, enough air movement with the inversion takes place to allow the smog layer to rise above ground level but the pollutants still cannot dissipate. This inversion can remain for days over an area, with the smog level only rising or lowering from ground level to a few hundred feet high. Meanwhile, the pollutant levels increase, causing eye irritation, respiratory problems, reduced visibility, plant damage and in some cases, even disease.

This inversion phenomenon was first noted in the Los Angeles, California area. The city lies in terrain resembling a basin and with certain weather conditions, a cold air mass is held in the basin while a warmer air mass covers it like a lid.

Because this type of condition was first documented as prevalent in the Los Angeles area, this type of trapped pollution was named Los Angeles Smog, although it occurs in other areas where a large concentration of automobiles are used and the air remains stagnant for any length of time.

HEAT TRANSFER

Consider the internal combustion engine as a machine in which raw materials must be placed so a finished product comes out. As in any machine operation, a certain amount of wasted material is formed. When we relate this to the internal combustion engine, we find that through the input of air and fuel, we obtain power during the combustion process to drive the vehicle. The by-product or waste of this power is, in part, heat and exhaust gases with which we must dispose.

The heat from the combustion process can rise to over 4000°F (2204°C). The dissipation of this heat is controlled by a ram air effect, the use of cooling fans to cause air flow and a liquid coolant solution surrounding the combustion area to transfer the heat of combustion through the cylinder walls and into the coolant. The coolant is then directed to a thin-finned, multi-tubed radiator, from which the excess heat is transferred to the atmosphere by 1 of the 3 heat transfer methods, conduction, convection or radiation.

The cooling of the combustion area is an important part in the control of exhaust emissions. To understand the behavior of the combustion and transfer of its heat, consider the air/fuel charge. It is ignited and the flame front burns progressively across the combustion chamber until the burning charge reaches the cylinder walls. Some of the fuel in contact with the walls is not hot enough to burn, thereby snuffing out or quenching the combustion process. This leaves unburned fuel in the combustion chamber. This unburned fuel is then forced out of the cylinder and into the exhaust system, along with the exhaust gases.

Many attempts have been made to minimize the amount of unburned fuel in the combustion chambers due to quenching, by increasing the coolant temperature and lessening the contact area of the coolant around the combustion area. However, design limitations within the combustion chambers prevent the complete burning of the air/fuel charge, so a certain amount of the unburned fuel is still expelled into the exhaust system, regardless of modifications to the engine.

AUTOMOTIVE EMISSIONS

Before emission controls were mandated on internal combustion engines, other sources of engine pollutants were discovered along with the exhaust emissions. It was determined that engine combustion exhaust produced approximately 60 percent of the total emission pollutants, fuel evaporation from the fuel tank and carburetor vents produced 20 percent, with the final 20 percent being produced through the crankcase as a by-product of the combustion process.

Exhaust Gases

The exhaust gases emitted into the atmosphere are a combination of burned and unburned fuel. To understand the exhaust emission and its composition, we must review some basic chemistry.

When the air/fuel mixture is introduced into the engine, we are mixing air, composed of nitrogen (78 percent), oxygen (21 percent) and other gases (1 percent) with the fuel, which is 100 percent hydrocarbons (HC), in a semi-controlled ratio. As the combustion process is accomplished, power is produced to move the vehicle while the heat of combustion is transferred to the cooling system. The exhaust gases are then composed of nitrogen, a diatomic gas (N_2), the same as was introduced in the engine, carbon dioxide (CO_2), the same gas that is used in beverage carbonation, and water vapor (H_2O). The nitrogen (N_2), for the most part, passes through the engine unchanged, while the oxygen (O_2) reacts (burns) with the hydrocarbons (HC) and produces the carbon dioxide (CO_2) and the water vapors (H_2O). If this chemical process would be the only process to take place, the exhaust emissions would be harmless. However, during the combustion process, other compounds are formed which are considered dangerous. These pollutants are hydrocarbons (HC), carbon monoxide (CO), oxides of nitrogen (NOx) oxides of sulfur (SOx) and engine particulates.

HYDROCARBONS

Hydrocarbons (HC) are essentially fuel which was not burned during the combustion process or which has escaped into the atmosphere through fuel evaporation. The main sources of incomplete combustion are rich air/fuel mixtures, low engine temperatures and improper spark timing. The main sources of hydrocarbon emission through fuel evaporation on most vehicles used to be the vehicle's fuel tank and carburetor float bowl.

To reduce combustion hydrocarbon emission, engine modifications were made to minimize dead space and surface area in the combustion chamber. In addition, the air/fuel mixture was made more lean through the improved control which feedback carburetion and fuel injection offers and by the addition of external controls to aid in further combustion of the hydrocarbons outside the engine. Two such methods were the addition of air injection systems, to inject fresh air into the exhaust manifolds and the installation of catalytic converters, units that are able to burn traces of hydrocarbons without affecting the internal combustion process or fuel economy.

To control hydrocarbon emissions through fuel evaporation, modifications were made to the fuel tank to allow storage of the fuel vapors during periods of engine shut-down. Modifications were also made to the air intake system so that at specific times during engine operation, these vapors may be purged and burned by blending them with the air/fuel mixture.

CARBON MONOXIDE

Carbon monoxide is formed when not enough oxygen is present during the combustion process to convert carbon (C) to carbon dioxide (CO_2). An increase in the carbon monoxide (CO) emission is normally accompanied by an increase in the hydrocarbon (HC) emission because of the lack of oxygen to completely burn all of the fuel mixture.

Carbon monoxide (CO) also increases the rate at which the photo chemical smog is formed by speeding up the conversion of nitric oxide (NO) to nitrogen dioxide (NO_2). To accomplish this, carbon monoxide (CO) combines with oxygen (O_2) and nitric oxide (NO) to produce carbon dioxide (CO_2) and nitrogen dioxide (NO_2). ($CO + O_2 + NO = CO_2 + NO_2$).

The dangers of carbon monoxide, which is an odorless and colorless toxic gas are many. When carbon monoxide is inhaled into the lungs and passed into the blood stream, oxygen is replaced by the carbon monoxide in the red blood cells, causing a reduction in the amount of oxygen supplied to the many parts of the body. This lack of oxygen causes headaches, lack of coordination, reduced mental alertness and, should the carbon monoxide concentration be high enough, death could result.

NITROGEN

Normally, nitrogen is an inert gas. When heated to approximately 2500°F (1371°C) through the combustion process, this gas becomes active and causes an increase in the nitric oxide (NO) emission.

Oxides of nitrogen (NOx) are composed of approximately 97–98 percent nitric oxide (NO). Nitric oxide is a colorless gas but when it is passed into the atmosphere, it combines with oxygen and forms nitrogen dioxide (NO_2). The nitrogen dioxide then combines with chemically active hydrocarbons (HC) and when in the presence of sunlight, causes the formation of photo-chemical smog.

Ozone

To further complicate matters, some of the nitrogen dioxide (NO_2) is broken apart by the sunlight to form nitric oxide and oxygen. (NO_2 + sunlight = NO + O). This single atom of oxygen then combines with diatomic (meaning 2 atoms) oxygen (O_2) to form ozone (O_3). Ozone is one of the smells associated with smog. It has a pungent and offensive odor, irritates the eyes and lung tissues, affects the growth of plant life and causes rapid deterioration of rubber products. Ozone can be formed by sunlight as well as electrical discharge into the air.

The most common discharge area on the automobile engine is the secondary ignition electrical system, especially when inferior quality spark plug cables are used. As the surge of high voltage is routed through the secondary cable, the circuit builds up an electrical field around the wire, which acts upon the oxygen in the surrounding air to form the ozone. The faint glow along the cable with the engine running that may be visible on a dark night, is called the "corona discharge." It is the result of the electrical field passing from a high along the cable, to a low in the surrounding air, which forms the ozone gas. The combination of corona and ozone has been a major cause of cable deterioration. Recently, different and better quality insulating materials have lengthened the life of the electrical cables.

Although ozone at ground level can be harmful, ozone is beneficial to the earth's inhabitants. By having a concentrated ozone layer called the "ozonosphere," between 10 and 20 miles (16–32 km) up in the atmosphere, much of the ultra violet radiation from the sun's rays are absorbed and screened. If this ozone layer were not present, much of the earth's surface would be burned, dried and unfit for human life.

OXIDES OF SULFUR

Oxides of sulfur (SOx) were initially ignored in the exhaust system emissions, since the sulfur content of gasoline as a fuel is less than $\frac{1}{10}$ of 1 percent. Because of this small amount, it was felt that it contributed very little to the overall pollution problem. However, because of the difficulty in solving the sulfur emissions in industrial pollution and the introduction of catalytic converters to automobile exhaust systems, a change was mandated. The automobile exhaust system, when equipped with a catalytic converter, changes the sulfur dioxide (SO_2) into sulfur trioxide (SO_3).

When this combines with water vapors (H_2O), a sulfuric acid mist (H_2SO_4) is formed and is a very difficult pollutant to handle since it is extremely corrosive. This sulfuric acid mist that is formed, is the same mist that rises from the vents of an automobile battery when an active chemical reaction takes place within the battery cells.

When a large concentration of vehicles equipped with catalytic converters are operating in an area, this acid mist may rise and be distributed over a large ground area causing land, plant, crop, paint and building damage.

PARTICULATE MATTER

A certain amount of particulate matter is present in the burning of any fuel, with carbon constituting the largest percentage of the particulates. In gasoline, the remaining particulates are the burned remains of the various other compounds used in its manufacture. When a gasoline engine is in good internal condition, the particulate emissions are low but as the engine wears internally, the particulate emissions increase. By visually inspecting the tail pipe emissions, a determination can be made as to where an engine defect may exist. An engine with light gray or blue smoke emitting from the tail pipe normally indicates an increase in the oil consumption through burning due to internal engine wear. Black smoke would indicate a defective fuel delivery system, causing the engine to operate in a rich mode. Regardless of the color of the smoke, the internal part of the engine or the fuel delivery system should be repaired to prevent excess particulate emissions.

Diesel and turbine engines emit a darkened plume of smoke from the exhaust system because of the type of fuel used. Emission control regulations are mandated for this type of emission and more stringent measures are being used to prevent excess emission of the particulate matter. Electronic components are being introduced to control the injection of the fuel at precisely the proper time of piston travel, to achieve the optimum in fuel ignition and fuel usage. Other particulate after-burning components are being tested to achieve a cleaner emission.

Good grades of engine lubricating oils should be used, which meet the manufacturer's specification. Cut-rate oils can contribute to the particulate emission problem because of their low flash or ignition temperature point. Such oils burn prematurely during the combustion process causing emission of particulate matter.

The cooling system is an important factor in the reduction of particulate matter. The optimum combustion will occur, with the cooling system operating at a temperature specified by the manufacturer. The cooling system must be maintained in the same manner as the engine oiling system, as each system is required to perform properly in order for the engine to operate efficiently for a long time.

Crankcase Emissions

Crankcase emissions are made up of water, acids, unburned fuel, oil fumes and particulates. These emissions are classified as hydrocarbons (HC) and are formed by the small amount of unburned, compressed air/fuel mixture entering the crankcase from the combustion area (between the cylinder walls and piston rings) during the compression and power strokes. The head of the compression and combustion help to form the remaining crankcase emissions.

Since the first engines, crankcase emissions were allowed into the atmosphere through a road draft tube, mounted on the lower side of the engine block. Fresh air came in through an open oil filler cap or breather. The air passed through the crankcase mixing with blow-by gases. The motion of the vehicle and the air blowing past the open end of the road draft tube caused a low pressure area (vacuum) at the end of the tube. Crankcase emissions were simply drawn out of the road draft tube into the air.

To control the crankcase emission, the road draft tube was deleted. A hose and/or tubing was routed from the crankcase to the intake manifold so the blow-by emission could be burned with the air/fuel mixture. However, it was found that intake manifold vacuum, used to draw the crankcase emissions into the manifold, would vary in strength at the wrong time and not allow the proper emission flow. A regulating valve was needed to control the flow of air through the crankcase.

Testing, showed the removal of the blow-by gases from the crankcase as quickly as possible, was most important to the longevity of the engine. Should large accumulations of blow-by gases remain and condense, dilution of the engine oil would occur to form water, soots, resins, acids and lead salts, resulting in the formation of sludge and varnishes. This condensation of the blow-by gases occurs more frequently on vehicles used in numerous starting and stopping conditions, excessive idling and when the engine is not allowed to attain normal operating temperature through short runs.

Evaporative Emissions

Gasoline fuel is a major source of pollution, before and after it is burned in the automobile engine. From the time the fuel is refined, stored, pumped and transported, again stored until it is pumped into the fuel tank of the vehicle, the gasoline gives off unburned hydrocarbons (HC) into the atmosphere. Through the redesign of storage areas and venting systems, the pollution factor was diminished, but not eliminated, from the refinery standpoint. However, the automobile still remained the primary source of vaporized, unburned hydrocarbon (HC) emissions.

Fuel pumped from an underground storage tank is cool but when exposed to a warmer ambient temperature, will expand. Before controls were mandated, an owner might fill the fuel tank with fuel from an underground storage tank and park the vehicle for some time in warm area, such as a parking lot. As the fuel would warm, it would expand and should no provisions or area be provided for the expansion, the fuel would spill out of the filler neck and onto the ground, causing hydrocarbon (HC) pollution and creating a severe fire hazard. To correct this condition, the vehicle manufacturers added overflow plumbing and/or gasoline tanks with built in expansion areas or domes.

However, this did not control the fuel vapor emission from the fuel tank. It was determined that most of the fuel evaporation occurred when the vehicle was stationary and the engine not operating. Most vehicles carry 5–25 gallons (19–95 liters) of gasoline. Should a large concentration of vehicles be parked in one area, such as a large parking lot, excessive fuel vapor emissions would take place, increasing as the temperature increases.

To prevent the vapor emission from escaping into the atmosphere, the fuel systems were designed to trap the vapors while the vehicle is stationary, by sealing the system from the atmosphere. A storage system is used to collect and hold the fuel vapors from the carburetor (if equipped) and the fuel tank when the engine is not operating. When the engine is started, the storage system is then purged of the fuel vapors, which are drawn into the engine and burned with the air/fuel mixture.

EMISSION CONTROLS

Crankcase Ventilation System

OPERATION

♦ See Figures 1 and 2

When the engine is running, a small portion of the gases which are formed in the combustion chamber leak by the piston rings and enter the crankcase. Since these gases are under pressure they tend to escape from the crankcase and enter into the atmosphere. If these gases are allowed to remain in the crankcase for any length of time, they would contaminate the engine oil and cause sludge to build up. If the gases are allowed to escape into the atmosphere, they would pollute the air, as they contain unburned hydrocarbons. The crankcase ventilation system recycles these gases back into the engine combustion chamber, where they are burned.

Crankcase gases are recycled in the following manner. While the engine is running, clean filtered air is drawn into the crankcase through the intake air filter and then through a hose leading to the oil filler cap or the valve cover . As the air passes through the crankcase it picks up the combustion gases and carries them out of the crankcase, up through the PCV valve, and into the intake mani-

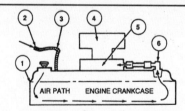

Item	Description
1	Valve Cover
2	To Fresh Air Source
3	Crankcase Ventilation Tube
4	Throttle Body
5	Intake Manifold
6	Positive Crankcase Ventilation Valve (PCV Valve)

91054G01

Fig. 1 Typical PCV air flow diagram

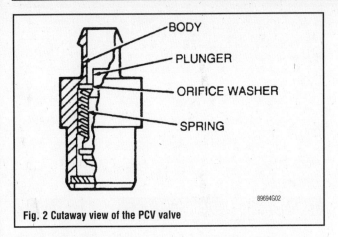

Fig. 2 Cutaway view of the PCV valve

Labels: BODY, PLUNGER, ORIFICE WASHER, SPRING

89694G02

fold. After they enter the intake manifold they are drawn into the combustion chamber and are burned.

The most critical component of the system is the PCV valve. This vacuum-controlled valve regulates the amount of gases which are recycled into the combustion chamber. At low engine speeds the valve is partially closed, limiting the flow of gases into the intake manifold. As engine speed increases, the valve opens to admit greater quantities of the gases into the intake manifold. If the valve should become blocked or plugged, the gases will be prevented from escaping the crankcase by the normal route. Since these gases are under pressure, they will find their own way out of the crankcase. This alternate route is usually a weak oil seal or gasket in the engine. As the gas escapes by the gasket, it also creates an oil leak. Besides causing oil leaks, a clogged PCV valve also allows these gases to remain in the crankcase for an extended period of time, promoting the formation of sludge in the engine.

COMPONENT TESTING

▶ **See Figure 3**

1. Remove the PCV valve from the valve cover grommet.
2. Shake the PCV valve.
  a. If the valve rattles when shaken, reinstall it and proceed to Step 3.
  b. If the valve does not rattle, it is sticking and must be replaced.
3. Start the engine and allow it to reach normal operating temperature.
4. Check the PCV valve for vacuum by placing your finger over the end of the valve.
  a. If vacuum exists, proceed to Step 5.
  b. If vacuum does not exist, check for loose hose connections, vacuum leaks or blockage. Correct as necessary.
5. Disconnect the fresh air intake hose from the air inlet tube (connects the air cleaner housing to the throttle body).
6. Place a stiff piece of paper over the hose end and wait 1 minute.
  a. If vacuum holds the paper in place, the system is OK; reconnect the hose.
  b. If the paper is not held in place, check for loose hose connections, vacuum leaks or blockage. Correct as necessary.

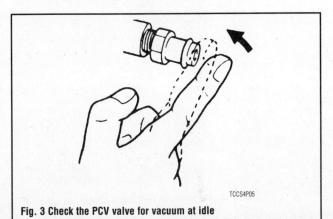

TCCS4P05

Fig. 3 Check the PCV valve for vacuum at idle

REMOVAL & INSTALLATION

Refer to Section 1 for removal and installation of the PCV valve. The PCV nipple should be replaced and inspected every 60,000 miles (96,000 km).

Evaporative Emission Controls

OPERATION

Changes in atmospheric temperature cause fuel tanks to breathe, that is, the air within the tank expands and contracts with outside temperature changes. If an unsealed system was used, when the temperature rises, air would escape through the tank vent tube or the vent in the tank cap. The air which escapes contains gasoline vapors.

The Evaporative Emission Control System provides a sealed fuel system with the capability to store and condense fuel vapors. When the fuel evaporates in the fuel tank, the vapor passes through the EVAP emission valve, through vent hoses or tubes to a carbon filled evaporative canister. When the engine is operating the vapors are drawn into the intake manifold and burned during combustion..

A sealed, maintenance free evaporative canister is used. The canister is filled with granules of an activated carbon mixture. Fuel vapors entering the canister are absorbed by the charcoal granules. A vent cap is located on the top of the canister to provide fresh air to the canister when it is being purged. The vent cap opens to provide fresh air into the canister, which circulates through the charcoal, releasing trapped vapors and carrying them to the engine to be burned.

Fuel tank pressure vents fuel vapors into the canister. They are held in the canister until they can be drawn into the intake manifold. The canister purge valve allows the canister to be purged at a pre-determined time and engine operating conditions.

Vacuum to the canister is controlled by the canister purge valve. The valve is operated by the PCM. The PCM regulates the valve by switching the ground circuit on and off based on engine operating conditions. When energized, the valve prevents vacuum from reaching the canister. When not energized the valve allows vacuum to purge the vapors from the canister.

During warm up and for a specified time after hot starts, the PCM energizes (grounds) the valve preventing vacuum from reaching the canister. When the engine temperature reaches the operating level of about 120°F (49°C), the PCM removes the ground from the valve allowing vacuum to flow through the canister and purges vapors through the throttle body. During certain idle conditions, the purge valve may be grounded to control fuel mixture calibrations.

The fuel tank is sealed with a pressure-vacuum relief filler cap. The relief valve in the cap is a safety feature, preventing excessive pressure or vacuum in the fuel tank. If the cap is malfunctioning, and needs to be replaced, ensure that the replacement is the identical cap to ensure correct system operation.

OBD-II EVAP System Monitor

1998–99 models have added system components due to the EVAP system monitor incorporated in the OBD-II engine control system. A pressure sensor is mounted on the fuel tank which measures pressure inside the tank, and a purge flow sensor measures the flow of the gases from the canister into the engine. The purge valve is now called the Vapor Management Valve (VMV). It performs the same functions as the purge valve, however it looks slightly different. A canister vent solenoid is mounted on the canister, taking the place of the vent cap, providing a source of fresh air to the canister.

The PCM can store trouble codes for EVAP system performance, a list of the codes is provided later in this section. Normal testing procedure can be used, see EVAP System Component Testing in this Section.

COMPONENT TESTING

Evaporative Emissions Canister

▶ **See Figure 4**

Generally, the only testing done to the canister is a visual inspection. Look the canister over and replace it with a new one if there is any evidence of cracks or other damage.

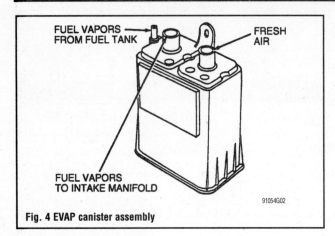

FUEL VAPORS FROM FUEL TANK

FRESH AIR

FUEL VAPORS TO INTAKE MANIFOLD

91054G02

Fig. 4 EVAP canister assembly

Evaporative Hoses and Tubes

Inspect all system hoses and tubes for signs of damage or cracks. Any damage or leakage must be repaired.

Evaporative Emissions Valve

▶ **See Figure 5**

Inspect the valve for open air passage through the orifice. The valve is molded directly to the fuel tank and is not serviceable separately. If the orifice is blocked, replace the fuel tank.

Canister Purge Valve/Vapor Management Valve

▶ **See Figure 6**

1. Remove the canister purge valve.
2. Measure the resistance between the two valve terminals.

a. If the resistance is between 30–36 ohms, proceed to the Step 3.
b. If the resistance is not between 30–36 ohms, replace the valve.
3. Attach a hand-held vacuum pump to the intake manifold vacuum side of the valve, then apply 16 in. Hg (53 kPa) of vacuum to the valve.

a. If the valve will not hold vacuum for at least 20 seconds replace it with a new one.
b. If the valve holds vacuum, proceed to Step 4. Keep the vacuum applied to the valve.
4. Using an external voltage source, apply 9–14 DC volts to the valve electrical terminals.

a. If the valve opens and the vacuum drops, the valve is working properly. Check power and ground circuits.
b. If the valve does not open and the vacuum remains, replace the valve is faulty.

REMOVAL & INSTALLATION

Evaporative Emissions Canister

1995–97 MODELS

▶ **See Figures 7 thru 13**

1. Raise and support the vehicle.
2. Remove the bolt retaining the canister and bracket assembly.
3. Label and disconnect the vapor hoses from the canister.
4. Remove the pushpin, and remove the canister from the bracket.
5. Installation is the reverse of removal. Tighten bolt to 43–63 inch lbs. (5–7 Nm)

1998–99 MODELS

1. Raise and support the vehicle.
2. Remove the vent hose retaining clips.
3. Loosen, but do not remove, the canister carrier rear retaining bolts.
4. Remove the front canister carrier rear retaining bolt.

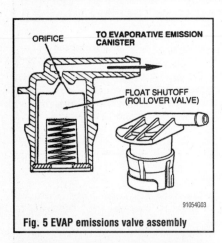

ORIFICE

TO EVAPORATIVE EMISSION CANISTER

FLOAT SHUTOFF (ROLLOVER VALVE)

91054G03

Fig. 5 EVAP emissions valve assembly

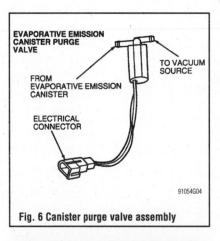

EVAPORATIVE EMISSION CANISTER PURGE VALVE

TO VACUUM SOURCE

FROM EVAPORATIVE EMISSION CANISTER

ELECTRICAL CONNECTOR

91054G04

Fig. 6 Canister purge valve assembly

91054P33

Fig. 7 Remove the retaining bolt from the canister's protective cover . . .

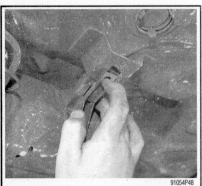

91054P48

Fig. 8 . . . and slide the retaining clip on the rear . . .

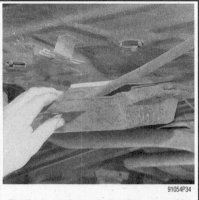

91054P34

Fig. 9 . . . to lower the canister assembly

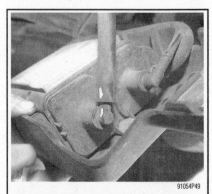

91054P49

Fig. 10 Matchmark the hoses for reinstallation

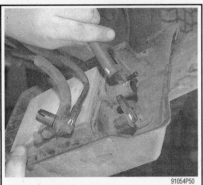

Fig. 11 Carefully remove the hoses from the canister

Fig. 12 Pry the retaining clips up . . .

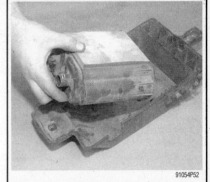

Fig. 13 . . . and lift the canister from the protective cover

5. Lower the canister carrier until the rear bolts support it.
6. Unplug the canister vent solenoid connector.
7. Remove the vapor tube connector from the canister.
8. Remove the rear carrier bolts and remove the carrier and canister.
9. Remove the canister vent solenoid from the canister.
10. Remove the canister from the carrier by prying upwards on the canister, and pulling the canister out.
11. Installation is the reverse of removal. Tighten the retaining bolts to 37 inch lbs. (6 Nm).

Evaporative Emissions Valve

1. Raise and support the vehicle.
2. Remove the fuel tank. See Section 5.
3. Disconnect the vapor hose from the valve.
4. Twist and remove the valve.
5. Installation is the reverse of removal.

Canister Purge Valve/Vapor Management Valve

1995–97 MODELS

1. Raise and support the vehicle.
2. Disconnect the electrical harness from the valve.
3. Disconnect the fuel vapor hoses and remove the valve.
4. Installation is the reverse of removal.

1998–99 MODELS

1. On 2.0L engine equipped vehicles:
   a. Remove the air cleaner outlet tube.
   b. Remove the air intake resonator.
2. On 2.5L engine equipped vehicles:
   a. Remove the ignition coil. See Section 2.
3. Disconnect the electrical harness from the valve.
4. Remove the valve retaining nuts.
5. Label and disconnect the vacuum and vapor hoses from the valve.
6. Remove the valve.
7. Installation is the reverse of removal.

Exhaust Gas Recirculation System

OPERATION

▶ See Figure 14

The Exhaust Gas Recirculation (EGR) system is designed to reintroduce exhaust gas into the combustion chambers, thereby lowering combustion temperatures and reducing the formation of Oxides of Nitrogen (NO_x).

The amount of exhaust gas that is reintroduced into the combustion cycle is determined by several factors, such as: engine speed, engine vacuum, exhaust system backpressure, coolant temperature, throttle position. All EGR valves are vacuum operated. The EGR vacuum diagram for your particular vehicle is displayed on the Vehicle Emission Control Information (VECI) label.

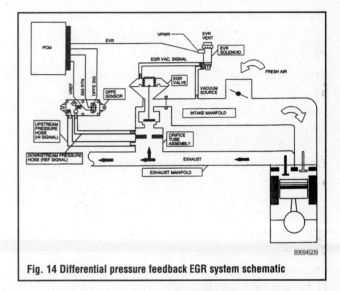

Fig. 14 Differential pressure feedback EGR system schematic

The EGR system is Differential Pressure Feedback EGR (DPFE) system, controlled by the Powertrain Control Module (PCM) and composed of the following components: DPFE sensor (also referred to as the backpressure transducer), EGR Vacuum Regulator (EVR) solenoid, EGR valve, and assorted hoses.

COMPONENT TESTING

DPFE Sensor

1. Disconnect the pressure hoses at the DPFE sensor.
2. Connect a hand vacuum pump to the downstream pickup marked **REF** on the sensor.
3. Using a multimeter, backprobe the SIG RTN circuit at the DPFE connector.
4. With the ignition **ON**, signal voltage should be 0.20–0.70 volts.
5. Apply 8–9 in. Hg of vacuum to the sensor. Voltage should be greater than 4 volts.
6. Quickly release the vacuum from the sensor. Voltage should drop to less than 1 volt in 3 seconds.
7. If the sensor does not respond as specified, check the power and ground circuits.
8. If power and ground circuits are functional, the sensor is faulty.

EVR Solenoid

1. Remove the EVR solenoid.
2. Attempt to lightly blow air into the EVR solenoid.
   a. If air blows through the solenoid, replace the solenoid with a new one.
   b. If air does not pass freely through the solenoid, continue with the test.
3. Apply battery voltage (approximately 12 volts) and a ground to the EVR

solenoid electrical terminals. Attempt to lightly blow air, once again, through the solenoid.

    a. If air does not pass through the solenoid, replace the solenoid with a new one.

    b. If air does not flow through the solenoid, the solenoid is OK.

4. If the solenoid is functional but the problem still exists, check the power and ground circuits.

EGR Valve

1. Install a tachometer on the engine, following the manufacturer's instructions.

2. Detach the engine wiring harness connector from the Idle Air Control (IAC) solenoid.

3. Disconnect and plug the vacuum supply hose from the EGR valve.

4. Start the engine, then apply the parking brake, block the rear wheels and position the transmission in Neutral.

5. Observe and note the idle speed.

➡**If the engine will not idle with the IAC solenoid disconnected, provide an air bypass to the engine by slightly opening the throttle plate or by creating an intake vacuum leak. Do not allow the idle speed to exceed typical idle rpm.**

6. Using a hand-held vacuum pump, slowly apply 5–10 in. Hg (17–34 kPa) of vacuum to the EGR valve nipple.

    a. If the idle speed drops more than 100 rpm with the vacuum applied and returns to normal after the vacuum is removed, the EGR valve is OK.

    b. If the idle speed does not drop more than 100 rpm with the vacuum applied and return to normal after the vacuum is removed, inspect the EGR valve for a blockage; clean it if a blockage is found. Replace the EGR valve if no blockage is found, or if cleaning the valve does not remedy the malfunction.

REMOVAL & INSTALLATION

DPFE Sensor

▸ **See Figures 15, 16, 17 and 18**

➡**The DPFE sensor is mounted on the firewall on the 2.0L engine, and on the upper intake on the 2.5L engine.**

1. Disconnect the negative battery cable.

2. On the 2.5L engine only, remove the air cleaner outlet tube and the IAC air tube.

3. Label and disconnect the wiring harness from the DPFE sensor.

4. Label and disconnect the vacuum hoses.

5. Remove the mounting screws and remove the DPFE sensor.

To install:

6. Position the DPFE sensor and tighten the mounting screws.

7. Attach all necessary hoses and wiring to the sensor.

8. On the 2.5L engine only, install the air cleaner outlet tube and IAC air tube.

9. Connect the negative battery cable.

EVR Solenoid

▸ **See Figures 19, 20, 21, 22 and 23**

➡**The EVR solenoid is mounted on the firewall on the 2.0L engine, and on the upper intake on the 2.5L engine.**

1. Disconnect the negative battery cable.

2. Label and detach the wiring harness connector from the EVR solenoid.

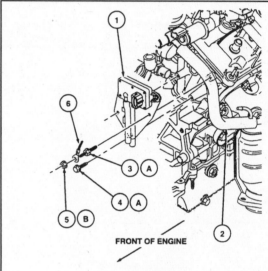

FRONT OF ENGINE

Item	Description
1	EGR Transducer
2	EGR Valve to Exhaust Manifold Tube
3	Stud Bolt
4	Bolt 2 Req'd)
5	Nut
6	Ignition Coil Ground Cable
A	Tighten to 8-12 N·m (71-106 Lb-In)
B	Tighten to 5-7 N·m (44-62 Lb-In)

91054G05

Fig. 15 DPFE sensor mounting—2.5L engine

91054P20

Fig. 16 Unplug the connector from the DPFE sensor

91054P21

Fig. 17 Remove the two retaining screws for the sensor

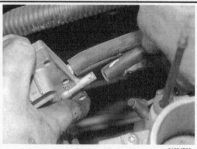

91054P22

Fig. 18 After the screws are removed, and the sensor can be moved, the sensor's hoses are more accessible. Make sure you matchmark the hoses for reinstallation

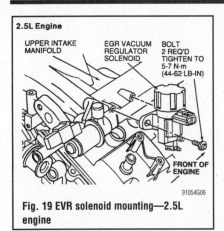

Fig. 19 EVR solenoid mounting—2.5L engine

Fig. 20 Unplug the connector from the EVR solenoid

Fig. 21 Remove the hoses from the EVR solenoid. The hoses are molded together and come off as one piece

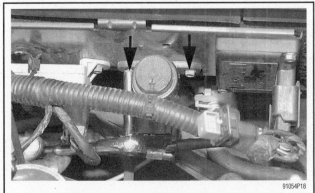

Fig. 22 Remove the two retaining bolts for the EVR solenoid and . . .

3. Detach the main emission vacuum control connector from the solenoid.

4. Remove the retaining bolts, and remove the solenoid.

To install:

5. Position the solenoid and install the retaining bolts.

6. Attach the main emission vacuum control connector and the wiring harness connector to the EVR solenoid.

7. Connect the negative battery cable.

EGR Valve

▸ **See Figures 24 thru 27, 50 thru 57**

1. Disconnect the negative battery cable.

2. On 2.0L engines, remove the air intake resonators.

3. On 2.5L engines, remove the air cleaner outlet tube.

4. Using a 22mm wrench or crowfoot, disconnect the EGR valve-to-exhaust manifold tube from the EGR valve.

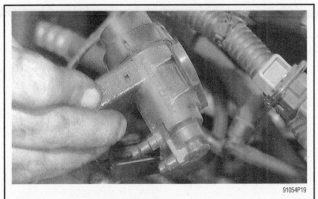

Fig. 23 . . . remove the EVR solenoid

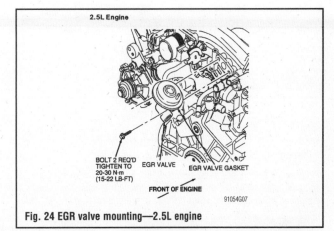

Fig. 24 EGR valve mounting—2.5L engine

Fig. 25 Remove the EGR tube from the bottom of the valve

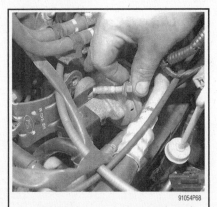

Fig. 26 Remove the valve retaining bolts

Fig. 27 The EGR valve gasket must be replaced

5. Remove the vacuum hose from the EGR valve.
6. Remove the EGR valve mounting fasteners, then separate the valve from the intake manifold.
7. Remove and discard the old EGR valve gasket, and clean the gasket mating surfaces on the valve and the intake manifold.

To install:

8. Install the EGR valve, along with a new gasket, on the upper intake manifold, then install and tighten the mounting bolts to 62–97 inch lbs.

(7–11 Nm) on the 2.0L engine, and 15–22 ft. lbs. (20–30 Nm) on the 2.5L engine.

9. Connect the EGR valve-to-exhaust manifold tube to the valve, then tighten the tube nut to 26–33 ft. lbs. (35–45 Nm).
10. Connect the vacuum hose to the EGR valve.
11. Install the air intake resonators or air cleaner outlet tube.
12. Connect the negative battery cable.

ELECTRONIC ENGINE CONTROLS

Powertrain Control Module

OPERATION

▶ See Figure 28

The Powertrain Control Module (PCM) performs many functions on your vehicle. The module accepts information from various engine sensors and computes the required fuel flow rate necessary to maintain the correct amount of air/fuel ratio throughout the entire engine operational range.

Based on the information that is received and programmed into the PCM's memory, the PCM generates output signals to control relays, actuators and solenoids. The PCM also sends out a command to the fuel injectors that meters the appropriate quantity of fuel. The module automatically senses and compensates for any changes in altitude when driving your vehicle.

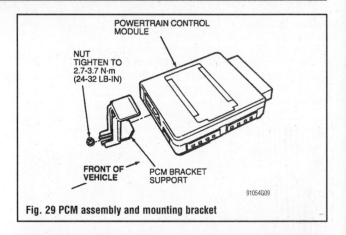

Fig. 29 PCM assembly and mounting bracket

Heated Oxygen Sensor (HO2S)

OPERATION

The oxygen (O2) sensor is a device which produces an electrical voltage when exposed to the oxygen present in the exhaust gases. The sensor is mounted in the exhaust system, usually in the manifold or a boss located on the down pipe before the catalyst.. The oxygen sensors used on the Ford Contour/Mercury Mystique/Mercury Cougar are electrically heated internally for faster switching when the engine is started cold. The oxygen sensor produces a voltage within 0 and 1 volt. When there is a large amount of oxygen present (lean mixture), the sensor produces a low voltage (less than 0.4v). When there is a lesser amount present (rich mixture) it produces a higher voltage (0.6–1.0v).The stoichiometric or correct fuel to air ratio will read between 0.4 and 0.6v. By monitoring the oxygen content and converting it to electrical voltage, the sensor acts as a rich-lean switch. The voltage is transmitted to the PCM.

Some models have two sensors, one before the catalyst and one after. This is done for a catalyst efficiency monitor that is a part of the OBD-II engine controls that are on 1996–99 year vehicles. The one before the catalyst measures the exhaust emissions right out of the engine, and sends the signal to the PCM about the state of the mixture as previously talked about. The second sensor reports the difference in the emissions after the exhaust gases have gone through the catalyst. This sensor reports to the PCM the amount of emissions reduction the catalyst is performing.

The oxygen sensor will not work until a predetermined temperature is reached, until this time the PCM is running in what as known as OPEN LOOP operation. OPEN LOOP means that the PCM has not yet begun to correct the air-to-fuel ratio by reading the oxygen sensor. After the engine comes to operating temperature, the PCM will monitor the oxygen sensor and correct the air/fuel ratio from the sensor's readings. This is what is known as CLOSED LOOP operation.

A heated oxygen sensor (HO2S) has a heating element that keeps the sensor at proper operating temperature during all operating modes. Maintaining correct sensor temperature at all times allows the system to enter into CLOSED LOOP operation sooner.

In CLOSED LOOP operation the PCM monitors the sensor input (along with other inputs) and adjusts the injector pulse width accordingly. During OPEN LOOP operation the PCM ignores the sensor input and adjusts the injector pulse to a preprogrammed value based on other inputs.

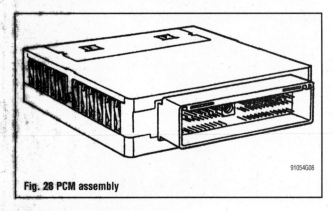

Fig. 28 PCM assembly

REMOVAL & INSTALLATION

▶ See Figure 29

➥When the battery has been disconnected, some abnormal driving symptoms may occur while the PCM relearns its fuel trim. The vehicle may need to be driven 10 miles (16 km) or more to relearn the fuel trim.

1. Disconnect the negative battery cable.
2. Remove the power steering fluid reservoir from its mount (without disconnecting the fluid lines), and position it out of the way.
3. Loosen the PCM harness connector retaining bolt.
4. Remove the engine harness connector from the PCM.
5. Lower the glove box door.
6. From inside the vehicle, remove the nut on the PCM support bracket and remove the bracket.
7. Remove the PCM.

To install:

8. Position the PCM into place.
9. Install the PCM support bracket and tighten the nut to 24–32 inch lbs. (3–4 Nm).
10. Reposition the glove box door.
11. Install the PCM harness connector and tighten the bolt to 32 inch lbs. (4 Nm).
12. Position the power steering fluid reservoir and tighten the retaining bolts.
13. Connect the negative battery cable.

TESTING

♦ See Figure 30

※※ WARNING

Do not pierce the wires when testing this sensor; this can lead to wiring harness damage. Backprobe the connector to properly read the voltage of the HO2S.

1. Disconnect the HO2S.
2. Measure the resistance between PWR and GND terminals of the sensor. Resistance should be approximately 6 ohms at 68°F (20°C). If resistance is not within specification, the sensor's heater element is faulty.
3. With the HO2S connected and engine running, measure the voltage with a Digital Volt-Ohmmeter (DVOM) between terminals **HO2S** and **SIG RTN** (GND) of the oxygen sensor connector. Voltage should fluctuate between 0.01–1.1 volts. If voltage fluctuation is slow or voltage is not within specification, the sensor may be faulty.

Fig. 30 The HO2S can be monitored with an appropriate and Datastream capable scan tool

REMOVAL & INSTALLATION

♦ See Figures 31 thru 39

➡An oxygen sensor wrench is available from Ford or aftermarket manufacturers to ease

1. Disconnect the negative battery cable.
2. Raise and support the vehicle safely.
3. Label and disconnect the HO2S from the engine control wiring harness.

➡Lubricate the sensor with penetrating oil prior to removal.

4. Remove the sensor using an oxygen sensor wrench or another suitable tool.

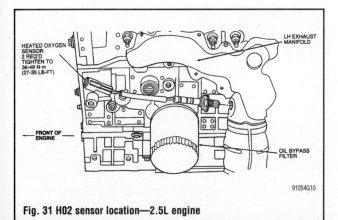

Fig. 31 HO2 sensor location—2.5L engine

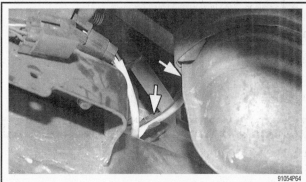

Fig. 32 Remove the HO2 sensor harness from the retaining clip and . . .

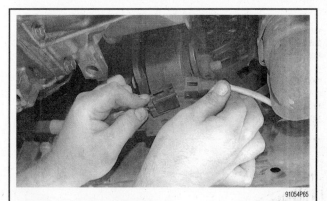

Fig. 33 . . . unplug the connector

Fig. 34 HO2 sensor is located on the exhaust manifold—1995 2.0L engine

Fig. 35 A special socket is recommended to remove the HO2 sensor(s). It can be purchased at most auto parts stores

Fig. 36 Place the harness into the slot in the socket and slide the socket down onto the sensor until the socket engages the sensor

Fig. 37 Carefully loosen the sensor by turning the socket counterclockwise with an appropriate drive tool

Fig. 38 After the sensor is removed from the manifold, take care in handling it if you plan to use it, if dropped they easily break

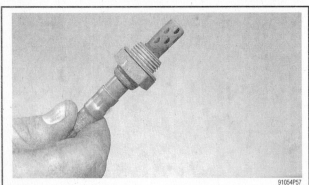

Fig. 39 Inspect the sensor for damage and build-up, replace if necessary

To install:

5. Install the sensor in the mounting boss and tighten to 27–33 ft. lbs. (37–45 Nm).
6. Connect the engine control wiring harness to the sensor.
7. Lower the vehicle.
8. Connect the negative battery cable.

Idle Air Control Valve

OPERATION

The Idle Air Control (IAC) valve adjusts the engine idle speed. The valve is located on the side of the throttle body. The valve is controlled by a duty cycle signal from the PCM and allows air to bypass the throttle plate in order to maintain the proper idle speed.

The IAC is located at the top of the upper intake manifold adjacent to the throttle body.

➡ Do not attempt to clean the IAC valve. Carburetor tune-up cleaners or any type of solvent cleaners will damage the internal components of the valve.

TESTING

▶ See Figure 40

1. Turn the ignition switch to the **OFF** position.
2. Disconnect the wiring harness from the IAC valve.
3. Measure the resistance between the terminals of the valve.

➡ Due to the diode in the solenoid, place the ohmmeter positive lead on the VPWR terminal and the negative lead on the ISC terminal.

4. Resistance should be 6–13 ohms.
5. If resistance is not within specification, the valve may be faulty.

REMOVAL & INSTALLATION

▶ See Figures 41, 42, 43 and 44

1. Disconnect the negative battery cable.
2. If your vehicle is equipped with the 2.0L engine, raise and support the vehicle.
3. Disconnnect the wiring harness from the IAC valve.
4. Remove the two retaining bolts.
5. Remove the IAC valve and discard the old gasket.

To install:

6. Clean the gasket mating surfaces thoroughly.
7. Using a new gasket, position the IAC valve on the throttle body.
8. Install and tighten the retaining bolts to 71–106 inch lbs. (8–12 Nm).
9. Connect the wiring harness to the IAC valve.

Fig. 40 The IAC can be monitored with an appropriate and Data-stream capable scan tool

Fig. 41 Unplug the connector from the IAC valve

Fig. 42 Remove the two retaining bolts and . . .

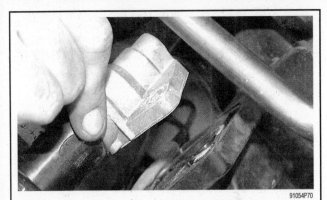

Fig. 43 . . . lift the IAC valve off of the intake manifold

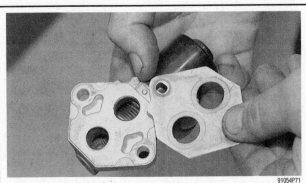

Fig. 44 The gasket must be replaced for the IAC valve or an air leak could occur possibly causing driveability problems

10. If raised, lower the vehicle.
11. Connect the negative battery cable.

Coolant Temperature Sensor

OPERATION

The Engine Coolant Temperature (ECT) sensor resistance changes in response to engine coolant temperature. The sensor resistance decreases as the coolant temperature increases, and increases as the coolant temperature decreases. This provides a reference signal to the PCM, which indicates engine coolant temperature. The signal sent to the PCM by the ECT sensor helps the PCM to determine spark advance, EGR flow rate, air/fuel ratio, and engine temperature. The ECT also is used for temperature gauge operation by sending it's signal to the instrument cluster.

The ECT is a two wire sensor, a 5-volt reference signal is sent to the sensor and the signal return is based upon the change in the measured resistance due to temperature.

TESTING

▶ See Figures 45, 46, 47, 48 and 49

1. Disconnect the engine wiring harness from the ECT sensor.
2. Connect an ohmmeter between the ECT sensor terminals.
3. With the engine cold and the ignition switch in the **OFF** position, measure and note the ECT sensor resistance.
4. Connect the engine wiring harness to the sensor.
5. Start the engine and allow the engine to reach normal operating temperature.
6. Once the engine has reached normal operating temperature, turn the engine **OFF**.
7. Once again, disconnect the engine wiring harness from the ECT sensor.
8. Measure and note the ECT sensor resistance with the engine hot.

Fig. 45 Unplug the ECT sensor to access the sensor

Fig. 46 Test the resistance of the ECT sensor across the two sensor pins

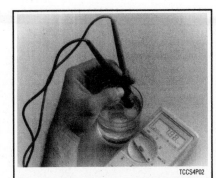

Fig. 47 Another method of testing the ECT is to submerge it in cold or hot water and check resistance

Fig. 48 The ECT can be monitored with an appropriate and Datastream capable scan tool

Temperature		Engine Coolant/Intake Air Temperature Sensor Values
°F	°C	Resistance (K ohms)
248	120	1.18
230	110	1.55
212	100	2.07
194	90	2.80
176	80	3.84
158	70	5.37
140	60	7.70
122	50	10.97
104	40	16.15
86	30	24.27
68	20	37.30
50	10	58.75

Fig. 49 ECT and IAT resistance-to-temperature specifications

9. Compare the cold and hot ECT sensor resistance measurements with the accompanying chart.

10. If readings do not approximate those in the chart, the sensor may be faulty.

REMOVAL & INSTALLATION

▶ See Figures 50 thru 64

1. Disconnect the negative battery cable.
2. Drain and recycle the engine coolant.

✳✳ CAUTION

Never open, service or drain the radiator or cooling system when hot; serious burns can occur from the steam and hot coolant. Also, when draining engine coolant, keep in mind that cats and dogs are attracted to ethylene glycol antifreeze and could drink any that is left in an uncovered container or in puddles on the ground. This will prove fatal in sufficient quantities. Always drain coolant into a sealable container. Coolant should be reused unless it is contaminated or is several years old.

3. On the 2.0L engine, remove the air intake resonators.
4. On the 2.5L engine, raise and support the vehicle.
5. Disconnect the ECT sensor connector.
6. Remove the ECT sensor from the thermostat housing (2.0L) or the water crossover tube (2.5L).

To install:

7. Coat the sensor threads with Teflon® sealant.
8. Thread the sensor into position and tighten to 10–14 ft lbs. (14–19 Nm) on the 2.5L engine and 89–120 inch lbs. (10–14 Nm) on the 2.0L engine.
9. Attach the ECT sensor connector.
10. On the 2.0L engine, install the air intake resonators.

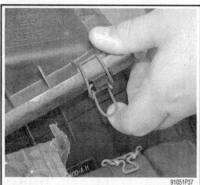

Fig. 50 Grasp and unfasten the retaining clips . . .

Fig. 51 . . . located in the following positions —2.0L engine, 2.5L similar

Fig. 52 The MAF connector is released by pressing down on the retaining spring—shown here already disconnected

Fig. 53 Label and disconnect the MAF sensor . . .

Fig. 54 . . . and the IAT sensor

Fig. 55 Loosen the clamp on the air cleaner tube

Fig. 56 Lift the air cleaner inlet tube slightly and slide the retaining tab on the air intake resonator out and . . .

Fig. 57 . . . remove the air cleaner inlet tube from the vehicle

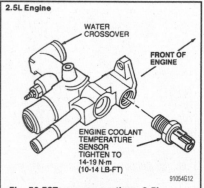

Fig. 58 ECT sensor mounting—2.5L engine

Fig. 59 Place a suitable size socket over the sensor. A special socket used for sensors, as shown here, can be used but is not necessary

Fig. 60 Carefully loosen the sensor from the plastic thermostat housing

Fig. 61 When loosened, remove the ECT sensor from the thermostat housing

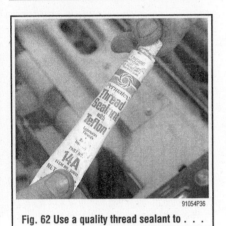

Fig. 62 Use a quality thread sealant to . . .

Fig. 63 . . . coat the threads of the ECT sensor before installation

Fig. 64 The ECT sensor must be tightened with a torque wrench to specifications or the plastic thermostat housing can crack

11. On the 2.5L engine, lower the vehicle.
12. Connect the negative battery cable.
13. Refill the engine cooling system.
14. Start the engine and check for coolant leaks.
15. Bleed the cooling system.

Intake Air Temperature Sensor

OPERATION

▶ **See Figure 65**

The Intake Air Temperature (IAT) sensor determines the air temperature inside the intake manifold. Resistance changes in response to the ambient air temperature. The sensor has a negative temperature coefficient. As the temperature of the sensor rises the resistance across the sensor decreases. This provides a signal to the PCM indicating the temperature of the incoming air charge. This sensor helps the PCM to determine spark timing and air/fuel ratio. Information from this sensor is added to the pressure sensor information to calculate the air mass being sent to the cylinders. The IAT is a two wire sensor, a 5-volt reference signal is sent to the sensor and the signal return is based upon the change in the measured resistance due to temperature.

TESTING

▶ **See Figures 66 and 67**

1. Turn the ignition switch **OFF**.
2. Disconnect the wiring harness from the IAT sensor.
3. Measure the resistance between the sensor terminals.
4. Compare the resistance reading with the accompanying chart.
5. If the resistance is not within specification, the IAT may be faulty.
6. Connect the wiring harness to the sensor.

Fig. 65 The tip of the IAT sensor has an exposed thermistor that changes the resistance of the sensor based upon the force of the air rushing past it

Fig. 66 Test the resistance of the IAT sensor across the two sensor pins

Fig. 67 The IAT sensor can be monitored with an appropriate and Data-stream capable scan tool

REMOVAL & INSTALLATION

2.0L Engine

▶ **See Figures 50 thru 57, 68 thru 71**

1. Disconnect the negative battery cable.
2. Unplug the MAF and IAT sensors connectors.
3. Release the retaining clips from the air cleaner cover.
4. Remove the air cleaner outlet tube from the resonator and remove the outlet tube and air cleaner cover assembly.
5. Remove the IAT sensor from the air intake resonator by carefully loosening it with the appropriate size tool.

To install:

6. Coat the sensor threads with Teflon® sealant.
7. Thread the sensor into the air intake resonator and tighten to 17 ft lbs. (23 Nm).
8. Install air cleaner outlet tube and cover into place and attach the retaining clips for the cover and tighten the hose clamps on the resonator.
9. Attach the connectors on the IAT and the MAF sensors.
10. Connect the negative battery cable.

2.5L Engine

▶ **See Figure 72**

1. Disconnect the negative battery cable.
2. Unplug the IAT sensor connector.
3. Rotate the IAT sensor 90° and remove the sensor from the air cleaner assembly.

To install:

4. Inspect the O-ring on the IAT sensor and replace if necessary.
5. Place the IAT sensor into the opening in the air cleaner assembly and rotate it 90°.
6. Attach the IAT sensor connector.
7. Connect the negative battery cable.

Mass Air Flow Sensor

OPERATION

▶ **See Figure 73**

The Mass Air Flow (MAF) sensor directly measures the mass of air being drawn into the engine. The sensor output is used to calculate injector pulse width. The MAF sensor is what is referred to as a hot-wire sensor. The sensor uses a thin platinum wire filament, wound on a ceramic bobbin and coated with glass, that is heated to 200°C (417°F) above the ambient air temperature and subjected to the intake airflow stream. A cold-wire is used inside the MAF sensor to determine the ambient air temperature.

Battery voltage from the EEC power relay, and a reference signal and a ground signal from the PCM are supplied to the MAF sensor. The sensor returns a signal proportionate to the current flow required to keep the hot-wire at the required temperature. The increased airflow across the hot-wire acts as a cooling fan, lowering the resistance and requiring more current to maintain the temperature of the wire. The increased current is measured by the voltage in the circuit, as current increases, voltage increases. As the airflow increases the signal return voltage of a normally operating MAF sensor will increase.

TESTING

▶ **See Figures 74, 75 and 76**

1. Using a multimeter, check for voltage by backprobing the MAF sensor connector.
2. With the key **ON**, and the engine **OFF**, verify that there is at least 10.5 volts between the VPWR and GND terminals of the MAF sensor connector. If voltage is not within specification, check power and ground circuits and repair as necessary.
3. With the key **ON**, and the engine **ON**, verify that there is at least 4.5 volts between the SIG and GND terminals of the MAF sensor connector. If voltage is

Fig. 68 Using the appropriate size socket, loosen the IAT sensor and . . .

Fig. 69 . . . remove the sensor from the air intake resonator

Fig. 70 Inspect the sensor tip if you plan to reinstall the original sensor

Fig. 71 Coat the threads of the IAT sensor before installing it

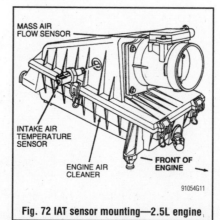
Fig. 72 IAT sensor mounting—2.5L engine

MASS AIR FLOW SENSOR

INTAKE AIR TEMPERATURE SENSOR

ENGINE AIR CLEANER

FRONT OF ENGINE

Fig. 73 The exposed hot wire of the MAF sensor

Fig. 74 Testing the VPWR circuit to the MAF sensor

Fig. 75 Testing the SIG circuit to the MAF sensor

Fig. 76 Testing the SIG RTN circuit to the MAF sensor

not within specification, check power and ground circuits and repair as necessary.

4. With the key **ON**, and the engine **ON**, check voltage between GND and SIG RTN terminals. Voltage should be approximately 0.34–1.96 volts. If voltage is not within specification, the sensor may be faulty.

REMOVAL & INSTALLATION

▶ **See Figures 50 thru 57, 77 thru 81**

1. Disconnect the negative battery cable.
2. Unplug the MAF and IAT sensors connectors.
3. Release the retaining clips from the air cleaner cover.
4. Remove the air cleaner outlet tube from the throttle body(2.5L) or resonator (2.0L)and remove the outlet tube and air cleaner cover assembly.
5. Loosen the hose clamps and remove the outlet tube from the MAF sensor.

6. Remove the MAF retaining clips (2.0L) or bolts (2.5L) from the air cleaner cover.
7. Carefully remove the MAF from the cover.
To install:
8. On the 2.5L engine:
   a. Replace the gasket between the MAF and the air cleaner cover.
   b. Install the MAF onto the air cleaner cover and tighten the retaining bolts to 25 inch lbs. (3.5 Nm).
9. On the 2.0L engine:
   a. Inspect the O-ring on the MAF and replace if necessary.
   b. Install the MAF onto the air cleaner cover and attach the retaining clips.
10. Install the outlet tube onto the MAF and tighten the hose clamps.
11. Install air cleaner outlet tube and cover into place and attach the retaining clips for the cover and tighten the hose clamps on the throttle body(2.5L) or resonator (2.0L).

Fig. 77 Loosen the hose clamp and . . .

Fig. 78 . . . slide the outlet hose off of the MAF sensor

Fig. 79 Unsnap the retaining clips and . . .

Fig. 80 . . . and remove the MAF sensor from the air cleaner cover

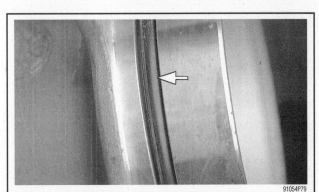

Fig. 81 Inspect the O-ring on the MAF sensor and replace if necessary

12. Attach the connectors on the IAT and the MAF sensors.
13. Connect the negative battery cable.

Throttle Position Sensor

OPERATION

The Throttle Position (TP) sensor is a potentiometer that provides a signal to the PCM that is directly proportional to the throttle plate position. The TP sensor is mounted on the side of the throttle body and is connected to the throttle plate shaft. The TP sensor monitors throttle plate movement and position, and transmits an appropriate electrical signal to the PCM. These signals are used by the PCM to adjust the air/fuel mixture, spark timing and EGR operation according to engine load at idle, part throttle, or full throttle. The TP sensor is not adjustable.

The TP sensor receives a 5 volt reference signal and a ground circuit from the PCM. A return signal circuit is connected to wiper that runs on a resistor internally on the sensor. The further the throttle is opened, the wiper moves along the resistor, at wide open throttle, the wiper essentially creates a loop between the reference signal and the signal return returning the full or nearly full 5 volt signal back to the PCM. At idle the signal return should be approximately 0.9 volts.

TESTING

▶ See Figures 82, 83, 84, 85 and 86

1. With the engine **OFF** and the ignition **ON**, check the voltage at the signal return circuit of the TP sensor by carefully backprobing the connector using a DVOM.
2. Voltage should be between 0.2 and 1.4 volts at idle.
3. Slowly move the throttle pulley to the wide open throttle (WOT) position and watch the voltage on the DVOM. The voltage should slowly rise to slightly less than 4.8v at Wide Open Throttle (WOT).

Fig. 82 Testing the SIG circuit to the TP sensor

Fig. 83 Testing the SIG RTN circuit of the TP sensor

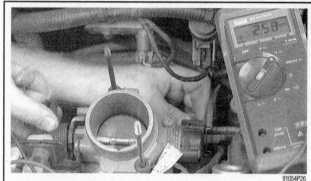
Fig. 84 Testing the operation of the potentiometer inside the TP sensor while slowly opening the throttle

Fig. 85 The TP sensor can be monitored with an appropriate and Data-stream capable scan tool

Fig. 86 Unplug the TP sensor connector

4. If no voltage is present, check the wiring harness for supply voltage (5.0v) and ground (0.3v or less), by referring to your corresponding wiring guide. If supply voltage and ground are present, but no output voltage from TP, replace the TP sensor. If supply voltage and ground do not meet specifications, make necessary repairs to the harness or PCM.

REMOVAL & INSTALLATION

▶ See Figures 50 thru 57, 86 and 87

1. Disconnect the negative battery cable.
2. On 2.0L engines, remove the air intake resonator.
3. On the 2.5L engine, remove the water pump pulley shield.
4. Disconnect the wiring harness from the TP sensor.
5. Remove the two sensor mounting screws, then pull the TP sensor off of the throttle shaft.

Fig. 87 Remove the two retaining bolts to remove the sensor

Fig. 88 The CMP sensor location—2.0L engine

To install:

6. Carefully slide the rotary tangs on the sensor into position over the throttle shaft, then rotate the sensor clockwise to the installed position..

☀ CAUTION

Failure to install the TP sensor in this manner may result in sensor damage or high idle speeds.

➡**The TP sensor is not adjustable.**

7. Install and tighten the sensor mounting screws to 27 inch lbs. (3 Nm).
8. Connect the wiring harness to the sensor.
9. On 2.0L engines, install the air intake resonator.
10. On the 2.5L engine, install the water pump pulley shield.
11. Connect the negative battery cable.

Camshaft Position Sensor

OPERATION

The camshaft position sensor (CMP) is a variable reluctance sensor that is triggered by a high point on the left-hand exhaust camshaft on the 2.5L engine and a high spot on the intake camshaft on the 2.0L engine. The CMP sends a signal relating camshaft position back to the PCM which is used by the PCM to control engine timing.

TESTING

1. Check voltage between the camshaft position sensor terminals PWR GND and CID.
2. With engine running, voltage should be greater than 0.1 volt AC and vary with engine speed.
3. If voltage is not within specification, check for proper voltage at the VPWR terminal.
4. If VPWR voltage is greater than 10.5 volts, sensor may be faulty.

REMOVAL & INSTALLATION

▶ **See Figures 50 thru 57, 88 and 89**

1. Disconnect the negative battery cable.
2. On 2.0L engines, remove the air intake resonator.
3. Unplug the connector from the CMP sensor.
4. Remove the retaining bolt and remove the CMP sensor.
To install:
5. Ensure the CMP sensor's mounting surface is clean, and the sensor's O-ring is in place.
6. Install the CMP sensor and tighten the retaining bolt to 13–17 ft. lbs. (18–23 Nm) on the 2.0L engine, and 71–106 inch lbs. (8–12 Nm) on the 2.5L engine.
7. Plug the CMP connector in.
8. On 2.0L engines, install the air intake resonator.
9. Connect the negative battery cable.

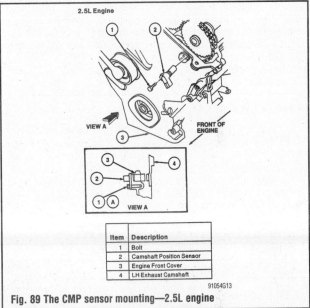

Item	Description
1	Bolt
2	Camshaft Position Sensor
3	Engine Front Cover
4	LH Exhaust Camshaft

Fig. 89 The CMP sensor mounting—2.5L engine

Crankshaft Position Sensor

Please refer to Section 2 for service information.

Knock Sensor

OPERATION

The operation of the Knock Sensor (KS) is to monitor preignition or engine knocks and send the signal to the PCM. The PCM responds by adjusting ignition timing until the knocks stop. The sensor works by generating a signal produced by the frequency of the knock as recorded by the piezoelectric ceramic disc inside the KS. The disc absorbs the shock waves from the knocks and exerts a pressure on the metal diaphragm inside the KS. This compresses the crystals inside the disc and the disc generates a voltage signal proportional to the frequency of the knocks ranging from zero to 1 volt.

TESTING

There is real no test for this sensor, the sensor produces it's own signal based on information gathered while the engine is running. The sensors also are usually inaccessible without major component removal. The sensors can be monitored with an appropriate scan tool using a data display or other data stream information. Follow the instructions included with the scan tool for information on accessing the data. The only test available is to test the continuity of the harness from the PCM to the sensor.

REMOVAL & INSTALLATION

▶ **See Figures 90 and 91**

➡ **The sensor is most easily accessed from underneath the vehicle.**

1. Disconnect the negative battery cable.
2. Raise and safely support the vehicle securely on jackstands.
3. Unplug the sensor connector.
4. Using the proper size socket, loosen and remove the knock sensor.

To install:

5. Carefully thread the sensor into the engine block.
6. Tighten the sensor to 11–15 ft lbs. (15–20 Nm) on 2.0L engines and 21–29 ft lbs. (29–39 Nm) on 2.5L engines.
7. Attach the sensor connector.
8. Lower the vehicle.
9. Connect the negative battery cable.

Fig. 90 The KS location as viewed from underneath the vehicle— 2.0L engine

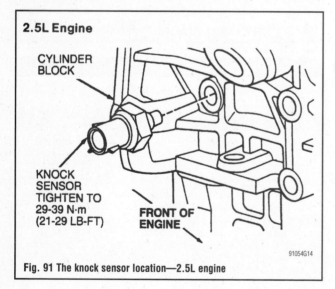

Fig. 91 The knock sensor location—2.5L engine

Vehicle Speed Sensor

OPERATION

▶ **See Figure 92**

The Vehicle Speed Sensor (VSS) is a magnetic pick-up sensor that sends a signal to the Powertrain Control Module (PCM) and the speedometer. The sensor measures the rotation of the output shaft on the transaxle and sends aa AC voltage signal to the PCM which determines the corresponding vehicle speed.

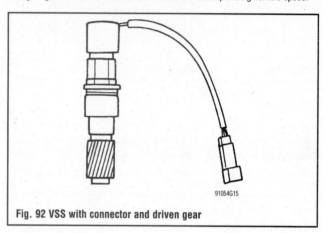

Fig. 92 VSS with connector and driven gear

TESTING

1. Disconnect the negative battery cable.
2. Disengage the wiring harness connector from the VSS.
3. Using a Digital Volt-Ohmmeter (DVOM), measure the resistance (ohmmeter function) between the sensor terminals. If the resistance is 190–250 ohms, the sensor is okay.

REMOVAL & INSTALLATION

1. Disconnect the negative battery cable.
2. On a manual transaxle equipped vehicle:
   a. Remove the air cleaner assembly.
3. On an automatic transaxle equipped vehicle:
   a. Raise and support the vehicle.
4. Unplug the VSS electrical connector.
5. Remove the speedometer cable (early models only).
6. Remove the retaining bolt from the VSS.
7. Lift the VSS out of the transaxle.
8. Remove the driven gear retainer and the drive gear.

To install:

9. Inspect the O-ring on the sensor and replace if necessary.
10. Install the driven gear and the retainer.
11. Place the VSS into the transaxle.
12. Tighten the retaining bolt to 43–53 inch lbs. (5–6 Nm).
13. Install the speedo cable (if necessary).
14. Attach the VSS electrical connector.
15. On a manual transaxle equipped vehicle:
    a. Install the air cleaner assembly.
16. On a automatic transaxle equipped vehicle:
    a. Lower the vehicle.
17. Connect the negative battery cable.

COMPONENT LOCATIONS

EMISSIONS AND ELECTRONIC ENGINE CONTROL COMPONENT LOCATIONS—2.0L ENGINE

1. Powertrain Control Module (PCM)—
   behind power steering reservoir
2. Differential Pressure Feedback EGR
   (DPFE) sensor
3. EGR Vacuum Regulator (EVR) solenoid
4. Ignition Control Module
5. Throttle Position (TP) sensor
6. Camshaft Position (CMP) sensor
7. Mass Air Flow (MAF) sensor
8. Engine Coolant Temperature (ECT) sensor
9. Crankshaft Position (CKP) sensor
10. Heated Oxygen Sensor (HO2S)—in exhaust manifold

91054P74

EMISSIONS AND ELECTRONIC ENGINE CONTROL COMPONENT LOCATIONS—2.5L ENGINE

1. Powertrain control module (PCM) behind power steering reservoir
2. EVAP test port
3. EGR vacuum regulator (EVR) solenoid
4. Exhaust gas recirculation (EGR) valve
5. Intake air temperature (IAT) sensor
6. Mass air flow (MAF) sensor
7. Position crankcase ventilation (PCV) valve
8. Throttle position (TP) sensor
9. Engine coolant temperature (ECT) sensor— under bypass tube

TROUBLE CODES

DIAGNOSTIC TROUBLE CODES	DEFINITIONS
111	System Pass
112	Intake Air Temp (IAT) sensor circuit below minimum voltage / 254°F indicated
113	Intake Air Temp (IAT) sensor circuit above maximum voltage / -40°F indicated
114	Intake Air Temp (IAT) sensor circuit voltage higher or lower than expected
116	Engine Coolant Temp (ECT) sensor circuit voltage higher or lower than expected
117	Engine Coolant Temp (ECT) sensor circuit below minimum voltage / 254°F indicated
118	Engine Coolant Temp (ECT) sensor circuit above maximum voltage / -40°F indicated
121	Closed throttle voltage higher or lower than expected
121	Throttle position voltage inconsistent with the MAF sensor
122	Throttle Position (TP) sensor circuit below minimum voltage
123	Throttle Position (TP) sensor circuit above maximum voltage
124	Throttle Position (TP) sensor voltage higher than expected
125	Throttle Position (TP) sensor voltage lower than expected
126	MAP / BARO sensor circuit voltage higher or lower than expected
128	MAP sensor vacuum hose damaged / disconnected
129	Insufficient MAP / Mass Air Flow (MAF) change during dynamic response test KOER
136	Lack of Heated Oxygen Sensor (HO2S-2) switch during KOER, indicates lean (Bank #2)
137	Lack of Heated Oxygen Sensor (HO2S-2) switch during KOER, indicates rich (Bank #2)
139	No Heated Oxygen Sensor (HO2S-2) switches detected (Bank #2)
141	Fuel system indicates lean
144	No Heated Oxygen Sensor (HO2S-1) switches detected (Bank #1)
157	Mass Air Flow (MAF) sensor circuit below minimum voltage
158	Mass Air Flow (MAF) sensor circuit above maximum voltage
159	Mass Air Flow (MAF) sensor circuit voltage higher or lower than expected
167	Insufficient throttle position change during dynamic response test KOER
171	Fuel system at adaptive limits, Heated Oxygen Sensor (HO2S-1) unable to switch (Bank #1)
172	Lack of Heated Oxygen Sensor (HO2S-1) switches, indicates lean (Bank #1)
173	Lack of Heated Oxygen Sensor (HO2S-1) switches, indicates rich (Bank #1)
175	Fuel system at adaptive limits, Heated Oxygen Sensor (HO2S-2) unable to switch (Bank #2)
176	Lack of Heated Oxygen Sensor (HO2S-2) switches, indicates lean (Bank #2)
177	Lack of Heated Oxygen Sensor (HO2S-2) switches, indicates rich (Bank #2)
179	Fuel system at lean adaptive limit at part throttle, system rich (Bank #1)
181	Fuel system at rich adaptive limit at part throttle, system lean (Bank #1)
184	Mass Air Flow (MAF) sensor voltage higher than expected
185	Mass Air Flow (MAF) sensor voltage lower than expected
186	Injector pulsewidth higher than expected (with BARO sensor)
186	Injector pulsewidth higher or mass air flow lower than expected (without BARO sensor)
187	Injector pulsewidth lower than expected (with BARO sensor)
187	Injector pulsewidth lower or mass air flow higher than expected (without BARO sensor)
188	Fuel system at lean adaptive limit at part throttle, system rich (Bank #2)
189	Fuel system at rich adaptive limit at part throttle, system lean (Bank #2)
193	Flexible Fuel (FF) sensor circuit failure

91054C01

EEC-IV Diagnostic Trouble Codes—1995 vehicles only

DIAGNOSTIC TROUBLE CODES	DEFINITIONS
457	Speed control command switch(s) circuit not functioning (KOEO IVSC test)
458	Speed control command switch(s) stuck / circuit grounded (KOEO IVSC test)
459	Speed control ground circuit open (KOEO IVSC test)
511	PCM Read Only Memory (ROM) test failure KOEO
512	PCM Keep Alive Memory (KAM) test failure
513	PCM internal voltage failure (KOEO)
519	Power Steering Pressure (PSP) switch circuit open KOEO
519	Power Steering Pressure (PSP) sensor circuit open
521	Power Steering Pressure (PSP) switch circuit did not change states KOER
521	Power Steering Pressure (PSP) sensor circuit did not change states KOER
522	Vehicle not in PARK or NEUTRAL during KOEO / PNP switch circuit open
524	Low speed fuel pump circuit open—battery to PCM
525	Indicates vehicle in gear / A / C on
527	Park / Neutral Position (PNP) switch circuit open—A / C on KOEO
528	Clutch Pedal Position (CPP) switch circuit failure
529	Data Communication Link (DCL) or PCM circuit failure
532	Cluster Control Assembly (CCA) circuit failure
533	Data Communication Link (DCL) or Electronic Instrument Cluster (EIC) circuit failure
536	Brake On / Off (BOO) circuit failure / not actuated during KOER
538	Insufficient RPM change during KOER dynamic response test
538	Invalid cylinder balance test due to throttle movement during test (SFI only)
538	Invalid cylinder balance test due to CID circuit failure
539	A / C on / Defrost on during Self-Test
542	Fuel pump secondary circuit failure
543	Fuel pump secondary circuit failure
551	Idle Air Control (IAC) circuit failure KOEO
552	Secondary Air Injection Bypass (AIRB) circuit failure KOEO
553	Secondary Air Injection Diverter (AIRD) circuit failure KOEO
554	Fuel Pressure Regulator Control (FPRC) circuit failure
556	Fuel pump relay primary circuit failure
557	Low speed fuel pump primary circuit failure
558	EGR Vacuum Regulator (EVR) circuit failure KOEO
559	Air Conditioning On (ACON) relay circuit failure KOEO
563	High Fan Control (HFC) circuit failure KOEO
564	Fan Control (FC) circuit failure KOEO
565	Canister Purge (CANP) circuit failure KOEO
566	3-4 shift solenoid circuit failure KOEO (A4LD)
567	Speed Control Vent (SCVNT) circuit failure (KOEO IVSC test)
568	Speed Control Vacuum (SCVAC) circuit failure (KOEO IVSC test)
569	Auxiliary Canister Purge (CANP2) circuit failure KOEO
571	EGRA solenoid circuit failure KOEO
572	EGRV solenoid circuit failure KOEO
578	A / C pressure sensor circuit shorted
579	Insufficient A / C pressure change

EEC-IV Diagnostic Trouble Codes—1995 vehicles only (continued)

91054C03

DIAGNOSTIC TROUBLE CODES	DEFINITIONS
211	Profile Ignition Pickup (PIP) circuit failure
212	Loss of Ignition Diagnostic Monitor (IDM) input to PCM / SPOUT circuit grounded
213	SPOUT circuit open
214	Cylinder Identification (CID) circuit failure
215	PCM detected coil 1 primary circuit failure (EI)
216	PCM detected coil 2 primary circuit failure (EI)
217	PCM detected coil 3 primary circuit failure (EI)
218	Loss of Ignition Diagnostic Monitor (IDM) signal-left side (dual plug EI)
219	Spark timing defaulted to 10 degrees-SPOUT circuit open (EI)
221	Spark timing error (EI)
222	Loss of Ignition Diagnostic Monitor (IDM) signal-right side (dual plug EI)
223	Loss of Dual Plug Inhibit (DPI) control (dual plug EI)
224	PCM detected coil 1, 2, 3 or 4 primary circuit failure (dual plug EI)
225	Knock not sensed during dynamic response test KOER
226	Ignition Diagnostic Module (IDM) signal not received (EI)
232	PCM detected coil 1, 2, 3 or 4 primary circuit failure (EI)
238	PCM detected coil 4 primary circuit failure (EI)
241	ICM to PCM IDM pulsewidth transmission error (EI)
244	CID circuit fault present when cylinder balance test requested
311	AIR system inoperative during KOER (Bank # 1 w / dual HO2S)
312	AIR misdirected during KOER
313	AIR not bypassed during KOER
314	AIR system inoperative during KOER (Bank # 2 w / dual HO2S)
326	EGR (PFE / DPFE) circuit voltage lower than expected
327	EGR (EGRP / EVP / PFE / DPFE) circuit below minimum voltage
328	EGR (EVP) closed valve voltage lower than expected
332	Insufficient EGR flow detected (EGRP / EVP / PFE / DPFE)
334	EGR (EVP) closed valve voltage higher than expected
335	EGR (PFE / DPFE) sensor voltage higher or lower than expected during KOEO
336	Exhaust pressure high / EGR (PFE / DPFE) circuit voltage higher than expected
337	EGR (EGRP / EVP / PFE / DPFE) circuit above maximum voltage
338	Engine Coolant Temperature (ECT) lower than expected (thermostat test)
339	Engine Coolant Temperature (ECT) higher than expected (thermostat test)
341	Octane adjust service pin open
381	Frequent A / C clutch cycling
411	Cannot control RPM during KOER low RPM check
412	Cannot control RPM during KOER high RPM check
415	Idle Air Control (IAC) system at maximum adaptive lower limit
416	Idle Air Control (IAC) system at upper adaptive learning limit
452	Insufficient input from Vehicle Speed Sensor (VSS) to PCM
453	Servo leaking down (KOER IVSC test)
454	Servo leaking up (KOER IVSC test)
455	Insufficient RPM increase (KOER IVSC test)
456	Insufficient RPM decrease (KOER IVSC test)

EEC-IV Diagnostic Trouble Codes—1995 vehicles only (continued)

91054C02

DIAGNOSTIC TROUBLE CODES	DEFINITIONS
581	Power to Fan circuit over current
582	Fan circuit open
583	Power to Fuel pump over current
584	VCRM Power ground circuit open (VCRM Pin 1)
585	Power to A/C clutch over current
586	A/C clutch circuit open
587	Variable Control Relay Module (VCRM) communication failure
593	Heated Oxygen Sensor Heater (HO2S HTR) circuit failure
617	1-2 shift error
618	2-3 shift error
619	3-4 shift error
621	Shift Solenoid 1 (SS1) circuit failure KOEO
622	Shift Solenoid 2 (SS2) circuit failure KOEO
623	Transmission Control Indicator Lamp (TCIL) circuit failure
624	Electronic Pressure Control (EPC) circuit failure
625	Electronic Pressure Control (EPC) driver open in PCM
626	Coast Clutch Solenoid (CCS) circuit failure KOEO
627	Torque Converter Clutch (TCC) solenoid circuit failure
628	Excessive converter clutch slippage
629	Torque Converter Clutch (TCC) solenoid circuit failure
631	Transmission Control Indicator Lamp (TCIL) circuit failure KOEO
632	Transmission Control Switch (TCS) circuit did not change states during KOER
633	4x4L switch closed during KOEO
634	Transmission Range (TR) voltage higher or lower than expected
636	Transmission Fluid Temperature (TFT) higher or lower than expected
637	Transmission Fluid Temperature (TFT) sensor circuit above maximum voltage / -40° F (-40° C) indicated / circuit open
638	Transmission Fluid Temperature (TFT) sensor circuit below minimum voltage / 290° F (143° C) indicated / circuit shorted
639	Insufficient input from Turbine Shaft Speed Sensor (TSS)
641	Shift Solenoid 3 (SS3) circuit failure
643	Torque Converter Clutch (TCC) circuit failure
645	Incorrect gear ratio obtained for first gear
646	Incorrect gear ratio obtained for second gear
647	Incorrect gear ratio obtained for third gear
648	Incorrect gear ratio obtained for fourth gear
649	Electronic Pressure Control (EPC) higher or lower than expected
651	Electronic Pressure Control (EPC) circuit failure
652	Torque Converter Clutch (TCC) solenoid circuit failure
653	Transmission Control Switch (TCS) did not change states during KOER
654	Transmission Range (TR) sensor not indicating PARK during KOEO
656	Torque Converter Clutch continuous slip error
657	Transmission overtemperature condition occurred
659	High vehicle speed in park indicated

91054C04

EEC-IV Diagnostic Trouble Codes—1995 vehicles only (continued)

DIAGNOSTIC TROUBLE CODES	DEFINITIONS
667	Transmission Range sensor circuit voltage below minimum voltage
668	Transmission Range circuit voltage above maximum voltage
675	Transmission Range sensor circuit voltage out of range
998	Hard fault present—FMEM MODE

91054C05

EEC-IV Diagnostic Trouble Codes—1995 vehicles only (continued)

Diagnostic Trouble Code (DTC) Definitions

DTC	Definitions
P0102	Mass Air Flow (MAF) sensor circuit low input
P0103	Mass Air Flow (MAF) sensor circuit high input
P0106	Barometric Pressure (BP) sensor circuit performance
P0107	Barometric Pressure (BP) sensor circuit low input
P0108	Barometric Pressure (BP) sensor circuit high input
P0112	Intake Air Temperature (IAT) sensor circuit low input
P0113	Intake Air Temperature (IAT) sensor circuit high input
P0117	Engine Coolant Temperature (ECT) sensor circuit low input
P0118	Engine Coolant Temperature (ECT) sensor circuit high input
P0121	In-range operating Throttle Position (TP) sensor circuit failure
P0122	Throttle Position (TP) sensor circuit low input
P0123	Throttle Position (TP) sensor circuit high input
P0125	Insufficient coolant temperature to enter closed loop fuel control
P0131	Upstream Heated Oxygen Sensor (HO2S 11) circuit out of range low voltage (Bank # 1)
P0133	Upstream Heated Oxygen Sensor (HO2S 11) circuit slow response (Bank # 1)
P0135	Upstream Heated Oxygen Sensor Heater (HTR 11) circuit malfunction (Bank # 1)
P0136	Downstream Heated Oxygen Sensor (HO2S 12) circuit malfunction (Bank # 1)
P0141	Downstream Heated Oxygen Sensor Heater (HTR 12) circuit malfunction (Bank # 1)
P0151	Upstream Heated Oxygen Sensor (HO2S 21) circuit out of range low voltage (Bank # 2)
P0153	Upstream Heated Oxygen Sensor (HO2S 21) circuit slow response (Bank # 2)
P0155	Upstream Heated Oxygen Sensor Heater (HTR 21) circuit malfunction (Bank # 2)
P0156	Downstream Heated Oxygen Sensor (HO2S 22) circuit malfunction (Bank # 2)
P0161	Downstream Heated Oxygen Sensor Heater (HTR 22) circuit malfunction (Bank # 2)
P0171	System (adaptive fuel) too lean (Bank # 1)
P0172	System (adaptive fuel) too rich (Bank # 1)
P0174	System (adaptive fuel) too lean (Bank # 2)
P0175	System (adaptive fuel) too rich (Bank # 2)
P0176	Fuel Composition sensor (FCS) circuit malfunction
P0182	Fuel Temperature sensor A circuit low input
P0183	Fuel Temperature sensor A circuit high input
P0187	Fuel Temperature sensor B circuit low input
P0188	Fuel Temperature sensor B circuit high input
P0191	Injector Pressure sensor circuit performance
P0192	Injector Pressure sensor circuit low input
P0193	Injector Pressure sensor circuit high input
P0222	Throttle Position Sensor B (TP-B) circuit low input
P0223	Throttle Position Sensor B (TP-B) circuit high input
P0230	Fuel Pump primary circuit malfunction
P0231	Fuel Pump secondary circuit low
P0232	Fuel Pump secondary circuit high
P0300	Random Misfire detected
P0301	Cylinder # 1 Misfire detected
P0302	Cylinder # 2 Misfire detected
P0303	Cylinder # 3 Misfire detected

Diagnostic Trouble Code (DTC) Definitions

DTC	Definitions
P0304	Cylinder # 4 Misfire detected
P0305	Cylinder # 5 Misfire detected
P0306	Cylinder # 6 Misfire detected
P0307	Cylinder # 7 Misfire detected
P0308	Cylinder # 8 Misfire detected
P0320	Ignition Engine Speed (Profile Ignition Pickup (PIP)) input circuit malfunction
P0325	Knock Sensor (KS) 1 circuit malfunction
P0326	Knock Sensor (KS) 1 circuit performance
P0331	Knock Sensor (KS) 2 circuit low input
P0331	Knock Sensor (KS) 2 circuit performance
P0340	Camshaft Position (CMP) sensor circuit malfunction (CID)
P0350	Ignition Coil primary circuit malfunction
P0351	Ignition Coil A primary circuit malfunction
P0352	Ignition Coil B primary circuit malfunction
P0353	Ignition Coil C primary circuit malfunction
P0354	Ignition Coil D primary circuit malfunction
P0385	Crankshaft Position (CKP) sensor malfunction
P0400	Exhaust Gas Recirculation (EGR) flow malfunction
P0401	Exhaust Gas Recirculation (EGR) flow insufficient detected
P0402	Exhaust Gas Recirculation (EGR) flow excess detected
P0411	Secondary Air Injection system incorrect upstream flow detected
P0412	Secondary Air Injection system switching valve A malfunction
P0413	Secondary Air Injection system switching valve A circuit open
P0414	Secondary Air Injection system switching valve A circuit shorted
P0416	Secondary Air Injection system switching valve B circuit open
P0417	Secondary Air Injection system switching valve B circuit shorted
P0420	Catalyst system efficiency below threshold (Bank # 1)
P0430	Catalyst system efficiency below threshold (Bank # 2)
P0440	Evaporative emission control system malfunction
P0442	Evaporative emission control system small leak detected
P0443	Evaporative emission control system purge control solenoid or vapor management valve circuit malfunction
P0446	Evaporative emission control system Canister Vent (CV) solenoid control malfunction
P0452	Evaporative emission control system Fuel Tank Pressure (FTP) sensor low input
P0453	Evaporative emission control system Fuel Tank Pressure (FTP) sensor high input
P0455	Evaporative emission control system control leak detected (gross leak)
P0500	Vehicle Speed Sensor (VSS) malfunction
P0503	Vehicle Speed Sensor (VSS) circuit intermittent
P0505	Idle Air Control (IAC) system malfunction
P0552	Power Steering Pressure (PSP) sensor circuit low input
P0553	Power Steering Pressure (PSP) sensor circuit high input
P0603	Powertrain Control Module (PCM) - Keep Alive Memory (KAM) test error
P0605	Powertrain Control Module (PCM) - Read Only Memory (ROM) test error
P0703	Brake On / Off (BOO) switch input malfunction

89694G37

89694G38

Diagnostic Trouble Code (DTC) Definitions

DTC	Definitions
P0704	Clutch Pedal Position (CPP) switch input circuit malfunction
P0707	Transmission Range (TR) sensor circuit low input
P0708	Transmission Range (TR) sensor circuit high input
P0712	Transmission Fluid Temperature (TFT) sensor circuit low input
P0713	Transmission Fluid Temperature (TFT) sensor circuit high input
P0715	Turbine Shaft Speed (TSS) sensor circuit malfunction
P0720	Output Shaft Speed (OSS) sensor circuit malfunction
P0721	Output Shaft Speed (OSS) sensor performance (noise)
P0731	Incorrect ratio for first gear
P0732	Incorrect ratio for second gear
P0733	Incorrect ratio for third gear
P0734	Incorrect ratio for fourth gear
P0736	Reverse incorrect gear ratio
P0741	Torque Converter Clutch (TCC) mechanical system performance
P0743	Torque Converter Clutch (TCC) electrical system malfunction
P0746	Electronic Pressure Control (EPC) solenoid performance
P0750	Shift Solenoid #1 (SS1) circuit malfunction
P0751	Shift Solenoid #1 (SS1) performance
P0755	Shift Solenoid #2 (SS2) circuit malfunction
P0756	Shift Solenoid #2 (SS2) performance
P0760	Shift Solenoid #3 (SS3) circuit malfunction
P0761	Shift Solenoid #3 (SS3) performance
P0781	1 to 2 shift error
P0782	2 to 3 shift error
P0783	3 to 4 shift error
P0784	4 to 5 shift error
P1000	OBD II Monitor Testing not complete
P1001	Key On Engine Running (KOER) Self-Test not able to complete. KOER aborted
P1100	Mass Air Flow (MAF) sensor intermittent
P1101	Mass Air Flow (MAF) sensor out of Self-Test range
P1112	Intake Air Temperature (IAT) sensor intermittent
P1116	Engine Coolant Temperature (ECT) sensor out of Self-Test range
P1117	Engine Coolant Temperature (ECT) sensor intermittent
P1120	Throttle Position (TP) sensor out of range low
P1121	Throttle Position (TP) sensor inconsistent with MAF Sensor
P1124	Throttle Position (TP) sensor out of Self-Test range
P1125	Throttle Position (TP) sensor circuit intermittent
P1127	Exhaust not warm enough, downstream Heated Oxygen Sensors (HO2Ss) not tested
P1128	Upstream Heated Oxygen Sensors (HO2Ss) swapped from bank to bank
P1129	Downstream Heated Oxygen Sensors (HO2Ss) swapped from bank to bank
P1130	Lack of upstream Heated Oxygen Sensor (HO2S 11) switch, adaptive fuel at limit (Bank #1)
P1131	Lack of upstream Heated Oxygen Sensor (HO2S 11) switch, sensor indicates lean (Bank #1)
P1132	Lack of upstream Heated Oxygen Sensor (HO2S 11) switch, sensor indicates rich (Bank #1)

EEC-V Diagnostic Trouble Codes—1996–99 vehicles only (continued)

89694G39

Diagnostic Trouble Code (DTC) Definitions

DTC	Definitions
P1137	Lack of downstream Heated Oxygen Sensor (HO2S 12) switch, sensor indicates lean (Bank #1)
P1138	Lack of downstream Heated Oxygen Sensor (HO2S 12) switch, sensor indicates rich (Bank #1)
P1150	Lack of upstream Heated Oxygen Sensor (HO2S 21) switch, adaptive fuel at limit (Bank #2)
P1151	Lack of upstream Heated Oxygen Sensor (HO2S 21) switch, sensor indicates lean (Bank #2)
P1152	Lack of upstream Heated Oxygen Sensor (HO2S 21) switch, sensor indicates rich (Bank #2)
P1157	Lack of downstream Heated Oxygen Sensor (HO2S 22) switch, sensor indicates lean (Bank #2)
P1158	Lack of downstream Heated Oxygen Sensor (HO2S 22) switch, sensor indicates rich (Bank #2)
P1220	Series Throttle Control system malfunction
P1224	Throttle Position Sensor B (TP-B) out of Self-Test range
P1230	Fuel Pump low speed malfunction
P1231	Fuel Pump secondary circuit low with high speed pump on
P1232	Low speed Fuel Pump primary circuit malfunction
P1233	Fuel Pump Driver Module disabled or offline
P1234	Fuel Pump Driver Module disabled or offline
P1235	Fuel Pump control out of Self-Test range
P1236	Fuel Pump control out of Self-Test range
P1237	Fuel Pump secondary circuit malfunction
P1238	Fuel Pump secondary circuit malfunction
P1260	THEFT detected - engine disabled
P1270	Engine RPM or vehicle speed limiter reached
P1285	Cylinder Head over temperature sensed
P1288	Cylinder Head Temperature (CHT) sensor out of Self-Test range
P1289	Cylinder Head Temperature (CHT) sensor circuit low input
P1290	Cylinder Head Temperature (CHT) sensor circuit high input
P1299	Engine over temperature condition
P1351	Ignition Diagnostic Monitor (IDM) circuit input malfunction
P1356	PIPs occurred while IDM pulsewidth indicates engine not turning
P1357	Ignition Diagnostic Monitor (IDM) pulsewidth not defined
P1358	Ignition Diagnostic Monitor (IDM) signal out of Self-Test range
P1359	Spark output circuit malfunction
P1390	Octane Adjust (OCT ADJ) out of Self-Test range
P1400	Differential Pressure Feedback EGR (DPFE) sensor circuit low voltage detected
P1401	Differential Pressure Feedback EGR (DPFE) sensor circuit high voltage detected
P1405	Differential Pressure Feedback EGR (DPFE) sensor upstream hose off or plugged
P1406	Differential Pressure Feedback EGR (DPFE) sensor downstream hose off or plugged
P1408	Exhaust Gas Recirculation (EGR) flow out of Self-Test range
P1409	Electronic Vacuum Regulator (EVR) control circuit malfunction
P1411	Secondary Air Injection system incorrect downstream flow detected
P1413	Secondary Air Injection system monitor circuit low voltage
P1414	Secondary Air Injection system monitor circuit high voltage

EEC-V Diagnostic Trouble Codes—1996–99 vehicles only (continued)

89694G40

Diagnostic Trouble Code (DTC) Definitions

DTC	Definitions
P1442	Evaporative emission control system small leak detected
P1443	Evaporative emission control system - vacuum system, purge control solenoid or vapor management valve malfunction
P1444	Purge Flow (PF) Sensor circuit low input
P1445	Purge Flow (PF) Sensor circuit high input
P1449	Evaporative emission control system unable to hold vacuum (Probe)
P1450	Unable to bleed up fuel tank vacuum
P1452	Unable to bleed up fuel tank vacuum
P1455	Evaporative emission control system control leak detected (gross leak)
P1460	Wide Open Throttle Air Conditioning Cut-off (WAC) circuit malfunction
P1461	Air Conditioning Pressure (ACP) sensor circuit low input
P1462	Air Conditioning Pressure (ACP) sensor circuit high input
P1463	Air Conditioning Pressure (ACP) sensor insufficient pressure change
P1464	Air condition (A/C) demand out of Self-Test range
P1469	Low air conditioning cycling period
P1473	Fan secondary high with fan(s) off
P1474	Low Fan Control primary circuit malfunction
P1479	High Fan Control primary circuit malfunction
P1480	Fan secondary low with low fan on
P1481	Fan secondary low with high fan on
P1483	Power to fan circuit overcurrent
P1484	Open power ground to Variable Load Control Module (VLCM)
P1500	Vehicle Speed Sensor (VSS) circuit intermittent
P1501	Vehicle Speed Sensor (VSS) out of Self-Test range
P1504	Idle Air Control (IAC) circuit malfunction
P1505	Idle Air Control (IAC) system at adaptive clip
P1506	Idle Air Control (IAC) overspeed error
P1507	Idle Air Control (IAC) underspeed error
P1512	Intake Manifold Runner Control (IMRC) malfunction (Bank #1 stuck closed)
P1513	Intake Manifold Runner Control (IMRC) malfunction (Bank #2 stuck closed)
P1516	Intake Manifold Runner Control (IMRC) input error (Bank #1)
P1517	Intake Manifold Runner Control (IMRC) input error (Bank #2)
P1518	Intake Manifold Runner Control (IMRC) malfunction (stuck open)
P1519	Intake Manifold Runner Control (IMRC) malfunction (stuck closed)
P1520	Intake Manifold Runner Control (IMRC) circuit malfunction
P1530	Air Condition (A/C) clutch circuit malfunction
P1537	Intake Manifold Runner Control (IMRC) malfunction (Bank #1 stuck open)
P1538	Intake Manifold Runner Control (IMRC) malfunction (Bank #2 stuck open)
P1539	Power to Air Condition (A/C) clutch circuit overcurrent
P1550	Power Steering Pressure (PSP) sensor out of Self-Test range
P1605	Powertrain Control Module (PCM) - Keep Alive Memory (KAM) test error
P1625	B(+) supply to Variable Load Control Module (VLCM) fan circuit malfunction
P1626	B(+) supply to Variable Load Control Module (VLCM) Air Condition (A/C) circuit malfunction
P1650	Power Steering Pressure (PSP) switch out of Self-Test range

89694G41

Diagnostic Trouble Code (DTC) Definitions

DTC	Definitions
P1651	Power Steering Pressure (PSP) switch input malfunction
P1701	Reverse engagement error
P1703	Brake On/Off (BOO) switch out of Self-Test range
P1705	Transmission Range (TR) Sensor out of Self-Test range
P1709	Park or Neutral Position (PNP) switch is not indicating neutral during KOEO Self-Test
P1711	Transmission Fluid Temperature (TFT) sensor out of Self-Test range
P1728	Transmission slip fault
P1729	4x4 Low switch error
P1741	Torque Converter Clutch (TCC) control error
P1742	Torque Converter Clutch (TCC) solenoid failed on (turns on MIL)
P1743	Torque Converter Clutch (TCC) solenoid failed on (turns on TCIL)
P1744	Torque Converter Clutch (TCC) system mechanically stuck in off position
P1746	Electronic Pressure Control (EPC) solenoid open circuit (low input)
P1747	Electronic Pressure Control (EPC) solenoid short circuit (high input)
P1749	Electronic Pressure Control (EPC) solenoid failed low
P1751	Shift Solenoid #1 (SS1) performance
P1754	Coast Clutch Solenoid (CCS) circuit malfunction
P1756	Shift Solenoid #2 (SS2) performance
P1761	Shift Solenoid #3 (SS3) performance
P1780	Transmission Control switch (TCS) circuit out of Self-Test range
P1781	4x4 Low switch out of Self-Test range
P1783	Transmission overtemperature condition
P1788	3-2 Timing/Coast Clutch Solenoid (3-2/CCS) circuit open
P1789	3-2 Timing/Coast Clutch Solenoid (3-2/CCS) circuit shorted
U1021	SCP indicating the lack of Air Condition (A/C) clutch status response
U1039	SCP indicating the vehicle speed signal missing or incorrect
U1051	SCP indicating the brake switch signal missing or incorrect
U1073	SCP indicating the lack of engine coolant fan status response
U1131	SCP indicating the lack of Fuel Pump status response
U1135	SCP indicating the ignition switch signal missing or incorrect
U1256	SCP indicating a communications error
U1451	Lack of response from Passive Anti-Theft system (PATS) module - engine disabled

89694G42

EEC-IV System

GENERAL INFORMATION

One part of the Powertrain Control Module (PCM) is devoted to monitoring both input and output functions within the system. This ability forms the core of the self-diagnostic system. If a problem is detected within a circuit, the controller will recognize the fault, assign it an identification code, and store the code in a memory section. Depending on the year and model, the fault code(s) may be represented by two or three-digit numbers. The stored code(s) may be retrieved during diagnosis.

While the EEC-IV system is capable of recognizing many internal faults, certain faults will not be recognized. Because the computer system sees only electrical signals, it cannot sense or react to mechanical or vacuum faults affecting engine operation. Some of these faults may affect another component which will set a code. For example, the PCM monitors the output signal to the fuel injectors, but cannot detect a partially clogged injector. As long as the output driver responds correctly, the computer will read the system as functioning correctly. However, the improper flow of fuel may result in a lean mixture. This would, in turn, be detected by the oxygen sensor and noticed as a constantly lean signal by the PCM. Once the signal falls outside the pre-programmed limits, the engine control assembly would notice the fault and set an identification code.

Failure Mode Effects Management (FMEM)

The PCM contains back-up programs which allow the engine to operate if a sensor signal is lost. If a sensor input is seen to be out of range—either high or low—the FMEM program is used. The processor substitutes a fixed value for the missing sensor signal. The engine will continue to operate, although performance and driveability may be noticeably reduced. This function of the controller is sometimes referred to as the limp-in or fail-safe mode. If the missing sensor signal is restored, the FMEM system immediately returns the system to normal operation. The dashboard warning lamp will be lit when FMEM is in effect.

Diagnostic Link Connector

▶ See Figures 93, 94 and 95

➡ Some of the vehicles covered by this manual utilize two Diagnostic Link Connectors (DLCs), both of which are in the same vicinity.

The Diagnostic Link Connector(s) (DLC) may be found in the following location:
- Under the hood near the firewall behind the driver's side strut tower.

The DLC is rectangular in design and capable of allowing access to 16 terminals. The connector has keying features that allow easy connection. The test equipment and the DLC have a latching feature to ensure a good mated connection.

Hardware Limited Operation Strategy (HLOS)

This mode is only used if the fault is too extreme for the FMEM circuit to handle. In this mode, the processor has ceased all computation and control; the entire system is run on fixed values. The vehicle may be operated but performance and driveability will be greatly reduced. The fixed or default settings provide minimal calibration, allowing the vehicle to be carefully driven in for service. The dashboard warning lamp will be lit when HLOS is engaged. Codes cannot be read while the system is operating in this mode.

HAND-HELD SCAN TOOLS

▶ See Figures 96, 97, 98 and 99

Although stored codes may be read through the flashing of the CHECK ENGINE or SERVICE ENGINE SOON lamp, the use of hand-held scan tools such as Ford's Self-Test Automatic Readout (STAR) tester or the second generation SUPER STAR II tester or their equivalent is highly recommended. There are many manufacturers of these tools; the purchaser must be certain that the tool is proper for the intended use.

The scan tool allows any stored faults to be read from the engine controller

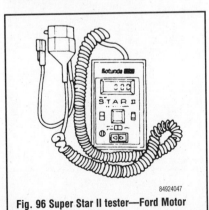

91054P01

Fig. 93 The DLC is located in the engine compartment near the driver's side strut tower. It is under the protective cover marked EEC TEST

91054P02

Fig. 94 Pull the DLC out of the protective cover

91054P03

Fig. 95 There are two parts to the DLC, the 6 pin self test connector and the smaller one pin STI (Self Test Input)

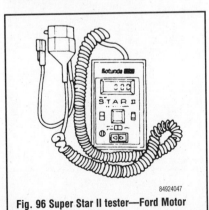

84924047

Fig. 96 Super Star II tester—Ford Motor Co.

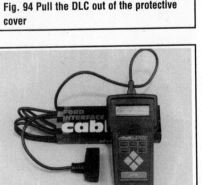

TCCS4P11

Fig. 97 Inexpensive scan tools, such as this Auto Xray®, are available to interface with your Ford vehicle

91054P14

Fig. 98 An economically friendly alternative is this Code Scanner® from SunPro. They are purchased according to manufacturer and are available at many parts stores

Fig. 99 The Code Scanner® from SunPro has no LCD display, just a LED that will flash out the codes and an audible buzzer to alert that the test is in progress

memory. Use of the scan tool provides additional data during troubleshooting, but does not eliminate the use of the charts. The scan tool makes collecting information easier, but the data must be correctly interpreted by an operator familiar with the system.

ELECTRICAL TOOLS

The most commonly required electrical diagnostic tool is the digital multimeter, also known as a Digital Volt Ohmmeter (DVOM), which permits voltage, resistance (ohms) and amperage to be read by one instrument. Many of the diagnostic charts require the use of a volt or ohmmeter during diagnosis.

The multimeter must be a high impedance unit, with 10 megaohms of impedance in the voltmeter. This type of meter will not place an additional load on the circuit it is testing; this is extremely important in low voltage circuits. The multimeter must be of high quality in all respects. It should be handled carefully and protected from impact or damage. Replace the batteries frequently in the unit.

Additionally, an analog (needle type) voltmeter may be used to read stored fault codes if the STAR tester is not available. The codes are transmitted as visible needle sweeps on the face of the instrument.

Almost all diagnostic procedures will require the use of a Breakout Box, a device which connects into the EEC-IV harness and provides testing ports for the 60 wires in the harness. Direct testing of the harness connectors at the terminals or by backprobing is not recommended; damage to the wiring and terminals is almost certain to occur.

Other necessary tools include a quality tachometer with inductive (clip-on) pickup, a fuel pressure gauge with system adapters and a vacuum gauge with an auxiliary source of vacuum.

Reading Codes

Diagnosis of a driveability problem requires attention to detail and following the diagnostic procedures in the correct order. Resist the temptation to begin extensive testing before completing the preliminary diagnostic steps. The preliminary or visual inspection must be completed in detail before diagnosis begins. In many cases this will shorten diagnostic time and often cure the problem without electronic testing.

VISUAL INSPECTION

This is possibly the most critical step of diagnosis. A detailed examination of all connectors, wiring and vacuum hoses can often lead to a repair without further diagnosis. Performance of this step relies on the skill of the technician performing it; a careful inspector will check the undersides of hoses as well as the integrity of hard-to-reach hoses blocked by the air cleaner or other components. Wiring should be checked carefully for any sign of strain, burning, crimping or terminal pull-out from a connector.

Checking connectors at components or in harnesses is required; usually, pushing them together will reveal a loose fit. Pay particular attention to ground circuits, making sure they are not loose or corroded. Remember to inspect connectors and hose fittings at components not mounted on the engine, such as the evaporative canister or relays mounted on the fender aprons. Any component or wiring in the vicinity of a fluid leak or spillage should be given extra attention during inspection.

Additionally, inspect maintenance items such as belt condition and tension, battery charge and condition and the radiator cap carefully. Any of these very simple items may affect the system enough to set a fault.

ELECTRONIC TESTING

If a code was set before a problem self-corrected (such as a momentarily loose connector), the code will be erased if the problem does not reoccur within 80 warm-up cycles. Codes will be output and displayed as numbers on the hand-held scan tool, such as 23. If the codes are being read on an analog voltmeter, the needle sweeps indicate the code digits. code 23 will appear as two needle pulses (sweeps) then, after a 1.6 second pause, the needle will pulse (sweep) three times.

Key On Engine Off (KOEO) Test

▶ **See Figures 100 thru 106**

1. Connect the scan tool to the self-test connectors. Make certain the test button is unlatched or up.
2. Start the engine and run it until normal operating temperature is reached.
3. Turn the engine **OFF** for 10 seconds.
4. Activate the test button on the STAR tester.

Fig. 100 Connect the scan tool to the DLC connector

Fig. 101 The scan tool menu will be displayed, follow the instructions included with the scan tool

Fig. 102 This PCM had no DTC's stored and passed the KOEO

Fig. 103 This PCM had a DTC 113 stored. Most scan tools will give a code definition on-screen as the Auto X-ray shown here informs what code 113 is for the IAT sensor

Fig. 104 If the A/C or Blower motor is left on, a code 539 will be tripped. Turn the A/C or blower motor off and retest

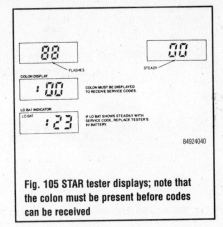

Fig. 105 STAR tester displays; note that the colon must be present before codes can be received

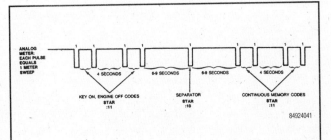

Fig. 106 Code transmission during KOEO test. Note that the continuous memory codes are transmitted after a pause and a separator pulse

5. Turn the ignition switch **ON** but do not start the engine.
6. The KOEO codes will be transmitted. Six to nine seconds after the last KOEO code, a single separator pulse will be transmitted. Six to nine seconds after this pulse, the codes from the Continuous Memory will be transmitted.
7. Record all service codes displayed. Do not depress the throttle on gasoline engines during the test.

Key On Engine Running (KOER) Test

▶ See Figures 96, 105 and 107

1. Make certain the self-test button is released or de-activated on the STAR tester.
2. Start the engine and run it at 2000 rpm for two minutes. This action warms up the oxygen sensor.
3. Turn the ignition switch **OFF** for 10 seconds.
4. Activate or latch the self-test button on the scan tool.
5. Start the engine. The engine identification code will be transmitted. This

is a single digit number representing ½ the number of cylinders in a gasoline engine. On the STAR tester, this number may appear with a zero, such as 20 = 2. The code is used to confirm that the correct processor is installed and that the self-test has begun.
6. If the vehicle is equipped with a Brake On/Off (BOO) switch, the brake pedal must be depressed and released after the ID code is transmitted.
7. If the vehicle is equipped with a Power Steering Pressure Switch (PSPS), the steering wheel must be turned at least ½ turn and released within 2 seconds after the engine ID code is transmitted.
8. Certain Ford vehicles will display a Dynamic Response code 6–20 seconds after the engine ID code. This will appear as one pulse on a meter or as a 10 on the STAR tester. When this code appears, briefly take the engine to wide open throttle. This allows the system to test the throttle position, MAF and MAP sensors.
9. All relevant codes will be displayed and should be recorded. Remember that the codes refer only to faults present during this test cycle. Codes stored in Continuous Memory are not displayed in this test mode.
10. Do not depress the throttle during testing unless a dynamic response code is displayed.

Reading Codes With Analog Voltmeter

▶ See Figures 108 and 109

In the absence of a scan tool, an analog voltmeter may be used to retrieve stored fault codes. Set the meter range to read DC 0–15 volts. Connect the + lead of the meter to the battery positive terminal and connect the -; lead of the meter to the self-test output pin of the diagnostic connector.

Follow the directions given previously for performing the KOEO and KOER tests. To activate the tests, use a jumper wire to connect the signal return pin on the diagnostic connector to the self-test input connector. The self-test input line is the separate wire and connector with or near the diagnostic connector.

The codes will be transmitted as groups of needle sweeps. This method may be used to read either 2 or 3-digit codes. The Continuous Memory codes are separated from the KOEO codes by 6 seconds, a single sweep and another 6 second delay.

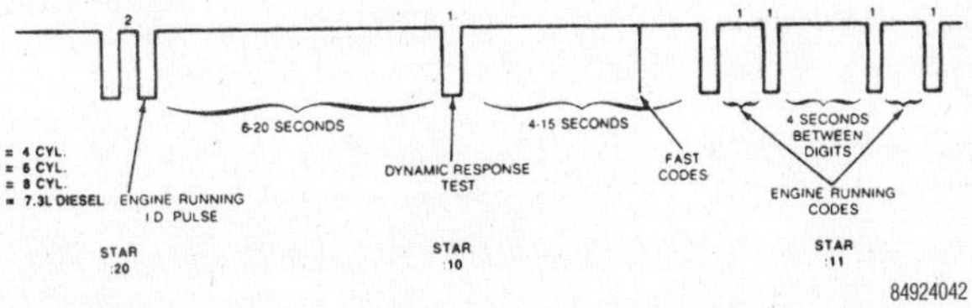

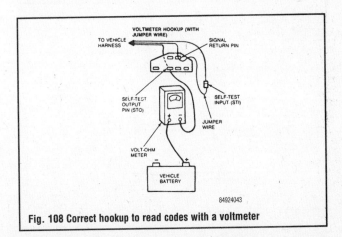

Fig. 107 Code transmission during KOER testing begins with the engine identification pulse and may include a dynamic response prompt

Fig. 108 Correct hookup to read codes with a voltmeter

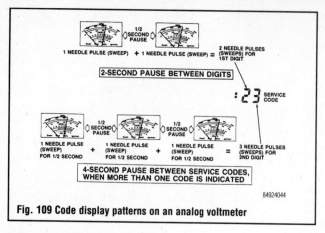

Fig. 109 Code display patterns on an analog voltmeter

Malfunction Indicator Lamp Method

♦ **See Figures 110 and 111**

The Malfunction Indicator Lamp (MIL) on the dashboard may also be used to retrieve the stored codes. This method displays only the stored codes and does not allow any system investigation. It should only be used in field conditions where a quick check of stored codes is needed.

Follow the directions given previously for performing the scan tool procedure. To activate the tests, use a jumper wire to connect the signal return pin on the diagnostic connector to the Self-Test Input (STI) connector. The self-test input line is the separate wire and connector with or near the diagnostic connector.

Codes are transmitted by place value with a pause between the digits; for example, code 32 would be sent as 3 flashes, a pause and 2 flashes. A slightly longer pause divides codes from each other. Be ready to count and record codes; the only way to repeat a code is to recycle the system. This method may

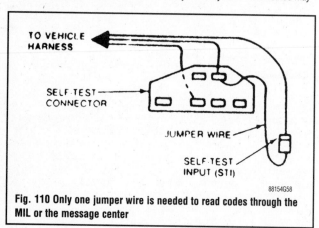

Fig. 110 Only one jumper wire is needed to read codes through the MIL or the message center

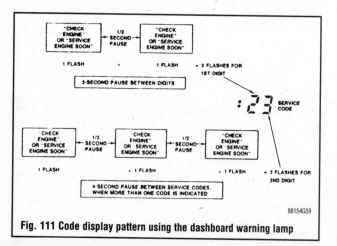

Fig. 111 Code display pattern using the dashboard warning lamp

be used to read either 2 or 3-digit codes. The Continuous Memory codes are separated from the other codes by 6 seconds, a single flash and another 6 second delay.

Other Test Modes

CONTINUOUS MONITOR OR WIGGLE TEST

Once entered, this mode allows the operator to attempt to recreate intermittent faults by wiggling or tapping components, wiring or connectors. The test may be performed during either KOEO or KOER procedures. The test requires the use of either an analog voltmeter or a hand-held scan tool.

To enter the continuous monitor mode during KOEO testing, turn the ignition switch **ON**. Activate the test, wait 10 seconds, then deactivate and reactivate the test; the system will enter the continuous monitor mode. Tap, move or wiggle the harness, component or connector suspected of causing the problem; if a fault is detected, the code will store in the memory. When the fault occurs, the dash warning lamp will illuminate, the STAR tester will light a red indicator (and possibly beep) and the analog meter needle will sweep once.

To enter this mode in the KOER test:
1. Start the engine and run it at 2000 rpm for two minutes. This action warms up the oxygen sensor.
2. Turn the ignition switch **OFF** for 10 seconds.
3. Start the engine.
4. Activate the test, wait 10 seconds, then deactivate and reactivate the test; the system will enter the continuous monitor mode.
5. Tap, move or wiggle the harness, component or connector suspected of causing the problem; if a fault is detected, the code will store in the memory.
6. When the fault occurs, the dash warning lamp will illuminate, the STAR tester will light a red indicator (and possibly beep) and the analog meter needle will sweep once.

OUTPUT STATE CHECK

This testing mode allows the operator to energize and de-energize most of the outputs controlled by the EEC-IV system. Many of the outputs may be checked at the component by listening for a click or feeling the item move or engage by a hand placed on the case. To enter this check:
1. Enter the KOEO test mode.
2. When all codes have been transmitted, depress the accelerator all the way to the floor and release it.
3. The output actuators are now all ON. Depressing the throttle pedal to the floor again switches the all the actuator outputs OFF.
4. This test may be performed as often as necessary, switching between ON and OFF by depressing the throttle.
5. Exit the test by turning the ignition switch **OFF**, disconnecting the jumper at the diagnostic connector or releasing the test button on the scan tool.

Clearing Codes

CONTINUOUS MEMORY CODES

These codes are retained in memory for 40 warm-up cycles. To clear the codes for purposes of testing or confirming repair, perform the code reading procedure. When the fault codes begin to be displayed, de-activate the test either by disconnecting the jumper wire (if using a meter, MIL or message center) or by releasing the test button on the hand scanner. Stopping the test during code transmission will erase the Continuous Memory. Do not disconnect the negative battery cable to clear these codes; the Keep Alive memory will be cleared and a new code, 19, will be stored for loss of PCM power.

KEEP ALIVE MEMORY

The Keep Alive Memory (KAM) contains the adaptive factors used by the processor to compensate for component tolerances and wear. It should not be routinely cleared during diagnosis. If an emissions related part is replaced during repair, the KAM must be cleared. Failure to clear the KAM may cause severe driveability problems since the correction factor for the old component will be applied to the new component.

To clear the Keep Alive Memory, disconnect the negative battery cable for at least 5 minutes. After the memory is cleared and the battery reconnected, the vehicle must be driven at least 10 miles (16 km) so that the processor may relearn the needed correction factors. The distance to be driven depends on the engine and vehicle, but all drives should include steady-throttle cruise on open roads. Certain driveability problems may be noted during the drive because the adaptive factors are not yet functioning.

EEC-V System

GENERAL INFORMATION

The Powertrain Control Module (PCM) is given responsibility for the operation of the emission control devices, cooling fans, ignition and advance and in some cases, automatic transmission functions. Because the EEC-V oversees both the ignition timing and the fuel injector operation, a precise air/fuel ratio will be maintained under all operating conditions. The PCM is a microprocessor or small computer which receives electrical inputs from several sensors, switches and relays on and around the engine.

Based on combinations of these inputs, the PCM controls outputs to various devices concerned with engine operation and emissions. The control module relies on the signals to form a correct picture of current vehicle operation. If any of the input signals is incorrect, the PCM reacts to whatever picture is painted for it. For example, if the coolant temperature sensor is inaccurate and reads too low, the PCM may see a picture of the engine never warming up. Consequently, the engine settings will be maintained as if the engine were cold. Because so many inputs can affect one output, correct diagnostic procedures are essential on these systems.

One part of the PCM is devoted to monitoring both input and output functions within the system. This ability forms the core of the self-diagnostic system. If a problem is detected within a circuit, the control module will recognize the fault, assign it an Diagnostic Trouble Code (DTC), and store the code in memory. The stored code(s) may be retrieved during diagnosis.

While the EEC-V system is capable of recognizing many internal faults, certain faults will not be recognized. Because the control module sees only electrical signals, it cannot sense or react to mechanical or vacuum faults affecting engine operation. Some of these faults may affect another component which will set a code. For example, the PCM monitors the output signal to the fuel injectors, but cannot detect a partially clogged injector. As long as the output driver responds correctly, the computer will read the system as functioning correctly. However, the improper flow of fuel may result in a lean mixture. This would, in turn, be detected by the oxygen sensor and noticed as a constantly lean signal by the PCM. Once the signal falls outside the pre-programmed limits, the control module would notice the fault and set an trouble code.

Additionally, the EEC-V system employs adaptive fuel logic. This process is used to compensate for normal wear and variability within the fuel system. Once the engine enters steady-state operation, the control module watches the oxygen sensor signal for a bias or tendency to run slightly rich or lean. If such a bias is detected, the adaptive logic corrects the fuel delivery to bring the air/fuel mixture towards a centered or 14.7:1 ratio. This compensating shift is stored in a non-volatile memory which is retained by battery power even with the ignition switched **OFF**. The correction factor is then available the next time the vehicle is operated.

MALFUNCTION INDICATOR LAMP

The Malfunction Indicator Lamp (MIL) is located on the instrument panel. The lamp is connected to the PCM and will alert the driver to certain malfunctions within the EEC-V system. When the lamp is illuminated, the PCM has detected a fault and stored an DTC in memory.

The light will stay illuminated as long as the fault is present. Should the fault self-correct, the MIL will extinguish but the stored code will remain in memory.

Under normal operating conditions, the MIL should illuminate briefly when the ignition key is turned **ON**. This is commonly known as a prove-out. As soon as the PCM receives a signal that the engine is cranking, the lamp should extinguish. The lamp should remain extinguished during the normal operating cycle.

Data Link Connector

▶ See Figure 112

The Data Link Connector (DLC) may be found in the following location:
- Under the driver's side dash , near the steering column.

The DLC is rectangular in design and capable of allowing access to 16 terminals. The connector has keying features that allow easy connection. The test equipment and the DLC have a latching feature to ensure a good mated connection.

Fig. 112 The diagnostic link connector is covered by a protective cap

ELECTRICAL TOOLS

The most commonly required electrical diagnostic tool is the Digital Multimeter, allowing voltage, resistance, and amperage to be read by one instrument. Many of the diagnostic charts require the use of a volt or ohmmeter during diagnosis.

The multimeter must be a high impedance unit, with 10 megaohms of impedance in the voltmeter. This type of meter will not place an additional load on the circuit it is testing; this is extremely important in low voltage circuits. The multimeter must be of high quality in all respects. It should be handled carefully and protected from impact or damage. Replace the batteries frequently in the unit.

Reading Codes

▶ See Figure 113

The EEC-V equipped engines utilize On Board Diagnostic II (OBD-II) DTC's, which are alpha-numeric (they use letters and numbers). The letters in the OBD-

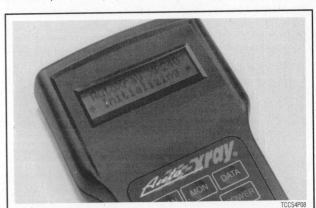

Fig. 113 When using a scan tool, make sure to follow all of the manufacturer's instructions carefully to ensure proper diagnosis

II DTC's make it highly difficult to convey the codes through the use of anything but a scan tool. Therefore, to read the codes on these vehicles it is necessary to utilize an OBD-II compatible scan tool.

Since each manufacturers scan tool is different, please follow the manufacturer's instructions for connecting the tool and obtaining code information.

Clearing Codes

CONTINUOUS MEMORY CODES

These codes are retained in memory for 40 warm-up cycles. To clear the codes for the purposes of testing or confirming repair, perform the code reading procedure. When the fault codes begin to be displayed, de-activate the test by either disconnecting the jumper wire (meter, MIL or message center) or releasing the test button on the hand scanner. Stopping the test during code transmission will erase the Continuous Memory. Do not disconnect the negative battery cable to clear these codes; the Keep Alive memory will be cleared and a new code, 19, will be stored for loss of PCM power.

KEEP ALIVE MEMORY

The Keep Alive Memory (KAM) contains the adaptive factors used by the processor to compensate for component tolerances and wear. It should not be routinely cleared during diagnosis. If an emissions related part is replaced during repair, the KAM must be cleared. Failure to clear the KAM may cause severe driveability problems since the correction factor for the old component will be applied to the new component.

To clear the Keep Alive Memory, disconnect the negative battery cable for at least 5 minutes. After the memory is cleared and the battery reconnected, the vehicle must be driven at least 10 miles so that the processor may relearn the needed correction factors. The distance to be driven depends on the engine and vehicle, but all drives should include steady-throttle cruise on open roads. Certain driveability problems may be noted during the drive because the adaptive factors are not yet functioning.

VACUUM DIAGRAMS

▶ **See Figures 114 thru 121**

Following are vacuum diagrams for most of the engine and emissions package combinations covered by this manual. Because vacuum circuits will vary based on various engine and vehicle options, always refer first to the vehicle emission control information label, if present. Should the label be missing, or

should the vehicle be equipped with a different engine from the vehicle's original equipment, refer to the diagrams below for the same or similar configuration.

If you wish to obtain a replacement emissions label, most manufacturers make the labels available for purchase. The labels can usually be ordered from a local dealer.

Fig. 114 The Emission Control Label contains information about the vehicle's emissions systems, along with other pertinent service information

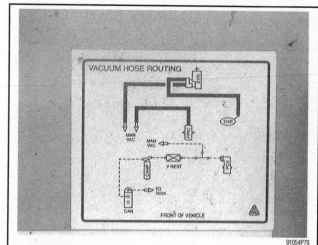

Fig. 115 A Vacuum diagram is usually located on the underside of the hood

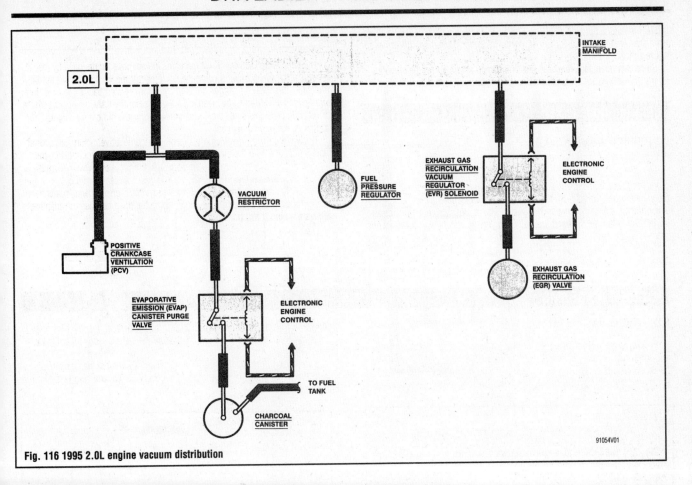

Fig. 116 1995 2.0L engine vacuum distribution

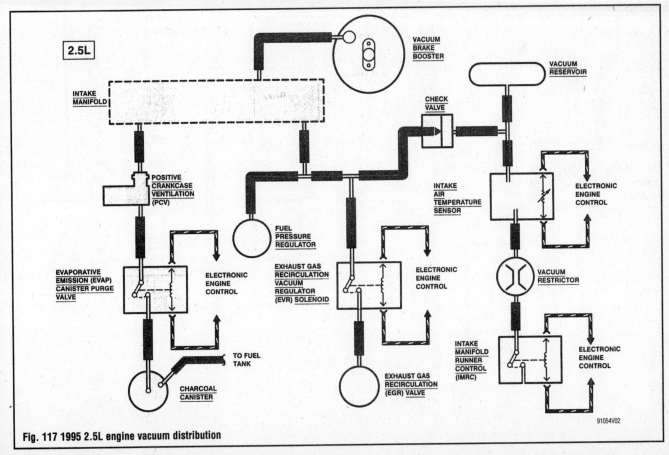

Fig. 117 1995 2.5L engine vacuum distribution

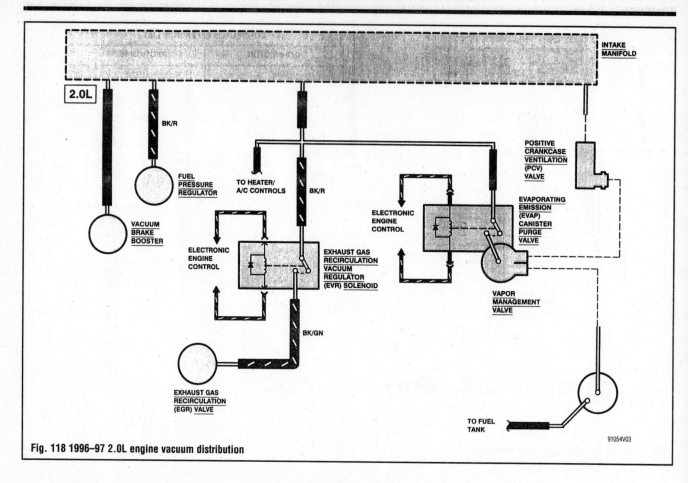

Fig. 118 1996–97 2.0L engine vacuum distribution

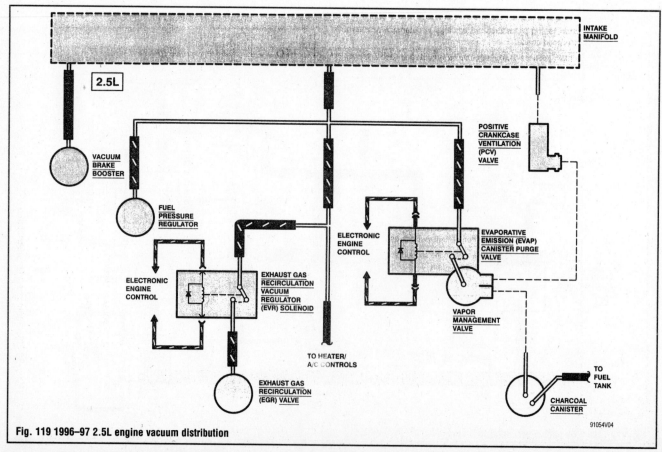

Fig. 119 1996–97 2.5L engine vacuum distribution

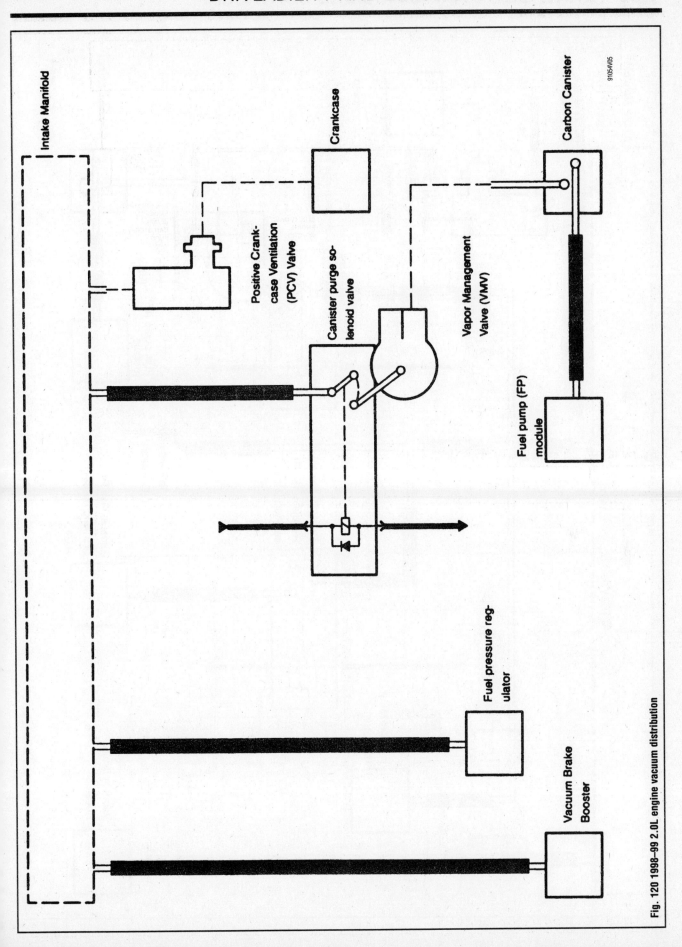

Fig. 120 1998–99 2.0L engine vacuum distribution

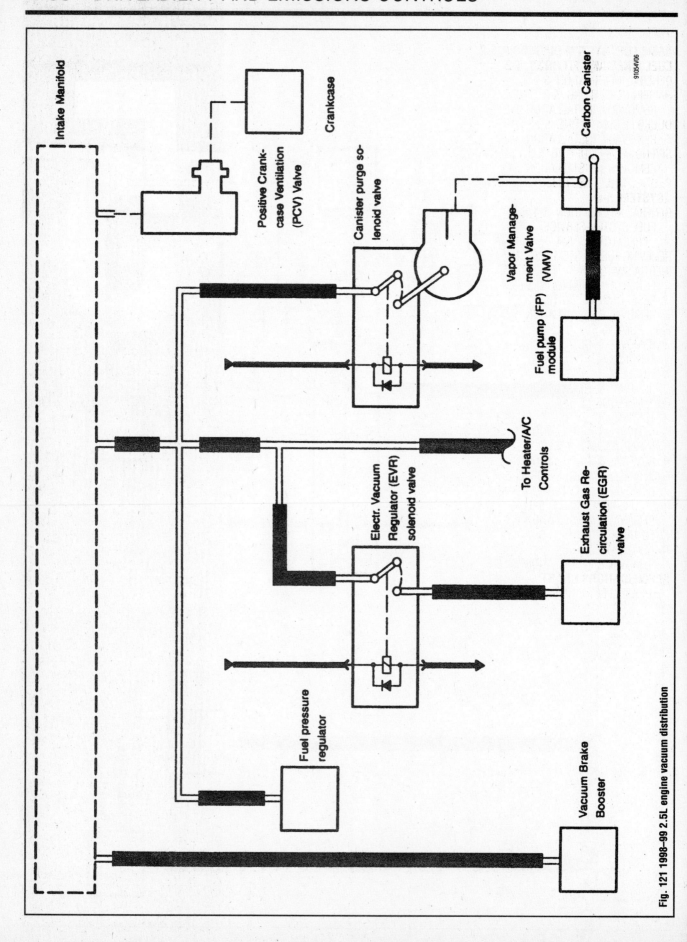

Fig. 121 1998–99 2.5L engine vacuum distribution

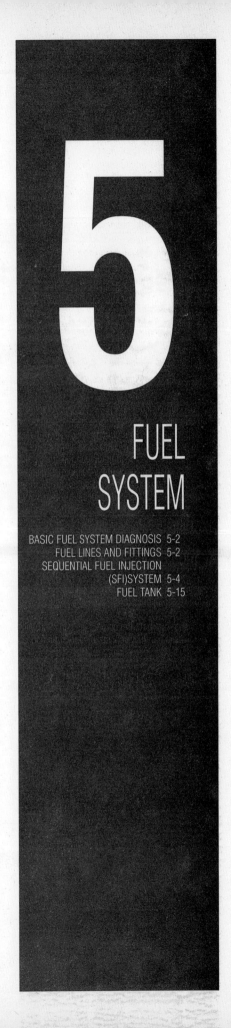

5

FUEL
SYSTEM

BASIC FUEL SYSTEM DIAGNOSIS

When there is a problem starting or driving a vehicle, two of the most important checks involve the ignition and the fuel systems. The questions most mechanics attempt to answer first, "is there spark?" and "is there fuel?" will often lead to solving most basic problems. For ignition system diagnosis and testing, please refer to the information on engine electrical components and ignition systems found earlier in this manual. If the ignition system checks out (there is spark), then you must determine if the fuel system is operating properly (is there fuel?).

FUEL LINES AND FITTINGS

General Information

➡**Quick-connect (push type) fuel line fittings must be disconnected using proper procedure or the fitting may be damaged. There are two types of retainers used on the push connect fittings. Line sizes of ⅜ and 5/16 in. diameter use a hairpin clip retainer. The ¼ in. diameter line connectors use a duck-bill clip retainer. In addition, some engines use spring-lock connections, secured by a garter spring, which require Ford Tool T81P-19623-G (or equivalent) for removal.**

✳✳ CAUTION

Observe all applicable safety precautions when working around fuel. Whenever servicing the fuel system, always work in a well ventilated area. Do not allow fuel spray or vapors to come in contact with a spark or open flame. Keep a dry chemical fire extinguisher near the work area. Always keep fuel in a container specifically designed for fuel storage; also, always properly seal fuel containers to avoid the possibility of fire or explosion.

Hairpin Clip Fitting

REMOVAL & INSTALLATION

◆ **See Figures 1 and 2**

1. Clean all dirt and grease from the fitting. Spread the two clip legs about ⅛ in. (3mm) each to disengage from the fitting and pull the clip outward from the fitting. Use finger pressure only; do not use any tools.
2. Grasp the fitting and hose assembly and pull away from the steel line. Twist the fitting and hose assembly slightly while pulling, if the assembly sticks.
3. Inspect the hairpin clip for damage, replacing the clip if necessary. Reinstall the clip in position on the fitting.
4. Inspect the fitting and inside of the connector to ensure freedom from dirt or obstruction. Install the fitting into the connector and push together. A click will be heard when the hairpin snaps into the proper connection. Pull on the line to insure full engagement.

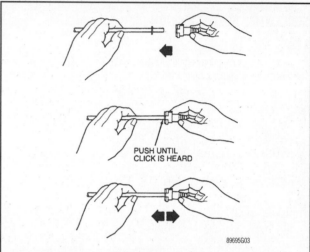
Fig. 2 When assembling the fitting, push the pipe into the fitting until a click is heard

Duckbill Clip Fitting

REMOVAL & INSTALLATION

◆ **See Figure 3**

1. A special tool is available from Ford and other manufacturers for removing the retaining clips. Use Ford Tool T90T-9550-B or C or equivalent. If the tool is not on hand, go onto step 2. Align the slot on the push connector disconnect tool with either tab on the retaining clip. Pull the line from the connector.
2. If the special clip tool is not available, use a pair of narrow 6-inch slip-jaw pliers with a jaw width of 0.2 in (5mm) or less. Align the jaws of the pliers with the openings of the fitting case and compress the part of the retaining clip

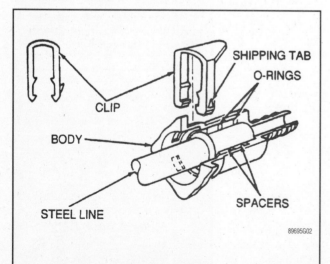
Fig. 1 Cutaway view of the hairpin clip fitting

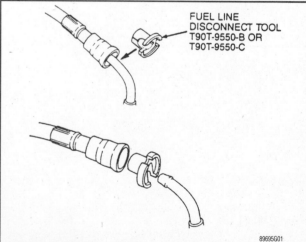
Fig. 3 A fuel line disconnect tool is required to properly separate a duckbill clip fitting

that engages the case. Compressing the retaining clip will release the fitting, which may be pulled from the connector. Both sides of the clip must be compressed at the same time to disengage.

3. Inspect the retaining clip, fitting end and connector. Replace the clip if any damage is apparent.

4. Push the line into the steel connector until a click is heard, indicating the clip is in place. Pull on the line to check engagement.

Spring Lock Coupling

REMOVAL & INSTALLATION

▶ See Figures 4 thru 13

The spring lock coupling is held together by a garter spring inside a circular cage. When the coupling is connected together, the flared end of the female fit-

ting slips behind the garter spring inside the cage of the male fitting. The garter spring and cage then prevent the flared end of the female fitting from pulling out of the cage. As an additional locking feature, most vehicles have a horseshoe-shaped retaining clip that improves the retaining reliability of the spring lock coupling.

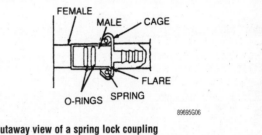

Fig. 4 Cutaway view of a spring lock coupling

Fig. 5 Remove the safety clip from the fuel lines, the clip is attached to a small wire that keeps it from getting lost

Fig. 6 This type of removal tool has a hinged center section that allows you to fit it around the fuel line

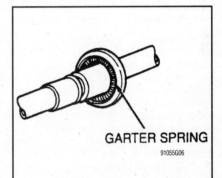

Fig. 7 The garter spring is located inside the fitting and holds the fitting together

Fig. 8 Slide the tool back to unseat the garter spring on the fitting, and pull back on the fuel line to separate them

Fig. 9 This type of removal tool snaps over the line

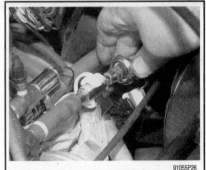

Fig. 10 Slide the tool back to unseat the garter spring on the fitting, and pull back on the fuel line to separate them

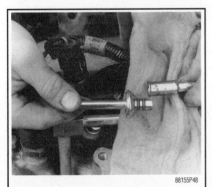

Fig. 11 Be sure to check the O-rings for damage; replace them if necessary

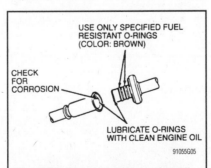

Fig. 12 The O-rings should be replaced if necessary with the specific ones used for the fuel system, a non-specific O-ring could leak

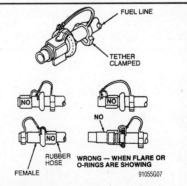

Fig. 13 The fitting should be inspected after assembly

SEQUENTIAL FUEL INJECTION (SFI) SYSTEM

General Information

The Sequential Fuel Injection (SFI) system includes a high pressure, inline electric fuel pump mounted in the fuel tank, a fuel supply manifold, a throttle body (meters the incoming air charge for the correct mixture with the fuel), a pressure regulator, fuel filters and both solid and flexible fuel lines. The fuel supply manifold includes 4 or 6 electronically-controlled fuel injectors, each mounted directly above an intake port in the intake manifold. Each injector fires once every other crankshaft revolution, in sequence with the engine firing order.

The fuel pressure regulator maintains a constant pressure drop across the injector nozzles. The regulator is referenced to intake manifold vacuum and is connected in parallel to the fuel injectors; it is positioned on the far end of the fuel rail. Any excess fuel supplied by the fuel pump passes through the regulator and is returned to the fuel tank via a return line.

➡**The pressure regulator reduces fuel pressure to 35–40 psi under normal operating conditions. At idle or high manifold vacuum condition, fuel pressure is further reduced to approximately 30 psi.**

The fuel pressure regulator is a diaphragm-operated relief valve, in which the inside of the diaphragm senses fuel pressure and the other side senses manifold vacuum. Normal fuel pressure is established by a spring preload applied to the diaphragm. Control of the fuel system is maintained through the Powertrain Control Module (PCM), although electrical power is routed through the fuel pump relay and an inertia switch. The fuel pump relay is normally located in the power distribution box, under the hood, and the inertia switch is located in the trunk. The inline fuel pump is mounted in the fuel tank.

The inertia switch opens the power circuit to the fuel pump in the event of a collision or roll over. Once tripped, the switch must be reset manually by pushing the reset button on the assembly.

➡**Check that the inertia switch is reset before diagnosing power supply problems to the fuel pump.**

The fuel injectors used with SFI system are electro-mechanical (solenoid) type, designed to meter and atomize fuel delivered to the intake ports of the engine. The injectors are mounted in the intake manifold and positioned so that their spray nozzles direct the fuel charge in front of the intake valves. The injector body consists of a solenoid-actuated pintle and needle-valve assembly. The control unit sends an electrical impulse that activates the solenoid, causing the pintle to move inward off the seat and allow the fuel to flow. The amount of fuel delivered is controlled by the length of time the injector is energized (pulse width), since the fuel flow orifice is fixed and the fuel pressure drop across the injector tip is constant. Correct atomization is achieved by contouring the pintle at the point where the fuel enters the pintle chamber.

➡**Exercise care when handling fuel injectors during service. Be careful not to lose the pintle cap and always replace O-rings to assure a tight seal.**

The injectors receive high-pressure fuel from the fuel supply manifold (fuel rail) assembly. The complete assembly includes a single, pre-formed tube with four or six connectors, the mounting flange for the pressure regulator, and mounting attachments to locate the manifold and provide the fuel injector retainers.

The fuel manifold is normally removed with the fuel injectors and pressure regulator attached. Fuel injector electrical connectors are plastic and have locking tabs that must be released when disconnecting the wiring harness.

FUEL SYSTEM SERVICE PRECAUTIONS

Safety is the most important factor when performing not only fuel system maintenance, but any type of maintenance. Failure to conduct maintenance and repairs in a safe manner may result in serious personal injury or death. Work on a vehicle's fuel system components can be accomplished safely and effectively by adhering to the following rules and guidelines.

• To avoid the possibility of fire and personal injury, always disconnect the negative battery cable unless the repair or test procedure requires that battery voltage by applied.

• Always relieve the fuel system pressure prior to disconnecting any fuel system component (injector, fuel rail, pressure regulator, etc.) fitting or fuel line connection. Exercise extreme caution whenever relieving fuel system pressure to avoid exposing skin, face and eyes to fuel spray. Please be advised that fuel under pressure may penetrate the skin or any part of the body that it contacts.

• Always place a shop towel or cloth around the fitting or connection prior to loosening to absorb any excess fuel due to spillage. Ensure that all fuel spillage is quickly remove from engine surfaces. Ensure that all fuel-soaked cloths or towels are deposited into a flame-proof waste container with a lid.

• Always keep a dry chemical (Class B) fire extinguisher near the work area.

• Do not allow fuel spray or fuel vapors to come into contact with a spark or open flame.

• Always use a second wrench when loosening or tightening fuel line connections fittings. This will prevent unnecessary stress and torsion to fuel piping. Always follow the proper torque specifications.

• Always replace worn fuel fitting O-rings with new ones. Do not substitute fuel hose where rigid pipe is installed.

Relieving Fuel System Pressure

▸ **See Figures 14 and 15**

✳ CAUTION

Observe all applicable safety precautions when working around fuel. Whenever servicing the fuel system, always work in a well ventilated area. Do not allow fuel spray or vapors to come in contact with a spark or open flame. Keep a dry chemical fire extinguisher near the work area. Always keep fuel in a container specifically designed for fuel storage; also, always properly seal fuel containers to avoid the possibility of fire or explosion.

All SFI fuel injected engines are equipped with a pressure relief valve located on the fuel supply manifold. Remove the fuel tank cap and attach fuel pressure gauge T80L-9974-B, or equivalent, to the valve to release the fuel pressure. Be sure to drain the fuel into a suitable container and to avoid gasoline spillage.

If a pressure gauge is not available, disconnect the vacuum hose from the fuel pressure regulator and attach a hand-held vacuum pump. Apply about 25 in. Hg (84 kPa) of vacuum to the regulator to vent the fuel system pressure into the fuel tank through the fuel return hose. Note that this procedure will remove the fuel pressure from the lines, but not the fuel. Take precautions to avoid the risk of fire and use clean rags to soak up any spilled fuel when the lines are disconnected.

An alternate method of relieving the fuel system pressure involves disconnecting the inertia switch with the engine running and waiting for the engine to stall. this procedure works, however it is not recommended and will set a DTC in the PCM but will not illuminate the MIL lamp.

Inertia Switch

GENERAL INFORMATION

This switch shuts off the fuel pump in the event of a collision. Once the switch has been tripped, it must be reset manually in order to start the engine.

The inertia switch is located on the driver's side of the vehicle behind the kick panel near the driver's feet.

RESETTING THE SWITCH

▸ **See Figure 16**

1. Turn the ignition switch **OFF**.
2. Ensure that there is no fuel leaking in the engine compartment, along any of the lines or at the tank. There should be no odor of fuel as well.
3. If no leakage and/or odor is apparent, reset the switch by pushing the reset button on the top of the switch.
4. Cycle the ignition switch from the **ON** to **OFF** positions several times, allowing five seconds at each position, to build fuel pressure within the system.

5. Again, check the fuel system for leaks. There should be no odor of fuel as well.

6. If there is no leakage and/or odor of fuel, it is safe to operate the vehicle. However, it is recommended that the entire system be checked by a professional, especially if the vehicle was in an accident severe enough to trip the inertia switch.

REMOVAL & INSTALLATION

1. Disconnect the negative battery cable.
2. Remove the driver's side kick panel.
3. Unplug the connector on the inertia switch.
4. Remove the retaining bolts and remove the switch.
To install:
5. Installation is the reverse of removal.

Fuel Pump

REMOVAL & INSTALLATION

▶ See Figures 17 thru 21

✳✳ CAUTION

Observe all applicable safety precautions when working around fuel. Whenever servicing the fuel system, always work in a well ventilated area. Do not allow fuel spray or vapors to come in contact with a spark or open flame. Keep a dry chemical fire extinguisher near the work area. Always keep fuel in a container specifically designed for fuel storage; also, always properly seal fuel containers to avoid the possibility of fire or explosion.

✳✳ CAUTION

The fuel injection system remains under pressure, even after the engine has been turned OFF. The fuel system pressure MUST BE relieved before disconnecting any fuel lines. Failure to do so may result in fire and/or personal injury.

1. Disconnect the negative battery cable.
2. Relieve the fuel pressure using the following procedure:
   a. Open the fuel tank filler cap to vent off pressure in the tank.
   b. Remove the air cleaner assembly.
   c. Connect a fuel pressure gauge to the fuel pressure relief valve located on the fuel rail.
   d. Open the manual valve on the fuel pressure gauge and drain the fuel through the drain tube into a suitable container.
   e. Remove the fuel pressure gauge.
   f. Secure the fuel fill cap and install the air cleaner assembly.
3. Remove the rear seat cushion.
4. Remove the plastic grommet from the floor pan.
5. Disconnect the fuel pump electrical harness.
6. Disconnect the fuel lines from the fuel pump by compressing the tabs

Fig. 14 The Schrader valve for the fuel system is located near the quick connect fittings for the fuel rail—2.0L engine

Fig. 15 Unscrew the protective cap to access the valve

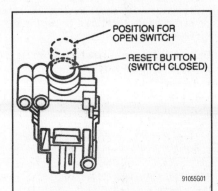
Fig. 16 The inertia switch reset button is located on the top of the switch

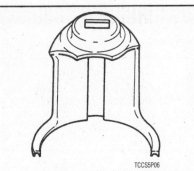
Fig. 17 A special tool is usually available to remove or install the fuel pump locking cam

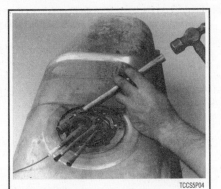
Fig. 18 A brass drift and a hammer can be used to loosen the fuel pump locking cam

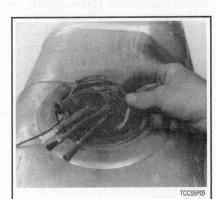
Fig. 19 Once the locking cam is released it can be removed to free the fuel pump

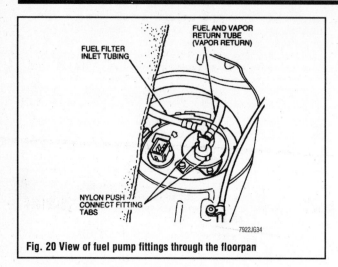

Fig. 20 View of fuel pump fittings through the floorpan

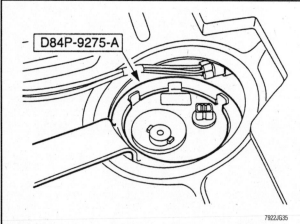

Fig. 21 Remove the locking ring from the fuel pump sender with a special wrench such as Fuel Tank Sender Wrench D84P-9275-A

on both sides of each nylon push connect fitting and easing the fuel line off of the fuel pump.

7. Using Fuel Tank Sender Wrench D84P-9275-A or equivalent, turn the fuel pump locking ring counterclockwise to loosen the ring.

➡**A drift punch or a screwdriver or other tool can be used to disengage the fuel pump locking ring, the special tool is not required.**

8. Remove the fuel pump locking ring.

9. Remove the fuel pump being careful not to damage the fuel gauge sending unit.

10. Place a shop towel over the opening in the fuel tank to prevent dirt from contaminating the fuel.

To install:

11. Remove the shop towel over the opening in the fuel tank and clean the groove for the fuel pump seal. Be careful not to allow dirt to enter the fuel tank.

12. Apply a light coat of grease onto a new O-ring seal and install into the groove of the fuel tank.

13. Carefully install the fuel pump into the tank to prevent damage to the fuel gauge sender or the fuel pick-up filter.

➡**It is recommended that the in-line fuel filter be replaced whenever a fuel pump is being replaced.**

14. Ensure that the flange of the fuel pump mounting plate is located properly in its keyway and that the O-ring has not shifted out of position.

15. Keep a light downward pressure on the fuel pump while installing the fuel pump locking retainer ring.

16. Install the ring ensuring that all of the locking tabs are under the fuel tank lock ring tabs. Turn the ring clockwise finger-tight.

17. Install the fuel tank sender wrench or equivalent, over the retainer ring and finish tightening until the retainer ring is resting against its stops.

18. Reconnect the fuel lines to the fuel pump.

19. Reinstall the fuel pump electrical harness connector.

20. Reinstall the plastic grommet into the floorpan.

21. Reinstall the rear seat cushion.

22. Reconnect the negative battery cable.

23. Start the engine and check for leaks and proper operation.

TESTING

▸ See Figures 14, 15 and 22

✳✳ CAUTION

Observe all applicable safety precautions when working around fuel. Whenever servicing the fuel system, always work in a well ventilated area. Do not allow fuel spray or vapors to come in contact with a spark or open flame. Keep a dry chemical fire extinguisher near the work area. Always keep fuel in a container specifically designed for fuel storage; also, always properly seal fuel containers to avoid the possibility of fire or explosion.

1. Check all hoses and lines for kinks and leaking. Repair as necessary.

2. Check all electrical connections for looseness and corrosion. Repair as necessary.

3. Turn the ignition key from the **OFF** position to the **RUN** position several times (do not start the engine) and verify that the pump runs briefly each time, (you will here a low humming sound from the fuel tank).

➡**Check that the inertia switch is reset before diagnosing power supply problems to the fuel pump.**

The use of a scan tool is required to perform these tests.

4. Turn the ignition key **OFF**.

5. Connect a suitable fuel pressure gauge to the fuel test port (Schrader valve) on the fuel rail.

6. Connect the scan tool and turn the ignition key **ON** but do not start the engine.

7. Following the scan tool manufacturer's instructions, enter the output test mode and run the fuel pump to obtain the maximum fuel pressure.

8. The fuel pressure should be between 30–40 psi (310–415 kPa).

9. If the fuel pressure is within specification the pump is working properly. If not, continue with the test.

10. Check the pump ground connection and service as necessary.

11. Turn the ignition key **ON**.

Fig. 22 Install a fuel pressure gauge onto the Schrader valve to check the fuel pressure

12. Using the scan tool, enter output test mode and turn on the fuel pump circuit.

13. Using a Digital Volt Ohmmeter (DVOM), check for voltage (approximately 10.5 volts) at the fuel pump electrical connector.

14. If the pump is getting a good voltage supply, the ground connection is good and the fuel pressure is not within specification, then replace the pump.

Throttle Body

REMOVAL & INSTALLATION

2.0L Engine

▶ See Figures 23 thru 37

1. Disconnect the negative battery cable.
2. Remove the air intake resonators..
3. Unplug the Throttle Position (TP) sensor electrical connection.
4. Disconnect the accelerator cable from the throttle lever.
5. If equipped with speed control, disconnect the speed control actuator.
6. Unfasten the throttle body retaining bolts and remove the throttle body.

➡If scraping is necessary to remove any gasket material, be careful not to damage the gasket mating surfaces or allow any foreign material to enter the intake manifold.

7. Remove the old gasket and clean any gasket residue from both mating surfaces.

To install:

8. Install a new gasket and the throttle body.
9. Install the throttle body retaining bolts and tighten them to 71–106 inch lbs. (8–12 Nm).
10. Connect the accelerator cable to the throttle lever.
11. If equipped with speed control, connect the speed control actuator.

12. Attach the Throttle Position (TP) sensor electrical connection.
13. Install the air intake resonators
14. Connect the negative battery cable.

2.5L Engine

▶ See Figure 38

1. Disconnect the negative battery cable.
2. Remove the air cleaner outlet tube.
3. Remove the water pump pulley shield retaining screws.
4. Unplug the Throttle Position (TP) sensor electrical connection and remove the harness retainer from the throttle body mounting stud..
5. Disconnect the accelerator cable from the throttle lever.
6. If equipped with speed control, disconnect the speed control actuator.
7. Unfasten the throttle body retaining bolts and remove the throttle body.

➡If scraping is necessary to remove any gasket material, be careful not to damage the gasket mating surfaces or allow any foreign material to enter the intake manifold.

8. Remove the old gasket and clean any gasket residue from both mating surfaces.

To install:

9. Install a new gasket and the throttle body.
10. Install the throttle body retaining bolts and tighten them to 71–106 inch lbs. (8–12 Nm).
11. Connect the accelerator cable to the throttle lever.
12. If equipped with speed control, connect the speed control actuator.
13. Attach the Throttle Position (TP) sensor electrical connection and connect the retainer to the throttle body stud.
14. Install the water pump pulley shield.
15. Connect the air cleaner outlet tube.
16. Connect the negative battery cable.

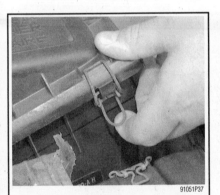
Fig. 23 Grasp and unfasten the retaining clips . . .

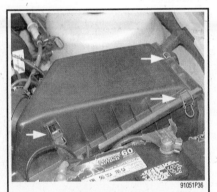
Fig. 24 . . . located in the following positions —2.0L engine, 2.5L similar

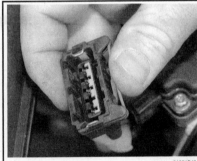
Fig. 25 The MAF connector is released by pressing down on the retaining spring—shown here already disconnected

Fig. 26 Label and disconnect the MAF sensor and . . .

Fig. 27 . . . the IAT sensor

Fig. 28 Loosen the clamp on the air cleaner tube

Fig. 29 Lift the air cleaner inlet tube slightly and slide the retaining tab on the air intake resonator out and . . .

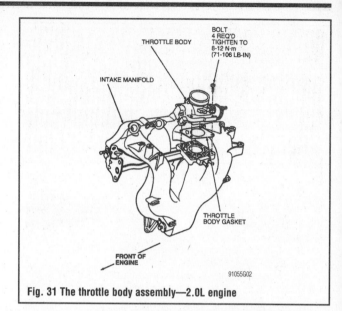

Fig. 31 The throttle body assembly—2.0L engine

Fig. 30 . . . remove the air cleaner inlet tube from the vehicle

Fig. 32 Remove the four throttle body air intake resonator retaining bolts

Fig. 33 Remove the throttle body air intake resonator from the engine

Fig. 34 Remove the accelerator cable from the throttle body

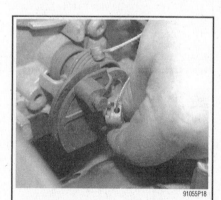

Fig. 35 Remove the speed control cable from the throttle body (if equipped)

Fig. 36 Remove the four throttle body retaining bolts

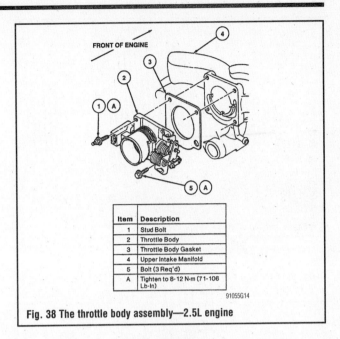

FRONT OF ENGINE

Item	Description
1	Stud Bolt
2	Throttle Body
3	Throttle Body Gasket
4	Upper Intake Manifold
5	Bolt (3 Req'd)
A	Tighten to 8-12 N·m (71-106 Lb-In)

Fig. 38 The throttle body assembly—2.5L engine

Fig. 37 Always replace the throttle body gasket or a air leak could occur and the vehicle will run poorly

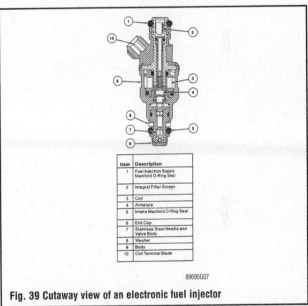

Item	Description
1	Fuel Injection Supply Manifold O-Ring Seal
2	Integral Filter Screen
3	Coil
4	Armature
5	Intake Manifold O-Ring Seal
6	End Cap
7	Stainless Steel Needle and Valve Body
8	Washer
9	Body
10	Coil Terminal Blade

Fig. 39 Cutaway view of an electronic fuel injector

Fuel Injector(s)

TESTING

♦ See Figures 39, 40 and 41

The easiest way to test the operation of the fuel injectors is to listen for a clicking sound coming from the injectors while the engine is running. This is accomplished using a mechanic's stethoscope, or a long screwdriver. Place the end of the stethoscope or the screwdriver (tip end, not handle) onto the body of the injector. Place the ear pieces of the stethoscope in your ears, or if using a screwdriver, place your ear on top of the handle. An audible clicking noise should be heard; this is the solenoid operating. If the injector makes this noise, the injector driver circuit and computer are operating as designed. Continue testing all the injectors this way.

❈❈ CAUTION

Be extremely careful while working on an operating engine, make sure you have no dangling jewelry, extremely loose clothes, power tool cords or other items that might get caught in a moving part of the engine.

All Injectors Clicking

If all the injectors are clicking, but you have determined that the fuel system is the cause of your driveability problem, continue diagnostics. Make sure that you have checked fuel pump pressure as outlined earlier in this section. An easy way to determine a weak or unproductive cylinder is a cylinder drop test. This is accomplished by removing one spark plug wire at a time, and seeing which cylinder causes the least difference in the idle. The one that causes the least change is the weak cylinder.

If the injectors were all clicking and the ignition system is functioning properly, remove the injector of the suspect cylinder and bench test it. This is accomplished by checking for a spray pattern from the injector itself. Install a fuel supply line to the injector (or rail if the injector is left attached to the rail) and momentarily apply 12 volts DC and a ground to the injector itself; a visible fuel spray should appear. If no spray is achieved, replace the injector and check the running condition of the engine.

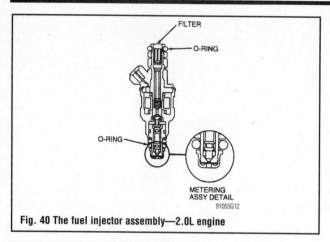

Fig. 40 The fuel injector assembly—2.0L engine

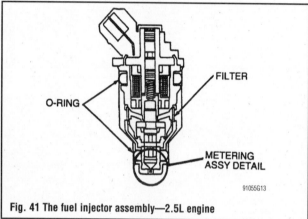

Fig. 41 The fuel injector assembly—2.5L engine

One or More Injectors Are Not Clicking

▶ See Figures 42, 43, 44 and 45

If one or more injectors are found to be not operating, testing the injector driver circuit and computer can be accomplished using a "noid" light. First, with the engine not running and the ignition key in the **OFF** position, remove the connector from the injector you plan to test, then plug the "noid" light tool into the injector connector. Start the engine and the "noid" light should flash, signaling that the injector driver circuit is working. If the "noid" light flashes, but the injector does not click when plugged in, test the injector's resistance. resistance should be between 11–18 ohms.

If the "noid" light does not flash, the injector driver circuit is faulty. Disconnect the negative battery cable. Unplug the "noid" light from the injector connector and also unplug the PCM. Check the harness between the appropriate pins on the harness side of the PCM connector and the injector connector. Resistance should be less than 5.0 ohms; if not, repair the circuit. If resistance is within specifications, the injector driver inside the PCM is faulty and replacement of the PCM will be necessary.

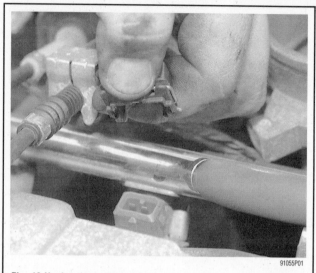

Fig. 42 Unplug the fuel injector connector

REMOVAL & INSTALLATION

2.0L Engine

▶ See Figures 23 thru 33, 46 thru 53

> ※※ **CAUTION**
>
> Fuel injection systems remain under pressure, even after the engine has been turned OFF. The fuel system pressure must be relieved before disconnecting any fuel lines. Failure to do so may result in fire and/or personal injury.

> ※※ **CAUTION**
>
> Observe all applicable safety precautions when working around fuel. Whenever servicing the fuel system, always work in a well ventilated area. Do not allow fuel spray or vapors to come in contact with a spark or open flame. Keep a dry chemical fire extinguisher near the work area. Always keep fuel in a container specifically designed for fuel storage; also, always properly seal fuel containers to avoid the possibility of fire or explosion.

1. Relieve the fuel system pressure.
2. Disconnect the negative battery cable.
3. Remove the fuel injection supply manifold (fuel rail).
4. Remove the injector retaining clips.
5. Grasp the fuel injectors body and pull up while gently rocking the fuel injector from side to side.

Fig. 43 Probe the two terminals of a fuel injector to check it's resistance

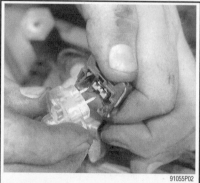

Fig. 44 Plug the correct "noid" light directly into the injector harness connector

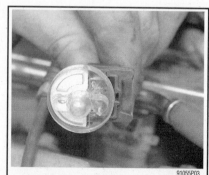

Fig. 45 If the correct "noid" light flashes while the engine is running, the injector driver circuit inside the PCM is working

Fig. 46 The fuel rail is held by three retaining bolts

Fig. 47 Remove the three fuel rail retaining bolts

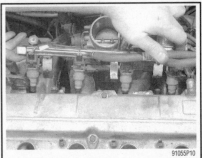

Fig. 48 Carefully lift the fuel rail up out of the intake manifold, if the fuel rail is tight coming out, slightly rock it side to side to loosen the injector O-rings

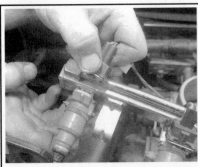

Fig. 49 Unplug the connector(s) from the fuel injector(s) by depressing the retaining springs

Fig. 50 The injectors are held to the fuel rail by steel clips, insert a small screwdriver behind the clips and . . .

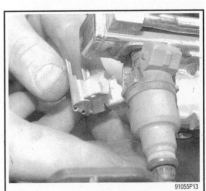

Fig. 51 . . . pry the clip from the injector and rail

Fig. 52 Wiggle the injector to release it from the fuel rail

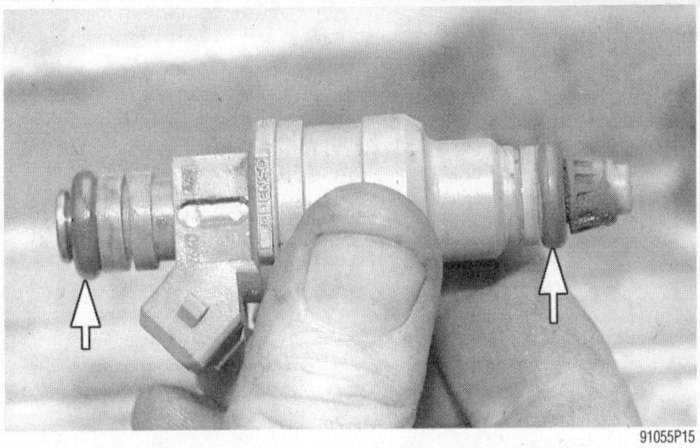

Fig. 53 Replace the O-rings or a fuel leak could occur

6. Once removed, inspect the fuel injector cap and body for signs of deterioration. Replace as required.

7. Remove the O-rings and discard. If an O-ring or end cap is missing, look in the intake manifold for the missing part.

To install:

8. Install new O-rings onto each injector and apply a small amount of clean engine oil to the O-rings.

9. Install the injectors using a slight twisting downward motion.

10. Install the injector retaining clips.

11. Install the fuel injection supply manifold (fuel rail).

12. Connect the negative battery cable.

13. Run the engine at idle for 2 minutes, then turn the engine **OFF** and check for fuel leaks and proper operation.

2.5L Engine

▶ See Figures 54 and 55

❊❊ CAUTION

Fuel injection systems remain under pressure, even after the engine has been turned OFF. The fuel system pressure must be relieved before disconnecting any fuel lines. Failure to do so may result in fire and/or personal injury.

1. Relieve the fuel system pressure.
2. Disconnect the negative battery cable.
3. Disconnect the fuel lines.
4. Remove the upper intake manifold.

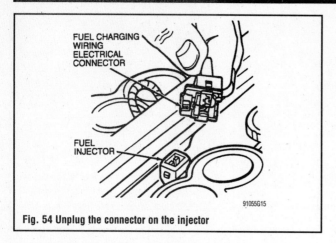

Fig. 54 Unplug the connector on the injector

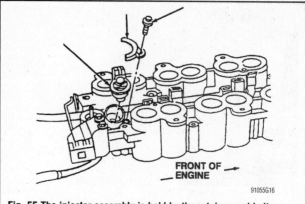

Fig. 55 The injector assembly is held by the retainer and bolt

5. Unplug the fuel injector connectors.
6. Remove the fuel injection supply manifold (fuel rail).
7. Remove the injector retaining clips.
8. Remove the injectors from the fuel rail using injector remover T94P-9000-AH or equivalent.
9. Once removed, inspect the fuel injector cap and body for signs of deterioration. Replace as required.
10. Remove the O-rings and discard. If an O-ring or end cap is missing, look in the intake manifold for the missing part.

To install:
11. Install new O-rings onto each injector and apply a small amount of clean engine oil to the O-rings.
12. Install the injectors into the fuel rail using a slight twisting downward motion.
13. Install the fuel injection supply manifold (fuel rail) but do not tighten the retaining bolts.
14. Install the injector retaining clips into lower intake manifold and tighten the fuel rail retaining bolts to 71–106 inch lbs. (8–12 Nm).
15. Make sure the fuel injector retainers are properly installed.
16. Attach the injector connectors.
17. Install the upper intake manifold.
18. Connect the negative battery cable.
19. Run the engine at idle for 2 minutes, then turn the engine **OFF** and check for fuel leaks and proper operation.

Fuel Rail Assembly

REMOVAL & INSTALLATION

2.0L Engine

◆ See Figures 23 thru 30, 32, 33, 42, 46, 47, 48, 56 and 57

❄❄ CAUTION

Fuel injection systems remain under pressure, even after the engine has been turned OFF. The fuel system pressure must be relieved before disconnecting any fuel lines. Failure to do so may result in fire and/or personal injury.

❄❄ CAUTION

Observe all applicable safety precautions when working around fuel. Whenever servicing the fuel system, always work in a well ventilated area. Do not allow fuel spray or vapors to come in contact with a spark or open flame. Keep a dry chemical fire extinguisher near the work area. Always keep fuel in a container specifically designed for fuel storage; also, always properly seal fuel containers to avoid the possibility of fire or explosion.

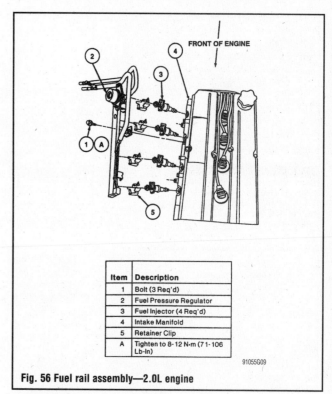

Item	Description
1	Bolt (3 Req'd)
2	Fuel Pressure Regulator
3	Fuel Injector (4 Req'd)
4	Intake Manifold
5	Retainer Clip
A	Tighten to 8-12 N-m (71-106 Lb-In)

Fig. 56 Fuel rail assembly—2.0L engine

1. Relieve the fuel system pressure.
2. Disconnect the negative battery cable.
3. Remove the air intake resonators.
4. Unplug the fuel injector electrical connections.
5. Disconnect the vacuum line from the fuel pressure regulator.
6. Disconnect the fuel lines spring lock coupling(s) using the appropriate tool.
7. Remove the retaining bolt from the fuel line retaining bracket.
8. Remove the fuel injection supply manifold (fuel rail) retaining bolts and remove the rail.

To install:
9. If replacing the fuel rail, remove the injectors and pressure regulator from the old fuel rail and install them to the new one as outlined in this Section.
10. Replace the injector O-rings.
11. Apply a small amount of clean engine oil to the injector O-rings.
12. Carefully position the fuel injection supply manifold on top of the fuel injectors. Push the fuel injection supply manifold down onto the injectors to fully seat the O-rings.
13. Install the fuel injection supply manifold retaining bolts and tighten them to 71–106 inch lbs. (8–12 Nm).

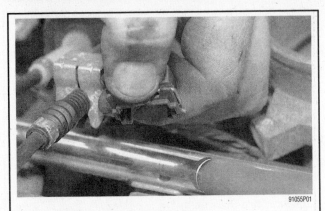

Fig. 57 Unplug the fuel injector connectors

14. Connect the fuel lines into the spring lock couplings and place the lines in the retaining bracket and tighten the retaining bolt.
15. Attach vacuum line to the fuel pressure regulator.
16. Attach the fuel injector electrical connections.
17. Install the air intake resonators..
18. Connect the negative battery cable.
19. Run the engine at idle for 2 minutes, then turn the engine **OFF** and check for fuel leaks and proper operation.

2.5L Engine

⬧ **See Figure 58**

❈❈ CAUTION

Fuel injection systems remain under pressure, even after the engine has been turned OFF. The fuel system pressure must be relieved before disconnecting any fuel lines. Failure to do so may result in fire and/or personal injury.

1. Relieve the fuel system pressure.
2. Disconnect the negative battery cable.
3. Remove the upper intake manifold.
4. Unplug the fuel injector electrical connections and move the injector wiring harness out of the way.
5. Disconnect the vacuum line from the fuel pressure regulator.
6. Disconnect the IMRC actuator cable from the stud on the linkage lever and bracket.
7. Disconnect the fuel lines spring lock coupling(s) using the appropriate tool and remove the fuel line bracket retaining bolt.
8. Remove the fuel injection supply manifold (fuel rail) retaining bolts.
9. Remove the IMRC linkage rod from the lower intake manifold by carefully prying the rod off using a suitable device.
10. Carefully remove the fuel rail assembly with the fuel injectors from the lower intake manifold.
To install:
11. If replacing the fuel rail, remove the injectors and pressure regulator from the old fuel rail and install them to the new one as outlined in this Section.
12. Replace the injector O-rings.
13. Apply a small amount of clean engine oil to the injector O-rings.
14. Carefully position the fuel injection supply manifold on top of the fuel injectors.
15. Install the injector retaining clips into lower intake manifold and tighten the fuel rail retaining bolts to 71–106 inch lbs. (8–12 Nm).
16. Make sure the fuel injector retainers are properly installed.
17. Install new bushings in the IMRC linkage rod and install the rod onto the lower intake manifold.
18. Install the IMRC actuator cable.
19. Attach vacuum line to the fuel pressure regulator.
20. Attach the fuel injector electrical connections.
21. Install the upper intake manifold.
22. Connect the spring lock coupling(s) using the appropriate tool and tighten the fuel line bracket retaining bolt.

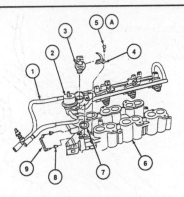

Item	Description
1	Fuel Injection Supply Manifold
2	Fuel Pressure Regulator
3	Fuel Injector (6 Req'd)
4	Fuel Injector Retainer (6 Req'd)
5	Bolt (7 Req'd)
6	Lower Intake Manifold (IMRC)
7	Fuel Injector Seal (6 Req'd)
8	IMRC Linkage Rod Bushings (2 Req'd)
9	IMRC Linkage Rod
A	Tighten to 8-12 N-m (71-106 Lb-In)

91055G21

Fig. 58 Fuel rail assembly—2.5L engine

23. Connect the negative battery cable.
24. Run the engine at idle for 2 minutes, then turn the engine **OFF** and check for fuel leaks and proper operation.

Fuel Pressure Regulator

REMOVAL & INSTALLATION

2.0L Engine

⬧ **See Figures 23 thru 30, 32, 33, 59 thru 63**

❈❈ CAUTION

Observe all applicable safety precautions when working around fuel. Whenever servicing the fuel system, always work in a well ventilated area. Do not allow fuel spray or vapors to come in contact with a spark or open flame. Keep a dry chemical fire extinguisher near the work area. Always keep fuel in a container specifically designed for fuel storage; also, always properly seal fuel containers to avoid the possibility of fire or explosion.

1. Properly relieve the fuel system pressure.
2. Disconnect the negative battery cable.
3. Remove the air intake resonators.
4. Disconnect the vacuum hose from the fuel pressure regulator.
5. Unfasten the two fuel pressure regulator retaining bolts.
6. Remove the fuel pressure regulator and the O-rings. Discard the O-rings.
To install:
7. Lubricate the new O-rings with a light engine oil.
8. Position a new O-rings onto the fuel pressure regulator.
9. Place the fuel pressure regulator into position and install the retainers. Tighten the retainers to 27–40 inch lbs. (3–5 Nm).
10. Connect the vacuum line to the fuel pressure regulator.
11. Install the air intake resonators.
12. Connect the negative battery cable.

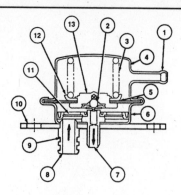

Item	Description
1	Engine Vacuum Reference Tube
2	Ball Seat
3	Spring
4	Upper Housing
5	Diaphragm
6	Lower Housing
7	Fuel Outlet Tube (Return)
8	Fuel Inlet Tube (Supply)
9	O-Ring Grooves
10	Mounting Plate
11	Fuel Filter Screen
12	Spring Seat
13	Valve Assy

91055G18

Fig. 59 Cutaway view of a vacuum type fuel pressure regulator—2.0L engine

13. Run the engine at idle for 2 minutes, then turn the engine **OFF** and check for fuel leaks and proper operation.

2.5L Engine

♦ See Figure 64

1. Properly relieve the fuel system pressure.
2. Disconnect the negative battery cable.
3. Remove the upper intake manifold.
4. Disconnect the vacuum hose from the fuel pressure regulator.
5. Unfasten the two fuel pressure regulator retaining bolts.
6. Remove the fuel pressure regulator and the O-rings. Discard the O-rings.

To install:

7. Lubricate the new O-rings with a light engine oil.
8. Position a new O-rings onto the fuel pressure regulator.
9. Remove the old return seal from the recess of the fuel rail and install a new seal.
10. Place the fuel pressure regulator into position and install the retainers. Tighten the retainers to 27–40 inch lbs. (3–5 Nm).
11. Connect the vacuum line to the fuel pressure regulator.
12. Install the upper intake manifold.
13. Connect the negative battery cable.
14. Run the engine at idle for 2 minutes, then turn the engine **OFF** and check for fuel leaks and proper operation.

Pressure Relief Valve

REMOVAL & INSTALLATION

♦ See Figures 65 and 66

1. Properly relieve the fuel system pressure.
2. Disconnect the negative battery cable.

91055P27

Fig. 60 Remove the vacuum hose from the pressure regulator

91055P28

Fig. 61 Remove the pressure regulator retaining bolts

91055P29

Fig. 62 Lift the pressure regulator up to remove it from the fuel rail

3. On the 2.0L engine remove the air intake resonators.
4. On the 2.5L engine remove the air outlet tube.
5. Remove the protective cap for the pressure relief valve.
6. Unscrew the fuel pressure relief valve.

To install:

7. Install the valve and tighten it to 66 inch lbs. (8 Nm).
8. Install the protective cap for the pressure relief valve.
9. On the 2.5L engine install the air outlet tube.
10. On the 2.0L engine install the air intake resonators.
11. Connect the negative battery cable.
12. Run the engine at idle for 2 minutes, then turn the engine **OFF** and check for fuel leaks and proper operation.

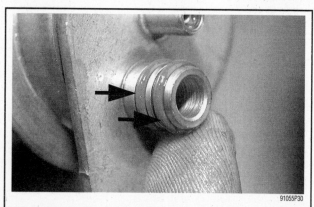

91055P30

Fig. 63 Replace the O-rings on the pressure regulator

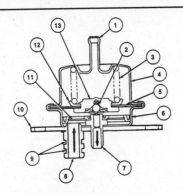

Item	Description
1	Engine Vacuum Reference Tube
2	Ball Seat
3	Spring
4	Upper Housing
5	Diaphragm
6	Lower Housing
7	Fuel Outlet (Return) Tube
8	Fuel Inlet (Supply) Tube
9	O-Ring Grooves
10	Mounting Plate
11	Fuel Filter Screen
12	Spring Seat
13	Valve Assembly

89695G08

Fig. 64 Cutaway view of a vacuum type fuel pressure regulator—2.5L engine

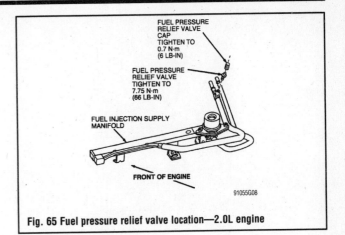

91055G08

Fig. 65 Fuel pressure relief valve location—2.0L engine

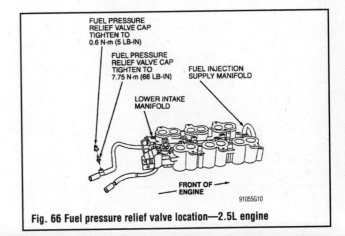

91055G10

Fig. 66 Fuel pressure relief valve location—2.5L engine

FUEL TANK

Tank Assembly

REMOVAL & INSTALLATION

♦ See Figures 67, 68, 69 and 70

✳✳ CAUTION

Observe all applicable safety precautions when working around fuel. Whenever servicing the fuel system, always work in a well ventilated area. Do not allow fuel spray or vapors to come in contact with a spark or open flame. Keep a dry chemical fire extinguisher near the work area. Always keep fuel in a container specifically designed for fuel storage; also, always properly seal fuel containers to avoid the possibility of fire or explosion.

1. Disconnect the negative battery cable.
2. Relieve the fuel pressure.
3. Remove the rear seat cushion.
4. Remove the plastic grommet from the floor pan.
5. Disconnect the fuel pump electrical harness.
6. Disconnect the fuel lines from the fuel pump by compressing the tabs on both sides of each nylon push connect fitting and easing the fuel line off of the fuel pump.
7. Raise and safely support the vehicle securely on jackstands.
8. Remove the muffler.
9. Remove the resonator and outlet pipe heat shields.
10. Disconnect the fuel lines and remove the fuel filter and base.
11. Loosen the fuel tank filler pipe clamp at the fuel tank.
12. Support the fuel tank using a hydraulic jack and a block of wood or other suitable device.

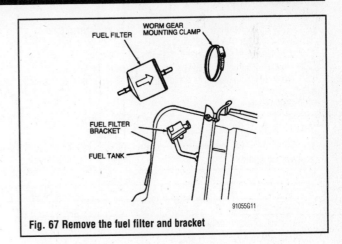

91055G11

Fig. 67 Remove the fuel filter and bracket

13. Remove the two fuel tank support strap bolts and position the straps out of the way.
14. Partially lower the fuel tank to access the fuel tank filler pipe vent tube and disconnect the vent tube and filler pipe from the tank.
15. Disconnect the fuel vapor tube from the tank.
16. Lower the tank from the vehicle.

To install:
17. If the tank is to be replaced:
   a. Drain the old tank and remove it from the jack or other device. Place the new tank on the jack or other device.
   b. Remove the retaining nuts and transfer the shields from the old tank to the new tank and tighten the nuts.

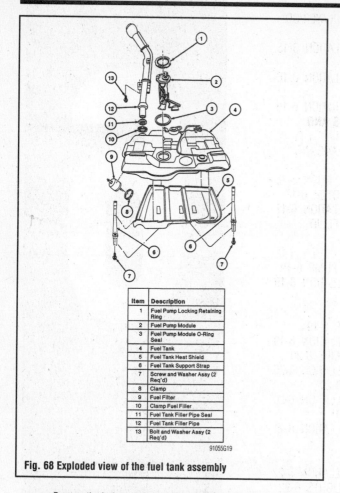

Item	Description
1	Fuel Pump Locking Retaining Ring
2	Fuel Pump Module
3	Fuel Pump Module O-Ring Seal
4	Fuel Tank
5	Fuel Tank Heat Shield
6	Fuel Tank Support Strap
7	Screw and Washer Assy (2 Req'd)
8	Clamp
9	Fuel Filter
10	Clamp Fuel Filler
11	Fuel Tank Filler Pipe Seal
12	Fuel Tank Filler Pipe
13	Bolt and Washer Assy (2 Req'd)

91055G19

Fig. 68 Exploded view of the fuel tank assembly

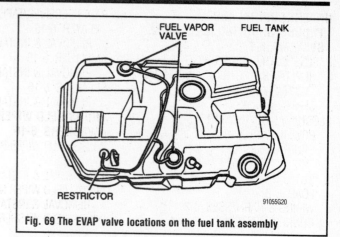

Fig. 69 The EVAP valve locations on the fuel tank assembly

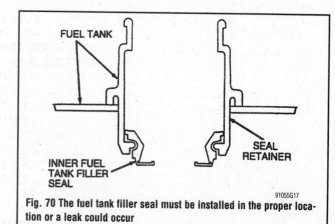

91055G17

Fig. 70 The fuel tank filler seal must be installed in the proper location or a leak could occur

c. Remove the fuel pump from the old tank and install it in the new tank.

d. Make sure the EVAP valves are installed in the new tank, if not, remove them from the old tank and install them in the new tank.

e. Make sure the inner fuel tank filler seal is in the correct position.

18. Raise the fuel tank into position.

19. Connect the fuel vapor tube to the tank.

20. Connect the filler pipe vent tube and filler pipe to the tank.

21. Position the fuel tank straps and tighten the retaining bolts to 21–30 ft lbs. (29–41 Nm).

22. Remove the hydraulic jack or other device.

23. Install the fuel filler pipe clamp and tighten.

24. Install the fuel filter and base and connect the fuel lines.

25. Install the resonator and outlet pipe heat shields.

26. Install the muffler.

27. Lower the vehicle.

28. Connect the fuel lines to the fuel pump.

29. Install the fuel pump electrical harness connector.

30. Install the plastic grommet into the floorpan.

31. Install the rear seat cushion.

32. Connect the negative battery cable.

33. Fill the tank with gas.

34. Cycle the ignition key several times from **OFF** to **ON** to build fuel pressure.

35. Start the engine and check for leaks and proper operation.

TORQUE SPECIFICATIONS

Components	English	Metric
Fuel rail retaining bolts	71-106 inch lbs.	8-12 Nm
Fuel tank retaining strap nuts	21-30 ft. lbs.	29-41 Nm
Pressure regulator retaining bolts	27-40 inch lbs.	3-5 Nm
Pressure relief valve	66 inch lbs.	8 Nm
Throttle body retaining bolts	71-106 inch lbs.	8-12 Nm

All torque values are for both the 2.0L and 2.5L engines

91055C01

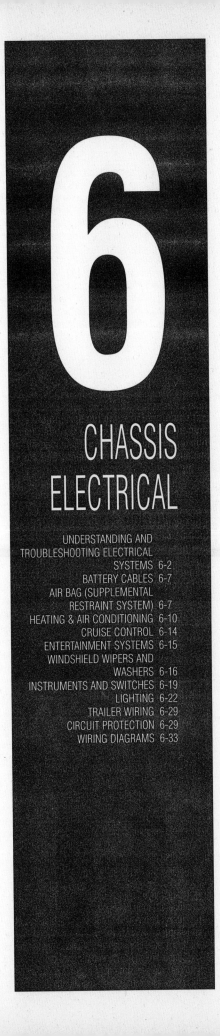

6

CHASSIS ELECTRICAL

UNDERSTANDING AND TROUBLESHOOTING ELECTRICAL SYSTEMS

Basic Electrical Theory

♦ See Figure 1

For any 12 volt, negative ground, electrical system to operate, the electricity must travel in a complete circuit. This simply means that current (power) from the positive (+) terminal of the battery must eventually return to the negative (-) terminal of the battery. Along the way, this current will travel through wires, fuses, switches and components. If, for any reason, the flow of current through the circuit is interrupted, the component fed by that circuit will cease to function properly.

Perhaps the easiest way to visualize a circuit is to think of connecting a light bulb (with two wires attached to it) to the battery—one wire attached to the negative (-) terminal of the battery and the other wire to the positive (+) terminal. With the two wires touching the battery terminals, the circuit would be complete and the light bulb would illuminate. Electricity would follow a path from the battery to the bulb and back to the battery. It's easy to see that with longer wires on our light bulb, it could be mounted anywhere. Further, one wire could be fitted with a switch so that the light could be turned on and off.

The normal automotive circuit differs from this simple example in two ways. First, instead of having a return wire from the bulb to the battery, the current travels through the frame of the vehicle. Since the negative (-) battery cable is attached to the frame (made of electrically conductive metal), the frame of the vehicle can serve as a ground wire to complete the circuit. Secondly, most automotive circuits contain multiple components which receive power from a single circuit. This lessens the amount of wire needed to power components on the vehicle.

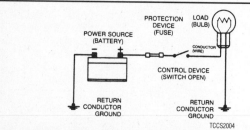

Fig. 1 This example illustrates a simple circuit. When the switch is closed, power from the positive (+) battery terminal flows through the fuse and the switch, and then to the light bulb. The light illuminates and the circuit is completed through the ground wire back to the negative (-) battery terminal. In reality, the two ground points shown in the illustration are attached to the metal frame of the vehicle, which completes the circuit back to the battery

HOW DOES ELECTRICITY WORK: THE WATER ANALOGY

Electricity is the flow of electrons—the subatomic particles that constitute the outer shell of an atom. Electrons spin in an orbit around the center core of an atom. The center core is comprised of protons (positive charge) and neutrons (neutral charge). Electrons have a negative charge and balance out the positive charge of the protons. When an outside force causes the number of electrons to unbalance the charge of the protons, the electrons will split off the atom and look for another atom to balance out. If this imbalance is kept up, electrons will continue to move and an electrical flow will exist.

Many people have been taught electrical theory using an analogy with water. In a comparison with water flowing through a pipe, the electrons would be the water and the wire is the pipe.

The flow of electricity can be measured much like the flow of water through a pipe. The unit of measurement used is amperes, frequently abbreviated as amps (a). You can compare amperage to the volume of water flowing through a pipe. When connected to a circuit, an ammeter will measure the actual amount of current flowing through the circuit. When relatively few electrons flow through a circuit, the amperage is low. When many electrons flow, the amperage is high.

Water pressure is measured in units such as pounds per square inch (psi); The electrical pressure is measured in units called volts (v). When a voltmeter is connected to a circuit, it is measuring the electrical pressure.

The actual flow of electricity depends not only on voltage and amperage, but also on the resistance of the circuit. The higher the resistance, the higher the force necessary to push the current through the circuit. The standard unit for measuring resistance is an ohm. Resistance in a circuit varies depending on the amount and type of components used in the circuit. The main factors which determine resistance are:

• **Material**—some materials have more resistance than others. Those with high resistance are said to be insulators. Rubber materials (or rubber-like plastics) are some of the most common insulators used in vehicles as they have a very high resistance to electricity. Very low resistance materials are said to be conductors. Copper wire is among the best conductors. Silver is actually a superior conductor to copper and is used in some relay contacts, but its high cost prohibits its use as common wiring. Most automotive wiring is made of copper.

• **Size**—the larger the wire size being used, the less resistance the wire will have. This is why components which use large amounts of electricity usually have large wires supplying current to them.

• **Length**—for a given thickness of wire, the longer the wire, the greater the resistance. The shorter the wire, the less the resistance. When determining the proper wire for a circuit, both size and length must be considered to design a circuit that can handle the current needs of the component.

• **Temperature**—with many materials, the higher the temperature, the greater the resistance (positive temperature coefficient). Some materials exhibit the opposite trait of lower resistance with higher temperatures (negative temperature coefficient). These principles are used in many of the sensors on the engine.

OHM'S LAW

There is a direct relationship between current, voltage and resistance. The relationship between current, voltage and resistance can be summed up by a statement known as Ohm's law.

Voltage (E) is equal to amperage (I) times resistance (R): $E = I \times R$

Other forms of the formula are $R = E/I$ and $I = E/R$

In each of these formulas, E is the voltage in volts, I is the current in amps and R is the resistance in ohms. The basic point to remember is that as the resistance of a circuit goes up, the amount of current that flows in the circuit will go down, if voltage remains the same.

The amount of work that the electricity can perform is expressed as power. The unit of power is the watt (w). The relationship between power, voltage and current is expressed as:

Power (w) is equal to amperage (I) times voltage (E): $W = I \times E$

This is only true for direct current (DC) circuits; The alternating current formula is a tad different, but since the electrical circuits in most vehicles are DC type, we need not get into AC circuit theory.

Electrical Components

POWER SOURCE

Power is supplied to the vehicle by two devices: The battery and the alternator. The battery supplies electrical power during starting or during periods when the current demand of the vehicle's electrical system exceeds the output capacity of the alternator. The alternator supplies electrical current when the engine is running. Just not does the alternator supply the current needs of the vehicle, but it recharges the battery.

The Battery

In most modern vehicles, the battery is a lead/acid electrochemical device consisting of six 2 volt subsections (cells) connected in series, so that the unit is capable of producing approximately 12 volts of electrical pressure. Each subsection consists of a series of positive and negative plates held a short distance apart in a solution of sulfuric acid and water.

The two types of plates are of dissimilar metals. This sets up a chemical reaction, and it is this reaction which produces current flow from the battery when its positive and negative terminals are connected to an electrical load . The power removed from the battery is replaced by the alternator, restoring the battery to its original chemical state.

The Alternator

On some vehicles there isn't an alternator, but a generator. The difference is that an alternator supplies alternating current which is then changed to direct current for use on the vehicle, while a generator produces direct current. Alternators tend to be more efficient and that is why they are used.

Alternators and generators are devices that consist of coils of wires wound together making big electromagnets. One group of coils spins within another set and the interaction of the magnetic fields causes a current to flow. This current is then drawn off the coils and fed into the vehicles electrical system.

GROUND

Two types of grounds are used in automotive electric circuits. Direct ground components are grounded to the frame through their mounting points. All other components use some sort of ground wire which is attached to the frame or chassis of the vehicle. The electrical current runs through the chassis of the vehicle and returns to the battery through the ground (-) cable; if you look, you'll see that the battery ground cable connects between the battery and the frame or chassis of the vehicle.

➡ **It should be noted that a good percentage of electrical problems can be traced to bad grounds.**

PROTECTIVE DEVICES

♦ **See Figure 2**

It is possible for large surges of current to pass through the electrical system of your vehicle. If this surge of current were to reach the load in the circuit, the surge could burn it out or severely damage it. It can also overload the wiring, causing the harness to get hot and melt the insulation. To prevent this, fuses, circuit breakers and/or fusible links are connected into the supply wires of the electrical system. These items are nothing more than a built-in weak spot in the system. When an abnormal amount of current flows through the system, these protective devices work as follows to protect the circuit:

• Fuse—when an excessive electrical current passes through a fuse, the fuse "blows" (the conductor melts) and opens the circuit, preventing the passage of current.

• Circuit Breaker—a circuit breaker is basically a self-repairing fuse. It will open the circuit in the same fashion as a fuse, but when the surge subsides, the circuit breaker can be reset and does not need replacement.

• Fusible Link—a fusible link (fuse link or main link) is a short length of special, high temperature insulated wire that acts as a fuse. When an excessive electrical current passes through a fusible link, the thin gauge wire inside the link melts, creating an intentional open to protect the circuit. To repair the circuit, the link must be replaced. Some newer type fusible links are housed in plug-in modules, which are simply replaced like a fuse, while older type fusible links must be cut and spliced if they melt. Since this link is very early in the

electrical path, it's the first place to look if nothing on the vehicle works, yet the battery seems to be charged and is properly connected.

✳✳ CAUTION

Always replace fuses, circuit breakers and fusible links with identically rated components. Under no circumstances should a component of higher or lower amperage rating be substituted.

SWITCHES & RELAYS

♦ **See Figures 3 and 4**

Switches are used in electrical circuits to control the passage of current. The most common use is to open and close circuits between the battery and the various electric devices in the system. Switches are rated according to the amount of amperage they can handle. If a sufficient amperage rated switch is not used in a circuit, the switch could overload and cause damage.

Some electrical components which require a large amount of current to operate use a special switch called a relay. Since these circuits carry a large amount of current, the thickness of the wire in the circuit is also greater. If this large wire were connected from the load to the control switch, the switch would have to carry the high amperage load and the fairing or dash would be twice as large to accommodate the increased size of the wiring harness. To prevent these problems, a relay is used.

Relays are composed of a coil and a set of contacts. When the coil has a current passed though it, a magnetic field is formed and this field causes the contacts to move together, completing the circuit. Most relays are normally open, preventing current from passing through the circuit, but they can take any electrical form depending on the job they are intended to do. Relays can be considered "remote control switches." They allow a smaller current to operate devices that require higher amperages. When a small current operates the coil, a larger current is allowed to pass by the contacts. Some common circuits which may use relays are the horn, headlights, starter, electric fuel pump and other high draw circuits.

LOAD

Every electrical circuit must include a "load" (something to use the electricity coming from the source). Without this load, the battery would attempt to deliver its entire power supply from one pole to another. This is called a "short circuit." All this electricity would take a short cut to ground and cause a great amount of damage to other components in the circuit by developing a tremendous amount of heat. This condition could develop sufficient heat to melt the insulation on all the surrounding wires and reduce a multiple wire cable to a lump of plastic and copper.

WIRING & HARNESSES

The average vehicle contains meters and meters of wiring, with hundreds of individual connections. To protect the many wires from damage and to keep

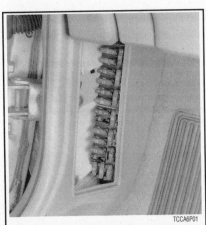

TCCA6P01

Fig. 2 Most vehicles use one or more fuse panels. This one is located on the driver's side kick panel

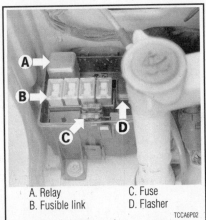

A. Relay   C. Fuse
B. Fusible link   D. Flasher

TCCA6P02

Fig. 3 The underhood fuse and relay panel usually contains fuses, relays, flashers and fusible links

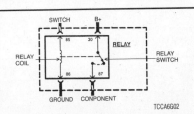

TCCA6G02

Fig. 4 Relays are composed of a coil and a switch. These two components are linked together so that when one operates, the other operates at the same time. The large wires in the circuit are connected from the battery to one side of the relay switch (B+) and from the opposite side of the relay switch to the load (component). Smaller wires are connected from the relay coil to the control switch for the circuit and from the opposite side of the relay coil to ground

them from becoming a confusing tangle, they are organized into bundles, enclosed in plastic or taped together and called wiring harnesses. Different harnesses serve different parts of the vehicle. Individual wires are color coded to help trace them through a harness where sections are hidden from view.

Automotive wiring or circuit conductors can be either single strand wire, multi-strand wire or printed circuitry. Single strand wire has a solid metal core and is usually used inside such components as alternators, motors, relays and other devices. Multi-strand wire has a core made of many small strands of wire twisted together into a single conductor. Most of the wiring in an automotive electrical system is made up of multi-strand wire, either as a single conductor or grouped together in a harness. All wiring is color coded on the insulator, either as a solid color or as a colored wire with an identification stripe. A printed circuit is a thin film of copper or other conductor that is printed on an insulator backing. Occasionally, a printed circuit is sandwiched between two sheets of plastic for more protection and flexibility. A complete printed circuit, consisting of conductors, insulating material and connectors for lamps or other components is called a printed circuit board. Printed circuitry is used in place of individual wires or harnesses in places where space is limited, such as behind instrument panels.

Since automotive electrical systems are very sensitive to changes in resistance, the selection of properly sized wires is critical when systems are repaired. A loose or corroded connection or a replacement wire that is too small for the circuit will add extra resistance and an additional voltage drop to the circuit.

The wire gauge number is an expression of the cross-section area of the conductor. Vehicles from countries that use the metric system will typically describe the wire size as its cross-sectional area in square millimeters. In this method, the larger the wire, the greater the number. Another common system for expressing wire size is the American Wire Gauge (AWG) system. As gauge number increases, area decreases and the wire becomes smaller. An 18 gauge wire is smaller than a 4 gauge wire. A wire with a higher gauge number will carry less current than a wire with a lower gauge number. Gauge wire size refers to the size of the strands of the conductor, not the size of the complete wire with insulator. It is possible, therefore, to have two wires of the same gauge with different diameters because one may have thicker insulation than the other.

It is essential to understand how a circuit works before trying to figure out why it doesn't. An electrical schematic shows the electrical current paths when a circuit is operating properly. Schematics break the entire electrical system down into individual circuits. In a schematic, usually no attempt is made to represent wiring and components as they physically appear on the vehicle; switches and other components are shown as simply as possible. Face views of harness connectors show the cavity or terminal locations in all multi-pin connectors to help locate test points.

CONNECTORS

▶ **See Figures 5 and 6**

Three types of connectors are commonly used in automotive applications—weatherproof, molded and hard shell.

• Weatherproof—these connectors are most commonly used where the connector is exposed to the elements. Terminals are protected against moisture and dirt by sealing rings which provide a weathertight seal. All repairs require the use of a special terminal and the tool required to service it. Unlike standard blade type terminals, these weatherproof terminals cannot be straightened once they are bent. Make certain that the connectors are properly seated and all of the sealing rings are in place when connecting leads.

Fig. 5 Hard shell (left) and weatherproof (right) connectors have replaceable terminals

TCCA6P03

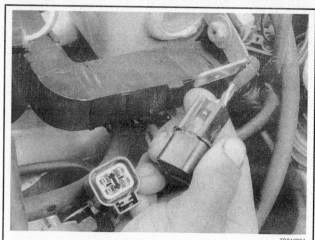

TCCA6P04

Fig. 6 Weatherproof connectors are most commonly used in the engine compartment or where the connector is exposed to the elements

• Molded—these connectors require complete replacement of the connector if found to be defective. This means splicing a new connector assembly into the harness. All splices should be soldered to insure proper contact. Use care when probing the connections or replacing terminals in them, as it is possible to create a short circuit between opposite terminals. If this happens to the wrong terminal pair, it is possible to damage certain components. Always use jumper wires between connectors for circuit checking and NEVER probe through weatherproof seals.

• Hard Shell—unlike molded connectors, the terminal contacts in hard-shell connectors can be replaced. Replacement usually involves the use of a special terminal removal tool that depresses the locking tangs (barbs) on the connector terminal and allows the connector to be removed from the rear of the shell. The connector shell should be replaced if it shows any evidence of burning, melting, cracks, or breaks. Replace individual terminals that are burnt, corroded, distorted or loose.

Test Equipment

Pinpointing the exact cause of trouble in an electrical circuit is most times accomplished by the use of special test equipment. The following describes different types of commonly used test equipment and briefly explains how to use them in diagnosis. In addition to the information covered below, the tool manufacturer's instructions booklet (provided with the tester) should be read and clearly understood before attempting any test procedures.

JUMPER WIRES

✳✳ CAUTION

Never use jumper wires made from a thinner gauge wire than the circuit being tested. If the jumper wire is of too small a gauge, it may overheat and possibly melt. Never use jumpers to bypass high resistance loads in a circuit. Bypassing resistances, in effect, creates a short circuit. This may, in turn, cause damage and fire. Jumper wires should only be used to bypass lengths of wire or to simulate switches.

Jumper wires are simple, yet extremely valuable, pieces of test equipment. They are basically test wires which are used to bypass sections of a circuit. Although jumper wires can be purchased, they are usually fabricated from lengths of standard automotive wire and whatever type of connector (alligator clip, spade connector or pin connector) that is required for the particular application being tested. In cramped, hard-to-reach areas, it is advisable to have insulated boots over the jumper wire terminals in order to prevent accidental grounding. It is also advisable to include a standard automotive fuse in any jumper wire. This is commonly referred to as a "fused jumper". By inserting an in-line fuse holder between a set of test leads, a fused jumper wire can be used for bypassing open circuits. Use a 5 amp fuse to provide protection against voltage spikes.

Jumper wires are used primarily to locate open electrical circuits, on either the ground (-) side of the circuit or on the power (+) side. If an electrical component fails to operate, connect the jumper wire between the component and a good ground. If the component operates only with the jumper installed, the ground circuit is open. If the ground circuit is good, but the component does not operate, the circuit between the power feed and component may be open. By moving the jumper wire successively back from the component toward the power source, you can isolate the area of the circuit where the open is located. When the component stops functioning, or the power is cut off, the open is in the segment of wire between the jumper and the point previously tested.

You can sometimes connect the jumper wire directly from the battery to the "hot" terminal of the component, but first make sure the component uses 12 volts in operation. Some electrical components, such as fuel injectors or sensors, are designed to operate on about 4 to 5 volts, and running 12 volts directly to these components will cause damage.

TEST LIGHTS

▶ See Figure 7

The test light is used to check circuits and components while electrical current is flowing through them. It is used for voltage and ground tests. To use a 12 volt test light, connect the ground clip to a good ground and probe wherever necessary with the pick. The test light will illuminate when voltage is detected. This does not necessarily mean that 12 volts (or any particular amount of voltage) is present; it only means that some voltage is present. It is advisable before using the test light to touch its ground clip and probe across the battery posts or terminals to make sure the light is operating properly.

✷✷ WARNING

Do not use a test light to probe electronic ignition, spark plug or coil wires. Never use a pick-type test light to probe wiring on computer controlled systems unless specifically instructed to do so. Any wire insulation that is pierced by the test light probe should be taped and sealed with silicone after testing.

Like the jumper wire, the 12 volt test light is used to isolate opens in circuits. But, whereas the jumper wire is used to bypass the open to operate the load, the 12 volt test light is used to locate the presence of voltage in a circuit. If the test light illuminates, there is power up to that point in the circuit; if the test light does not illuminate, there is an open circuit (no power). Move the test light in successive steps back toward the power source until the light in the handle illuminates. The open is between the probe and a point which was previously probed.

The self-powered test light is similar in design to the 12 volt test light, but contains a 1.5 volt penlight battery in the handle. It is most often used in place of a multimeter to check for open or short circuits when power is isolated from the circuit (continuity test).

The battery in a self-powered test light does not provide much current. A weak battery may not provide enough power to illuminate the test light even when a complete circuit is made (especially if there is high resistance in the circuit). Always make sure that the test battery is strong. To check the battery, briefly touch the ground clip to the probe; if the light glows brightly, the battery is strong enough for testing.

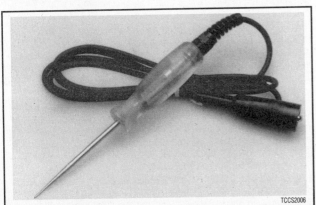

TCCS2006

Fig. 7 A 12 volt test light is used to detect the presence of voltage in a circuit

➡**A self-powered test light should not be used on any computer controlled system or component. The small amount of electricity transmitted by the test light is enough to damage many electronic automotive components.**

MULTIMETERS

Multimeters are an extremely useful tool for troubleshooting electrical problems. They can be purchased in either analog or digital form and have a price range to suit any budget. A multimeter is a voltmeter, ammeter and ohmmeter (along with other features) combined into one instrument. It is often used when testing solid state circuits because of its high input impedance (usually 10 megaohms or more). A brief description of the multimeter main test functions follows:

• Voltmeter—the voltmeter is used to measure voltage at any point in a circuit, or to measure the voltage drop across any part of a circuit. Voltmeters usually have various scales and a selector switch to allow the reading of different voltage ranges. The voltmeter has a positive and a negative lead. To avoid damage to the meter, always connect the negative lead to the negative (-) side of the circuit (to ground or nearest the ground side of the circuit) and connect the positive lead to the positive (+) side of the circuit (to the power source or the nearest power source). Note that the negative voltmeter lead will always be black and that the positive voltmeter will always be some color other than black (usually red).

• Ohmmeter—the ohmmeter is designed to read resistance (measured in ohms) in a circuit or component. Most ohmmeters will have a selector switch which permits the measurement of different ranges of resistance (usually the selector switch allows the multiplication of the meter reading by 10, 100, 1,000 and 10,000). Some ohmmeters are "auto-ranging" which means the meter itself will determine which scale to use. Since the meters are powered by an internal battery, the ohmmeter can be used like a self-powered test light. When the ohmmeter is connected, current from the ohmmeter flows through the circuit or component being tested. Since the ohmmeter's internal resistance and voltage are known values, the amount of current flow through the meter depends on the resistance of the circuit or component being tested. The ohmmeter can also be used to perform a continuity test for suspected open circuits. In using the meter for making continuity checks, do not be concerned with the actual resistance readings. Zero resistance, or any ohm reading, indicates continuity in the circuit. Infinite resistance indicates an opening in the circuit. A high resistance reading where there should be none indicates a problem in the circuit. Checks for short circuits are made in the same manner as checks for open circuits, except that the circuit must be isolated from both power and normal ground. Infinite resistance indicates no continuity, while zero resistance indicates a dead short.

✷✷ WARNING

Never use an ohmmeter to check the resistance of a component or wire while there is voltage applied to the circuit.

• Ammeter—an ammeter measures the amount of current flowing through a circuit in units called amperes or amps. At normal operating voltage, most circuits have a characteristic amount of amperes, called "current draw" which can be measured using an ammeter. By referring to a specified current draw rating, then measuring the amperes and comparing the two values, one can determine what is happening within the circuit to aid in diagnosis. An open circuit, for example, will not allow any current to flow, so the ammeter reading will be zero. A damaged component or circuit will have an increased current draw, so the reading will be high. The ammeter is always connected in series with the circuit being tested. All of the current that normally flows through the circuit must also flow through the ammeter; if there is any other path for the current to follow, the ammeter reading will not be accurate. The ammeter itself has very little resistance to current flow and, therefore, will not affect the circuit, but it will measure current draw only when the circuit is closed and electricity is flowing. Excessive current draw can blow fuses and drain the battery, while a reduced current draw can cause motors to run slowly, lights to dim and other components to not operate properly.

Troubleshooting Electrical Systems

When diagnosing a specific problem, organized troubleshooting is a must. The complexity of a modern automotive vehicle demands that you approach any problem in a logical, organized manner. There are certain troubleshooting techniques, however, which are standard:

• Establish when the problem occurs. Does the problem appear only under certain conditions? Were there any noises, odors or other unusual symptoms? Isolate the problem area. To do this, make some simple tests and observations, then eliminate the systems that are working properly. Check for obvious problems, such as broken wires and loose or dirty connections. Always check the obvious before assuming something complicated is the cause.

• Test for problems systematically to determine the cause once the problem area is isolated. Are all the components functioning properly? Is there power going to electrical switches and motors. Performing careful, systematic checks will often turn up most causes on the first inspection, without wasting time checking components that have little or no relationship to the problem.

• Test all repairs after the work is done to make sure that the problem is fixed. Some causes can be traced to more than one component, so a careful verification of repair work is important in order to pick up additional malfunctions that may cause a problem to reappear or a different problem to arise. A blown fuse, for example, is a simple problem that may require more than another fuse to repair. If you don't look for a problem that caused a fuse to blow, a shorted wire (for example) may go undetected.

Experience has shown that most problems tend to be the result of a fairly simple and obvious cause, such as loose or corroded connectors, bad grounds or damaged wire insulation which causes a short. This makes careful visual inspection of components during testing essential to quick and accurate troubleshooting.

Testing

OPEN CIRCUITS

▶ See Figure 8

This test already assumes the existence of an open in the circuit and it is used to help locate the open portion.
1. Isolate the circuit from power and ground.
2. Connect the self-powered test light or ohmmeter ground clip to the ground side of the circuit and probe sections of the circuit sequentially.
3. If the light is out or there is infinite resistance, the open is between the probe and the circuit ground.
4. If the light is on or the meter shows continuity, the open is between the probe and the end of the circuit toward the power source.

SHORT CIRCUITS

➡Never use a self-powered test light to perform checks for opens or shorts when power is applied to the circuit under test. The test light can be damaged by outside power.

1. Isolate the circuit from power and ground.
2. Connect the self-powered test light or ohmmeter ground clip to a good ground and probe any easy-to-reach point in the circuit.
3. If the light comes on or there is continuity, there is a short somewhere in the circuit.
4. To isolate the short, probe a test point at either end of the isolated circuit (the light should be on or the meter should indicate continuity).

5. Leave the test light probe engaged and sequentially open connectors or switches, remove parts, etc. until the light goes out or continuity is broken.
6. When the light goes out, the short is between the last two circuit components which were opened.

VOLTAGE

This test determines voltage available from the battery and should be the first step in any electrical troubleshooting procedure after visual inspection. Many electrical problems, especially on computer controlled systems, can be caused by a low state of charge in the battery. Excessive corrosion at the battery cable terminals can cause poor contact that will prevent proper charging and full battery current flow.
1. Set the voltmeter selector switch to the 20V position.
2. Connect the multimeter negative lead to the battery's negative (-) post or terminal and the positive lead to the battery's positive (+) post or terminal.
3. Turn the ignition switch **ON** to provide a load.
4. A well charged battery should register over 12 volts. If the meter reads below 11.5 volts, the battery power may be insufficient to operate the electrical system properly.

VOLTAGE DROP

▶ See Figure 9

When current flows through a load, the voltage beyond the load drops. This voltage drop is due to the resistance created by the load and also by small resistances created by corrosion at the connectors and damaged insulation on the wires. The maximum allowable voltage drop under load is critical, especially if there is more than one load in the circuit, since all voltage drops are cumulative.
1. Set the voltmeter selector switch to the 20 volt position.
2. Connect the multimeter negative lead to a good ground.
3. Operate the circuit and check the voltage prior to the first component (load).
4. There should be little or no voltage drop in the circuit prior to the first component. If a voltage drop exists, the wire or connectors in the circuit are suspect.
5. While operating the first component in the circuit, probe the ground side of the component with the positive meter lead and observe the voltage readings. A small voltage drop should be noticed. This voltage drop is caused by the resistance of the component.
6. Repeat the test for each component (load) down the circuit.
7. If a large voltage drop is noticed, the preceding component, wire or connector is suspect.

RESISTANCE

▶ See Figures 10 and 11

✳✳ WARNING

Never use an ohmmeter with power applied to the circuit. The ohmmeter is designed to operate on its own power supply. The normal 12 volt electrical system voltage could damage the meter!

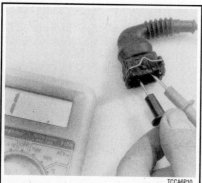
Fig. 8 The infinite reading on this multimeter indicates that the circuit is open

TCCA6P10

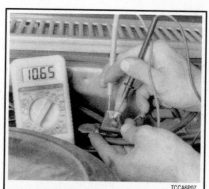
Fig. 9 This voltage drop test revealed high resistance (low voltage) in the circuit

TCCA6P07

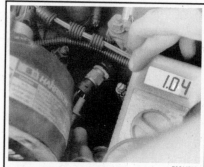
Fig. 10 Checking the resistance of a coolant temperature sensor with an ohmmeter. Reading is 1.04 kilohms

TCCA6P08

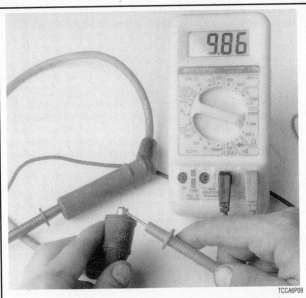

Fig. 11 Spark plug wires can be checked for excessive resistance using an ohmmeter

1. Isolate the circuit from the vehicle's power source.
2. Ensure that the ignition key is **OFF** when disconnecting any components or the battery.
3. Where necessary, also isolate at least one side of the circuit to be checked, in order to avoid reading parallel resistances. Parallel circuit resistances will always give a lower reading than the actual resistance of either of the branches.
4. Connect the meter leads to both sides of the circuit (wire or component) and read the actual measured ohms on the meter scale. Make sure the selector switch is set to the proper ohm scale for the circuit being tested, to avoid misreading the ohmmeter test value.

Wire and Connector Repair

Almost anyone can replace damaged wires, as long as the proper tools and parts are available. Wire and terminals are available to fit almost any need. Even the specialized weatherproof, molded and hard shell connectors are now available from aftermarket suppliers.

Be sure the ends of all the wires are fitted with the proper terminal hardware and connectors. Wrapping a wire around a stud is never a permanent solution and will only cause trouble later. Replace wires one at a time to avoid confusion. Always route wires exactly the same as the factory.

➡**If connector repair is necessary, only attempt it if you have the proper tools. Weatherproof and hard shell connectors require special tools to release the pins inside the connector. Attempting to repair these connectors with conventional hand tools will damage them.**

BATTERY CABLES

Disconnecting the Cables

When working on any electrical component on the vehicle, it is always a good idea to disconnect the negative (-) battery cable. This will prevent potential damage to many sensitive electrical components such as the Powertrain Control Module (PCM), radio, alternator, etc.

➡**Any time you disengage the battery cables, it is recommended that you disconnect the negative (-) battery cable first. This will prevent your accidentally grounding the positive (+) terminal to the body of the vehicle when disconnecting it, thereby preventing damage to the above mentioned components.**

Before you disconnect the cable(s), first turn the ignition to the **OFF** position. This will prevent a draw on the battery which could cause arcing (electricity trying to ground itself to the body of a vehicle, just like a spark plug jumping the gap) and, of course, damaging some components such as the alternator diodes.

When the battery cable(s) are reconnected (negative cable last), be sure to check that your lights, windshield wipers and other electrically operated safety components are all working correctly. If your vehicle contains an Electronically Tuned Radio (ETR), don't forget to also reset your radio stations. Ditto for the clock.

AIR BAG (SUPPLEMENTAL RESTRAINT SYSTEM)

General Information

▶ **See Figures 12, 13 and 14**

The Air Bag system or Supplemental Restraint System (SRS) is designed to provide additional protection for front seat occupants when used in conjunction with a seat belt. The system is an electronically controlled, mechanically operated system. The system contains two basic subsytems: the air bag module(s) (the actual air bag(s) themselves), and the electrical system. The system consists of:

- The crash sensors
- The safing sensor
- The air bag module(s)
- The diagnostic monitor
- The instrument cluster indicator
- The sliding contacts (clock spring assembly)

The system is operates as follows: The system remains out of sight until activated in an accident that is determined to be the equivalent of hitting a parked car of the same size and weight at 28 mph (40 km/h) with the vehicle receiving severe front end damage. This determination is made by crash and safing sensors mounted on the vehicle which when an sufficient impact occurs, close their contacts completing the electrical circuit and inflating the air bags. When not activated the system is monitored by the air bag diagnostic monitor and system readiness is indicated by the lamp located on the instrument cluster. Any fault detected by the diagnostic monitor will illuminate the lamp and store a Diagnostic Trouble Code (DTC).

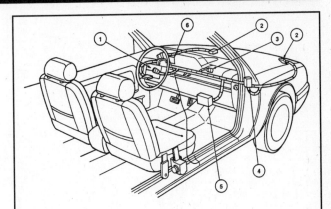

Item	Description
1	Driver Side Air Bag Module
2	Primary Crash Front Air Bag Sensor and Bracket
3	Passenger Side Air Bag Module
4	Rear Air Bag Sensor and Bracket
5	Air Bag Diagnostic Monitor
6	Air Bag Warning Indicator (Part of 04320)

91056G16

Fig. 12 The air bag system component locations—1995–97 models

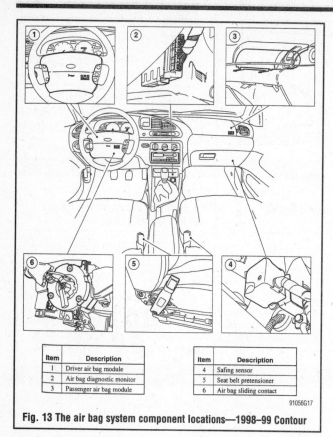

Item	Description
1	Driver air bag module
2	Air bag diagnostic monitor
3	Passenger air bag module

Item	Description
4	Safing sensor
5	Seat belt pretensioner
6	Air bag sliding contact

91056G17

Fig. 13 The air bag system component locations—1998–99 Contour

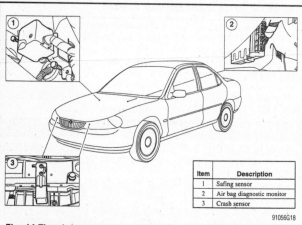

Item	Description
1	Safing sensor
2	Air bag diagnostic monitor
3	Crash sensor

91056G18

Fig. 14 The air bag system component locations—1998–99 Mystique. Cougar similar

Air Bag Module(s)

▶ See Figures 15 and 16

The air bag module(s) are located in the steering wheel and the passenger side of the instrument panel, if equipped with a passenger side air bag. The modules are molded to fit into their designated areas, the driver's side is located in the center of the steering wheel. The passenger side module is molded to fit into the instrument panel and is located above the glove box, it is generally unnoticeable until deflated.

The module contain four parts: an inflator, a bag, a container, and the cover. The purpose of the inflator is to generate the gas needed to fill the air bag, it consists of a high strength steel casing containing a propellant that is activated by an igniter. The igniter is fired by the electrical signal received when the safing sensor closes. When the igniter is fired, the propellant discharge is ignited and fills the bag. As the bag fills, invisible "split seams" in the cover tear open allowing the bag to inflate and cushion the forward motion of the occupant and protect against serious injury.

Diagnostic Monitor

▶ See Figure 17

The diagnostic monitor is located behind the center of the instrument panel, under the radio. The diagnostic monitor serves no purpose in the firing of the air bag(s). The main purpose of the diagnostic monitor is to monitor the operational status of the system through continual checks of the system's circuits. In the event of a fault detected, the diagnostic monitor will illuminate the air bag indicator and flash out a DTC. All codes are double digit and if a code is flashed, it can be read as follows: a flash-flash-flash, one-second pause, flash-flash, three-second pause, is a code 32. If numerous codes are stored, they will flash after the three second pause, if only one code is stored, the same flash sequence will begin again. In the event of a air bag indicator bulb failure, an audible tone will be emitted from the diagnostic monitor. this tone is a series of five sets of five beeps, this is code 55 indicating the indicator bulb is out and in addition the air bag system may require service.

The diagnostic monitor also contains the back-up power supply. In the event of a impact severing the battery or other electrical sources to the air bag system, the back up power supply contains enough power to deploy the air bag(s). The diagnostic monitor contains several small capacitors that store power. The back-up power supply must be discharged before air bag service can be performed.

Crash Sensors

▶ See Figure 18

The crash sensors are located in the front of the vehicle on either side of the front radiator support. In the event of a head-on impact (or at least a ¾ frontal impact, the sensing mass inside the sensor breaks away from the bias magnet. The sensor mass rolls along a cylinder toward two electrical contacts, if the deceleration is sufficient, the sensing mass will bridge the contacts and complete the primary deployment circuit to the air bag module.

The mounting and orientation of the sensors is vital to system operation. The sensors should be inspected by a qualified individual after any impact where the

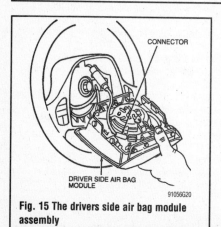

Fig. 15 The drivers side air bag module assembly

CONNECTOR

DRIVER SIDE AIR BAG MODULE

91056G20

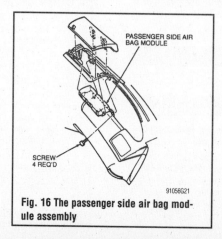

Fig. 16 The passenger side air bag module assembly

PASSENGER SIDE AIR BAG MODULE

SCREW 4 REQ'D

91056G21

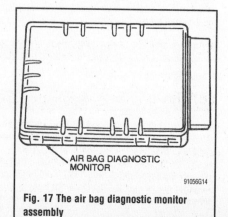

Fig. 17 The air bag diagnostic monitor assembly

AIR BAG DIAGNOSTIC MONITOR

91056G14

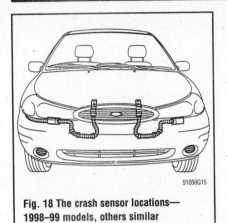

Fig. 18 The crash sensor locations—1998–99 models, others similar

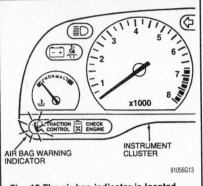

Fig. 19 The air bag indicator is located here on 1995–97 models

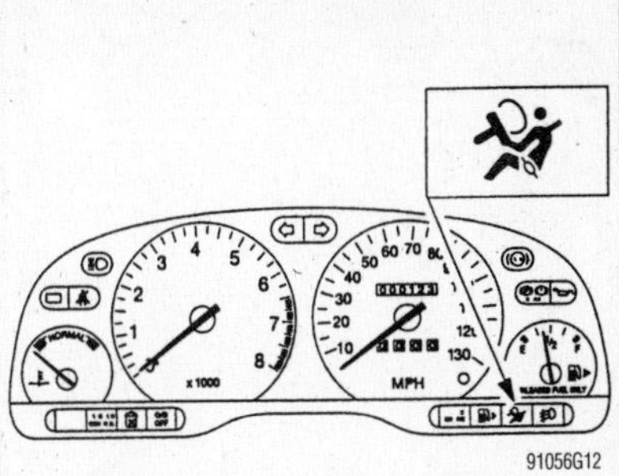

Fig. 20 The air bag indicator is located here on 1998–99 models

sensors could have been damaged. If any structural damage is evident, the area must be repaired to its original condition, otherwise the sensor orientation could be compromised. If the sensor(s) have received damage, they must be replaced.

Safing Sensor

The safing sensor is located behind the kick panel on the passenger side, below the instrument panel. The safing sensor operates identical to the crash sensor, except for the calibration. This is accomplished using a slightly weaker bias magnet. If the safing sensor contacts close simultaneously with the crash sensor, the air bag(s) will be deployed.

The safing sensor is essentially a safety for the air bag system. It protects the bag(s) from deploying due to an electrical short. The safing sensor is used to verify the force of a collision and complete the air bag(s) deployment. The sensor is located inside the passenger compartment so that a forceful enough impact could be detected, and a false signal from the crash sensor would not deploy the air bag(s) at an inappropriate time.

Air Bag Indicator

▶ See Figures 19 and 20

The air bag indicator is located on the instrument cluster and illuminates when activated by the diagnostic monitor. The indicator illuminates when the key is placed in the ignition and turned to **RUN**, this is the bulb prove-out. The indicator will stay illuminated after the vehicle is started while the diagnostic monitor checks the system for faults, if no faults are detected, the indicator will go out after about 6 seconds. If the indicator does not go out after 6 seconds, a fault has been detected in the system, a DTC will be flashed using the indicator.

Sliding Contact

▶ See Figure 21

The clock spring assembly is located in the steering column, behind the steering wheel. The function of the clock spring assembly is to keep the electrical connection intact while the steering wheel is rotated while the driver is turning the wheel to steer the vehicle.

System Service

▶ See Figure 22

✴✴ CAUTION

Some vehicles are equipped with an air bag system. The system must be disabled before performing service on or around air bag system components, steering column, instrument panel components, wiring and sensors. Failure to follow safety and disabling procedures could result in accidental air bag deployment, possible personal injury and unnecessary SRS system repairs.

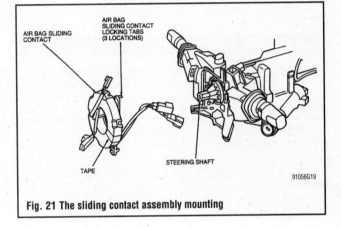

Fig. 21 The sliding contact assembly mounting

SERVICE PRECAUTIONS

▶ See Figures 23 and 24

Whenever working around, or on, the air bag supplemental restraint system, ALWAYS adhere to the following warnings and cautions.

• Always wear safety glasses when servicing an air bag vehicle and when handling an air bag module.

• Carry a live air bag module with the bag and trim cover facing away from your body, so that an accidental deployment of the air bag will have a small chance of personal injury.

• Place an air bag module on a table or other flat surface with the bag and trim cover pointing up.

• Wear gloves, a dust mask and safety glasses whenever handling a deployed air bag module. The air bag surface may contain traces of sodium hydroxide, a by-product of the gas that inflates the air bag and which can cause skin irritation.

• Ensure to wash your hands with mild soap and water after handling a deployed air bag.

• All air bag modules with discolored or damaged cover trim must be replaced, not repainted.

• All component replacement and wiring service must be made with the negative and positive battery cables disconnected from the battery for a minimum of one minute prior to attempting service or replacement.

• NEVER probe the air bag electrical terminals. Doing so could result in air bag deployment, which can cause serious physical injury.

• If the vehicle is involved in a fender-bender which results in a damaged front bumper or grille, have the air bag sensors inspected by a qualified automotive technician to ensure that they were not damaged.

• If at any time, the air bag light indicates that the computer has noted a problem, have your vehicle's SRS serviced immediately by a qualified automotive technician. A faulty SRS can cause severe physical injury or death.

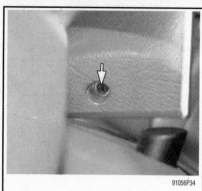

Fig. 22 The driver's side air bag is usually retained with tamper proof bolts

Fig. 23 Be sure to observe any precaution labels on the vehicle regarding the air bag system

Fig. 24 This label is placed on all passenger side air bag equipped vehicles warning of placing children in rear facing car seats

DISARMING THE SYSTEM

✳✳ CAUTION

The air bag system must be disarmed before performing service around air bag components or wiring. Failure to do so may cause accidental deployment of the air bag, resulting in unnecessary repairs and/or personal injury.

1. Position the vehicle with the front wheels in a straight ahead position.
2. Disconnect the negative battery cable.
3. Disconnect the positive battery cable.
4. Wait at least one minute for the air bag back-up power supply to drain before continuing.
5. Proceed with the repair.
6. Once complete, connect the battery cables, negative cable last.
7. Check the functioning of the air bag system by turning the ignition key to the **RUN** position and visually monitoring the air bag indicator lamp in the instrument cluster. The indicator lamp should illuminate for approximately six seconds, then turn **OFF**. If the indicator lamp does not illuminate, stays on, or flashes at any time, a fault has been detected by the air bag diagnostic monitor.

ARMING THE SYSTEM

1. Connect the positive battery cable.
2. Connect the negative battery cable.
3. Stand outside the vehicle and carefully turn the ignition to the **RUN** position. Be sure that no part of your body is in front of the air bag module on the steering wheel, to prevent injury in case of an accidental air bag deployment.
4. Ensure the air bag indicator light turns off after approximately 6 seconds. If the light does not illuminate at all, does not turn off, or starts to flash, have the system tested by a qualified automotive technician. If the light does turn off after 6 seconds and does not flash, the SRS is working properly.

HEATING & AIR CONDITIONING

Blower Motor

REMOVAL & INSTALLATION

▶ **See Figures 25, 26, 27 and 28**

1. Disconnect the negative battery cable.
2. Remove the push pins and remove the upper footwell panel from under the passenger side of the instrument panel.
3. Unplug the connector from the blower motor.
4. Carefully lift the retaining lug on the blower motor flange and rotate the motor counterclockwise approximately 30° to disengage it from the evaporator housing.
5. Remove the blower motor from the evaporator housing.

To install:
6. Inspect the gasket on the housing, replace if necessary.
7. Place the blower motor into the evaporator housing and rotate the motor clockwise until the retaining lug engages.
8. Attach the blower motor connector.
9. Install the upper footwell panel.
10. Connect the negative battery cable.

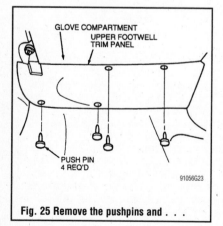

Fig. 25 Remove the pushpins and . . .

Fig. 26 . . . remove the upper footwell panel from under the passenger side of the instrument panel

Fig. 27 The blower motor is mounted vertically into the evaporator housing

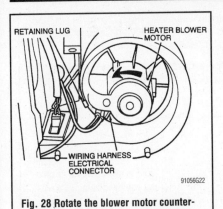

Fig. 28 Rotate the blower motor counter-clockwise to disengage the retaining lug

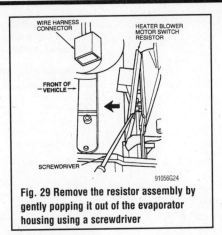

Fig. 29 Remove the resistor assembly by gently popping it out of the evaporator housing using a screwdriver

Fig. 30 The heater hoses are best accessed from underneath the vehicle

Blower Motor Switch Resistor Assembly

REMOVAL & INSTALLATION

▶ **See Figures 25 and 29**

1. Disconnect the negative battery cable.
2. Remove the push pins and remove the upper footwell panel from under the passenger side of the instrument panel.
3. Unplug the connector from the blower motor resistor assembly.
4. Insert a screwdriver approximately 0.2 inch (5mm) under the edge of the resistor assembly to disengage it from the evaporator housing.
5. Remove the resistor assembly.

To install:

6. Position the resistor assembly into the housing and snap it into place.
7. Attach the resistor connector.
8. Install the upper footwell panel.
9. Connect the negative battery cable.

Heater Core

REMOVAL & INSTALLATION

▶ **See Figures 30, 31, 32 and 33**

1. Disconnect the negative battery cable.
2. Remove the center console.
3. Disarm the air bag system and remove the air bag diagnostic monitor and bracket.
4. Remove the screw retaining the air transfer duct to the heater outlet floor duct.
5. Push the transfer duct inside of the heater outlet floor duct.
6. Remove the three screws retaining the heater outlet floor duct to the heater core cover and release the retaining tabs on each side of the duct and remove the duct.

7. Raise and safely support the vehicle securely on jackstands.
8. Disconnect the heater hoses from the heater core and plug the heater core tubes and the hoses to prevent coolant loss.
9. Disconnect the vacuum supply hose (the black hose) from the vacuum source in the engine compartment.
10. Lower the vehicle.
11. Disconnect the vacuum supply hose (the black hose) from the A/C vacuum reservoir tank.
12. Release the four retaining tabs, remove the two clips and remove the heater core cover containing the heater core.
13. Remove the heater dash panel seal and the vacuum hose from the heater core cover.
14. Remove the retaining screw and remove the heater core bracket from the cover.
15. Remove the heater core from the cover.
16. Remove the heater core case seal from the heater core.

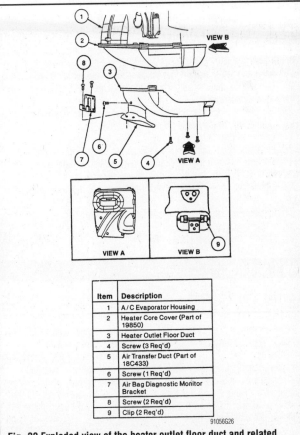

Item	Description
1	A/C Evaporator Housing
2	Heater Core Cover (Part of 19850)
3	Heater Outlet Floor Duct
4	Screw (3 Req'd)
5	Air Transfer Duct (Part of 18C433)
6	Screw (1 Req'd)
7	Air Bag Diagnostic Monitor Bracket
8	Screw (2 Req'd)
9	Clip (2 Req'd)

Fig. 32 Exploded view of the heater outlet floor duct and related components

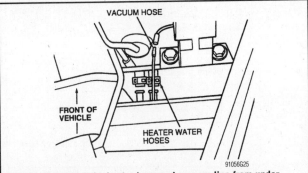

Fig. 31 Disconnect the heater hose and vacuum line from underneath the vehicle.

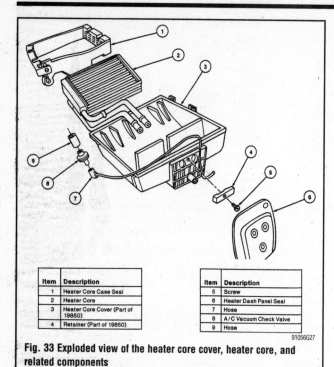

Fig. 33 Exploded view of the heater core cover, heater core, and related components

Item	Description
1	Heater Core Case Seal
2	Heater Core
3	Heater Core Cover (Part of 19850)
4	Retainer (Part of 19850)

Item	Description
5	Screw
6	Heater Dash Panel Seal
7	Hose
8	A/C Vacuum Check Valve
9	Hose

91056G27

To install:

17. Install the heater core case seal on the heater core.
18. Install the heater core into the cover.
19. Install the retaining screw and install the heater core bracket onto the cover.
20. Install the heater dash panel seal and the vacuum hose onto the heater core cover.
21. Engage the four retaining tabs, install the two clips and install the heater core cover containing the heater core.
22. Connect the vacuum supply hose (the black hose) to the A/C vacuum reservoir tank.
23. Raise and safely support the vehicle securely on jackstands.
24. Connect the vacuum supply hose (the black hose) to the vacuum source in the engine compartment.
25. Remove the plugs from the hoses and the core tubes (if installing old core).
26. Connect the heater hoses onto the heater core.
27. Lower the vehicle.
28. Install the heater outlet floor duct, engage the retaining tabs and tighten the three screws retaining the heater outlet floor duct to the heater core cover.
29. Push the transfer duct out of the heater outlet floor duct.
30. Tighten the screw retaining the air transfer duct to the heater outlet floor duct.
31. Install the air bag diagnostic monitor and bracket.
32. Install the center console.
33. Connect the negative battery cable.

Air Conditioning Components

REMOVAL & INSTALLATION

Repair or service of air conditioning components is not covered by this manual, because of the risk of personal injury or death, and because of the legal ramifications of servicing these components without the proper EPA certification and experience. Cost, personal injury or death, environmental damage, and legal considerations (such as the fact that it is a federal crime to vent refrigerant into the atmosphere), dictate that the A/C components on your vehicle should be serviced only by a Motor Vehicle Air Conditioning (MVAC) trained, and EPA certified automotive technician.

➡️If your vehicle's A/C system uses R-12 refrigerant and is in need of recharging, the A/C system can be converted over to R-134a refrigerant

(less environmentally harmful and expensive). Refer to Section 1 for additional information on R-12 to R-134a conversions, and for additional considerations dealing with your vehicle's A/C system.

Vacuum Actuator Motors

REMOVAL & INSTALLATION

Air Inlet Duct Door

▸ See Figure 34

1. Disconnect the negative battery cable.
2. Open the glove box, push in on the sides of the glove box, and lower the glove box to the floor.
3. If equipped, remove the three retaining screws from the radio power amplifier bracket and move the amplifier out of the way.
4. If equipped, move the electronic door lock module to improve the access to the vacuum motor retaining screws.
5. Remove the two vacuum motor-to-air inlet duct retaining screws.
6. Disconnect the vacuum motor from the A/C outside air intake lever and remove the vacuum hose.
7. Remove the vacuum control motor.

To install:

8. Place the vacuum motor into place and connect the lever and the vacuum hose.
9. Install the vacuum motor-to-air inlet duct retaining screws.
10. Reposition and install the electronic door lock module and the radio power amplifier.
11. Install the glovebox.
12. Connect the negative battery cable.

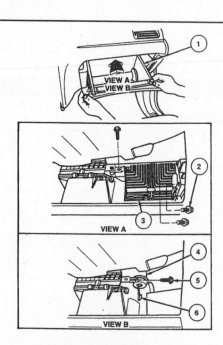

Item	Description
1	Glove Compartment
2	Screw (3 Req'd)
3	Radio Power Booster Equalizer Amplifier Bracket
4	Vacuum Control Motor
5	Screw (2 Req'd)
6	A/C Outside Air Intake Control Lever

91056G30

Fig. 34 Air damper door vacuum motor exploded view

Air Damper Door

▶ **See Figure 35**

1. Disconnect the negative battery cable.
2. Remove the instrument panel. See Section 10.
3. Disconnect the vacuum harness from the vacuum motor.
4. Remove the two vacuum motor-to-evaporator housing retaining nuts.
5. Carefully disconnect the heater outlet control lever from the vacuum motor.
6. Remove the vacuum motor.

To install:

7. Place the vacuum motor into place and connect the lever.
8. Install the vacuum motor-to-evaporator housing retaining nuts.
9. Connect the vacuum harness to the vacuum motor.
10. Install the instrument panel.
11. Connect the negative battery cable.

Defroster Door

▶ **See Figures 35 and 36**

1. Disconnect the negative battery cable.
2. Unplug the courtesy lamp from the instrument panel steering column cover (knee bolster panel).
3. On Mystique only, open the storage compartment door.
4. Remove the five panel retaining screws and remove the cover.
5. Disconnect the vacuum harness from the vacuum motor.
6. Remove the two vacuum motor-to-evaporator housing retaining nuts.
7. Carefully disconnect the heater outlet control lever from the vacuum motor.
8. Remove the vacuum motor.

To install:

9. Place the vacuum motor into place and connect the lever.
10. Install the vacuum motor-to-evaporator housing retaining nuts.

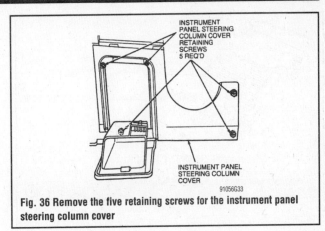

Fig. 36 Remove the five retaining screws for the instrument panel steering column cover

11. Connect the vacuum harness to the vacuum motor.
12. Install the instrument panel steering column cover.
13. Attach the courtesy lamp to the instrument panel steering column cover.
14. Connect the negative battery cable.

Blend Door Actuator

REMOVAL & INSTALLATION

▶ **See Figure 37**

1. Disconnect the negative battery cable.
2. Remove the two lower retaining screws from the blend door actuator.

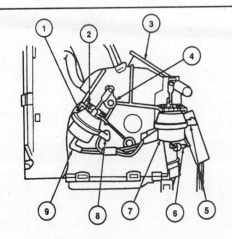

Item	Description
1	Windshield Defroster Door Vacuum Control Motor
2	Nut (2 Req'd)
3	A/C Evaporator Housing
4	Heater Air Outlet Control Lever
5	Vacuum Hose Harness, Gray
6	Vacuum Hose Harness, Blue
7	Heater Air Damper Door Vacuum Control Motor
8	Vacuum Hose Harness, Red
9	Vacuum Hose Harness, Yellow

91056G31

Fig. 35 Air damper and defroster doors vacuum motor and related components

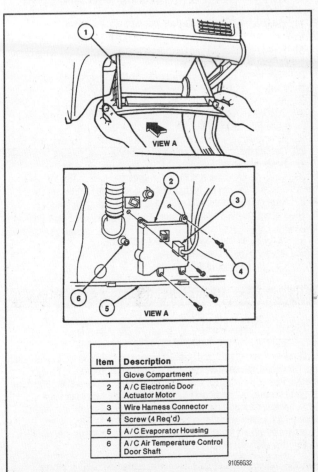

Item	Description
1	Glove Compartment
2	A/C Electronic Door Actuator Motor
3	Wire Harness Connector
4	Screw (4 Req'd)
5	A/C Evaporator Housing
6	A/C Air Temperature Control Door Shaft

91056G32

Fig. 37 The blend door actuator and accompanying components

3. Open the glove box, push in on the sides of the glove box, and lower the glove box to the floor.

4. Unplug the wire harness connector from the blend door actuator.

5. Remove the two upper retaining screws from the blend door actuator.

6. Remove the blend door actuator from the evaporator housing.

To install:

7. Place the blend door actuator onto the evaporator housing and tighten the two upper retaining screws.

8. Attach the wire harness connector to the blend door actuator.

9. Install the glovebox.

10. Install the two lower retaining screws onto the blend door actuator.

11. Connect the negative battery cable.

Control Panel

REMOVAL & INSTALLATION

♦ **See Figures 38 and 39**

1. Disconnect the negative battery cable.

2. On the contour, remove the radio from the instrument panel. On the Mystique and Cougar, remove the radio and in-dash CD player (if equipped).

3. Open the ash tray and remove the two retaining screws for the control opening finish panel.

4. Carefully pull the panel away from the instrument panel to unseat the retaining clips. Unplug the dimmer switch connector and place the panel in a safe location.

5. Remove the two retaining screws (Contour) or four retaining screws (Mystique and Cougar) and remove the control panel from the instrument panel opening.

6. Label and unplug the wiring connectors from the control panel.

7. Unplug the vacuum hose harness from the control panel.

To install:

8. Attach the wiring and vacuum connections to the control panel.

9. Place the control panel into the opening in the instrument panel and tighten the retaining screws.

10. Attach the dimmer switch connector and snap the finish panel into place on the instrument cluster.

11. Tighten the two retaining screws at the ash tray opening and install the ash tray.

12. Install the radio and/or radio/CD player as removed.

13. Connect the negative battery cable.

CRUISE CONTROL

♦ **See Figure 40**

1995–95 Contour, Mystique and Cougar vehicles were available with a speed control system. This system automatically controls the speed of the vehicle when cruising at a stable highway speed. The speed control system consists of the following:

- Speed control amplifier/servo assembly
- Speed control cable
- Vehicle Speed Sensor (VSS)
- Speed control actuator switch
- Stop light switch
- Deactivator switch
- Clutch pedal position switch (manual transmissions only)

The speed control system operates independently of engine vacuum and, therefore, does not utilize any vacuum lines.

The speed control amplifier integrates the system electronics, thereby eliminating any other electronic control modules in the vehicle. The amplifier controls the vehicle's speed via a cable attached to the throttle body lever.

The speed control actuator switch assembly is mounted on the steering wheel and allows the driver to control the system's operation. The switch assembly contains five control buttons for system functioning, namely: ON, OFF, RESUME, SET ACCEL, COAST.

The system will continue to control the vehicle's speed until the OFF button is used, or the brake pedal or clutch pedal (manual transmissions only) is depressed.

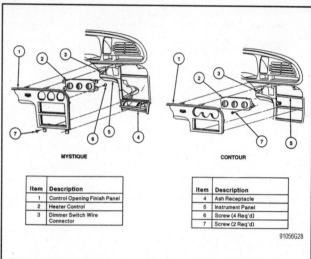

Item	Description
1	Control Opening Finish Panel
2	Heater Control
3	Dimmer Switch Wire Connector

Item	Description
4	Ash Receptacle
5	Instrument Panel
6	Screw (4 Req'd)
7	Screw (2 Req'd)

91056G28

Fig. 38 HVAC control panel mountings—Contour and Mystique shown, Cougar similar

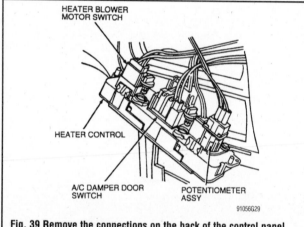

91056G29

Fig. 39 Remove the connections on the back of the control panel

91056P03

Fig. 40 The speed control amplifier/servo assembly is located behind the driver's side strut tower in the engine compartment

CRUISE CONTROL TROUBLESHOOTING

Problem	Possible Cause
Will not hold proper speed	Incorrect cable adjustment
	Binding throttle linkage
	Leaking vacuum servo diaphragm
	Leaking vacuum tank
	Faulty vacuum or vent valve
	Faulty stepper motor
	Faulty transducer
	Faulty speed sensor
	Faulty cruise control module
Cruise intermittently cuts out	Clutch or brake switch adjustment too tight
	Short or open in the cruise control circuit
	Faulty transducer
	Faulty cruise control module
Vehicle surges	Kinked speedometer cable or casing
	Binding throttle linkage
	Faulty speed sensor
	Faulty cruise control module
Cruise control inoperative	Blown fuse
	Short or open in the cruise control circuit
	Faulty brake or clutch switch
	Leaking vacuum circuit
	Faulty cruise control switch
	Faulty stepper motor
	Faulty transducer
	Faulty speed sensor
	Faulty cruise control module

Note: Use this chart as a guide. Not all systems will use the components listed.

TCCA6C01

ENTERTAINMENT SYSTEMS

Radio Receiver/Tape Player/CD Player

REMOVAL & INSTALLATION

♦ See Figures 41, 42, 43, 44 and 45

1. Disconnect the negative battery cable.

➡ Do not use excessive force when installing the radio removal tool. This will damage the retaining clips, making radio chassis removal difficult and may cause other internal damage.

2. Install Radio Removal Tool (T87P-19061-A) or equivalent into the radio face place. Push the tool in approximately 1 in. (25mm) to release the retaining clips.
3. Apply a slight spreading force on both sides and pull the radio chassis out of the instrument panel.
4. Disconnect the radio wiring harness and antenna cable.
5. Remove the radio chassis.
To install:
6. Position the radio chassis in the vehicle.
7. Connect the radio wiring harness and antenna cable.
8. Push the radio chassis inward until the retaining clips are fully engaged.
9. Connect the negative battery cable.

Fig. 41 There are two small holes located on either side of the radio chassis

91056P57

Fig. 42 Insert the special radio removal tool and push outward to . . .

91056P58

Fig. 43 . . . disengage the retaining clips and slide the radio out of the instrument panel

91056P59

Fig. 44 When the radio is free of the dash, unplug the electrical connectors and the . . .

Fig. 45 . . . antenna connection

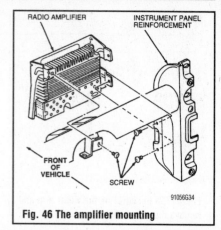
Fig. 46 The amplifier mounting

Amplifier

REMOVAL & INSTALLATION

▶ See Figure 46

➡ Only vehicles equipped with a premium sound system contain an amplifier.

1. Disconnect the negative battery cable.
2. Open the glove box, push in on the sides of the glove box, and lower the glove box to the floor.
3. Remove the three amplifier-to-instrument panel reinforcement retaining screws.
4. Pull the amplifier out and unplug the electrical connectors.
5. Remove the amplifier.

To install:
6. Attach the electrical connectors to the amplifier.
7. Place the amplifier into position and tighten the retaining screws.
8. Install the glove box.
9. Connect the negative battery cable.

Speakers

REMOVAL & INSTALLATION

➡ All Contour and Mystique models are equipped with four speakers, one in each door.

Door Speakers

▶ See Figures 47, 48 and 49

1. Disconnect the negative battery cable.
2. Remove the door trim panel.
3. Remove the three screws attaching the speaker to the door panel.
4. Lift the speaker from the door panel and disconnect the electrical harness.
5. Remove the speaker.

To install:
6. Connect the electrical harness to the speaker.
7. Place the speaker into the opening in the door panel.
8. Tighten the attaching screws to 8 inch lbs. (0.9 Nm).
9. Install the door trim panel.
10. Connect the negative battery cable.

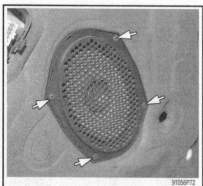
Fig. 47 Remove the four speaker retaining screws and . . .

Fig. 48 . . . pull the speaker out of the door to . . .

Fig. 49 . . . access and unplug the electrical connector

WINDSHIELD WIPERS AND WASHERS

Windshield Wiper Blade and Arm

REMOVAL & INSTALLATION

▶ See Figures 50, 51, 52 and 53

1. Disconnect the negative battery cable.
2. Raise the covers over the wiper arm retaining nuts.

3. Remove the retaining nuts on the wiper arm pivots.
4. Matchmark the wiper arms to the pivot for reinstallation.
5. Lift each wiper arm and free it from the pivot shafts.

➡ The wiper arms will most likely be stuck, a useful tool for removal of the wiper arms is a battery terminal puller. The battery terminal puller exerts force on the pivot and raises the arm, otherwise prying and other techniques could do damage to the wiper arms, trim, windshield, or painted surfaces of the vehicle.

Fig. 50 Lift the cover on the wiper arm and remove the nut on the wiper arm pivot

Fig. 51 Matchmark the wiper arm to the pivot for reinstallation

Fig. 52 A useful tool to prevent damage is to use a battery terminal puller to remove the wiper arms

Fig. 53 After the arm is sufficiently loose, lift it straight up off of the pivot

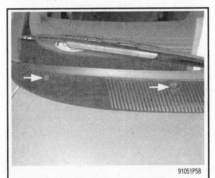

Fig. 54 The passenger side panel is retained by two upper trim screws as indicated by the arrows

Fig. 55 Gently pry the covers off of the trim screws and . . .

To install:
6. Place the wiper arm onto the pivot aligning the matchmarks.
7. Tighten the retaining nuts to 18 ft. lbs (25 Nm).
8. Fasten the retaining nut covers.
9. Connect the negative battery cable.

Windshield Wiper Motor

REMOVAL & INSTALLATION

♦ See Figures 50 thru 70

1. Disconnect the negative battery cable.
2. Remove the wiper arms from the front of the vehicle.
3. Open the hood and remove the hood weather-strip from the cowl top extension.

4. Remove the upper fastener caps and remove the 5 screws.
5. Remove the lower screws that secure the cowl vent screens to the upper cowl panel.
6. Lift the passenger side cowl vent screen away from the upper cowl panel and remove.
7. Lift the drivers side cowl vent screen away from the upper cowl panel and remove.
8. Remove the bolt retaining the wiper motor output arm to the wiper motor crankshaft.
9. Matchmark the crank arm to the motor.
10. Remove the 3 bolts retaining the wiper motor to its mounting plate.
11. Remove the wiper motor assembly from mounting plate.
12. Disconnect the wiring harness connector at the wiper motor.
13. Remove the wiper motor.
To install:
14. Reconnect the wiring harness to the wiper motor.

Fig. 56 . . . remove the screws using an appropriate tool

Fig. 57 Grasp the end of the weather-stripping and gently pull up and towards the center of the vehicle to unseat it

Fig. 58 Remove the three panel lower retaining bolts as indicated

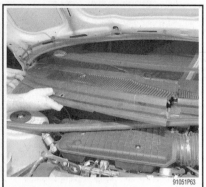

Fig. 59 Carefully lift the panel up to remove it from the vehicle

Fig. 60 The drivers side panel is also held by two upper screws

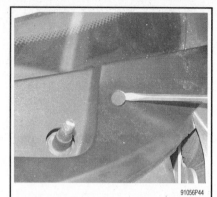

Fig. 61 Again pry the clips up and . . .

Fig. 62 . . . remove the screws using a screwdriver or other suitable tool

Fig. 63 Remove the drivers side weather-stripping and . . .

Fig. 64 . . . remove the lower retaining bolts to . . .

Fig. 65 . . . remove the driver's side panel

Fig. 66 Remove the wiper linkage-to-wiper motor crankshaft retaining bolt

Fig. 67 Matchmark the linkage arm to the motor

Fig. 68 Remove the three motor retaining bolts and . . .

Fig. 69 . . . remove the wiper motor from the linkage and . . .

Fig. 70 . . . unplug the electrical connector from the motor

15. Mount the wiper motor to the mounting plate and torque the 3 bolts to 71–106 inch lbs. (8–12 Nm).

16. Position the wiper motor output arm to the wiper motor crankshaft and torque the nut to 19 ft. lbs. (26 Nm).

17. Check that the position of the wiper motor output arm is indexed properly with the mark made during the removal procedure.

18. Reinstall the drivers side cowl vent screen.

19. Reinstall the passenger side cowl vent screen.

20. Secure the 5 screws securing the cowl vent screens and reinstall the upper fastener caps.

21. Reinstall the lower screws retaining the cowl vent screens to the upper cowl panel.

22. Reinstall the hood weather-strip to the cowl top extension.

23. Make sure that the wiper motor is in the park position before installing the wiper arms.

24. Reinstall the wiper arms and retaining nuts. Only snug the nuts at this time.

25. Reconnect the negative battery cable.

26. Run the wiper motor at low speed and check the wiper arms for proper positioning.

27. If the wiper arm positioning is correct, continue to torque the wiper arm retaining nuts to 18 ft. lbs. (25 Nm). If not, re–index the wiper arms, check their positioning and then tighten the retaining nuts.

28. Check for proper operation of the wiper motor at all speeds.

Windshield Washer Fluid Reservoir

REMOVAL & INSTALLATION

▶ **See Figures 71 and 72**

1. Disconnect the negative battery cable.
2. Raise and support the vehicle.

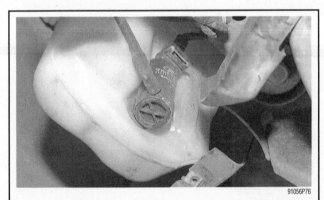

Fig. 71 The windshield washer fluid reservoir and pump assembly

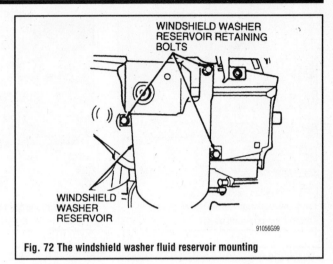

Fig. 72 The windshield washer fluid reservoir mounting

3. Remove the passenger side front fender splash shield.

4. Remove the three retaining bolts for the windshield washer fluid reservoir.

5. Slide the reservoir forward and disconnect the washer pump hose and the pump wiring harness.

6. Remove the reservoir from the vehicle.

To install:

7. Connect the washer pump hose and the pump wiring harness.

8. Place the reservoir into position and tighten the three retaining bolts.

9. Install the splash shield.

10. Lower the vehicle.

11. Connect the negative battery cable.

Windshield Washer Pump

REMOVAL & INSTALLATION

1. Disconnect the negative battery cable.
2. Remove the windshield washer fluid reservoir as outlined above.
3. Drain any washer fluid in the reservoir into an appropriate container.
4. Twist the pump from the reservoir to remove.

To install:

5. Inspect the pump seal on the reservoir, replace if necessary.
6. Twist the pump into place until seated on the seal.
7. Install the windshield washer fluid reservoir.
8. Refill the washer fluid reservoir.
9. Connect the negative battery cable.

INSTRUMENTS AND SWITCHES

Instrument Cluster

REMOVAL & INSTALLATION

▶ **See Figures 73 thru 82**

1. Disconnect the negative battery cable.
2. Remove the instrument cluster finish panel retaining screw covers.
3. Remove the six instrument cluster finish panel retaining screws.
4. Remove the instrument cluster finish panel.
5. Remove the five instrument cluster retaining screws.
6. Pull the cluster out to access the connectors on back and unplug them.
7. Remove the cluster from the vehicle.

To install:

8. Attach the connectors to the instrument cluster.

Fig. 73 The instrument cluster finish panel is retained by bolts under various switches and covers

Fig. 74 Pry the covers, clock assembly, and any applicable switches necessary to access the retaining bolts

Fig. 75 Unplug the rear defroster and the . . .

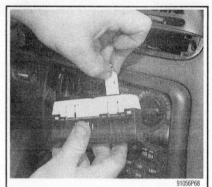

Fig. 76 . . . clock assembly and any other optional switches on the vehicle

Fig. 77 When removed, the retaining bolts are accessible through the openings

Fig. 78 Remove the three upper retaining screws and . . .

Fig. 79 . . . remove the panel from the instrument panel

Fig. 80 Remove the five retaining screws for the instrument cluster and . . .

Fig. 81 Pull the cluster out to . . .

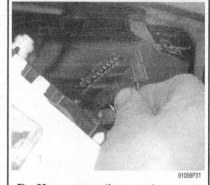

Fig. 82 . . . access the connectors on back and unplug them

9. Place the cluster into the dash opening and tighten the five retaining screws.
10. Install the instrument cluster finish panel and tighten the retaining screws.
11. Install the instrument cluster finish panel retaining screw covers.
12. Connect the negative battery cable.

Gauges/Warning Lamps

REMOVAL & INSTALLATION

▶ See Figures 83 thru 88

1. Disconnect the negative battery cable.
2. Remove the instrument cluster.
3. Remove the retaining screws for the instrument cluster lens and cover assembly. Remove the cover and lens.

4. Remove the retaining screws for the gauge or warning lamp to be replaced and remove the gauge or warning lamp.

To install:
5. Place the gauge or warning lamp into place and tighten the retaining screws.
6. Install the instrument cluster lens and cover assembly.
7. Install the instrument cluster.
8. Connect the negative battery cable.

Headlight Switch

REMOVAL & INSTALLATION

▶ See Figures 89 and 90

1. Disconnect the negative battery cable.
2. Remove the knee bolster panel on the driver's side of the instrument panel.

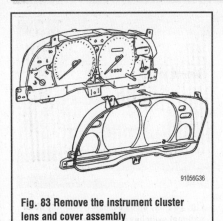

Fig. 83 Remove the instrument cluster lens and cover assembly

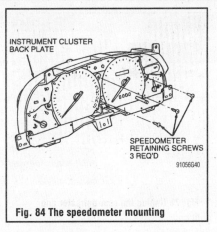

Fig. 84 The speedometer mounting

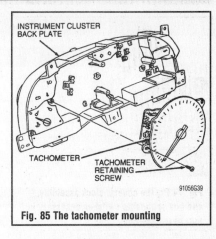

Fig. 85 The tachometer mounting

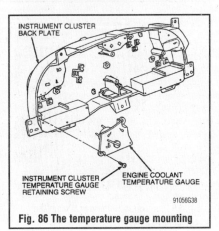

Fig. 86 The temperature gauge mounting

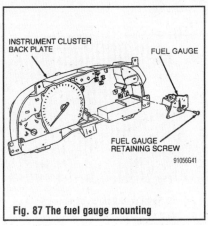

Fig. 87 The fuel gauge mounting

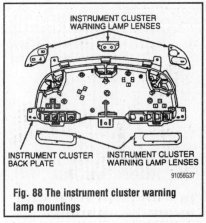

Fig. 88 The instrument cluster warning lamp mountings

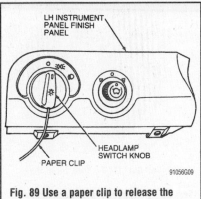

Fig. 89 Use a paper clip to release the knob from the headlight switch shaft

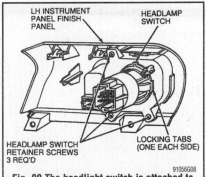

Fig. 90 The headlight switch is attached to the finish panel, and is retained by three screws

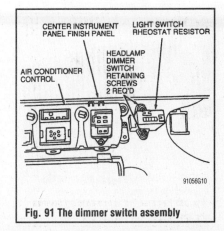

Fig. 91 The dimmer switch assembly

3. Remove the left hand finish panel from the instrument panel.
4. Unplug the headlamp switch connector.
5. Slide a small pin into the hole on the bottom of the headlight switch knob to release the locking tab, and remove the knob from the headlight switch shaft.
6. Remove the three headlamp switch-to-panel retaining screws and remove the switch assembly.
7. Press the locking tabs on the headlamp switch and remove the switch from the headlamp switch retainer.

To install:
8. Press the headlamp switch into the retainer until the locking tabs engage.
9. Install the headlamp switch assembly onto the panel and tighten the three headlamp switch-to-panel retaining screws.
10. Attach the headlamp switch connector.
11. Install the finish panel.
12. Install the knee bolster panel.
13. Connect the negative battery cable.

Dimmer Switch

REMOVAL & INSTALLATION

♦ **See Figure 91**

1. Disconnect the negative battery cable.
2. Remove the center finish panel from the instrument panel.
3. Remove the two retaining screws from the dimmer switch.
4. Pull the dimmer switch out, unplug the electrical connector and remove the dimmer switch.

To install:
5. Attach the connector to the dimmer switch.
6. Install and tighten the two dimmer switch retaining screws.
7. Install the center finish panel.
8. Connect the negative battery cable.

LIGHTING

Headlights

REMOVAL & INSTALLATION

▶ **See Figures 92 thru 97**

1. Disconnect the negative battery cable.
2. Open the vehicle's hood and secure it in an upright position.
3. Rotate the bulb and socket assembly counterclockwise to release the retaining tabs.

✳✳ WARNING

Do not touch the glass bulb with your fingers. Oil from your fingers can severely shorten the life of the bulb. If necessary, wipe off any dirt or oil from the bulb with rubbing alcohol before completing installation.

4. Careful raise the bulb with the wiring still connected.
5. Unplug the wiring connector from the bulb

To install:

6. Attach the electrical connector.
7. Carefully lower the bulb into the lens.
8. Rotate the bulb clockwise to engage the retaining tabs on the bulb.
9. Connect the negative battery cable.
10. To ensure that the replacement bulb functions properly, activate the applicable switch to illuminate the bulb which was just replaced. (If this is a combination low and high beam bulb, be sure to check both intensities.) If the replacement light bulb does not illuminate, either it too is faulty or there is a problem in the bulb circuit or switch. Correct if necessary.

AIMING THE HEADLIGHTS

▶ **See Figures 98, 99 and 100**

The headlights must be properly aimed to provide the best, safest road illumination. The lights should be checked for proper aim and adjusted as necessary. Certain state and local authorities have requirements for headlight aiming; these should be checked before adjustment is made.

✳✳ CAUTION

About once a year, when the headlights are replaced or any time front end work is performed on your vehicle, the headlight should be accurately aimed by a reputable repair shop using the proper equipment. Headlights not properly aimed can make it virtually impossible to see and may blind other drivers on the road, possibly causing an accident. Note that the following procedure is a temporary fix, until you can take your vehicle to a repair shop for a proper adjustment.

Headlight adjustment may be temporarily made using a wall, as described below, or on the rear of another vehicle. When adjusted, the lights should not glare in oncoming car or truck windshields, nor should they illuminate the passenger compartment of vehicles driving in front of you. These adjustments are rough and should always be fine-tuned by a repair shop which is equipped with headlight aiming tools. Improper adjustments may be both dangerous and illegal.

For most of the vehicles covered by this manual, horizontal and vertical aiming of each sealed beam unit is provided by two adjusting screws which move the retaining ring and adjusting plate against the tension of a coil spring. There is no adjustment for focus; this is done during headlight manufacturing.

Fig. 92 The headlight bulb is accessed from inside the engine compartment

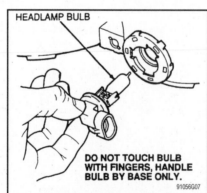
Fig. 93 Turn the headlight bulb counterclockwise to release the retaining tabs

Fig. 94 Carefully lift the bulb out of the lens

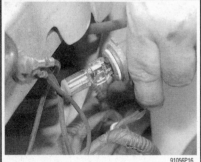
Fig. 95 Make sure you do not touch the glass bulb with your fingers, grasp the bulb around the base of the socket

Fig. 96 Unplug the connector from the bulb

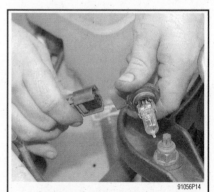
Fig. 97 Attach the bulb to the connector and install it into the lens assembly

➡Because the composite headlight assembly is bolted into position, no adjustment should be necessary or possible. Some applications, however, may be bolted to an adjuster plate or may be retained by adjusting

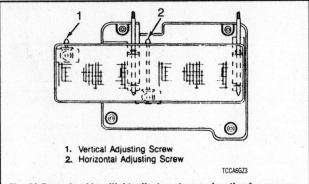

1. Vertical Adjusting Screw
2. Horizontal Adjusting Screw

TCCA6GZ3

Fig. 98 Example of headlight adjustment screw location for composite headlamps

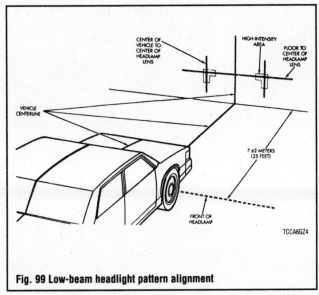

TCCA6GZ4

Fig. 99 Low-beam headlight pattern alignment

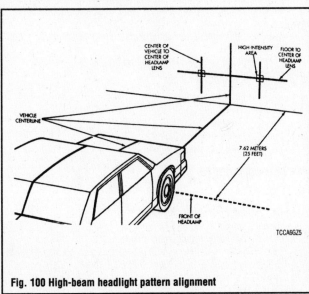

TCCA6GZ5

Fig. 100 High-beam headlight pattern alignment

screws. If so, follow this procedure when adjusting the lights, BUT always have the adjustment checked by a reputable shop.

Before removing the headlight bulb or disturbing the headlamp in any way, note the current settings in order to ease headlight adjustment upon reassembly. If the high or low beam setting of the old lamp still works, this can be done using the wall of a garage or a building:

1. Park the vehicle on a level surface, with the fuel tank about ½ full and with the vehicle empty of all extra cargo (unless normally carried). The vehicle should be facing a wall which is no less than 6 feet (1.8m) high and 12 feet (3.7m) wide. The front of the vehicle should be about 25 feet from the wall.

2. If aiming is to be performed outdoors, it is advisable to wait until dusk in order to properly see the headlight beams on the wall. If done in a garage, darken the area around the wall as much as possible by closing shades or hanging cloth over the windows.

3. Turn the headlights **ON** and mark the wall at the center of each light's low beam, then switch on the brights and mark the center of each light's high beam. A short length of masking tape which is visible from the front of the vehicle may be used. Although marking all four positions is advisable, marking one position from each light should be sufficient.

4. If neither beam on one side is working, and if another like-sized vehicle is available, park the second one in the exact spot where the vehicle was and mark the beams using the same-side light. Then switch the vehicles so the one to be aimed is back in the original spot. It must be parked no closer to or farther away from the wall than the second vehicle.

5. Perform any necessary repairs, but make sure the vehicle is not moved, or is returned to the exact spot from which the lights were marked. Turn the headlights **ON** and adjust the beams to match the marks on the wall.

6. Have the headlight adjustment checked as soon as possible by a reputable repair shop.

Signal and Marker Lights

REMOVAL & INSTALLATION

Front Turn Signal and Parking Lights

▶ See Figures 101, 102, 103, 104 and 105

1. Disconnect the negative battery cable.
2. Open and support the hood.
3. Remove the one retaining bolt for the parking lamp assembly from the radiator support.
4. Slide the parking lamp assembly out of the vehicle.
5. Unplug the connector for the lamp.
6. Turn the bulb and socket counterclockwise ¼ of a turn to release it from the lens.
7. Turn the bulb counterclockwise ¼ of a turn to release it from the socket.

91056P18

Fig. 101 Loosen the retaining bolt for the lamp assembly and . . .

Fig. 102 . . . remove the bolt and carefully pull the lamp assembly out of the fender

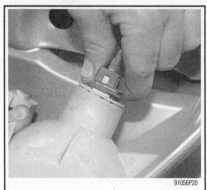

Fig. 103 Squeeze the retaining spring and unplug the connector

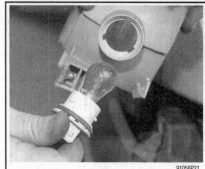

Fig. 104 Rotate the socket assembly counterclockwise ¼ of a turn and remove it from the lens

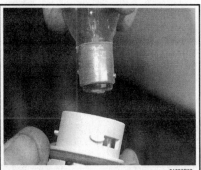

Fig. 105 Rotate the bulb counterclockwise ¼ of a turn and remove the bulb from the socket

Fig. 106 Open the bulb access door inside the trunk

Fig. 107 Unplug the connector from the socket

To install:

8. Place a new bulb into the socket and turn the bulb ¼ of a turn clockwise to engage the retaining tabs.

9. Place the bulb and socket assembly into the opening of the lens and turn it ¼ of a turn clockwise to engage it into the lens.

10. Attach the connector for the lamp.

11. Slide the lamp assembly into the opening in the fender.

12. Tighten the retaining bolt.

13. Connect the negative battery cable.

14. Verify the operation of the lamp.

15. Close the hood.

Rear Turn Signal, Brake and Tail Lights

▶ **See Figures 106, 107, 108 and 109**

1. Disconnect the negative battery cable.

2. Open the trunklid.

3. Open the lamp access door inside the luggage compartment.

4. Unplug the connector for the lamp.

5. Turn the socket counterclockwise ¼ of a turn to release it from the lens.

6. Turn the bulb counterclockwise ¼ of a turn to release it from the socket.

To install:

7. Place a new bulb into the socket and turn the bulb ¼ of a turn clockwise to engage the bulb into the socket.

8. Place the socket into the opening of the lens and turn the socket ¼ of a turn clockwise to engage it into the lens.

9. Attach the connector for the lamp.

10. Close the access door.

11. Connect the negative battery cable.

12. Verify the operation of the lamp.

Back-up Light

CONTOUR

▶ **See Figures 110, 111, 112 and 113**

1. Disconnect the negative battery cable.

2. Open trunklid.

3. If equipped, remove the trim on the underside of the trunklid.

4. Unplug the connector for the lamp.

5. Turn the socket counterclockwise ¼ of a turn to release it from the lens.

6. Turn the bulb counterclockwise ¼ of a turn to release it from the socket.

To install:

7. Place a new bulb into the socket and turn the bulb ¼ of a turn clockwise to engage the bulb into the socket.

8. Place the socket into the opening of the lens and turn the socket ¼ of a turn clockwise to engage it into the lens.

9. Attach the connector for the lamp.

10. If equipped, install the trim on the trunklid.

11. Connect the negative battery cable.

12. Verify the operation of the lamp.

MYSTIQUE AND COUGAR

▶ **See Figure 114**

1. Disconnect the negative battery cable.

2. Open the trunklid.

3. Open the lamp access door on the trunklid.

4. Turn the socket counterclockwise ¼ of a turn to release it from the lens.

5. Pull the bulb straight out to release it from the socket.

To install:

6. Place a new bulb into the socket and lightly press it into place.

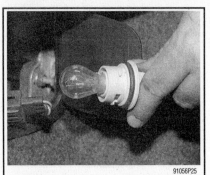

Fig. 108 Rotate the socket assembly counterclockwise ¼ of a turn and remove it from the lens

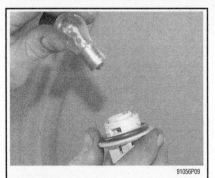

Fig. 109 Rotate the bulb counterclockwise ¼ of a turn and remove the bulb from the socket

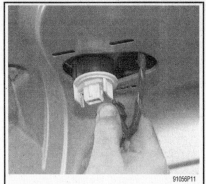

Fig. 110 Unplug the connector on the socket

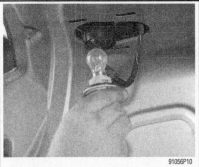

Fig. 111 Rotate the socket assembly counterclockwise ¼ of a turn and remove it from the lens

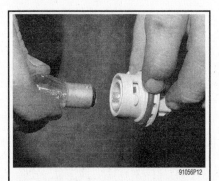

Fig. 112 Rotate the bulb assembly counterclockwise ¼ of a turn and remove it from the socket

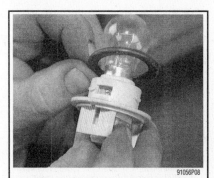

Fig. 113 Inspect the gasket on the socket and replace if necessary, or a water leak could occur damaging the bulb

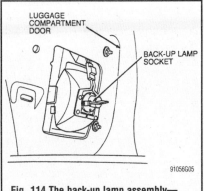

Fig. 114 The back-up lamp assembly—Mystique and Cougar

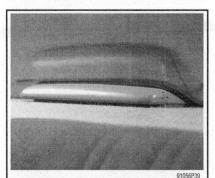

Fig. 115 The high mount brake lamp is mounted on the rear package shelf and is accessible from the back seat of the vehicle

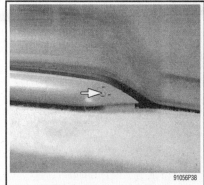

Fig. 116 The lamp cover is retained by two tabs, one on each side of the cover

7. Place the socket into the opening of the lens and turn the socket ¼ of a turn clockwise to engage it into the lens.
8. Close the access door.
9. Connect the negative battery cable.
10. Verify the operation of the lamp.

High-mount Brake Light

▶ See Figures 115, 116, 117, 118 and 119

➡There are several small bulbs located in the high-mount brake light, replace each bulb as necessary.

1. Disconnect the negative battery cable.
2. Press and release the tabs on the lamp cover.
3. Remove the lamp cover from the lens.
4. Turn the socket(s) counterclockwise ¼ of a turn to release them from the lens.

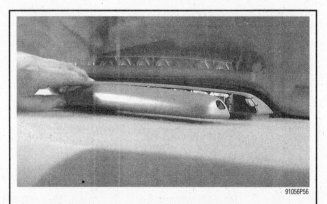

Fig. 117 Depress the retaining tabs and remove the lamp cover

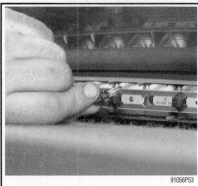

Fig. 118 Rotate the socket assembly out of the lamp

Fig. 119 Pull the bulb straight out to disengage it from the socket

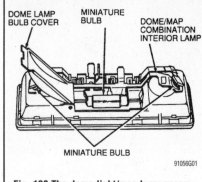

Fig. 120 The dome light/map lamp assembly

5. Pull the bulb(s) straight out to release them from the socket.

To install:

6. Place a new bulb into the socket and lightly press it into place.

7. Place the socket into the opening of the lens and turn the socket ¼ of a turn clockwise to engage it into the lens.

8. Place the lamp cover into place and ensure the retaining tabs engage.

9. Connect the negative battery cable.

10. Verify the operation of the lamp.

Dome Light/Map Lamp

▶ **See Figures 120, 121, 122, 123 and 124**

1. Disconnect the negative battery cable.

2. Carefully pry the dome/map lamp assembly from the headliner.

3. For the dome light, remove the bulb from the terminals by gently pulling the bulb upward.

4. For the map lamp(s), slide retaining spring to the side and remove the bulb from the lens.

To install:

5. For the dome light, gently press the bulb into the terminals on the lens.

6. For the map lamp(s), install the bulb into the lens and slide retaining spring over the bulb.

7. Snap lamp assembly into the headliner.

8. Connect the negative battery cable.

9. Verify the operation of the lamp.

License Plate Lights

CONTOUR

▶ **See Figures 125, 126 and 127**

1. Disconnect the negative battery cable.

2. Remove the two retaining screws for the lamp lens.

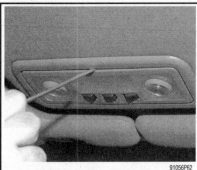

Fig. 121 Using a small screwdriver or other suitable tool, pry the lamp assembly out of the headliner

Fig. 122 Lower the assembly down

Fig. 123 To replace the map lamp bulbs, slide the retaining spring to the side and . . .

Fig. 124 . . . remove the bulb from the lamp assembly

Fig. 125 Remove the two lamp lens retaining screws and . . .

Fig. 126 . . . lower the lens to access the bulb

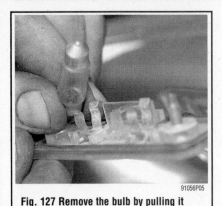

Fig. 127 Remove the bulb by pulling it from the terminals on the lens

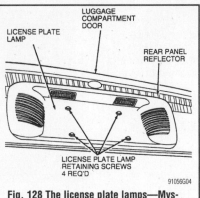

Fig. 128 The license plate lamps—Mystique and Cougar

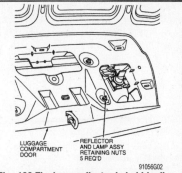

Fig. 129 The lamp reflector is held by five nuts located on the underside of the trunklid

3. Lower the lens from the trunklid.
4. Grasp the bulb and remove it from the terminals on the lens.

To install:

5. Place the bulb into place on the lens and lightly press into the terminals on the lens.
6. Place the lens into position on the trunklid and tighten the two retaining screws.
7. Connect the negative battery cable.
8. Verify the operation of the lamp.

MYSTIQUE AND COUGAR

▶ **See Figures 128 and 129**

1. Disconnect the negative battery cable.
2. Remove the rear lamp reflector panel from the trunklid.
3. Remove the two retaining screws for the license plate lamp lens.
4. Grasp the bulb and remove it from the terminals on the lens.

To install:

5. Place the bulb into place on the lens and lightly press into the terminals on the lens.
6. Place the lens into position on the panel and tighten the two retaining screws.
7. Install the rear lamp reflector panel onto the trunklid.
8. Connect the negative battery cable.
9. Verify the operation of the lamp.

Fog/Driving Lights

REMOVAL & INSTALLATION

Lamp assembly

▶ **See Figure 130**

1. Disconnect the negative battery cable.
2. Remove the radiator air deflector.

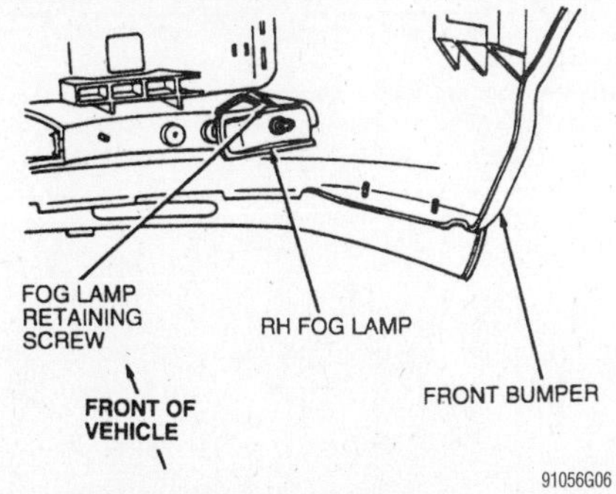

Fig. 130 The foglamp assembly—Passenger side

3. Unplug the fog lamp connectors.
4. From behind the bumper cover, remove the three screws (Contour only) or one screw (Mystique and Cougar) retaining each foglamp to the bumper cover.
5. Remove the lamp assembly from the vehicle.

To install:

6. Place the foglamp assembly into place and tighten the screws on the Contour to 4–5 ft lbs. (6–7 Nm). On the Mystique and Cougar, tighten the screw to 25–26 inch lbs. (3 Nm).
7. Attach the foglamp connectors.
8. Install the radiator air deflector.
9. Connect the negative battery cable.

Bulb Replacement

1. Disconnect the negative battery cable.
2. Unplug the fog lamp connector(s).
3. Turn the bulb ¼ of a turn counterclockwise and remove the bulb and socket.
4. Pull the bulb straight out to remove it from the socket.

To install:

5. Gently push a new bulb into the socket assembly.
6. Place the bulb and socket assembly into the foglamp and turn it ¼ of a turn clockwise to engage the socket into the foglamp.
7. Attach the foglamp connector(s).
8. Connect the negative battery cable.

INSTALLING AFTERMARKET AUXILIARY LIGHTS

➡ **Before installing any aftermarket light, make sure it is legal for road use. Most acceptable lights will have a DOT approval number. Also check your local and regional inspection regulations. In certain areas, aftermarket lights must be installed in a particular manner or they may not be legal for inspection.**

1. Disconnect the negative battery cable.
2. Unpack the contents of the light kit purchased. Place the contents in an open space where you can easily retrieve a piece if needed.
3. Choose a location for the lights. If you are installing fog lights, below the bumper and apart from each other is desirable. Most fog lights are mounted below or very close to the headlights. If you are installing driving lights, above the bumper and close together is desirable. Most driving lights are mounted between the headlights.
4. Drill the needed hole(s) to mount the light. Install the light, and secure using the supplied retainer nut and washer. Tighten the light mounting hardware, but not the light adjustment nut or bolt.
5. Install the relay that came with the light kit in the engine compartment, in a rigid area, such as a fender. Always install the relay with the terminals facing down. This will prevent water from entering the relay assembly.
6. Using the wire supplied, locate the ground terminal on the relay, and connect a length of wire from this terminal to a good ground source. You can drill a hole and screw this wire to an inside piece of metal; just scrape the paint away from the hole to ensure a good connection.

7. Locate the light terminal on the relay; and attach a length of wire between this terminal and the fog/driving lamps.

8. Locate the ignition terminal on the relay, and connect a length of wire between this terminal and the light switch.

9. Find a suitable mounting location for the light switch and install. Some examples of mounting areas are a location close to the main light switch, auxiliary light position in the dash panel, if equipped, or in the center of the dash panel.

10. Depending on local and regional regulations, the other end of the switch can be connected to a constant power source such as the battery, an ignition opening in the fuse panel, or a parking or headlight wire.

11. Locate the power terminal on the relay, and connect a wire with an in-line fuse of at least 10 amperes between the terminal and the battery.

12. With all the wires connected and tied up neatly, connect the negative battery cable.

13. Turn the lights ON and adjust the light pattern, if necessary.

AIMING

1. Park the vehicle on level ground, so it is perpendicular to and, facing a flat wall about 25 ft. (7.6m) away.

2. Remove any stone shields, if equipped, and switch ON the lights.

3. Loosen the mounting hardware of the lights so you can aim them as follows:

a. The horizontal distance between the light beams on the wall should be the same as between the lights themselves.

b. The vertical height of the light beams above the ground should be 4 in. (10cm) less than the distance between the ground and the center of the lamp lenses for fog lights. For driving lights, the vertical height should be even with the distance between the ground and the center of the lamp.

4. Tighten the mounting hardware.

5. Test to make sure the lights work correctly, and the light pattern is even.

Instrument Cluster Light bulbs

REMOVAL & INSTALLATION

♦ **See Figures 131 and 132**

1. Disconnect the negative battery cable.
2. Remove the instrument cluster as outlined in this section.

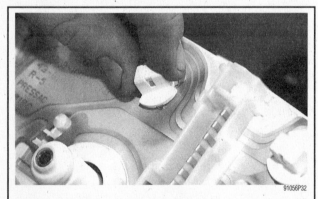

Fig. 131 Turn the socket counterclockwise to remove it

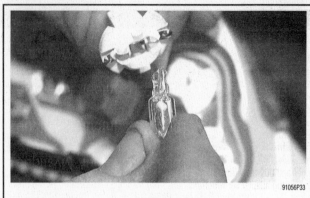

Fig. 132 Pull the bulb straight out to remove it

3. Turn the desired bulb socket counter clockwise to remove it from the cluster.

4. Grasp the bulb and pull it straight out to remove it from the socket.

To install:

5. Place a new bulb into the socket and lightly press it into place.

6. Place the socket into the cluster and turn the socket clockwise to engage it into the cluster.

7. Install the instrument cluster.

8. Connect the negative battery cable.

Function	Trade Number
Tail lamp, brakelamp, turn lamp	1157
Backup lamp	1156
Front park, turn lamp	2357NA

Headlamp
    Low beam
    High beam
	
	9006
	9005

Fog Lamp	893
License plate lamp	C5W
High-mount brakelamp	2723
Dome/Map lamp	**
Door courtesy lamp	168
Engine compartment lamp	89
Floor console	168
Luggage compartment lamp	**
Glove box	168
Instrument courtesy lamps	**
High beam indicator	51A
I/P Ashtray lamp	Not available at time of printing. See your dealer for replacement.
Radio illumination	*
Clock	**
Warning lights (all)	51A
Turn signal indicator	51A
"PRND21"	161
Heater or heater A/C	Not available at time of printing. See your dealer for replacement.
Light switch illumination	161

*Refer bulb replacement to a Ford authorized radio service center.
NA means Natural Amber
**Refer bulb replacement to a Ford authorized dealer.

91056C05

TRAILER WIRING

Wiring the vehicle for towing is fairly easy. There are a number of good wiring kits available and these should be used, rather than trying to design your own.All trailers will need brake lights and turn signals as well as tail lights and side marker lights. Most areas require extra marker lights for overwide trailers. Also, most areas have recently required back-up lights for trailers, and most trailer manufacturers have been building trailers with back-up lights for several years.Additionally, some Class I, most Class II and just about all Class III and IV trailers will have electric brakes. Add to this number an accessories wire, to operate trailer internal equipment or to charge the trailer's battery, and you can have as many as seven wires in the harness.Determine the equipment on your trailer and buy the wiring kit necessary. The kit will contain all the wires needed, plus a plug adapter set which includes the female plug, mounted on the bumper or hitch, and the male plug, wired into, or plugged into the trailer harness.When installing the kit, follow the manufacturer's instructions. The color coding of the wires is usually standard throughout the industry. One point to note: some domestic vehicles, and most imported vehicles, have separate turn signals. On most domestic vehicles, the brake lights and rear turn signals operate with the same bulb. For those vehicles without separate turn signals, you can purchase an isolation unit so that the brake lights won't blink whenever the turn signals are operated.One, final point, the best kits are those with a spring loaded cover on the vehicle mounted socket. This cover prevents dirt and moisture from corroding the terminals. Never let the vehicle socket hang loosely; always mount it securely to the bumper or hitch.

CIRCUIT PROTECTION

Fuses

REPLACEMENT

▶ **See Figures 133, 134 and 135**

Fuses are located either in the engine compartment or passenger compartment fuse and relay panels. If a fuse blows, a single component or single circuit will not function properly.
1. Remove the fuse or relay box cover.
2. Inspect the fuses to determine which is faulty.
3. Unplug and discard the fuse.
4. Inspect the box terminals and clean if corroded. If any terminals are damaged, replace the terminals.
5. Plug in a new fuse of the same amperage rating.

✳✳ WARNING

Never exceed the amperage rating of a blown fuse. If the replacement fuse also blows, check for a problem in the circuit.

6. Check for proper operation of the affected component or circuit.

Maxi-Fuses (Fusible Links)

Maxi-fuses are located in the engine compartment relay box. If a maxi-fuse blows, an entire circuit or several circuits will not function properly.

REPLACEMENT

1. Remove the fuse and relay box cover.
2. Inspect the fusible links to determine which is faulty.

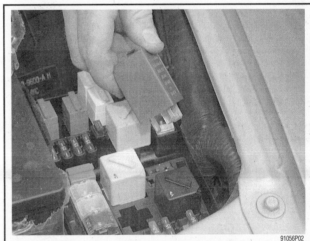

Fig. 134 The engine compartment fuse or power distribution box contains a combination of fuses, maxi-fuses, relays, and diodes. Most can be removed by simply pulling upward

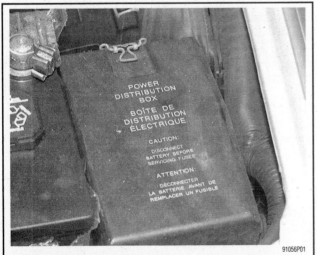

Fig. 133 The engine compartment fuse or power distribution box, is located adjacent to the battery in the engine compartment

Fig. 135 The interior fuse box is located under the driver's side of the instrument panel, it can be lowered for easier access by releasing retaining clips

3. Unplug and discard the fusible link.
4. Inspect the box terminals and clean if corroded. If any terminals are damaged, replace the terminals.
5. Plug in a new fusible link of the same amperage rating.

✳✳ WARNING

Never exceed the amperage rating of a blown maxi-fuse. If the replacement fuse also blows, check for a problem in the circuit(s).

6. Check for proper operation of the affected circuit(s).

Circuit Breakers

RESETTING AND/OR REPLACEMENT

Circuit breakers are located inside the fuse panel. They are automatically reset when the problem corrects itself, is repaired, or the circuit cools down to allow operation again.

Fusible Link

▶ **See Figure 136**

The fuse link is a short length of wire, integral with the engine compartment wiring harness and should not be confused with standard wire. The fusible link wire gauge is smaller than the circuit which it protects. Under no circumstances should a fuse link replacement repair be made using a length of standard wire cut from bulk stock or from another wiring harness.

Fusible link wire is covered with a special thick, non-flammable insulation. An overload condition causes the insulation to blister. If the overall condition continues, the wire will melt. To check a fusible link, look for blistering insula-

FUSIBLE LINK COLOR CODING	
WIRE LINK SIZE	**INSULATION COLOR**
20 GA	Blue
18 GA	Brown or Red
16 GA	Black or Orange
14 GA	Green
12 GA	Gray

90986G89

Fig. 136 Common fusible link color coding

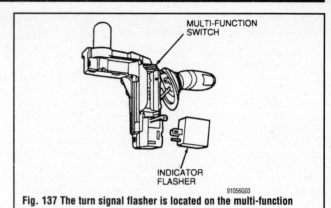

MULTI-FUNCTION
SWITCH

INDICATOR
FLASHER

91056G03

Fig. 137 The turn signal flasher is located on the multi-function switch in the steering column

tion. If the insulation is okay, pull gently on the wire. If the fusible link stretches, the wire has melted.

Fusible links are often identified by the color coding of the insulation. Refer to the accompanying illustration for wire link size and color.

Flashers

REPLACEMENT

Turn Signal Flasher

▶ **See Figure 137**

1. Disconnect the negative battery cable.
2. Remove the upper and lower steering column shrouds.
3. Pull the flasher from the back of the multi-function switch.

To install:

4. Install a new flasher in the multi-function switch.
5. Install the column shrouds.
6. Connect the negative battery cable.

Hazard Warning Flasher

1. Disconnect the negative battery cable.
2. Remove the knee bolster panel from the underside of the driver's side of the instrument panel.
3. Grasp and pull the flasher from the connector located near the top of the steering column.

To install:

4. Install a new flasher in the connector.
5. Install the knee bolster panel.
6. Connect the negative battery cable.

INTERIOR FUSE PANEL

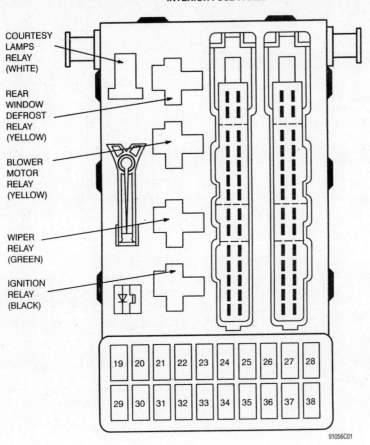

91056C01

	FUSE	AMPS	CIRCUITS PROTECTED
19	MIRROR HEATER	7.5	POWER/HEATED MIRROR DEFROST GRIDS
20	WIPER (C.B.)	10	WINDSHIELD WIPER/WASHER SYSTEM
21	POWER WINDOWS	40	POWER WINDOWS, POWER MOONROOF
22	ABS MODULE	7.5	ABS MODULE, SPEED CONTROL CUT OUT RELAY
23	BACKUP LAMP	15	PNP SWITCH, TR SENSOR, HEATER – A/C MODE SWITCH, SPEED CONTROL MODULE, GEARSHIFT LEVER UNIT, AIR TEMPERATURE ACTUATOR
24	STOP LAMP	15	INSTRUMENT CLUSTER, BOO SWITCH, BRAKE PEDAL SWITCH, CLUTCH PEDAL SWITCH
25	DOOR LOCK	20	POWER DOOR LOCKS, REMOTE ENTRY, PANIC ALARM
26	MAIN LIGHT	7.5	MAIN LIGHT SWITCH, HEADLAMP SWITCH, FOG LAMP SWITCH, COMBINATION SWITCH
27	CIGAR LIGHTER	15	CIGAR LIGHTER
28	SEATS	30	AUDIO SYSTEM AMPLIFIER, POWER SEATS
29	REAR WINDOW HEATER	30	REAR WINDOW DEFROST GRID, REAR WINDOW DEFROST SWITCH
30	ELECTRONICS	7.5	INSTRUMENT CLUSTER, AIR BAG DIAGNOSTIC MODULE, POWER ANTENNA, INSTRUMENT INTERFACE MODULE
31	ILLUMINATION	7.5	INSTRUMENT ILLUMINATON, LICENSE LAMP, INSTRUMENT INTERFACE MODULE
32	RADIO	7.5	CLOCK, RADIO, RADIO/CD
33	SIDE LIGHTS (LEFT)	7.5	LEFT FRONT PARK/TURN LAMPS, LEFT REAR COMBINATION LAMPS
34	COURTESY LAMPS	7.5	DOME/MAP LAMPS, VANITY MIRRORS, LUGGAGE COMPART-MENT LAMP, ENGINE COMPARTMENT AND GLOVE BOX LAMPS
35	SIDE LIGHTS (RIGHT)	7.5	RIGHT FRONT PARK/TURN LAMPS, RIGHT REAR COMBINA-TION LAMPS
36	AIR BAG	10	AIR BAG DIAGOSTIC MONITOR
37	BLOWER MOTOR	30	BLOWER SWITCH, BLOWER MOTOR RELAY, BLOWER MOTOR RESISTORS
38	NOT USED	—	

91056C02

ENGINE COMPARTMENT FUSE BOX

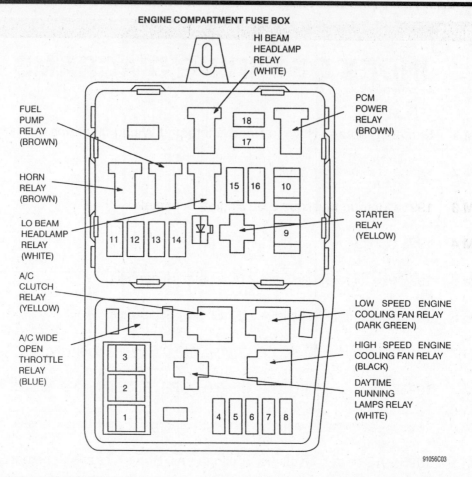

91056C03

	MAXI-FUSE	AMPS	CIRCUITS PROTECTED
1	MAIN	80	CENTRAL TIMER MODULE, ALL CIRCUITS EXCEPT ENGINE COOLING FANS, ABS SYSTEM, IGNITION SWITCH, PCM
2	ENGINE COOLING FAN	60	ENGINE COOLING FANS
3	ABS/HEATER BLOWER	60	ABS HYDRAULIC UNIT, BLOWER MOTOR RELAY
9	PCM	20	POWERTRAIN CONTROL MODULE
10	IGNITION SWITCH	20	IGNITION SWITCH
	FUSE	**AMPS**	**CIRCUITS PROTECTED**
4	IGNITION/DRL	20	GENERATOR, IGNITION COIL, PCM POWER RELAY
5	FOG LAMP	15	FOG LAMP RELAY
6	NOT USED	—	
7	ABS	30	ABS HYDRAULIC UNIT
8	NOT USED	—	
11	PCM MEMORY	3	PCM MEMORY CIRCUITS
12	HORN/HAZARD	15	HORN RELAY, HAZARD SWITCH (COMBINATION SWITCH)
13	HO2S	15	HEATED OXYGEN SENSORS
14	FUEL PUMP	15	INERTIA FUEL SHUT OFF SWITCH, PCM
15	RIGHT LO BEAM	10	RIGHT LO BEAM HEADLAMP
16	LEFT LO BEAM	10	LEFT LO BEAM HEADLAMP
17	RIGHT HI BEAM	10	RIGHT HI BEAM HEADLAMP, DRL RELAY
18	LEFT HI BEAM	10	LEFT HI BEAM HEADLAMP

91056C04

WIRING DIAGRAMS

INDEX OF WIRING DIAGRAMS

91056W01

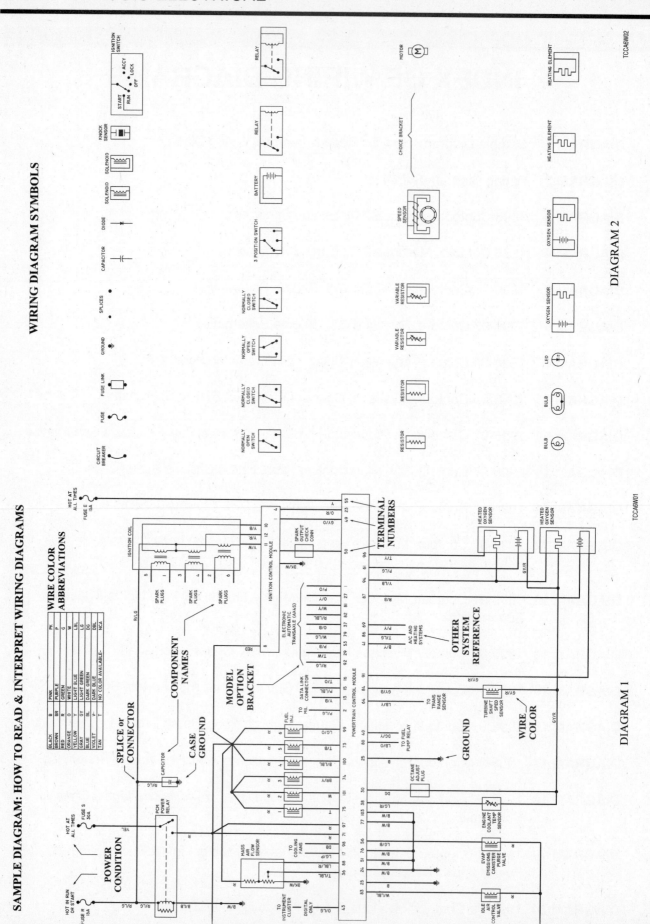

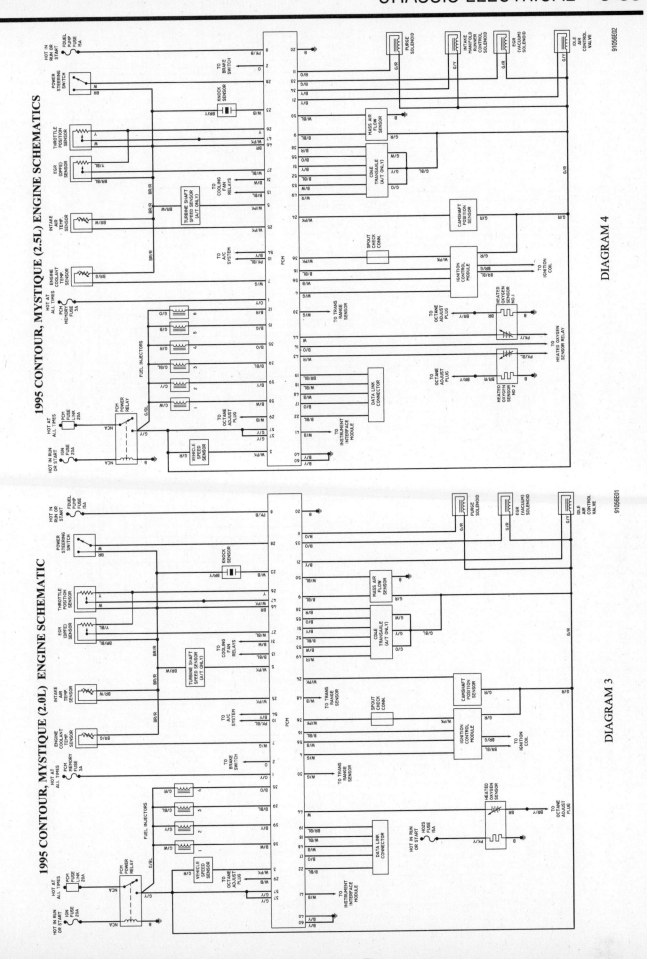

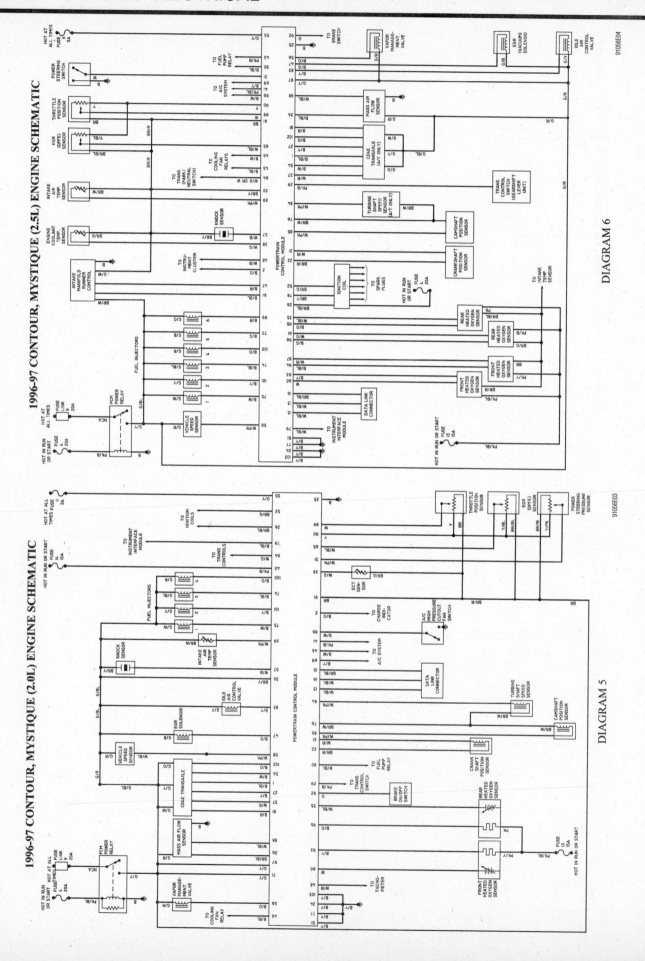

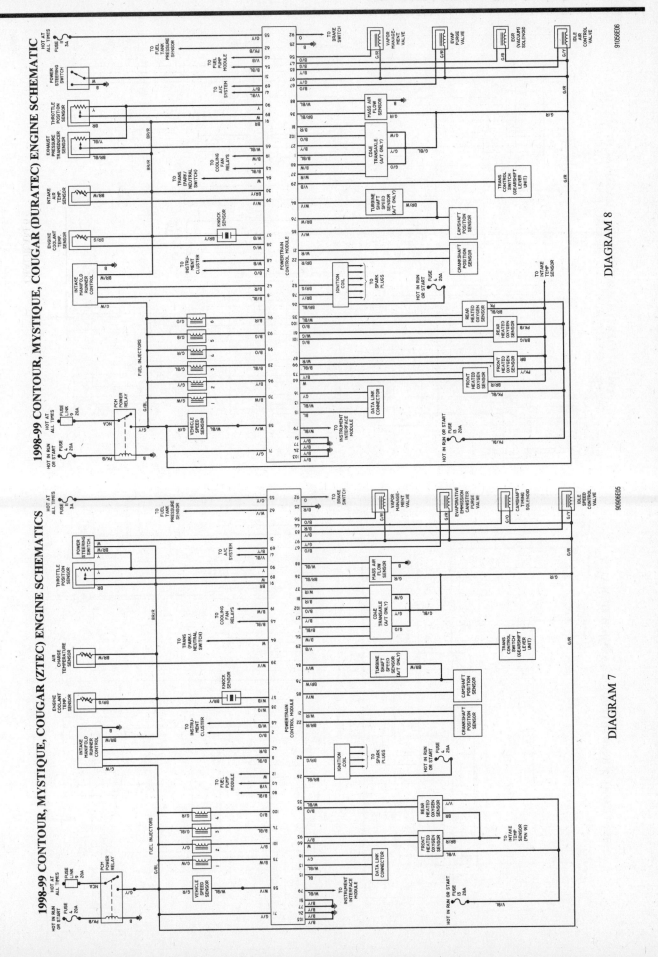

1998-99 CONTOUR, MYSTIQUE, COUGAR (DURATEC) ENGINE SCHEMATIC

DIAGRAM 8

1998-99 CONTOUR, MYSTIQUE, COUGAR (ZTEC) ENGINE SCHEMATICS

DIAGRAM 7

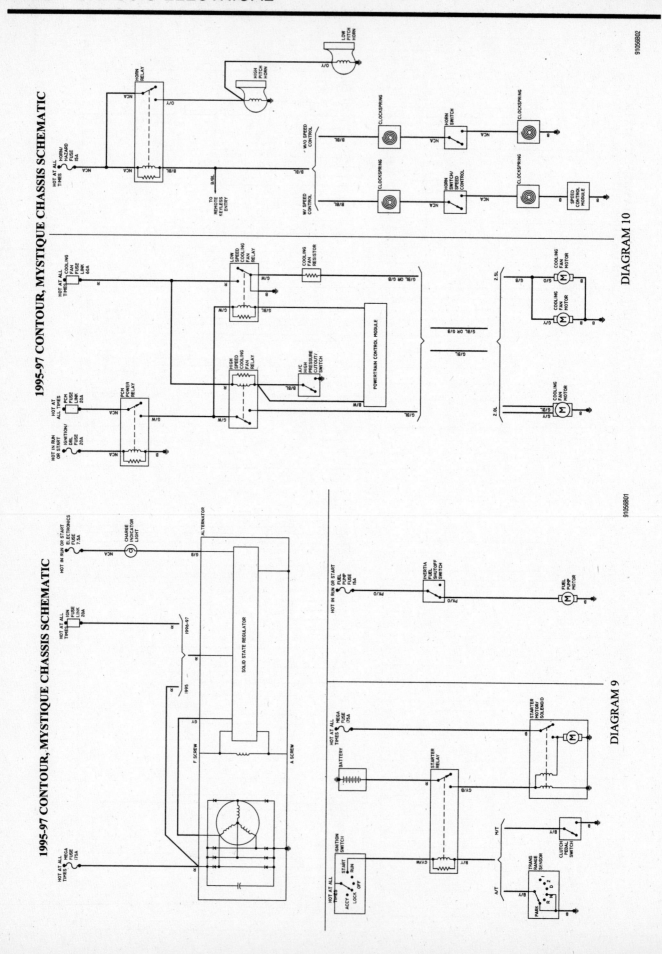

1995-97 CONTOUR, MYSTIQUE CHASSIS SCHEMATIC

DIAGRAM 10

1995-97 CONTOUR, MYSTIQUE CHASSIS SCHEMATIC

DIAGRAM 9

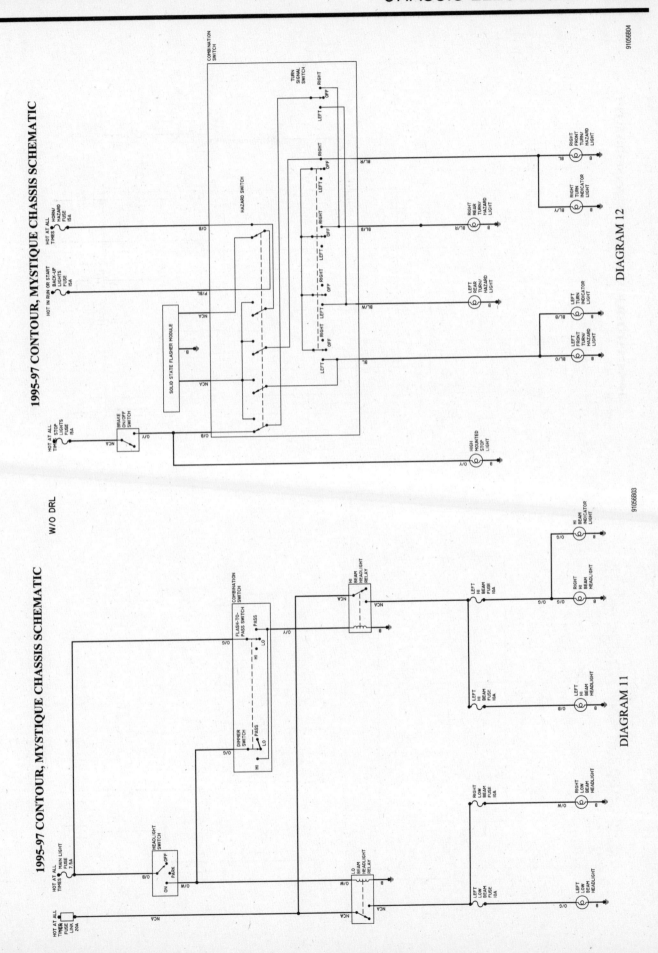

DIAGRAM 12

1995-97 CONTOUR, MYSTIQUE CHASSIS SCHEMATIC

W/O DRL

DIAGRAM 11

1995-97 CONTOUR, MYSTIQUE CHASSIS SCHEMATIC

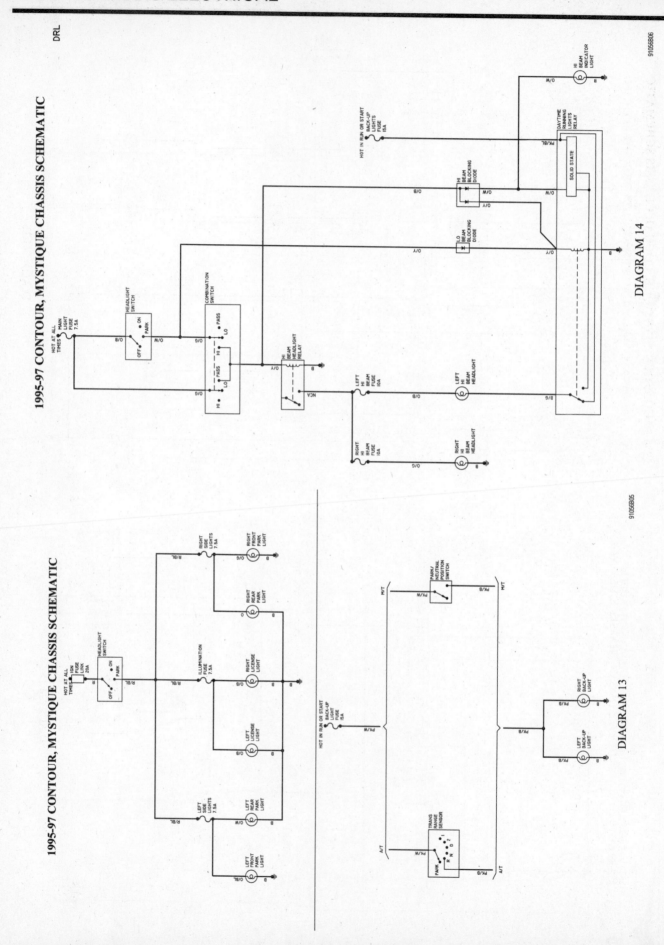

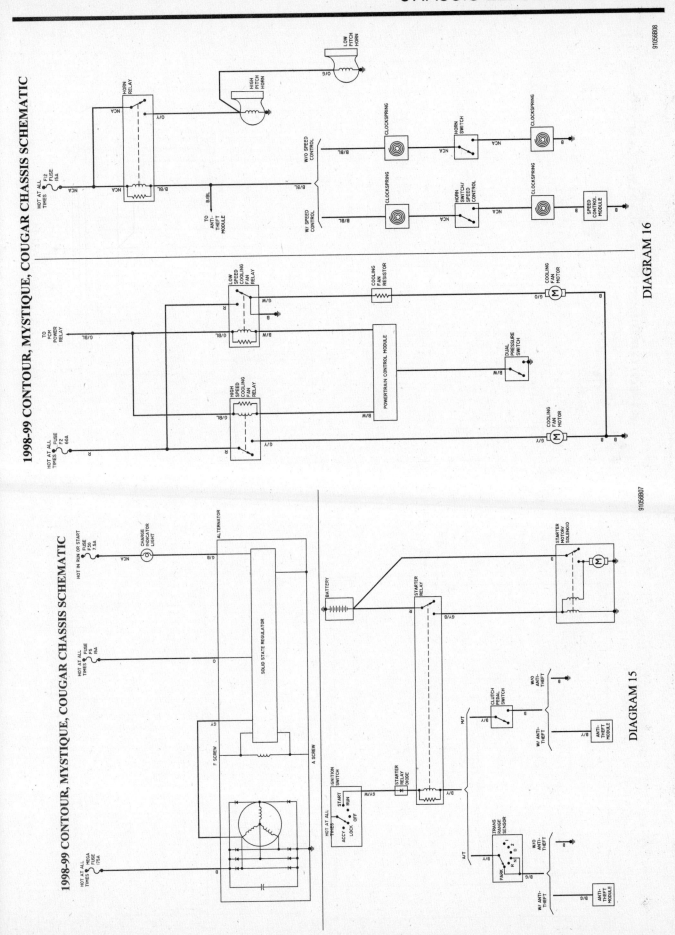

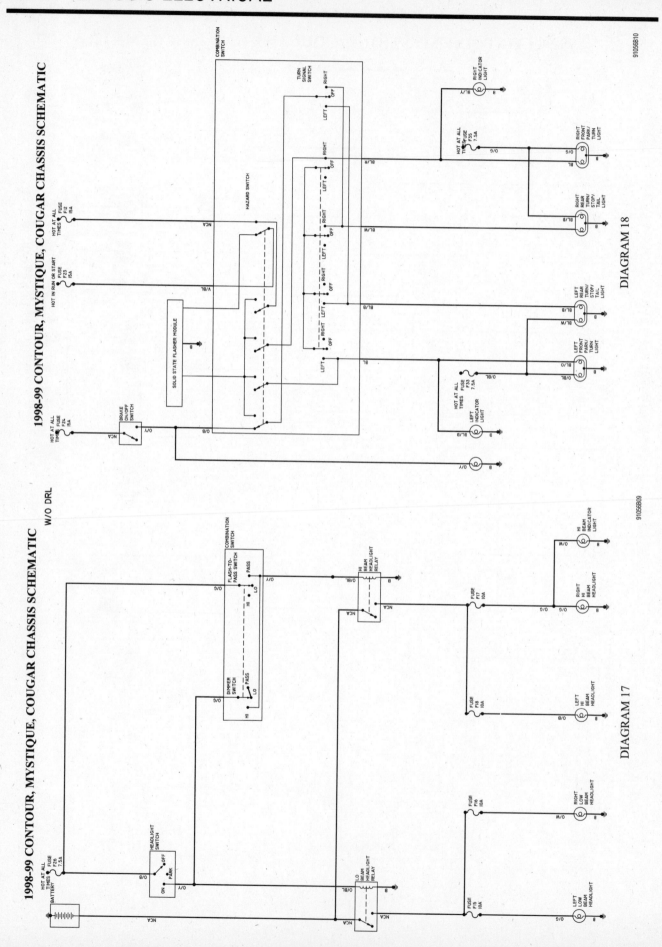

1998-99 CONTOUR, MYSTIQUE, COUGAR CHASSIS SCHEMATIC

DIAGRAM 18

91056B10

W/O DRL

1998-99 CONTOUR, MYSTIQUE, COUGAR CHASSIS SCHEMATIC

DIAGRAM 17

91056B09

1998-99 CONTOUR, MYSTIQUE, COUGAR CHASSIS SCHEMATICS

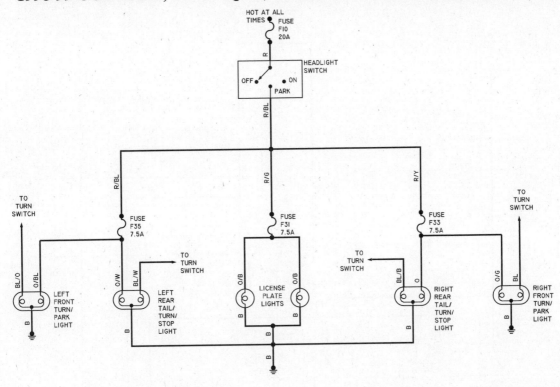

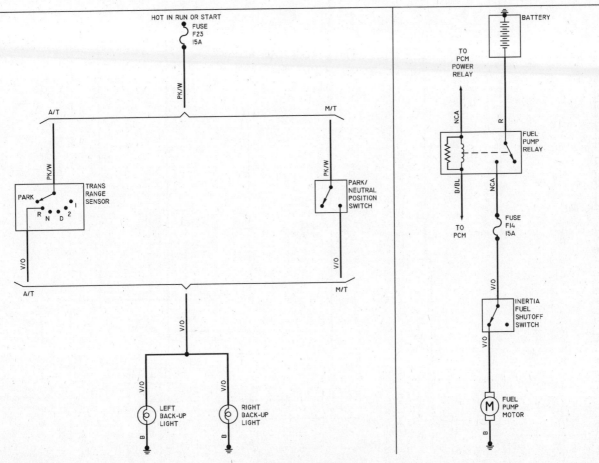

DIAGRAM 19

91056B11

1998-99 CONTOUR, MYSTIQUE, COUGAR CHASSIS SCHEMATIC

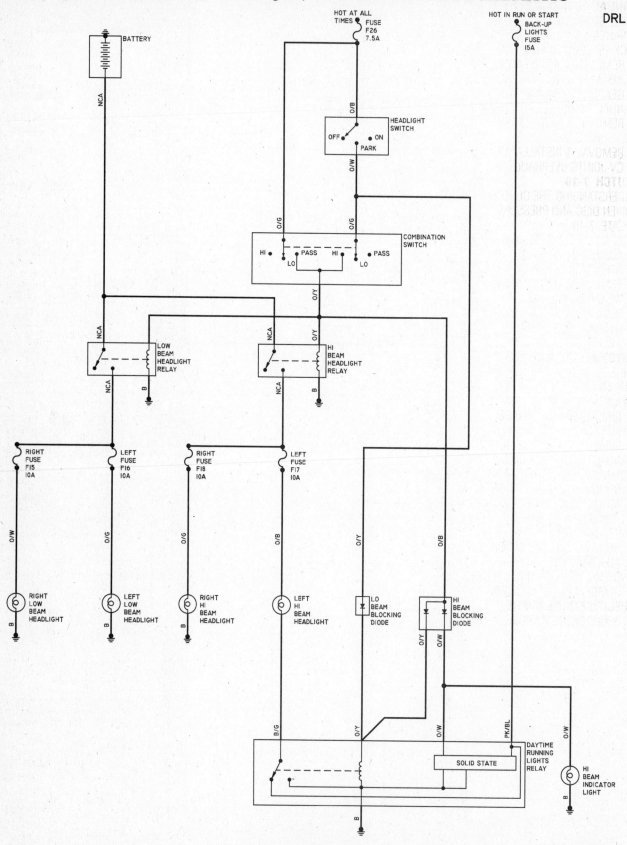

DRL

DIAGRAM 20

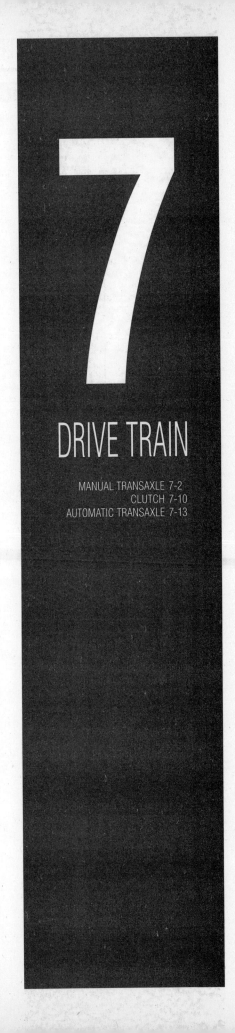

7
DRIVE TRAIN

MANUAL TRANSAXLE

Understanding the Manual Transaxle

Because of the way an internal combustion engine breathes, it can produce torque, or twisting force, only within a narrow speed range. Most modern, overhead valve pushrod engines must turn at about 2500 rpm to produce their peak torque. By 4500 rpm they are producing so little torque that continued increases in engine speed produce no power increases. The torque peak on overhead camshaft engines is generally much higher, but much narrower.

The manual transaxle and clutch are employed to vary the relationship between engine speed and the speed of the wheels so that adequate engine power can be produced under all circumstances. The clutch allows engine torque to be applied to the transaxle input shaft gradually, due to mechanical slippage. Consequently, the vehicle may be started smoothly from a full stop. The transaxle changes the ratio between the rotating speeds of the engine and the wheels by the use of gears. The gear ratios allow full engine power to be applied to the wheels during acceleration at low speeds and at highway/passing speeds.

In a front wheel drive transaxle, power is usually transmitted from the input shaft to a mainshaft or output shaft located slightly beneath and to the side of the input shaft. The gears of the mainshaft mesh with gears on the input shaft, allowing power to be carried from one to the other. All forward gears are in constant mesh and are free from rotating with the shaft unless the synchronizer and clutch is engaged. Shifting from one gear to the next causes one of the gears to be freed from rotating with the shaft and locks another to it. Gears are locked and unlocked by internal dog clutches which slide between the center of the gear and the shaft. The forward gears employ synchronizers; friction members which smoothly bring gear and shaft to the same speed before the toothed dog clutches are engaged.

Back-Up Light Switch

REMOVAL & INSTALLATION

1. Disconnect the negative battery cable.
2. Remove the air cleaner assembly.
3. Remove the two back-up light switch-to-control selector lever retaining bolts.
4. Unplug the back-up light switch connector.
5. Remove the switch.

To install:

6. Attach the back-up light switch connector.
7. Install the switch and tighten the retaining bolts to 15–21 ft. lbs. (20–29 Nm).
8. Install the air cleaner assembly.
9. Connect the negative battery cable.

Adjustments

GEARSHIFT LINKAGE

♦ **See Figures 1, 2, 3, 4 and 5**

1. Raise and safely support the vehicle securely on jackstands.
2. Loosen the shift linkage clamp bolt and place the transaxle in neutral.
3. Lower the vehicle.
4. Unsnap the gear shift boot bezel from the console and slide the boot up the gear shift lever.
5. Disconnect the shift lever housing insulator from the retainer and slide it up the gear shift lever.
6. Install gear shift lever aligning tool T94P-7025-FH onto the gear shift lever and rotate the top of the tool clockwise.
7. Raise and safely support the vehicle securely on jackstands.
8. Locate the access hole in the center of the underbody heat shield. Install shifter aligning tool T96P-7B140-A through the access hole and into the shift lever housing.

➡ **It may be necessary to move the shift linkage slightly to align tool T96P-7B140-A with the internal shift lever.**

9. Screw tool T96P-7B140-A into the shift lever housing until the hex portion of the tool bottoms lightly on the shift lever housing.
10. Tighten the shift linkage clamp bolt to 141 inch lbs. (16 Nm).
11. Remove tool T96P-7B140-A.
12. Lower the vehicle.
13. Remove tool T94P-7025-FH by turning it counterclockwise.
14. Install the shift lever housing insulator and the shift boot bezel.

Manual Transaxle Assembly

REMOVAL & INSTALLATION

♦ **See Figures 6, 7, 8, 9 and 10**

1. Disconnect the battery cables, negative cable first.
2. Remove the battery.
3. Secure the radiator and fan shroud to the radiator support using safety wire.
4. Loosen the front strut upper retaining nuts a total of five turns to allow room for the removal of the halfshafts. Do not remove the nuts.
5. Remove the Mass Air Flow sensor (MAF) and the air cleaner assembly. Remove the air cleaner lower bracket.
6. Install an engine support device and support the engine.

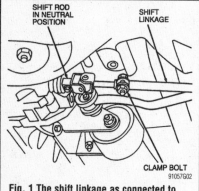

Fig. 1 The shift linkage as connected to the transaxle

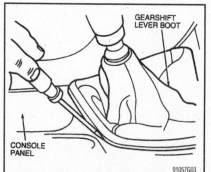

Fig. 2 Release the shifter boot bezel from the console and slide it up the gear shift lever

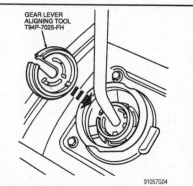

Fig. 3 Place the aligning tool onto the gear shift lever

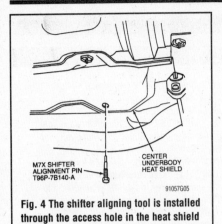

Fig. 4 The shifter aligning tool is installed through the access hole in the heat shield

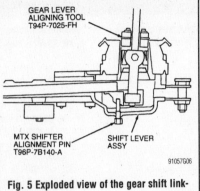

Fig. 5 Exploded view of the gear shift linkage adjustment

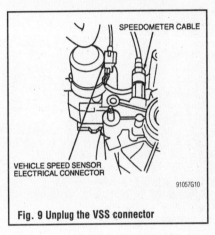

Fig. 6 Remove the ground strap and unplug the back-up lamp connector

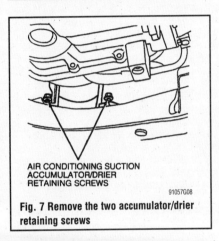

Fig. 7 Remove the two accumulator/drier retaining screws

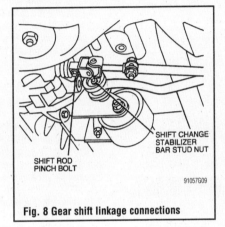

Fig. 8 Gear shift linkage connections

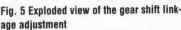

Fig. 9 Unplug the VSS connector

7. Disconnect the back-up lamp switch.

8. Remove the bolts securing the ground strap to the transaxle housing.

9. Remove the engine and transmission support insulator (mount).

10. Disconnect the hydraulic line and rubber grommet from the support insulator bracket.

11. Remove the rubber inspection cover from the transaxle clutch housing.

12. Remove the retaining clip and remove the hydraulic line fitting at the clutch slave cylinder.

13. Remove the upper transaxle to engine bolt.

14. Remove the two upper starter motor retaining bolts with the ground strap.

15. If equipped with the 2.0L engine, remove the exhaust manifold heat shield and the catalytic converter retaining nuts at the exhaust manifold.

16. Remove the wheel and tire assemblies.

17. Remove the accessory drive belt pulley cover.

18. Raise and safely support the vehicle.

19. If equipped with the 2.0L engine, remove the oil level dipstick. Remove the catalytic converter to engine bracket strap and the retaining bolts to the half-shaft bracket.

20. Remove the catalytic converter.

21. If equipped with the 2.5L engine, remove the water pump pulley shield. Remove the front Y-pipe nuts and the rear Y-pipe to catalytic converter nuts and remove the Y-pipe.

22. Disconnect the Vehicle Speed Sensor (VSS).

23. Remove the speedometer cable.

24. Remove the nine screws securing the lower radiator air deflector and remove the deflector.

25. Push the shift rod forward and remove the shift rod pinch bolt.

26. Pull the shift rod back and remove it from the transaxle.

27. Remove the shift control stabilizer bar nut at the stud and remove the stabilizer bar.

28. Remove the shift control stabilizer bar and bracket from the right engine support insulator bracket.

29. Remove the underbody heat shield from under the shift control.

30. Reposition the shift rod and stabilizer bar to allow transaxle removal.

31. Remove the two screws securing the A/C accumulator to the sub-frame.

32. Remove the halfshafts and the intermediate shaft.

33. Remove the bolts and the right engine support insulator mounting nuts and remove the bracket from the transaxle.

34. Remove the left engine support insulator through-bolt.

35. Lower the vehicle.

36. Adjust the three bar engine support or equivalent, to relieve tension on the right front engine support bracket.

37. Remove the right front engine support bracket through-bolt.

38. Raise and safely support the vehicle.

39. Disconnect the steering column from the steering gear at the pinch bolt.

40. Remove the catalytic converter.

41. Disconnect the tie rod ends from the steering knuckles and discard the cotter pins.

42. Remove the lower control arm to ball joint pinch bolts and separate the lower control arms from the ball joints.

43. Separate the sway bar (stabilizer bar) links from the sway bar.

44. Remove the splash shield at the front of the sub-frame.

45. Remove the through-bolt from the left front engine support insulator and remove the right front engine support insulator and mounting bracket.

46. Disconnect the power steering oil cooler hoses at the right front of the sub-frame and drain the power steering fluid.

47. Remove the A/C accumulator retaining bracket screws from the sub-frame.

48. Remove the four bolts retaining the lower radiator supports to the sub-frame. Rotate the radiator supports forward.

49. Remove the two screws retaining the bumper cover braces to the left and right sides of the sub-frame. Rotate the bumper cover braces forward.

50. Position a suitable support device with wood blocks approximately 40 inches (1,016mm) in length secured to the lift under the sub-frame.

51. Remove the four sub-frame to body retaining bolts.

52. Allow the sub-frame to lower slightly and disconnect the power steering pressure and return hoses from the rack and pinion (steering gear).

53. Finish lowering the sub-frame and move aside.

54. Lower the vehicle.

55. Loosen the front mount retaining nuts five turns.
56. Place a floor jack and a block of wood under the transaxle and raise the transaxle enough to release the tension on the three bar engine support, or equivalent.
57. Back off on the three bar engine support adjustment to allow downward travel of the transaxle.
58. Slowly lower the transaxle until it reaches the limits of the front engine mount movement.
59. Adjust the three bar engine support or equivalent, to hold the transaxle in this position.
60. Remove the floor jack and wood block.
61. Raise the vehicle and safely support.
62. Position a suitable transmission jack to the transaxle and secure.
63. Remove the last starter motor retaining bolt and hang the starter off to the side using safety wire.
64. Remove the two bolts retaining the engine oil pan to the transaxle.
65. Remove the remaining bolts.
66. Separate the transaxle from the engine and carefully remove from the vehicle.

To install:
67. If removed, place the transaxle on the transmission jack and secure.
68. Apply a film of grease to the input shaft splines.
69. If removed, install the right engine support insulator bracket to the transaxle case. Tighten the bolts to 62 ft. lbs. (84 Nm).
70. If removed, install the shift stabilizer bar mounting bracket to the right transaxle support insulator bracket stud and transaxle case. Tighten the nut and bolt to 28–38 ft. lbs. (38–51 Nm).
71. Carefully raise the transaxle into position with the engine.
72. If required, use an 18mm socket to rotate the engine to line up the splines on the clutch disc with the input shaft.
73. Reinstall two lower side and two lower transaxle retaining bolts. Tighten the retaining bolts to 30 ft. lbs. (40 Nm).
74. Reinstall the starter motor and the lower bolt. Tighten the starter motor lower bolt to 35 ft. lbs. (48 Nm).
75. Lower the vehicle.
76. Using the floor jack and a block of wood positioned at the engine and transaxle mating area, raise the assembly into position.
77. Adjust the three bar engine support to maintain the engine in the correct position.
78. Remove the floor jack and the block of wood. Reinstall the upper transaxle retaining bolts.
79. Tighten the retaining bolts to 28–38 ft. lbs. (38–51 Nm).
80. Reinstall the nuts retaining the front engine support bracket. Tighten the retaining nuts to 61 ft. lbs. (83 Nm).
81. Reinstall the upper starter motor retaining bolts. Tighten the retaining bolts to 35 ft. lbs. (48 Nm).
82. Reinstall the ground strap to the transaxle retaining bolt.
83. Reconnect the back-up lamp switch.
84. Reinstall the engine and transaxle support insulator.
85. Raise and safely support the vehicle.
86. Reinstall the left and right halfshafts and the intermediate shaft.

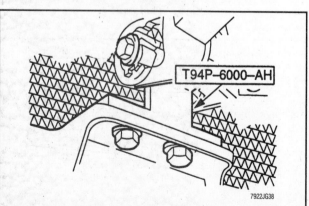

Fig. 10 The Powertrain Alignment Gauge (T94P-6000-AH) tool must be installed in the correct position to ensure proper engine/transaxle orientation

87. If removed, place the sub-frame on the powertrain lift, or equivalent with wood blocks approximately 40 inches (1,016mm) in length secured to the lift under the sub-frame.
88. Raise the sub-frame and connect the power steering pressure and return hoses to the rack and pinion.
89. Align the sub-frame to the body. Route the power steering hoses into position at the rear of the engine.
90. Reinstall the four sub-frame retaining bolts loosely.
91. Install Sub-Frame Alignment Pin Set T95P-2100-AH or equivalent into the sub-frame and body alignment holes. After aligning the holes, slightly tighten the four sub-frame retaining bolts.
92. After the sub-frame alignment is complete, tighten the four sub-frame retaining bolts to 81–110 ft. lbs. (110–150 Nm). Remove the alignment tools.
93. Reinstall the A/C accumulator bracket to the sub-frame and tighten the screws to 48–72 inch. lbs. (6–8 Nm).
94. Reconnect the power steering oil cooler hoses to the right front side of the sub-frame.
95. Install Powertrain Alignment Gauge T94P-6000-AH or equivalent to the left-front engine support bracket and the sub-frame. Tighten the two retaining bolts to 20 ft. lbs. (27 Nm) and snug the through-bolt.
96. Reinstall the right engine support insulator with retaining bolts to the sub-frame and through-bolt. Tighten the two retaining bolts to sub-frame to 30–41 ft. lbs. (41–55 Nm) and the through-bolt to 75–102 ft. lbs. (103–137 Nm).
97. Observe the position of the right engine support insulator. It must be centered in the bracket and in perfect alignment front to rear. Remove the powertrain alignment gauge.
98. Reinstall the left engine support insulator to the sub-frame with two retaining bolts. Tighten the retaining bolts to 84 inch. lbs. (10 Nm).
99. Observe the position of the left engine support insulator to ensure perfect alignment front to rear. Retighten the bolts to 30–41 ft. lbs. (41–55 Nm). Reinstall the left engine support insulator through-bolt and tighten to 75–102 ft. lbs. (103–137 Nm).
100. Reinstall the left and right lower control arms to the steering knuckles. Install new pinch bolts and nuts. Tighten the pinch bolts to 70 ft. lbs. (84 Nm).
101. Reconnect the steering yoke to the steering gear shaft. Tighten the steering yoke retaining bolt to 15–20 ft. lbs. (20–27 Nm).
102. Reinstall the sway bar (stabilizer bar) links. Reinstall the retaining nuts and tighten to 37 ft. lbs. (50 Nm).
103. Reinstall the left and right tie rod ends to the steering knuckles. Tighten the castellated nuts to 18–22 ft. lbs. (25–30 Nm). Install new cotter pins.
104. Reinstall the front bumper cover braces and tighten the bolts securely. Reinstall the splash shield to the sub-frame.
105. Reinstall the two retaining screws and the A/C accumulator to the sub-frame.
106. Reinstall the radiator supports to the sub-frame. Tighten the bolts to 71–97 inch lbs. (8–11 Nm).
107. Reinstall the splash shield at the front of the sub-frame.
108. Reinstall the front wheel and tire assemblies. Tighten the lug nuts to 62 ft. lbs. (85 Nm).
109. Reinstall the shift rod to transaxle gearshift shaft. Reinstall the retaining bolt and tighten to 14–18 ft. lbs. (19–25 Nm).
110. Reinstall the shift control stabilizer bar to its mounting stud. Reinstall the mounting nut and tighten to 28–38 ft. lbs. (38–51 Nm).
111. Reinstall the underbody heat shield under the shift control.
112. Reconnect the VSS.
113. Reinstall the speedometer cable.
114. If equipped with 2.5L engine, install the Y-pipe to the exhaust manifolds and the catalytic converter using new gaskets. Reinstall the water pump pulley shield.
115. If equipped with 2.0L engine, install the catalytic converter between the exhaust manifold and the exhaust pipe using new gaskets. Reinstall the exhaust manifold heat shield and the oil level dipstick. Tighten the retaining bolts to 71–106 inch lbs. (8–11 Nm).
116. Reinstall the support bracket strap to the catalytic converter and engine.
117. Reinstall the bracket to the catalytic converter and the intermediate halfshaft bearing bracket.
118. Reinstall the lower radiator air deflector.
119. Reinstall the belt pulley cover by sliding it up and under the front fender splash shield.
120. Check the transmission fluid level and add fluid as required.

121. Lower the vehicle.
122. Remove the three bar engine support, or equivalent.
123. Reinstall the wire loom retainers removed during the transaxle removal.
124. Reinstall the hydraulic line to the clutch slave cylinder and install the clip.
125. Reinstall the rubber inspection cover to the clutch housing and the hydraulic line to the retaining grommet.
126. Remove the upper strut mounting nuts and replace with new locknuts. Tighten the strut mounting nuts to 34 ft. lbs. (46 Nm).
127. Reinstall the air cleaner lower bracket.
128. Reinstall the MAF sensor and the air cleaner assembly.
129. Remove the wire retaining the radiator and fan shroud to the radiator support.
130. Reinstall the battery and cables, negative cable last.
131. Adjust the shift linkage and bleed the hydraulic clutch system as required.
132. Road test the vehicle and check for proper operation.

Halfshafts

REMOVAL & INSTALLATION

➡️**Do not begin this procedure without a new wheel hub retaining nut(s), a new lower control arm to steering knuckle pinch bolt and new retainer circlips for the CV-joints. Once removed, these parts lose their torque holding or retention capabilities and must not be reused.**

Left Side

◆ **See Figures 11, 12 and 13**

1. Raise and safely support the vehicle.
2. Remove the left front wheel and tire assembly.
3. Snug two of the lug nuts back onto the rotor.
4. Insert the tapered end of a prybar or steel rod into one of the cooling slots of the disc brake rotor and place the bar against the disc brake anchor plate, to keep the rotor from turning.
5. Loosen and remove the wheel hub retaining nut. Discard the nut.
6. Remove the nut of the stabilizer bar link and separate the stabilizer bar from the strut using a tie rod end removal tool.
7. Remove the cotter pin and castellated nut that secures the tie rod end to the steering knuckle. Discard the cotter pin.
8. Using a tie rod end removal tool, separate the tie rod end from the steering knuckle.
9. Remove the lower control arm to steering knuckle pinch bolt and nut.
10. Using a prybar or similar tool, separate the lower control arm ball joint from the steering knuckle.

✳️✳️ WARNING

Never use a hammer to separate the halfshaft from the front wheel hub as damage to the threads or internal components may result.

11. Separate the outer CV-joint and halfshaft from the wheel hub using Front Hub Remover/Replacer T81P-1104-C and its associated components, or equivalent.
12. Install a suitable slide hammer and adapter between the inner CV-joint and the transaxle case.

➡️**If the right halfshaft has already been removed, install Differential Rotator T81P-4026-A or equivalent into the right side of the differential before removing the left shaft to maintain alignment within the differential.**

13. Attach the corresponding extension and slide hammer to the CV-joint puller and remove the halfshaft with both CV-joints as an assembly from the transaxle case.
14. Remove the assembly from the vehicle.

To install:
15. Replace the driveshaft bearing retainer circlip. Start one end of the circlip into the groove and work the circlip over the housing end and into the groove. This will avoid over expanding the circlip.
16. Carefully align the splines of the inner CV-joint (install the halfshaft and both CV-joints as an assembly) with the splines in the transaxle case and push it into the differential side gear until the circlip is felt to seat.

➡️**A non-metallic mallet may be used to aid in seating the inner CV-joint into the differential side gear of the transaxle case. Only tap on the outboard CV-joint stub shaft.**

17. Position the outer CV-joint with halfshaft and carefully align the splines of the outer CV-joint with the splines of the wheel hub.
18. Push the CV-joint shaft into the wheel hub as far as possible.
19. Reinstall the front suspension lower control arm ball joint into the steering knuckle.
20. Reinstall a new lower control arm to knuckle pinch bolt and nut. Tighten the nut to 70 ft. lbs. (84 Nm).
21. Insert the tapered end of a prybar into one of the cooling slots in the disc brake rotor and jamb to prevent the rotor from turning.
22. Install a new wheel hub retaining nut onto the exposed threads of the outer CV-joint and manually thread the nut on as far as possible.
23. Finish running the nut up and tighten to 210 ft. lbs. (290 Nm).
24. Remove the steel rod or prybar.
25. Reinstall the tie rod end on the steering knuckle. Reinstall the castellated nut and tighten to 18–22 ft. lbs. (25–30 Nm). Install a new cotter pin.
26. Reinstall the stabilizer bar links. Tighten the nut to 37 ft. lbs. (50 Nm).
27. Reinstall the wheel and tire assembly. Tighten the lug nuts to 62 ft. lbs. (85 Nm).
28. Lower the vehicle.
29. Road test the vehicle and check for proper operation.

Right Side and Intermediate

◆ **See Figures 14 thru 33**

1. While the wheel is still on the ground, loosen the axle shaft retaining nut using a suitable socket and drive tool.
2. Raise and safely support the vehicle.
3. Remove the right front wheel and tire assembly.

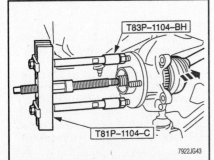

Fig. 11 Use a puller such as Front Hub Remover/Replacer T81P-1104-C to press the halfshaft out of the hub assembly

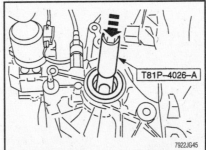

Fig. 12 If the right halfshaft has been removed, install Differential Rotator T81P-4026-A or equivalent into the differential before removing the left halfshaft

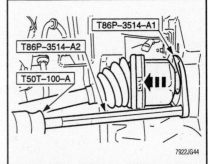

Fig. 13 Use a slide hammer with the special adapter to pull the inner CV-joint from the transaxle

4. Snug two of the lug nuts back onto the rotor.

5. Remove the wheel hub retaining nut. Discard the retaining nut.

6. Remove the nut of the stabilizer bar link and separate the stabilizer bar from the strut using a tie rod end removal tool.

7. Remove the cotter pin and castellated nut that secures the tie rod end to the steering knuckle. Discard the cotter pin.

8. Using a tie rod end removal tool, separate the tie rod end from the steering knuckle.

9. Remove the lower control arm-to-wheel spindle pinch bolt and nut.

10. Using a prybar or similar tool, separate the lower control arm ball joint from the steering knuckle.

Fig. 14 While the wheel is still on the ground is the best time to loosen the axle shaft retaining nut

✳✳ WARNING

Never use a hammer to separate the halfshaft from the front wheel hub as damage to the threads or internal components may result.

11. Separate the outer CV-joint and halfshaft from the wheel hub using an appropriate hub remover.

12. Install a suitable slide hammer and adapter between the inner CV-joint and the intermediate halfshaft.

13. Using the extension and slide hammer on the CV-joint puller, separate the right halfshaft with CV-joints from the intermediate halfshaft.

14. Remove the right side halfshaft from the vehicle.

15. If intermediate shaft removal is required, proceed as follows:

   a. Remove the intermediate shaft and bearing shield.

   b. On the 2.0L engine, the exhaust clamp and two bolts will need to be removed to allow removal of the intermediate shaft.

   c. Remove the intermediate shaft from the vehicle.

   d. If the intermediate shaft support bracket needs to be removed, locate the three bolts securing the support bracket and remove the bolts.

   e. Remove the support bracket.

To install:

16. If the intermediate shaft was removed, reinstall as follows:

   a. If the support bracket was removed, reinstall with the three bolts and tighten to 15–23 ft. lbs. (21–32 Nm).

   b. Carefully align the splines of the intermediate shaft with the splines of the differential side gears in the transaxle case.

   c. Push the shaft into the case until it is fully seated. The inner CV-joint is to be installed with the halfshaft and outer CV-joint attached as an assembly.

   d. Reinstall the two nuts onto the intermediate shaft support bracket and bearing shield. Tighten the nuts to 17–22 ft. lbs. (24–30 Nm).

   e. On the 2.0L engine, install the two bolts and the exhaust clamp.

17. Replace the bearing retainer circlip on the intermediate shaft. Start one end of the circlip into the groove and work the circlip over the housing end into the groove. This will prevent over-expanding the circlip.

Fig. 15 Remove the nut retaining the stabilizer bar link to the strut and . . .

Fig. 16 . . . remove the stabilizer bar link from the strut

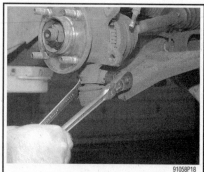

Fig. 17 Loosen the lower control arm-to-wheel spindle pinch bolt and nut using the appropriate tools and . . .

Fig. 18 . . . remove the bolt tand nut from the spindle

Fig. 19 Remove the cotter pin from the outer tie rod end

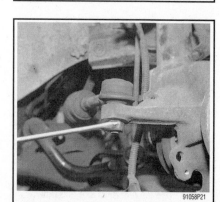

Fig. 20 Remove the nut from the outer tie rod end

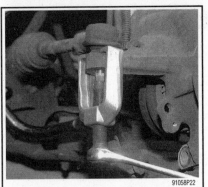

Fig. 21 Using the proper removal tool, remove the tie rod end from the spindle

Fig. 22 . . . remove the tie rod end from the spindle

Fig. 23 Using a prybar or other suitable tool, pry the ball joint out of the spindle

Fig. 24 Lightly tapping the shaft with a hammer can aid in . . .

Fig. 25 . . . removing it from the intermediate shaft

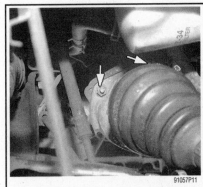

Fig. 26 Remove the nuts on the intermediate shaft bearing shield and . . .

Fig. 27 . . . remove it from the intermediate shaft

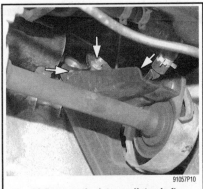

Fig. 28 Remove the intermediate shaft support bracket bolts

Fig. 29 Remove the intermediate shaft support bracket and . . .

Fig. 30 . . . remove the intermediate shaft

Fig. 31 Inspect the intermediate shaft splines

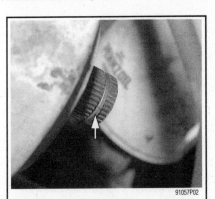

Fig. 32 Replace the CV joint retaining circlip on the intermediate shaft

18. Carefully align the splines of the inner CV-joint with the splines of the intermediate shaft. The inner CV-joint is to be installed as an assembly with the right halfshaft and outer CV-joint.

19. Push the inner CV-joint onto the intermediate shaft until it is fully seated.

20. Carefully align the splines of the outer CV-joint with the wheel hub and push the CV-joint into the hub as far as possible.

21. Reinstall the lower control arm ball joint into the steering knuckle.

22. Reinstall a new lower control arm to knuckle pinch bolt and nut. Tighten to 70 ft. lbs. (84 Nm).

23. Install a new wheel hub retaining nut onto the exposed threads of the outer CV-joint and manually thread the nut on as far as possible.

24. Reinstall the tie rod end into the steering knuckle. Reinstall the castellated nut and tighten to 18–22 ft. lbs. (25–30 Nm). Install a new cotter pin.

25. Reinstall the stabilizer bar link and nut. Tighten to 37 ft. lbs. (50 Nm).

26. Reinstall the right front wheel and tire assembly. Tighten the lug nuts to 62 ft. lbs. (85 Nm).

27. Lower the vehicle.

28. Tighten the wheel hub retaining nut to 210 ft. lbs. (290 Nm).

29. Road test the vehicle and check for proper operation.

CV-JOINTS OVERHAUL

▶ **See Figures 34 thru 47**

These vehicles use several different types of joints. Engine size, transaxle type, whether the joint is an inboard or outboard joint, even which side of the vehicle is being serviced could make a difference in joint type. Be sure to properly identify the joint before attempting joint or boot replacement. Look for identification numbers at the large end of the boots and/or on the end of the metal retainer bands.

The 3 types of joints used are the Birfield Joint, (B.J.), the Tripod Joint (T.J.) and the Double Offset Joint (D.O.J.).

➡**Do not disassemble a Birfield joint. Service with a new joint or clean and repack using a new boot kit.**

The distance between the large and small boot bands is important and should be checked prior to and after boot service. This is so the boot will not be installed either too loose or too tight, which could cause early wear and cracking, allowing the grease to get out and water and dirt in, leading to early joint failure.

➡**The driveshaft joints use special grease; do not add any grease other than that supplied with the kit.**

Double Offset Joint

The Double Offset Joint (D.O.J.) is bigger than other joints and, in these applications, is normally used as an inboard joint.

1. Remove the halfshaft from the vehicle.

2. Side cutter pliers can be used to cut the metal retaining bands. Remove the boot from the joint outer race.

3. Locate and remove the large circlip at the base of the joint. Remove the outer race (the body of the joint).

4. Remove the small snapring and take off the inner race, cage and balls as an assembly. Clean the inner race, cage and balls without disassembling.

5. If the boot is to be reused, wipe the grease from the splines and wrap the splines in vinyl tape before sliding the boot from the shaft.

6. Remove the inner (D.O.J.) boot from the shaft. If the outer (B.J.) boot is to be replaced, remove the boot retainer rings and slide the boot down and off of the shaft at this time.

To install:

7. Be sure to tape the shaft splines before installing the boots. Fill the inside of the boot with the specified grease. Often the grease supplied in the replacement parts kit is meant to be divided in half, with half being used to lubricate the joint and half being used inside the boot.

8. Install the cage onto the halfshaft so the small diameter side of the cage is installed first. With a brass drift pin, tap lightly and evenly around the inner

Fig. 33 After the vehicle has been lowered, tighten the axle tight to specification using a torque wrench

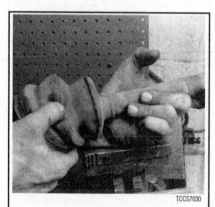

Fig. 34 Check the CV-boot for wear

Fig. 35 Removing the outer band from the CV-boot

Fig. 36 Removing the inner band from the CV-boot

Fig. 37 Removing the CV-boot from the joint housing

Fig. 38 Clean the CV-joint housing prior to removing boot

race to install the race until it comes into contact with the rib of the shaft. Apply the specified grease to the inner race and cage and fit them together. Insert the balls into the cage.

9. Install the outer race (the body of the joint) after filling with the specified grease. The outer race should be filled with this grease.

10. Tighten the boot bands securely. Make sure the distance between the boot bands is correct.

11. Install the halfshaft to the vehicle.

Except Double Offset Joint

1. Disconnect the negative battery cable. Remove the halfshaft.

2. Use side cutter pliers to remove the metal retaining bands from the boot(s) that will be removed. Slide the boot from the T.J. case.

3. Remove the snapring and the tripod joint spider assembly from the half-shaft. Do not disassemble the spider and use care in handling.

4. If the boot is be reused, wrap vinyl tape around the spline part of the shaft so the boot(s) will not be damaged when removed. Remove the dynamic damper, if used, and the boots from the shaft.

To install:

5. Double check that the correct replacement parts are being installed. Wrap vinyl tape around the splines to protect the boot and install the boots and damper, if used, in the correct order.

6. Install the joint spider assembly to the shaft and install the snapring.

7. Fill the inside of the boot with the specified grease. Often the grease supplied in the replacement parts kit is meant to be divided in half, with half being used to lubricate the joint and half being used inside the boot. Keep grease off the rubber part of the dynamic damper (if used).

8. Secure the boot bands with the halfshaft in a horizontal position. Make sure distance between boot bands is correct.

9. Install the halfshaft to the vehicle and reconnect the negative battery cable.

Fig. 39 Removing the CV-joint housing assembly

Fig. 40 Removing the CV-joint

Fig. 41 Inspecting the CV-joint housing

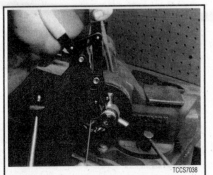

Fig. 42 Removing the CV-joint outer snapring

Fig. 43 Checking the CV-joint snapring for wear

Fig. 44 CV-joint snapring (typical)

Fig. 45 Removing the CV-joint assembly

Fig. 46 Removing the CV-joint inner snapring

Fig. 47 Installing the CV-joint assembly (typical)

CLUTCH

Understanding The Clutch

✳✳ CAUTION

The clutch driven disc may contain asbestos, which has been determined to be a cancer causing agent. Never clean clutch surfaces with compressed air! Avoid inhaling any dust from any clutch surface! When cleaning clutch surfaces, use a commercially available brake cleaning fluid.

The purpose of the clutch is to disconnect and connect engine power at the transaxle. A vehicle at rest requires a lot of engine torque to get all that weight moving. An internal combustion engine does not develop a high starting torque (unlike steam engines) so it must be allowed to operate without any load until it builds up enough torque to move the vehicle. Torque increases with engine rpm. The clutch allows the engine to build up torque by physically disconnecting the engine from the transaxle, relieving the engine of any load or resistance.

The transfer of engine power to the transaxle (the load) must be smooth and gradual; if it weren't, drive line components would wear out or break quickly. This gradual power transfer is made possible by gradually releasing the clutch pedal. The clutch disc and pressure plate are the connecting link between the engine and transaxle. When the clutch pedal is released, the disc and plate contact each other (the clutch is engaged) physically joining the engine and transaxle. When the pedal is pushed inward, the disc and plate separate (the clutch is disengaged) disconnecting the engine from the transaxle.

Most clutches utilize a single plate, dry friction disc with a diaphragm-style spring pressure plate. The clutch disc has a splined hub which attaches the disc

to the input shaft. The disc has friction material where it contacts the flywheel and pressure plate. Torsion springs on the disc help absorb engine torque pulses. The pressure plate applies pressure to the clutch disc, holding it tight against the surface of the flywheel. The clutch operating mechanism consists of a release bearing, fork and cylinder assembly.

The release fork and actuating linkage transfer pedal motion to the release bearing. In the engaged position (pedal released) the diaphragm spring holds the pressure plate against the clutch disc, so engine torque is transmitted to the input shaft. When the clutch pedal is depressed, the release bearing pushes the diaphragm spring center toward the flywheel. The diaphragm spring pivots the fulcrum, relieving the load on the pressure plate. Steel spring straps riveted to the clutch cover lift the pressure plate from the clutch disc, disengaging the engine drive from the transaxle and enabling the gears to be changed.

The clutch is operating properly if:
• It will stall the engine when released with the vehicle held stationary.
• The shift lever can be moved freely between 1st and reverse gears when the vehicle is stationary and the clutch disengaged.

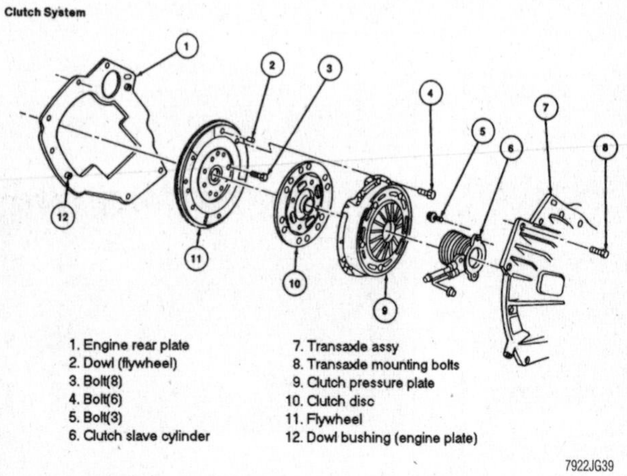

Driven Disc and Pressure Plate

REMOVAL & INSTALLATION

◆ **See Figures 48 thru 63**

1. Disconnect the negative battery cable.
2. Raise and safely support the vehicle.
3. Remove the starter motor.
4. Disconnect the hydraulic coupling for the slave cylinder at the transaxle by sliding the sleeve on the tube towards the slave cylinder and applying a slight pulling force to the tube.
5. Remove the transaxle.
6. Mark the assembled position of the clutch and pressure plate to the flywheel if it is to be reinstalled.

➡**The clutch pressure plate is only held in place by the retaining bolts. No dowel pins are used, therefore the pressure plate must be supported when removing the retaining bolts.**

7. Loosen the pressure plate bolts evenly until the pressure plate spring pressure is released, then finish removing the bolts while supporting the clutch and pressure plate assembly.
8. Remove the clutch and pressure plate from the vehicle.
9. Inspect the flywheel, slave cylinder and other components for wear or damage.
To install:
10. Clean the pressure plate and flywheel surfaces.
11. Install the clutch disc using an appropriate clutch aligning tool.

➡**If the clutch disc and pressure plate are being reused, align the marks made during disassembly.**

12. Install an appropriate flywheel holding tool to hold the flywheel.

Clutch System

1. Engine rear plate
2. Dowel (flywheel)
3. Bolt(8)
4. Bolt(6)
5. Bolt(3)
6. Clutch slave cylinder
7. Transaxle assy
8. Transaxle mounting bolts
9. Clutch pressure plate
10. Clutch disc
11. Flywheel
12. Dowel bushing (engine plate)

7922JG39

Fig. 48 Exploded view of the clutch disc, pressure plate and related component mounting

---

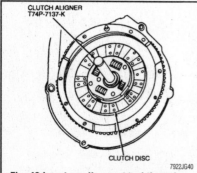

CLUTCH ALIGNER
T74P-7137-K

CLUTCH DISC

7922JG40

Fig. 49 Insert an alignment tool through the clutch disc to ensure that it is centered after the pressure plate is installed

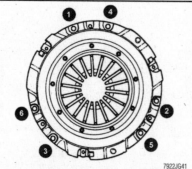

7922JG41

Fig. 50 Tighten the pressure plate bolts gradually and in the sequence shown to ensure correct clutch operation

TCCS7142

Fig. 51 Typical clutch alignment tool, note how the splines match the transmission's input shaft

Fig. 52 Loosen and remove the clutch and pressure plate bolts evenly, a little at a time . . .

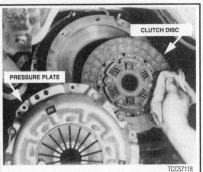

Fig. 53 . . . then carefully removing the clutch and pressure plate assembly from the flywheel

Fig. 54 Check across the flywheel surface, it should be flat

Fig. 55 If necessary, lock the flywheel in place and remove the retaining bolts . . .

Fig. 56 . . . then remove the flywheel from the crankshaft in order replace it or have it machined

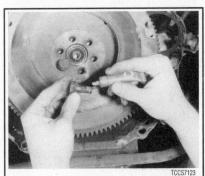

Fig. 57 Upon installation, it is usually a good idea to apply a threadlocking compound to the flywheel bolts

Fig. 58 Check the pressure plate for excessive wear

Fig. 59 Be sure that the flywheel surface is clean, before installing the clutch

Fig. 60 Use the clutch alignment tool to align the clutch disc during assembly

Fig. 61 Pressure plate-to-flywheel bolt holes should align

Fig. 62 You may want to use a threadlocking compound on the clutch assembly bolts

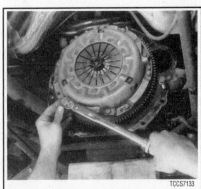

Fig. 63 Be sure to use a torque wrench to tighten all bolts

13. Install the pressure plate and start the retaining bolts.
14. Tighten the retaining bolts evenly and in sequence to 13–18 ft. lbs. (18–26 Nm).
15. Remove the clutch aligner tool.
16. Reinstall the transaxle.
17. Reconnect the slave cylinder tube coupling by pushing the male coupling into the slave cylinder female coupling.
18. Lower the vehicle.
19. Reconnect the negative battery cable.
20. Bleed the hydraulic clutch system, if required.
21. Check the clutch system for proper operation.

ADJUSTMENTS

Because the clutch system is hydraulic, the clutch pedal free-play is self-adjusting and requires no additional maintenance.

Master Cylinder

REMOVAL & INSTALLATION

▶ **See Figures 64 and 65**

1. Disconnect the negative battery cable.
2. Lower the storage compartment door located to the lower left side of the steering column by depressing the locking tabs.
3. Remove the lower instrument panel by removing 3 retaining screws and 2 retaining clips.
4. Lower the fuse box and disconnect the 2 multi-plugs and remove the multi–plugs from the fuse box.
5. Unhook the fuse box from its support.
6. Unplug the 5 electrical connectors from the back of the fuse box and remove the fuse box.
7. Remove the spring clip retaining the clutch master cylinder to the clutch pedal.
8. Remove the spring clip retaining the clutch slave cylinder tube to the clutch master cylinder.

➡**Place a fender cover or equivalent on the floor to protect the carpet from the hydraulic fluid.**

9. Disconnect the clutch slave cylinder tube and brake master cylinder fluid reservoir tube from the clutch master cylinder and plug the tubes.
10. Remove the 2 nuts retaining the clutch master cylinder to the bracket and remove the clutch master cylinder from the vehicle.
To install:
11. Reinstall the clutch master cylinder to the bracket and install the 2 retaining nuts. Torque the retaining nuts to 90 inch. lbs. (10 Nm).

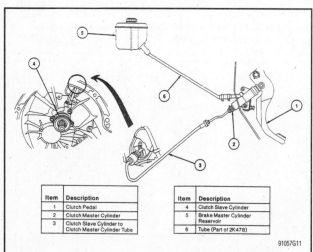

Item	Description		Item	Description
1	Clutch Pedal		4	Clutch Slave Cylinder
2	Clutch Master Cylinder		5	Brake Master Cylinder Reservoir
3	Clutch Slave Cylinder to Clutch Master Cylinder Tube		6	Tube (Part of 2K478)

91057G11

Fig. 64 Hydraulic clutch system found on the Contour/Mystique/Cougar

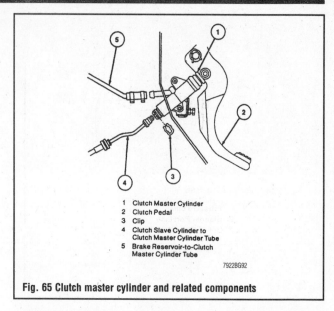

1 Clutch Master Cylinder
2 Clutch Pedal
3 Clip
4 Clutch Slave Cylinder to Clutch Master Cylinder Tube
5 Brake Reservoir-to-Clutch Master Cylinder Tube

7922BG92

Fig. 65 Clutch master cylinder and related components

12. Reinstall the clutch slave cylinder tube to the clutch master cylinder and install the spring clip. Reconnect the brake master cylinder fluid reservoir tube to the clutch master cylinder.
13. Reinstall the spring clip retaining the clutch master cylinder to the clutch pedal.
14. Reconnect the 5 electrical connectors to the back of the fuse box and position the fuse box.
15. Reconnect the fuse box to its support.
16. Reconnect the 2 multi-plugs to the fuse box.
17. Raise the fuse box into its normal position.
18. Reinstall the lower instrument panel using the retaining screws and clips.
19. Close the lower storage compartment door.
20. Reconnect the negative battery cable.
21. Bleed the hydraulic clutch system.
22. Check for proper clutch system operation.

Slave Cylinder

REMOVAL & INSTALLATION

▶ **See Figure 66**

1. Disconnect the negative battery cable.
2. Raise and safely support the vehicle.
3. Disconnect the hydraulic coupling for the clutch slave cylinder at the transaxle by removing the clip and then sliding the sleeve on the tube towards the clutch slave cylinder while applying a slight pulling force to the tube.
4. Remove the transaxle.
5. From inside the transaxles bellhousing, remove the 3 clutch slave cylinder retaining bolts and remove the clutch slave cylinder.
6. Remove the clutch slave cylinder bleed tube.
To install:
7. Place the clutch slave cylinder over the input shaft splines and position the clutch slave cylinder.
8. Reinstall the clutch slave cylinder retaining bolts. Torque the retaining bolts to 7–14 ft. lbs. (9–19 Nm).
9. Reinstall the bleed tube. Torque the bleed tube fitting to 10 ft. lbs. (14 Nm).
10. Reinstall the transaxle.
11. Reconnect the slave cylinder tube coupling by pushing the male coupling into the slave cylinder female coupling and then installing the clip.
12. Lower the vehicle.
13. Reconnect the negative battery cable.
14. Bleed the hydraulic clutch system, if required.
15. Check for proper clutch operation.

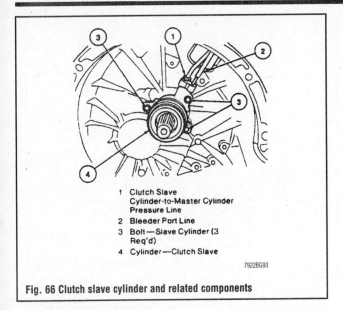

1 Clutch Slave
   Cylinder-to-Master Cylinder
   Pressure Line
2 Bleeder Port Line
3 Bolt—Slave Cylinder (3
   Req'd)
4 Cylinder—Clutch Slave

7922BG93

Fig. 66 Clutch slave cylinder and related components

HYDRAULIC SYSTEM BLEEDING

♦ See Figure 67

1. Disconnect the negative battery cable.
2. Remove the air cleaner outlet tube and the Mass Air Flow (MAF) sensor.
3. Clean the top of the brake master cylinder fluid reservoir before opening it.

➡The brake master cylinder fluid reservoir is also the reservoir for the hydraulic clutch master cylinder.

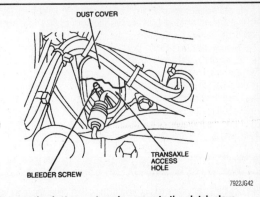

DUST COVER

TRANSAXLE
ACCESS
HOLE

BLEEDER SCREW

7922JG42

Fig. 67 Remove the dust cover to gain access to the clutch slave cylinder bleeder valve

4. Be sure that there is adequate fluid in the master cylinder fluid reservoir before attempting to bleed the system. Check the fluid level throughout the bleeding procedure.
5. Remove the rubber inspection cover from the bell housing.
6. Connect a hose to the bleeder valve fitting on the clutch slave cylinder. Submerge the other end of the hose into a container of clean brake fluid.
7. Push the clutch pedal down while opening the bleeder on the clutch slave cylinder. Watch for air bubbles escaping from the hydraulic system.
8. Close the bleeder before releasing the clutch pedal.
9. Repeat the procedure until no more air bubbles are seen.
10. Reinstall the rubber inspection cover to the bell housing.
11. Top off the brake master cylinder fluid reservoir and install the diaphragm and cap securely.
12. Reinstall the MAF sensor and air cleaner outlet tube.
13. Reconnect the negative battery cable.
14. Check the clutch for proper operation.

AUTOMATIC TRANSAXLE

Understanding the Automatic Transaxle

The automatic transaxle allows engine torque and power to be transmitted to the front wheels within a narrow range of engine operating speeds. It will allow the engine to turn fast enough to produce plenty of power and torque at very low speeds, while keeping it at a sensible rpm at high vehicle speeds (and it does this job without driver assistance). The transaxle uses a light fluid as the medium for the transmission of power. This fluid also works in the operation of various hydraulic control circuits and as a lubricant. Because the transaxle fluid performs all of these functions, trouble within the unit can easily travel from one part to another. For this reason, and because of the complexity and unusual operating principles of the transaxle, a very sound understanding of the basic principles of operation will simplify troubleshooting.

Adjustments

SHIFT CONTROL LINKAGE

♦ See Figures 68, 69 and 70

1. With the engine OFF, place the gearshift lever in the D position.
2. Verify that the vehicle is in the D position by viewing the MLP (TR) sensor. The alignment marks will be aligned with the D arrow on the sensor body.
3. Have an assistant hold the gearshift lever in the D position.
4. Raise and safely support the vehicle securely on jackstands.
5. Remove the transaxle shift cable from the shift arm using a screwdriver.

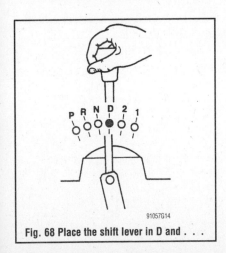

P R N D 2 1

91057G14

Fig. 68 Place the shift lever in D and . . .

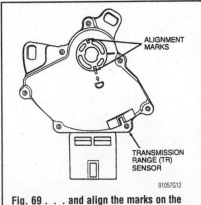

ALIGNMENT
MARKS

TRANSMISSION
RANGE (TR)
SENSOR

91057G12

Fig. 69 . . . and align the marks on the MLP/TR sensor with the D

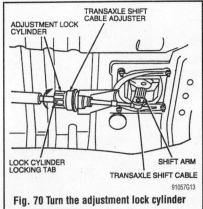

TRANSAXLE SHIFT
CABLE ADJUSTER

ADJUSTMENT LOCK
CYLINDER

LOCK CYLINDER
LOCKING TAB

SHIFT ARM

TRANSAXLE SHIFT CABLE

91057G13

Fig. 70 Turn the adjustment lock cylinder counterclockwise

6. Depress the two locking tabs on the adjustment lock cylinder and rotate the lock cylinder counterclockwise. The shift cable is now unlocked and free to slide in the retainer.

7. Make sure the assistant is holding the gearshift lever in the **D** position.

8. Grasp the cable forward of the adjustment lock cylinder and move as necessary to align the cable eye with the pin on the shift arm.

9. Install the shift end to the shift arm by pressing on by hand. Rotate the adjustment lock cylinder clockwise until it snaps into place.

10. Lower the vehicle.

11. Shift the transaxle through all the ranges to make sure the shift linkage is adjusted and the indicator is aligned.

Fluid Pan

REMOVAL & INSTALLATION

The CD4E transaxle in the Contour/Mystique/Cougar has no service procedure for the transaxle pan and filter removal. The filter is located in the center of the transaxle and can only be removed at transaxle disassembly. the pan should only be removed for repair or adjustment of the transaxle is necessary.

Manual Lever Position Switch/Transmission Range Sensor

REMOVAL & INSTALLATION

♦ **See Figures 71, 72, 73, 74 and 75**

➡**The manual lever position sensor (transmission range sensor) is only used on vehicles equipped with an automatic transaxle. It performs several tasks, it acts as the neutral safety switch, the back-up light switch, and also is an input to the PCM of gear position.**

1. Disconnect the negative battery cable.
2. Place the transmission manual control lever in the **NEUTRAL** position.

3. Remove the engines air intake resonators and Mass Air Flow (MAF) sensor.

4. Disconnect the electrical harness connector from the manual lever position sensor, which is located on top of the automatic transaxle.

5. Remove the 2 retaining bolts and remove the manual lever position sensor.

To install:

6. Make sure that the transmission manual control lever is in the **NEUTRAL** position.

7. Reinstall the manual lever position sensor and loosely install the 2 retaining bolts.

8. Align the sensor slots using Transmission Range Sensor Tool T94P–70010–AH, or equivalent.

9. Torque the retaining bolts to 84–108 inch. lbs. (9–12 Nm).

10. Reinstall the electrical harness connector to the sensor.

11. Reinstall the MAF sensor and the air intake resonator.

12. Reconnect the negative battery cable.

13. Engage the parking brake and check for proper operation and adjustment of the manual lever position sensor as follows:

   a. Check that the engine will only crank in the **PARK** or **NEUTRAL** positions.

   b. Check that the back–up lamps only work in the **REVERSE** position.

ADJUSTMENT

♦ **See Figures 75 and 76**

1. Disconnect the negative battery cable.
2. Place the transmission manual control lever in the **NEUTRAL** position.
3. Remove the engines air intake resonators and Mass Air Flow (MAF) sensor.
4. Loosen the 2 retaining bolts on the manual lever position sensor.
5. Make sure that the transmission manual control lever is in the **NEUTRAL** position.
6. Align the sensor slots using Transmission Range Sensor Tool T94P–70010–AH, or equivalent.
7. Torque the retaining bolts to 84–108 inch. lbs. (9–12 Nm).

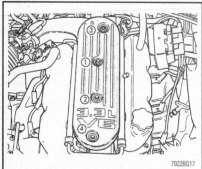

Fig. 71 View of the manual lever position sensor

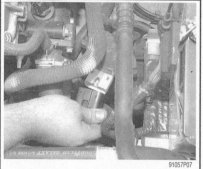

Fig. 72 Unplug the connector from the MLP sensor

Fig. 73 Remove the two retaining bolts and . . .

Fig. 74 . . . remove the sensor from the transaxle

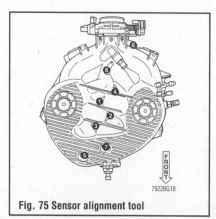

Fig. 75 Sensor alignment tool

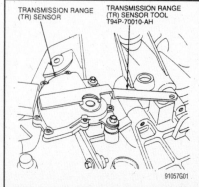

Fig. 76 Sensor alignment tool as installed

8. Reinstall the MAF sensor and the air intake resonators.

9. Reconnect the negative battery cable.

10. Engage the parking brake and check for proper operation and adjustment of the manual lever position sensor as follows:

a. Check that the engine will only crank in the **PARK** or **NEUTRAL** positions.

b. Check that the back–up lamps only work in the **REVERSE** position.

Automatic Transaxle Assembly

REMOVAL & INSTALLATION

▶ **See Figures 77, 78, 79 and 80**

1. Disconnect the negative battery cable.

2. Disconnect the positive battery cable and remove the battery.

3. On vehicles equipped with the 2.0L engine, remove the oil level dipstick and the exhaust manifold heat shield.

4. On vehicles equipped with the 2.5L engine, remove the water pump pulley shield.

5. Secure the radiator and fan shroud with safety wire to the radiator support.

6. Remove the air cleaner assembly and mounting bracket.

7. Loosen the left and right upper strut mounting nuts five turns to allow room for removal of the halfshafts. Do not remove the nuts completely.

8. Disconnect the shift cable and remove the two retaining bolts securing the shift cable bracket to the transaxle case.

9. Disconnect the Transmission Range (TR) sensor.

10. Remove the TR sensor.

11. Disconnect the 10-pin harness from the transaxle.

12. Support the engine with a suitable support device designed for transverse mounted engines.

13. Remove the upper transaxle support insulator bracket mounting nuts.

14. Remove the three bolts retaining the upper transaxle support insulator to the inner fenderwell and remove the insulator.

15. Remove the upper bell housing to engine retaining bolts.

16. Raise and safely support the vehicle.

17. Remove the wheel and tire assemblies.

18. Disconnect the steering column from the rack and pinion by removing the pinch bolt.

19. Disconnect the tie rod ends from the steering knuckles. Discard the cotter pins.

20. Remove the ball joint to lower control arm pinch bolts and separate the ball joints from the lower control arms.

21. Remove the sway bar (stabilizer bar) link nuts and separate the sway bar links from the stabilizer bar.

22. Remove the splash shield at the front of the sub-frame.

23. Remove the through-bolts retaining the left and right front engine support insulators to the sub-frame.

24. Disconnect the power steering oil cooler hoses at the right front sub-frame and drain the power steering system.

25. Remove the two screws retaining the bumper cover braces to the sub-frame. Rotate the bumper cover braces forward.

26. Remove the radiator air deflector.

27. Remove the four bolts retaining the left and right lower radiator support brackets to the front of the sub-frame. Rotate the radiator supports forward.

28. Disconnect and remove the exhaust system components necessary for transaxle removal.

29. Remove the two bolts retaining the A/C accumulator to the sub-frame, located at the drivers side front corner of the vehicle.

30. Remove the bolt retaining the transaxle cooler line bracket to the front of the sub-frame.

31. Position a suitable lifting device with wood blocks approximately 40 inches (1,016mm) in length secured to the lift under the sub-frame.

32. Remove the four sub-frame to body retaining bolts. Lower the sub-frame slightly and disconnect the power steering pressure and return hoses from the rack and pinion.

33. Finish lowering the sub-frame and set aside.

34. Disconnect the Turbine Shaft Speed (TSS) sensor at the transaxle oil pump.

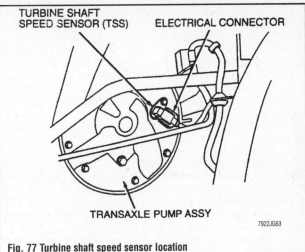

Fig. 77 Turbine shaft speed sensor location

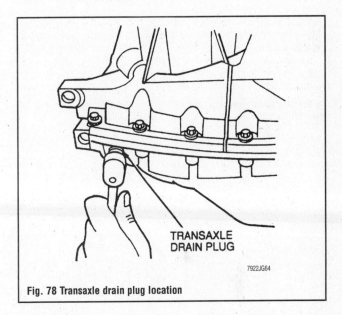

Fig. 78 Transaxle drain plug location

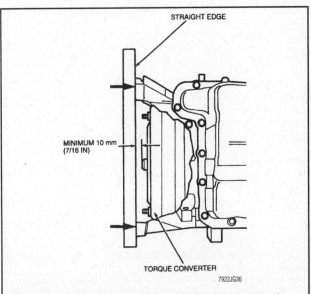

Fig. 79 Be sure that the torque converter is properly seated in the transaxle

35. Drain the transaxle oil into a suitable container for recycling.
36. Disconnect the transaxle cooler inlet line at the transaxle case.
37. Remove the transaxle cooler inlet line from the bracket at the transaxle oil pump.
38. Disconnect the transaxle cooler outlet line at the transaxle case.
39. Disconnect the transaxle cooler inlet and outlet lines at the radiator and remove from the vehicle.
40. Remove the left halfshaft and the right halfshaft and intermediate shaft from the vehicle.
41. Remove the speedometer cable and disconnect the Vehicle Speed Sensor (VSS).
42. Remove the inspection cover from the transaxle to engine spacer plate located at the right-rear corner of the engine.
43. Rotate the torque converter to align each of the four torque converter to flywheel retaining nuts and remove the nuts.
44. Lower the vehicle.
45. Remove the upper right engine support insulator (engine mount) bracket nuts.
46. Lower the engine and transaxle assembly using the three bar engine support until the transaxle assembly is level with the left frame member.
47. On vehicles equipped with A/C, lower the engine until the A/C compressor is below the right frame member.
48. Raise and safely support the vehicle.
49. Support the transaxle on a transmission jack and secure the transaxle to the jack.
50. Remove the starter motor retaining nuts and remove the starter.
51. Remove the lower transaxle to engine retaining bolts.
52. Separate the transaxle from the engine.

➡**Use care when removing the transaxle to prevent the torque converter from falling out.**

53. Carefully lower the transaxle from the vehicle.
To install:
54. Be sure that the torque converter is fully engaged in the transaxle.
55. There should be approximately a 7/16 inch (10mm) air gap between a straightedge across the bell housing flange and the torque converter.
56. If removed, place the transaxle on the transmission jack and secure.

➡**Use care not to allow the torque converter to fall out of the transaxle when tilted.**

57. Raise the transaxle into position and align with the engine.
58. Align the torque converter studs with the mating holes in the flywheel.
59. Once the transaxle is fitted to the engine, install the lower transaxle to engine retaining bolts. Tighten the retaining bolts to 41–50 ft. lbs. (55–68 Nm).
60. Rotate the torque converter and install the four converter to flywheel retaining nuts. Tighten the retaining nuts to 23–39 ft. lbs. (31–53 Nm).
61. Remove the transmission jack.
62. Reinstall the transaxle to engine separator plate.
63. Reinstall the electrical connector to the TSS.
64. If removed, place the sub-frame on the powertrain lift, or equivalent with wood blocks approximately 40 inches (1,016mm) in length secured to the lift under the sub-frame.
65. Raise the sub-frame and connect the power steering pressure and return hoses to the rack and pinion.
66. Align the sub-frame. Route the power steering hoses into position at the rear of the engine.
67. Reinstall the four sub-frame retaining bolts loosely.
68. Install Sub-Frame Alignment Pin Set T95P-2100-AH or equivalent into the sub-frame and body alignment holes. After aligning the holes, slightly tighten the four sub-frame retaining bolts.

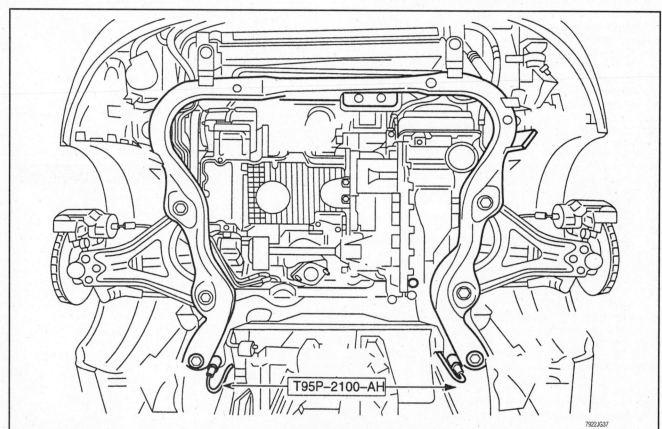

T95P–2100–AH

7922JG37

Fig. 80 To properly align the sub-frame, install sub-frame alignment pins such as Sub-Frame Alignment Pin Set T95P-2100-AH—manual and automatic transaxles

69. After the sub-frame alignment is complete, tighten the four sub-frame retaining bolts to 81–110 ft. lbs. (110–150 Nm). Remove the alignment tools.

70. Reinstall the A/C accumulator bracket to the sub-frame and tighten the screws to 48–72 inch. lbs. (6–8 Nm).

71. Reconnect the power steering oil cooler hoses to the right front side of the sub-frame.

72. Install Powertrain Alignment Gauge T94P-6000-AH or equivalent to the left-front engine support bracket and the sub-frame. Tighten the two retaining bolts to 20 ft. lbs. (27 Nm) and snug the through-bolt.

73. Reinstall the right engine support insulator with retaining bolts to the sub-frame and through-bolt. Tighten the two sub-frame retaining bolts to 30–41 ft. lbs. (41–55 Nm) and the through-bolt to 75–102 ft. lbs. (103–137 Nm).

74. Observe the position of the right engine support insulator. It must be centered in the bracket and in perfect alignment front to rear. Remove the powertrain alignment gauge.

75. Reinstall the left engine support insulator to the sub-frame with two retaining bolts. Tighten the retaining bolts to 84 inch. lbs. (10 Nm).

76. Observe the position of the left engine support insulator to ensure perfect alignment front to rear. Retighten the bolts to 30–41 ft. lbs. (41–55 Nm). Reinstall the left engine support insulator through-bolt and tighten to 75–102 ft. lbs. (103–137 Nm).

77. Reinstall the transaxle cooler inlet and outlet lines.

78. Reinstall the lower radiator support brackets to the sub-frame. Tighten the bolts to 20 ft. lbs. (27 Nm).

79. Reconnect the speedometer cable and the VSS.

80. Reinstall the exhaust system.

81. Reinstall the left halfshaft using a new circlip.

82. Reinstall the intermediate halfshaft and tighten the two retaining nuts to 20 ft. lbs. (27 Nm).

83. Reinstall the right-side halfshaft.

84. Reinstall the left and right lower control arms to the steering knuckles.

85. Install new pinch bolts and nuts. Tighten the pinch bolts to 70 ft. lbs. (84 Nm).

86. Reinstall the sway bar (stabilizer bar) links. Reinstall the retaining nuts and tighten to 37 ft. lbs. (50 Nm).

87. If equipped, install the ABS wiring loom retainer to the sway bar link stud. Tighten the retaining nuts to 35 ft. lbs. (47 Nm).

88. Reinstall the left and right tie rod ends to the steering knuckles. Tighten the castellated nuts to 18–22 ft. lbs. (25–30 Nm). Install new cotter pins.

89. Reinstall the front bumper cover braces and tighten the bolts securely. Reinstall the splash shield to the sub-frame.

90. Reinstall the wheel and tire assemblies. Tighten the lug nuts to 62 ft. lbs. (85 Nm).

91. Lower the vehicle.

92. Reconnect the steering yoke to the steering gear shaft. Tighten the steering yoke retaining bolt to 15–20 ft. lbs. (20–27 Nm).

93. Reinstall the upper transaxle to engine retaining bolts. Tighten the retaining bolts to 41–50 ft. lbs. (55–68 Nm).

94. Remove the safety wire securing the radiator and fan shroud to the radiator support.

95. Reinstall all wiring retaining clips that were disturbed during transaxle removal.

96. Raise the engine and transaxle assembly into position using the three bar engine support or similar tool.

97. Reinstall the engine and transmission support insulator to the left front fender apron. Tighten the bolts to 40–55 ft. lbs. (54–75 Nm).

98. Reinstall new locknuts retaining the engine and transmission support insulator to the transaxle. Tighten the locknuts to 40–55 ft. lbs. (54–75 Nm).

99. Reinstall the front engine support insulator.

100. If equipped with 2.5L engine, install the power steering line retaining bracket to the front engine support insulator. Tighten the new locknuts to 56–76 ft. lbs. (77–103 Nm). Reinstall the water pump pulley shield.

101. If equipped with the 2.0L engine, install the exhaust manifold heat shield and oil level dipstick. Tighten the retaining bolts to 71–106 inch lbs. (8–12 Nm).

102. Remove the engine support.

103. Reinstall the TR sensor and adjust.

104. Reattach the 10-pin harness connector to the transaxle.

105. Reinstall the TR sensor electrical connector.

106. Reinstall the starter motor and retaining bolts. Tighten the starter motor retaining bolts to 43–58 ft. lbs. (59–79 Nm) for the 2.5L engine or 15–20 ft. lbs. (20–27 Nm) for the 2.0L engine.

107. Reinstall the shift cable mounting bracket. Tighten the retaining bolts to 15–19 ft. lbs. (20–25 Nm).

108. Reinstall the shift cable to the manual lever by pressing the cable end onto the stud until a click is heard.

109. Reinstall the battery tray, battery and the battery hold-down.

110. Reinstall new upper strut mounting nuts. Tighten the strut mounting nuts to 34 ft. lbs. (46 Nm).

111. Fill the power steering remote oil reservoir.

112. Reconnect the battery cables, negative cable last.

113. Fill the transaxle with the proper type and amount of transmission fluid.

114. Run the engine and check the transaxle for leaks.

115. Recheck the transmission fluid level.

➥**Whenever the vehicle sub-frame is removed or lowered, the wheel alignment should be checked.**

116. Check the alignment and adjust if necessary.

117. Road test the vehicle to check for proper transmission operation.

ADJUSTMENTS

There are no adjustments possible on the CD4E automatic transaxle. The transaxle is electronically controlled and monitored by the PCM.

Halfshafts

REMOVAL & INSTALLATION

The halfshaft removal and installation and overhaul are the same as a manual transaxle. Please refer to Manual Transaxle in this Section.

TORQUE SPECIFICATIONS

Components	English	Metric
A/C accumulator-to-subframe bolts	48-72 inch lbs.	6-8 Nm
Automatic transaxle		
Shift cable mounting bracket	15-19 ft. lbs.	20-25 Nm
Starter bolts		
2.0L engine	15-20 ft. lbs.	20-27 Nm
2.5L engine	43-58 ft. lbs.	59-79 Nm
Transaxle-to-engine bolts	41-50 ft. lbs.	55-68 Nm
Torque converter-to-flywheel nuts	23-39 ft. lbs.	31-53 Nm
Ball joint-to-steering knuckle	70 ft. lbs.	84 Nm
Clutch bleed tube	10 ft. lbs.	14 Nm
Clutch slave cylinder retaining bolts	7-14 ft. lbs.	9-19 Nm
Engine support insulators		
Engine and transaxle support insulator-to-left front fender apron	40-55 ft. lbs.	54-75 Nm
Lower insulator-to-subframe	30-41 ft. lbs.	41-55 Nm
Through bolts	75-102 ft. lbs.	103-107 Nm
Left insulator-to-subframe	84 inch lbs.	10 Nm
Front engine support bracket	61 ft. lbs.	83 Nm
Intermediate shaft support bracket bolts	15-23 ft. lbs.	21-32 Nm
Intermediate shaft support bracket and bearing shield nuts	17-22 ft. lbs.	24-30 Nm
Manual lever positioning switch/TR sensor retaining bolts	84-108 inch lbs.	9-12 Nm
Manual transaxle		
Shift linkage clamp	141 inch lbs.	16 Nm
Shift rod-to-gearshift shaft	14-18 ft. lbs.	19-25 Nm
Shift stabilizer bar mounting bracket-to-mounting stud	28-38 ft. lbs.	38-51 Nm
Shift stabilizer bar mounting bracket-to-support insulator	28-38 ft. lbs.	38-51 Nm
Shift stabilizer bar mounting bracket-to-transaxle	28-38 ft. lbs.	38-51 Nm
Transaxle-to-engine bolts	30 ft. lbs.	40 Nm
Starter bolts	35 ft. lbs.	48 Nm
Powertrain alignment gauge bolts	20 ft. lbs.	27 Nm
Pressure plate bolts	13-1 ft. lbs.	18-26 Nm
Radiator supports-to-subframe	71-97 inch lbs.	8-11 Nm
Steering yoke-to-steering gear shaft	15-20 ft. lbs.	20-27 Nm
Subframe bolts	81-110 ft. lbs	110-150 Nm
Sway bar links	37 ft. lbs.	50 Nm
Tie-rod end castellated nuts	18-22 ft. lbs.	25-30 Nm
Wheel hub retaining nut	210 ft. lbs.	290 Nm

91057C01

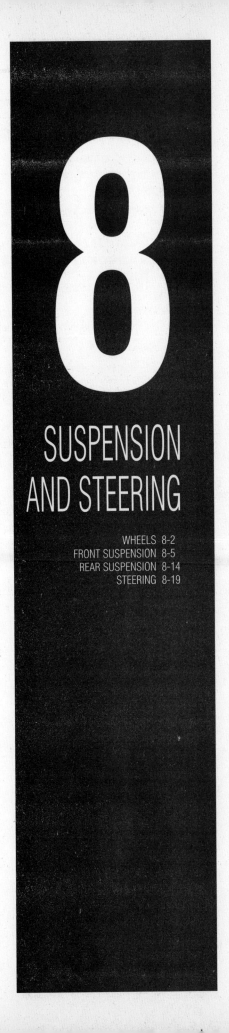

8

SUSPENSION AND STEERING

WHEELS

Wheel Assembly

REMOVAL & INSTALLATION

♦ **See Figures 1 thru 8**

1. Park the vehicle on a level surface.
2. Remove the jack, tire iron and, if necessary, the spare tire from their storage compartments.
3. Check the owner's manual or refer to Section 1 of this manual for the jacking points on your vehicle. Then, place the jack in the proper position.
4. If equipped with lug nut trim caps, remove them by either unscrewing or pulling them off the lug nuts, as appropriate. Consult the owner's manual, if necessary.
5. If equipped with a wheel cover or hub cap, insert the tapered end of the tire iron in the groove and pry off the cover.
6. Apply the parking brake and block the diagonally opposite wheel with a wheel chock or two.

➡ **Wheel chocks may be purchased at your local auto parts store, or a block of wood cut into wedges may be used. If possible, keep one or two of the chocks in your tire storage compartment, in case any of the tires has to be removed on the side of the road.**

7. If equipped with an automatic transmission/transaxle, place the selector lever in **P** or Park; with a manual transmission/transaxle, place the shifter in Reverse.
8. With the tires still on the ground, use the tire iron/wrench to break the lug nuts loose.

➡ **If a nut is stuck, never use heat to loosen it or damage to the wheel and bearings may occur. If the nuts are seized, one or two heavy hammer blows directly on the end of the bolt usually loosens the rust. Be careful, as continued pounding will likely damage the brake drum or rotor.**

9. Using the jack, raise the vehicle until the tire is clear of the ground. Support the vehicle safely using jackstands.
10. Remove the lug nuts, then remove the tire and wheel assembly.
To install:
11. Make sure the wheel and hub mating surfaces, as well as the wheel lug studs, are clean and free of all foreign material. Always remove rust from the wheel mounting surface and the brake rotor or drum. Failure to do so may cause the lug nuts to loosen in service.
12. Install the tire and wheel assembly and hand-tighten the lug nuts.
13. Using the tire wrench, tighten all the lug nuts, in a crisscross pattern, until they are snug.
14. Raise the vehicle and withdraw the jackstand, then lower the vehicle.
15. Using a torque wrench, tighten the lug nuts in a crisscross pattern to 62 ft. lbs. (85 Nm). Check your owner's manual or refer to Section 1 of this manual for the proper tightening sequence.

✳✳ WARNING

Do not overtighten the lug nuts, as this may cause the wheel studs to stretch or the brake disc (rotor) to warp.

16. If so equipped, install the wheel cover or hub cap. Make sure the valve stem protrudes through the proper opening before tapping the wheel cover into position.

Fig. 1 Place the jack at the proper lifting point on your vehicle

Fig. 2 Before jacking the vehicle, block the diagonally opposite wheel with one or, preferably, two chocks

Fig. 3 With the vehicle still on the ground, break the lug nuts loose using the wrench end of the tire iron

Fig. 4 After the lug nuts have been loosened, raise the vehicle using the jack until the tire is clear of the ground

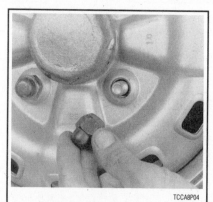

Fig. 5 Remove the lug nuts from the studs

Fig. 6 Remove the wheel and tire assembly from the vehicle

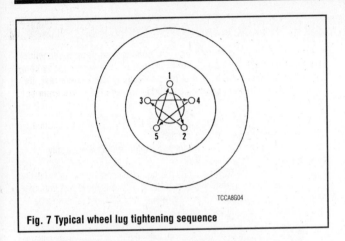
Fig. 7 Typical wheel lug tightening sequence

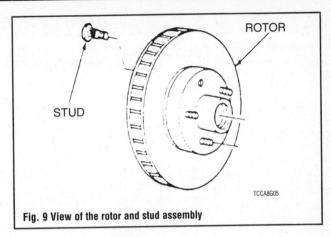
Fig. 9 View of the rotor and stud assembly

Fig. 8 With the wheels on the ground, tighten the lug nuts to specification using a torque wrench

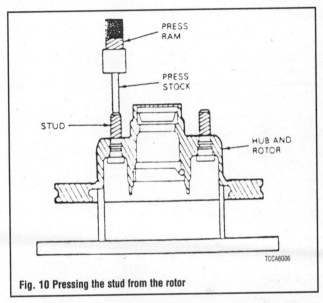
Fig. 10 Pressing the stud from the rotor

17. If equipped, install the lug nut trim caps by pushing them or screwing them on, as applicable.

18. Remove the jack from under the vehicle, and place the jack and tire iron/wrench in their storage compartments. Remove the wheel chock(s).

19. If you have removed a flat or damaged tire, place it in the storage compartment of the vehicle and take it to your local repair station to have it fixed or replaced as soon as possible.

INSPECTION

Inspect the tires for lacerations, puncture marks, nails and other sharp objects. Repair or replace as necessary. Also check the tires for treadwear and air pressure as outlined in Section 1 of this manual.

Check the wheel assemblies for dents, cracks, rust and metal fatigue. Repair or replace as necessary.

Wheel Lug Studs

REMOVAL & INSTALLATION

With Disc Brakes

▶ See Figures 9, 10 and 11

1. Raise and support the appropriate end of the vehicle safely using jackstands, then remove the wheel.

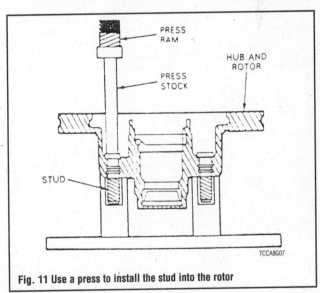
Fig. 11 Use a press to install the stud into the rotor

2. Remove the brake pads and caliper. Support the caliper aside using wire or a coat hanger. For details, please refer to Section 9 of this manual.

3. Remove the outer wheel bearing and lift off the rotor. For details on

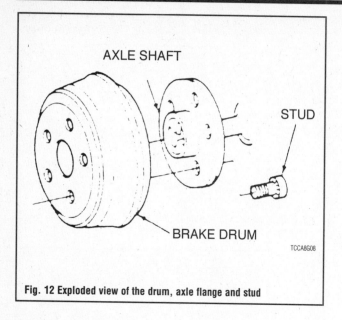

Fig. 12 Exploded view of the drum, axle flange and stud

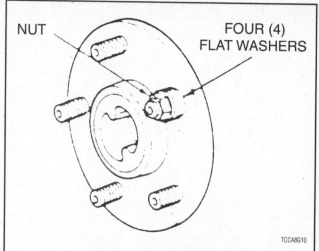

Fig. 14 Force the stud onto the axle flange using washers and a lug nut

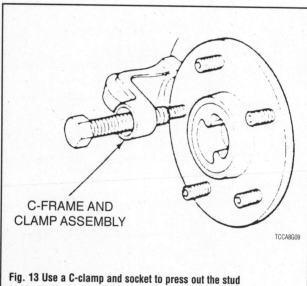

Fig. 13 Use a C-clamp and socket to press out the stud

wheel bearing removal, installation and adjustment, please refer to Section 1 of this manual.

4. Properly support the rotor using press bars, then drive the stud out using an arbor press.

➡If a press is not available, CAREFULLY drive the old stud out using a blunt drift. MAKE SURE the rotor is properly and evenly supported or it may be damaged.

To install:

5. Clean the stud hole with a wire brush and start the new stud with a hammer and drift pin. Do not use any lubricant or thread sealer.

6. Finish installing the stud with the press.

➡If a press is not available, start the lug stud through the bore in the hub, then position about 4 flat washers over the stud and thread the lug nut. Hold the hub/rotor while tightening the lug nut, and the stud should be drawn into position. MAKE SURE THE STUD IS FULLY SEATED, then remove the lug nut and washers.

7. Install the rotor and adjust the wheel bearings.
8. Install the brake caliper and pads.
9. Install the wheel, then remove the jackstands and carefully lower the vehicle.
10. Tighten the lug nuts to the proper torque.

With Drum Brakes

▶ **See Figures 12, 13 and 14**

1. Raise the vehicle and safely support it with jackstands, then remove the wheel.
2. Remove the brake drum.
3. If necessary to provide clearance, remove the brake shoes, as outlined in Section 9 of this manual.
4. Using a large C-clamp and socket, press the stud from the axle flange.
5. Coat the serrated part of the stud with liquid soap and place it into the hole.

To install:

6. Position about 4 flat washers over the stud and thread the lug nut. Hold the flange while tightening the lug nut, and the stud should be drawn into position. MAKE SURE THE STUD IS FULLY SEATED, then remove the lug nut and washers.

7. If applicable, install the brake shoes.
8. Install the brake drum.
9. Install the wheel, then remove the jackstands and carefully lower the vehicle.
10. Tighten the lug nuts to the proper torque.

FRONT SUSPENSION

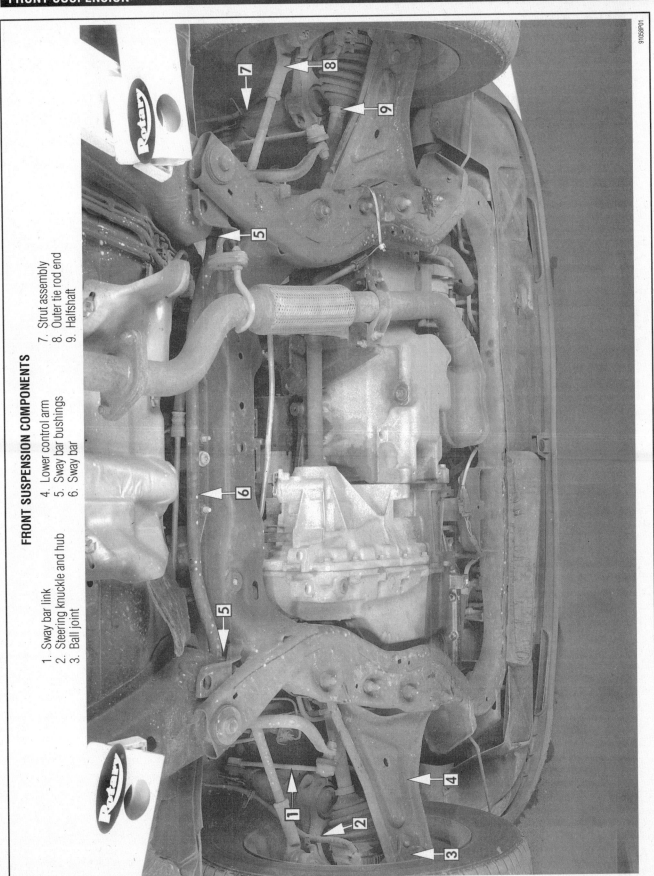

FRONT SUSPENSION COMPONENTS

1. Sway bar link
2. Steering knuckle and hub
3. Ball joint
4. Lower control arm
5. Sway bar bushings
6. Sway bar
7. Strut assembly
8. Outer tie rod end
9. Halfshaft

91058P01

MacPherson Strut and Spring Assembly

REMOVAL & INSTALLATION

▶ **See Figures 15 thru 26**

1. Disconnect the negative battery cable.
2. Raise and safely support the vehicle.
3. Remove the wheel and tire assembly.
4. Lower the vehicle enough to gain access to the strut retaining nut.
5. From inside the engine compartment, hold the strut piston with an 8mm Allen head wrench while removing the top retaining nut.
6. Raise and safely support the vehicle.
7. Disconnect the sway bar link from the strut.
8. Remove the brake hose and anti-lock wiring from the strut bracket.
9. Remove the steering knuckle-to-strut pinch bolt.

10. Work the strut out of the steering knuckle and lower the strut out of the strut tower.
11. Remove the strut/coil spring assembly from the vehicle.
To install:
12. Position the strut/coil spring assembly into the strut tower and fit the lower portion of the strut into the steering knuckle.
13. Reinstall the knuckle to strut pinch bolt. Do not tighten the bolt at this time.
14. Partially lower and safely support the vehicle.
15. Reinstall the top strut mounting nut.
16. Use an 8mm Allen head wrench to prevent the strut piston rod from turning while tightening the mounting nut to 34 ft. lbs. (46 Nm).
17. Tighten the knuckle to strut pinch bolt to 40 ft. lbs. (54 Nm).
18. Raise and safely support the vehicle.
19. Reinstall the sway bar link. Be careful not to damage the ball joint seal. Replace the sway bar link if the seal is damaged.
20. Tighten the sway bar link retaining nut to 37 ft. lbs. (50 Nm).

Fig. 15 A hollow socket and an Allen wrench are needed to remove the retaining nut

Fig. 16 Hold the strut piston with an Allen wrench while removing the retaining nut

Fig. 17 Remove the nut retaining the sway bar link to the strut and . . .

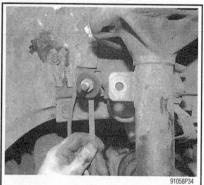
Fig. 18 . . . remove the sway bar link from the strut

Fig. 19 Remove the brake hose and wheel speed sensor from the brackets

Fig. 20 Remove the cotter pin from the outer tie rod end

Fig. 21 Remove the nut from the outer tie rod end

Fig. 22 Using the proper removal tool, remove the tie rod end from the spindle

Fig. 23 . . . remove the tie rod end from the spindle

Fig. 24 Remove the steering knuckle-to-strut pinch bolt and . . .

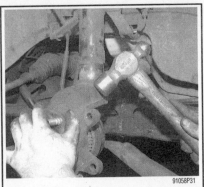

Fig. 25 Remove the steering knuckle from the strut tube and . . .

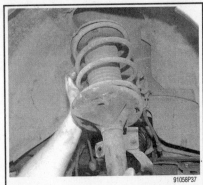

Fig. 26 . . . and remove the strut from the vehicle

21. Position the brake hose and the anti-lock wiring to the strut bracket.
22. Reinstall the wheel and tire assembly. Tighten the lug nuts to 62 ft. lbs. (85 Nm).
23. Lower the vehicle.
24. Connect the negative battery cable.
25. Check the front wheel alignment.
26. Road test the vehicle and check for proper operation.

OVERHAUL

▶ **See Figures 27 thru 36**

1. Remove the strut assembly as described in this Section.

✳✳ CAUTION

Do not attempt to remove the coil spring from the strut without first compressing the coil spring with the appropriate tool.

2. Install a suitable spring compressor to the coil spring and compress the spring until the spring tension is relieved from the spring seat.
3. Remove the thrust bearing retainer nut.
4. Remove the thrust bearing, spring seat and dust shield.
5. Remove the coil spring from the strut.
6. Remove the jounce bumper from the strut.
7. Replace the coil spring or the strut as needed.

To install:
8. Reinstall the jounce bumper to the strut.
9. Position the coil spring to the strut.
10. Compress the coil spring if removed from the spring compressor.
11. Reinstall the dust shield, spring seat and thrust bearing.
12. The coil spring must seat in the notch of the spring seat.
13. Reinstall the thrust bearing retainer nut. Tighten the nut to 44 ft. lbs. (59 Nm).
14. Install the strut assembly into the vehicle.

Lower Ball Joint

INSPECTION

1. Raise and the vehicle and place jacks under the front lower control arms to minimize the load on the front suspension.
2. Grasp the tire at the top and the bottom and gently push in and pull out, doing the opposite of each hand (one hand pushes in, the other pulls outward). If excessive movement is detected, verify the ball joint has excessive play and

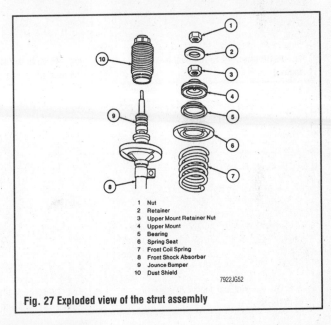

1. Nut
2. Retainer
3. Upper Mount Retainer Nut
4. Upper Mount
5. Bearing
6. Spring Seat
7. Front Coil Spring
8. Front Shock Absorber
9. Jounce Bumper
10. Dust Shield

Fig. 27 Exploded view of the strut assembly

Fig. 28 Mount the strut in a suitable vise and install a strut spring compressor

Fig. 29 Tighten the spring compressor to . . .

Fig. 30 . . . compress the spring to remove the bearing retaining nut

Fig. 31 Remove the bearing retaining nut using the hollow socket and an Allen wrench

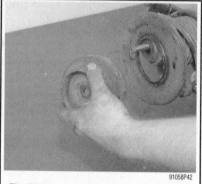

Fig. 32 After the retaining nut is removed, remove the thrust bearing

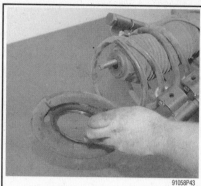

Fig. 33 Remove the spring seat from the strut

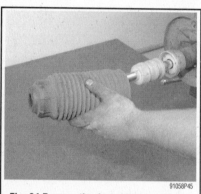

Fig. 34 Remove the dust shield from the strut

Fig. 35 Slide the compressed spring off of the strut

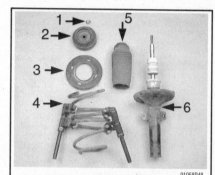

Fig. 36 1) Thrust bearing retaining nut 2) Thrust bearing 3) Spring seat 4) Coil spring 5) Dust shield 6) Strut tube

replace as necessary. However, worn wheel bearings will cause excessive movement also, and should be replaced if defective.

REMOVAL & INSTALLATION

▶ See Figures 37 and 38

1. Disconnect the negative battery cable.
2. Raise and safely support the vehicle securely on jackstands.
3. Remove the front wheel(s).
4. Remove the lower control arm as outlined in this Section.
5. Drill a 0.118 inch (3mm) hole in each rivet retaining the ball joint to the control arm.
6. Drill a 0.354 inch (9mm) hole in each rivet to a depth of 0.472 inch (12mm).
7. Using a 0.275–0.314 inch (7–8mm) in diameter punch, knock the rivets out of the control arm and remove the ball joint.
   To install:
8. Position the ball joint into the lower control arm.

9. Install three bolts and nuts (supplied with the replacement ball joint) into the rivet holes and tighten the nuts to 65 ft. lbs (85 Nm).
10. Install the control arm into the vehicle.
11. Install the front wheel(s).
12. Lower the vehicle.
13. Connect the negative battery cable.

Sway Bar

REMOVAL & INSTALLATION

▶ See Figures 39 thru 44

1. Disconnect the negative battery cable.
2. Raise and safely support the vehicle.
3. Remove the front wheel and tire assemblies.

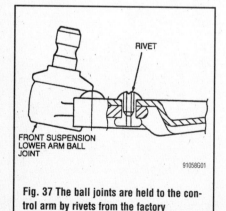

Fig. 37 The ball joints are held to the control arm by rivets from the factory

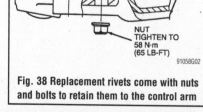

Fig. 38 Replacement rivets come with nuts and bolts to retain them to the control arm

Fig. 39 Remove the nut retaining the sway bar link to the strut and . . .

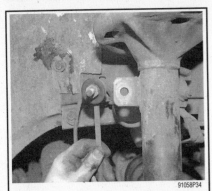

Fig. 40 . . . remove the sway bar link from the strut

Fig. 41 The sway bar link as mounted to the sway bar

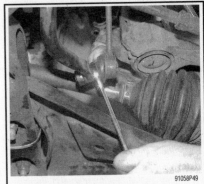

Fig. 42 Using two wrenches remove the sway bar link from the sway bar and . . .

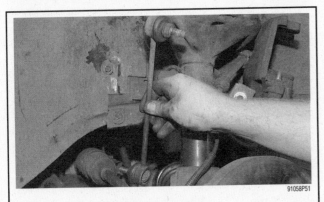

Fig. 43 . . . remove the link from the vehicle

Fig. 44 The sway bar bushings are mounted to the rear of the subframe and held by two bolts

4. Remove the left and right sway bar (stabilizer bar) link retaining nuts and the sway bar links from the bracket on the strut housings.

5. Remove the sway bar links from the sway bar and set aside.

6. If necessary, use a ball joint remover to separate the sway bar link from the sway bar.

7. Remove the 4 sway bar insulator bracket to subframe bolts (2 on each side).

➡ It may be necessary to lower the subframe to access the sway bar insulator bracket to subframe bolts. Support the rear of the subframe with a suitable device and remove the two rear subframe bolts only and slowly lower the subframe down to access the bolts.

8. Remove the sway bar from the vehicle.

To install:

9. Position the sway bar (stabilizer bar) into the vehicle.

10. Reinstall the 4 mounting bracket to subframe bolts.

11. Torque the bolts to 37 ft. lbs. (50 Nm).

12. Attach the sway bar links to each side of the sway bar and to each strut bracket.

➡ If the sway bar link boot seals are damaged, the link must be replaced.

13. Reinstall the 4 retaining nuts and torque to 37 ft. lbs. (50 Nm).

14. Reinstall the wheel and tire assemblies. Torque the lug nuts to 62 ft. lbs. (85 Nm).

15. Lower the vehicle.

16. Connect the negative battery cable.

17. Road test the vehicle and check for proper operation.

Lower Control Arm

REMOVAL & INSTALLATION

◆ See Figures 45 thru 51

Right Side

1. Disconnect the negative battery cable.

2. Raise and safely support the vehicle.

3. Remove the wheel and tire assembly.

4. Remove the lower ball joint to steering knuckle pinch bolt.

5. Separate the lower control arm ball joint from the steering knuckle.

6. Remove the 4 lower control arm bushing to front subframe nuts and bolts.

7. Remove the right side lower control arm.

To install:

8. Place the right side lower control arm to the front subframe.

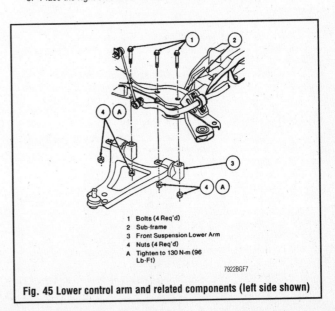

1 Bolts (4 Req'd)
2 Sub-frame
3 Front Suspension Lower Arm
4 Nuts (4 Req'd)
A Tighten to 130 N·m (96 Lb-Ft)

Fig. 45 Lower control arm and related components (left side shown)

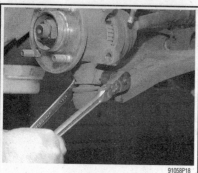

Fig. 46 Loosen the lower control arm-to-knuckle pinch bolt and nut using the appropriate tools and . . .

Fig. 47 . . . remove the bolt and nut from the knuckle

Fig. 48 Using a prybar or other suitable tool, pry the ball joint out of the knuckle

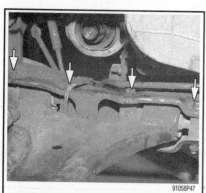

Fig. 49 The control arm is held by four retaining bolts on the subframe

Fig. 50 Remove the control arm-to-subframe retaining bolts and . . .

Fig. 51 . . . and remove the control arm from the vehicle

9. Reinstall the mounting bolts with the threads pointed down. Torque the mounting bolts to 96 ft. lbs. (130 Nm).

10. Reinstall the lower ball joint stud to the steering knuckle.

11. Reinstall the lower ball joint to steering knuckle pinch bolt. Torque the pinch bolt to 70 ft. lbs. (84 Nm).

12. Reinstall the wheel and tire assembly. Torque the lug nuts to 62 ft. lbs. (85 Nm).

13. Lower the vehicle.

14. Connect the negative battery cable.

15. Check the wheel alignment.

16. Road test the vehicle and check for proper operation.

Left Side

1. Disconnect the negative battery cable.

2. Support the radiator and fan shroud using safety wire to the radiator support.

3. If equipped with 2.0L (VIN 3) engine, remove the heat shield and the catalytic converter retaining nuts from the exhaust manifold.

4. Raise and safely support the vehicle.

5. Remove the catalytic converter.

6. Disconnect the steering column lower yoke.

7. If equipped with a manual transaxle, disconnect the gearshift rod and clevis.

8. Remove the front lower radiator cover.

9. Remove the radiator supports.

10. Remove the ball joint to steering knuckle pinch bolt.

11. Separate the lower control arm from the steering knuckle.

12. Disconnect the power steering cooler lines at the right–hand side of the front subframe.

13. Disconnect the sway bar link from the front sway bar.

14. Remove the through-bolts from the front and rear engine mounts.

15. Position a transmission jack or equivalent, under the front subframe.

16. Remove the subframe mounting bolts.

17. Remove the 4 lower control arm bushing to front subframe mounting nuts.

18. Lower the front subframe enough to allow removal of the lower control arm mounting bolts.

19. Remove the mounting bolts and remove the lower control arm.

To install:

20. Position the lower control arm into the front subframe.

21. Reinstall the mounting bolts with the threads pointed down.

22. Raise the front subframe into position.

23. Reinstall the lower control arm to subframe mounting bolts. Torque the mounting bolts and nuts to 96 ft. lbs. (130 Nm).

24. Reinstall the subframe mounting bolts. Torque the bolts to 81–110 ft. lbs. (110–150 Nm).

25. Remove the transmission jack or equivalent.

26. Reinstall the front and rear engine mount through-bolts. Torque the through-bolts to 40–55 ft. lbs. (54–75 Nm).

27. Connect the power steering cooler lines to the right–hand side of the subframe.

28. Position the lower control arm ball joint stud to the steering knuckle.

29. Reinstall the pinch bolt and torque to 70 ft. lbs. (84 Nm).

30. Connect the sway bar link to the front sway bar. Torque the bar link to 37 ft. lbs. (50 Nm).

31. Reinstall the radiator support.

32. Reinstall the front lower radiator cover.

33. Reinstall the catalytic converter.

34. Lower the vehicle.

35. If equipped with 2.0L (VIN 3) engine, install the heat shield and the catalytic converter retaining nuts.

36. Raise and safely support the vehicle.

37. If equipped with a manual transaxle, install the gearshift rod and clevis.

38. Connect the steering column lower yoke.

39. Reinstall the wheel and tire assembly. Torque the lug nuts to 62 ft. lbs. (85 Nm).

40. Lower the vehicle.

41. Remove the safety wire supporting the radiator.

42. Connect the negative battery cable.

→ Whenever the vehicle subframe is removed or lowered, the wheel alignment should be checked.

43. Check the wheel alignment.
44. Road test the vehicle and check for proper operation.

CONTROL ARM BUSHING REPLACEMENT

♦ See Figure 52

If the control arm bushings require replacement, the lower control arm assembly must be replaced, as the control arm bushings are not separately serviceable.

Fig. 52 The control arm bushings are part of the control arm assembly

Steering Knuckle, Front Hub And Wheel Bearing Assembly

REMOVAL & INSTALLATION

♦ See Figures 53 thru 62

→ Before proceeding, be sure to have available new pinch bolts for the steering knuckle to lower ball joint and steering knuckle to strut as well as a new wheel hub retaining nut.

1. Disconnect the negative battery cable.
2. Raise and safely support the vehicle.
3. Remove the wheel and tire assembly.
4. Remove the disc brake caliper and rotor.
5. Support the disc brake caliper with safety wire. Do not let the caliper hang by the brake hose.
6. Remove the anti-lock brake sensor retaining bolt and remove the sensor from the steering knuckle.
7. Remove the outer tie rod end cotter pin and remove the castellated nut. Discard the cotter pin.
8. Separate the outer tie rod end from the steering knuckle using an appropriate tie rod end remover.
9. Remove the wheel hub retaining nut. Discard the nut.
10. Separate the halfshaft from the wheel hub using Front Hub Remover/Replacer T81P-1104-C or equivalent, and the related adapters.
11. Once removed, support the end of the halfshaft.
12. Remove the steering knuckle to lower ball joint pinch bolt.
13. Remove the steering knuckle to strut pinch bolt.

Fig. 53 Loosen the lower control arm-to-knuckle pinch bolt and nut using the appropriate tools and . . .

Fig. 54 . . . remove the bolt and nut from the knuckle

Fig. 55 Using a prybar or other suitable tool, pry the ball joint out of the knuckle

Fig. 56 Remove the steering knuckle-to-strut pinch bolt

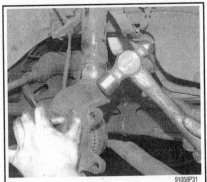

Fig. 57 Lightly tap the knuckle from the strut tube and . . .

Fig. 58 . . . remove the knuckle/hub/bearing assembly from the vehicle

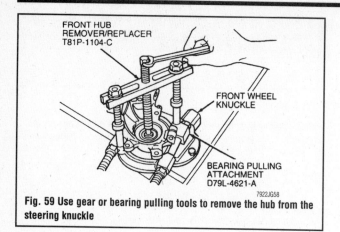

Fig. 59 Use gear or bearing pulling tools to remove the hub from the steering knuckle

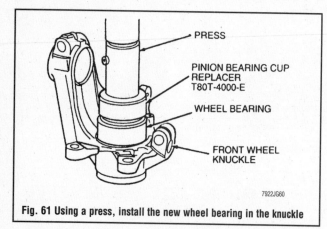

Fig. 60 The wheel bearing is retained in the knuckle by two snaprings, as shown

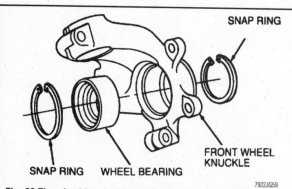

Fig. 61 Using a press, install the new wheel bearing in the knuckle

14. Work the steering knuckle off of the lower ball joint and out of the lower strut tube.
15. Remove the steering knuckle from the vehicle.
16. Place the steering knuckle assembly onto a suitable workbench.
17. Install Front Hub Remover/Replacer T81P-1104-C or equivalent with the appropriate adapters and separate the hub from the steering knuckle.
18. Remove the inner and outer snap rings securing the wheel bearing.
19. Remove the wheel bearing from the steering knuckle. Drive or press the old wheel bearing out as required.

To install:

20. Install the outer snap ring into the steering knuckle.
21. Install the wheel bearing using a hydraulic press with the appropriate size bearing cup adapter.
22. Reinstall the inner snap ring in the steering knuckle.

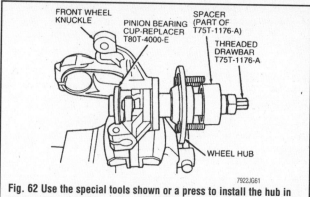

Fig. 62 Use the special tools shown or a press to install the hub in the knuckle assembly

23. Reinstall the hub to the steering knuckle using Threaded Drawbar T75T-1176-A or equivalent.
24. Carefully align the splines of the outer CV-joint with the splines in the hub.
25. Position the steering knuckle to the lower ball joint stud.
26. Position the steering knuckle to the lower strut tube.
27. Install a new steering knuckle to lower ball joint pinch bolt. Tighten the bolt to 70 ft. lbs. (84 Nm).
28. Install a new steering knuckle to strut pinch bolt. Tighten the bolt to 40 ft. lbs. (54 Nm).
29. Reinstall the anti-lock brake sensor and retaining bolt. Tighten the retaining bolt to 84 inch. lbs. (10 Nm).
30. Reinstall the disc brake rotor and caliper assembly.
31. Reinstall a new wheel hub retaining nut. Tighten the retaining nut to 210 ft. lbs. (290 Nm).

➡**Do not use an impact gun to tighten the wheel hub retaining nut or damage to the wheel bearing may result.**

32. Attach the tie rod end to the steering knuckle. Install the castellated nut and tighten the nut to 18–22 ft. lbs. (25–30 Nm). Install a new cotter pin.
33. Reinstall the wheel and tire assembly. Tighten the lug nuts to 62 ft. lbs. (85 Nm).
34. Lower the vehicle.
35. Connect the negative battery cable.
36. Pump the brake pedal several times to position the disc brake pads before attempting to move the vehicle.
37. Road test the vehicle and check for proper operation.

ADJUSTMENT

The front wheel bearings consist of a cartridge design and are permanently lubricated and sealed requiring no further maintenance. The bearings are pre-set and cannot be adjusted. If any part of a wheel bearing assembly is defective, the unit must be replaced. It is critical that the wheel hub retainer is properly tightened to 210 ft. lbs. (290 Nm) and that a new wheel hub retainer is always used.

Wheel Alignment

If the tires are worn unevenly, if the vehicle is not stable on the highway or if the handling seems uneven in spirited driving, the wheel alignment should be checked. If an alignment problem is suspected, first check for improper tire inflation and other possible causes. These can be worn suspension or steering components, accident damage or even unmatched tires. If any worn or damaged components are found, they must be replaced before the wheels can be properly aligned. Wheel alignment requires very expensive equipment and involves minute adjustments which must be accurate; it should only be performed by a trained technician. Take your vehicle to a properly equipped shop.

Following is a description of the alignment angles which are adjustable on most vehicles and how they affect vehicle handling. Although these angles can apply to both the front and rear wheels, usually only the front suspension is adjustable.

CASTER

▶ **See Figure 63**

Looking at a vehicle from the side, caster angle describes the steering axis rather than a wheel angle. The steering knuckle is attached to a control arm or strut at the top and a control arm at the bottom. The wheel pivots around the line between these points to steer the vehicle. When the upper point is tilted back, this is described as positive caster. Having a positive caster tends to make the wheels self-centering, increasing directional stability. Excessive positive caster makes the wheels hard to steer, while an uneven caster will cause a pull to one side. Overloading the vehicle or sagging rear springs will affect caster, as will raising the rear of the vehicle. If the rear of the vehicle is lower than normal, the caster becomes more positive.

CAMBER

▶ **See Figure 64**

Looking from the front of the vehicle, camber is the inward or outward tilt of the top of wheels. When the tops of the wheels are tilted in, this is negative camber; if they are tilted out, it is positive. In a turn, a slight amount of negative camber helps maximize contact of the tire with the road. However, too much negative camber compromises straight-line stability, increases bump steer and torque steer.

TOE

▶ **See Figure 65**

Looking down at the wheels from above the vehicle, toe angle is the distance between the front of the wheels, relative to the distance between the back of the wheels. If the wheels are closer at the front, they are said to be toed-in or to have negative toe. A small amount of negative toe enhances directional stability and provides a smoother ride on the highway.

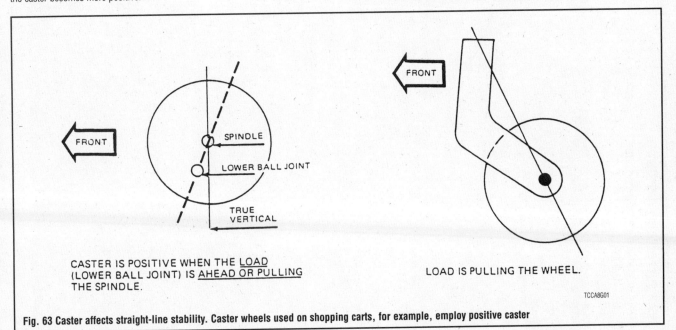

CASTER IS POSITIVE WHEN THE <u>LOAD</u> (LOWER BALL JOINT) IS <u>AHEAD OR PULLING</u> THE SPINDLE.

LOAD IS PULLING THE WHEEL.

TCCA8G01

Fig. 63 Caster affects straight-line stability. Caster wheels used on shopping carts, for example, employ positive caster

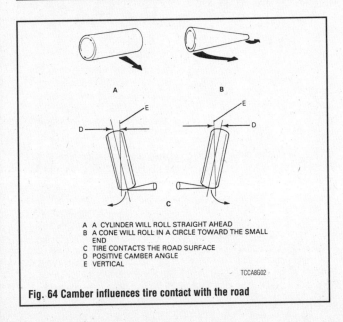

A   A CYLINDER WILL ROLL STRAIGHT AHEAD
B   A CONE WILL ROLL IN A CIRCLE TOWARD THE SMALL END
C   TIRE CONTACTS THE ROAD SURFACE
D   POSITIVE CAMBER ANGLE
E   VERTICAL

TCCA8G02

Fig. 64 Camber influences tire contact with the road

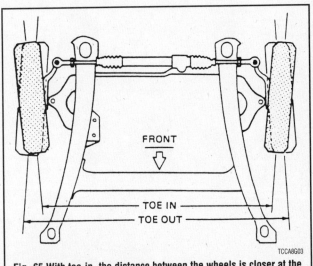

TCCA8G03

Fig. 65 With toe-in, the distance between the wheels is closer at the front than at the rear

REAR SUSPENSION

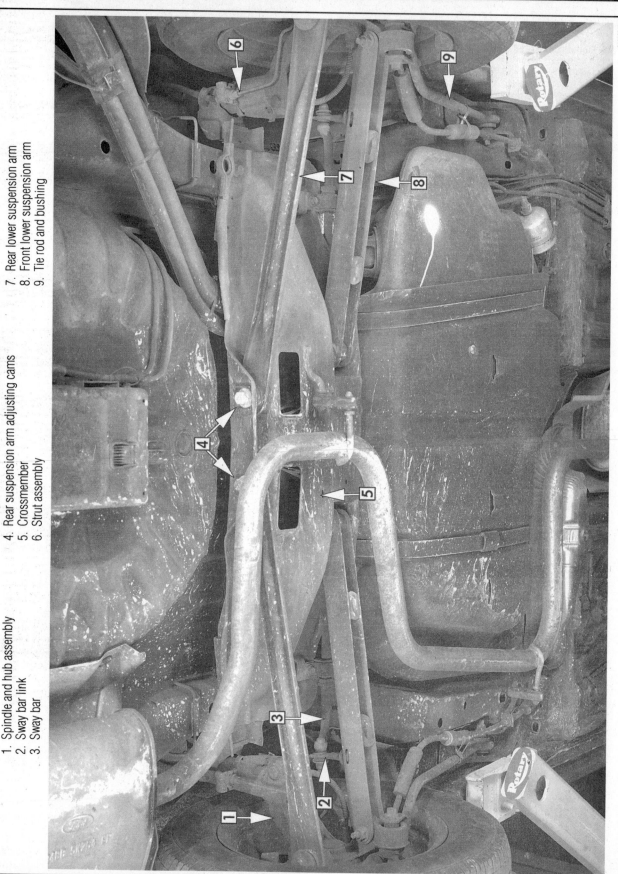

REAR SUSPENSION COMPONENTS

1. Spindle and hub assembly
2. Sway bar link
3. Sway bar
4. Rear suspension arm adjusting cams
5. Crossmember
6. Strut assembly
7. Rear lower suspension arm
8. Front lower suspension arm
9. Tie rod and bushing

MacPherson Strut And Spring Assembly

REMOVAL & INSTALLATION

▶ **See Figures 66, 67, 68, 69 and 70**

1. Disconnect the negative battery cable.
2. Raise and safely support the vehicle.
3. Remove the wheel and tire assembly.
4. Remove the anti-lock sensor wiring from the strut bracket.
5. Remove the anti-lock sensor mounting bolt and remove the sensor.
6. Disconnect the rear brake hose fitting from the brake tube. Plug the brake lines.
7. Remove the retainer and the rear brake hose from the strut.
8. Remove the tie strap retaining the parking brake rear cable and conduit to the rear suspension tie rod.
9. Disconnect the rear sway bar link and bushings from the rear control arm (suspension arm).
10. Disconnect the rear suspension tie rod from the wheel spindle.

➡ **The front and rear control arms (suspension arms) must be supported prior to the removal of the upper or lower strut attachments.**

11. Position a jack stand under the front and rear control arms.
12. Remove the spindle to strut pinch bolt.
13. Separate the spindle from the strut by tapping down on the wheel spindle.
14. Compress the coil spring using an appropriate strut spring compressor.
15. Remove the two top retaining bolts and remove the strut assembly.

To install:

16. With the coil spring compressed, install the strut assembly into position.
17. Reinstall the two rear strut bracket mounting bolts. Tighten the rear strut bracket mounting bolts to 17–22 ft. lbs. (23–30 Nm).
18. Position the strut to the wheel spindle.
19. Reinstall the spindle-to-strut pinch bolt. Tighten the pinch bolt to 52–72 ft. lbs. (70–98 Nm).

20. Remove the strut spring compressor.
21. Reinstall the rear suspension tie rod and bushing. Tighten the bolt to 75–102 ft. lbs. (102–135 Nm).
22. Remove the jackstand.
23. Attach the rear brake hose to the strut.
24. Reinstall the rear brake anti-lock sensor and retaining bolt. Tighten the retaining bolt to 84 inch. lbs. (9 Nm).
25. Reinstall the anti-lock wiring to the strut.
26. Secure the parking brake cable and conduit to the rear suspension tie rod with a tie strap.
27. Unplug and connect the rear brake hose fitting to the brake tube. Tighten the fitting securely.
28. Bleed the brake system.
29. Reinstall the wheel and tire assembly. Tighten the lug nuts to 62 ft. lbs. (85 Nm).
30. Lower the vehicle.
31. Connect the negative battery cable.
32. Check the rear wheel alignment.
33. Road test the vehicle and check for proper operation.

OVERHAUL

▶ **See Figure 71**

1. Remove the strut from the vehicle.
2. Place the strut assembly on a suitable workbench.
3. Compress the coil spring enough to relieve the tension on the spring seat.
4. Remove the top mount nut, rear strut bracket, bushing and spring seat.
5. Remove the coil spring and slowly relieve the tension on the spring if it is not to be reinstalled.
6. Remove the dust shield and the jounce bumper if the strut is being replaced.

To install:

7. If removed, install the jounce bumper and dust shield to the strut.

Fig. 66 The rear strut has a tight clearance along the strut tower; a special spring compressor is needed to remove it

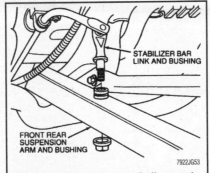

Fig. 67 For rear strut removal, disconnect the sway bar link from the control arm . . .

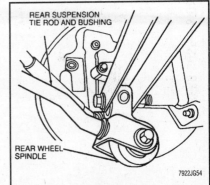

Fig. 68 . . . and separate the tie rod from the rear wheel spindle

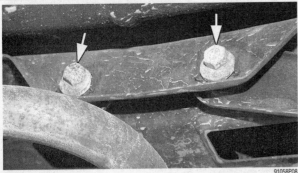

Fig. 69 Remove the rear strut pinch bolt to release the strut assembly from the spindle

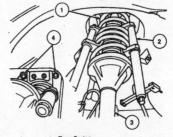

1. Rear Spring
2. Strut Spring Compressor
3. Shock Absorber
4. Mounting Nuts

Fig. 70 Compress the coil spring, then unthread the two top retaining bolts and remove the strut from the vehicle

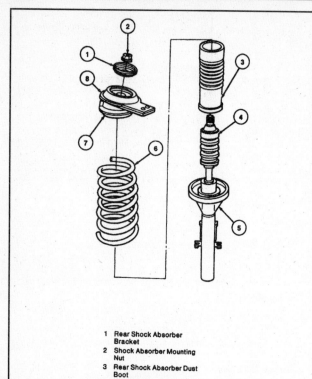

1 Rear Shock Absorber Bracket
2 Shock Absorber Mounting Nut
3 Rear Shock Absorber Dust Boot
4 Rear Suspension Jounce Bumper
5 Shock Absorber
6 Rear Spring
7 Spring Seat
8 Shock Absorber Bushing

7922JG57

Fig. 71 Exploded view of the rear strut assembly

8. Reinstall the coil spring and compress the spring if not already done.

9. Reinstall the spring seat, bushing, rear strut bracket and the top mount nut. Tighten the top mount nut to 30–43 ft. lbs. (41–58 Nm).

10. Install the strut into the vehicle.

Control Arms

REMOVAL & INSTALLATION

Front Lower Arm

▶ **See Figures 72, 73 and 74**

1. Disconnect the negative battery cable.
2. Raise and safely support the vehicle securely on jackstands.

3. Remove the rear wheel(s).

4. Remove the nut and disconnect the sway bar end from the arm and bushings.

5. Remove the bolt and nut and remove the arm and bushings from the spindle.

6. Position a jack under the rear subframe.

7. Lower the rear subframe so that the arm-to-crossmember bolt will clear the fuel tank.

8. Remove the arm-to-crossmember bolt and remove the front lower control arm.

To install:

9. Install the arm and bushing into the crossmember. Install the arm-to-crossmember bolt and nut. the bolt head must face the fuel tank. Do not tighten the bolt at this time.

10. Install the arm and bushings onto the spindle. Install the bolt and nut but do not tighten at this time.

11. Connect the rear sway bar link and bushings onto the arm and tighten the nut to 22–30 ft. lbs. (30–40 Nm).

12. Install the rear wheel(s).

13. Place a jack or other suitable device under the wheel of the removed control arm. Raise the suspension to load the vehicle weight onto the wheel.

14. Tighten the arm-to-spindle bolt to 52–79 ft. lbs. (70–98 Nm).

15. Tighten the arm-to-crossmember bolt to 52–79 ft. lbs. (70–98 Nm).

16. Lower the vehicle.

17. Check the alignment.

Rear Lower Arm

▶ **See Figures 74 and 75**

1. Disconnect the negative battery cable.
2. Raise and safely support the vehicle securely on jackstands.
3. Remove the rear wheel(s).
4. Remove the bolt and nut and remove the arm and bushings from the spindle.
5. Mark the location of the adjuster cam on the crossmember.
6. Remove the arm-to-crossmember bolt and remove the rear lower control arm.

To install:

7. Install the arm and bushing into the crossmember. Install the adjuster cam through bolt and align the mark on the adjuster cam and install the nut finger tight. Do not tighten the bolt at this time.

8. Install the arm and bushings onto the spindle. Install the bolt and nut but do not tighten at this time.

9. Install the rear wheel(s).

10. Place a jack or other suitable device under the wheel of the removed control arm. Raise the suspension to load the vehicle weight onto the wheel.

11. Tighten the arm-to-spindle bolt to 52–79 ft. lbs. (70–98 Nm).

12. Tighten the arm-to-crossmember bolt to 52–79 ft. lbs. (70–98 Nm).

13. Lower the vehicle.

14. Check the alignment.

91058P14

Fig. 72 The rear sway bar link-to-control arm connection

91058P15

Fig. 73 The front control arm-to-spindle connection

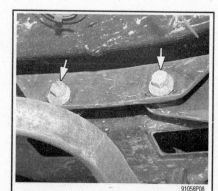

91058P08

Fig. 74 The rear control arm-to-crossmember connections

Fig. 75 The rear control arm-to-spindle connection

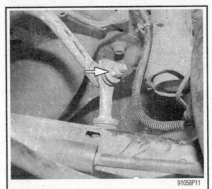

Fig. 76 The rear sway bar link-to-sway bar connection

Fig. 77 The rear sway bar link-to-control arm connection

Sway Bar

REMOVAL & INSTALLATION

▶ See Figures 76, 77, 78 and 79

1. Disconnect the negative battery cable.
2. Raise and safely support the vehicle.
3. Remove the sway bar (stabilizer bar) link nut from the lower control arm on each side of the sway bar.
4. Rotate the sway bar to separate the sway bar links from the lower control arms.

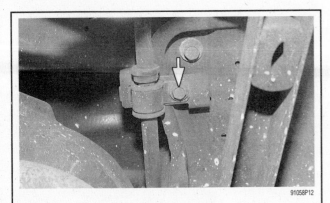

Fig. 78 The rear sway bar bushing and bracket

1	Bolt (4 Req'd)
2	Stabilizer Bar Bracket (2 Req'd)
3	Stabilizer Bar Insulator (2 Req'd)
4	Rear Stabilizer Bar
5	Rear Crossmember
6	Stabilizer Bar End

7922BGG9

Fig. 79 Sway bar and related components

5. Remove the sway bar bracket bolts and remove the brackets.
6. Remove the sway bar from the vehicle.
7. If the sway bar is being replaced, remove the sway bar links by prying them off of the studs on each end of the sway bar and remove the rubber insulators from the sway bar.

To install:

8. Connect the rubber insulators and the sway bar links if removed.
9. Place the sway bar into position.
10. Reinstall the sway bar brackets. Torque the bracket bolts to 14–19 ft. lbs. (19–26 Nm).
11. Fit the sway bar link ends to the lower control arms.
12. Reinstall the sway bar link bushings if removed, and the sway bar link nuts. Torque the sway bar link nuts to 22–30 ft. lbs. (30–40 Nm).
13. Lower the vehicle.
14. Connect the negative battery cable.
15. Road test the vehicle and check for proper operation.

Hub & Bearings

REMOVAL & INSTALLATION

➡The wheel bearings are contained within the wheel hub and must be replaced as an assembly.

With Rear Disc Brakes

1. Disconnect the negative battery cable.
2. Raise and safely support the vehicle.
3. Remove the wheel and tire assembly.
4. Remove the anti-lock sensor retaining bolt and remove the sensor.
5. Remove the rear disc brake caliper and rotor.

➡Do not use an impact gun to remove the hub retainer nut.

6. Remove the hub retainer nut.
7. Slide the hub and wheel bearing assembly off of the spindle and remove.

To install:

8. Reinstall the hub and bearing assembly to the spindle.
9. Reinstall the hub retainer nut. Tighten the hub retainer nut to 170–192 ft. lbs. (230–260 Nm).

➡Do not use an impact gun to tighten the hub retainer nut.

10. Reinstall the rear disc brake rotor and caliper.
11. Reinstall the anti-lock sensor. Tighten the retaining bolt for the sensor to 84–96 inch. lbs. (9–11 Nm).
12. Reinstall the wheel and tire assembly. Tighten the wheel nuts to 62 ft. lbs. (85 Nm).
13. Lower the vehicle until the wheels are supporting the vehicles weight. This will properly load the suspension.
14. Tighten the spindle-to-control arm bolt to 52–79 ft. lbs. (70–98 Nm).
15. Tighten the tie rod-to-spindle bolt to 75–102 ft. lbs. (102–135).
16. Finish lowering the vehicle.
17. Road test the vehicle and check for proper operation.

With Rear Drum Brakes

▶ See Figures 80, 81, 82, 83 and 84

➡The wheel bearings are contained within the wheel hub and must be replaced as an assembly.

1. Disconnect the negative battery cable.
2. Raise and safely support the vehicle.
3. Remove the wheel and tire assembly.
4. Remove the anti-lock sensor retaining bolt and remove the sensor.
5. Remove the brake drum retainer and the brake drum.
6. Remove the hub retaining nut dust cover.

➡Do not use an impact gun to remove the hub retainer nut.

7. Remove the wheel hub retainer nut.
8. Slide the hub and bearing assembly off of the spindle.

To install:

9. Reinstall the hub and bearing assembly to the spindle.
10. Reinstall the hub retainer nut. Tighten the retainer nut to 170–192 ft. lbs. (230–260 Nm).

☀ WARNING

Do not use an impact gun to tighten the hub retainer nut, otherwise the bearings may be damaged.

11. Install the hub retaining nut dust cover.
12. Reinstall the brake drum.
13. Check the brake shoes for proper adjustment.
14. Reinstall the anti-lock sensor and the retaining bolt. Tighten the retaining bolt to 7–8 ft. lbs. (9–11 Nm).
15. Reinstall the wheel and tire assembly. Tighten the wheel nuts to 62 ft. lbs. (85 Nm).
16. Lower the vehicle until the wheels are supporting the vehicles weight. This will properly load the suspension.
17. Tighten the spindle-to-control arm bolt to 52–79 ft. lbs. (70–98 Nm).

18. Tighten the tie rod-to-spindle bolt to 75–102 ft. lbs. (102–135 Nm).
19. Finish lowering the vehicle.
20. Road test the vehicle and check for proper operation.

ADJUSTMENT

The rear wheel bearings are not adjustable. If the bearings make noise or become loose, they must be replaced.

Spindle

REMOVAL & INSTALLATION

With Rear Disc Brakes

1. Disconnect the negative battery cable.
2. Raise and safely support the vehicle.
3. Remove the wheel and tire assembly.
4. Remove the anti-lock sensor retaining bolt and remove the sensor.
5. Remove the rear disc brake caliper and rotor.

➡Do not use an impact gun to remove the hub retainer nut.

6. Remove the hub retainer nut.
7. Slide the hub and wheel bearing assembly off of the spindle and remove.
8. Remove the disc brake dust shield.
9. Disconnect the rear tie rod and bushing from the spindle.
10. Disconnect the rear control arm (suspension arm) from the spindle. Remove the front control arm (suspension arm) from the spindle.
11. Remove the strut-to-spindle pinch bolt.
12. Separate the spindle from the strut and remove from the vehicle.

To install:

13. Reinstall the spindle to the to the strut. Tighten the pinch nut to 52–72 ft. lbs. (70–98 Nm).
14. Connect the rear control arm (suspension arm) to the spindle. Connect

Fig. 80 Using suitable tools loosen and . . .

Fig. 81 . . . remove the hub retaining nut dust cover

Fig. 82 Using suitable tools, loosen and . . .

Fig. 83 . . . remove the hub retaining nut

Fig. 84 Carefully slide the hub and bearing assembly off of the spindle

the front control arm (suspension arm) to the spindle. Tighten the bolt, but do not tighten at this time.

15. Connect the rear tie rod and bushing to the spindle. Tighten the bolt, but do not tighten at this time.
16. Reinstall the disc brake dust shield.
17. Reinstall the hub and bearing assembly to the spindle.
18. Reinstall the hub retainer nut. Tighten the hub retainer nut to 170–192 ft. lbs. (230–260 Nm).

➡**Do not use an impact gun to tighten the hub retainer nut.**

19. Reinstall the rear disc brake rotor and caliper.
20. Reinstall the anti-lock sensor. Tighten the retaining bolt for the sensor to 84–96 inch. lbs. (9–11 Nm).
21. Reinstall the wheel and tire assembly. Tighten the wheel nuts to 62 ft. lbs. (85 Nm).
22. Lower the vehicle until the wheels are supporting the vehicles weight. This will properly load the suspension.
23. Tighten the spindle-to-control arm bolt to 52–79 ft. lbs. (70–98 Nm).
24. Tighten the tie rod-to-spindle bolt to 75–102 ft. lbs. (102–135 Nm).
25. Finish lowering the vehicle.
26. Road test the vehicle and check for proper operation.

With Rear Drum Brakes

1. Disconnect the negative battery cable.
2. Raise and safely support the vehicle.
3. Remove the wheel and tire assembly.
4. Remove the anti-lock sensor retaining bolt and remove the sensor.
5. Remove the brake drum retainer and the brake drum.

➡**Do not use an impact gun to remove the hub retainer nut.**

6. Remove the wheel hub retainer nut.
7. Slide the hub and bearing assembly off of the spindle.
8. Remove the four backing plate bolts and move the backing plate out of the way. Be careful not to damage the brake line to the wheel cylinder.

9. Disconnect the rear tie rod and bushing from the spindle.
10. Disconnect the rear control arm (suspension arm) from the spindle. Remove the front control arm (suspension arm) from the spindle.
11. Remove the strut-to-spindle pinch bolt.
12. Separate the spindle from the strut and remove.
To install:
13. Reinstall the spindle to the strut. Tighten the pinch bolt to 52–72 ft. lbs. (70–98 Nm).
14. Connect the rear control arm (suspension arm) to the spindle. Connect the front control arm (suspension arm) to the spindle.
15. Connect the rear tie rod and bushing to the spindle. Do not tighten the bolt at this time.
16. Place the backing plate into position. Reinstall the four backing plate bolts and tighten to 33–40 ft. lbs. (45–54 Nm).
17. Reinstall the hub and bearing assembly to the spindle.
18. Reinstall the hub retainer nut. Tighten the retainer nut to 170–192 ft. lbs. (230–260 Nm).

✳✳ WARNING

Do not use an impact gun to tighten the hub retainer nut, otherwise the bearings may be damaged.

19. Reinstall the brake drum.
20. Check the brake shoes for proper adjustment.
21. Reinstall the anti-lock sensor and the retaining bolt. Tighten the retaining bolt to 7–8 ft. lbs. (9–11 Nm).
22. Reinstall the wheel and tire assembly. Tighten the wheel nuts to 62 ft. lbs. (85 Nm).
23. Lower the vehicle until the wheels are supporting the vehicles weight. This will properly load the suspension.
24. Tighten the spindle-to-control arm bolt to 52–79 ft. lbs. (70–98 Nm).
25. Tighten the tie rod-to-spindle bolt to 75–102 ft. lbs. (102–135 Nm).
26. Finish lowering the vehicle.
27. Road test the vehicle and check for proper operation.

STEERING

Steering Wheel

▸ See Figure 85

REMOVAL & INSTALLATION

▸ See Figures 86, 87, 88 and 89

✳✳ CAUTION

The Supplemental Inflatable Restraint (SIR) system must be disarmed before performing service around SIR system components or

SIR system wiring. Failure to do so may cause accidental deployment of the air bag, resulting in unnecessary SIR system repairs and/or personal injury.

1. Position the vehicle with the front wheels in a straight ahead position.
2. Disconnect both battery cables, negative cable last.

✳✳ CAUTION

WAIT at least 1 minute for the air bag backup power supply to deplete its stored energy before continuing.

3. Disconnect the air bag backup power supply.
4. Remove the 2 air bag retaining screws from the steering column side of the steering wheel. Turn the steering wheel 90 degrees from center to remove 1 screw and then turn the steering wheel 180 degrees to gain access to the 2nd screw.

✳✳ CAUTION

When carrying a live air bag, make sure the bag and trim cover are pointed away from the body. In the unlikely event of an accidental deployment, the bag will then deploy with minimal chance of injury. When placing a live air bag on a bench or other surface, always face the bag and trim cover up, away from the surface. This will reduce the motion of the module if it is accidentally deployed.

5. Carefully remove the air bag module from the steering wheel and disconnect the electrical connector.
6. Remove the air bag module from the vehicle and place on a bench with the trim cover facing up.
7. Center the front wheels to the straight ahead position.
8. Disconnect the speed control wiring harness from the steering wheel.
9. Remove the steering wheel retaining bolt.

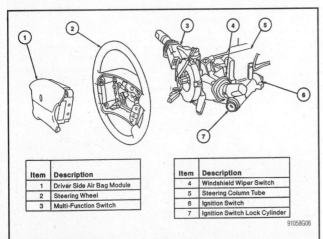

Item	Description
1	Driver Side Air Bag Module
2	Steering Wheel
3	Multi-Function Switch

Item	Description
4	Windshield Wiper Switch
5	Steering Column Tube
6	Ignition Switch
7	Ignition Switch Lock Cylinder

91058G06

Fig. 85 Upper steering column components

Fig. 86 The driver's side air bag is usually retained with tamper proof screws

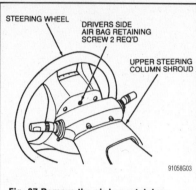

Fig. 87 Remove the air bag retaining screws

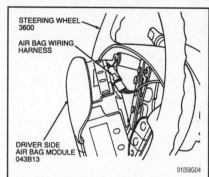

Fig. 88 Carefully remove the air bag from the steering wheel to access the wiring connector

10. Carefully lift the steering wheel off of the shaft while routing the air bag sliding contact wire harness through the steering wheel opening.

11. Remove the steering wheel from the vehicle.

To install:

12. Ensure that the vehicles front wheels are in a straight ahead position.

➡ **If the air bag was deployed due to an accident, the steering column must also be replaced.**

13. Feed the air bag sliding contact wire harness through the steering wheel opening and position the steering wheel on the steering shaft.

14. Make sure that the shaft alignment marks are aligned and that the air bag contact wire is not pinched.

15. Install a new steering wheel retaining bolt.

16. Torque the retaining bolt to 37 ft. lbs. (50 Nm).

17. Reconnect the speed control wiring harness to the steering wheel and snap the connector assembly into the steering wheel clip.

18. Reconnect the air bag wiring harness to the air bag module and install the air bag to the steering wheel. Torque the air bag retaining screws to 8–10 ft. lbs. (11–13 Nm).

19. Reconnect the air bag backup power supply.

20. Reconnect both battery cables, negative cable last.

21. Prove out the air bag system by turning the ignition key to the **RUN** position and visually monitoring the air bag indicator lamp in the instrument cluster. The indicator lamp should illuminate for approximately 6 seconds and then turn off. If the indicator lamp does not illuminate, stays on, or flashes at any time, a fault has been detected by the air bag diagnostic monitor.

Multi-Function Switch (Turn Signal Switch)

REMOVAL & INSTALLATION

▶ **See Figures 90 and 91**

1. Disconnect the negative battery cable.

2. Remove the upper steering column cover.

3. Release the locking tab securing the multi-function switch to the steering column.

4. Slide the switch from the steering column.

5. Unplug the wiring harness connector from the multi-function switch.

To Install:

6. If the multi-function switch is being replaced, transfer the indicator flasher from the old switch.

7. Reconnect the wiring harness connector to the multi-function switch.

8. Slide the switch into position and make sure the locking tab is fully seated.

9. Reinstall the upper steering column cover.

10. Reconnect the negative battery cable.

11. Check the multi-function switch for proper operation.

Wiper/Washer Switch

REMOVAL & INSTALLATION

▶ **See Figures 90 and 92**

1. Disconnect the negative battery cable.

2. Remove the upper steering column cover.

3. Release the locking tab securing the wiper/washer switch to the steering column.

4. Slide the switch from the steering column.

5. Unplug the wiring harness connector from the wiper/washer switch.

To Install:

6. Attach the wiring harness connector to the wiper/washer switch.

7. Slide the switch into position and make sure the locking tab is fully seated.

8. Reinstall the upper steering column cover.

9. Reconnect the negative battery cable.

10. Check the wiper/washer switch for proper operation.

Fig. 89 The steering wheel is retained by a single bolt in the center

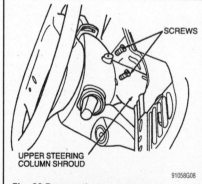

Fig. 90 Remove the two screws and remove the upper column cover

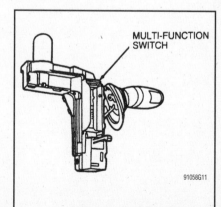

Fig. 91 Multi-function switch assembly

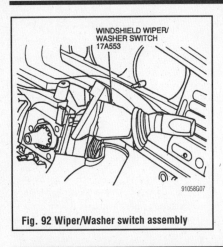

Fig. 92 Wiper/Washer switch assembly

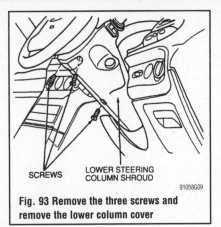

Fig. 93 Remove the three screws and remove the lower column cover

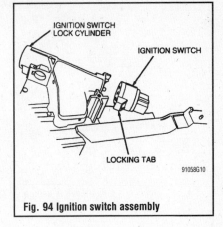

Fig. 94 Ignition switch assembly

Ignition Switch

REMOVAL & INSTALLATION

▶ **See Figures 90, 93 and 94**

1. Disconnect the negative battery cable.
2. Remove the 2 upper steering column cover screws and remove the cover.

➡ **It is not necessary to remove the steering wheel for this procedure.**

3. Remove the 3 lower steering column cover retaining screws and remove the cover.
4. Disconnect the electrical harness connector at the ignition switch.
5. Depress the locking tabs and remove the ignition switch.

To install:

6. Place the new ignition switch into position and push into place making sure that the switch is held securely.
7. Reconnect the electrical harness connector to the ignition switch.
8. Reinstall the lower steering column cover and its retaining screws.
9. Reinstall the upper steering column cover and its retaining screws.
10. Reconnect the negative battery cable.
11. Check for proper ignition switch operation.

Ignition Lock Cylinder

REMOVAL & INSTALLATION

Functional Lock Cylinder

▶ **See Figure 95**

1. Disconnect the negative battery cable.
2. Remove the upper and lower steering column covers.
3. Turn the ignition lock to the accessory position.
4. Insert a 0.125 (3.17mm) wire pin or small drift punch in the hole at the top of the cylinder housing and depress the retaining pin while pulling out the lock cylinder.

To Install:

5. Turn the new lock cylinder to accessory position and while pressing the retaining pin in, insert the lock cylinder into the housing.
6. Turn the key to the **OFF** position the release the retaining pin.
7. Try the lock cylinder operation in all positions.
8. Reinstall the steering column covers.
9. Reconnect the negative battery cable.

Non-Functional Lock Cylinder

1. Disconnect the negative battery cable.
2. Remove the upper and lower steering column covers.
3. Insert a 0.125 (3.17mm) drill bit in the hole at the top of the cylinder housing and drill out the retaining pin.

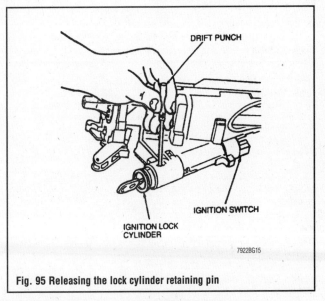

Fig. 95 Releasing the lock cylinder retaining pin

➡ **Be careful not to drill into the lock cylinder housing.**

4. Pull out the lock cylinder.
5. Clean out all the metal shavings and check the tube for damage. If damaged, the housing must be replaced.

To Install:

6. Turn the new lock cylinder to accessory position and while pressing the retaining pin in, insert the lock cylinder into the housing.
7. Turn the key to the **OFF** position the release the retaining pin.
8. Try the lock cylinder operation in all positions.
9. Reinstall the steering column covers.
10. Reconnect the negative battery cable.

Tie Rods

REMOVAL & INSTALLATION

Outer Tie Rod Ends

▶ **See Figures 96 thru 102**

1. Disconnect the negative battery cable.
2. Remove the wheel and tire assembly.
3. Remove the cotter pin and the castellated nut from the outer tie rod end. Discard the cotter pin.
4. Separate the outer tie rod end from the steering knuckle using an appropriate tie rod end remover.
5. Hold the outer tie rod end with a wrench and loosen the tie rod end jam nut.

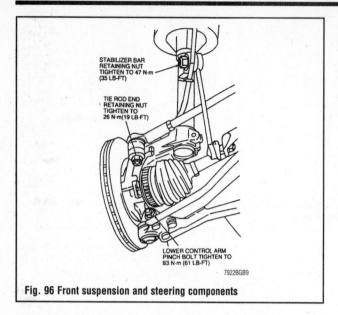

Fig. 96 Front suspension and steering components

11. Place the outer tie rod end stud into the steering knuckle. Set the front wheels in a straight ahead position.

12. Install a new castellated nut onto the outer tie rod end stud.

13. Torque the nut to 21 ft. lbs. (28 Nm).

14. Continue to tighten the castellated nut until a new cotter pin can be inserted through the hole in the stud. Install a new cotter pin.

15. If required, repeat the procedure for the opposite side.

16. Reinstall the wheel and tire assembly. Torque the lug nuts to 62 ft. lbs. (85 Nm).

17. Reconnect the negative battery cable.

18. Check the alignment and set the toe adjustment to specification.

19. Torque the outer tie rod end jam nut to 35–50 ft. lbs. (48–68 Nm).

Inner Tie Rods

◊ See Figure 103

1. Remove the front subframe and the rack and pinion (steering gear).

2. Remove the rack and pinion from the front subframe and secure to a bench mounted holding fixture.

3. Working on one side, remove the outer tie rod end making sure to record the number of turn required for removal.

4. Remove the outer tie rod end jam nut.

5. Remove the outer clamp securing the inner tie rod bellows to the tie rod spindle.

6. Loosen the larger inner clamp using a wrench or screwdriver and remove the bellows.

7. Position the rack and pinion so that several teeth of the rack are exposed.

8. Hold the rack with an adjustable wrench on the end teeth only while loosening the inner tie rod nut (ball joint nut) with a pipe wrench.

9. Once the inner tie rod is loose, remove by hand.

10. Remove the inner tie rod from the vehicle and inspect the rack and pinion for seal leakage. Replace the rack and pinion if there is excessive leakage from the rack seals.

To install:

11. Install a new inner tie rod assembly.

6. Note the depth that the outer tie rod end jam nut is located.

7. Remove the outer tie rod end from the inner tie rod spindle. Count and record the number of turns required to remove the outer tie rod end.

8. Remove the outer tie rod end from the vehicle.

To install:

9. Clean the threads on the inner tie rod spindle (front wheel spindle connecting rod).

10. Thread the new outer tie rod end onto the inner tie rod. Use the same number of turns recorded during disassembly. The jam nut should also indicate that the new outer tie rod end is positioned properly.

Fig. 97 Remove the cotter pin from the outer tie rod end

Fig. 98 Remove the nut from the outer tie rod end

Fig. 99 Using the proper removal tool . . .

Fig. 100 . . . remove the tie rod end from the spindle

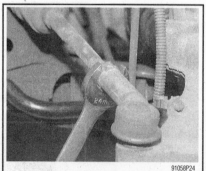

Fig. 101 It is easier to remove the jam nut if you place the tie rod socket into the knuckle so that the tie rod resists turning

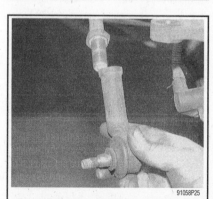

Fig. 102 Remove the tie rod end from the inner tie rod by turning it counterclockwise

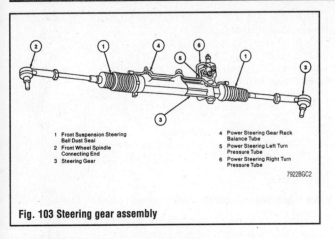

Fig. 103 Steering gear assembly

1 Front Suspension Steering Ball Dust Seal	4 Power Steering Gear Rack Balance Tube
2 Front Wheel Spindle Connecting End	5 Power Steering Left Turn Pressure Tube
3 Steering Gear	6 Power Steering Right Turn Pressure Tube

12. Turn the rack and pinion against the left stop.

13. While holding the rack with an adjustable wrench nearest the rack end, tighten the inner tie rod nut (ball joint nut) using a pipe wrench.

14. Apply a small amount of grease to the lip of the bellows where it clamps to the inner tie rod spindle to allow the shaft to turn without twisting the bellows.

15. Install the bellows with the larger inner clamp and tighten with a wrench or screwdriver.

16. Install a new outer clamp using needlenose pliers.

17. Install the jam nut onto the tie rod spindle.

18. Apply a small amount of grease to the outer tie rod threads and install the outer tie rod end using the same number of threads recorded during disassembly.

19. Repeat the procedure for the opposite side.

20. Reinstall the rack and pinion to the front subframe and install the front subframe to the vehicle.

21. Reconnect the negative battery cable.

➡ **Whenever the vehicle subframe is removed or lowered, the wheel alignment should be checked.**

22. Check the alignment and set the toe adjustment to specification.

23. Torque the outer tie rod end jam nut to 35–50 ft. lbs. (48–68 Nm).

Power Steering Rack and Pinion

REMOVAL & INSTALLATION

◆ **See Figures 104, 105, 106 and 107**

1. Disconnect the negative battery cable.

2. Working inside the vehicle, remove the clamp plate bolt retaining the steering column shaft to the flexible coupling.

3. Rotate the clamp plate to separate it from the shaft of the flexible coupling.

4. Remove the floor seal being careful not to damage the sealing lip.

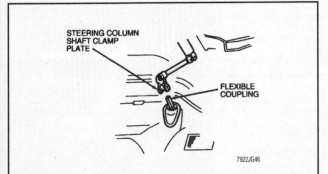

Fig. 104 Disconnect the steering column shaft from the flexible coupling

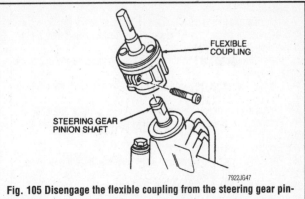

Fig. 105 Disengage the flexible coupling from the steering gear pinion shaft

5. Remove the pinch bolt securing the flexible coupling to the rack and pinion (steering gear) pinion shaft and remove the flexible coupling.

6. Remove as much of the power steering fluid as possible from the power steering auxiliary reservoir using a suction gun or similar method.

7. Disconnect the power steering return hose from the power steering pump auxiliary reservoir.

➡ **The front sub-frame must be removed in order to allow removal of the rack and pinion (steering gear).**

8. If equipped with the 2.0L engine, remove the oil level dipstick and the exhaust manifold shield.

9. If equipped with the 2.5L engine, remove the water pump pulley shield.

10. Secure the radiator and fan shroud assembly to the radiator support using safety wire.

11. Install an appropriate engine support device to the engine lifting eyes and support the engine/transaxle assembly.

12. Raise and safely support the vehicle.

13. Remove the catalytic converter.

14. Remove the front wheel and tire assemblies.

15. Separate the left and right sway bar links from the front sway bar.

16. Separate the left and right outer tie rod ends from the steering knuckles. Discard the cotter pins.

17. Remove the pinch bolts and separate the front suspension lower control arms from the steering knuckles at the ball joints.

18. Remove the splash shield at the front of the sub-frame.

19. If equipped with an automatic transaxle, remove the retaining through-bolts from the left and right front engine support insulators (engine mounts) to the sub-frame.

20. If equipped with a manual transaxle, remove the through-bolt from the left front engine support insulator and remove the right front engine support insulator and mounting bracket.

21. Disconnect the power steering oil cooler hoses at the right front of the sub-frame and drain the power steering system.

22. Remove the A/C accumulator retaining screws from the front sub-frame.

23. Remove the four bolts retaining the lower radiator supports to the front sub-frame. Rotate the radiator supports forward.

24. Remove the two screws retaining the bumper cover braces to the left and right sides of the front sub-frame and rotate the cover braces forward.

25. Position an appropriate lifting device and two wood blocks approximately 40 inches in length attached to the sub-frame to support the sub-frame for removal from the vehicle.

➡ **Be sure that the lifting device and wood blocks are correctly positioned for safe removal of the sub-frame.**

26. Remove the four sub-frame to body retaining bolts.

27. Lower the sub-frame slightly and disconnect the power steering pressure and return hoses from the rack and pinion.

28. Finish lowering the sub-frame.

29. Remove the six bolts and the steering gear cover plate from the sub-frame.

30. Disconnect the power steering pressure and return hose unions from the steering gear.

31. Remove the two bolts retaining the steering gear to the sub-frame and remove the rack and pinion.

To install:

32. If the rack and pinion (steering gear) is being replaced, remove the inner tie rods and boots from the old unit and install on the new one, if they are in good condition.

33. Install new plastic seals on the power steering pressure and return line fittings as required.

34. Reinstall the rack and pinion to the sub-frame and install the retaining bolts.

35. Tighten the two rack and pinion retaining bolts to 101 ft. lbs. (137 Nm).

36. Reconnect the power steering and return hose unions to the rack and pinion.

37. Tighten the unions to 23 ft. lbs. (31 Nm).

38. Reinstall the rack and pinion cover plate and install the six retaining bolts.

39. Tighten the retaining bolts to 37 ft. lbs. (50 Nm).

40. If lowered, raise and safely support the vehicle.

41. If removed, position the front sub-frame onto the powertrain lift and raise.

42. Reinstall the power steering pressure and return hoses to the rack and pinion.

43. Position the front sub-frame to the body.

44. Route the power steering hoses to their correct positions.

45. Loosely install the four sub-frame to body bolts.

46. Install Sub-Frame Alignment Pin Set T94P-2100-AH or equivalent, into the front sub-frame to body alignment holes.

47. Slightly tighten the four sub-frame to body retaining bolts.

48. Move the sub-frame to complete the alignment.

49. Tighten the four sub-frame to body retaining bolts to 81–110 ft. lbs. (110–150 Nm).

50. Remove the alignment tools.

51. Reinstall the A/C bracket retaining screw to the sub-frame and secure.

52. Reconnect the power steering oil cooler hoses to the front of the sub-frame.

53. Install the Powertrain Alignment Gauge T94P-6000-AH or equivalent, to the left front engine support bracket and the sub-frame.

54. Tighten the two retaining bolts to 20 ft. lbs. (27 Nm) and snug the through-bolt.

55. Lower the vehicle.

56. Remove the engine support from the top of the engine compartment.

57. Reconnect the power steering return hose to the power steering pump auxiliary reservoir.

58. Working inside the vehicle, install the flexible coupling to the steering gear pinion shaft and install the pinch bolt.

59. Tighten the pinch bolt to 21 ft. lbs. (28 Nm).

60. Reinstall the floor seal.

61. Align the steering column shaft clamp plate with the flexible coupling and install the clamp plate bolt. Tighten the clamp plate bolt to 18 ft. lbs. (24 Nm).

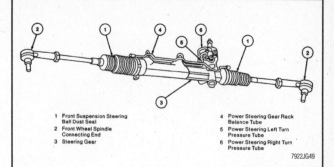

1 Front Suspension Steering Ball Dust Seal	4 Power Steering Gear Rack Balance Tube
2 Front Wheel Spindle Connecting End	5 Power Steering Left Turn Pressure Tube
3 Steering Gear	6 Power Steering Right Turn Pressure Tube

7922JG49

Fig. 107 Power rack and pinion steering gear assembly component identification

62. Partially raise and safely support the vehicle.

63. Install the right front engine support insulator (engine mount). Tighten the two retaining bolts to 30–41 ft. lbs. (41–55 Nm) and the through-bolt to 75–102 ft. lbs. (103–137 Nm).

64. Check the position of the right front engine mount (support insulator). It must be centered in the transaxle bracket and in perfect front to rear alignment.

65. Remove the two retaining bolts and the through-bolt securing the powertrain alignment gauge and remove the powertrain alignment gauge.

66. Reinstall the left front engine mount to the front sub-frame using the two retaining bolts. Tighten the retaining bolts to 84 inch lbs. (10 Nm).

67. Check the position of the left front engine mount to ensure perfect front to rear alignment.

68. Retighten the two retaining bolts to 30–40 ft. lbs. (41–55 Nm).

69. Reinstall the left front engine mount through-bolt. Tighten the through-bolt to 75–102 ft. lbs. (103–137 Nm).

70. Reinstall the sway bar link to the front sway bar. Tighten the retaining nuts to 35–48 ft. lbs. (47–65 Nm).

71. Reconnect the left and right lower control arms to the ball joints and install the pinch bolts. Tighten the pinch bolts to 37–43 ft. lbs. (50–58 Nm).

72. Reinstall the catalytic converter.

73. Reinstall both tie rod ends to the steering knuckles. Install new cotter pins.

74. Reinstall the wheel and tire assemblies and tighten the lug nuts to 63 ft. lbs. (85 Nm).

75. Reinstall the front bumper cover braces to both sides of the sub-frame.

76. Reinstall the radiator supports and the splash shield to the sub-frame.

77. Lower the vehicle.

78. Remove the safety wire supporting the radiator and fan shroud assembly.

79. If equipped with the 2.0L engine, install the exhaust manifold shield and the oil level dipstick.

80. If equipped with the 2.5L engine, install the water pump pulley shield and secure.

81. Fill the power steering system with the proper fluid.

82. Reconnect the negative battery cable.

83. Run the engine and check for leaks and proper operation.

➡ **Whenever the vehicle sub-frame is removed or lowered, the wheel alignment should be checked.**

84. Bleed the power steering system, if needed.

Power Steering Pump

REMOVAL & INSTALLATION

2.0L Engine

♦ See Figure 108

1. Disconnect the negative battery cable.
2. Remove the exhaust manifold heat shield.
3. Remove the power steering reservoir pump hose from the power steering pump bracket and engine lifting bracket.

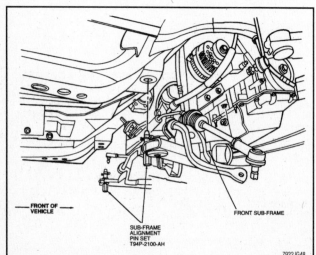

Fig. 106 Install alignment pins such as Sub-Frame Alignment Pin Set T94P-2100-AH into the sub-frame to ensure correct positioning

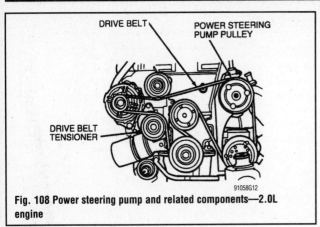

Fig. 108 Power steering pump and related components—2.0L engine

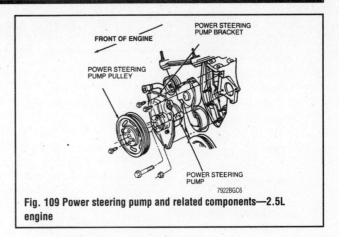

Fig. 109 Power steering pump and related components—2.5L engine

4. Disconnect the power steering return hose and the power steering reservoir pump hose from the power steering pump.
5. Allow the fluid to drain into an appropriate container.
6. Raise and safely support the vehicle.
7. Remove the lower drive belt guard.
8. Remove the accessory drive belt.
9. Lower the vehicle.
10. Remove the 3 bolts from the traction assist module and move aside.
11. Rotate the power steering pump pulley to gain access to the 3 power steering pump retaining bolts and remove the bolts.
12. Remove the bolt at the back of the power steering pump.
13. Remove the power steering pump from the vehicle.
14. If required, remove the power steering pump pulley using an appropriate power steering pump pulley remover.

To install:

15. If the pulley was removed from the power steering pump, install the pulley using an appropriate power steering pump pulley replacer.
16. The power steering pulley must be flush or within 0.010 inch (0.25mm) of the end of the pump shaft.
17. Reinstall the power steering pump and install the single retaining bolt at the rear of the pump. Do not tighten the bolt at this time.
18. Rotate the power steering pump pulley to install the 3 retaining bolts into the front of the power steering pump. Torque all 4 bolts to 18 ft. lbs. (25 Nm).
19. Position the traction assist module and install the 3 retaining bolts. Torque the retaining bolts to 53 inch lbs. (6 Nm).
20. Raise and safely support the vehicle.
21. Reinstall the accessory drive belt.
22. Reinstall the lower drive belt guard.
23. Lower the vehicle.
24. Reconnect the power steering pressure hose and the power steering reservoir pump hose to the power steering pump.
25. Torque the pressure hose fitting to 48 ft. lbs. (65 Nm).
26. Reinstall the power steering pressure hose to the power steering pump bracket and engine lifting bracket.
27. Reinstall the exhaust manifold heat shield.
28. Reconnect the negative battery cable.
29. Fill the power steering system with the proper fluid.
30. Run the engine and check for leaks and proper operation.
31. Bleed the power steering system of air if necessary.

2.5L Engine

▶ See Figure 109

1. Disconnect the negative battery cable.
2. Remove the retaining bolt securing the power steering pressure hose to the upper engine mount.
3. Disconnect the power steering pressure hose from the power steering pump and allow the fluid to drain into a proper container.
4. Move the power steering pressure hose aside.
5. Move the ignition wire organizer aside.
6. Remove the front engine support insulator (engine mount). This requires the use of an engine support brace.
7. Loosen but do not remove the 4 power steering pump pulley bolts.

8. Remove the accessory drive belt.
9. Remove the 4 bolts and the power steering pump pulley.
10. Disconnect the power steering reservoir pump hose from the power steering pump.
11. Remove the power steering pressure hose clamp from the power steering pump bracket.
12. Remove the 6 retaining nuts and 5 retaining bolts from the power steering pump bracket.
13. Remove the power steering pump and bracket from the vehicle.

To install:

14. Reinstall the power steering pump and bracket into the vehicle.
15. Reinstall the 6 retaining nuts and 5 retaining bolts. Torque the nuts and bolts to 18 ft. lbs. (25 Nm).
16. Reinstall the power steering pressure hose clamp to the power steering pump bracket.
17. Reconnect the power steering reservoir pump hose to the power steering pump.
18. Reinstall the power steering pump pulley and the 4 retaining bolts, finger tight.
19. Reinstall the accessory drive belt.
20. Torque the power steering pump pulley bolts to 97 inch lbs. (11 Nm).
21. Reinstall the front engine support insulator (engine mount) and remove the engine support brace.
22. Reposition the ignition wire organizer.
23. Reconnect the power steering pressure hose to the power steering pump. Torque the pressure hose fitting to 48 ft. lbs. (65 Nm).
24. Reinstall the power steering pressure hose to the front engine support insulator.
25. Reconnect the negative battery cable.
26. Fill the power steering system.
27. Run the engine and check for leaks and proper operation.
28. Bleed the power steering system of air if necessary.

BLEEDING

1. Disable the ignition system.
2. Raise the vehicle until the front tires are just off of the ground and safely support. Make sure that the transaxle is not in gear.
3. Fill the power steering pump auxiliary reservoir.
4. Crank the engine for 30 seconds without turning the steering wheel and recheck the fluid level. Add fluid if needed.
5. Crank the engine for 30 seconds while turning the steering wheel lock to lock. Check the fluid level and fill if needed.

❄❄ WARNING

Do not hold the steering wheel against a stop for more than 5 seconds as damage to the steering pump could result.

6. Lower the vehicle.
7. Restore the ignition system.
8. Start the vehicle and check that the power steering system is free of air. If not, repeat the procedure or purge the system of air using an external vacuum source.

TORQUE SPECIFICATIONS

Components	English	Metric
A/C accumulator-to-subframe bolts	48-72 inch lbs.	6-8 Nm
Air bag retaining screws	8-10 ft. lbs.	11-13 Nm
Engine support insulators		
Engine and transaxle support insulator-to-left front fender apron	40-55 ft. lbs.	54-75 Nm
Lower insulator-to-subframe	30-41 ft. lbs.	41-55 Nm
Through bolts	75-102 ft. lbs.	102-135 Nm
Left insulator-to-subframe	84 inch lbs.	10 Nm
Front engine support bracket	61 ft. lbs.	84 Nm
Front Suspension		
Ball joint-to-steering knuckle	70 ft. lbs.	84 Nm
Control arm mounting bolts	96 ft. lbs.	130 Nm
Knuckle-to-strut bolts	40 ft. lbs.	54 Nm
Replacement ball joint-to-control arm bolts	65 ft. lbs.	88 Nm
Strut		
Thrust bearing retainer nut	44 ft. lbs.	59 Nm
Top mounting nut	34 ft. lbs.	46 Nm
Sway bar-to-subframe bolts	37 ft. lbs.	50 Nm
Sway bar links	37 ft. lbs.	50 Nm
Tie-rod end castellated nuts	18-22 ft. lbs.	25-30 Nm
Wheel hub retaining nut	210 ft. lbs.	290 Nm
Intermediate halfshaft support bracket bolts	15-23 ft. lbs.	21-32 Nm
Intermediate halfshaft support bracket and bearing shield nuts	17-22 ft. lbs.	24-30 Nm
Power rack and pinion		
Rack-to-subframe retaining bolts	101 ft. lbs.	137 Nm
Rack and pinion cover plate retaining bolts	37 ft. lbs.	50 Nm
Power steering hose unions	23 ft. lbs.	31 Nm
Power steering pump		
2.0L engine		
Pressure hose fitting	48 ft. lbs.	65 Nm
Pulley retaining bolts	18 ft. lbs.	25 Nm
Pump retaining bolts	18 ft. lbs.	25 Nm
Traction assist module retaining bolts	53 inch lbs.	6 Nm
2.5L engine		
Pressure hose fitting	48 ft. lbs.	65 Nm
Pulley retaining bolts	97 inch lbs.	11 Nm
Pump retaining bolts	18 ft. lbs.	25 Nm
Powertrain alignment gauge bolts	20 ft. lbs.	27 Nm
Radiator supports-to-subframe	71-97 inch lbs.	8-11 Nm
Rear suspension		
Front lower control arm-to-spindle	52-79 ft. lbs.	70-98 Nm
Front lower control arm-to-crossmember	52-79 ft. lbs.	70-98 Nm
Rear lower control arm-to-spindle	52-79 ft. lbs.	70-98 Nm
Rear lower control arm-to-crossmember	52-79 ft. lbs.	70-98 Nm
Strut		
Bracket mounting bolts	17-22 ft. lbs.	23-30 Nm
Strut-to-spindle bolt	52-72 ft. lbs.	70-98 Nm
Top mount nut	30-43 ft. lbs.	41-58 Nm
Sway bar mounts	14-19 ft. lbs.	19-26 Nm
Sway bar links	22-30 ft. lbs.	30-40 Nm
Tie rod-to-spindle	75-102 ft. lbs.	102-135 Nm
Wheel hub retaining nut	170-192 ft. lbs.	230-260 Nm
Steering wheel retaining bolt	37 ft. lbs.	50 Nm
Steering yoke-to-steering gear shaft	15-20 ft. lbs.	20-27 Nm
Subframe bolts	81-110 ft. lbs.	110-150 Nm
Wheel lug nuts	62 ft. lbs.	85 Nm

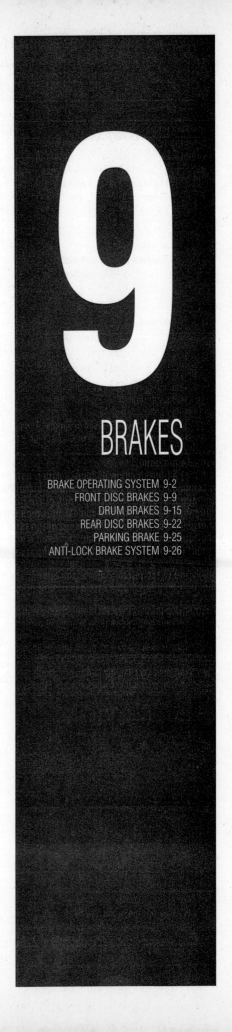

9

BRAKES

BRAKE OPERATING SYSTEM

Basic Operating Principles

Hydraulic systems are used to actuate the brakes of all modern automobiles. The system transports the power required to force the frictional surfaces of the braking system together from the pedal to the individual brake units at each wheel. A hydraulic system is used for two reasons.

First, fluid under pressure can be carried to all parts of an automobile by small pipes and flexible hoses without taking up a significant amount of room or posing routing problems.

Second, a great mechanical advantage can be given to the brake pedal end of the system, and the foot pressure required to actuate the brakes can be reduced by making the surface area of the master cylinder pistons smaller than that of any of the pistons in the wheel cylinders or calipers.

The master cylinder consists of a fluid reservoir along with a double cylinder and piston assembly. Double type master cylinders are designed to separate the front and rear braking systems hydraulically in case of a leak. The master cylinder coverts mechanical motion from the pedal into hydraulic pressure within the lines. This pressure is translated back into mechanical motion at the wheels by either the wheel cylinder (drum brakes) or the caliper (disc brakes).

Steel lines carry the brake fluid to a point on the vehicle's frame near each of the vehicle's wheels. The fluid is then carried to the calipers and wheel cylinders by flexible tubes in order to allow for suspension and steering movements.

In drum brake systems, each wheel cylinder contains two pistons, one at either end, which push outward in opposite directions and force the brake shoe into contact with the drum.

In disc brake systems, the cylinders are part of the calipers. At least one cylinder in each caliper is used to force the brake pads against the disc.

All pistons employ some type of seal, usually made of rubber, to minimize fluid leakage. A rubber dust boot seals the outer end of the cylinder against dust and dirt. The boot fits around the outer end of the piston on disc brake calipers, and around the brake actuating rod on wheel cylinders.

The hydraulic system operates as follows: When at rest, the entire system, from the piston(s) in the master cylinder to those in the wheel cylinders or calipers, is full of brake fluid. Upon application of the brake pedal, fluid trapped in front of the master cylinder piston(s) is forced through the lines to the wheel cylinders. Here, it forces the pistons outward, in the case of drum brakes, and inward toward the disc, in the case of disc brakes. The motion of the pistons is opposed by return springs mounted outside the cylinders in drum brakes, and by spring seals, in disc brakes.

Upon release of the brake pedal, a spring located inside the master cylinder immediately returns the master cylinder pistons to the normal position. The pistons contain check valves and the master cylinder has compensating ports drilled in it. These are uncovered as the pistons reach their normal position. The piston check valves allow fluid to flow toward the wheel cylinders or calipers as the pistons withdraw. Then, as the return springs force the brake pads or shoes into the released position, the excess fluid reservoir through the compensating ports. It is during the time the pedal is in the released position that any fluid that has leaked out of the system will be replaced through the compensating ports.

Dual circuit master cylinders employ two pistons, located one behind the other, in the same cylinder. The primary piston is actuated directly by mechanical linkage from the brake pedal through the power booster. The secondary piston is actuated by fluid trapped between the two pistons. If a leak develops in front of the secondary piston, it moves forward until it bottoms against the front of the master cylinder, and the fluid trapped between the pistons will operate the rear brakes. If the rear brakes develop a leak, the primary piston will move forward until direct contact with the secondary piston takes place, and it will force the secondary piston to actuate the front brakes. In either case, the brake pedal moves farther when the brakes are applied, and less braking power is available.

All dual circuit systems use a switch to warn the driver when only half of the brake system is operational. This switch is usually located in a valve body which is mounted on the firewall or the frame below the master cylinder. A hydraulic piston receives pressure from both circuits, each circuit's pressure being applied to one end of the piston. When the pressures are in balance, the piston remains stationary. When one circuit has a leak, however, the greater pressure in that circuit during application of the brakes will push the piston to one side, closing the switch and activating the brake warning light.

In disc brake systems, this valve body also contains a metering valve and, in some cases, a proportioning valve. The metering valve keeps pressure from traveling to the disc brakes on the front wheels until the brake shoes on the rear wheels have contacted the drums, ensuring that the front brakes will never be used alone. The proportioning valve controls the pressure to the rear brakes to lessen the chance of rear wheel lock-up during very hard braking.

Warning lights may be tested by depressing the brake pedal and holding it while opening one of the wheel cylinder bleeder screws. If this does not cause the light to go on, substitute a new lamp, make continuity checks, and, finally, replace the switch as necessary.

The hydraulic system may be checked for leaks by applying pressure to the pedal gradually and steadily. If the pedal sinks very slowly to the floor, the system has a leak. This is not to be confused with a springy or spongy feel due to the compression of air within the lines. If the system leaks, there will be a gradual change in the position of the pedal with a constant pressure.

Check for leaks along all lines and at wheel cylinders. If no external leaks are apparent, the problem is inside the master cylinder.

DISC BRAKES

Instead of the traditional expanding brakes that press outward against a circular drum, disc brake systems utilize a disc (rotor) with brake pads positioned on either side of it. An easily-seen analogy is the hand brake arrangement on a bicycle. The pads squeeze onto the rim of the bike wheel, slowing its motion. Automobile disc brakes use the identical principle but apply the braking effort to a separate disc instead of the wheel.

The disc (rotor) is a casting, usually equipped with cooling fins between the two braking surfaces. This enables air to circulate between the braking surfaces making them less sensitive to heat buildup and more resistant to fade. Dirt and water do not drastically affect braking action since contaminants are thrown off by the centrifugal action of the rotor or scraped off the by the pads. Also, the equal clamping action of the two brake pads tends to ensure uniform, straight line stops. Disc brakes are inherently self-adjusting. There are three general types of disc brake:

- Fixed caliper.
- Floating caliper.
- Sliding caliper.

The fixed caliper design uses two pistons mounted on either side of the rotor (in each side of the caliper). The caliper is mounted rigidly and does not move.

The sliding and floating designs are quite similar. In fact, these two types are often lumped together. In both designs, the pad on the inside of the rotor is moved into contact with the rotor by hydraulic force. The caliper, which is not held in a fixed position, moves slightly, bringing the outside pad into contact with the rotor. There are various methods of attaching floating calipers. Some pivot at the bottom or top, and some slide on mounting bolts. In any event, the end result is the same.

DRUM BRAKES

Drum brakes employ two brake shoes mounted on a stationary backing plate. These shoes are positioned inside a circular drum which rotates with the wheel assembly. The shoes are held in place by springs. This allows them to slide toward the drums (when they are applied) while keeping the linings and drums in alignment. The shoes are actuated by a wheel cylinder which is mounted at the top of the backing plate. When the brakes are applied, hydraulic pressure forces the wheel cylinder's actuating links outward. Since these links bear directly against the top of the brake shoes, the tops of the shoes are then forced against the inner side of the drum. This action forces the bottoms of the two shoes to contact the brake drum by rotating the entire assembly slightly (known as servo action). When pressure within the wheel cylinder is relaxed, return springs pull the shoes back away from the drum.

Most modern drum brakes are designed to self-adjust themselves during application when the vehicle is moving in reverse. This motion causes both shoes to rotate very slightly with the drum, rocking an adjusting lever, thereby causing rotation of the adjusting screw. Some drum brake systems are designed to self-adjust during application whenever the brakes are applied. This on-board adjustment system reduces the need for maintenance adjustments and keeps both the brake function and pedal feel satisfactory.

POWER BOOSTERS

Virtually all modern vehicles use a vacuum assisted power brake system to multiply the braking force and reduce pedal effort. Since vacuum is always available when the engine is operating, the system is simple and efficient. A vacuum diaphragm is located on the front of the master cylinder and assists the driver in applying the brakes, reducing both the effort and travel he must put into moving the brake pedal.

The vacuum diaphragm housing is normally connected to the intake manifold by a vacuum hose. A check valve is placed at the point where the hose enters the diaphragm housing, so that during periods of low manifold vacuum brakes assist will not be lost.

Depressing the brake pedal closes off the vacuum source and allows atmospheric pressure to enter on one side of the diaphragm. This causes the master cylinder pistons to move and apply the brakes. When the brake pedal is released, vacuum is applied to both sides of the diaphragm and springs return the diaphragm and master cylinder pistons to the released position.

If the vacuum supply fails, the brake pedal rod will contact the end of the master cylinder actuator rod and the system will apply the brakes without any power assistance. The driver will notice that much higher pedal effort is needed to stop the car and that the pedal feels harder than usual.

Vacuum Leak Test

1. Operate the engine at idle without touching the brake pedal for at least one minute.

2. Turn off the engine and wait one minute.
3. Test for the presence of assist vacuum by depressing the brake pedal and releasing it several times. If vacuum is present in the system, light application will produce less and less pedal travel. If there is no vacuum, air is leaking into the system.

System Operation Test

1. With the engine **OFF**, pump the brake pedal until the supply vacuum is entirely gone.
2. Put light, steady pressure on the brake pedal.
3. Start the engine and let it idle. If the system is operating correctly, the brake pedal should fall toward the floor if the constant pressure is maintained.

Power brake systems may be tested for hydraulic leaks just as ordinary systems are tested.

✳✳ WARNING

Clean, high quality brake fluid is essential to the safe and proper operation of the brake system. You should always buy the highest quality brake fluid that is available. If the brake fluid becomes contaminated, drain and flush the system, then refill the master cylinder with new fluid. Never reuse any brake fluid. Any brake fluid that is removed from the system should be discarded.

Troubleshooting the Brake System

Problem	Cause	Solution
Low brake pedal (excessive pedal travel required for braking action.)	• Excessive clearance between rear linings and drums caused by inoperative automatic adjusters	• Make 10 to 15 alternate forward and reverse brake stops to adjust brakes. If brake pedal does not come up, repair or replace adjuster parts as necessary.
	• Worn rear brakelining	• Inspect and replace lining if worn beyond minimum thickness specification
	• Bent, distorted brakeshoes, front or rear	• Replace brakeshoes in axle sets
	• Air in hydraulic system	• Remove air from system. Refer to Brake Bleeding.
Low brake pedal (pedal may go to floor with steady pressure applied.)	• Fluid leak in hydraulic system	• Fill master cylinder to fill line; have helper apply brakes and check calipers, wheel cylinders, differential valve tubes, hoses and fittings for leaks. Repair or replace as necessary.
	• Air in hydraulic system	• Remove air from system. Refer to Brake Bleeding.
	• Incorrect or non-recommended brake fluid (fluid evaporates at below normal temp)	• Flush hydraulic system with clean brake fluid. Refill with correct-type fluid.
	• Master cylinder piston seals worn, or master cylinder bore is scored, worn or corroded	• Repair or replace master cylinder
Low brake pedal (pedal goes to floor on first application—o.k. on subsequent applications.)	• Disc brake pads sticking on abutment surfaces of anchor plate. Caused by a build-up of dirt, rust, or corrosion on abutment surfaces	• Clean abutment surfaces
Fading brake pedal (pedal height decreases with steady pressure applied.)	• Fluid leak in hydraulic system	• Fill master cylinder reservoirs to fill mark, have helper apply brakes, check calipers, wheel cylinders, differential valve, tubes, hoses, and fittings for fluid leaks. Repair or replace parts as necessary.
	• Master cylinder piston seals worn, or master cylinder bore is scored, worn or corroded	• Repair or replace master cylinder
Decreasing brake pedal travel (pedal travel required for braking action decreases and may be accompanied by a hard pedal.)	• Caliper or wheel cylinder pistons sticking or seized	• Repair or replace the calipers, or wheel cylinders
	• Master cylinder compensator ports blocked (preventing fluid return to reservoirs) or pistons sticking or seized in master cylinder bore	• Repair or replace the master cylinder
	• Power brake unit binding internally	• Test unit according to the following procedure: (a) Shift transmission into neutral and start engine (b) Increase engine speed to 1500 rpm, close throttle and fully depress brake pedal (c) Slow release brake pedal and stop engine (d) Have helper remove vacuum check valve and hose from power unit. Observe for backward movement of brake pedal. (e) If the pedal moves backward, the power unit has an internal bind—replace power unit

TCCA9C01

Troubleshooting the Brake System (cont.)

Problem	Cause	Solution
Spongy brake pedal (pedal has abnormally soft, springy, spongy feel when depressed.)	• Air in hydraulic system	• Remove air from system. Refer to Brake Bleeding.
	• Brakeshoes bent or distorted	• Replace brakeshoes
	• Brakelining not yet seated with drums and rotors	• Burnish brakes
	• Rear drum brakes not properly adjusted	• Adjust brakes
Hard brake pedal (excessive pedal pressure required to stop vehicle. May be accompanied by brake fade.)	• Loose or leaking power brake unit vacuum hose	• Tighten connections or replace leaking hose
	• Incorrect or poor quality brakelining	• Replace with lining in axle sets
	• Bent, broken, distorted brakeshoes	• Replace brakeshoes
	• Calipers binding or dragging on mounting pins. Rear brakeshoes dragging on support plate.	• Replace mounting pins and bushings. Clean rust or burrs from rear brake support plate ledges and lubricate ledges with molydisulfide grease. NOTE: If ledges are deeply grooved or scored, do not attempt to sand or grind them smooth—replace support plate.
	• Caliper, wheel cylinder, or master cylinder pistons sticking or seized	• Repair or replace parts as necessary
	• Power brake unit vacuum check valve malfunction	• Test valve according to the following procedure: (a) Start engine, increase engine speed to 1500 rpm, close throttle and immediately stop engine (b) Wait at least 90 seconds then depress brake pedal (c) If brakes are not vacuum assisted for 2 or more applications, check valve is faulty
	• Power brake unit has internal bind	• Test unit according to the following procedure: (a) With engine stopped, apply brakes several times to exhaust all vacuum in system (b) Shift transmission into neutral, depress brake pedal and start engine (c) If pedal height decreases with foot pressure and less pressure is required to hold pedal in applied position, power unit vacuum system is operating normally. Test power unit. If power unit exhibits a bind condition, replace the power unit.
	• Master cylinder compensator ports (at bottom of reservoirs) blocked by dirt, scale, rust, or have small burrs (blocked ports prevent fluid return to reservoirs).	• Repair or replace master cylinder CAUTION: Do not attempt to clean blocked ports with wire, pencils, or similar implements. Use compressed air only.
	• Brake hoses, tubes, fittings clogged or restricted	• Use compressed air to check or unclog parts. Replace any damaged parts.
	• Brake fluid contaminated with improper fluids (motor oil, transmission fluid, causing rubber components to swell and stick in bores	• Replace all rubber components, combination valve and hoses. Flush entire brake system with DOT 3 brake fluid or equivalent.
	• Low engine vacuum	• Adjust or repair engine

TCCA9C02

Troubleshooting the Brake System (cont.)

Problem	Cause	Solution
Grabbing brakes (severe reaction to brake pedal pressure.)	• Brakelining(s) contaminated by grease or brake fluid	• Determine and correct cause of contamination and replace brakeshoes in axle sets
	• Parking brake cables incorrectly adjusted or seized	• Adjust cables. Replace seized cables.
	• Incorrect brakelining or lining loose on brakeshoes	• Replace brakeshoes in axle sets
	• Caliper anchor plate bolts loose	• Tighten bolts
	• Rear brakeshoes binding on support plate ledges	• Clean and lubricate ledges. Replace support plate(s) if ledges are deeply grooved. Do not attempt to smooth ledges by grinding.
	• Incorrect or missing power brake reaction disc	• Install correct disc
	• Rear brake support plates loose	• Tighten mounting bolts
Dragging brakes (slow or incomplete release of brakes)	• Brake pedal binding at pivot	• Loosen and lubricate
	• Power brake unit has internal bind	• Inspect for internal bind. Replace unit if internal bind exists.
	• Parking brake cables incorrectly adjusted or seized	• Adjust cables. Replace seized cables.
	• Rear brakeshoe return springs weak or broken	• Replace return springs. Replace brakeshoe if necessary in axle sets.
	• Automatic adjusters malfunctioning	• Repair or replace adjuster parts as required
	• Caliper, wheel cylinder or master cylinder pistons sticking or seized	• Repair or replace parts as necessary
	• Master cylinder compensating ports blocked (fluid does not return to reservoirs).	• Use compressed air to clear ports. Do not use wire, pencils, or similar objects to open blocked ports.
Vehicle moves to one side when brakes are applied	• Incorrect front tire pressure	• Inflate to recommended cold (reduced load) inflation pressure
	• Worn or damaged wheel bearings	• Replace worn or damaged bearings
	• Brakelining on one side contaminated	• Determine and correct cause of contamination and replace brakelining in axle sets
	• Brakeshoes on one side bent, distorted, or lining loose on shoe	• Replace brakeshoes in axle sets
	• Support plate bent or loose on one side	• Tighten or replace support plate
	• Brakelining not yet seated with drums or rotors	• Burnish brakelining
	• Caliper anchor plate loose on one side	• Tighten anchor plate bolts
	• Caliper piston sticking or seized	• Repair or replace caliper
	• Brakelinings water soaked	• Drive vehicle with brakes lightly applied to dry linings
	• Loose suspension component attaching or mounting bolts	• Tighten suspension bolts. Replace worn suspension components.
	• Brake combination valve failure	• Replace combination valve
Chatter or shudder when brakes are applied (pedal pulsation and roughness may also occur.)	• Brakeshoes distorted, bent, contaminated, or worn	• Replace brakeshoes in axle sets
	• Caliper anchor plate or support plate loose	• Tighten mounting bolts
	• Excessive thickness variation of rotor(s)	• Refinish or replace rotors in axle sets

TCCA9C03

Brake Light Switch

REMOVAL & INSTALLATION

▶ **See Figure 1**

1. Disconnect the negative battery cable.
2. Unplug the connector on the brake light switch.
3. Rotate the switch 90° counterclockwise and pull outward to remove it.

To install:

4. Place the switch into place and rotate it 90° clockwise.
5. Attach the connector to the brake light switch.
6. Connect the negative battery cable.

Master Cylinder

REMOVAL & INSTALLATION

▶ **See Figures 2, 3, 4, 5 and 6**

✳✳ CAUTION

Brake fluid contains polyglycol ethers and polyglycols. Avoid contact with the eyes and wash your hands thoroughly after handling brake fluid. If you do get brake fluid in your eyes, flush your eyes with clean, running water for 15 minutes. If eye irritation persists, or if you have taken brake fluid internally, IMMEDIATELY seek medical assistance.

1. Disconnect the negative battery cable.
2. Apply the brake pedal several times to exhaust all vacuum in the brake booster.

3. Disconnect the fluid level indicator connector.
4. If equipped with a manual transmission, remove the hose for the hydraulic clutch master cylinder.
5. Remove the brake lines from the primary and secondary outlet ports on the master cylinder.
6. Remove the 2 nuts securing the master cylinder to the power brake booster.
7. Slide the master cylinder forward and remove it from the vehicle.

To install:

8. Prior to installation, bench bleed the new master cylinder as follows:

   a. Secure the master cylinder in a soft-jawed vise. Be careful not to damage or distort the master cylinder housing.

   b. Attach short lengths of brake tubing to the master cylinder outlet ports, positioning the ends of the tubing inside the master cylinder reservoir.

   c. Fill the master cylinder reservoir with fresh clean brake fluid, making sure the ends of the brake tubing are submerged.

   d. Using a suitable tool to push on the master cylinder piston, stroke the piston in the master cylinder bore until no more air bubbles are seen in the master cylinder fluid reservoir.

   e. Remove the short lengths of brake tubing and install temporary plugs in the master cylinder cylinder outlet ports, to keep fluid from spilling.

   f. Reinstall the cap on the fluid reservoir and remove the master cylinder from the vise.

9. Position the master cylinder onto the studs of the power brake booster.
10. Reinstall the 2 retaining nuts and torque to 15–18 ft. lbs. (21–29 Nm).
11. Reinstall the primary and secondary brake lines to the master cylinder outlet ports and torque to 10–18 ft. lbs. (14–22 Nm).
12. If equipped with a manual transmission, connect the hose to the hydraulic clutch master cylinder.
13. Reconnect the brake warning indicator switch connector.
14. Fill the master cylinder with the proper brake fluid to just below the full line.

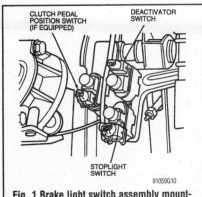

Fig. 1 Brake light switch assembly mounting

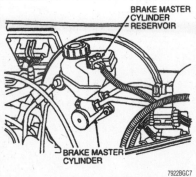

Fig. 2 View of master cylinder and components

Fig. 3 Unplug the fluid level indicator connector

Fig. 4 Remove the brake lines from the master cylinder

Fig. 5 Remove the two master cylinder-to-booster retaining nuts . . .

Fig. 6 . . . and remove the master cylinder from the vehicle

✳✳ WARNING

Clean, high quality brake fluid is essential to the safe and proper operation of the brake system. You should always buy the highest quality brake fluid that is available. If the brake fluid becomes contaminated, drain and flush the system, then refill the master cylinder with new fluid. Never reuse any brake fluid. Any brake fluid that is removed from the system should be discarded. Also, do not allow any brake fluid to come in contact with a painted surface; it will damage the paint.

15. Bleed the brake system starting with the right rear wheel and working to the left front. Top off the master cylinder when complete.
16. Road test the vehicle and check for proper brake system operation.

BENCH BLEEDING

✳✳ CAUTION

Brake fluid contains polyglycol ethers and polyglycols. Avoid contact with the eyes and wash your hands thoroughly after handling brake fluid. If you do get brake fluid in your eyes, flush your eyes with clean, running water for 15 minutes. If eye irritation persists, or if you have taken brake fluid internally, IMMEDIATELY seek medical assistance.

✳✳ WARNING

All new master cylinders should be bench bled prior to installation. Bleeding a new master cylinder on the vehicle is not a good idea. With air trapped inside, the master cylinder piston may bottom in the bore and possibly cause internal damage.

1. Secure the master cylinder in a bench vise using soft jaws.
2. Remove the master cylinder reservoir cap.
3. Manufacture or purchase bleeding tubes and install them on the master cylinder as illustrated.
4. Fill the master cylinder reservoir with clean, fresh brake fluid until the level is within 0.25 in. of the reservoir top.

➡Ensure the bleeding tubes are below the level of the brake fluid, otherwise air may get into the system making your bleeding efforts ineffective.

5. Use a blunt tipped rod (a long socket extension works well) to slowly depress the master cylinder piston. Make sure the piston travels full its full stroke.
6. As the piston is depressed, bubbles will come out of the bleeding tubes. Continue depressing and releasing the piston until all bubbles cease.
7. Refill the master cylinder with fluid.

✳✳ WARNING

Clean, high quality brake fluid is essential to the safe and proper operation of the brake system. You should always buy the highest quality brake fluid that is available. If the brake fluid becomes contaminated, drain and flush the system, then refill the master cylinder with new fluid. Never reuse any brake fluid. Any brake fluid that is removed from the system should be discarded. Also, do not allow any brake fluid to come in contact with a painted surface; it will damage the paint.

8. Remove the bleeding tubes.
9. Install the master cylinder reservoir cap.
10. Install the master cylinder on the vehicle.

Power Brake Booster

REMOVAL & INSTALLATION

▶ See Figures 7, 8 and 9

✳✳ CAUTION

Brake fluid contains polyglycol ethers and polyglycols. Avoid contact with the eyes and wash your hands thoroughly after handling brake fluid. If you do get brake fluid in your eyes, flush your eyes with clean, running water for 15 minutes. If eye irritation persists, or if you have taken brake fluid internally, IMMEDIATELY seek medical assistance.

1. Disconnect the negative battery cable.
2. Remove the master cylinder assembly.
3. Disconnect the vacuum supply hose from the booster.
4. Remove the four brake booster retaining nuts.
5. Gently pull the booster forward, and while holding the booster assembly away from the firewall, have an assistant remove the push rod retainer from the push rod.
6. Remove the booster assembly.
   To install:
7. Position the brake booster onto the vehicle and have an assistant guide the push rod onto the retainer.
8. Place the booster onto the mounting studs and tighten the retaining nuts to 29 ft. lbs. (40 Nm).
9. Connect the vacuum supply hose to the booster.
10. Install the master cylinder assembly.
11. Connect the negative battery cable.
12. Bleed the brake system.

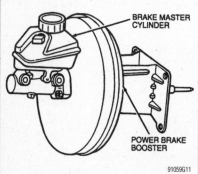

Fig. 7 Brake booster assembly with master cylinder attached

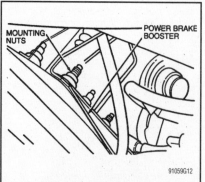

Fig. 8 The brake booster is held by four retaining bolts

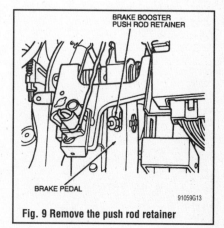

Fig. 9 Remove the push rod retainer

Brake Pressure Control Valves

REMOVAL & INSTALLATION

➡This procedure applies only to vehicles without Anti-Lock brakes. On vehicles with Anti-Lock brakes, the valve is contained inside the Anti-Lock hydraulic control unit. If equipped, the brake pressure control valves are located on the outlet ports of the master cylinder.

❋❋ CAUTION

Brake fluid contains polyglycol ethers and polyglycols. Avoid contact with the eyes and wash your hands thoroughly after handling brake fluid. If you do get brake fluid in your eyes, flush your eyes with clean, running water for 15 minutes. If eye irritation persists, or if you have taken brake fluid internally, IMMEDIATELY seek medical assistance.

1. Remove the brake lines from the pressure control valves.
2. Unscrew the valves from the master cylinder.

To install:

3. Install the valves into the master cylinder.
4. Install the brake lines into the valves.
5. Bleed the brake system.

Brake Hoses and Lines

Metal lines and rubber brake hoses should be checked frequently for leaks and external damage. Metal lines are particularly prone to crushing and kinking under the vehicle. Any such deformation can restrict the proper flow of fluid and therefore impair braking at the wheels. Rubber hoses should be checked for cracking or scraping; such damage can create a weak spot in the hose and it could fail under pressure.

Any time the lines are removed or disconnected, extreme cleanliness must be observed. Clean all joints and connections before disassembly (use a stiff bristle brush and clean brake fluid); be sure to plug the lines and ports as soon as they are opened. New lines and hoses should be flushed clean with brake fluid before installation to remove any contamination.

REMOVAL & INSTALLATION

◆ **See Figures 10 thru 16**

1. Disconnect the negative battery cable.
2. Raise and safely support the vehicle on jackstands.
3. Remove any wheel and tire assemblies necessary for access to the particular line you are removing.
4. Thoroughly clean the surrounding area at the joints to be disconnected.

Fig. 10 Rear brake hose connection location on strut

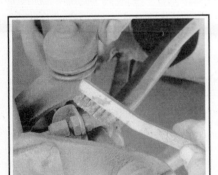

Fig. 11 Use a brush to clean the fittings of any debris

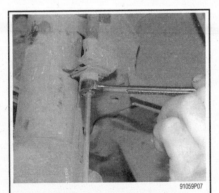

Fig. 12 Using a flare nut wrench, loosen the connection

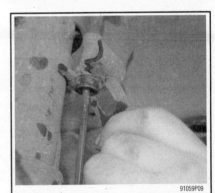

Fig. 13 The connection is held to the strut by a clip

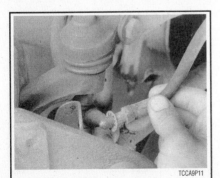

Fig. 14 Any gaskets/crush washers should be replaced with new ones during installation

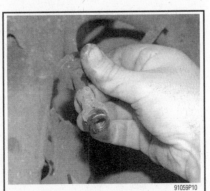

Fig. 15 Inspect the female end of the fitting before reconnecting the lines

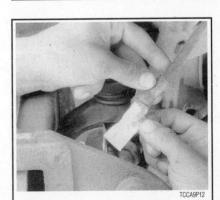

Fig. 16 Tape or plug the line to prevent contamination

Brake fluid contains polyglycol ethers and polyglycols. Avoid contact with the eyes and wash your hands thoroughly after handling brake fluid. If you do get brake fluid in your eyes, flush your eyes with clean, running water for 15 minutes. If eye irritation persists, or if you have taken brake fluid internally, IMMEDIATELY seek medical assistance.

5. Place a suitable catch pan under the joint to be disconnected.

6. Using two wrenches (one to hold the joint and one to turn the fitting), disconnect the hose or line to be replaced.

7. Disconnect the other end of the line or hose, moving the drain pan if necessary. Always use a back-up wrench to avoid damaging the fitting.

8. Disconnect any retaining clips or brackets holding the line and remove the line from the vehicle.

➡ If the brake system is to remain open for more time than it takes to swap lines, tape or plug each remaining clip and port to keep contaminants out and fluid in.

To install:

9. Install the new line or hose, starting with the end farthest from the master cylinder. Connect the other end, then confirm that both fittings are correctly threaded and turn smoothly using finger pressure. Make sure the new line will not rub against any other part. Brake lines must be at least ½ in. (13mm) from the steering column and other moving parts. Any protective shielding or insulators must be reinstalled in the original location.

❊❊❊ **WARNING**

Make sure the hose is NOT kinked or touching any part of the frame or suspension after installation. These conditions may cause the hose to fail prematurely.

10. Using two wrenches as before, tighten each fitting.

11. Install any retaining clips or brackets on the lines.

12. If removed, install the wheel and tire assemblies, then carefully lower the vehicle to the ground.

13. Refill the brake master cylinder reservoir with clean, fresh brake fluid, meeting DOT 3 specifications. Properly bleed the brake system.

❊❊❊ **WARNING**

Clean, high quality brake fluid is essential to the safe and proper operation of the brake system. You should always buy the highest quality brake fluid that is available. If the brake fluid becomes contaminated, drain and flush the system, then refill the master cylinder with new fluid. Never reuse any brake fluid. Any brake fluid that is removed from the system should be discarded. Also, do not allow any brake fluid to come in contact with a painted surface; it will damage the paint.

14. Connect the negative battery cable.

Bleeding the Brake System

▶ See Figures 17, 18 and 19

Brake fluid contains polyglycol ethers and polyglycols. Avoid contact with the eyes and wash your hands thoroughly after handling brake fluid. If you do get brake fluid in your eyes, flush your eyes with clean, running water for 15 minutes. If eye irritation persists, or if you have taken brake fluid internally, IMMEDIATELY seek medical assistance.

When any part of the hydraulic system has been disconnected for repair or replacement, air may get into the lines and cause spongy pedal action (because air can be compressed and brake fluid cannot). To correct this condition, it is necessary to bleed the hydraulic system so to be sure all air is purged.

When bleeding the brake system, bleed one brake cylinder at a time, beginning at the cylinder with the longest hydraulic line (farthest from the master cylinder) first. ALWAYS Keep the master cylinder reservoir filled with brake fluid during the bleeding operation. Never use brake fluid that has been drained from the hydraulic system, no matter how clean it is.

The primary and secondary hydraulic brake systems are separate and are bled independently. During the bleeding operation, do not allow the reservoir to run dry. Keep the master cylinder reservoir filled with brake fluid.

1. Clean all dirt from around the master cylinder fill cap, remove the cap and fill the master cylinder with brake fluid until the level is within ¼ in. (6mm) of the top edge of the reservoir.

2. Clean the bleeder screws at all 4 wheels. The bleeder screws are located on the back of the brake backing plate (drum brakes) and on the top of the brake calipers (disc brakes).

3. Attach a length of rubber hose over the bleeder screw and place the other end of the hose in a glass jar, submerged in brake fluid.

4. Open the bleeder screw ½–¾ turn. Have an assistant slowly depress the brake pedal.

5. Close the bleeder screw and tell your assistant to allow the brake pedal to return slowly. Continue this process to purge all air from the system.

6. When bubbles cease to appear at the end of the bleeder hose, close the bleeder screw and remove the hose.

7. Check the master cylinder fluid level and add fluid accordingly. Do this after bleeding each wheel.

❊❊❊ **WARNING**

Clean, high quality brake fluid is essential to the safe and proper operation of the brake system. You should always buy the highest quality brake fluid that is available. If the brake fluid becomes contaminated, drain and flush the system, then refill the master cylinder with new fluid. Never reuse any brake fluid. Any brake fluid that is removed from the system should be discarded. Also, do not allow any brake fluid to come in contact with a painted surface; it will damage the paint.

8. Repeat the bleeding operation at the remaining 3 wheels, ending with the one closet to the master cylinder.

9. Fill the master cylinder reservoir to the proper level.

91059P30

Fig. 17 Remove the bleeder screw cap

91059P31

Fig. 18 Install a hose and container to the bleeder screw

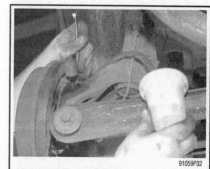

91059P32

Fig. 19 Slowly crack open the bleeder screw while an assistant presses down the brake pedal

FRONT DISC BRAKES

♦ See Figure 20

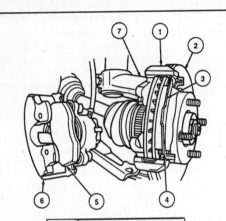

Item	Description
1	Front Disc Brake Caliper Anchor Plate
2	Front Disc Brake Rotor
3	Brake Shoe and Lining Clip (Part of 2001)
4	Outboard Brake Shoe and Lining
5	Inboard Brake Shoe and Lining
6	Disc Brake Caliper
7	Front Wheel Knuckle

91059G14

Fig. 20 Front disc brake exploded view

Brake Pads

REMOVAL & INSTALLATION

♦ See Figures 21 thru 34

✳ CAUTION

Older brake pads or shoes may contain asbestos, which has been determined to be cancer causing agent. Never clean the brake surfaces with compressed air! Avoid inhaling any dust from any brake surface! When cleaning brake surfaces, use a commercially available brake cleaning fluid.

1. Remove ½ of the brake fluid from the master cylinder reservoir.
2. Raise and safely support the vehicle.
3. Remove the wheel and tire assembly.
4. Remove the outer disc brake pad spring clip (anti-rattle clip).
5. Remove the 2 locating pin covers and remove the locating pins.
6. Free the hose from its mounting on the strut.
7. Lift the caliper off of the brake rotor and tie it off to prevent damage to the brake hose.
8. Remove the outboard disc brake pad from the anchor plate.
9. Remove the inboard disc brake pad from the brake caliper.

To install:

10. If installing new disc brake pads, use a C-clamp or similar tool to push the caliper piston into the caliper bore. This will allow room for the new pads.
11. Place the inboard disc brake pad into the caliper.
12. Place the outboard disc brake pad into position in the anchor plate.
13. Position the disc brake caliper onto the rotor.
14. Reinstall the 2 locating pins and torque to 20 ft. lbs. (28 Nm).
15. Reinstall the caliper locating pin covers.

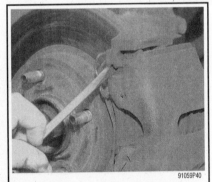

91059P40

Fig. 21 Remove the brake pad spring by prying one end from the caliper

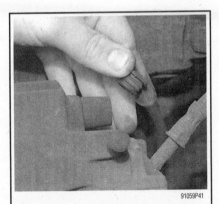

91059P41

Fig. 22 Remove the locating pin covers

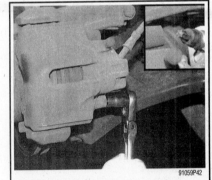

91059P42

Fig. 23 The locating pins are a T40 Torx headed bolt

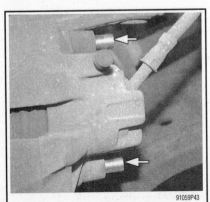

91059P43

Fig. 24 Remove the locating pins and . . .

91059P44

Fig. 25 . . . remove the caliper from the anchor plate

91059P63

Fig. 26 Use mechanicís wire or a similar device to support the caliper out of the way

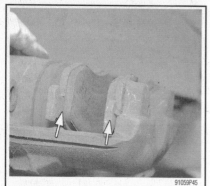

Fig. 27 The pads will most likely stay in the caliper

Fig. 28 Remove the pads from the caliper

Fig. 29 Thoroughly clean the caliper and . . .

Fig. 30 . . . the anchor plate of any dust, dirt or build-up

Fig. 31 The caliper piston can be depressed using a special tool, such as this one from Lisle® or . . .

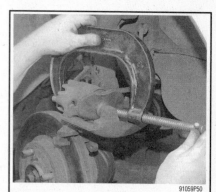

Fig. 32 . . . a large C-clamp will also work

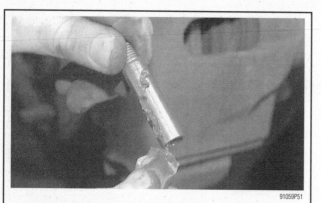

Fig. 33 Lubricate the locating pins with a quality lubricant

16. Secure the brake hose to its support on the strut.

17. Reinstall the disc brake pad spring clip.

18. Reinstall the wheel and tire assembly. Torque the lug nuts to 62 ft. lbs. (85 Nm).

19. Lower the vehicle.

20. Pump the brake pedal several times to achieve a good pedal before attempting to move the vehicle.

21. Check the brake fluid level in the master cylinder fluid reservoir and add fluid as necessary.

22. Road test the vehicle and check for proper brake system operation.

INSPECTION

▶ See Figure 35

Inspect the brake pads for wear using a ruler or Vernier caliper. Compare measurements to the brake specifications chart. If the lining is thinner than

Fig. 34 A quality disc brake quiet or equivalent should be applied to the new pads

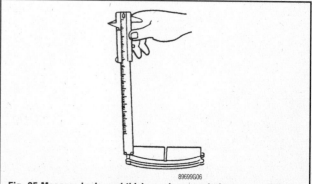

Fig. 35 Measure brake pad thickness in several places around the pad with a ruler or Vernier caliper

specification or there is evidence of the lining being contaminated by brake fluid or oil, make the necessary repairs and replace all brake pad assemblies (a complete axle set).

Brake Caliper

REMOVAL & INSTALLATION

▶ See Figures 36 thru 42

1. Raise and safely support the vehicle.
2. Remove the wheel and tire assembly.
3. Remove the outer disc brake pad spring clip (anti-rattle clip).
4. Remove the 2 locator pin covers and remove the locator pins.

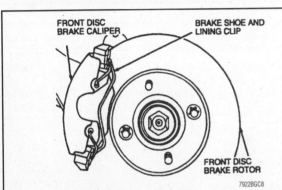

Fig. 36 Position of disc brake pad (brake shoe and lining) spring clip

✳✳ CAUTION

Brake fluid contains polyglycol ethers and polyglycols. Avoid contact with the eyes and wash your hands thoroughly after handling brake fluid. If you do get brake fluid in your eyes, flush your eyes with clean, running water for 15 minutes. If eye irritation persists, or if you have taken brake fluid internally, IMMEDIATELY seek medical assistance.

5. Free the hose from its mounting on the strut.
6. Lift the caliper off of the brake rotor.
7. Remove the inboard disc brake pad from the caliper.
8. If the brake caliper is to be removed from the vehicle, place a pan under the caliper to catch the brake fluid for proper disposal. Disconnect the brake hose at the caliper and allow to drain.

✳✳ CAUTION

Brake fluid contains polyglycol ethers and polyglycols. Avoid contact with skin and eyes.

9. Remove the brake caliper.
10. If the caliper is not to be serviced, tie off the caliper to prevent strain on the brake hose.
To install:
11. If removed, install the brake hose onto the caliper. Torque the fitting to 10 ft. lbs. (14 Nm).
12. Position the inboard disc brake pad into the caliper.
13. Make sure that the outboard disc brake pad is positioned properly.
14. Reinstall the caliper over the brake rotor and position onto the caliper anchor plate.
15. Reinstall the 2 caliper locator pins and torque to 20 ft. lbs. (28 Nm).
16. Reinstall the caliper locator pin covers.

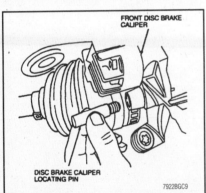

Fig. 37 View of disc brake caliper locating pin

Fig. 38 A flare nut wrench is recommended to loosen the brake caliper hose connection

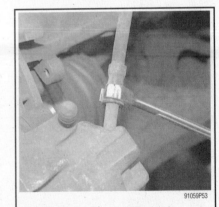

Fig. 39 Loosen the connection and . . .

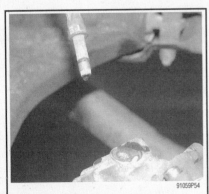

Fig. 40 . . . remove the line from the caliper

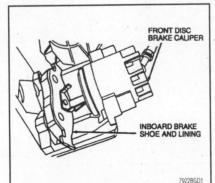

Fig. 41 View of inboard disc brake pad (brake shoe and lining)

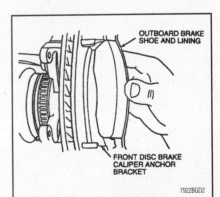

Fig. 42 Positioning the outboard disc brake pad (brake shoe and lining)

17. Reinstall the outer disc brake pad spring clip.
18. Reconnect the brake hose to the front strut.
19. Bleed the brake system of air. Top off the master cylinder when complete.

✳✳ WARNING

Clean, high quality brake fluid is essential to the safe and proper operation of the brake system. You should always buy the highest quality brake fluid that is available. If the brake fluid becomes contaminated, drain and flush the system, then refill the master cylinder with new fluid. Never reuse any brake fluid. Any brake fluid that is removed from the system should be discarded. Also, do not allow any brake fluid to come in contact with a painted surface; it will damage the paint.

20. If the brake pedal feels spongy, repeat the brake bleeding procedure.
21. Reinstall the wheel and tire assembly. Torque the lug nuts to 62 ft. lbs. (85 Nm).
22. Lower the vehicle.
23. Pump the brake pedal several times to position the brake pads before attempting to move the vehicle.
24. Road test the vehicle and check for proper brake system operation.

OVERHAUL

▶ See Figures 43 thru 50

➡Some vehicles may be equipped dual piston calipers. The procedure to overhaul the caliper is essentially the same with the exception of multiple pistons, O-rings and dust boots.

1. Remove the caliper from the vehicle and place on a clean workbench.

✳✳ CAUTION

NEVER place your fingers in front of the pistons in an attempt to catch or protect the pistons when applying compressed air. This could result in personal injury!

➡Depending upon the vehicle, there are two different ways to remove the piston from the caliper. Refer to the brake pad replacement procedure to make sure you have the correct procedure for your vehicle.

2. The first method is as follows:
   a. Stuff a shop towel or a block of wood into the caliper to catch the piston.

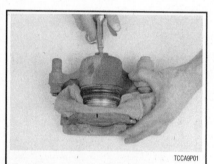

TCCA9P01

Fig. 43 For some types of calipers, use compressed air to drive the piston out of the caliper, but make sure to keep your fingers clear

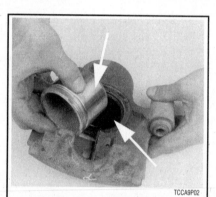

TCCA9P02

Fig. 44 Withdraw the piston from the caliper bore

TCCA9P03

Fig. 45 On some vehicles, you must remove the anti-rattle clip

TCCSA9P04

Fig. 46 Use a prytool to carefully pry around the edge of the boot . . .

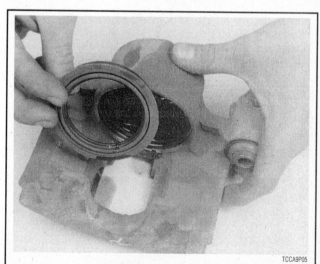

TCCA9P05

Fig. 47 . . . then remove the boot from the caliper housing, taking care not to score or damage the bore

Fig. 48 Use extreme caution when removing the piston seal; DO NOT scratch the caliper bore

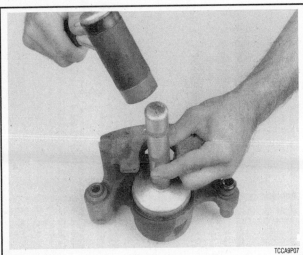

Fig. 49 Use the proper size driving tool and a mallet to properly seal the boots in the caliper housing

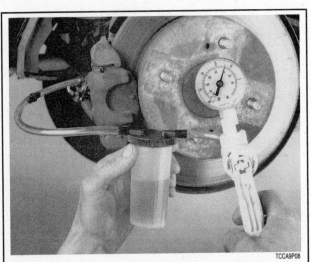

Fig. 50 There are tools, such as this Mighty-Vac, available to assist in proper brake system bleeding

b. Remove the caliper piston using compressed air applied into the caliper inlet hole. Inspect the piston for scoring, nicks, corrosion and/or worn or damaged chrome plating. The piston must be replaced if any of these conditions are found.

3. For the second method, you must rotate the piston to retract it from the caliper.

4. If equipped, remove the anti-rattle clip.

5. Use a prytool to remove the caliper boot, being careful not to scratch the housing bore.

6. Remove the piston seals from the groove in the caliper bore.

7. Carefully loosen the brake bleeder valve cap and valve from the caliper housing.

8. Inspect the caliper bores, pistons and mounting threads for scoring or excessive wear.

9. Use crocus cloth to polish out light corrosion from the piston and bore.

10. Clean all parts with denatured alcohol and dry with compressed air.

To assemble:

11. Lubricate and install the bleeder valve and cap.

12. Install the new seals into the caliper bore grooves, making sure they are not twisted.

13. Lubricate the piston bore.

14. Install the pistons and boots into the bores of the calipers and push to the bottom of the bores.

15. Use a suitable driving tool to seat the boots in the housing.

16. Install the caliper in the vehicle.

17. Install the wheel and tire assembly, then carefully lower the vehicle.

18. Properly bleed the brake system.

Brake Disc (Rotor)

REMOVAL & INSTALLATION

◆ See Figures 51, 52 and 53

1. Raise and safely support the vehicle.

2. Remove the wheel and tire assembly.

3. Remove the outer disc brake pad spring clip (anti-rattle clip).

4. Remove the 2 locator pin covers and remove the locator pins.

5. Free the brake hose from its mounting on the strut.

6. Lift the caliper off of the brake rotor and tie it off to prevent damage to the brake hose.

7. Remove the outboard disc brake pad from the anchor plate.

8. Remove the 2 bolts securing the anchor plate and remove the anchor plate.

9. Remove the disc brake rotor.

10. Inspect the brake rotor surfaces for scoring, wear or other damage. Machine or replace the brake rotor as necessary.

Fig. 51 Remove the anchor plate retaining bolts . . .

Fig. 52 . . . and remove the anchor plate

Fig. 53 View of front caliper anchor plate and bolts

To install:

11. If using a new disc brake rotor, thoroughly clean the surfaces to remove any protective coating before assembly.

12. Position the disc brake rotor onto the wheel hub.

13. Reinstall the anchor plate and secure with the 2 bolts. Torque the bolts to 88 ft. lbs. (120 Nm).

14. Set the outboard disc brake pad into position on the anchor plate.

15. Position the caliper over the brake rotor and install it to the anchor plate with the 2 locator pins. Torque the locator pins to 20 ft. lbs. (28 Nm).

16. Reinstall the brake caliper locator pin covers.

17. Secure the brake hose to its support on the strut.

18. Reinstall the disc brake pad spring clip.

19. Reinstall the wheel and tire assembly. Torque the lug nuts to 62 ft. lbs. (85 Nm).

20. Lower the vehicle.

21. Pump the brake pedal several times to achieve a good pedal before attempting to move the vehicle.

22. Road test the vehicle and check the brake system for proper operation.

INSPECTION

▶ **See Figures 54 and 55**

Rotor thickness should be measured any time a brake inspection is done. Rotor thickness can be measured using a brake rotor micrometer or Vernier caliper. Measure the rotor thickness in several places around the rotor. Compare the thickness to the specifications chart found at the end of this section.

The run-out of the brake rotor should be checked any time a vibration during braking occurs. Excessive run-out can be caused by a build-up of rust scale or other particles on the rotor or hub surfaces. Remove the rotor and thoroughly clean the hub and rotor-to-hub mounting surface on the back of the rotor. Mount a dial indicator to a suspension member and zero the indicator stylus on the face of the rotor. Rotate the rotor 360 degrees by hand and record the run-out.

Compare measurements to the brake specifications chart. If the thickness and run-out do not meet specifications, replace the rotor.

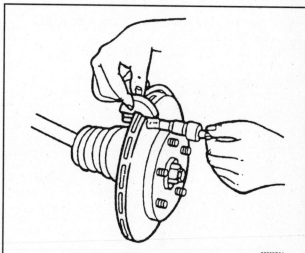

Fig. 54 Check brake rotor thickness in several places around the rotor

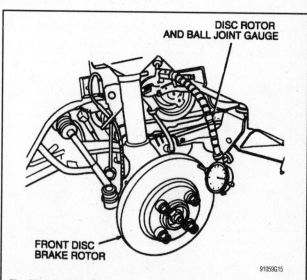

DISC ROTOR
AND BALL JOINT GAUGE

FRONT DISC
BRAKE ROTOR

Fig. 55 mount the dial indicator and zero the indicator

DRUM BRAKES

DRUM BRAKE COMPONENTS—ASSEMBLED

1. Wheel cylinder
2. Adjusting strut and quadrant
3. Parking brake cable
4. Shoe retracting springs
5. Parking brake return spring
6. Brake shoe retaining pin and spring
7. Brake shoe
8. Brake shoe and parking brake lever
9. Anchor block
10. Backing plate

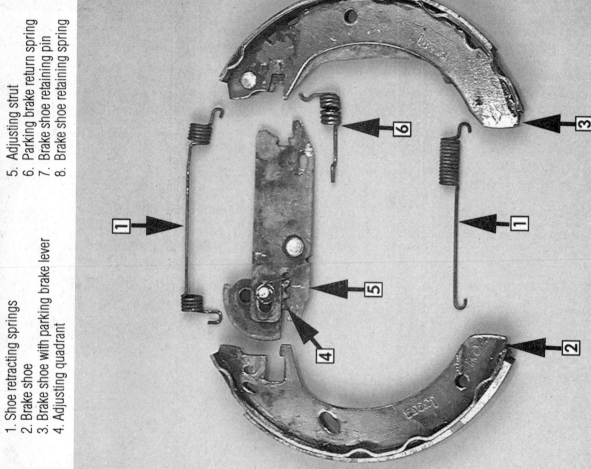

DRUM BRAKE COMPONENTS—DISASSEMBLED

1. Shoe retracting springs
2. Brake shoe
3. Brake shoe with parking brake lever
4. Adjusting quadrant
5. Adjusting strut
6. Parking brake return spring
7. Brake shoe retaining pin
8. Brake shoe retaining spring

Brake Drums

REMOVAL & INSTALLATION

▶ See Figures 56, 57 and 58

1. Raise and safely support the vehicle.
2. Remove the wheel and tire assembly.
3. Remove the brake drum retainers, if installed.
4. Grasp the brake drum and remove.
5. If the drum will not slide off with light force, then the brake shoes will need to be backed off as follows:

    a. Remove the rubber plug on the backing plate and insert a screwdriver or small brake adjusting tool into the slot to contact the brake strut and quadrant.

    b. A forward motion of the tool will separate the quadrant from the knurled wheel and allow the brake shoes to retract.

    c. Remove the brake drum.

To install:

6. Make sure the brake drum and shoes are clean of any oils or protective coatings.
7. Position the brake drum onto the wheel hub.
8. Install new brake drum retainers if available.
9. Reinstall the wheel and tire assembly. Torque the lug nuts to 62 ft. lbs. (85 Nm).
10. Lower the vehicle.
11. Work the parking brake control several times to adjust the rear brake shoes.
12. Pump the brake pedal several times to assure a good pedal before attempting to move the vehicle.
13. Road test the vehicle and check for proper brake system operation.

INSPECTION

▶ See Figures 59, 60 and 61

Check that there are no cracks or chips in the braking surface. Excessive bluing indicates overheating and a replacement drum is needed. The drum can be machined to remove minor damage and to establish a rounded braking surface on a warped drum. Never exceed the maximum oversize of the drum when machining the braking surface.

The brake drum inside diameter and run-out can be measured using a brake drum micrometer. The drum should be measured every time a brake inspection is performed. Take the inside diameter readings at points 90° apart from each other on the drum to measure the run-out. The maximum inside diameter is stamped on the rim of the drum or on the inside above the lug nut stud holes and is also contained in the brake specifications chart at the end of this section.

Brake Shoes

INSPECTION

▶ See Figure 62

Inspect the brake shoes for wear using a ruler or Vernier caliper. Compare measurements to the brake specifications chart. If the lining is thinner than specification or there is evidence of the lining being contaminated by brake fluid or oil, repair the leak and replace all brake shoe assemblies (a complete axle set). In addition to the shoes inspect all springs and brake shoe hardware for wear and replace as necessary.

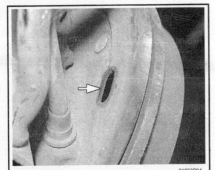

Fig. 56 The shoes can be backed off through this slot located in the backing plate

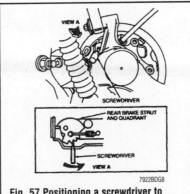

Fig. 57 Positioning a screwdriver to release the brake shoes

Fig. 58 Remove the drum from the hub

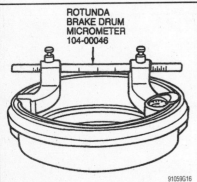

Fig. 59 Measure the drum using a micrometer especially for drums

Fig. 60 The drum MAX DIAMETER specification is stamped on the drum either on the inside or . . .

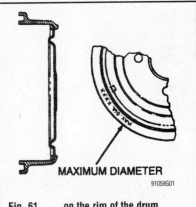

MAXIMUM DIAMETER

Fig. 61 . . . on the rim of the drum

REMOVAL & INSTALLATION

♦ See Figures 63 thru 79

✳✳ CAUTION

Older brake pads or shoes may contain asbestos, which has been determined to be cancer causing agent. Never clean the brake surfaces with compressed air! Avoid inhaling any dust from any brake surface! When cleaning brake surfaces, use a commercially available brake cleaning fluid.

➡When servicing drum brakes, only dissemble and assemble one side at a time, leaving the remaining side intact for reference.

1. Raise and safely support the vehicle.
2. Remove the rear wheel and tire assembly.
3. Remove the brake drum retainers, if equipped.
4. Grasp the brake drum and remove.
5. If the drum will not slide off with light force, then the brake shoes will need to be backed off:
   a. Remove the rubber plug on the backing plate and insert a screwdriver or small brake adjusting tool into the slot to contact the brake strut and quadrant.

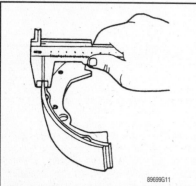

Fig. 62 Measure brake shoe thickness in several places around the shoe

Fig. 63 The shoes can be backed off through this slot located in the backing plate

Fig. 64 Remove the shoe hold down springs and . . .

Fig. 65 . . . pull the retainer out of the rear of the backing plate

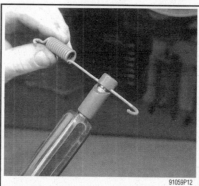

Fig. 66 A useful tool is a spring removal tool such as this one from Lisle®

Fig. 67 Remove the upper . . .

Fig. 68 . . . and lower retracting springs

Fig. 69 Remove the forward . . .

Fig. 70 . . . and rear brake shoes from the backing plate

Fig. 71 Remove the adjusting quadrant and strut assembly

Fig. 72 Remove the parking brake cable from the actuating lever

Fig. 73 Thoroughly clean the contact points on the backing plate with a brush or other suitable device . . .

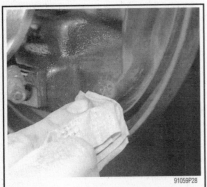

Fig. 74 . . . and wipe them clean of any possible contaminants

Fig. 75 Lubricating points on the backing plate

Fig. 76 Apply a high temp grease to the shoe contact points on the backing plate

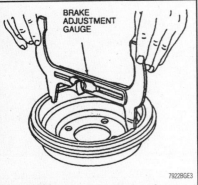

Fig. 77 Measuring the brake drum inner diameter

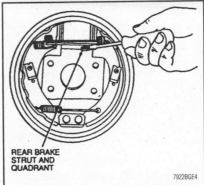

Fig. 78 Adjusting the brake shoes to fit the drum

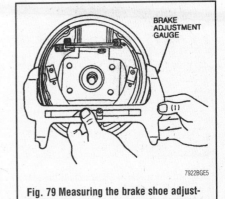

Fig. 79 Measuring the brake shoe adjustment

   b. A forward motion of the screwdriver will separate the quadrant from the knurled wheel and allow the brake shoes to retract.

   c. Remove the brake drum.

6. Remove the brake shoe hold down springs and the brake shoe hold down pins.

7. Remove the brake shoe retracting springs.

8. Disengage the parking brake cable and conduit from the parking brake lever.

9. Remove the brake shoes.

10. Disengage the rear brake strut and quadrant from the rear brake shoe.

11. Remove the parking brake rear cable and conduit from the parking brake cable anchor on the trailing brake shoe.

   To install:

12. Lubricate the rear brake shoe contact points on the backing plate with an appropriate grease.

13. Engage the parking brake rear cable and conduit into the parking brake cable anchor on the trailing brake shoe.

14. Position the trailing brake shoe on the backing plate.

15. Engage the rear brake strut and quadrant.

16. Reinstall the parking brake rear spring.

17. Reinstall the brake shoe hold down spring pin and the hold down spring.

18. Insert the leading brake shoe into the slot on the rear brake strut and quadrant.

19. Reinstall the brake shoe hold down pin and hold down spring.

20. Reinstall the brake shoe retracting springs.

21. Adjust the brake shoes by first measuring the inside drum diameter with an appropriate brake adjustment gauge.

22. Insert a small screwdriver or similar tool into the knurled quadrant of the brake strut and quadrant to adjust the brake shoes to the same measurement of the brake drum by expanding the brake strut and quadrant.

23. Trial fit the brake drum. The shoes should just contact the drum surface when properly adjusted.

24. Make sure that the brake drum and brake shoes are clean of any oils or protective coatings.

25. Reinstall the brake drum.

26. Reinstall new drum retainers, if available.

27. Reconnect the parking brake rear cable and conduit to the parking brake lever. It may be necessary to back off on the parking brake cable adjustment to allow for the new brake shoes.

28. Reinstall the wheel and tire assembly. Torque the lug nuts to 62 ft. lbs. (85 Nm).

29. Lower the vehicle.

30. Work the parking brake control several times to complete the brake shoe adjustment and to check the parking brake adjustment as well.

31. Pump the brake pedal several times to assure a good pedal.

32. Road test the vehicle and check for proper brake system operation.

ADJUSTMENTS

▶ **See Figures 77, 78 and 79**

The rear brakes are automatically adjusted while driving the vehicle. The brakes are also adjusted each time the parking brake is applied. Manual brake adjustment is only required after the brake shoes or hardware has been replaced, or the adjuster has been replaced.

1. Remove the brake drum as described in this section..

2. Remove any excessive dust and dirt present on the brakes using the appropriate methods.

3. Using a brake adjustment gauge, measure the inside diameter of the brake drum.

4. Insert a screwdriver into the knurled quadrant to release the brake shoes.

5. Adjust the brake shoes to the same diameter as the drum by placing the brake adjustment gauge on the shoes and expanding the strut and quadrant.

6. Install the brake drum as described in this section.

Wheel Cylinders

REMOVAL & INSTALLATION

▶ **See Figures 80 thru 85**

✳ CAUTION

Brake fluid contains polyglycol ethers and polyglycols. Avoid contact with the eyes and wash your hands thoroughly after handling brake fluid. If you do get brake fluid in your eyes, flush your eyes with clean, running water for 15 minutes. If eye irritation persists, or if you have taken brake fluid internally, IMMEDIATELY seek medical assistance.

1. Raise and safely support the vehicle.

2. Remove the rear wheel and tire assembly.

3. Remove the brake drum retainers, if equipped.

4. Grasp the brake drum and remove.

5. If the drum will not slide off with light force, then the brake shoes need to be backed off.

   a. Remove the rubber plug on the backing plate and insert a screwdriver or small brake adjusting tool into the slot to contact the brake strut and quadrant.

   b. A forward motion of the screwdriver will separate the quadrant from the knurled wheel and allow the brake shoes to retract.

   c. Remove the brake drum.

6. Remove the brake shoe hold down springs and the brake shoe hold down pins.

7. Remove the brake shoe retracting springs.

8. Disengage the parking brake cable and conduit from the parking brake lever.

9. Remove the brake shoes.

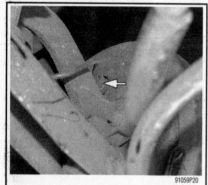

Fig. 80 The brake line connects to the rear of the wheel cylinder

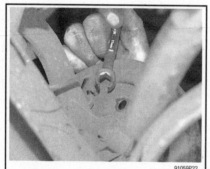

Fig. 81 Use an appropriate size wrench to remove the brake line from the wheel cylinder

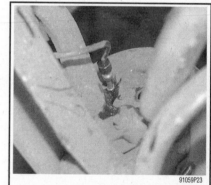

Fig. 82 When the line is sufficiently loosened, brake fluid will flow out of the fitting

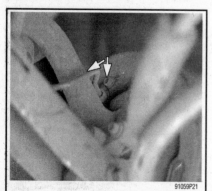

Fig. 83 The wheel cylinder is held by two retaining bolts

Fig. 84 After the bolts are removed, the wheel cylinder can be removed from the backing plate

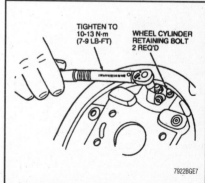

Fig. 85 Using a torque wrench to secure the wheel cylinder retaining bolts

10. Disengage the rear brake strut and quadrant from the rear brake shoe.

11. Remove the parking brake rear cable and conduit from the parking brake cable anchor on the training brake shoe.

12. Disconnect the brake line at the wheel cylinder.

13. Remove the 2 bolts securing the wheel cylinder to the backing plate and remove the wheel cylinder.

To install:

14. Reinstall the wheel cylinder to the brake backing plate and install the 2 retaining bolts. Torque the retaining bolts to 84–108 inch. lbs. (10–13 Nm).

15. Reconnect the brake line to the wheel cylinder and torque the fitting to 10–18 ft. lbs. (14–24 Nm).

16. Lubricate the rear brake shoe contact points on the backing plate with an appropriate grease.

17. Engage the parking brake rear cable and conduit into the parking brake cable anchor on the trailing brake shoe.

18. Position the trailing brake shoe on the backing plate.

19. Engage the rear brake strut and quadrant.

20. Reinstall the parking brake rear spring.

21. Reinstall the brake shoe hold down spring pin and the hold down spring.

22. Insert the leading brake shoe into the slot on the rear brake strut and quadrant.

23. Reinstall the brake shoe hold down pin and hold down spring.

24. Reinstall the brake shoe retracting springs.

25. Adjust the brake shoes by first measuring the inside drum diameter with an appropriate brake adjustment gauge.

26. Insert a small screwdriver into the knurled quadrant of the brake strut and quadrant to adjust the brake shoes to the same measurement of the brake drum by expanding the brake strut and quadrant.

27. Trial fit the brake drum. The shoes should just contact the drum surface when properly adjusted.

28. Make sure that the brake drum and brake shoes are clean of any oils or protective coatings.

29. Reinstall the brake drum.

30. Reinstall new drum retainers, if available.

31. Reconnect the parking brake rear cable and conduit to the parking brake lever. It may be necessary to back off on the parking brake cable adjustment to allow for the new brake shoes.

32. Bleed the brake system of air until a firm pedal is achieved. Top off the brake fluid in the master cylinder.

❋❋ WARNING

Clean, high quality brake fluid is essential to the safe and proper operation of the brake system. You should always buy the highest quality brake fluid that is available. If the brake fluid becomes contaminated, drain and flush the system, then refill the master cylin-der with new fluid. Never reuse any brake fluid. Any brake fluid that is removed from the system should be discarded. Also, do not allow any brake fluid to come in contact with a painted surface; it will damage the paint.

33. Reinstall the wheel and tire assembly. Torque the lug nuts to 62 ft. lbs. (85 Nm).

34. Lower the vehicle.

35. Work the parking brake control several times to complete the brake shoe adjustment and to check the parking brake adjustment as well.

36. Pump the brake pedal several times to assure a good pedal.

37. Road test the vehicle and check the brake system for proper operation.

OVERHAUL

◆ **See Figures 86 thru 95**

❋❋ CAUTION

Brake fluid contains polyglycol ethers and polyglycols. Avoid contact with the eyes and wash your hands thoroughly after handling brake fluid. If you do get brake fluid in your eyes, flush your eyes with clean, running water for 15 minutes. If eye irritation persists, or if you have taken brake fluid internally, IMMEDIATELY seek medical assistance.

TCCA9P13

Fig. 86 Remove the outer boots from the wheel cylinder

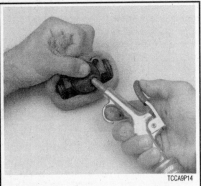

TCCA9P14

Fig. 87 Compressed air can be used to remove the pistons and seals

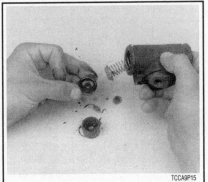

TCCA9P15

Fig. 88 Remove the pistons, cup seals and spring from the cylinder

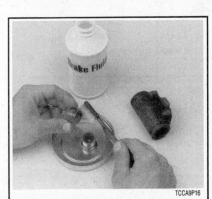

TCCA9P16

Fig. 89 Use brake fluid and a soft brush to clean the pistons . . .

Fig. 90 . . . and the bore of the wheel cylinder

Fig. 91 Once cleaned and inspected, the wheel cylinder is ready for assembly

Fig. 92 Lubricate the cup seals with brake fluid

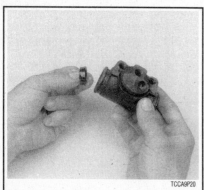

Fig. 93 Install the spring, then the cup seals in the bore

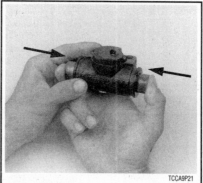

Fig. 94 Lightly lubricate the pistons, then install them

Fig. 95 The boots can now be installed over the wheel cylinder ends

Wheel cylinder overhaul kits may be available, but often at little or no savings over a reconditioned wheel cylinder. It often makes sense with these components to substitute a new or reconditioned part instead of attempting an overhaul.

If no replacement is available, or you would prefer to overhaul your wheel cylinders, the following procedure may be used. When rebuilding and installing wheel cylinders, avoid getting any contaminants into the system. Always use clean, new, high quality brake fluid. If dirty or improper fluid has been used, it will be necessary to drain the entire system, flush the system with proper brake fluid, replace all rubber components, then refill and bleed the system.

1. Remove the wheel cylinder from the vehicle and place on a clean workbench.

2. First remove and discard the old rubber boots, then withdraw the pistons. Piston cylinders are equipped with seals and a spring assembly, all located behind the pistons in the cylinder bore.

3. Remove the remaining inner components, seals and spring assembly. Compressed air may be useful in removing these components. If no compressed air is available, be VERY careful not to score the wheel cylinder bore when removing parts from it. Discard all components for which replacements were supplied in the rebuild kit.

4. Wash the cylinder and metal parts in denatured alcohol or clean brake fluid.

✳✳ WARNING

Never use a mineral-based solvent such as gasoline, kerosene or paint thinner for cleaning purposes. These solvents will swell rubber components and quickly deteriorate them.

5. Allow the parts to air dry or use compressed air. Do not use rags for cleaning, since lint will remain in the cylinder bore.

6. Inspect the piston and replace it if it shows scratches.

7. Lubricate the cylinder bore and seals using clean brake fluid.

8. Position the spring assembly.

9. Install the inner seals, then the pistons.

10. Insert the new boots into the counterbores by hand. Do not lubricate the boots.

11. Install the wheel cylinder.

REAR DISC BRAKES

Brake Pads

REMOVAL & INSTALLATION

◆ See Figures 96, 97 and 98

✳✳ CAUTION

Older brake pads or shoes may contain asbestos, which has been determined to be cancer causing agent. Never clean the brake surfaces with compressed air! Avoid inhaling any dust from any brake surface! When cleaning brake surfaces, use a commercially available brake cleaning fluid.

1. Remove ½ of the brake fluid from the master cylinder reservoir.

2. Raise and safely support the vehicle.

3. Remove the wheels.

4. Remove the cotter pin and guide pin.

5. Remove the caliper locating pin cover and remove the locating pin.

6. Swing the rear disc brake caliper away from the brake rotor and anchor plate. There is no need to remove the parking brake cable or brake hose.

7. Remove the inner and outer disc brake pads.

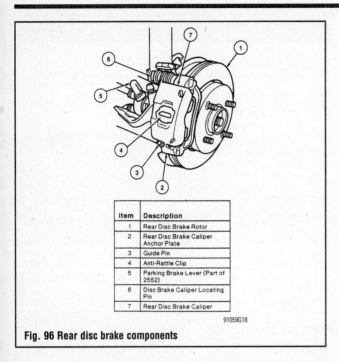

Item	Description
1	Rear Disc Brake Rotor
2	Rear Disc Brake Caliper Anchor Plate
3	Guide Pin
4	Anti-Rattle Clip
5	Parking Brake Lever (Part of 2552)
6	Disc Brake Caliper Locating Pin
7	Rear Disc Brake Caliper

91059G18

Fig. 96 Rear disc brake components

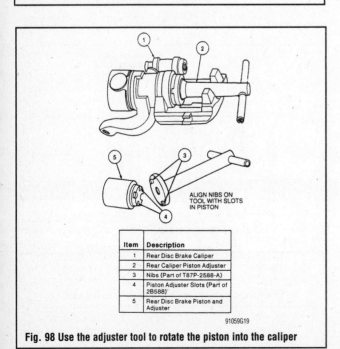

91059G17

Fig. 97 Removing the parking brake cable

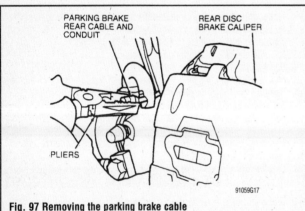

Item	Description
1	Rear Disc Brake Caliper
2	Rear Caliper Piston Adjuster
3	Nibs (Part of T87P-2588-A)
4	Piston Adjuster Slots (Part of 2B588)
5	Rear Disc Brake Piston and Adjuster

91059G19

Fig. 98 Use the adjuster tool to rotate the piston into the caliper

To install:

8. If installing new disc brake pads, use rear caliper piston adjuster T87P–2588–A or similar tool, to rotate the rear disc brake piston clockwise, retracting the caliper piston. This will allow room for the new brake pads.

9. Install the inner and outer disc brake pads.

10. Swing the rear disc brake caliper back into position over the disc brake pads.

11. Clean the locating pin threads and apply 1 drop of a thread locking agent or similar sealer.

12. Apply a small amount of disc brake caliper slide grease to the shaft of the locating pin.

13. Reinstall the locating pin and torque to 30 ft. lbs. (41 Nm).

14. Reinstall the guide pin and the cotter pin.

15. Adjust the parking brake by operating the parking brake control several times.

16. Reinstall the wheel and tire assembly. Torque the lug nuts to 62 ft. lbs. (85 Nm).

17. Lower the vehicle.

18. Adjust the parking brake by operating the parking brake control several times.

19. Pump the brake pedal several times to achieve a good pedal before attempting to move the vehicle.

20. Check the brake fluid level in the master cylinder fluid reservoir and add fluid as necessary.

21. Road test the vehicle and check for proper brake system operation.

INSPECTION

▶ **See Figure 99**

Inspect the brake pads for wear using a ruler or Vernier caliper. Compare measurements to the brake specifications chart. If the lining is thinner than specification or there is evidence of the lining being contaminated by brake fluid or oil, make the necessary repairs and replace all brake pad assemblies (a complete axle set).

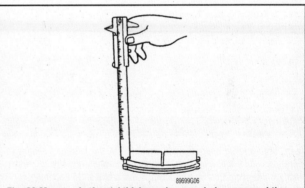

89699G06

Fig. 99 Measure brake pad thickness in several places around the pad with a ruler or Vernier caliper

Brake Caliper

REMOVAL & INSTALLATION

▶ **See Figure 100**

1. Raise and safely support the vehicle.
2. Remove the wheel and tire assembly.
3. Remove the parking brake rear cable and conduit from the parking brake lever at the disc brake caliper, using a pair of pliers.
4. Remove the cotter pin and guide pin.
5. Remove the caliper locating pin cover and remove the locating pin.
6. Lift the rear disc brake caliper off of the anchor plate.
7. Place a pan under the caliper to catch any lost brake fluid. Dispose of properly.

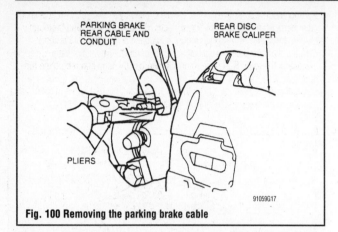

Fig. 100 Removing the parking brake cable

❋❋ CAUTION

Brake fluid contains polyglycol ethers and polyglycols. Avoid contact with the eyes and wash your hands thoroughly after handling brake fluid. If you do get brake fluid in your eyes, flush your eyes with clean, running water for 15 minutes. If eye irritation persists, or if you have taken brake fluid internally, IMMEDIATELY seek medical assistance.

8. Crack open the rear brake hose fitting and allow the brake fluid to drain.
9. Finish removing the rear brake hose and washers from the caliper. Discard the washers.
10. Remove the disc brake caliper.

To install:
11. Reconnect the rear brake hose to the caliper using new washers.
12. Fit the rear disc brake caliper over the rotor and position onto the anchor plate.
13. Reinstall the caliper locating pin and torque to 30 ft. lbs. (41 Nm).
14. Reinstall the caliper locating pin cover.
15. Reinstall the guide pin and the cotter pin.
16. Reinstall the parking brake rear cable and conduit onto the parking brake lever.
17. Adjust the parking brake by operating the parking brake control several times.
18. Properly bleed the brake system of air. Top off the master cylinder when complete.

❋❋ WARNING

Clean, high quality brake fluid is essential to the safe and proper operation of the brake system. You should always buy the highest quality brake fluid that is available. If the brake fluid becomes contaminated, drain and flush the system, then refill the master cylinder with new fluid. Never reuse any brake fluid. Any brake fluid that is removed from the system should be discarded. Also, do not allow any brake fluid to come in contact with a painted surface; it will damage the paint.

19. If the brake pedal feels spongy, repeat the brake bleeding procedure.
20. Reinstall the wheel and tire assembly. Torque the lug nuts to 62 ft. lbs. (85 Nm).
21. Lower the vehicle.
22. Pump the brake pedal several times to position the brake pads before attempting to move the vehicle.
23. Road test the vehicle and check for proper brake system operation.

OVERHAUL

Brake caliper overhaul is covered under Front Disc Brakes, earlier in this section.

Brake Disc (Rotor)

REMOVAL & INSTALLATION

◗ See Figure 101

1. Raise and safely support the vehicle.
2. Remove the wheel and tire assembly.
3. Remove the parking brake rear cable and conduit from the parking brake lever at the disc brake caliper using a pair of pliers.
4. Remove the cotter pin and guide pin.
5. Remove the caliper locating pin cover and remove the locating pin.
6. Lift the rear disc brake caliper off of the anchor plate.
7. Secure the caliper using wire to prevent damage to the brake hose.
8. Remove the inner and outer disc brake pads.
9. Remove the 2 bolts securing the anchor plate. Remove the anchor plate.
10. Remove the retainers on the wheel studs securing the brake rotor to the hub (if not already removed).
11. Remove the brake rotor.
12. Inspect the brake rotor surfaces for scoring, wear or other damage. Machine or replace the disc brake rotor as necessary.

To install:
13. If the rotor is being replaced, make sure that the new rotor is thoroughly cleaned of its protective coating.
14. Lubricate the area of the wheel hub that the rotor fits to with a suitable grease.
15. Install the rear disc rotor onto the wheel hub using new retainers.
16. Fit the caliper anchor plate and secure with the 2 bolts after applying 1 drop of threadlock sealer to the threads of each bolt.
17. Torque the retaining bolts to 43 ft. lbs. (59 Nm).
18. Reinstall the inner and outer disc brake pads.
19. Reinstall the rear disc brake caliper.
20. Fit the caliper locating pin and torque to 30 ft. lbs. (41 Nm).
21. Reinstall the caliper locating pin cover.
22. Reinstall the guide pin and the cotter pin.
23. Reinstall the parking brake rear cable and conduit onto the parking brake lever.
24. Adjust the parking brake by operating the parking brake control several times.
25. Reinstall the wheel and tire assembly. Torque the lug nuts to 62 ft. lbs. (85 Nm).
26. Lower the vehicle.
27. Pump the brake pedal several times to achieve a good pedal before attempting to move the vehicle.
28. Road test the vehicle and check the brake system for proper operation.

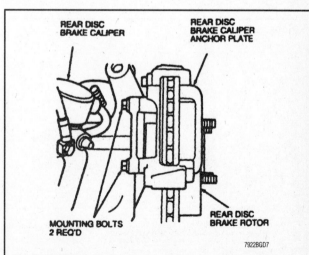

Fig. 101 Location of rear caliper anchor plate retaining bolts

INSPECTION

▶ **See Figures 102 and 103**

Rotor thickness should be measured any time a brake inspection is done. Rotor thickness can be measured using a brake rotor micrometer or Vernier caliper. Measure the rotor thickness in several places around the rotor. Compare the thickness to the specifications chart found at the end of this section.

The run-out of the brake rotor should be checked any time a vibration during braking occurs. Excessive run-out can be caused by a build-up of rust scale or other particles on the rotor or hub surfaces. Remove the rotor and thoroughly clean the hub and rotor-to-hub mounting surface on the back of the rotor. Mount a dial indicator to a suspension member and zero the indicator stylus on the face of the rotor. Rotate the rotor 360 degrees by hand and record the run-out.

Compare measurements to the brake specifications chart. If the thickness and run-out do not meet specifications, replace the rotor.

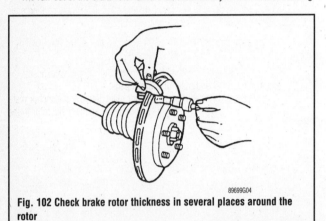

Fig. 102 Check brake rotor thickness in several places around the rotor

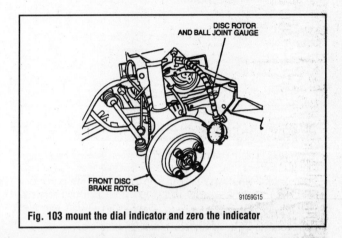

Fig. 103 mount the dial indicator and zero the indicator

PARKING BRAKE

Cable(s)

REMOVAL & INSTALLATION

Front Cable

▶ **See Figures 104, 105 and 106**

1. Fully release the parking brake.
2. Raise and safely support the vehicle.
3. Loosen and lower the exhaust system and remove the heat shields.
4. Disengage the rear parking brake cables from the equalizer.
5. Lower the vehicle.
6. Remove the console for removal of the cable.
7. Route the parking brake cable and equalizer through the hole in the floor pan.

8. Disconnect the parking brake cable and equalizer from the parking brake control and remove the parking brake cable.

To install:

9. Position the parking brake cable and equalizer to the parking brake control.
10. Release the cable tension as follows:
    a. Press down on the pawl of the parking brake control while pulling on the parking brake cable and equalizer.

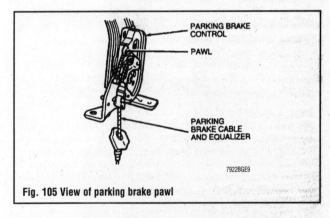

Fig. 105 View of parking brake pawl

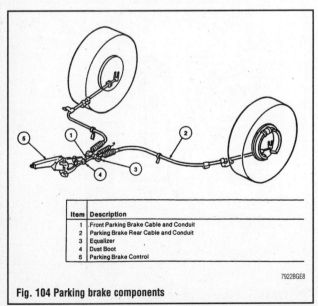

Item	Description
1	Front Parking Brake Cable and Conduit
2	Parking Brake Rear Cable and Conduit
3	Equalizer
4	Dust Boot
5	Parking Brake Control

Fig. 104 Parking brake components

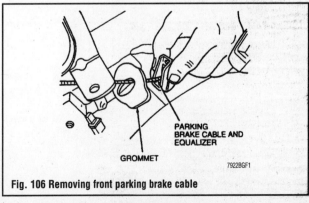

Fig. 106 Removing front parking brake cable

b. Press down hard on the pawl while releasing the tension on the cable. The cable will stay released as long as no tension is applied to the cable or as long as the parking brake control handle is not moved.

11. Route the parking brake cable and equalizer through the hole in the floor pan.

12. Reinstall the grommet into the opening.

13. Raise and safely support the vehicle.

14. Reconnect the parking brake rear cables to the equalizer.

15. Reinstall the heat shields and reposition the exhaust system.

16. Lower the vehicle.

17. Reinstall the console.

18. Operate the parking brake control several times to set the parking brake adjuster.

19. Check the parking brake for proper operation.

Rear Cable

WITH REAR DISC BRAKES

1. Fully release the parking brake control.
2. Raise and safely support the vehicle.
3. Loosen the exhaust system and remove the heat shields.
4. Disengage the rear parking brake cable from the equalizer.
5. Remove the rear parking brake cable from its routing brackets.
6. Remove the rear parking brake cable and conduit from the rear disc brake caliper using pliers.

To install:

7. Reconnect the rear parking brake cable and conduit to the rear disc brake caliper.
8. Position the rear parking brake cable into its routing brackets.
9. Attach the rear parking brake cable and conduit to the equalizer.
10. Reinstall the heat shields and reposition the exhaust system.
11. Lower the vehicle.
12. Operate the parking brake control several times to adjust the parking brake cable tension.
13. Check the parking brake for proper operation.

WITH REAR DRUM BRAKES

1. Fully release the parking brake control.
2. Raise and safely support the vehicle.
3. Loosen the exhaust system and remove the heat shields.
4. Disengage the rear parking brake cable to be removed from the equalizer.
5. Remove the rear parking brake cable from its routing brackets.
6. Remove the rear wheel of the cable being serviced.
7. Remove the brake drum to gain access to the parking brake cable anchor.
8. Disengage the cable end from the parking brake cable anchor (parking brake lever).
9. Press the prongs on the cable conduit attaching the cable to the backing plate using the box end of a ½ inch wrench.
10. With the prongs compressed, pull the cable and conduit out of the backing plate and remove the cable.

To install:

11. Push the new cable end for the brake side into the backing plate until the prongs on the conduit are fully seated.
12. Reconnect the rear parking brake cable to the parking brake cable anchor (parking brake lever).
13. Reinstall the brake drum.
14. Reinstall the wheel and torque the lug nuts to 62 ft. lbs. (85 Nm).
15. Reinstall the rear parking brake cable into its routing brackets.
16. Reconnect the parking brake cable to the equalizer.
17. Reinstall the heat shields and reposition the exhaust system.
18. Lower the vehicle.
19. Operate the parking brake control several times to adjust the parking brake cable tension.
20. Check the parking brake for proper operation.

ADJUSTMENT

The parking brake cable is adjusted by operating the parking brake control handle several times.

ANTI-LOCK BRAKE SYSTEM

General Information

♦ See Figure 107

The 4-Wheel Anti-lock Brake System (ABS) is an electronically operated, all wheel brake control system. Major components include the vacuum power brake booster, master cylinder, the wheel speed sensors, and the Hydraulic Control Unit (HCU) which contains the control module, a relay, and the pressure control valves.

The system is designed to retard wheel lockup during periods of high wheel slip when braking. Retarding wheel lockup is accomplished by modulating fluid pressure to the wheel brake units. When the control module detects a variation in voltage across the wheel speed sensors, the ABS is activated. The control module opens and closes various valves located inside the HCU. These valves, called dump and isolation valves, modulate the hydraulic pressure to the wheels by applying and venting the pressure to the brake fluid circuits.

PRECAUTIONS

• Certain components within the ABS system are not intended to be serviced or repaired individually.

• Do not use rubber hoses or other parts not specifically specified for and ABS system. When using repair kits, replace all parts included in the kit. Partial or incorrect repair may lead to functional problems and require the replacement of components.

• Lubricate rubber parts with clean, fresh brake fluid to ease assembly. Do not use shop air to clean parts; damage to rubber components may result.

• Use only DOT 3 brake fluid from an unopened container.

• If any hydraulic component or line is removed or replaced, it may be necessary to bleed the entire system.

• A clean repair area is essential. Always clean the reservoir and cap thoroughly before removing the cap. The slightest amount of dirt in the fluid may

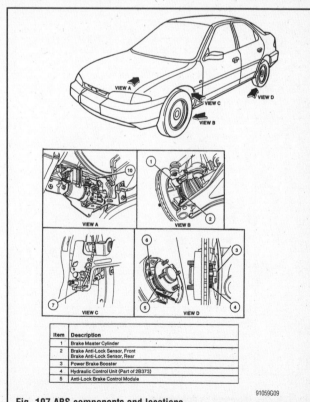

Item	Description
1	Brake Master Cylinder
2	Brake Anti-Lock Sensor, Front Brake Anti-Lock Sensor, Rear
3	Power Brake Booster
4	Hydraulic Control Unit (Part of 2B373)
5	Anti-Lock Brake Control Module

91059G09

Fig. 107 ABS components and locations

plug an orifice and impair the system function. Perform repairs after components have been thoroughly cleaned; use only denatured alcohol to clean components. Do not allow ABS components to come into contact with any substance containing mineral oil; this includes used shop rags.

• The Anti-Lock control unit is a microprocessor similar to other computer units in the vehicle. Ensure that the ignition switch is **OFF** before removing or installing controller harnesses. Avoid static electricity discharge at or near the controller.

• If any arc welding is to be done on the vehicle, the control unit should be unplugged before welding operations begin.

TESTING

♦ See Figures 108, 109, 110 and 111

The ABS module performs system tests and self-tests during startup and normal operation. The valves, wheel sensors and fluid level circuits are monitored for proper operation. If a fault is found, the ABS will be deactivated and the amber ANTI LOCK light will be lit until the ignition is turned OFF. When the light is lit, the Diagnostic Trouble Code (DTC) may be obtained. Under normal operation, the light will stay on for about 2 seconds while the ignition switch is in the ON position and will go out shortly after.

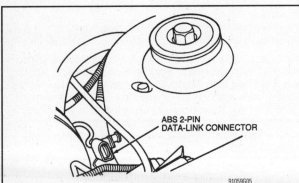

ABS 2-PIN
DATA-LINK CONNECTOR

91059G05

Fig. 108 The ABS diagnostic connector location on 1995 models only

The Diagnostic Trouble Codes (DTC) are an alphanumeric code and a scan tool, such as Rotunda NGS Tester 007-00500 or its equivalent, is required to retrieve the codes. Refer to the manufacturer's instructions for operating the tool and retrieving the codes.

The data link connector (DLC) for the ABS on 1995 models is located in the engine compartment on the inboard side of the driver's side strut tower. The data link connector (DLC) for the ABS on 1996–99 models is the OBDII connector located under the driver's side of the instrument panel, underneath the steering column.

ON-BOARD DIAGNOSTIC TROUBLE CODE INDEX

DTC	Source	Action
C1011 C1012 C1013 C1211 C1212 C1213	Open or short circuit—RH front ABS solenoid valve.	GO to Pinpoint Test B.
C1026 C1027 C1028 C1195 C1196 C1197	Open or short circuit—LH front ABS solenoid valve.	GO to Pinpoint Test B.
C1056 C1057 C1058 C1247 C1248 C1249	Open or short circuit—RH rear ABS solenoid valve.	GO to Pinpoint Test B.
C1071 C1072 C1073 C1243 C1244 C1245	Open or short circuit—LH rear ABS solenoid valve.	GO to Pinpoint Test B.
C1138 B2143	EE PROM Failure	GO to Pinpoint Test B.
C1401 C1402 C1403	Open or short circuit—RH Traction Control solenoid front valve	GO to Pinpoint Test B.
C1411 C1412 C1413	Open or short circuit—LH front Traction Control solenoid valve.	GO to Pinpoint Test B.
C1081 C1082 C1083 C1085 C1111 C1112 C1113 C1114	Failure, caused by high / low battery voltage, relay, main fuse, wire harness, or damaged anti-lock brake control module.	GO to Pinpoint Test C.
C1084 C1110 C1115 C1440	Reference voltage failure caused by high / low battery voltage, main fuse, wire harness or damaged anti-lock brake control module.	GO to Pinpoint Test D.
C1091 C1151 C1161 C1171 C1181 C1148 C1158 C1168 C1178 C1236 C1235 C1233 C1234	Open or short circuit, front sensor, rear sensor, harness, damaged teeth on brake anti-lock sensor, sensor air gap too small / large, damaged anti-lock brake control module.	GO to Pinpoint Test E.

91059G03

Fig. 110 ABS Diagnostic Trouble Codes

ON-BOARD DIAGNOSTIC TROUBLE CODE INDEX

DTC	Source	Action
C1090 C1237	Open or short circuit, rear sensor, wire harness, damaged anti-lock brake control module.	GO to DTC C1237.
C1095	Pump motor running continuously or inoperative, triggered by anti-lock brake control module.	GO to DTC C1095.
C1120 C1671	Reference voltage failure caused by high / low battery voltage, main fuse, wire harness or damaged anti-lock brake control module.	GO to DTC C1671.
C1137	Interrupted or defective power circuit. Replace anti-lock brake relay if DTC repeats.	GO to DTC C1137.
C1495	Traction control actuator throttle cable position sensor, wire harness or damaged anti-lock brake control module.	GO to DTC C1495.

91059G02

Fig. 109 ABS Diagnostic Trouble Codes

ON-BOARD DIAGNOSTIC TROUBLE CODE INDEX

DTC	Source	Action
C1146 C1147 C1148 C1149 C1150 C1152 C1153	Open or short circuit, RH front sensor, wire harness, damaged teeth on front brake anti-lock sensor, sensor air gap too small/large, damaged anti-lock brake control module.	GO to Pinpoint Test E.
C1156 C1157 C1158 C1159 C1160 C1162 C1163	Open or short circuit, LH front sensor, wire harness, damaged teeth on front brake anti-lock sensor, sensor air gap too small/large, damaged anti-lock brake control module.	GO to Pinpoint Test E.
C1166 C1167 C1168 C1169 C1170 C1172 C1173	Open or short circuit, RH rear sensor, wire harness, damaged teeth on front brake anti-lock sensor, sensor air gap too small/large, damaged anti-lock brake control module.	GO to Pinpoint Test E.
C1176 C1177 C1178 C1179 C1180 C1182 C1183	Open or short circuit, LH rear sensor, wire harness, damaged teeth on front brake anti-lock sensor, sensor air gap too small/large, damaged anti-lock brake control module.	GO to Pinpoint Test E.
C1491 C1492 C1493 C1451 C1452 C1453	Traction control actuator open/shorted. Damaged anti-lock brake control module.	GO to Pinpoint Test F.
C1414	Unidentifiable system identifier. Replace anti-lock brake control module if DTC repeats.	GO to DTC C1414.

91059G04

Fig. 111 ABS Diagnostic Trouble Codes

Hydraulic Control Unit Assembly

REMOVAL & INSTALLATION

♦ **See Figures 112, 113 and 114**

1. Disconnect the negative battery cable.
2. Remove the master cylinder.
3. Remove the brake booster assembly.

✲✲ CAUTION

Brake fluid contains polyglycol ethers and polyglycols. Avoid contact with the eyes and wash your hands thoroughly after handling brake fluid. If you do get brake fluid in your eyes, flush your eyes with clean, running water for 15 minutes. If eye irritation persists, or if you have taken brake fluid internally, IMMEDIATELY seek medical assistance.

4. Remove the two brake master cylinder-to-HCU brake lines.
5. Remove the four HCU-to-wheel brake lines.
6. Unplug the two electrical connectors.
7. Remove the four HCU mounting bracket retaining bolts.
8. Remove the HCU assembly from the vehicle.
9. Remove the nuts from the insulators and remove the HCU from the mounting bracket.
10. Remove the two insulator studs and the insulator ring from the HCU.

To install:

11. Position the two insulator studs and the insulator ring onto the HCU.
12. Position the HCU onto the mounting bracket and install the insulator retaining nuts.
13. Position the HCU into place and tighten the mounting bracket mounting bolts.
14. Install the four HCU brake lines.
15. Attach the two electrical connectors.
16. Install the two brake master cylinder-to-HCU brake lines.
17. Install the brake booster assembly.
18. Install the master cylinder.
19. Connect the negative battery cable.
20. Bleed the brake system.

✲✲ WARNING

Clean, high quality brake fluid is essential to the safe and proper operation of the brake system. You should always buy the highest quality brake fluid that is available. If the brake fluid becomes contaminated, drain and flush the system, then refill the master cylinder with new fluid. Never reuse any brake fluid. Any brake fluid that is removed from the system should be discarded. Also, do not allow any brake fluid to come in contact with a painted surface; it will damage the paint.

Speed Sensors

REMOVAL & INSTALLATION

Front Wheel Sensor

♦ **See Figures 115 thru 120**

1. Raise and safely support the vehicle.
2. Remove the sensor retaining bolt and sensor from the front wheel knuckle.
3. Disconnect the sensor wire from the strut bracket.
4. Unplug the sensor connector.
5. Remove the sensor wires from the routing clips.
6. Remove the screw for the fender trim and gently bend the trim back to access the connector.
7. Unplug the connector and remove the sensor.

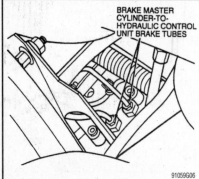

91059G06

Fig. 112 Remove the master cylinder-to-HCU brake lines

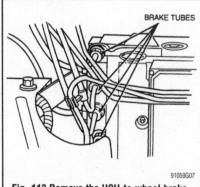

91059G07

Fig. 113 Remove the HCU-to-wheel brake lines

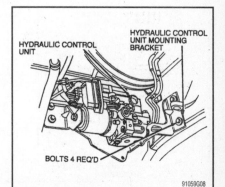

91059G08

Fig. 114 The HCU mounting bracket and retaining bolts

Fig. 115 Remove the sensor retaining screw . . .

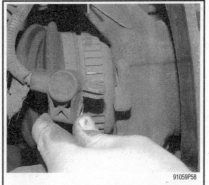

Fig. 116 . . . and remove the sensor from the knuckle

Fig. 117 The sensor wire is retained to the strut by two clips

Fig. 118 The sensor wire is routed using the clips located here

Fig. 119 Remove the fender trim screw and . . .

Fig. 120 . . . carefully pull back on the trim to access the sensor connector

To Install:

8. Properly route the sensor and attach the routing clips.
9. Attach the speed sensor to the vehicle harness.
10. Install the fender trim retaining screw.
11. Reconnect the sensor wire to the strut housing.
12. Reinstall the speed sensor and torque the retaining bolt to 84 inch. lbs. (10 Nm).
13. Lower the vehicle.
14. Road test the vehicle.

Rear Wheel Sensor

♦ See Figures 121 thru 126

1. Disconnect the negative battery cable.
2. Remove the rear seat cushion by pulling upward on the front of the cushion.

3. Disconnect the sensor connector and feed the wire through the floor-pan.
4. Raise and safely support the vehicle.
5. Disconnect the wire from the routing brackets.
6. Remove the sensor retaining bolt and remove the sensor.
To Install:
7. Install the speed sensor and torque the retaining bolt 84 inch. lbs. (10 Nm).
8. Feed the sensor wire through the floorpan and connect the wire to the routing brackets.
9. Lower the vehicle.
10. Reconnect the wiring connector and install the rear seat cushion.
11. Reconnect the negative battery cable.
12. Road test the vehicle.

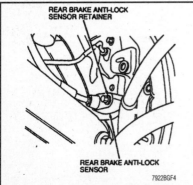

Fig. 121 Rear wheel anti-lock wheel sensor

Fig. 122 Unplug the sensor connector located under the rear seat

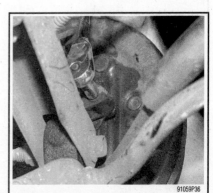

Fig. 123 Loosen the sensor retaining bolt and . . .

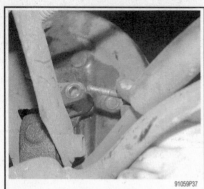

Fig. 124 . . . remove the sensor retaining bolt

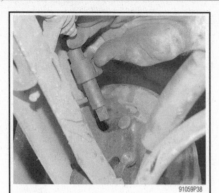

Fig. 125 Remove the sensor from the backing plate

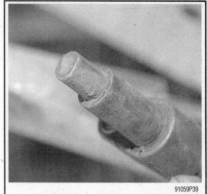

Fig. 126 Inspect the sensor tip for damage

Tone (Exciter) Ring

REMOVAL & INSTALLATION

Front

The front exciter rings are located on the outer cv joints. Refer to Section 8 for hub removal.

Rear

▶ **See Figure 127**

The rear exciter rings are located on the hubs. Refer to Section 8 for hub removal.

Bleeding the ABS System

The bleeding procedure for vehicles with conventional braking systems and ABS is the same. Refer to the brake bleeding procedure earlier in this section.

Fig. 127 The rear exciter ring is located on the back of the hub assembly

BRAKE SPECIFICATIONS
FORD CONTOUR, MERCURY MYSTIQUE, COUGAR (1999)
All measurements in inches unless noted

Year	Model		Master Cylinder Bore	Brake Disc Original Thickness	Brake Disc Minimum Thickness	Brake Disc Maximum Runout	Brake Drum Diameter Original Inside Diameter	Brake Drum Diameter Max. Wear Limit	Brake Drum Diameter Maximum Machine Diameter	Minimum Lining Thickness Front	Minimum Lining Thickness Rear
1995	Contour	F	NA	0.950	0.870	0.006	—	—	—	0.125	—
		R	—	0.790	0.710	0.006	8.00	—	—	—	0.125
	Mystique	F	NA	0.950	0.870	0.006	—	—	—	0.125	—
		R	—	0.790	0.710	0.006	8.00	—	—	—	0.125
1996	Contour	F	NA	0.950	0.870	0.006	—	—	—	0.125	—
		R	—	0.790	0.710	0.006	8.00	NA	8.04	—	0.125
	Mystique	F	NA	0.950	0.870	0.006	—	—	—	0.125	—
		R	—	0.790	0.710	0.006	8.00	NA	8.04	—	0.125
1997	Contour	F	NA	0.950	0.870	0.006	—	—	—	0.125	—
		R	—	0.790	0.710	0.006	8.00	NA	8.04	—	0.125
	Mystique	F	NA	0.950	0.870	0.006	—	—	—	0.125	—
		R	—	0.790	0.710	0.006	8.00	NA	8.04	—	0.125
1998	Contour	F	NA	0.950	0.870	0.006	—	—	—	0.125	—
		R	—	0.790	0.710	0.006	8.00	NA	8.04	—	0.125
	Mystique	F	NA	0.950	0.870	0.006	—	—	—	0.125	—
		R	—	0.790	0.710	0.006	8.00	NA	8.04	—	0.125
1999	Contour	F	NA	0.950	0.870	0.006	—	—	—	0.125	—
		R	—	0.790	0.710	0.006	8.00	NA	8.04	—	0.125
	Cougar	F	NA	0.950	0.870	0.006	—	—	—	0.125	—
		R	—	0.790	0.710	0.006	8.00	NA	8.04	—	0.125
	Mystique	F	NA	0.950	0.870	0.006	—	—	—	0.125	—
		R	—	0.790	0.710	0.006	8.00	NA	8.04	—	0.125

NOTE: Follow specifications stamped on rotor or drum if figures differ from those in this chart.
NA - Not Available
F - Front
R - Rear

91059C01

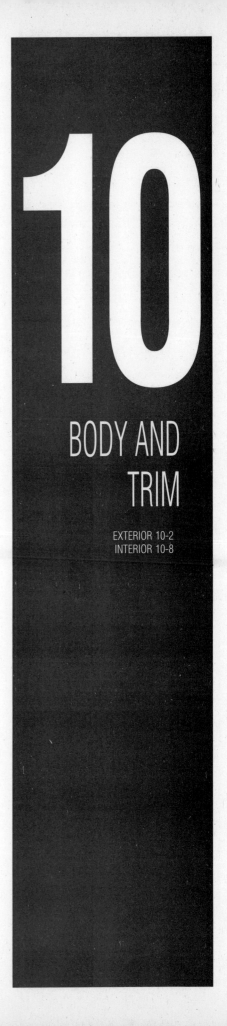

10

BODY AND TRIM

EXTERIOR

Doors

REMOVAL & INSTALLATION

♦ **See Figures 1, 2, 3, 4 and 5**

➡**Front and rear doors may be removed using the same procedure.**

1. Disconnect the negative battery cable.
2. Support the door, by placing a floor jack and a piece of wood underneath the door.
3. Remove the bolts from the door stop arm.
4. Rotate the collar on the main wiring harness connector to unplug it. Unplug any other applicable wiring connectors.
5. Matchmark the location of the hinges on the door.
6. Remove the hinge bolts and remove the door assembly.

To install:

7. Position the door into place and finger tighten the hinge bolts.
8. Align the door with the hinge marks made earlier and tighten the bolts to 19–25 ft. lbs. (25–35 Nm).
9. Attach the wiring connectors.
10. Attach the door stop arm and tighten the bolts to 89 inch lbs. (10 Nm).
11. Remove the supporting jack.
12. Connect the negative battery cable.

ADJUSTMENT

Inspect the door-to-body gap. The gap should be even and minimal around the entire door opening area and the door should open and close smoothly. If it the door has uneven gaps or opening and closing the door does not feel smooth, an adjustment is most likely necessary.

Door Alignment

1. Determine which hinge should be loosened to move the door in the desired direction.
2. Loosen the hinge bolts just enough to permit movement of the door with a padded prybar (if necessary).
3. Move the door to the desired position and tighten the hinge bolts to 19–25 ft. lbs. (25–35 Nm).
4. Repeat the procedure until the door is aligned as desired.

Door Latch Striker

♦ **See Figure 6**

1. Loosen the striker plate retaining bolts.
2. Rotate the striker until the door opens smoothly.
3. Tighten the striker bolts to 17–20 ft. lbs. (22–28 Nm).
4. Repeat if necessary.

Hood

REMOVAL & INSTALLATION

♦ **See Figures 7 thru 12**

➡**The help of an assistant is recommended when removing or installing the hood.**

1. Disconnect the negative battery cable.
2. Open and support the hood.
3. Protect the body with covers to prevent damage to the paint.
4. Use a marker or scribe marks around the hinge locations for reference during installation.

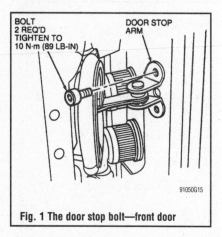

Fig. 1 The door stop bolt—front door

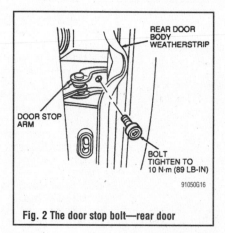

Fig. 2 The door stop bolt—rear door

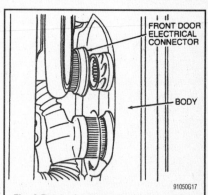

Fig. 3 Rotate the connector to remove the wire harness from the door

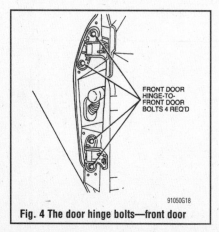

Fig. 4 The door hinge bolts—front door

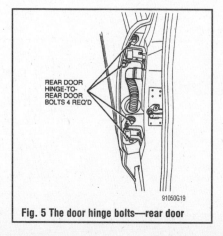

Fig. 5 The door hinge bolts—rear door

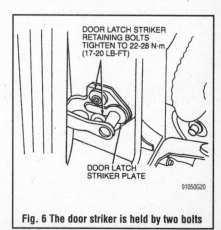

Fig. 6 The door striker is held by two bolts

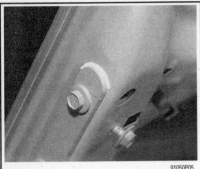
Fig. 7 Mark the location of the hinges on the hood

Fig. 8 The connector for the hood lamp is located behind the driver's side strut tower, near the cruise control servo assembly

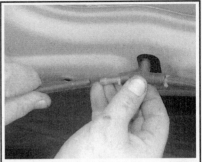
Fig. 9 Detach the washer hoses from the jet nipples and . . .

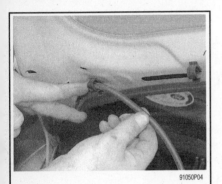
Fig. 10 . . . slide the hoses out of the retainers

Fig. 11 If equipped, remove the ground wire from the hood

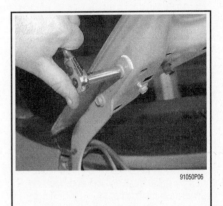
Fig. 12 Remove the hinge bolts

5. Unplug any electrical connections and windshield washer hoses that would interfere with hood removal.

6. While an assistant helps secure the hood, unfasten the attaching bolts, then remove the hood from the vehicle.

To install:

7. Place the hood into position. Install and partially tighten attaching bolts.

8. Adjust the hood with the reference marks and tighten the attaching bolts to 18 ft. lbs. (24 Nm).

9. Check the hood for an even fit between the fenders and for flush fit with the front of the fenders. Also, check for a flush fit with the top of the cowl and fenders. If necessary, adjust the hood latch.

10. Attach any electrical connections or windshield washer hoses removed to facilitate hood removal.

ALIGNMENT

The hood can be adjusted fore and aft and side to side by loosening the hood-to-hinge attaching bolts and reposition the hood. To raise or lower the hood, loosen the hinge hood on body attaching bolts and raise or lower the hinge as necessary.

The hood lock can be moved from side-to-side and up and down and laterally to obtain a snug hood fit by loosening the lock attaching screws and moving as necessary.

Trunk Lid

REMOVAL & INSTALLATION

▶ See Figures 13, 14 and 15

1. Disconnect the negative battery cable.
2. Open the trunk lid and cover the surrounding body panels with suitable protective covers.
3. Remove the hinge wiring trim from the driver's side hinge.
4. Remove the release cable guide by depressing the three sprung locators.

5. Remove the trunk lid trim panel (if equipped).
6. Unplug the wire harness connectors and remove the harness from the trunk lid.
7. Matchmark the location of the hinges on the trunk lid.
8. Have an assistant hold the trunk lid on one side and remove the hinge bolts.
9. Remove the hinge bolts on the opposite side while holding the trunk lid.
10. Remove the trunk lid from the vehicle.

To install:

11. Using an assistant position the trunk lid into place.
12. Install the hinge bolts finger tight.
13. Line up the marks on the hinges and tighten the hinge bolts to 89 inch lbs. (10 Nm).
14. Install the harness into the trunk lid and attach the connectors.
15. Install the trim panel.
16. Install the release cable and guide.
17. Install the driver's side hinge wiring trim.
18. Connect the negative battery cable.
19. Check alignment and correct as necessary.

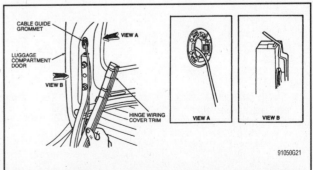
Fig. 13 Remove the hinge wiring trim and the release cable guide

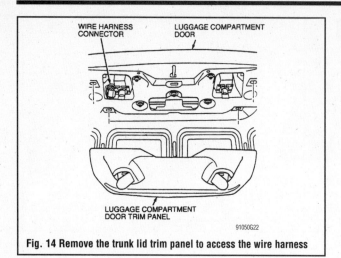

Fig. 14 Remove the trunk lid trim panel to access the wire harness

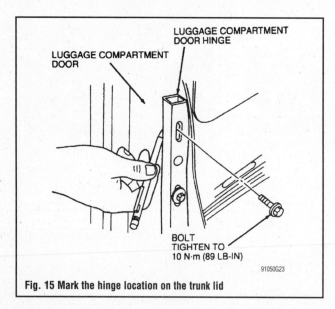

Fig. 15 Mark the hinge location on the trunk lid

ALIGNMENT

The trunk lid should be inspected for fit along the trunk lid edges and the height in relation to the adjacent body panels. The trunk lid adjustment can be

made fore-and-aft and side-to-side. the fore and aft adjustment is made by tightening the hinge center bolt. The side-to-side movement is made by loosening the hinge bolts and moving the trunk lid to the desired position. The trunk lid should be inspected for fit along the trunk lid edges and the height in relation to the adjacent body panels.

Grille

REMOVAL & INSTALLATION

♦ See Figures 16, 17, 18 and 19

1. Disconnect the negative battery cable.
2. Open and support the hood.
3. Remove the grille retaining screws and remove the grille.

To install:

4. Position the grille and tighten the retaining screws to 11–16 inch lbs (1.2–1.8 Nm).
5. Lower the hood.
6. Connect the negative battery cable.

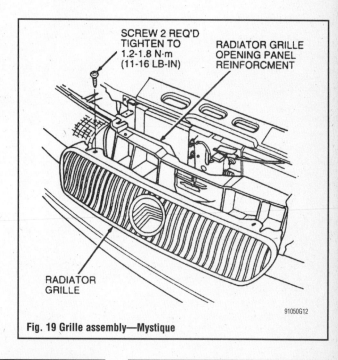

Fig. 19 Grille assembly—Mystique

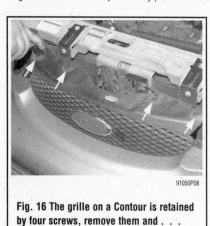

Fig. 16 The grille on a Contour is retained by four screws, remove them and . . .

Fig. 17 . . . remove the grille from the vehicle

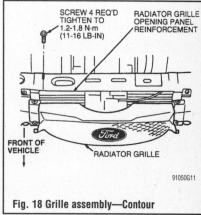

Fig. 18 Grille assembly—Contour

Outside Mirrors

REMOVAL & INSTALLATION

Manual Mirror

▶ See Figure 20

1. Disconnect the negative battery cable.
2. Remove the screw cover and the retaining screw for the outside A/C side window demister and hose.
3. Loosen the setscrew retaining the mirror control knob.
4. Remove the three mirror retaining screws.
5. Remove the mirror.

To install:

6. Place the mirror into position and install the retaining screws to 53–71 inch lbs. (6–8 Nm).
7. Tighten the control knob setscrew.
8. Install the retaining screw and screw cover.
9. Connect the negative battery cable.

Power Mirror

▶ See Figures 21 thru 26

1. Disconnect the negative battery cable.
2. Remove the screw cover and the retaining screw for the mirror cover.
3. Unplug the connector for the power mirror.
4. Remove the three mirror retaining screws.
5. Remove the mirror.

To install:

6. Place the mirror into position and install the retaining screws to 53–71 inch lbs. (6–8 Nm).
7. Attach the connector for the power mirror.
8. Install the mirror cover, retaining screw, and screw cover.
9. Connect the negative battery cable.

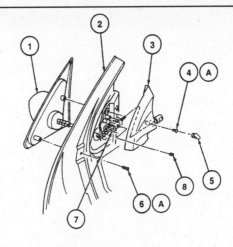

Item	Description
1	Outside Rear View Mirror
2	Front Door
3	Rear View Mirror Mounting Hole Cover
4	Screw
5	Screw Hole Cover Plug
6	Screw
7	Front Door Glass Defroster Plenum
A	Tighten to 6-8 N·m (53-71 Lb-In)

91050G10

Fig. 20 The manual mirror assembly

91050P16

Fig. 21 Pry the screw cover off of the mirror cover, due to the design, it is nearly impossible not to destroy the screw cover

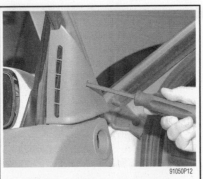

91050P12

Fig. 22 Remove the mirror cover retaining screw and . . .

91050P11

Fig. 23 . . . remove the mirror cover

91050P29

Fig. 24 Unplug the connector for the power mirror

91050P30

Fig. 25 The mirror assembly is held by three retaining bolts

91050P28

Fig. 26 After the bolts are removed, pull the mirror off of the door to remove the mirror assembly

Antenna

REPLACEMENT

Fixed Antenna

▶ **See Figures 27 and 28**

1. Disconnect the negative battery cable.
2. Remove the push pins retaining the passenger side trunk trim panel and remove the panel.

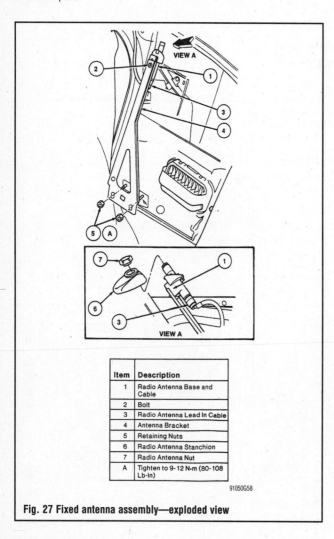

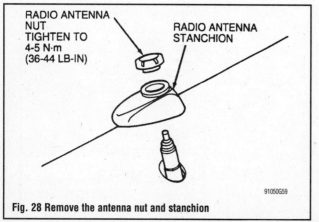

Item	Description
1	Radio Antenna Base and Cable
2	Bolt
3	Radio Antenna Lead In Cable
4	Antenna Bracket
5	Retaining Nuts
6	Radio Antenna Stanchion
7	Radio Antenna Nut
A	Tighten to 9-12 N·m (80-108 Lb-In)

91050G58

Fig. 27 Fixed antenna assembly—exploded view

RADIO ANTENNA NUT TIGHTEN TO 4-5 N·m (36-44 LB-IN)

RADIO ANTENNA STANCHION

91050G59

Fig. 28 Remove the antenna nut and stanchion

3. Remove the antenna mast by loosening it at the bottom and turning it counterclockwise until it is separated.
4. Remove the radio antenna nut and antenna stanchion (the small hole cover located on the top of the body panel).
5. Remove the one bolt retaining the antenna to the bracket.
6. Unplug the antenna cable and remove the antenna base and short cable.

To install:

7. Place the base and cable into position and tighten the retaining bolt.
8. Attach the antenna cable.
9. Install the stanchion and the radio antenna nut. Tighten the nut to 31–44 inch lbs. (4–5 Nm).
10. Install the antenna mast.
11. Install the trim panel and the push pins.
12. Connect the negative battery cable.

Power Antenna

▶ **See Figure 29**

1. Disconnect the negative battery cable.
2. Remove the push pins retaining the passenger side trunk trim panel and remove the panel.
3. Remove the radio antenna nut and antenna stanchion (the small hole cover located on the top of the body panel).
4. Unplug the antenna cable.
5. Unplug the antenna power connection.
6. Unplug the antenna module connector.
7. Disconnect the plastic drain tube from the rubber grommet.
8. Remove the two lower retaining bolts and remove the antenna assembly.

To install:

9. If replacing the antenna assembly, transfer the lower mounting bracket, drain tube and power antenna module to the new antenna.

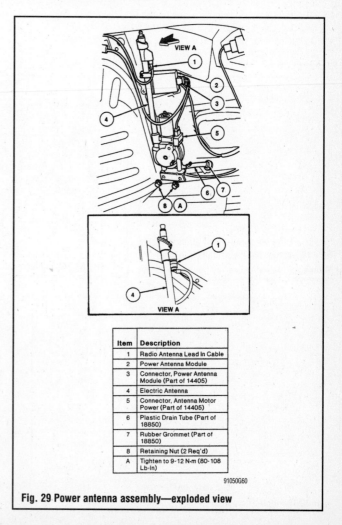

Item	Description
1	Radio Antenna Lead In Cable
2	Power Antenna Module
3	Connector, Power Antenna Module (Part of 14405)
4	Electric Antenna
5	Connector, Antenna Motor Power (Part of 14405)
6	Plastic Drain Tube (Part of 18850)
7	Rubber Grommet (Part of 18850)
8	Retaining Nut (2 Req'd)
A	Tighten to 9-12 N·m (80-108 Lb-In)

91050G60

Fig. 29 Power antenna assembly—exploded view

10. Position the antenna assembly and tighten the lower retaining bolts.
11. Connect the plastic drain tube.
12. Attach the antenna cable, module connector, and power connector.
13. Install the stanchion and the radio antenna nut. Tighten the nut to 31–44 inch lbs. (4–5 Nm).
14. Install the trim panel and the push pins.
15. Connect the negative battery cable.

Fenders

REMOVAL & INSTALLATION

▶ **See Figures 30 and 31**

1. Disconnect the negative battery cable.
2. Open the hood and support the hood with the prop rod.
3. Remove the cowl vent panels.
4. Remove the front fender splash shield(s).
5. Remove the parking lamp(s).
6. Remove the two front fender-to-front sidemember retaining screws located in front of the wheel opening.
7. Remove the screw at the base of the front fender body behind the wheel opening and remove the shim if necessary.
8. Remove the two retaining screws from the front fender body-to-radiator grille opening panel reinforcement.
9. Remove the two screws from the rear of the front fender at the A-pillar.
10. Remove the six screws from the top of the fender along the top of the apron and front sidemember. Remove the shims if necessary.
11. Remove the fender.

To install:
12. Position the fender into place and finger tighten the six screws (and shims if removed) on the top of the fender.
13. Install the remaining screws (and shims if removed) finger tight.

14. Align the fender and install shims if necessary to properly align the fender.
15. Tighten all the fender retaining screws to 89–124 inch lbs. (10–14 Nm).
16. Install the parking lamps.
17. Install the front fender splash shields.
18. Install the cowl vent panels.
19. Lower the hood.
20. Connect the negative battery cable.

Power Sunroof

REMOVAL & INSTALLATION

Sunroof Switch

▶ **See Figure 32**

1. Disconnect the negative battery cable.
2. Remove the sunroof switch from the panel by carefully prying the switch out.
3. Unplug the switch connectors and remove the switch

To install:
4. Installation is the reverse of removal.

Sunroof Motor

▶ **See Figures 33 and 34**

1. Disconnect the negative battery cable.
2. Remove the sunroof switch panel.
3. Remove the three motor retaining bolts.
4. Lower the sunroof motor and unplug the connectors.
5. Remove the motor assembly.

To install:
6. Attach the connectors to the motor.
7. Place the motor into position and tighten the retaining bolts.

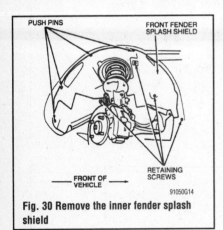

Fig. 30 Remove the inner fender splash shield

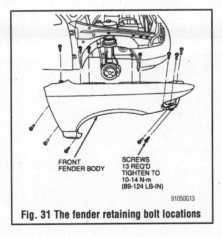

Fig. 31 The fender retaining bolt locations

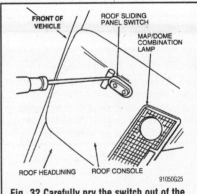

Fig. 32 Carefully pry the switch out of the panel

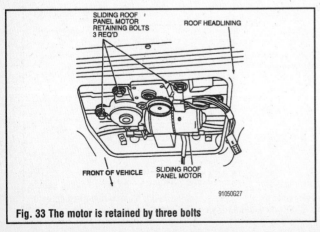

Fig. 33 The motor is retained by three bolts

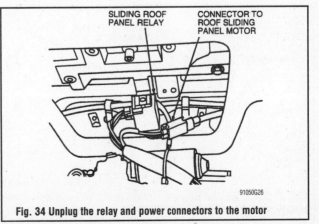

Fig. 34 Unplug the relay and power connectors to the motor

8. Connect the negative battery cable.
9. Verify the operation of the motor.
10. Install the sunroof switch panel.

Sunroof Assembly

▶ **See Figures 35 and 36**

1. Disconnect the negative battery cable.
2. Remove the headliner.
3. Disconnect and remove the drain hoses from the each corner of the roof opening panel frame.

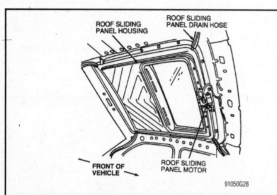

Fig. 35 Remove the drain hoses from each corner of the sunroof and unplug the motor

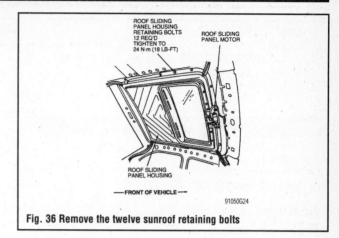

Fig. 36 Remove the twelve sunroof retaining bolts

4. Unplug the sunroof panel motor connector.
5. Remove the twelve sliding sunroof-to- roof retaining bolts.
6. Remove the sunroof assembly.

To install:

7. Place the sunroof assembly into position.
8. Install the twelve sliding sunroof-to- roof retaining bolts and tighten them to 18 ft. lbs. (24 Nm).
9. Attach the sunroof panel motor connector.
10. Connect the drain hose to the roof opening panel frame.
11. Install the headliner.
12. Connect the negative battery cable.

INTERIOR

Instrument Panel and Pad

REMOVAL & INSTALLATION

▶ **See Figures 37 thru 46**

✳ CAUTION

Some models covered by this manual are equipped with a Supplemental Restraint System (SRS), which uses an air bag. Whenever working near any of the SRS components, such as the impact sensors, the air bag module, steering column and instrument panel, disable the SRS, as described in Section 6.

1. Disconnect the negative battery cable.
2. Remove the cowl panel covers.
3. Disconnect the upper speedometer cable from the lower speedometer cable
4. Remove the center console as outlined in this Section.
5. Remove the steering column.

6. Remove the instrument cluster. Refer to Section 6.
7. Remove the radio and CD player (if equipped). Refer to Section 6.
8. Remove the heater control panel. Refer to Section 6.
9. Remove the driver's side switch plate finish panel.
10. Push in on the glove compartment door tabs and lower the door.
11. Unfasten the glove compartment hinge-to-instrument panel screws and remove the glove compartment.
12. Remove the center body pillar trim panel.
13. Unplug the connections on the firewall under the passenger side kick panel.
14. Pull the passenger side front door opening weatherstrip off of the front of the door opening.
15. Remove the passenger side instrument panel mounting bolt cover.
16. Remove the two retaining screws at the edge of the glove compartment opening.
17. Unplug the two main connections at the interior fuse panel.
18. Unplug the five connectors on the back of the fuse box.
19. Unplug the three connectors on the stoplight switch.
20. Remove the rubber grommet from the upper speedometer cable at the instrument panel.

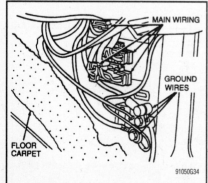

Fig. 37 Unplug the connections behind the passenger side kick panel

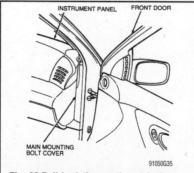

Fig. 38 Pull back the weather-stripping and remove the mounting bolt cover on the passenger side

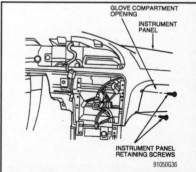

Fig. 39 Remove the two retaining screws located at the edge of the glove compartment opening

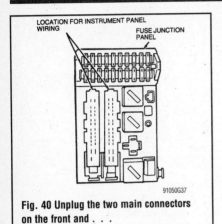

Fig. 40 Unplug the two main connectors on the front and . . .

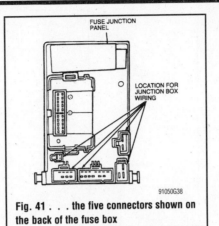

Fig. 41 . . . the five connectors shown on the back of the fuse box

Fig. 42 Remove the rubber grommet from the upper speedometer cable

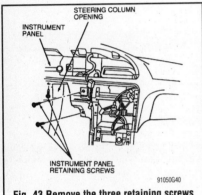

Fig. 43 Remove the three retaining screws at the steering column opening

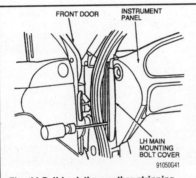

Fig. 44 Pull back the weather-stripping and remove the mounting bolt cover on the driver's side

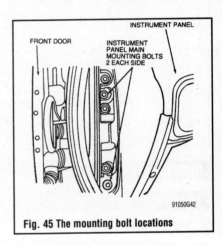

Fig. 45 The mounting bolt locations

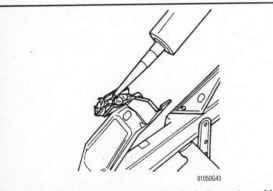

Fig. 46 Apply a small bead of silicone to the instrument panel brace to aid in the reduction of squeaks

21. From underneath the instrument panel, pry the upper speedometer cable out of the center bracket at the instrument panel.

22. Remove the three retaining screws in the steering column opening.

23. Pull the driver's door opening weatherstrip off of the front of the door opening.

24. Remove the driver's side instrument panel mounting bolt cover.

25. Remove the passenger side air bag-to-instrument panel reinforcement bolts.

26. Cut the wire ties retaining the demister hoses to the instrument panel reinforcement.

27. Unplug the connections for the radio amplifier.

28. Remove the four instrument panel mounting bolts that were located under the covers (two bolts on each side).

➡ It is recommended that two people remove the instrument panel from the vehicle.

29. Carefully lift the instrument panel away and remove the instrument panel from the vehicle.

To install:

30. If the instrument panel is being replaced, transfer any necessary components and hardware to the new panel.

31. Apply a ⅛ of an inch (10 mm) bead of silicone to the instrument panel brace.

32. Place the panel into position.

33. Install the instrument panel mounting bolts.

34. The balance of the installation is the reverse of removal.

35. Connect the negative battery cable.

Center Console

REMOVAL & INSTALLATION

With Armrest

◆ **See Figures 47, 48 and 49**

1. Disconnect the negative battery cable.
2. Remove the ashtray.
3. Remove the gearshift lever knob.
4. Carefully pry gearshift control lever plate away from the console.
5. Remove the four screws (two on each side) retaining the front of the console to the instrument panel.
6. Remove the two screws retaining the console to the instrument panel through the ashtray opening.

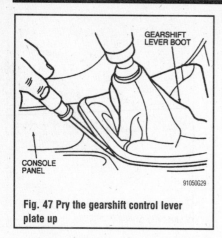

Fig. 47 Pry the gearshift control lever plate up

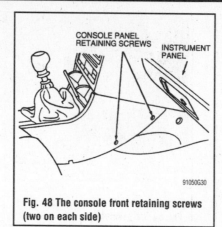

Fig. 48 The console front retaining screws (two on each side)

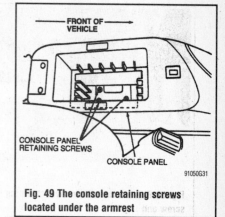

Fig. 49 The console retaining screws located under the armrest

7. Open the lid for the storage compartment located inside the console. Remove the three screws retaining the console to the floor pan.

8. Raise the console and carefully ease the parking brake handle boot over the brake lever.

9. Unplug the connectors for the cigarette lighter.

10. Remove the console.

To install:

11. Lower the console and attach the cigarette lighter connectors.

12. Slide the brake lever through the parking brake handle boot.

13. Attach the retaining screws for the console.

14. Install the gearshift control lever plate.

15. Install the gearshift knob.

16. Install the ashtray.

17. Connect the negative battery cable.

Without Armrest

♦ **See Figures 50 and 51**

1. Disconnect the negative battery cable.

2. Remove the two screws retaining the console to the floor pan.

3. Remove the gearshift lever knob.

4. Remove the console cup holder.

5. Remove the three screws retaining the rear of the console to the floor pan.

6. Raise the console and carefully ease the parking brake handle boot over the brake lever.

7. Remove the console.

To install:

8. Lower the console and slide the brake lever through the parking brake handle boot.

9. Install the console retaining screws.

10. Install the cup holder.

11. Install the gearshift knob.

12. Connect the negative battery cable.

Door Panels

REMOVAL & INSTALLATION

♦ **See Figures 52 thru 67**

1. Disconnect the negative battery cable.

2. Remove the screw cover, screw and mirror mounting cover.

3. If equipped with manual windows, remove the window regulator arm, by releasing the clip using an appropriate tool.

4. Remove the cover on the inside door handle.

5. Remove the screws retaining the inside door handle to the door panel.

6. Pull out the inside release handle cup and unplug the connectors from the switches (if equipped). Remove the front door release handle cup assembly.

7. Remove any necessary door panel retaining screw covers.

8. Remove the retaining screws from the door panel.

9. Lift the door panel straight up to release the retaining tabs.

To install:

10. Slide the door panel down and ensure all the retaining tabs are engaged.

11. Tighten the door panel retaining screws. Install any screw covers that were removed.

12. Attach any unplugged connectors onto the inside handle cup assembly.

13. Place the cup into position and snap it into place.

14. Install the inside handle and tighten the retaining screws. Install the handle cover.

15. If equipped install the manual window regulator arm.

16. Install the mirror cover, retaining screw and screw cover.

17. Connect the negative battery cable.

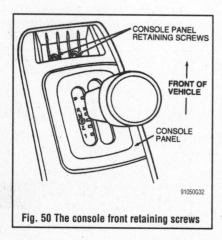

Fig. 50 The console front retaining screws

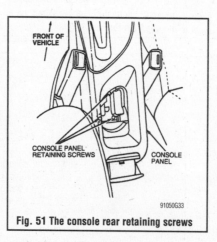

Fig. 51 The console rear retaining screws

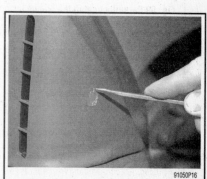

Fig. 52 Pry the screw cover off of the mirror cover, due to the design, it is nearly impossible not to destroy the screw cover

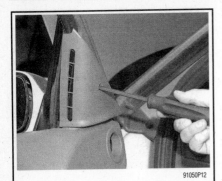

91050P12

Fig. 53 Remove the mirror cover retaining screw and . . .

91050P11

Fig. 54 . . . remove the mirror cover

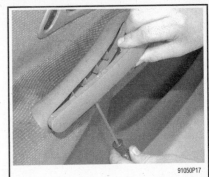

91050P17

Fig. 55 Remove the inside handle cover by carefully prying it off

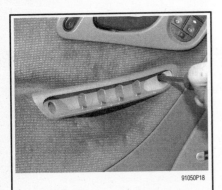

91050P18

Fig. 56 Remove the inside handle retaining screws and . . .

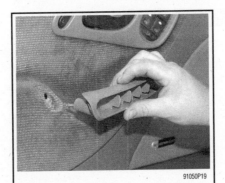

91050P19

Fig. 57 . . . remove the inside handle

91050P22

Fig. 58 Gently remove the inside release handle cup and switch assembly

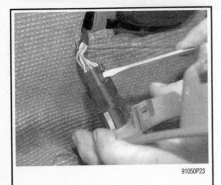

91050P23

Fig. 59 Carefully unplug the connector on the power door lock switch

91050P24

Fig. 60 The power window switch assembly stays connected and is pushed out of the cup from the rear

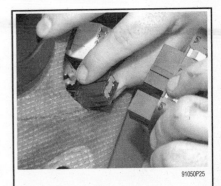

91050P25

Fig. 61 After the power window switch is removed from the cup, unplug it

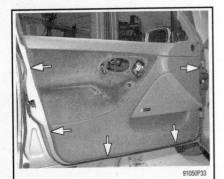

91050P33

Fig. 62 The location of the door panel retaining screws

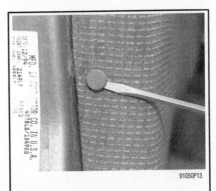

91050P13

Fig. 63 Remove the screw covers on the rear and . . .

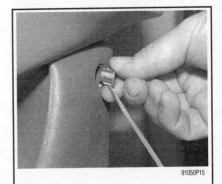

91050P15

Fig. 64 . . . the front of the door panel

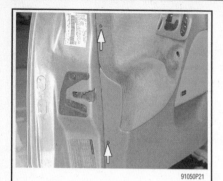

Fig. 65 Remove the two rear retaining screws

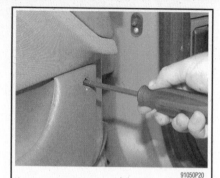

Fig. 66 Remove the retaining screw on the front of the door panel

Fig. 67 Lift the door panel straight up to remove it from the door

Door Handle/Latch Assembly

REMOVAL & INSTALLATION

▶ See Figures 68, 69 and 70

1. Disconnect the negative battery cable.
2. Remove the door panel.
3. Remove the door speaker.
4. Unplug the connector for the door open warning switch.
5. If equipped, unplug the connector for the lock cylinder illumination lamp.
6. Remove the two retaining nuts for the outside door handle and outside door handle bezel-to-door. Lower the outside door handle bezel.
7. If equipped with power locks, unplug the door lock actuator.
8. Unplug door handle illumination lamp connector.

9. Remove the two screws retaining front door latch remote control and link to the door.
10. Remove the three screws retaining door latch to the door.
11. Slide the handle/latch assembly to the front of the opening in the door and rotate the handle/latch assembly out of the door.

To install:

12. Insert the handle/latch assembly into the door and rotate it into position.
13. Install the three screws retaining door latch to the door.
14. Install the two screws retaining front door latch remote control and link to the door.
15. Attach the connectors for the power door lock actuator and the door handle illumination lamp.
16. Install the outside door handle bezel and tighten the two retaining nuts for the outside door handle and outside door handle bezel-to-door.
17. If equipped, attach the connector for the lock cylinder illumination lamp.
18. Attach the connector for the door open warning switch.
19. Install the door speaker.
20. Install the door panel.
21. Connect the negative battery cable.

Door Lock Cylinder

REMOVAL & INSTALLATION

▶ See Figures 71 and 72

1. Disconnect the negative battery cable.
2. Remove the door handle/latch assembly.
3. Press in on the locking tab retaining the lock cylinder to outside handle.
4. Remove the lock cylinder from the outside handle and feed the illumination wire through the opening in the handle.

To install:

5. Route the illumination wire through the handle and install the lock cylinder.

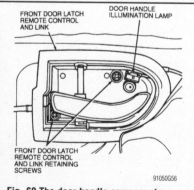

Fig. 68 Remove the door handle retaining nuts

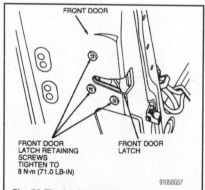

Fig. 69 The door handle components located on the inside of the door

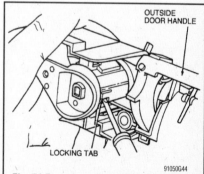

Fig. 70 The latch assembly is retained by three screws

Fig. 71 Press in on the locking tab retaining the lock cylinder to outside handle and . . .

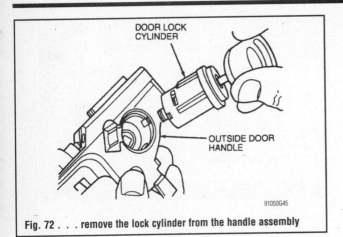

Fig. 72 . . . remove the lock cylinder from the handle assembly

6. Snap the locking tab into place retaining the lock cylinder to the outside handle.
7. Install the door handle/latch assembly.
8. Connect the negative battery cable.

Trunk Lid Lock Cylinder

REMOVAL & INSTALLATION

▶ See Figures 73 and 74

1. Pull the trunk lid lock cable upward from the bracket and slide it out of the lock cylinder plate.
2. Pull the lock cylinder retaining clip upward to release the lock cylinder plate.

3. Remove the lock cylinder plate.
4. Installation is the reverse of removal.

Power Door Lock Actuator

REMOVAL & INSTALLATION

▶ See Figure 75

1. Disconnect the negative battery cable.
2. Remove the door handle/latch assembly.
3. Remove the two actuator retaining screws from the door latch assembly
4. Remove the actuator.
5. Installation is the reverse of removal.

Door Glass

REMOVAL & INSTALLATION

Front Door

▶ See Figures 76, 77, 78, 82 and 83

1. Disconnect the negative battery cable.
2. Remove the door panel and watershield.
3. Remove the outside mirror assembly.
4. For manual windows, place the window regulator handle onto the regulator.
5. For power windows, connect the battery cable and connect the switch.
6. Lower the window to align the regulator-to-glass retaining bolts with the holes in the door.
7. Remove the regulator handle or disconnect the battery cable and unplug the switch.

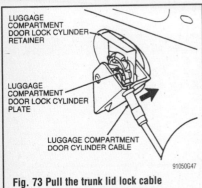

Fig. 73 Pull the trunk lid lock cable upward from the bracket and slide it out of the lock cylinder plate

Fig. 74 Pull the lock cylinder retaining clip upward

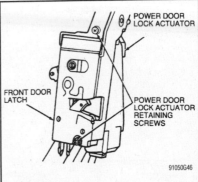

Fig. 75 The door lock actuator is retained by two screws

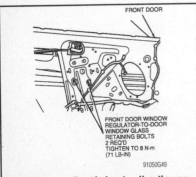

Fig. 76 Lower the window to align the regulator-to-glass retaining bolts with the holes in the door

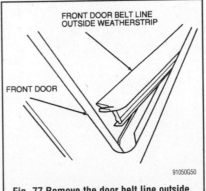

Fig. 77 Remove the door belt line outside weatherstrip from the door

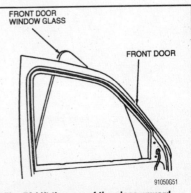

Fig. 78 Lift the rear of the glass upward and remove the glass from the door

8. Remove the two regulator-to-glass retaining bolts.

9. Have an assistant hold the glass, carefully pry the regulator from the glass.

10. Remove the door belt line outside weatherstrip from the door.

11. Rasie the rear of the glass upward and remove the glass from the door.

To install:

12. Lower the glass into the door.

13. Have an assistant hold the glass, and install the regulator onto the glass.

14. Finger-tighten the regulator-to-glass retaining bolts.

15. Install the door belt line outside weatherstrip.

16. Align the glass and tighten the regulator-to-glass retaining bolts to 71 inch lbs. (8 Nm).

17. Install the outside mirror assembly.

18. Install the watershield and door panel.

19. Connect the negative battery cable.

Rear Door

♦ **See Figures 76, 77, 79, 80 and 81**

1. Disconnect the negative battery cable.

2. Remove the door panel and watershield.

3. Carefully pry inside door trim from the rear door.

4. Carefully pry outside door trim from the rear door.

5. For manual windows, place the window regulator handle onto the regulator.

6. For power windows, connect the battery cable and connect the switch.

7. Lower the window to align the regulator-to-glass retaining bolts with the holes in the door.

8. Remove the regulator handle or disconnect the battery cable and unplug the switch.

9. Have an assistant hold the glass, and remove the regulator-to-glass retaining bolts.

10. Remove the door belt line outside weatherstrip from the door.

11. Have your assistant raise the glass to a near closed position.

12. Loosen, but do not remove the regulator retaining bolts.

13. Slide the top regulator retaining bolts forward in their slots in the door.

14. Slide the bottom regulator retaining bolts upward and out of the inner door panel. The door regulator most likely will drop to the bottom of the door, if it does not, push it down.

15. Lower the rear door glass into the door past the bottom of the window run inside of the rear door.

16. Raise the glass past the rear window runs and out of the door.

To install:

17. Lower the glass into the door.

18. Have an assistant hold the glass while raising the regulator from the bottom of the door.

19. Position the regulator and tighten the retaining bolts for the regulator.

20. Lower the glass down and align the glass with the regulator.

21. Finger-tighten the regulator-to-glass retaining bolts.

22. Install the door belt line outside weatherstrip.

23. Tighten the regulator-to-glass retaining bolts to 71 inch lbs. (8 Nm).

24. Install the outside door trim onto the rear door.

25. Install the inside door trim onto the rear door.

26. Install the watershield and door panel.

27. Connect the negative battery cable.

Door Window Regulator

REMOVAL & INSTALLATION

Front Door

♦ **See Figures 82 and 83**

1. Disconnect the negative battery cable.

2. Remove the door glass as outlined in this section.

3. Loosen, but do not remove the regulator retaining bolts.

4. Remove the window motor retaining bolts (if equipped).

5. Slide the regulator bolts forward in their slots.

6. Unplug the window motor connector.

7. Remove the regulator from the door.

To install:

8. Install the regulator and attach the window motor connector.

9. Tighten the window motor bolts.

10. Tighten the regulator bolts.

11. Install the door glass.

12. Connect the negative battery cable.

Rear Door

♦ **See Figure 84**

1. Disconnect the negative battery cable.

2. Remove the door glass as outlined in this section.

3. Unplug the window motor connector.

4. Remove the regulator from the door.

To install:

5. Install the regulator and attach the window motor connector.

6. Install the door glass.

7. Connect the negative battery cable.

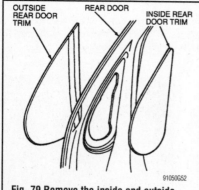

Fig. 79 Remove the inside and outside door trim panels

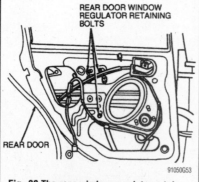

Fig. 80 The rear window regulator retaining bolt locations

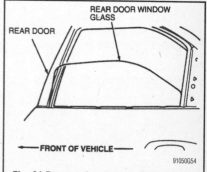

Fig. 81 Remove the glass by tilting the glass toward the vehicle and inside of the top run

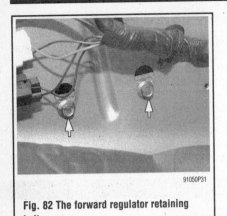

Fig. 82 The forward regulator retaining bolts

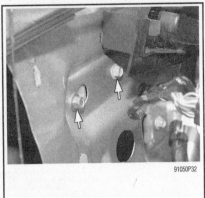

Fig. 83 The rear regulator retaining bolts

Fig. 84 Remove the window regulator from the rear door

Electric Window Motor

REMOVAL & INSTALLATION

▶ See Figure 85

➡On some models it may be necessary to remove the window regulator from the vehicle. If so, remove the regulator as described in the Section and remove the retaining bolts from the motor and remove the motor. Installation is the reverse of removal.

1. Disconnect the negative battery cable.
2. Remove the door panel and watershield.
3. Remove the window motor retaining bolts.
4. Carefully remove the motor from the regulator and unplug the connector.

To install:

5. Attach the connector for the window motor and carefully place the drive gear of the motor into the regulator, making sure the teeth align.
6. Tighten the motor retaining bolts.
7. Connect the negative battery cable.
8. Verify the motor operation.
9. Install the door panel and watershield.

Windshield and Fixed Glass

REMOVAL & INSTALLATION

If your windshield, or other fixed window, is cracked or chipped, you may decide to replace it with a new one yourself. However, there are two main reasons why replacement windshields and other window glass should be installed only by a professional automotive glass technician: safety and cost.

The most important reason a professional should install automotive glass is for safety. The glass in the vehicle, especially the windshield, is designed with safety in mind in case of a collision. The windshield is specially manufactured from two panes of specially-tempered glass with a thin layer of transparent plastic between them. This construction allows the glass to "give" in the event that a part of your body hits the windshield during the collision, and prevents the glass from shattering, which could cause lacerations, blinding and other harm to passengers of the vehicle. The other fixed windows are designed to be tempered so that if they break during a collision, they shatter in such a way that there are no large pointed glass pieces. The professional automotive glass technician knows how to install the glass in a vehicle so that it will function optimally during a collision. Without the proper experience, knowledge and tools, installing a piece of automotive glass yourself could lead to additional harm if an accident should ever occur.

Cost is also a factor when deciding to install automotive glass yourself. Performing this could cost you much more than a professional may charge for the same job. Since the windshield is designed to break under stress, an often life saving characteristic, windshields tend to break VERY easily when an inexperienced person attempts to install one. Do-it-yourselfers buying two, three or even four windshields from a salvage yard because they have broken them during installation are common stories. Also, since the automotive glass is designed to prevent the outside elements from entering your vehicle, improper installation can lead to water and air leaks. Annoying whining noises at highway speeds from air leaks or inside body panel rusting from water leaks can add to your stress level and subtract from your wallet. After buying two or three windshields, installing them and ending up with a leak that produces a noise while driving and water damage during rainstorms, the cost of having a professional do it correctly the first time may be much more alluring. We here at Chilton, therefore, advise that you have a professional automotive glass technician service any broken glass on your vehicle.

WINDSHIELD CHIP REPAIR

▶ See Figures 86 thru 100

➡Check with your state and local authorities on the laws for state safety inspection. Some states or municipalities may not allow chip repair as a viable option for correcting stone damage to your windshield.

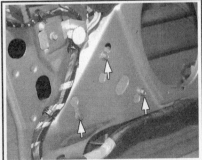

Fig. 85 The window motor is retained by the three bolts shown here

Fig. 86 Small chips on your windshield can be fixed with an aftermarket repair kit, such as the one from Loctite®

Fig. 87 To repair a chip, clean the windshield with glass cleaner and dry it completely

Fig. 88 Remove the center from the adhesive disc and peel off the backing from one side of the disc . . .

Fig. 89 . . . then press it on the windshield so that the chip is centered in the hole

Fig. 90 Be sure that the tab points upward on the windshield

Fig. 91 Peel the backing off the exposed side of the adhesive disc . . .

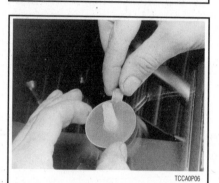

Fig. 92 . . . then position the plastic pedestal on the adhesive disc, ensuring that the tabs are aligned

Fig. 93 Press the pedestal firmly on the adhesive disc to create an adequate seal . . .

Fig. 94 . . . then install the applicator syringe nipple in the pedestal's hole

Although severely cracked or damaged windshields must be replaced, there is something that you can do to prolong or even prevent the need for replacement of a chipped windshield. There are many companies which offer windshield chip repair products, such as Loctite's® Bullseye™ windshield repair kit. These kits usually consist of a syringe, pedestal and a sealing adhesive. The syringe is mounted on the pedestal and is used to create a vacuum which pulls the plastic layer against the glass. This helps make the chip transparent. The adhesive is then injected which seals the chip and helps to prevent further stress cracks from developing. Refer to the sequence of photos to get a general idea of what windshield chip repair involves.

➥Always follow the specific manufacturer's instructions.

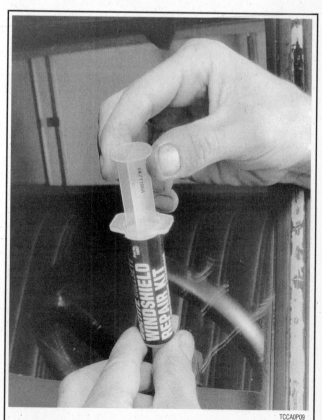

Fig. 95 Hold the syringe with one hand while pulling the plunger back with the other hand

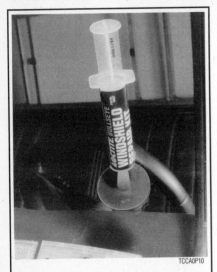

Fig. 96 After applying the solution, allow the entire assembly to sit until it has set completely

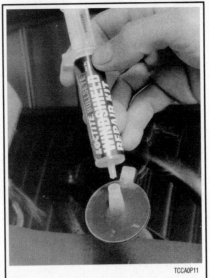

Fig. 97 After the solution has set, remove the syringe from the pedestal . . .

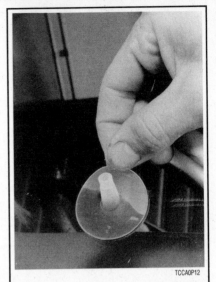

Fig. 98 . . . then peel the pedestal off of the adhesive disc . . .

Fig. 99 . . . and peel the adhesive disc off of the windshield

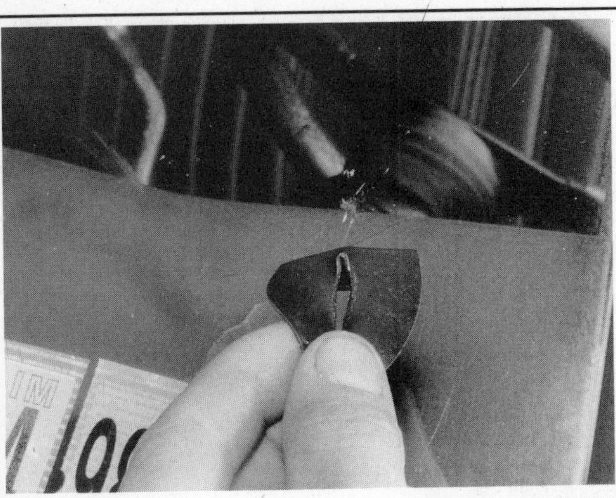

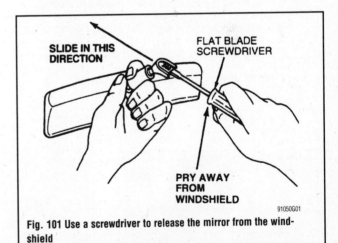

Fig. 100 The chip will still be slightly visible, but it should be filled with the hardened solution

Inside Rear View Mirror

REPLACEMENT

▶ See Figure 101

1. Grasp the rear view mirror firmly.
2. Insert a small flatblade screwdriver into the screwless mount slot until the spring clip is contacted.
3. Push on the spring clip with the tool and pull the mirror to remove it from the mounting bracket.
   To install:
4. Install the mirror onto the mounting bracket until it firmly fits in place.

SLIDE IN THIS DIRECTION

FLAT BLADE SCREWDRIVER

PRY AWAY FROM WINDSHIELD

91050G01

Fig. 101 Use a screwdriver to release the mirror from the windshield

Seats

REMOVAL & INSTALLATION

Front

▶ See Figures 102, 103, 104 and 105

1. Disconnect the negative battery cable.
2. Remove the side shield from the seat.

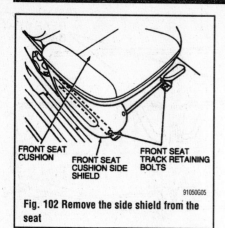

Fig. 102 Remove the side shield from the seat

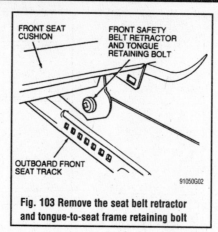

Fig. 103 Remove the seat belt retractor and tongue-to-seat frame retaining bolt

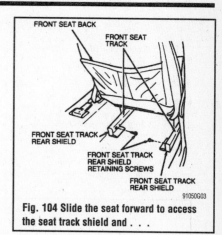

Fig. 104 Slide the seat forward to access the seat track shield and . . .

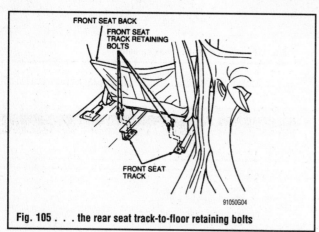

Fig. 105 . . . the rear seat track-to-floor retaining bolts

3. Remove the seat belt retractor and tongue-to-seat frame retaining bolt. Slide the seat belt upward from behind the seat.

4. Slide the seat forward.

5. Unfasten the two retaining screws (one from each side) attaching the seat track shield on the track and remove the shield.

6. Unfasten the four (two each side) rear seat track-to-floor mounting bolts.

7. Slide the seat rearward.

8. Remove the two (one from each side) front seat track-to-floor mounting bolts.

9. Unplug the power seat electrical connection (if equipped).

10. Remove the front seat.

To install:

11. Install the seat and attach the power seat electrical connection (if equipped).

12. Install the two front seat track-to-floor mounting bolts. Tighten the bolts to 15–19 ft. lbs. (20–26 Nm).

13. Slide the seat forward.

14. Install the four rear seat track-to-floor mounting bolts. Tighten the bolts to 15–19 ft. lbs. (20–26 Nm).

15. Install the seat track shield on the track and tighten the retaining screws.

16. Slide the seat rearward.

17. Install the seat belt retractor and tongue-to-seat frame retaining bolt.

18. Install the side shield from the seat.

19. Connect the negative battery cable.

Rear

SEAT CUSHION

♦ **See Figures 106 and 107**

1. Pull upward on the front of the seat cushion to release the two rear seat cushion retaining clips which attach the front of the seat cushion to the floor.

2. Guide the seat belts and latches through the seat cushion.

3. Remove the seat cushion.

To install:

4. Place the seat cushion into position, making sure the safety belt buckles are through the rear seat cushion openings..

5. Align the cushion's retaining pins with the retaining clips and push down on the cushion, making sure the clips are firmly engaged.

REAR SEAT BACK

♦ **See Figure 108**

1. Remove the rear seat cushion.

2. Remove the two rear seat back retaining bolts from the bottom of the seat back.

Fig. 106 Lift the seat cushion straight up to release the retaining clips from the floor

Fig. 107 Guide the seat belts through the holes in the cushion

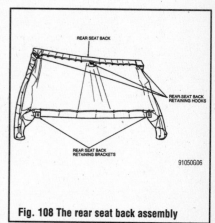

Fig. 108 The rear seat back assembly

3. Lift the seat back upward to release the retaining hooks and remove the seat back.

4. Installation is the reverse of removal. Tighten the retaining bolts to 23–35 ft. lbs. (31–48 Nm).

60/40 SPLIT REAR SEAT BACK

▶ See Figures 109 and 110

1. Fold the rear seat back down.
2. Remove the push pins retaining the lower trim to the rear of the seat back(s).
3. Fold the seat back trim up to access the seat back retaining bolts.
4. Remove the retaining bolts and remove the seat back(s).

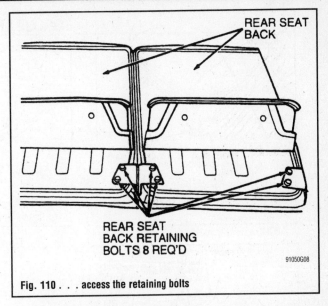

Fig. 110 . . . access the retaining bolts

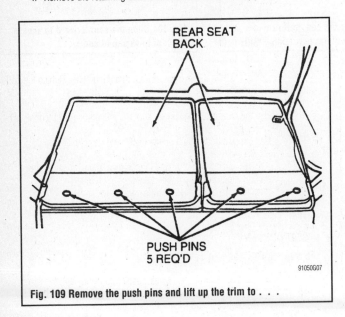

Fig. 109 Remove the push pins and lift up the trim to . . .

5. Installation is the reverse of removal. Tighten the retaining bolts to 15–19 ft. lbs. (20–26 Nm).

Power Seat Motor

REMOVAL & INSTALLATION

1. Disconnect the negative battery cable.
2. Remove front seats as outlined.
3. Remove the seat motor retaining bolts and remove seat motor.
4. Installation is the reverse of removal.

TORQUE SPECIFICATIONS

Components	English	Metric
Antenna nut	31-44 inch lbs.	4-5 Nm
Door hinge bolts	19-25 ft. lbs.	25-35 Nm
Door stop arm bolts	89 inch lbs.	10 Nm
Door striker bolts	17-20 ft. lbs.	22-28 Nm
Fender retaining screws	89-124 inch lbs.	10-14 Nm
Front seat retaining bolts	15-19 ft. lbs.	20-26 Nm
Grille retaining screws	11-16 inch lbs.	1.2-1.8 Nm
Hood hinge bolts	18 ft. lbs.	24 Nm
Outside mirror retaining bolts	53-71 inch lbs.	6-8 Nm
Rear seat		
Rear seat back	23-35 ft. lbs.	31-48 Nm
60/40 split rear seat back	15-19 ft. lbs.	20-26 Nm
Trunk lid hinge bolts	89 inch lbs.	10 Nm
Window regulator-to-door glass retaining bolts	71 inch lbs.	8 Nm

91050C01

GLOSSARY

AIR/FUEL RATIO: The ratio of air-to-gasoline by weight in the fuel mixture drawn into the engine.

AIR INJECTION: One method of reducing harmful exhaust emissions by injecting air into each of the exhaust ports of an engine. The fresh air entering the hot exhaust manifold causes any remaining fuel to be burned before it can exit the tailpipe.

ALTERNATOR: A device used for converting mechanical energy into electrical energy.

AMMETER: An instrument, calibrated in amperes, used to measure the flow of an electrical current in a circuit. Ammeters are always connected in series with the circuit being tested.

AMPERE: The rate of flow of electrical current present when one volt of electrical pressure is applied against one ohm of electrical resistance.

ANALOG COMPUTER: Any microprocessor that uses similar (analogous) electrical signals to make its calculations.

ARMATURE: A laminated, soft iron core wrapped by a wire that converts electrical energy to mechanical energy as in a motor or relay. When rotated in a magnetic field, it changes mechanical energy into electrical energy as in a generator.

ATMOSPHERIC PRESSURE: The pressure on the Earth's surface caused by the weight of the air in the atmosphere. At sea level, this pressure is 14.7 psi at 32°F (101 kPa at 0°C).

ATOMIZATION: The breaking down of a liquid into a fine mist that can be suspended in air.

AXIAL PLAY: Movement parallel to a shaft or bearing bore.

BACKFIRE: The sudden combustion of gases in the intake or exhaust system that results in a loud explosion.

BACKLASH: The clearance or play between two parts, such as meshed gears.

BACKPRESSURE: Restrictions in the exhaust system that slow the exit of exhaust gases from the combustion chamber.

BAKELITE: A heat resistant, plastic insulator material commonly used in printed circuit boards and transistorized components.

BALL BEARING: A bearing made up of hardened inner and outer races between which hardened steel balls roll.

BALLAST RESISTOR: A resistor in the primary ignition circuit that lowers voltage after the engine is started to reduce wear on ignition components.

BEARING: A friction reducing, supportive device usually located between a stationary part and a moving part.

BIMETAL TEMPERATURE SENSOR: Any sensor or switch made of two dissimilar types of metal that bend when heated or cooled due to the different expansion rates of the alloys. These types of sensors usually function as an on/off switch.

BLOWBY: Combustion gases, composed of water vapor and unburned fuel, that leak past the piston rings into the crankcase during normal engine operation. These gases are removed by the PCV system to prevent the buildup of harmful acids in the crankcase.

BRAKE PAD: A brake shoe and lining assembly used with disc brakes.

BRAKE SHOE: The backing for the brake lining. The term is, however, usually applied to the assembly of the brake backing and lining.

BUSHING: A liner, usually removable, for a bearing; an anti-friction liner used in place of a bearing.

CALIPER: A hydraulically activated device in a disc brake system, which is mounted straddling the brake rotor (disc). The caliper contains at least one piston and two brake pads. Hydraulic pressure on the piston(s) forces the pads against the rotor.

CAMSHAFT: A shaft in the engine on which are the lobes (cams) which operate the valves. The camshaft is driven by the crankshaft, via a belt, chain or gears, at one half the crankshaft speed.

CAPACITOR: A device which stores an electrical charge.

CARBON MONOXIDE (CO): A colorless, odorless gas given off as a normal byproduct of combustion. It is poisonous and extremely dangerous in confined areas, building up slowly to toxic levels without warning if adequate ventilation is not available.

CARBURETOR: A device, usually mounted on the intake manifold of an engine, which mixes the air and fuel in the proper proportion to allow even combustion.

CATALYTIC CONVERTER: A device installed in the exhaust system, like a muffler, that converts harmful byproducts of combustion into carbon dioxide and water vapor by means of a heat-producing chemical reaction.

CENTRIFUGAL ADVANCE: A mechanical method of advancing the spark timing by using flyweights in the distributor that react to centrifugal force generated by the distributor shaft rotation.

CHECK VALVE: Any one-way valve installed to permit the flow of air, fuel or vacuum in one direction only.

CHOKE: A device, usually a moveable valve, placed in the intake path of a carburetor to restrict the flow of air.

CIRCUIT: Any unbroken path through which an electrical current can flow. Also used to describe fuel flow in some instances.

CIRCUIT BREAKER: A switch which protects an electrical circuit from overload by opening the circuit when the current flow exceeds a predetermined level. Some circuit breakers must be reset manually, while most reset automatically.

COIL (IGNITION): A transformer in the ignition circuit which steps up the voltage provided to the spark plugs.

COMBINATION MANIFOLD: An assembly which includes both the intake and exhaust manifolds in one casting.

COMBINATION VALVE: A device used in some fuel systems that routes fuel vapors to a charcoal storage canister instead of venting them into the atmosphere. The valve relieves fuel tank pressure and allows fresh air into the tank as the fuel level drops to prevent a vapor lock situation.

COMPRESSION RATIO: The comparison of the total volume of the cylinder and combustion chamber with the piston at BDC and the piston at TDC.

CONDENSER: 1. An electrical device which acts to store an electrical charge, preventing voltage surges. 2. A radiator-like device in the air conditioning system in which refrigerant gas condenses into a liquid, giving off heat.

CONDUCTOR: Any material through which an electrical current can be transmitted easily.

CONTINUITY: Continuous or complete circuit. Can be checked with an ohmmeter.

COUNTERSHAFT: An intermediate shaft which is rotated by a mainshaft and transmits, in turn, that rotation to a working part.

CRANKCASE: The lower part of an engine in which the crankshaft and related parts operate.

CRANKSHAFT: The main driving shaft of an engine which receives reciprocating motion from the pistons and converts it to rotary motion.

CYLINDER: In an engine, the round hole in the engine block in which the piston(s) ride.

CYLINDER BLOCK: The main structural member of an engine in which is found the cylinders, crankshaft and other principal parts.

CYLINDER HEAD: The detachable portion of the engine, usually fastened to the top of the cylinder block and containing all or most of the combustion chambers. On overhead valve engines, it contains the valves and their operating parts. On overhead cam engines, it contains the camshaft as well.

DEAD CENTER: The extreme top or bottom of the piston stroke.

DETONATION: An unwanted explosion of the air/fuel mixture in the combustion chamber caused by excess heat and compression, advanced timing, or an overly lean mixture. Also referred to as "ping".

DIAPHRAGM: A thin, flexible wall separating two cavities, such as in a vacuum advance unit.

DIESELING: A condition in which hot spots in the combustion chamber cause the engine to run on after the key is turned off.

DIFFERENTIAL: A geared assembly which allows the transmission of motion between drive axles, giving one axle the ability to turn faster than the other.

DIODE: An electrical device that will allow current to flow in one direction only.

DISC BRAKE: A hydraulic braking assembly consisting of a brake disc, or rotor, mounted on an axle, and a caliper assembly containing, usually two brake pads which are activated by hydraulic pressure. The pads are forced against the sides of the disc, creating friction which slows the vehicle.

DISTRIBUTOR: A mechanically driven device on an engine which is responsible for electrically firing the spark plug at a predetermined point of the piston stroke.

DOWEL PIN: A pin, inserted in mating holes in two different parts allowing those parts to maintain a fixed relationship.

DRUM BRAKE: A braking system which consists of two brake shoes and one or two wheel cylinders, mounted on a fixed backing plate, and a brake drum, mounted on an axle, which revolves around the assembly.

DWELL: The rate, measured in degrees of shaft rotation, at which an electrical circuit cycles on and off.

ELECTRONIC CONTROL UNIT (ECU): Ignition module, module, amplifier or igniter. See Module for definition.

ELECTRONIC IGNITION: A system in which the timing and firing of the spark plugs is controlled by an electronic control unit, usually called a module. These systems have no points or condenser.

END-PLAY: The measured amount of axial movement in a shaft.

ENGINE: A device that converts heat into mechanical energy.

EXHAUST MANIFOLD: A set of cast passages or pipes which conduct exhaust gases from the engine.

FEELER GAUGE: A blade, usually metal, or precisely predetermined thickness, used to measure the clearance between two parts.

FIRING ORDER: The order in which combustion occurs in the cylinders of an engine. Also the order in which spark is distributed to the plugs by the distributor.

FLOODING: The presence of too much fuel in the intake manifold and combustion chamber which prevents the air/fuel mixture from firing, thereby causing a no-start situation.

FLYWHEEL: A disc shaped part bolted to the rear end of the crankshaft. Around the outer perimeter is affixed the ring gear. The starter drive engages the ring gear, turning the flywheel, which rotates the crankshaft, imparting the initial starting motion to the engine.

FOOT POUND (ft. lbs. or sometimes, ft.lb.): The amount of energy or work needed to raise an item weighing one pound, a distance of one foot.

FUSE: A protective device in a circuit which prevents circuit overload by breaking the circuit when a specific amperage is present. The device is constructed around a strip or wire of a lower amperage rating than the circuit it is designed to protect. When an amperage higher than that stamped on the fuse is present in the circuit, the strip or wire melts, opening the circuit.

GEAR RATIO: The ratio between the number of teeth on meshing gears.

GENERATOR: A device which converts mechanical energy into electrical energy.

HEAT RANGE: The measure of a spark plug's ability to dissipate heat from its firing end. The higher the heat range, the hotter the plug fires.

HUB: The center part of a wheel or gear.

HYDROCARBON (HC): Any chemical compound made up of hydrogen and carbon. A major pollutant formed by the engine as a byproduct of combustion.

HYDROMETER: An instrument used to measure the specific gravity of a solution.

INCH POUND (inch lbs.; sometimes in.lb. or in. lbs.): One twelfth of a foot pound.

INDUCTION: A means of transferring electrical energy in the form of a magnetic field. Principle used in the ignition coil to increase voltage.

INJECTOR: A device which receives metered fuel under relatively low pressure and is activated to inject the fuel into the engine under relatively high pressure at a predetermined time.

INPUT SHAFT: The shaft to which torque is applied, usually carrying the driving gear or gears.

INTAKE MANIFOLD: A casting of passages or pipes used to conduct air or a fuel/air mixture to the cylinders.

JOURNAL: The bearing surface within which a shaft operates.

KEY: A small block usually fitted in a notch between a shaft and a hub to prevent slippage of the two parts.

MANIFOLD: A casting of passages or set of pipes which connect the cylinders to an inlet or outlet source.

MANIFOLD VACUUM: Low pressure in an engine intake manifold formed just below the throttle plates. Manifold vacuum is highest at idle and drops under acceleration.

MASTER CYLINDER: The primary fluid pressurizing device in a hydraulic system. In automotive use, it is found in brake and hydraulic clutch systems and is pedal activated, either directly or, in a power brake system, through the power booster.

MODULE: Electronic control unit, amplifier or igniter of solid state or integrated design which controls the current flow in the ignition primary circuit based on input from the pick-up coil. When the module opens the primary circuit, high secondary voltage is induced in the coil.

NEEDLE BEARING: A bearing which consists of a number (usually a large number) of long, thin rollers.

OHM: (Ω) The unit used to measure the resistance of conductor-to-electrical flow. One ohm is the amount of resistance that limits current flow to one ampere in a circuit with one volt of pressure.

OHMMETER: An instrument used for measuring the resistance, in ohms, in an electrical circuit.

OUTPUT SHAFT: The shaft which transmits torque from a device, such as a transmission.

OVERDRIVE: A gear assembly which produces more shaft revolutions than that transmitted to it.

OVERHEAD CAMSHAFT (OHC): An engine configuration in which the camshaft is mounted on top of the cylinder head and operates the valve either directly or by means of rocker arms.

OVERHEAD VALVE (OHV): An engine configuration in which all of the valves are located in the cylinder head and the camshaft is located in the cylinder block. The camshaft operates the valves via lifters and pushrods.

OXIDES OF NITROGEN (NOx): Chemical compounds of nitrogen produced as a byproduct of combustion. They combine with hydrocarbons to produce smog.

OXYGEN SENSOR: Use with the feedback system to sense the presence of oxygen in the exhaust gas and signal the computer which can reference the voltage signal to an air/fuel ratio.

PINION: The smaller of two meshing gears.

PISTON RING: An open-ended ring with fits into a groove on the outer diameter of the piston. Its chief function is to form a seal between the piston and cylinder wall. Most automotive pistons have three rings: two for compression sealing; one for oil sealing.

PRELOAD: A predetermined load placed on a bearing during assembly or by adjustment.

PRIMARY CIRCUIT: the low voltage side of the ignition system which consists of the ignition switch, ballast resistor or resistance wire, bypass, coil, electronic control unit and pick-up coil as well as the connecting wires and harnesses.

PRESS FIT: The mating of two parts under pressure, due to the inner diameter of one being smaller than the outer diameter of the other, or vice versa; an interference fit.

RACE: The surface on the inner or outer ring of a bearing on which the balls, needles or rollers move.

REGULATOR: A device which maintains the amperage and/or voltage levels of a circuit at predetermined values.

RELAY: A switch which automatically opens and/or closes a circuit.

RESISTANCE: The opposition to the flow of current through a circuit or electrical device, and is measured in ohms. Resistance is equal to the voltage divided by the amperage.

RESISTOR: A device, usually made of wire, which offers a preset amount of resistance in an electrical circuit.

RING GEAR: The name given to a ring-shaped gear attached to a differential case, or affixed to a flywheel or as part of a planetary gear set.

ROLLER BEARING: A bearing made up of hardened inner and outer races between which hardened steel rollers move.

ROTOR: 1. The disc-shaped part of a disc brake assembly, upon which the brake pads bear; also called, brake disc. 2. The device mounted atop the distributor shaft, which passes current to the distributor cap tower contacts.

SECONDARY CIRCUIT: The high voltage side of the ignition system, usually above 20,000 volts. The secondary includes the ignition coil, coil wire, distributor cap and rotor, spark plug wires and spark plugs.

SENDING UNIT: A mechanical, electrical, hydraulic or electro-magnetic device which transmits information to a gauge.

SENSOR: Any device designed to measure engine operating conditions or ambient pressures and temperatures. Usually electronic in nature and designed to send a voltage signal to an on-board computer, some sensors may operate as a simple on/off switch or they may provide a variable voltage signal (like a potentiometer) as conditions or measured parameters change.

SHIM: Spacers of precise, predetermined thickness used between parts to establish a proper working relationship.

SLAVE CYLINDER: In automotive use, a device in the hydraulic clutch system which is activated by hydraulic force, disengaging the clutch.

SOLENOID: A coil used to produce a magnetic field, the effect of which is to produce work.

SPARK PLUG: A device screwed into the combustion chamber of a spark ignition engine. The basic construction is a conductive core inside of a ceramic insulator, mounted in an outer conductive base. An electrical charge from the spark plug wire travels along the conductive core and jumps a preset air gap to a grounding point or points at the end of the conductive base. The resultant spark ignites the fuel/air mixture in the combustion chamber.

SPLINES: Ridges machined or cast onto the outer diameter of a shaft or inner diameter of a bore to enable parts to mate without rotation.

TACHOMETER: A device used to measure the rotary speed of an engine, shaft, gear, etc., usually in rotations per minute.

THERMOSTAT: A valve, located in the cooling system of an engine, which is closed when cold and opens gradually in response to engine heating, controlling the temperature of the coolant and rate of coolant flow.

TOP DEAD CENTER (TDC): The point at which the piston reaches the top of its travel on the compression stroke.

TORQUE: The twisting force applied to an object.

TORQUE CONVERTER: A turbine used to transmit power from a driving member to a driven member via hydraulic action, providing changes in drive ratio and torque. In automotive use, it links the driveplate at the rear of the engine to the automatic transmission.

TRANSDUCER: A device used to change a force into an electrical signal.

TRANSISTOR: A semi-conductor component which can be actuated by a small voltage to perform an electrical switching function.

TUNE-UP: A regular maintenance function, usually associated with the replacement and adjustment of parts and components in the electrical and fuel systems of a vehicle for the purpose of attaining optimum performance.

TURBOCHARGER: An exhaust driven pump which compresses intake air and forces it into the combustion chambers at higher than atmospheric pressures. The increased air pressure allows more fuel to be burned and results in increased horsepower being produced.

VACUUM ADVANCE: A device which advances the ignition timing in response to increased engine vacuum.

VACUUM GAUGE: An instrument used to measure the presence of vacuum in a chamber.

VALVE: A device which control the pressure, direction of flow or rate of flow of a liquid or gas.

VALVE CLEARANCE: The measured gap between the end of the valve stem and the rocker arm, cam lobe or follower that activates the valve.

VISCOSITY: The rating of a liquid's internal resistance to flow.

VOLTMETER: An instrument used for measuring electrical force in units called volts. Voltmeters are always connected parallel with the circuit being tested.

WHEEL CYLINDER: Found in the automotive drum brake assembly, it is a device, actuated by hydraulic pressure, which, through internal pistons, pushes the brake shoes outward against the drums.

MASTER

INDEX